BEYOND NEW

Beyond New Age

Exploring Alternative Spirituality

Edited by Steven Sutcliffe and Marion Bowman

Edinburgh University Press

Edinburgh University Press Ltd
22 George Square, Edinburgh

Typeset in Goudy Old Style
by Hewer Text Ltd, Edinburgh, and
printed and bound in Great Britain by
MPG Books Ltd, Bodmin

A CIP record for this book is
available from the British Library

ISBN 0 7486 0998 9 (paperback)

Contents

Contents

Introduction

This volume of original essays grew directly out of our frustration with the cavalier use to which the label 'New Age' has been put in recent decades, both in the popular media and by many scholars of religions. A vast range of 'alternative' or 'spiritual' phenomena may sport this label, which – however convenient it may be as a shorthand device – is far from exact phenomenologically (cf. Bednarowski, 1991; York, 1997). It is used to cover everything from well-established New Religious Movements to contemporary popular spiritualities and recent developments in specific religions, and may be applied with comparatively little historical and structural specificity (Sutcliffe, 1998). In short, it seems to us that it is high time to problematise the term, while simultaneously beginning more thorough and wide-ranging excavations of, and differentiations between, the kinds of religiosity that the label has sought to identify. The 'beyond' of the title, then, carries no moral or theological judgement, but simply points to the historical dimension of the field in question, which both predates and will survive the term or emblem 'New Age'. That is, 'New Age' turns out to be merely a particular codeword in a larger field of modern religious experimentation.

We have chosen the loose term 'alternative spirituality' to describe the subject matter of the essays in this volume, although with some reservations and qualifications, as we briefly explain below. In most cases, the contributors were asked to restrict their focus to mainland Britain, our intention being that the British experience over the last century or so might act as a small case study for the growth and development of a genre of alternative spirituality in the modern world.

The subject-matter reflects recent historical currents and contemporary manifestations of this genre. Clearly our choice is far from exhaustive, but we think these papers identify some key features. In claiming that a more or less distinctive field of phenomena is indicated here, we are aware that we are positing a degree of homogeneity amongst disparate phenomena over and above that often argued for by activists and practitioners within particular constitutive currents. However, without wishing here to enter into the debate concerning the relative merits of etic/'outsider' versus emic/ 'insider' categorisation, we simply see a host of similarities and interconnections between emic modes and structures of discourse and praxis which suggest a common stance and attitude. This is avowedly and selfconsciously one in dynamic tension with – if not outright opposition to – the hitherto dominant ideas and structures of 'official' religion and secular science alike. Put simply, these currents invariably understand themselves to be 'alternative', either strongly (they are explicitly dissenting) or weakly (they are merely variant or optional). Finer differentiations – which in due course will certainly be required – we leave to others. At the same time, we think that these kinds of individualistic, flexible and acculturating spirituality are now of considerable cultural significance.

Inspection of this collection's contents reveals a variety of topics and approaches. Sociological, anthropological, historical and ethnographical perspectives mould often overlapping accounts of Theosophy (Tingay), the seminal reduction of religion to psychology by Jung (Segal), seekers, gurus, artists and other virtuosi (Sutcliffe, Green), the allure of certain landscapes and settlements (Bowman, Monteith, York), alternative healing modes (Hamilton, Hedges and Beckford), the dynamics of contemporary magical and Pagan identities (Greenwood, Harvey) and humanistic and secularised spirituality (Bruce, Heelas, Puttick). Since each chapter is effectively a self-contained and self-explanatory essay, we do not propose to spend time here on formal introductions. Rather, we wish to propose a handful of themes and frames through which to approach these intertwined episodes in the growth and development of alternative spirituality.

EPISTEMOLOGICAL AND METHODOLOGICAL ISSUES

We envisage this book not only as a valuable and thought-provoking resource for those studying and teaching in the field of contemporary religion, but as a stimulus for epistemological and methodological debate. The chapters in this volume reflect an increased scholarly interest in the experiences and perceptions of the growing number of religious practitioners whose spiritual lives in industrial and post-industrial society have lain, and lie, in less established, informal groupings. The need to review and reflect on how we talk about religion and spirituality in the light of late-twentieth-century trends – especially the growth of 'privatised' or 'customised' forms, and 'seeking' – is amply demonstrated here. A reappraisal is taking place, both within academia and more generally, of how we think about, classify and study religion. Many aspects of vernacular religion and contemporary spirituality fall outside the traditional purlieu of academic studies of religion, to the detriment of a rounded understanding of religious and spiritual culture(s). However, as scholars in a variety of disciplines have become aware of the changes in belief and praxis, it is becoming increasingly difficult to characterise what is 'mainstream'. To see religious experimentation, customisation and change as 'deviant' behaviour is no longer appropriate.

Methodologically, more cross-disciplinary and inter-disciplinary approaches are being developed to take into account the changing forms and expressions of religion. Some traditional means of information-gathering, such as counting numbers in churches or on membership lists, for example, are simply inappropriate for many of the looser, more personal, uninstitutionalised forms of contemporary spirituality. Indeed, it might be argued that such methods have always been problematical as measurements of individual belief. If Davie (1994) has argued that an important trend in contemporary religion is 'believing without belonging', implicit in this is the comparatively under-explored corollary of 'belonging without believing' – through custom and social pressures – which suggests that there are limitations in 'number-crunching' alone. Hence the contributions to this volume reflect a spectrum of information-gathering techniques, including historical, textual and archival studies, quantitative research and qualitative approaches such as interview and participant-observation.

Additionally, the scholar's role in the research process and her or his impact on the area researched continue to be areas for exploration. In the arena of contemporary spirituality, where the spiritual search is in part a literary activity, a significant proportion of informants are also avid readers of both emic and academic works. Informants may double as conscious representatives or academic scholars of their chosen path; the same person may be not only an informant, but the researcher's academic or public audience. The issue of reflexivity is thus becoming increasingly complex, and researchers must remain aware of their evolving role within the research 'ecosystem'. Furthermore, the traditional assumption of many scholars outside departments of theology that disbelief or scepticism constitutes an 'objective' stance in relation to belief studies is being challenged increasingly (Hufford, 1995). Hence the representation of 'reality' in a cultural context which acknowledges multiple possible realities is not just an 'academic' issue, for there are issues of legitimacy and power involved in whatever definition of 'normative' is counted as authoritative – and in who makes that judgment.

AN HISTORICAL PERSPECTIVE

There is in fact very little in contemporary spirituality that was not already present and available in the 1920s and 1930s, in the Edwardian era, at the *fin-de-siècle* or even earlier. Certainly there are exceptions: the 'secular myth' of flying saucers (Segal), and witchcraft/Wicca (Greenwood), for example, both emerge only in mid-century. But 'seeking' (Sutcliffe) has long been an established spiritual *modus operandi*, particularly amongst the more leisured and financially comfortable. Indeed, a strong case can be made for the urban Victorian *fin-de-siècle* as a seedbed for seekers: think of the metaphysical and geographical wanderings of Aleister Crowley (1875–1947), who proclaimed a 'new aeon' in 1904, or of H.P. Blavatsky (1831–91; see Tingay, Chapter 2). Similarly, sites such as Glastonbury and Iona (Bowman, Monteith, Chapters 5 and 6), and colonies for art and lifestyle experiment (Green, Chapter 3), have been foci for adventurous groups throughout the twentieth century, as have Druidry and *ad hoc* nature worship (Harvey, Chapter 9) since the Romantic era. Vernacular therapies and heterodox healing systems (Hedges and Beckford, Chapter 10; Hamilton, Chapter 11) have a similarly lengthy historical pedigree (Cooter [ed.], 1988). For example, the London publisher Rider had a series entitled 'Mind and Body Handbooks' in print before World War I, with titles like *Nature's Help to Happiness*, *The Power of Self-Suggestion*, *How to Keep Fit: an Unconventional Manual*, and *Studies in Self-Healing, or Cure by Meditation* (Colville, 1911: end pages). And its journal the *Occult Review* (published for some fifty years from 1905) was concurrently addressing most of the subject-matter to be found in contemporary magazines like *Kindred Spirit* (founded 1987), or on 'New Age' and 'Mind Body and Spirit' bookshelves today:

> Occultism, Hypnotism, Magic, Psychic Phenomena, Telepathy, Reincarnation, World Memory, Planetary Influence, Dreams, Multiple Personality, The Occult in English Literature, Religious Mysticism, &c., &c. (advertisement in Colville, 1911: end pages)

The same point could be made by reference to the Findhorn community in Scotland, a rural colony of several hundred seekers (Sutcliffe, forthcoming, 2000). All of Rider's themes and more featured, and feature, in the eclectic religiosity which informs this famous experiment in alternative spirituality begun in 1962. Predominating interests at Findhorn since the founders first came together in the mid-1950s have veered between gnostic meditation and mediumistic contact (including UFOs), positive thinking, the study of occult philosophies and healing and 'growth' activities. In the 1960s Findhorn was known chiefly for its organic – even magical – garden; in the 1970s, as a 'New Age' centre; and more recently, as a 'spiritual community'. Whatever its official title, Findhorn's underlying concerns remain more or less constant, only taking on different nuances and impressions according to shifting trends in spirituality and contemporary culture.

Historical perspective shows that the prevailing stance in all cases – amongst *fin-de-siècle* seekers and post-Sixties therapists alike; in the Edwardian journalism of the *Occult Review* as in today's *Kindred Spirit*; in diverse enclaves and centres – concerns the exploration and application of personal religiosity. Typically termed 'spirituality', such religiosity can be seen as a practical and flexible resource for the everyday world that is simultaneously goal-oriented action, re-sensitisation to the realms of the 'magical' and 'unexplained' and a label for a popular psychological–expressivist hermeneutic.

VERNACULAR RELIGION

Some very helpful insights in relation to alternative spirituality can be found in the study of vernacular religion. Related to 'folk' and 'popular' definitions of religion, this broad field has been delineated in different ways in different academic disciplines (Yoder, 1974), but more often than not it has simply been ignored. Ignoring a field of study is a way of demoting it, making value judgements as to what constitutes 'worthy' objects of study. We feel that it is important to question some of the implicit and explicit assumptions both generally and in the academy as to what constitutes 'real' or 'proper' belief, both in relation to vernacular religion and contemporary spirituality.

Some of the neglect of popular belief has sprung from a rather 'literalist', text-oriented attitude that suspects or dismisses material culture, ritual or custom. Academic studies of religions, or religions as taught in schools and colleges, for example, sometimes tend to be 'bookish' versions of traditions. While this may be seen as a necessary pedagogic device, both students and the traditions themselves are done a great disservice if we give the impression that this skeletal form is all there is to it. The diversity within religious traditions, the role of vernacular religion and the individual 'spin' on religion are all there and deserve to be acknowledged. That converts to belief systems as varied as Buddhism, Islam, and Paganism consistently say 'It's not a religion, it's a way of life' speaks volumes about a previously impoverished understanding of what 'religion' is and how it functions in everyday life. Meanwhile, more functionalist studies of religion have largely ignored aspects of belief and praxis which have not obviously promoted their presuppositions concerning the purpose of religion. Religion is as likely to be divisive as cohesive; individuals shape religion as well as being shaped by it.

Academic studies of religion, then, have tended to concentrate on 'official' religion, concerned primarily with theology, philosophy and group ritual. 'Popular' and 'folk' views and practices outside this fairly narrow focus have been treated as quaint, mistaken, superstitious or deviant, depending on the context. However, the reality and diversity of religion resides in 'the totality of all those views and practices of religion that exist among the people apart from and alongside the strictly theological and liturgical forms of the official religion' (Yoder, 1974: 14): a convenient definition of 'folk' religion. Some have used this term in a derogatory sense, but it might more positively be seen as a way of designating an integral aspect of religious culture which acknowledges the practice as well as the theory of religion.

While Yoder's definition developed in a Christian milieu, it can be applied in any tradition in which there is a sense (emically or etically) of there being a hegemonic official or authentic 'version' (Vrijhof and Waardenburg, 1979). Furthermore, as Primiano (1995: 41) has commented, 'One of the hallmarks of the study of religion by folklorists has been their attempt to do justice to belief and lived experience'. Particular aspects of folklore studies which complement the study of religion and alternative spirituality include: the refusal to privilege written over oral forms; the understanding that 'folk', 'popular' or 'unofficial' beliefs are an integral part of people's conceptual world and not simply wilful aberrations; the recognition that belief spills over into every aspect of behaviour; and the appreciation of the dynamic nature of 'tradition', which has been characterised by folklorist Henry Glassie as 'the creation of the future out of the past' (1995: 395).

In addition, folklorists' attention to the use of narrative in various forms, particularly as legend (stories which are told as true) and memorate (stories based on personal experience), are invaluable in relation to alternative religious phenomena, providing insights into the world view of groups and individuals for whom there is no offical spokesperson or recognised 'canon' of literature. Particularly helpful here is Bennett's (1989: 291) characterisation of the multifunctional 'belief story' as an informal story which enunciates and validates the current beliefs and experiences of a given community. Here, the 'grand narrative' which frames different world views is refracted through many little, everyday, not-so-grand narratives: aetiological legends (how the robin got a red breast; how the stones got to Stonehenge; 'Karma!'), corroborative legends ('Twas only the statue on his dashboard saved him'; 'Synchronicity!'; 'When the Pupil is ready the Master appears'), or personal experience narratives ('we had a miracle down here just the other week'; '. . . and then I realised I had been a Scot in a previous life').

It might be argued that the term 'folk' religion, precisely because of its possible negative or judgemental connotations, should be abandoned in favour of 'vernacular' religion (see Chapter 5) – 'religion as it is lived: as humans encounter, understand, interpret and practise it' (Primiano, 1995: 44). But whatever precise term is chosen – vernacular, folk, popular – it is evident that subject-matter and theory overlap considerably with those of the scholar of alternative spirituality.

RELIGION AND THE INDIVIDUAL

There is much talk of the contemporary 'privatisation' of religion. Un-doubtedly, the outward appearance of religion has changed and there is – in Britain, Western Europe and America – more consumer choice in religion than ever before. One of the features that has made the twentieth-century tapestry of religion so interesting is that more people have greater access to more forms of religion simultaneously than at any other period. While some use 'spiritual supermarket' as a derogatory term, it can be seen as an accurate reflection of the current situation, with the emphasis on variety and choice. Thus, in our *fin-de-siècle* emporium, Irish Catholic nuns are enhancing their devotions with Buddhist meditation, Anglicans are learn-ing spiral dances and Druids are teaching Neuro Linguistic Programming. Individual religion or spirituality in the modern world can be a very personal package, and this must be taken into account in formulating a useful model of religion. One such working model (Bowman, 1992) under-stands 'religion' as the sum of 'official', vernacular or folk, and individual cultural forms and expressions. It is a dynamic interaction of beliefs, practices, attitudes, rationales, narratives, perceptions of efficacy and personal experience.

The language of alternative spirituality in the 1980s and 1990s empha-sised 'taking responsibility for your own spiritual life', 'doing what feels right', 'seeing what works for you'. But we should not assume that such 'picking and mixing' is anything new: several essays in the present collection demonstrate quite the reverse. Nor is this phenomenon limited to 'alter-native' spirituality. Realistic observation suggests that this is precisely what people always do – or at least incline towards – in their splicings and conjoinings of deities, saints, calendar customs, doctrines and rites (Tho-mas, 1971; Hempton, 1988; Hutton, 1996). As always, efficacy and personal experience form the empirical basis of people's faith. Hence what is different about contemporary spirituality, it might be argued, is not the role of individual or vernacular religion, but the relative strength and social significance of official religion. In the most customised developments, the individual is fed by and feeds upon a gamut of traditions, old and new, in line with the decline of any one widely accepted or recognised official form.

'SPIRITUALITY'

Spirituality . . . has become a kind of buzz-word of the age . . . 'I'm trying to cultivate my spiritual side', people say; or, 'I'm learning to connect with my spirituality' . . . The spiritual search, whatever that may mean – and it means myriad things to different people – has become a dominant feature of late twentieth-century life. (Brown, 1998: 1)

By now it should be clear that what is articulated in the following pages is less a matter of 'religion', officially conceived, than of 'spirituality'. Certainly this term is now in common use: A. King (1996: 343), for example, remarks upon its 'extraordinary popularity . . . and . . . proliferation . . . in courses, conferences, discussions, journals and books'. Spirituality – at least in the alternative and vernacular forms portrayed in this volume – can be understood as an emic repackaging of popular and vernacular religion to suit the peculiar conditions of industrial and post-industrial societies. In broad terms, what characterises its discourse and practice?

To begin with, a historical–comparative perspective reveals the absence – or at best, the merely weak presence – of the kinds of empirical feature associated with 'official' religion (and also the 'new' religion embodied in New Religious Movements), such as distinctive buildings, a dominant founder-figure, a foundational book or a uniquely authoritative 'canon', an acknowledged creed and determined body of ritual, and a more or less clear and unambiguous self-presentation. Only diluted versions of these various institutions are present in alternative spirituality: special rooms and 'spaces', multiple pioneers and gurus, a spectrum of texts, small groups and workshops, flexible ritual work. Self-presentation is a perennial issue: Pagans refute the 'New Age' tag, Heathens refute the 'Pagan' tag. Few wish now to be associated with generic labels like 'occultism', a pursuit endorsed by early influential figures such as Dion Fortune or Alice Bailey, say; but many happily embrace 'Celtic'. Perhaps a common feature is the preference for ideals of self-determination and agency over more 'official' constraints of institutional membership and ideological boundary.

Furthermore, the rhetoric of spirituality tends to spurn religion(s).

Recalling his early adulthood, one prominent writer and workshop leader writes: 'I had little respect for the religious institutions and priestly hierarchies' (Bloom, 1990: 2), and remembers his school vicar as 'an extraordinarily boring man!' (Bloom, 1993: 18). One activist even speaks of religion as 'one of the greatest forces for evil at work in the world today' (Thompson, in Spangler and Thompson, 1991: 176). By way of contrast, Shallcrass (1996: 65) notes that 'many druids have preferred to portray Druidry as a philosophy, an ethical code, or a way of life, rather than a religion' (1996: 66), his own preferred term being 'spiritual path' (idem). Indeed, from Hodgkinson's (1993: 108) self-help perspective: 'You can be genuinely spiritual without ever going near a church or place of worship and, conversely, go to church, synagogue or mosque several times a week without ever understanding what spirituality is all about.'

Nor is this kind of juxtaposition a recent phenomenon. Findhorn founder Dorothy Maclean (1980: 12–13) opted for 'spiritual unfoldment' as the focus of her life in the late 1940s, and went on to explore many 'spiritual' groups (the inverted commas are hers) of the day. One 1930s editorial in the *Occult Review* proposed setting up a 'Spiritual League' to 'weld together . . . scattered spiritual units'[1] (meaning groups and individuals); another noted the increasing popularity of 'the type of literature which deals with the spiritual quest'[2]. And H.P. Blavatsky's former secretary, G.R.S. Mead, included a chapter entitled 'On the Track of Spirituality' in his book *Some Mystical Adventures* (Mead, 1910: 148*ff.*), published before World War I.

These early thoughts chime well with a certain strand of gnostic-psychological experience within the field:

> By 'spiritual experience' I do not mean abnormal happenings – these may or may not occur – but a life of rest, of poise and balance, of peaceful understanding, an inner recognition of the great truths and great powers which are hidden all around us, and which, when brought within the immediate consciousness of a man, lead to his co-operating with them in the divine scheme of things. (Mead, 1910: 297)

U. King (1997: 667–8) has continued in this vein, understanding 'spirituality' to be a 'universal codeword' with 'emphasis placed on the subject, on the discovery of the self and a more differentiated understanding of human psychology'. This is hardly the language of 'official' religion, and indeed it is a moot point if there is traditional theological content at all in the more secularised spiritualities discussed here (see Puttick, Bruce and Heelas, Chapters 12–14), which – as King suggests – wrap what little 'god talk' they contain in strategies and explanations from the worlds of psychology and therapy.

Hence 'spirituality' implies a kind of 'halfway house' between on the one hand 'official', heavily institutionalised religion, and on the other, the variegated lifestyles and niche cultures of modernity. It promises its exponents the best of both worlds – the religious and the profane – while remaining always somewhat equivocal and contingent with regard to 'ultimate' allegiances. That is, a particular 'spiritual path' might just as easily take in bodywork and psychotherapy as, say, more fully-blown denominational rituals, serially or even concurrently. The determinant factors in each case stem from the interplay between the personal tastes and inclinations of individuals, 'softer' cultural trends, and 'harder' socioeconomic forces. Precisely because of its adaptation to this vortex of influences, spirituality represents not only a pragmatic, but a strategically powerful, resource for mobile individuals in the modern world.

But just as 'religion' as an abstract category is open to critique (McCutcheon, 1995; Fitzgerald, 1997), it might be as well to problematise our representation of 'spirituality' from the beginning. Is it not more accurately the case that, rather than a monolithic 'spirituality', there are actually any number of variegated 'spiritual cultures' abroad in the modern world? Finer analysis will in due course certainly be required, but several of the more prominent varieties – if we take this line – are already addressed in one way or another in this book: Theosophical, Jungian, 'New Age', Pagan, Celtic, Expressivist, Humanistic and Holistic. These categories in turn beg the final question: in what way can the spirituality portrayed in this collection be said to be 'alternative'?

CONTEXTUALISING 'ALTERNATIVE'

One of our aims in this book is to put 'alternative spirituality' in perspective, both in terms of where it has come from and where it seems to be heading. For assuredly, these spiritual trends have not appeared from nowhere; their seeds were planted long ago. A number of chapters (e.g. Green, Tingay) show how late-nineteenth and early-twentieth-century ideas and praxis have 'trickled down'. What in recent scholarly history has been frequently considered marginal or eccentric (be it Theosophy, Jungian psychology, vernacular religion, or the idea of 'spiritual growth' and 'personal development') can be seen at the end of the twentieth century to have contributed to the world views of significant numbers of practitioners. Considerable acculturation has ensued.

Hence any talk of 'alternative' spirituality begs the question of normativity in contemporary religion. But the older model of 'mainstream' religion(s), based on a particular view of 'official', 'real', 'proper', 'legitimate' or 'functional' religion, has been widely problematised – for reasons we have in part indicated above. It is now inappropriate to regard such phenomena as vernacular religion, New Religious Movements, alternative spirituality and the individual spiritual quest either through the lens of one version – the official version – of one religious tradition, or through the lens of a sociology of deviancy. They are all part of the contemporary religious scene, and as such equally worthy objects of study.

The flip side of the coin is that we must review the boundaries of what can now be considered 'alternative'. Certainly, from Theosophy to 1990s Paganism, everything carries to some degree a charge of emic dissidence and opposition *vis-à-vis* prominent cultural formations, whether religious or secular. But there is also a weaker sense of 'alternative' as that which is merely 'variant' or 'other', an interpretation which highlights issues of choice and option noted earlier. Modern expressions of alternative spirituality can usefully be situated on a continuum between these different stances, where 'alternative' represents at one pole opposition, and at the other, option. Charted chronologically, it might even be possible to detect periods of ebb and flow between respective tendencies. With regard to the present situation, burgeoning scholarly teaching and research interests in New Religious Movements, New Age, Paganism and contemporary spirituality would seem to bear out the claim that, contrary to predictions that 'New Age' would 'go mainstream', 'now it's as if the mainstream is going New Age' (cited in Ferguson, 1994: 16). Genuine challenge or creeping acculturation? Time will tell.

In any case, forms of religion and modes of religiosity continue to change and evolve. The 'novelty' of much of what is happening is to some extent illusory. Some aspects were simply unobserved or not thought worthy of comment in the past. Media exposure, global communications, popularisation and commodification are presenting beliefs, groups, practices, ideas and artefacts to a new and wider audience, as well as putting a fresh 'spin' on them. In this regard it is location and profile, rather than content and structure, that have changed. The existence of a New Age Foundation Diploma in Tasseography (teacup reading) which is said to 'further your development as a New Age Counsellor'; the repackaging of spiritual healing as Reiki; the popularisation of shamanic, magical and other *virtuoso* techniques and roles: these and countless other strategies are indicative of the trend towards formalising and marketing traditions that were previously informally or privately transmitted and practised, or pursued in quite different cultural contexts.

NOTES

1. 'Linking Up', *Occult Review* LVI/1 (July, 1932): 2–7.
2. *The London Forum* (temporary title of *Occult Review*) LXII/4 (October, 1935): 219.

BIBLIOGRAPHY

Bednarowski, M., 1991: 'Literature of the New Age: a Review of Representative Sources', *Religious Studies Review* 17/3: 209–16.

Bennett, G., 1989: ' "Belief Stories": The Forgotten Genre', *Western Folklore* 48: 4: 289–311.

Bloom, W., 1990: *Sacred Times: A New Approach to Festivals* (Forres: Findhorn Press).

—— 1993: 'Practical Spiritual Practice', *One Earth* (Findhorn Foundation) 12: 18–21.

Bowman, M., 1992: 'Phenomenology, Fieldwork and Folk Religion', British Association for the Study of Religions Occasional Paper No. 6.

Brown, M., 1998: *The Spiritual Tourist: A Personal Odyssey Through the Outer Reaches of Belief* (London: Bloomsbury).

Colville, W., 1911: *Ancient Mysteries and Modern Revelations* (London: William Rider).

Cooter, R., ed., 1988: *Studies in the History of Alternative Medicine* (London: Macmillan).

Davie, G., 1994: *Religion in Britain since 1945 – Believing without Belonging* (Oxford: Blackwell).

Ferguson, M., 1994: 'Whatever happened to the Age of Aquarius?', *Kindred Spirit* 3(4): 14–16.

Fitzgerald, T., 1997: 'A Critique of "Religion" as a Cross-cultural Category', *Method and Theory in the Study of Religion* 9/2: 91–110.

Glassie, H., 1995: 'Tradition', *Journal of American Folklore* 108: 395–412.

Hempton, D., 1988: 'Popular Religion 1800–1986', in Thomas, T., ed., *The British: Their Religious Beliefs and Practices 1800–1986* (London: Routledge, pp. 181–210).

Hodgkinson, L., 1993: *The Personal Growth Book: Dozens of Ways to Develop your Inner Self* (London: Piatkus).

Hufford, D., 1995: 'The Scholarly Voice and the Personal Voice: Reflexivity in Belief Studies', *Western Folklore* 54 (1): 57–76.

Hutton, R., 1996: *The Stations of the Sun: A History of the Ritual Year in Britain* (Oxford: Oxford University Press).

King, A., 1996: 'Spirituality: Transformation and Metamorphosis', *Religion* 26 (4): 343–51.

King, U., 1997: 'Spirituality' in Hinnells, J., ed., *A New Handbook of Living Religions* (Oxford: Blackwell, pp. 667–81).

Maclean, D., 1980: *To Hear the Angels Sing* (Forres: Findhorn Press).

McCutcheon, R., 1995: 'The Category "Religion" in Recent Publications: a Critical Survey', *Numen* 42/3: 284–309.

Mead, G., 1910: *Some Mystical Adventures* (London: John M. Watkins).

Primiano, L., 1995: 'Vernacular Religion and the Search for Method in Religious Folklife', *Western Folklore* 54: 37–56.

Shallcrass, P., 1996: 'Druidry Today', in Hardman, C., and Harvey, G., eds, *Paganism Today* (London: Thorsons, pp. 65–80).

Spangler, D., and Thompson, W., 1991: *Reimagination of the World: a Critique of the New Age, Science and Popular Culture* (Santa Fe, NM: Bear and Co).

Sutcliffe, S., 1998: ' "New Age" in Britain: an Ethnographical and Historical Exploration', unpublished PhD thesis, The Open University.

Sutcliffe, S., 'A Colony of Seekers: Findhorn in the 1990s', *Journal of Contemporary Religion* (forthcoming 2000).

Thomas, K., 1971: *Religion and the Decline of Magic* (London: Weidenfeld and Nicolson).

Vrijhof, P., and Waardenburg, J., (eds), 1979: *Official and Popular Religion: Analysis of a Theme for Religious Studies* (The Hague: Mouton).

Yoder, D., 1974: 'Toward a Definition of Folk Religion', *Western Folklore* 33/1: 2–15.

York, M., 1997: 'New Age and the Late Twentieth Century' (review article), *Journal of Contemporary Religion* 12 (3): 401–19.

Part 1: People

1

'Wandering Stars':
Seekers and Gurus in the Modern World
Steven Sutcliffe

I was born under a wanderin' star
(Lee Marvin, 1969: *Paint Your Wagon*)

INTRODUCTION: THE HINTERLANDS OF RELIGION

Lee Marvin's paean to the wandering life reflects an American expansivity –
or restlessness – of spirit, as common to the Pilgrim Fathers as it is to the
cowboy movie. Veteran 'New Age' protagonist David Spangler is describing
something similar when he says that 'it's restful for the eye to move from up
close to a receding horizon, which draws the spirit out'.[1] In the post-war period
such behaviour typifies the wanderings of the Beats – whom Prothero (1996:
19) calls 'wandering seekers of mystical visions and transcendence' – as well as
the 'freaks' and hippies, for whom life 'on the road' – to invoke the title of Jack
Kerouac's late-1950s novel – could now unfold just as well psychologically
(and chemically) as geographically. Ken Kesey, for example, roamed the USA
in the 1960s with his Beat/Dada ensemble 'The Merry Pranksters', travelling
in a bus with the word 'Further' rather than any particular placename on its
destination board (Webb, 1976: 444–6). Others preferred to head east in
significant numbers, leading one activist, Michael Murphy, founder in 1962
of the Esalen Institute in California, to describe a 'third wave' of post-war
seekers after the Beats and hippies: the orientalised *sadhak* (from *sadhu/*
Sanskrit, 'holy person'), whose focus is now less drug-aided 'inner' exploration
than meditative consciousness (cited in Brown, 1998: 194).

Seeking, sampling, exploring – or, more bluntly, 'shopping', 'touring',
'scavenging': whatever the precise term used, these kinds of spiritual
bricolage have become increasingly commonplace, even mainstream, strategies in post-1960s America and modern cultures in general. Roof (1993)
even characterises a whole generation in these terms: the post-war 'baby
boomers', he claims, are a 'generation of seekers'.

As in the USA, so in Britain (and elsewhere in Europe),[2] where post-war countercultural and popular cultural developments have stimulated latent currents of 'seekership'. Consider two brief British examples. At the end of the 1960s, 'Gandalf's Garden' in Chelsea, London, described itself as an 'experimental, spiritually hip community evolving a lifestyle and producing a mystical scene magazine' (Strachan [ed.], 1970: 20). It included a:

> shop and meeting place selling hand-made goods, occult books, exotic teas and health snacks; also free food and free notice board, yoga classes and weekly mantra meditations, talks, gurus, occultists, yogis, seekers for the miraculous. (ibid.: 20)

The excited jumble of phenomena in this entry from an early directory of multiple religiosity in and on the fringes of the British counterculture reflects the fierce cultural flux of the day, in which multiple realms and identities were flung together in a blitz of cultural mix-and-match. A little later, in the counterculture's wake, ordered – even serial – explorations became commonplace. Consider my own serendipitous quest of the 1980s:

> I became a regular reader of *Peace News* . . . and the anarchist periodical *Freedom*. Under the influence of books by the dissident psychiatrists R.D. Laing and David Cooper, I moved [from Bristol] to Edinburgh to work as a volunteer in a community house . . . I adopted a wholefood and vegetarian lifestyle, and lived in communal and co-operative households. I consulted . . . the *I Ching* and Tarot cards, I undertook a sporadic Zen meditation practice, I struggled with T'ai Chi Chuan. I seriously considered converting to Tibetan Buddhism. I became apprenticed to a craft shoemaker who followed Rudolf Steiner's Anthroposophy. Later still I investigated Gestalt therapy, assertiveness training and men's consciousness-raising groups . . . In short, I sought. (Sutcliffe, 1998: 1–2)

In the 1990s such hypersyncretic splicings of ideas and techniques scarcely raise an eyebrow. The annual 'Mind–Body–Spirit' festival,[3] for example, has writ large the themes and activities of 'Gandalf's Garden', while a dizzying range of vernacular variations upon my own psycho-spiritual samplings is daily enacted, in both strong and weak forms, amongst the population at large. Some practitioners congregate at specialist sites, such as the Findhorn community, 'a sort of spiritual supermarket, where you can pick and mix and try to find something which suits you',[4] or they may have felt themselves 'drawn' mysteriously by the 'spiritual magnet' of Glastonbury (Bowman, 1993: 29–30); or they may congregate at St James's, Piccadilly, London, for 'Alternatives' evenings (York, 1995: 230–1, 234–5). Others browse the bookshops, where nearly one-fifth of all religious titles published in the UK in the 1990s has been classified as 'occult' (Bruce, 1996: 199). There is also plenty of opportunity to attend lectures, learn specific techniques of visualisation, meditation and other ritual work in small groups and through sympathetic networks, and sample workshops – sometimes residential – in a plethora of skills, from Reiki healing to firewalking.[5] As William Bloom (1993a: 82), an activist associated both with Findhorn and 'Alternatives', puts it:

> Not so many decades ago . . . most seekers would have been limited to what their local church or temple had to offer. Today we need not be restricted to the teachings of the religion and culture into which we were born. *All the spiritual traditions and cosmologies are now available to us.* (my emphasis)

Nor is this pick-and-mix approach peculiar to alternative enclaves or to consumer subcultures. Particularly since the 1893 'World's Parliament of Religions' in Chicago, hyperecumenicalism has created considerable opportunities for inter-faith exchange (Braybrooke, 1992), and the exploration by 'singular seekers'[6] of the differing liturgies and lifestyles of various denominations has become a far from atypical feature of modern Christianity. To take one popular example, *At a Service Near You* (Gledhill, 1996), a volume based on the author's attendance at around two hundred different church services in the UK, is lightheartedly likened in the foreword to 'an ecclesiastical version of *The Good Pub Guide*' (*ibid.*: vii).

Elsewhere the discourse of 'spirituality' has entered popular culture. In Sunday newspapers and consumer magazines, Hollywood actress Shirley MacLaine has spoken of her 'spiritual search',[7] and classical musician Evelyn Glennie has described herself as a 'spiritual person . . . fascinated by all sorts of religions', her strategy being to 'pick from them what I want'.[8] In his contributions to a reader on 'New Age' which accompanied a Channel Four television series, William Bloom (1991: 221, xvi) writes of 'our instinctive spirituality' and of the 'right to explore spirituality in total freedom'.

A marked feature of these developments is that the preferred terms are 'spirituality' and 'spiritual' rather than 'religion' and 'religious'. Eileen Caddy, a founder of the Findhorn community, makes this distinction when she recalls of Peter, her husband-to-be in the 1950s, that ' "religious" was not the way to describe him. I knew he didn't go to church, but I sensed a commitment to something spiritual' (Caddy, 1988: 19). Spirituality, understood as an expressive and holistic mode of personal behaviour encouraging strategic interaction on the part of the practitioner between natural and supernatural realms, is an attractive proposition for modern individualists, since its fuzzy boundaries and malleable praxis allow it to occupy ambiguous, multivalent ground between realms elsewhere more clearly categorisable (and hence potentially open to stigma) as 'religious' and 'secular'.[9]

Thus the way in which religion has been expressed in the modern world by individuals and what we might call 'elective collectives' – specialist groups, communities, enclaves – has gradually become detached both from doctrinal regularity and from strong institutional structure. Increasingly, people wishing to express or practise a style of religiosity appropriate to the quickened tempo and cultural promiscuity of high modernity might recognise Lee Marvin's popular song as being curiously relevant to their own situation at the counter of pick-and-mix religion – that 'world of options, lifestyles, and preferences' (Bruce, 1996: 233). Indeed, a veritable 'spiritual supermarket' (Bloom, 1993a: 82) is now available, in which hitherto unfamiliar, exotic or avant-garde figures – spiritual teachers and 'gurus' (Storr, 1996; Rawlinson, 1997) – have pitched their stalls alongside more mainstream authorities. Emulating the mythologised lifestyles of the wandering songster on the American frontier, or the post-war Beats and hippies, many contemporary religionists have become peripatetic and hypermobile.

SEEKERS AND GURUS AS 'SPIRITUAL VIRTUOSI'

In its most pedestrian sense 'quest' connotes simply 'seeking' or 'search'; but does it not already . . . evoke an atmosphere of romance, of poetry, of things spiritual? (Mead, 1910: 285–6)

However, these post-war developments, whether countercultural or popular-cultural, were in fact anticipated from around the latter half of the nineteenth century by the careers of individuals involved in the closely interrelated networks of spiritualism, psychic research, theosophy, occultism and ceremonial magic that together make up the core historical constituencies of alternative spirituality.[10] For example, the Theosophist scholar G.R.S. Mead identified a variety of alternative religious functionaries active within what he saw as a 'rising psychic tide' in Edwardian London. These included:

seers and soothsayers and prophets, pythonesses, sibyls and prophetesses, tellers of dreams and of omens, mantics of every description and by every sort of contrivance; astrologists and even alchemists; professors of magical arts and ceremonies; cosmologists and revelationists. (Mead, 1913: 236)

Mead himself founded in 1909 the appropriately named 'Quest Society', the motto of which was 'Seek, and ye shall find' and the objective 'To promote investigation and comparative study of religion, philosophy, and science, on the basis of experience' (Mead, 1910: 285). This last clause was crucial, for Mead emphasised in his inaugural address to the society in Kensington Town Hall that 'we are not in search of knowledge only . . . our seeking is also for deeper and intenser life' (ibid., 290).

The Quest Society endured into the inter-war years, ending its days in the early 1930s as the 'Search Society'. By now much else was afoot: Landau's (1945; orig. 1935) seminal record of 'modern mystics, masters and teachers' active in Europe included such figures as the Theosophical 'children' Rudolf Steiner and Jiddu Krishnamurti; the mage/philosopher pairing of Gurdjieff and Ouspensky; and one of the first Indian gurus in Britain, Meher Baba. Tellingly, Landau explains in the new edition of his book that its bestselling success stems from the fact that 'people are always eager to learn from the spiritual experiences of a fellow seeker' (ibid.: 7).

Now, as I have argued elsewhere (Sutcliffe, 1997), the 'seeker' is an essential component in modern alternative religiosity: indeed, the inherent fissiparity of seekership both explains the brittleness and extreme change-ability of these circles whilst allowing for a minimum collective behavioural norm. Seekers may be broadly defined as 'popular *virtuosi* able and willing to select, synthesise and exchange amongst an increasing diversity of religious and secular options and perspectives' (ibid., 105). Seekers are of course active to a degree within all religions. However, amongst traditional and even new religions, the seeker as a pure type is necessarily in the minority, being merely one amongst several far more structurally embedded models of religious participation (think of the roles of 'member', 'regular', 'convert') within securely institutionalised and firmly boundaried symbolic systems.

It is within the far more fluid and deregulated arena of alternative spirituality that the act of seeking and the role of seeker flourish. Consider two cases briefly. The career of Glasgow-born painter Benjamin Creme (b.1922) exemplifies certain strains of alternative spirituality, its cross-fertilisation of 'oriental' and occult sources culminating in supernatural contact of a most heterodox kind:

[Creme] devoured the writings of Gurdjieff, Ouspensky, the Swamis Viveka-nanda, Sivananda and Yogananda; and, of course, Blavatsky and [Alice] Bailey. He studied meditation techniques, and came to the conclusion that he had mediumistic and healing powers . . . One day in 1959 . . . [he] received his first telepathic communication from one of the Hierarchy of Masters. (Brown, 1998: 12)

Since 1982, when Creme placed advertisements in newspapers announcing the imminent appearance of one of these 'Masters' – 'The Christ', no less – on the world stage, he has lectured and published extensively on his 'telepathic' contacts. With functional similarity, but considerable difference in content and outcome, consider the post-countercultural odyssey of Philip Shallcrass, a Pagan Druid. His story of how he became a 'priest of the Goddess' (Shallcrass, 1998: 159*ff*.) takes in 'childhood experience of the spirit world' and his trials as a 'would-be medicine man' (including use of hallucinogenic drugs), before describing his exploration of ritual magic, entry into a Wiccan coven, peripatetic 'solo Druidry' and, finally, his founding of the British Druid Order.

As is immediately evident, a notable feature of 'seekership' (Campbell, 1972: 123) is a tendency for more experienced seekers to make available what they have accumulated by way of ideas and techniques to others who – just like themselves – are exploring alternative emporia where vernacular religion and alternative spirituality converge. In fact, insofar as seekers become models for action and a source of advice to others on the scene, they themselves come to function as 'exemplary persons' – an 'exemplary person' in this sense being 'one who by subtle, often nonverbal means shows he is "turned on" and is able to "turn on" others just by the radiance of his presence' (Ellwood, 1973: xv). 'Turning on' implies some kind of *transmission* of wisdom and expertise, the means of which may vary considerably: for example, 'specific training', 'making a technique of transformation available', 'initiation', and 'passing on a blessing' (Rawlinson, 1997: 35). In any case, the 'journeyman' seeker is on the way to becoming, in some measure at least, a 'guru',[11] albeit one whose catchphrase is far more likely to be something like 'try it' (Caddy, 1992: 11) or 'do what turns you on' (Bloom, 1993b: 19), rather than the well-documented authoritarianism of some fully-fledged religious leaders. That is, the authority of this variety of guru is likely to be far more attenuated than the latter's. Nevertheless, such gurus may still engender 'lineages' of their own, offering a diluted transmission through talks, workshops, retreats and the printed word, all the time trawling those same networks spun and maintained by seekers (York, 1995; Sutcliffe, 1997). Joyce Collin-Smith's experience, for example, gently exemplifies the situation: serially involved with Ouspenskian circles and Maharishi Mahesh Yogi (amongst others) in the 1950s and 1960s, she later began to offer her own classes in astrology. She describes herself as 'a kind of freelance, moving as I thought best, learning and occasionally giving talks, in the spheres with which I had made myself familiar' (Collin-Smith 1988: 197). And bumping into 'old associates' from earlier stages is part of the process: 'Clearly we were all joined together on "La Ronde" . . . our pathways were to cross and recross down the years' (ibid., 111).

As weak forms of institutionalisation periodically crystallise, a tension develops on the part of the seeker between the impulse to seek – that is, to keep on the move both geographically and metaphysically – and the need to stay put long enough adequately to receive the goods – the transmission – on offer in any particular instance. The same applies, in reverse, to the guru, who needs seekers' attention at least long enough to put across a message – by which time, of course, the different parties may have found a mutual need for each other that survives the powerfully fissiparous impulses of this arena of spiritual transactions.

To help flesh out these skeleton types of seeker and guru, let us consider in a little more detail the mid-century careers of two such 'spiritual virtuosi': Mary Swainson and J.G. Bennett.[12]

THE SEEKER: MARY SWAINSON

> Sometimes I was over-critical, so that I rejected a system of teaching because its idiom repelled me; at other times I was not critical enough. (Swainson, 1977: 204)

Mary Swainson (b.1908) grew up as an only child in Somerset vicarages. She studied geography at Exeter University in the late 1920s, and educational psychology at Oxford during the Second World War. Around this time she also underwent psychotherapeutic analysis (Swainson, 1977: 33*ff*). At Leicester University in the late 1940s she began a student counselling service, amongst the first of its kind in Britain. But alongside this distinguished mainstream career, Swainson had other interests. At Exeter she had become interested in psychical research (ibid., 203), and by the mid-1930s, she tells us, she had begun to 'read systematically the evidence and theories behind so-called "occult" knowledge':

> Beginning with Steiner, Ouspensky, Alice Bailey and Theosophy, the Christian Mystics and the classical Eastern sources, I studied some of the many different idioms which reiterate the Ageless Wisdom. Steadily I built up my own library. (ibid.)

As with Benjamin Creme, heterodox reading legitimated and then developed her interests. She recalls: 'Through reading . . . I found companionship, intellectual validation, and deepening of my previous gropings' (ibid.). But, as she notes in a remark typical of the folk epistemology of seekership, 'reading is only head-learning; the wisdom needs to be sifted, applied, and deeply felt' (ibid.).

And so her search came quietly out of the closet:

I discovered the existence of groups and societies in the outer world where one could speak openly of these matters. Part of several vacations I spent in London, exploring, testing out everything from spiritualism to psychic science. (ibid., 204)

After a few years of apparently open-ended exploration, Swainson made a commitment of sorts, if through a remarkably casual train of events:

I was browsing in a public library. Somehow my hand seemed led to touch an unknown book (many seekers have had this experience). It turned out to be the first publication of an esoteric group which, at long last, 'felt right' for me. (ibid.)

For some twenty years after the Second World War Swainson went to 'annual retreats where we were trained carefully in group meditation and spiritual experience' (ibid., 205). Significantly Swainson remarks that 'now I was no longer alone; at any time I could contact group members, and some of my most long-standing friendships have come in this way' (ibid.). In other words, she had balanced the intense solo dynamic of seekership through the peer-group confirmation of a social network.

Yet her commitment to this 'esoteric group' is a qualified one:

Quite early I was told (from the higher world) that 'We would not restrict you in any way', and *always* advised to follow my own inner light. It felt inwardly right to branch out, continuing to explore all possible schools and movements. (ibid.)

And branch out she did. She studied a 'postal course' called *An Introduction to Spiritual Science*, and in the 1950s and 1960s frequented the College of Psychic Studies in London, which she calls a 'gold-mine for all seekers' (ibid., 206). Like others, Swainson sampled Subud, an Indonesian mystical practice which became available in England through the efforts of the seeker-guru J.G. Bennett (see below), and she also explored systems of alternative healing like Radionics (ibid.).

She also met Ruth White (ibid., 207*ff.*) and became involved in the 1960s in the extended study of the content and methods of the communication claimed by White between herself and her discarnate spirit guide, 'Gildas'. A constituency of readers and students of the 'Gildas' material grew up over the decade, numbering some three hundred by 1969 (ibid., 214), and comprising a highly de-traditionalised mix of social roles and identities, including 'academics engaged in psychic research, educationists, psychologists of various schools, hippies, occultists, housewives [and] spiritualists' (White and Swainson, 1971: 33). In the course of disseminating this material more publicly in the early 1970s, Swainson came into contact with other significant small groups and organisations of the day, such as the Churches' Fellowship for Psychical and Spiritual Studies, the Seekers Trust, and Sir George Trevelyan's various activities (Swainson, 1977: 209–9). Many of these groups had been preoccupied with the idea of a 'New Age' and are a prime historical source of the so-called 'New Age movement' of the post-1970s (Sutcliffe, 1998). Swainson has continued her interests into the 1990s, when amongst other things she has been an adviser to a contemporary alternative health magazine, *Caduceus*.

The seeker as guru: J.G. Bennett

> The idea of search entered my consciousness. There was something that must be found, before there could be anything to be done. (Bennett, 1962: 46)

Writing of spiritual healing, Mary Swainson (1977: 206) remarks: 'As is usual in learning any skill . . . it is part of the process to be a patient first'. Translating this methodology, we could say that only those who have themselves sought – and who perhaps still seek – know the needs of other seekers. So we are here chiefly concerned with those gurus who explicitly acknowledge their status as time-served seekers, since it is the symbiotic relationship between seeker and guru that provides a rare element of structural predictability in the arena of alternative spirituality as a whole. Such a guru is J.G. Bennett (1897–1974), the 'thinker, writer, teacher' (Hinnells, 1991: 50) and 'spiritual maverick' (Rawlinson, 1997: 183).

Bennett's career must be understood in the light of a distinctive religiosity developed in the inter-war years under the influence of the Greek–Armenian 'modern-day gnostic and enigma' G.I. Gurdjieff, who:

> determined to find the explanation to various unusual phenomena such as faith-healing, clairvoyance and telepathy, began to search from a very early age, sometimes alone, and sometimes with a group he refers to as 'the seekers after truth'. (Hinnells, 1991: 137)

A former associate of Gurdjieff's in Russia, the 'searcher and teacher' P.D. Ouspensky (ibid., 313–4) had also travelled widely – in Egypt, Ceylon and India, for example. From 1921, Ouspensky gave public talks in London about his and Gurdjieff's ideas, to which many writers, intellectuals and liberal socialites of the day were attracted. To these came J.G. Bennett, who had previously become interested in Islamic mysticism while working for British Intelligence in Turkey after the 1914–18 war (Bennett, 1962: 37*ff.*) and who had already met there both Gurdjieff and Ouspensky, *en route* to Europe.

Bennett dramatically begins his autobiography – appropriately subtitled *The Story of a Search* – with an account of a near-death experience he underwent on being wounded towards the end of the war (Bennett, 1962: 13–14). He summarises this experience as 'as much a birth as a death – though I did not realize until much later that I had indeed died and been born again'. But, invalided out of action, Bennett became 'troubled' (ibid., 15): 'Why was I still alive? So many of my schoolfellows . . . had been killed and not I. Why not?'

Now in Istanbul, and reflecting upon the impression made upon him by devout Muslims, Bennett again became preoccupied with large philosophical questions such as 'What did I really wish to attain in my lifetime?' (ibid., 45). Far from being a solution, religion itself seemed to Bennett problematic: 'Everywhere I could see mutual exclusion, the denial of another's truth, the rejection of another's faith' (ibid.). He ruminates: 'I could not believe that any one religion could have the only truth and the whole truth. I could not turn for help to those who lived by the very exclusions that I wished to abolish in myself' (ibid.). Bennett's resolution of this quandary amounts to a seeker's creed: 'I vowed that I would never rest until I could find . . . the source of all religion and the unity of mankind' (ibid., 45–6). Bennett's ensuing 'spiritual quest' (ibid., 221) was to preoccupy him for the rest of his life, leading him from Sufism, through the teachings of Gurdjieff and Ouspensky, to Subud and various other teachers, and finally to Catholicism.

Rawlinson (1997: 185) has aptly characterised Bennett as 'a man of considerable intellect, fascinated by systems and formulæ, but given to sudden lurches'. Nevertheless, at the same time as he ransacked the esoteric systems of the day, Bennett acted as guru to other seekers. For example, he led his own study groups in and around London in the 1930s, based on his own interpretations of Gurdjieffian and Ouspenskian ideas. These endeavours culminated in the establishment of households for work and study: at Coombe Springs in South London in 1946, and in the Cotswolds in the early 1970s. In these models of what Bennett termed 'a spiritual community' (ibid., 224) he and his associates explored his own eclectic version of 'the Work' (as Gurdjieff's system was called). They were not short of interested participants: around two hundred associates in the late 1940s, and over four hundred a decade later (ibid., 251, 330).

THE SIGNIFICANCE OF SEEKERS AND GURUS

'I'm trying to cultivate my spiritual side', people say; or, 'I'm learning to connect with my spirituality.' (Brown, 1998: 1)

The roles of seeker and guru adopted by Swainson and Bennett were certainly not unique, but they were comparatively unusual in their day.

Since the 1960s, however, these roles have increasingly been acted out *en masse*. Evidence for this can be found in Roof's (1993) depiction of a post-war 'generation of seekers'; in Rawlinson's (1997) detailed compendium of contemporary gurus; in my own ethnographies of 'New Age' in Scotland in the 1990s (Sutcliffe, 1998); and in the narratives of virtuoso voyagers like St John (1977) in Human Potential circles, Forsyth (1993) amongst healers and psychics, McGrath (1996) in American 'New Age' circles, and Brown (1998) as a 'spiritual tourist'.

But apart from their intrinsic interest as modern religious identities, in what ways does the study of these 'wandering stars' contribute to an understanding of religion – specifically alternative spiritualities – in the modern world?

First, these variant models of religious praxis are becoming more widely available in the culture at large, closely tied in with notions of 'pick-and-mix' religion (Bruce, 1996: 233) and the predilections of the 'spiritual market consumer' (York, 1995: 1). Recall, for example, Shirley MacLaine's 'spiritual search' and Evelyn Glennie's self-identification as a 'spiritual person', cited earlier. In this regard, Campbell (1982: 235) persuasively argues that the real significance of the NRMs of the 1970s and 1980s lies in their role as harbingers of a 'more diffuse phenomenon . . . an ethos or cluster of values and beliefs which accords a general place to spirituality'. Indeed, Campbell (ibid., 236) notes the existence of a population of what he calls 'incipient seekers' – ' a sizeable number of people sympathetically disposed towards some form of spirituality but not participating members of any particular church'. More recently, Rose (1998: 15) has found that around two-thirds of his sample of subscribers to the Mind–Body–Spirit/'New Age' magazine *Kindred Spirit* 'follow more than one teaching at any one time', leading him to conclude that 'New Age spiritual practice is very much a self-led quest' (ibid.).

A fine example of the kind of personal stance exemplified by the seeker – and, because variegated and curious, structurally convenient for the guru also – is a response at the Findhorn community to my question 'How, if at all, would you describe your religious identity?' A single white-collar German woman in her mid-thirties replied:

> At the moment I tend towards eastern religions but I don't follow anything specific, I like to pick out what is true for me and follow that and use it.[13]

Almost every word and phrase in this brief statement reflects key facets of seekership. 'At the moment' makes clear the radically contingent nature of the respondent's choice, while the phrases 'tend towards' and 'don't follow anything specific' confirm a stance in some tension with traditional models of religious commitment. Espousing 'eastern religions' – although now a well-established alternative to both Christian denominations and secular world views – still remains an affirmation of religious heterodoxy in many if not most western cultures. To 'pick out' establishes the self-selection principle, while 'true for me' clearly implies a relativist stance on what has previously been considered a matter of life and death. Finally, to 'follow *that*' (i.e. only those bits 'true for me'), and to '*use* it', completes a picture of individualistic spiritual pragmatism that is ruthlessly accommodated to the cultural flux of the modern world.

And this is my second point: 'spiritual virtuosi' embody in the religious orbit the tensions and opportunisms of the modern social and economic order. J.G. Bennett, for example, was acutely sensitive to the bigger picture. In war-torn Istanbul he grappled with the seminal questions of a diaspora world:

> Where was I at home? In England, where I was born? In America, where my mother came from? In Turkey, where I felt at ease? Somewhere in Asia, where there might be a source of truth of which I knew nothing? (Bennett, 1962: 45-6)

The vivid multiculturality of post-war Turkey prompts some simple but crucial reflections:

> All day long I was dealing with different races: English, French, Italian, Greek, Armenian, Turkish, Kurdish, Russian, Arab, Jew and people so mixed as to be of no race at all. Each and every one was convinced of the superiority of his own people. How could anyone be right and all the rest wrong? (ibid., 46)

Around the same time, at Gurdjieff's experimental community near Paris, the grandly-entitled 'Institute for the Harmonious Development of Man', a tough regime of manual labour and neo-behaviourist psychology sought to prepare individuals' psyches for a Europe in transition. In a 1924 article in the *New York Times*, a resident described the principle of 'irregularity' operative in the community:

> It is a place where habits are changed, fixed ideas are broken up, mechanical routines do not exist, and adaptability to ever-changing forms and modes of life is practised. (Pogson, 1987: 75)

The writer might have been describing the post-war condition of the continent itself. In any case, a visitor to this international community might be received by 'anybody, the editor of a London paper, a Harley

Street specialist, a court musician or a Russian lawyer' (ibid., 75–6). Nationalities, professions and occupations were all manifestly displaced in this experiment in 'harmonious development'.

Spiritual strategy or religious disarray? Assessments differ. Whereas Lofland and Stark (1965: 868–9) emphasise the seeker's 'difficulties' and 'discontent' – his 'floundering about among religions' – Straus (1976: 252) understands the seeker as a radical subject 'acting creatively . . . to construct a satisfying life' and tactically exploiting opportunities for 'life-change' (ibid., 253). In this view, far from being a victim of circumstance, and rather more than a merely passive exemplification of wider social trends, the seeker is in fact an opportunist and a strategist looking to turn to good advantage the perceived shortcomings of the day – the structural atomisation, social fragmentation, and de-traditionalisation of this 'age of extremes' (Hobsbawm, 1995).

But whether losers or winners, seekers actively – deliberately – undermine institutional forms, and this is my third point regarding their significance in the study of contemporary religion. As the inherent fissiparity of historical movements which have encouraged seekership demonstrates – Theosophy, Spiritualism, ceremonial magical orders, say – or as a more recent phenomenon – 'New Age' – reveals through its repeated failure to achieve the minimum profile of a viable religious movement (Sutcliffe, 1997), seekers either struggle to maintain organisational structures or repudiate them altogether. This is of course to turn on its head Weber's well-known statement that 'every hierocratic and official authority of a "church" . . . fights principally against all virtuoso-religion and against its autonomous development' (Gerth and Mills, 1970: 288). The tides have turned: virtuosity now has the upper hand, actively subverting institutionalisation *per se* rather than simply agitating for new or improved institutions (as do most NRMs).

The lack of concrete structure to regulate the diffuse collectivity of synthesisers, scavengers, and shoppers that constitutes the historical arena of seekers and gurus also helps to explain precisely why there is so much overlap, repetition and recycling of ideas and practices in these domains, as well as confusion and contention amongst practitioners and observers alike as to where, exactly, to draw the boundaries between sympathetic and contiguous currents such as Theosophy and Spiritualism in the late nineteenth century,[14] modern occultism and popular Indian religiosity,[15] or Paganism and 'New Age' in recent decades.[16]

Now, the experiential, autodidactic and amateurist models of study and learning favoured by the majority of seekers and gurus only contribute to these fuzzy structural contours, since the main thrust of their folk epistemology is towards the de-differentiation, de-classification and de-regulation of formal categories of knowledge and status. Hence, the basic message of the alternative healing and human potential networks of the 1980s, according to Ross (1992: 539), is that 'everyone has the potential to become the engineer/architect/designer of his or her own environment'. Nevertheless such populist claims on access to special states of consciousness and subtle experience are likely to sit awkwardly with the practical demands of the elite-oriented, highly-skilled methodology required actually to attain them in most religious traditions. So while something akin to a mass culture of virtuosity – as proposed by, amongst others, Bloom (1990: 8) when he writes 'I advise people not to be cowardly about their own spiritual authority', or Edwards (1993: 192) in her call for 'everyone to become a shaman, a metaphysician, a dream-weaver, a walker-between-worlds' – may yet take hold as a result of the increasing ideological dissemination in popular culture of the *idea* of spiritual virtuosity, its simultaneous dilution in potency may be inevitable, given that – as Weber baldly puts it – '"heroic" or "virtuoso" religiosity is opposed to mass religiosity' (Gerth and Mills 1970: 287). Thus, when the hero of a fictional reworking of Aleister Crowley's circle refers to himself as a 'spiritual aristocrat' (Wilson, 1963: 77), or when 'New Age' activist Spangler (1996: 46) describes himself as a 'freelance mystic', these identities gain allure and charisma precisely to the degree that they belong to a virtuosic avant-garde, and *not* to the popular mainstream. However, even if what actually obtains is not some 'universalization of charisma' but individualistic, user-friendly 'spiritual' praxis – variegated complexes of personal behaviour that are neither overtly religious nor resoundingly secular, but certainly heavily psychologised[17] – then such behaviour still has little to gain from cumbersome corporate institutions.

In fact the phenomenology of seekership and spiritual virtuosity in general correlates well with that 'disembedding of social institutions' which Giddens (1991: 16–21) claims to be a major characteristic of modernity. This we may understand as the sum of various social trends which prise both organisation and individual from existing loyalties, commitments and other marked indices of social 'belonging', through the inculcation of an ideology of autonomy and radical agency. Status, class, career, place and pattern of residence, peer-group, relationships, sexuality, self-identity: all may be to a greater or lesser degree thrown open to revision and reconfiguration.

Let me briefly indicate what I mean. In terms of social mobility – that is, movement between social classes – there has been considerable traffic in the post-war years, both inter- and intra-generational (Abercrombie *et al.*, 1988: 198*ff.*). The net effect is inevitably to soften the social cement binding individuals on the basis of occupation and attendant social mores. The well-known decline of heavy industry, and the concomitant growth in the information, service and leisure industries, only exacerbates this effect. Handy (1985: 8), for example, suggests we now pursue a 'portfolio of activities and relationships' in order to secure 'the package of things we want out of work and life'. Notice that this is effectively the 'supermarket' principle of contemporary spiritualities. Commitments – in work as in spirituality – become serial, perhaps even multiple;[18] but always provisional.

Also significant is a trend towards single households. More than a quarter (27%) of British households in 1996–7 were occupied by single people (ONS, 1998: 42), almost double the figure at the beginning of the 1960s. In England alone, the number of single-person owner-occupied homes trebled between 1977–8 and 1996–7 (ibid., 177). Significantly, the fastest growth area here was amongst younger people (under the age of forty-five). Now the evidence suggests that seeking, and alternative spirituality in general, is – at least post-1960s – largely an arena of younger single people. For example, York (1995: 191,183) reproduces figures from an 'occult' survey conducted in 1989 by the Leeds shop and contact centre 'The Sorcerer's Apprentice' which indicate that half its respondents were single people, and as many as 89% had become interested in occultism before the age of twenty-five: a very youthful and mobile constituency. York (1995: 191) also found from his own survey, in London, of a small Pagan group and a larger 'New Age' event that over half of each group comprised single people. Furthermore, 90% of attendees at the latter were aged between 18 and 49 (ibid., 180). At a larger Pagan gathering, over three-quarters of the assembly were also within this age-range (ibid.). Elsewhere, Rose (1998: 8) has found that nearly three-quarters (73%) of his sample of subscribers to *Kindred Spirit* were aged between 25 and 54. Younger single people, then, are particularly well-represented within contemporary alternative spiritualities, and in terms of their potential to 'disembed' (through age, relative lack of dependents and general mobility) are clearly well-positioned to exploit a seeker's lifestyle.

A related point concerns trends in sexual relationships that correlate with the 'soloist' lifestyle of contemporary seeking. The sharp fall in the marriage rate – particularly since 1970 – and the rise in cohabitation in the 1980s and 1990s is well-known. But two-fifths of the total number of marriages in 1995 were actually *remarriages* (ONS, 1998: 50), indicating that the numbers of first-time entrants into the marriage arena are dwindling. Indeed, 'serial' marriages and 'polyamoury' are amongst future behavioural models being forecast in the late 1990s:[19] self-explanatory modes of relationship which again bear comparison with my models of 'serial' and 'multiple' seeking (Sutcliffe, 1997).

CONCLUSION

I do my thing, and you do your thing.
I am not in this world to live up to your expectations
And you are not in this world to live up to mine.
You are you and I am I
and if by chance we find each other, it's beautiful.
If not, it can't be helped. (Perls, 1969: 4)

This well-known 'gestalt prayer' may be understood as a more psychologically-nuanced formulation of the theme of Lee Marvin's popular song with which this chapter began. More widely, it typifies the pragmatic grassroots ethos of spiritual virtuosity and its chief agents, the seekers and gurus: that is, if it works, good; if not, move on. Active down the century in specific – often adjoining – microcultures, more recently these individuals, like other cultural dissidents, are increasingly 'coming out', so to speak, in popular and mainstream culture.

The sum is that the 'spiritual culture' of individuals is now one of the few remaining constants in post-traditional religious life, for the whittling away of institutional bulk has the effect of exposing the individuals at the heart of the social process. Thus has a traditionally massive (in the sense of material structure and concrete presence) social institution – 'religion' – metamorphosed into a buzzing hive of virtuosic individualists: the 'wandering stars' of the title.

Some have already understood this. In 1922, Gurdjieff was asked by a participant at the Institute why, as part of their work, they were erecting temporary buildings rather than more enduring structures. The guru explained that this was because 'in a very short time everything will be different – everyone will be elsewhere. Nothing can be built permanently at this moment' (Pogson, 1987: 83).

NOTES

1. Opening address by Spangler (15 April 1995) at a conference at the Findhorn Community in Moray, Scotland, entitled 'The Western Mysteries: Which Way Today?'.
2. See the discussion of Amsterdam as a European countercultural centre in York, Chapter 7.
3. See Hamilton, Chapter 11.
4. Resident, quoted in 'Clan of the Outsiders', J. Hancox, The Guardian (8 July 1992), 'Society' section, p. 23.
5. See, for example, the ethnographies in Sutcliffe (1998).
6. See my typology of singular, serial and multiple seeking in Sutcliffe (1997). The singular seeker 'has inherited a tradition or . . . made a self-conscious decision to commit to one' (ibid.: 106), which s/he then pursues with self-conscious commitment and reflexivity.

7. Interview: 'The Force is With Her', *Scotland on Sunday*, 9 July 1997, 'Spectrum' section, p. 3.
8. Interview: 'Good Vibrations', *Face to Face* (Bank of Scotland consumer magazine), Summer 1997, p. 12.
9. Cf. King (1997: 667): 'Today the notion of spirituality is applied across different religious traditions; it is used inside and outside particular religions as well as in many inter-faith and secular contexts.'
10. Cf. Landau (1945), Howe (1972), Webb (1976), Oppenheim (1985), and Heelas (1996). Washington (1993) and Rawlinson (1997) take the founding of the Theosophical Society in 1875 by Blavatsky and Olcott (see Tingay, Chapter 2) as the defining moment in alternative spirituality.
11. See the exploratory models of Washington (1993), Storr (1996) and Rawlinson (1997), which variously naturalise this Sanskrit term. According to Hinnells (1988: 138), 'guru', originally indicating 'a brahman who instructed young brahmans in the sacred lore', 'has come to mean a religious teacher of any kind who has undertaken to give personal instruction to a pupil or disciple.' Storr (1996: xi) adopts the very broad definition of 'spiritual teacher', adding that 'most [gurus] claim the possession of special spiritual insight based on personal revelation'. Washington's (1993) sceptical narrative of personalities in the Theosophical and Gurdjieff–Ouspenskian lineages is implicitly a case study of the 'western guru', a phrase the author attributes to Andrew Rawlinson (ibid., viii), who for his part characterises gurus as 'western teachers in eastern traditions' (Rawlinson, 1997). My own use of 'guru' here suggests popular/vernacular ramifications: seekers and gurus as a 'folk' current within religious alternativism.
12. These figures – little-known in scholarly circles – exemplify significant currents within the field. But they do not exhaust it: only lack of space prevents me from casting a wider net.
13. From a questionnaire I conducted amongst a small group at Findhorn in February 1995.
14. See, for example, Blavatsky's (1972: 27–33) polemic against Spiritualism.
15. For example, is H.P. Blavatsky primarily an 'occult' (Hanegraaff, 1996), 'eastern' (Rawlinson, 1997), or synthetic (Bevir, 1994) figure?
16. York, 1995; Pearson, 1998.
17. Hence Ferguson (1982: 91) writes of 'psychotechnologies' – 'systems for a deliberate change in consciousness'; Rawlinson (1997: 34–5), of 'spiritual psychology'; Segal (Chapter 4), of Jung's seminal 'psychologising of religion'.
18. Cf. my models of serial and multiple seeking in Sutcliffe (1997: 107,108): 'the serial seeker represents a psychological differentiation of the singular act of seeking: now there are distracting, potentially rivalrous *foci* . . . rather than one steady *focus*. A serial seeker [has] changed direction, or affiliation, more than once'; and 'multiple seeking is typically a multidirectional and synchronic activity . . . a number of religions or facets thereof are filtered and explored more-or-less simultanously'.
19. By Henley Centre for Forecasting and others: see 'Loves and Marriage', *The Guardian*, 21 July 1998, 'G2' section, pp. 2–3.

BIBLIOGRAPHY

Abercrombie, Nicholas *et al.*, 1988: *Contemporary British Society* (Cambridge: Polity Press).

Bennett, J.G., 1962: *Witness: The Story of a Search* (London: Hodder and Stoughton).

Bevir, Mark, 1994: 'The West Turns Eastward: Madame Blavatsky and the Transformation of the Occult Tradition', *Journal of the American Academy of Religion* LXII/3: 747–67.

Blavatsky, H.P., 1972 [1889]: *The Key to Theosophy* (Pasadena, CA: Theosophical University Press).

Bloom, William, 1990: *Sacred Times: a New Approach to Festivals* (Forres: Findhorn Press).

—— 1991: *The New Age* (London: Channel Four/Rider).

—— 1993a: *First Steps: an Introduction to Spiritual Practice* (Forres: Findhorn Press).

—— 1993b: 'Practical Spiritual Practice', *One Earth* 12, pp. 8–21.

Bowman, Marion, 1993: 'Drawn to Glastonbury', in Ian Reader and Tony Walter, eds, *Pilgrimage in Contemporary Culture* (London: Macmillan, pp. 29–62).

Braybrooke, Marcus, 1992: *Pilgrimage of Hope: One Hundred Years of Global Interfaith Dialogue* (London: SCM).

Brown, Mick, 1998: *The Spiritual Tourist: A Personal Odyssey Through the Outer Reaches of Belief* (London: Bloomsbury).

Bruce, Steve, 1996: *Religion in the Modern World: from Cathedrals to Cults* (Oxford: Oxford University Press).

Caddy, Eileen, 1988: *Flight Into Freedom* (Shaftesbury, Dorset: Element).

—— 1992: *God Spoke to Me* (Forres: Findhorn Press).

Campbell, Colin, 1972: 'The Cult, the Cultic Milieu and Secularization', in Hill, M. (ed.) *A Sociological Yearbook of Religion in Britain 5* (London: SCM).

Campbell, Colin, C., 1982: 'Some Comments on the New Religious Movements, the New Spirituality and Post-Industrial Society', in E. Barker (ed.) *New Religious Movements: A Perspective for Understanding Society* (New York: Edwin Mellen, pp. 232–42).

Collin-Smith, Joyce, 1988: *Call No Man Master* (Bath: Gateway).

Edwards, Gill, 1993: *Stepping into the Magic: A New Approach to Everyday Life* (London: Piatkus).

Ellwood, Robert S., 1973: *Religious and Spiritual Groups in Modern America* (Englewood Cliffs, NJ: Prentice-Hall).

Ferguson, Marilyn, 1982: *The Aquarian Conspiracy: Personal and Social Transformation in the 1980s* (St. Albans: Granada).

Forsyth, Lori, 1993: *Journey Towards Healing* (Nairn, Moray: Balnain Books).

Gerth, H.H., and Mills, C.W. (eds), 1970/1948: *From Max Weber: Essays in Sociology* (London: Routledge and Kegan Paul).

Giddens, Anthony, 1991: *Modernity and Self-Identity: Self and Society in the Late Modern Age* (Cambridge: Polity Press).

Gledhill, Ruth, 1996: *At a Service near You: British Churches – the Good, the Bad and the Ugly* (London: Hodder and Stoughton).

Handy, Charles, 1985: *The Future of Work: a guide to a changing society* (Oxford: Blackwell).

Heelas, Paul, 1996: *The New Age Movement: the Celebration of the Self and the Sacralization of Modernity* (Oxford: Blackwell).

Hinnells, John (ed.) 1988: *The Penguin Dictionary of Religions* (Harmondsworth: Penguin).

—— 1991: *Who's Who of World Religions* (London: Macmillan).

Hobsbawm, Eric, 1995 [1994]: *Age of Extremes: The Short Twentieth Century 1914–1991* (London: Abacus).

Howe, Ellic, 1972: *The Magicians of the Golden Dawn* (London: Routledge and Kegan Paul).

King, Ursula, 1997: 'Spirituality', in J. Hinnells (ed.), *A New Handbook of Living Religions* (Oxford: Blackwell, pp. 667–81).

Landau, Rom, 1945/1935: *God is My Adventure: a book on Modern Mystics, Masters and Teachers* (London: Faber).

Lofland, John, and Stark, R., 1965: 'Becoming a World-Saver: A Theory of Conversion to a Deviant Perspective', *American Sociological Review* 30: 862–75.

McGrath, Melanie, 1996 [1995]: *Motel Nirvana: Dreaming of the New Age in the American Desert* (London: Flamingo).

Mead, G.R.S., 1910: *Some Mystical Adventures*, London: John M. Watkins.

—— 1913: *Quests Old and New* (London: G. Bell).

ONS (Office for National Statistics), 1998: *Social Trends 28* (London: The Stationery Office).

Oppenheim, Janet, 1985: *The Other World: Spiritualism and Psychical Research in England 1850–1914* (New York: Cambridge University Press).

Pearson, Joanne, 1998: 'Assumed Affinities: Wicca and the New Age', in Pearson *et al.* (eds) pp. 45–56.

Pearson, Joanne *et al.* (eds), 1998: *Nature Religion Today: Paganism in the Modern World* (Edinburgh: Edinburgh University Press).

Perls, Frederick S., 1969: *Gestalt Therapy Verbatim* (Moab, UT: Real People Press).

Pogson, Beryl, 1987 [1961]: *Maurice Nicoll: A Portrait* (New York: Fourth Way Books).

Prothero, Stephen, 1996: 'Introduction', in C. Tonkinson (ed.), *Big Sky Mind: Buddhism and the Beat Generation* (London: Thorsons, pp. 1–20).

Rawlinson, Andrew, 1997: *The Book of Enlightened Masters: Western Teachers in Eastern Traditions* (Chicago: Open Court).

Roof, Wade C., 1993: *A Generation of Seekers: the Spiritual Journeys of the Baby Boom Generation* (San Francisco: HarperCollins).

Rose, Stuart, 1998: 'An Examination of the New Age Movement: who is involved and what constitutes its Spirituality', *Journal of Contemporary Religion* 13/1: 5–22.

Ross, Andrew, 1992: 'New Age Technoculture', in L. Grossberg *et al.* (eds) *Cultural Studies* (London: Routledge, pp. 531–55).

Shallcrass, Philip, 1998: 'A Priest of the Goddess', in J. Pearson *et al.* (eds) 1998, pp. 157–69.

Spangler, David, 1996: *Pilgrim in Aquarius* (Forres: Findhorn Press).

Strachan, Francoise (ed.), 1970: *The Aquarian Guide to Occult, Mystical, Religious, Magical London and Around* (London: Aquarian Press).

Straus, Roger, 1976: 'Changing Oneself: Seekers and the Creative Transformation of Life Experience', in J. Lofland, *Doing Social Life* (New York: John Wiley, pp. 252–72).

St John, John, 1977: *Travels in Inner Space: One Man's Exploration of Encounter Groups, Meditation and Altered States of Consciousness* (London: Victor Gollancz).

Storr, Anthony, 1996: *Feet of Clay: A Study of Gurus* (London: HarperCollins).

Sutcliffe, Steven, 1997: 'Seekers, Networks and "New Age" ', *Scottish Journal of Religious Studies* 15/2: 97–114.

—— 1998: ' "New Age" in Britain: an Ethnographical and Historical Exploration', unpublished PhD dissertation, The Open University.

Swainson, Mary, 1977: *The Spirit of Counsel* (Sudbury, Suffolk: Neville Spearman).

Washington, Peter, 1993: *Madame Blavatsky's Baboon: Theosophy and the Emergence of the Western Guru* (London: Secker and Warburg).

Webb, James, 1976: *The Occult Establishment* (La Salle, IL: Open Court).

White, Ruth, and Swainson M. 1971: *Gildas Communicates* (London: Neville Spearman).

Wilson, Colin, 1963: *Man Without a Shadow: the Diary of an Existentialist* (London: Arthur Barker).

York, Michael, 1995: *The Emerging Network: A Sociology of the New Age and Neo-Pagan Movements* (Lanham, MD: Rowman and Littlefield).

Madame Blavatsky's Children: Theosophy and Its Heirs

Kevin Tingay

INTRODUCTION

The Theosophical Society (hereafter 'TS') has for most of its history been the object of opprobrium from mainstream Christianity, and either ridiculed or ignored as a movement of marginal interest by students of religion until recent years. Yet the writings of Theosophists appear as a constant backdrop to many of the alternative spiritual traditions of the twentieth century. The society can be seen as the major institutional culmination of the growth of interest in occultism in the nineteenth century and its influence continues to be felt in our own times. The history and significance of the movement await a major study but work is beginning to be published which has moved on from the propaganda and polemic which has often characterised comment on Theosophy and its ramifications over the past one hundred and twenty years.[1]

The key themes of modern Theosophy are to be found in the writings of H.P. Blavatsky and her followers. They are not original to her and she did not claim that they were. She gathered together ideas which she thought represented the tradition of an 'Ancient Wisdom', and which she believed had been expressed though the ages in widely dispersed circumstances. We summarise them as follows for brevity's sake:

- The existence of a perennial wisdom tradition
- Its esoteric or gnostic character
- Its manifestation through exoteric religious traditions
- The existence of adepts or 'Masters of the Wisdom'
- Reincarnation and the law of karma
- A view of the human constitution as functioning in a series of interpenetrating 'bodies' from physical, etheric, emotional, mental, to 'higher self'
- An evolution of the spirit undergirding physical evolution
- A vision of universal brotherhood
- Western acceptance of Asian spiritual traditions
- Techniques of clairvoyance, divination and healing

The prime founder of the Theosophical movement was born Helena Petrovna Hahn in Ekaterinoslav in the Ukraine in 1831. She was by all accounts an unconventional child of her class, and did not fit at all into the pattern set for a young Russian woman of the minor aristocracy. She took a great interest in the folklore and popular religious practices of the local peasant community, especially psychic phenomena, magic and shamanism. Three weeks before her seventeenth birthday she was married to Nikifor Blavatsky, often described as an elderly military officer, but in fact a middle-aged provincial governor in Armenia. After a few weeks, however, Helena abandoned her husband and in 1848, the 'Year of Revolutions', began a series of travels and adventures which resulted in the foundation of the Theosophical movement twenty seven years later.

No child was born to this union. Indeed Blavatsky later wrote that the marriage was never consummated and that a combination of her distaste for sex and gynaecological problems precluded any consideration of child-bearing. Some biographers have asserted that she did in fact give birth to a son, Yuri, in 1861, and that the child died in infancy. This has always been denied by Blavatsky and by Theosophical biographers. The name of Blavatsky was not to be lost to posterity by lack of issue, however, as Madame Blavatsky, or 'HPB' as she is referred to in Theosophical and occultist circles, lives on through a far-reaching series of activities. This essay outlines how the life and activities of this curious Russian woman, of no formal education, have been perpetuated in writings that have remained in print over the century since her death on 8 May 1891, and in a host of organisations expressing what we now call 'alternative spiritualities' from then until the present day. It will dwell no more on the details of her earlier life, fascinating though it was, but will describe something of what followed from it. Blavatsky travelled in Europe, the Middle East and Central Asia in search of spiritual wisdom. Contacts with the early Spiritualist movement led her to the United States where, in 1874, she met Colonel Henry Olcott (1832–1907) who was also investigating Spiritualism. These two drew together a small group to discuss how they might facilitate the study of occultism and related matters.

THE BIRTH OF THE THEOSOPHICAL SOCIETY

The Theosophical Society was founded in 1875 in New York. Blavatsky contributed a charismatic enthusiasm for the occult and claimed to have access to teachings on the subject which had hitherto been concealed. Olcott, who had a background in law and administration, provided an organisational impetus for the movement. He became its first president and remained in that office until his death. The founders travelled to India in 1879 and in 1882 established the headquarters of the now flourishing society at Adyar near Madras. The society had been established as a response to the growing interest in occultism, Spiritualism and comparative religion which had developed in the latter half of the nineteenth century. The reasons for the move to India are not obviously apparent, but it proved fruitful in terms of the growth of the movement, enabling links to be established with both Hindus and Buddhists, and bringing it closer to those 'Masters of the Wisdom' whom the founders believed to reside in the Himalayas. From that time onwards the spirituality of Theosophists was clearly rooted in eastern rather than western esoteric traditions.

The original single object of the society at the time of its foundation was 'to collect and diffuse a knowledge of the laws which govern the universe.' After some modification its objects were established in 1896 as:

1. to form a nucleus of the Universal Brotherhood of Humanity, without distinction of race, creed, sex, caste or colour
2. to encourage the study of comparative religion, philosophy and science
3. to investigate unexplained laws of nature and the powers latent in man[2]

But the society was not an assembly in the tradition of nineteenth-century literary or scientific societies. Blavatsky claimed that she had been instructed in an Ancient Wisdom that underlay the teachings and practices of all the world's faiths, and that that instruction had come from hidden adepts – the Masters of the Wisdom. These adepts were alleged to be human beings who had reached the peak of human evolution through many reincarnations and were the custodians of this wisdom. Two such beings – Koot Hoomi and Morya – had chosen her to proclaim the teachings to a world that was deemed ready for their reception. The Theosophical Society was the mechanism by which this plan was to be achieved.[3]

From its earliest days the movement had to cope with the inbuilt tension between the wide-ranging scope of its three objects and the apparently definitive teachings of Blavatsky and her hidden teachers. Despite its claims not to be a religious body it has in fact provided for many of its members doctrinal and ethical teachings traditionally associated with religion. In common with many movements of the period, the society's predominant public activity was to arrange lectures and publish literature, both being directed to the propagation of the teachings and the recruitment of members. Meetings for members generally took the form of lectures or the group study of Theosophical texts. Though the TS itself did not for the most part provide devotional or liturgical activities, these did in fact emerge in a number of associated movements.

GROWTH, DISAGREEMENT AND SCHISM

The development of the movement became progressively more complex. In an attempt to provide a provisional taxonomy, I classify the groups that have links with Blavatsky's initiative as follows:

1. *Controlled movements*: groups whose membership is drawn wholly from the parent society but have their own organisational structures
2. *Schismatic movements*: groups which use the term 'Theosophy' in their title or claim to present or interpret Blavatsky's teachings directly, but have separated themselves from the parent society
3. *Derivative movements*: groups founded by one-time members of the parent society, and which embody some aspect of Theosophical teaching but whose members may now disavow or minimise the importance of the Theosophical connection.
4. *Influenced movements*: groups whose membership and leadership is largely drawn from the parent society, but are open to, and include, others.

The parent TS, with its headquarters in India, has remained the major component of the movement. It reached its peak of membership in the 1920s, when numbers reached 45,000. Its current worldwide membership is around 30,000.[4] The basic group within the society is the 'Lodge'. This appellation reflects discussion in the earliest days of the movement, when the organisational pattern of Freemasonry was examined as a possible model for the TS (masonic lodges being semi-secret groups into which members are ritually initiated). In the event, it was decided that a rather more open system of membership was appropriate, though, as we shall see, the appeal of initiation into inner groups has been a constant attraction to Theosophists. As the movement grew, the lodges were organised into national self-governing sections. Representatives of these sections serve on a general council under an international president. The president resides at the international headquarters in India and is elected by individual voting by all the membership. In countries where there are few members they may be directly attached to the headquarters. The fact that the foundational writings of the movement were in English was important in its initial growth throughout the English-speaking world. In this we include India, which was the arena for the greatest recruitment and has remained so to the present day. The annual reports of the society demonstrate that the Indian section is the only major part of the society which has shown growth since World War II.

With the death of Blavatsky in 1891, the mantle of leadership passed to another remarkable woman, Annie Besant. Having rejected Christianity, Besant became involved in radical Secularism and Socialism, but was converted to Theosophy after reading Blavatsky's *The Secret Doctrine* which she had been asked to review by W.T. Stead, the editor of *The Review of Reviews*. With her skills of oratory and organisation, Besant built up the movement and remained a focus for the devotion of its membership until her death in 1933. She was elected president in 1907 on the death of Olcott.[5] Her powerful personality and gifts of popularising Theosophical teachings transformed the society from one centred on the metropolitan salon to a movement which drew its membership from a surprisingly wide range of society. But these same gifts were also a contributory factor to the first major schism in the movement.

What later became generally known as the Theosophical Society (Pasadena) came into being in the United States in 1892, after a dispute which was centred around the claims to authority by Annie Besant and the American W.Q. Judge. Both claimed to be receiving guidance from the Masters and to be the legitimate successor to Blavatsky, although neither could sustain a working relationship with the other. After Judge's death in 1896 the leadership of his group of American Theosophists passed to yet another charismatic woman, Katherine Tingley. Under her inspiration a community was established at Point Loma, San Diego, California. By the early 1940s, however, this group had to move to smaller premises at Pasadena. The United Lodge of Theosophists, formed in 1909, represented a further split from the Point Loma Society. Both these remain separate organisations and claim to remain true to the original teachings of Blavatsky. Though both groups exist in many parts of the world their membership has never been anything like as large as the parent society. A number of smaller groups have split off at later stages, but have generally not outlived the individuals who led the schism. In more recent years the influence of Besant (and her collaborator C. W. Leadbeater) has declined somewhat within the movement and there has been some co-operation between the former rival Theosophical movements (as in the celebration of the centenary of the publication of Blavatsky's *The Secret Doctrine* in 1988). Besant and Leadbeater, who wrote in an accessible but simplistic style on such topics as reincarnation, after-death states, the human aura and the chakras, still remain popular among some members of the parent society. They are often referred to in contemporary 'New Age' writings, and continue to sell to a constituency beyond Theosophy.

ALTERNATIVE INTERPRETATIONS

A further group of 'children' came into being who did not lay a claim to be Theosophical by name, but claimed to be valid interpreters of the same occult tradition. They may appropriately be termed 'derivative movements', having been founded by individuals who were once members of the TS. The Hermetic Society (led by Anna Kingsford) and The Quest Society (founded by G.R.S. Mead) have long since ceased activities, but the Anthroposophical movement had its origins in the German Section of the TS. The bulk of its membership left the TS with its then general secretary, Rudolf Steiner, just before the World War I. It has since grown into a completely separate movement and now plays down its Theosophical roots.[6]

A TS member in the 1920s, Alice La Trobe-Bateman (later Bailey) claimed to have communication from the Masters who were guiding events from their Himalayan retreats. This precipitated one of the periodic crises of authority that punctuates Theosophical history. How are the genuine spokespersons for the Masters to be recognised? Bailey set up The Arcane School and over the next twenty years acted as a 'channel' for the teachings of the Master Djwal Khul, which rival those of Blavatsky in their length. From this group have derived a further series of groups, such as that of Benjamin Creme who proclaims the imminent return of the Lord Maitreya, a familiar messianic theme from the Theosophy of the 1920s. The 'I AM' Movement (begun by Guy Ballard) and its successor, The Summit Lighthouse, now the Church Universal and Triumphant (headed by Mark and Elizabeth Prophet) appropriated to themselves the direct guidance of the Theosophical Masters. We might ask ourselves whether these exalted beings are flattered or frustrated by the diversity of their disciples.

Melton (1989) has catalogued numerous other groups with Theosophical origins or links in North America. In England we might note that the Buddhist Society, one of the pioneering groups in English Buddhism, had its origins in the Buddhist Lodge of the TS and its enthusiastic young leader, Christmas Humphreys. The Society of the Inner Light, founded by Dion Fortune, had its origins in the Christian Mystic Lodge of the TS in London, as did one of the later manifestations of the Order of the Golden Dawn. Both these developments occurred in the 1920s, but links with other esoteric groups had also taken place in the 1890s when the Rosicrucian Society and the original Order of the Golden Dawn had enjoyed an overlap of membership with the TS.

ESOTERIC ELABORATIONS

The aforementioned three objects of the Theosophical Society did not mention Masters of the Wisdom or concealed teachings directly and there have always been members who did not concern themselves too much with these matters. For those who did, however, provision was made from the start of the movement for detailed teachings of an occult nature and the possibility of being put in closer contact with the Masters. The 'ES' (at various times these initials stood for the 'Esoteric Section', the 'Eastern School' or 'Esoteric School' of Theosophy) had its origins in the personal pupils of Blavatsky. They had to follow an ascetic spiritual regime and to declare confidence in the legitimacy of Blavatsky and her successors as the approved agents of the Masters, and to commit themselves to work for the society to the best of their abilities. Membership of this inner group has provided the leadership of the TS in most parts of the world until the present day. Other controlled groups – that is, those which restricted themselves to TS members – included at various times The Temple of the Rosy Cross (1912), The Krotona Drama (1921), The Egyptian Rite of the Ancient Mysteries (1930), The Temple of the Motherhood of God (c.1924), and the Ritual of the Mystic Star (1935), all of which offered ceremonial expression to Theosophy. Some of these were short-lived, while others endured for longer periods. In the social field the Theosophical Order of Service (1908) co-ordinated work of a philanthropic nature. The Theosophical Fraternity in Education (1916) was the focus for progressive developments in schools and evolved into the wider New Education Fellowship. Less successful was the Theosophical World University project (1925) which envisaged a chain of progressive centres of higher learning around the world. It never developed further than a series of public lectures and some vague and grandiose planning. A number of activities for children enjoyed greater popularity in the period up to 1930. Lotus Circles (1892), the Order of the Golden Chain (1899) and the International Order of the Round Table (1908) provided opportunities for children of different ages to be exposed to the ethical and spiritual teachings of Theosophy. Since the 1930s the first two of these groups have been subsumed into the Order of the Round Table, which still functions in several countries and uses ceremonies based on the Arthurian legends. The bulk of its membership comes from the children of Theosophical families.

Those movements I have designated 'controlled' had links with the TS built into their individual constitutions, but there were two larger movements which sought, amongst other things, to explore Theosophy through ceremonial expression. They had no formal links with Theosophy and did recruit some of their membership from outside Theosophy, but its influence remained as a vital component and hence they can fairly be described as 'influenced' movements. These two groups were The Liberal Catholic Church (hereafter 'LCC') and The Order of International Co-Freemasonry (generally referred to as 'Co-Masonry'). The LCC derived from an attempt to establish a branch of the Dutch Old Catholic Church in England in 1908. This attracted a number of Theosophists who enthusiastically adopted a rich catholic liturgical practice and interpreted it from an esoteric viewpoint. This appealed to those who had reluctantly left established churches as a result of their Theosophical interests, but also antagonised members who saw Theosophy as a rejection of Christianity. The LCC developed a hierarchy of bishops (who have generally been Theosophists) in many parts of the world has endured a number of schisms, and has reflected the general decline in Theosophical membership in its own decline in numbers. C.W. Leadbeater, an Anglican clergyman prior to becoming a disciple of Blavatsky, became a bishop in this church in 1916 and subsequently wrote prolifically on ecclesiastical topics. His *Science of the Sacraments* offered the student of Christian liturgy his clairvoyant Theosophical insights into what was going on in the inner worlds during the celebration of Mass and the administration of the sacraments.

The Co-Masonic Order had its origins in France and is still governed from Paris. In 1882 a French masonic lodge decided to initiate a woman. This resulted in their being expelled by their governing authority and they established a masonic order of their own which admitted men and women on equal terms. Annie Besant was initiated in 1902 and the movement expanded through her enthusiasm, particularly in the English-speaking Theosophical world. Since World War II this order has recruited less from the Theosophical movement and, like the LCC, has declined in recent years. In France, however, where the Theosophical influence was only peripheral, it has continued to grow. Several of the later generation of Theosophical leaders were active in this movement and have written on masonic symbolism, and in some cases the masonic ritual was elaborated along Theosophical lines. Some freemasons from lodges of the United Grand Lodge of England and the Grand Lodge of Scotland associated themselves with the new order, but the ruling authorities of those bodies did not take kindly to this feminine development and forbade their members from having any contact with it. Some men did in fact throw in their lot with the new body and assisted in its growth. After a few years of activity, in which several new lodges were founded in Great Britain, a faction of initiates who did not find themselves in sympathy with the Theosophical influence separated themselves. Their endeavours evolved into two separate orders of Freemasonry for women only which continue to the present day and have no connection with their co-masonic forebears.

THE EMERGENCE OF A WORLD TEACHER

One of the most remarkable fruits of the Theosophical enterprise was the promotion of Jiddu Krishnamurti. At the time of his death in 1989 his name was probably more widely known than Madame Blavatsky or any other Theosophical leader. His thinking attracted the attention of a wider and more significant circle of people than did Theosophical teachings in any of their traditional forms. His story may briefly be summarised as follows.

In 1909, Jiddu Narayaniah, a Brahmin employee of the TS came to live on the headquarters estate at Adyar. He was a widower with four sons and lived in rather straitened circumstances. C.W. Leadbeater, observing the fourteen-year-old Krishnamurti, one of the four, claimed that he had a remarkable 'aura' which indicated that he was a person of great spiritual significance. The boy's education, hitherto non-existent, was taken in hand by a number of Theosophists, European and Indian. In 1911 a movement was started called The Order of the Star in the East (OSE) whose object was to prepare for 'the near coming of a great Spiritual teacher'. Krishnamurti was the 'Head of the Order' and the implicit suggestion was that he would be the 'vehicle' for the embodiment of the 'World Teacher' at some stage in the near future.[7] This movement was again organised quite separately from the TS but attracted most of its leading figures. Those who were disturbed by this messianic tendency left, Rudolf Steiner being the most prominent. After World War I the OSE began to take off, perhaps a fitting part of a post-war spirit of hope and optimism. Many people joined, including members of mainstream churches and other religious bodies who had no connection with Theosophy. Krishnamurti, now well-groomed and, when in the West, dressed in the height of fashion by his patrons, proved an irresistible and exotic attraction to the earnest seekers of the time. Centres for his work were established in Ommen (Holland), Sydney (Australia) and Ojai (California), and the OSE functioned as an adjunct to Theosophical activities in many countries of the world, and was often administered from TS premises.

However, as time went by, Krishnamurti considered that a spirit of self-aggrandisement bordering on hysteria was developing among his followers, some of whom saw themselves as 'apostles' to the new messiah. In 1929 he disavowed the role of 'World Teacher', dissolved the Order of the Star and embarked on a career as an independent spiritual teacher. He continued to attract a devoted coterie of disciples, but his teaching strongly attacked the need for gurus or any form of organisation as a basis for the understanding of truth. Many Theosophists left the society, and Annie Besant, now in her old age, never really recovered from the blow and died in 1933. Other Theosophists adjusted to the new situation by suggesting that 'the Coming had gone wrong' perhaps though the agency of the 'dark powers'.[8] In more recent times the current president of the Adyar Society, Radha Burnier, has led it away from the Besant/Leadbeater style towards a spirit more in accord with Krishnamurti's approach. Before his death Krishnamurti revisited the Adyar estate where he had spent his childhood and which he had not entered for over fifty years. His lectures, seminars and writings attracted a growing audience in the post-war years, and he engaged in dialogue with a wide circle of respected scientists, philosophers and educators.[9]

THEOSOPHISTS AT WORK IN THE WORLD

Such was the organisational fruit of Blavatsky's endeavours, manifested in movements that attempted in some way or another to express the inner or spiritual aspect of her teachings. How far she saw her movement as having a wider social function is a matter of debate, but the influence of Annie Besant propelled many of the members into social action. Amongst the 'progressive' causes which they espoused were alternative medicine, vegetarianism, animal welfare, progressive education, female suffrage, the Garden City movement and the struggle for Indian independence. We should also note some influence on artistic and literary trends in the period from 1880 to 1914.[10]

The excitements of the 1920s were followed by a period of retrenchment after the departure of Krishnamurti and the death of Annie Besant, and through the difficult years of World War II. A resolution, originally passed by the general council of the society in 1924 and regularly reproduced in *The Theosophist*, its international journal since the 1930s, illustrates the movement away from dogmatic pronouncements by authoritarian leaders towards a more dispersed pattern of authority:

As the Theosophical Society has spread far and wide over the world, and as members of all religions have become members of it without surrendering the special dogmas, teachings and beliefs of their respective faiths, it is thought desirable to emphasise the fact that there is no doctrine, no opinion, by whomsoever taught or held, that is any way binding on any member of the Society, none which any member is not free to accept or reject. Approval of its three Objects is the sole condition of membership. No teacher, or writer, from H.P. Blavatsky downwards, has any authority to impose his teachings or opinions on members. Every member has a equal right to attach himself to any school of thought which he may choose, but has no right to force his choice on any other. Neither a candidate for any office nor any voter can be rendered ineligible to stand or to vote because of any opinion he may hold, or because of membership of any school of thought to which he may belong. Opinions or beliefs neither bestow privileges nor inflict penalties. The Members of the General Council earnestly request every member of The Theosophical Society to maintain, defend and act upon these fundamental principles of the Society, and also fearlessly to exercise his own right of liberty of thought, and of expression thereof, within the limits of courtesy and consideration for others.

In common with other movements with a mission in a pre-electronic age, Theosophy used the printed word to embody its teachings. A great volume of books, pamphlets, and periodical literature poured from the presses. Their sales went beyond the membership of the specifically Theosophical, which might lead us to suppose that there were many more who took an interest in esoteric ideas than actually joined organisations, a situation which I suspect applies as much today as it did a century ago. The writings of Blavatsky remain in print, as do many by Annie Besant and C. W. Leadbeater. The TS, which still runs publishing houses in India, the USA and elsewhere, has produced a wide range of books over the past one hundred years. We summarise the genres, with examples, as follows:

- Foundational texts of H.P. Blavatsky – *Isis Unveiled* (1877), *The Secret Doctrine* (1888) and *The Key to Theosophy* (1889)
- Channelled/'received' texts – *The Mahatma Letters* (written in the 1880s, published 1923)[11]
- Descriptions of supersensible experiences or observations – *Man, Visible and Invisible* (1902) and other titles by C.W. Leadbeater.
- Translations and commentaries on classical oriental texts – *The Bhagavad Gita* translated by Annie Besant
- Cosmological and anthropological schemas and accounts of past lives – *Man, Whence, How and Whither* (1913) by Besant and Leadbeater
- Guides to spiritual practices, meditation, yoga, etc.
- 'Esoteric' Christianity – *Esoteric Christianity* (1905) by Besant, *The Christian Creed* (1917) by Leadbeater[12]

The other movements already noted engendered a corresponding volume of printed material. Perhaps the greatest number of Blavatsky's 'children' are these now largely neglected texts which expressed the hopes and fears of their earnest authors.[13]

Our opening summary of Theosophical interests and our outline of the movements and activities over the past one hundred and twenty years points to the place where Blavatsky's children mostly seem to dwell in our own times – the New Age. Blavatsky is not the only mother of that age but surely one of the most significant. The movements and activities which she and her successors instigated provided a comprehensive range of opportunities for seekers of esoteric spirituality. The parent society might be likened to a Clapham Junction for occult travellers, who entered from various directions and travelled on to several destinations beyond. Some were quite famous names, and there has always been a faithful core of members who saw it as the centre of their spiritual world, but today the Theosophical Society is a rather faded shadow of its grand former self. For the seeker after ancient wisdom, there is now a bewildering variety of alternative transport. A century ago Theosophy had the major share of the market; now it is almost submerged by the brightly packaged products of the New Age. In 1889 H.P. Blavatsky wrote some words towards the end of her book *The Key to Theosophy* which now have a prophetic ring:

> Every such attempt as the Theosophical Society has hitherto ended in failure, because, sooner or later, it has degenerated into a sect, set up hard-and-fast dogmas of its own, and so lost by imperceptible degrees that vitality which living truth alone can impart. You must remember that all our members have been bred and born in some creed or religion, that all are more or less of their generation both physically and mentally, and consequently that their judgement is but too likely to be warped and unconsciously biased by some or all of these influences. If, then, they cannot be freed from such inherent bias, or at least taught to recognise it instantly and so avoid being led away by it, the result can only be that the Society will drift off on to some sandbank of thought or another, and there remain a stranded carcass to moulder and die. (Blavatsky, 1893: 193)

NOTES

1. Several biographies of the chief founder H.P. Blavatsky have been produced since her death in 1891. Most adopt a partisan attitude for or against the proposition that she was a major spiritual teacher of the nineteenth-century. Amongst more recent works are Meade (1980) (*against*), Fuller (1988), and Cranston (1993) (*for*). The co-founder of the Society, H.S. Olcott, has been memorialised from within the movement by Murphet (1972), and his place in the revival of Buddhism in Asia has been analysed by Prothero (1996). Studies of the history of the Theosophical movement as a whole have been written from within the parent society by Ransom (1938), from the Pasadena position by Ryan (1975), and from the traditionally anonymous standpoint of the independent United Lodge of Theosophists in *The Theosophical Movement* (1951). A general academic survey of the subject is to be found in Campbell (1980), and particular studies have been made of Theosophy in Australia (Roe, 1986), New Zealand (Ellwood, 1993), and Russia (Carlson, 1993). A popular work which accepts uncritically the accusations that Blavatsky was a 'fraud', but nevertheless goes on to chart some of the links between Theosophy and other twentieth-century movements, has been written by Washington

(1993). Detailed academic studies of the movements and personalities which predated the foundation of the TS but whose influences are significant are to be found in Godwin (1994) and Faivre (1994).

2. Ransom (1938:545*ff*).

3. Letters alleged to be from these Masters were published by Barker in 1923. Details of physical and clairvoyant contacts with various Masters appear through much of Theosophical literature up to the 1950s. Johnson (1994) attempts to correlate Blavatsky's descriptions with identifiable historical figures.

4. Annual Reports of the Theosophical Society, Adyar, from 1908 to date.

5. Her life has been comprehensively recorded by Nethercot (1961, 1963), who is the only biographer to have seriously addressed the Theosophical phase of her career.

6. Leviton (1994) addresses in some depth the distinctiveness of Steiner's thought and the reasons for his parting from the Theosophical Society.

7. Nethercot (1963:160).

8. Schuller (1997) analyses the responses to these events.

9. A personal account of his life can be found in the works of Mary Lutyens, who spent her childhood with him, and remained a close friend and associate throughout his life.

10. Nethercot (1961, 1963) provides the most accessible source of reference for these activities.

11. *The Mahatma Letters* were purported to have been 'precipitated' by occult means from the Masters to A.P. Sinnett, Blavatsky and others. Other Theosophists have from time to time made claims to the reception of what is now referred to as 'channelled' communications from the same source.

12. Esoteric Christianity, so-called, generally turns out to be old gnosticism in new clothing. Theosophists from Blavatsky onwards subscribe to the theory that the Church throughout the ages has conspired to keep the true message of Jesus Christ a closely guarded secret.

13. No comprehensive bibliography covers the whole of the period of Theosophical history, but Gomes (1994) covers the period up to 1900.

BIBLIOGRAPHY

Barker, A. Trevor, 1923: *The Mahatma Letters to A.P. Sinnett* (London: T. Fisher Unwin).

Blau, Evelyne, 1995: *Krishnamurti – 100 years* (New York: Stewart, Chabori and Chang).

Blavatsky, Helena P., 1893: *The Key to Theosophy*, 3rd edn (London: Theosophical Publishing Society).

Campbell, Bruce J., 1980: *Ancient Wisdom Revived – A History of the Theosophical Movement* (Berkeley: University of California Press).

Carlson, Maria, 1993: *'No Religion Higher Than Truth' – A History of the Theosophical Movement in Russia 1875–1922* (Princeton: Princeton University Press).

Cranston, Sylvia, 1993: *H.P.B. – The Extraordinary Life and Influence of Helena Blavatsky* (New York: Putnam).

Ellwood, Robert S., 1993: *Islands of the Dawn – The Story of Alternative Spirituality in New Zealand* (Honolulu: University of Hawaii).

Faivre, Antoine, 1994: *Access to Modern Esotericism* (New York: State University of New York Press).

Fuller, Jean Overton, 1988: *Blavatsky and her Teachers* (London: East-West Publications).

Godwin, Joscelyn, 1994: *The Theosophical Enlightenment* (New York: State University of New York Press).

Gomes, Michael, 1994: *Theosophy in the Nineteenth Century: an Annotated Bibliography* (New York: Garland).

Johnson, K. Paul, 1994: *The Masters Revealed* (New York: State University of New York Press).

Leviton, Richard, 1994: *The Imagination of Pentecost – Rudolf Steiner & Contemporary Spirituality* (Hudson, NY: Anthroposophic Press).

Lutyens, Mary, 1990: *The Life and Death of Krishnamurti* (London: John Murray).

Meade, Marion, 1980: *Madame Blavatsky – The Woman behind the Myth* (New York: Putnam).

Melton, J. Gordon, 1989: *The Encyclopaedia of American Religions* (Detroit: Gale Research).

Murphet, Howard, 1972: *Hammer on the Mountain – The Life of Henry Steel Olcott (1832–1907)* (Wheaton, IL.: Theosophical Publishing House).

Nethercot, Arthur H., 1961: *The First Four Lives of Annie Besant* (London: Rupert Hart-Davis).

—— 1963: *The Last Five Lives of Annie Besant* (London: Rupert Hart-Davis).

Prothero, Stephen, 1996: *The White Buddhist – The Asian Odyssey of Henry Steel Olcott* (Bloomington: Indiana University Press).

Ransom, Josephine, 1938: *A Short History of the Theosophical Society* (Adyar: Theosophical Publishing House).

Roe, Jill, 1986: *Beyond Belief – Theosophy in Australia 1879–1939* (Kensington, NSW: University of New South Wales Press).

Ryan, Charles J., 1975: *H.P. Blavatsky and the Theosophical Movement* (San Diego: Point Loma Publications).

Schuller, Govert, 1997: *Krishnamurti and the World Teacher Project: Some Theosophical Perceptions*, Theosophical History Occasional Papers, Vol.V (Fullerton, CA.: Theosophical History).

The Theosophical Movement 1875–1950–1952 (Los Angeles: The Cunningham Press).

Washington, Peter, 1993: *Madame Blavatsky's Baboon – Theosophy and the Emergence of the Western Guru* (London: Bloomsbury).

3

New Centres of Life

Martin Green

INTRODUCTION

At the turn of the twentieth century new centres of life were generated in various parts of Western civilisation. A 'centre of life' for the purpose of this essay is a place where people meet to share new ideas and try to realise them; but it may also be a place people pass through, many of the groups discussed here being loosely organised and peripatetic. The ideas of this period were new in a variety of ways; they fostered people's sense of possibility – fed the sense that they could begin, as individuals or as small groups, to lead their lives in the way they wanted to. Simply by acts of will, faith and courage they could, for instance, defy the state and elude the iron cage of modernisation. Such an ambition could be regarded as tending towards anarchism, but there are many kinds of anarchism ranging from violent terrorism to peaceable Gandhian communities.

Most of these centres of life were in some sense religious, and their religion could be divided into two main kinds. One was Christian in its spirituality, or, to be more specific, Quaker/pacifist and was strongly represented in the peace movements. In the early twentieth century, and among more speculative minds, this spirituality often took over Hindu and Buddhist ideas. This orientalist tendency crystallised in, for example, the teachings of the Theosophical Society. But even when this religion's vocabulary remained Christian, it rarely attached itself primarily to institutions or theologies.

The other strain of religion we can call 'pagan' – partly because that term was current in this period, 1880–1920. This was attached to eroticism, and thereby to feminism. The latter was not necessarily pagan in this sense, but the case of Emma Goldman, in whom these ideas did come together, was in some ways typical. Born in Russia, and spending most of her life in America, Goldman edited *Mother Earth*, preached paganism, and practised anarchism. Though she acknowledged her fellow countryman Peter Kropotkin as her master, especially in the matter of anarchism, she felt herself separated from him by both his nonviolence and his refusal to speak for erotic values. There was also an angry debate between two male anarchists at the end of the first decade of this century: Otto Gross, a Freudian psychoanalyst, speaking for sexual liberation, and Gustav Landauer, a Zionist, speaking for marriage and village anarchism. The two men belonged to the German-speaking centre of Europe, and the Russians, Goldman and Kropotkin, also belonged to that mid-European culture. This paper will be concerned primarily with England's 'New Age', but from an international point of view German culture was always central.

Pagans tended to make much of aesthetic and occultist values; so, somewhat paradoxically, they looked back to picturesque medieval Christendom. But both Paganism and Quaker/pacifist Christianity were attracted to the simple life, to nature and often to nature cure, to folk and orientalist medicines. As important as these positive attractions was the negative distrust of western 'scientific' medicine, which represented contemporary civilisation at its most prestigious. Many kinds of art and philosophy reflected both strains of religion.

These centres of new life, taken together as a network, constituted a *New Age* - another phrase of the times, often applied both favourably and unfavourably in the years 1880 to 1910 or 1920. A 'New Age' is a period of more-than-ordinary life-experiment, spontaneity and social hope - when there is a general readiness to believe that life can be significantly changed by the conviction of an individual or a small group without their disposing of great force or devising big institutions or elaborate theories.

The greatest leaders of such teaching at the beginning of the 1880–1920 period were Tolstoy and Ruskin - long mocked for their 'idealism', by liberals as well as conservatives, but later acknowledged as the two great teachers of the next generation, which included Gandhi and others. The communities Gandhi founded in South Africa, Phoenix and Tolstoy Farm, were comparable with the English and German examples to be discussed here. These were all forms of protest against 'the world' in all its compromises.

We can begin with an example which was central to Europe both geographically and intellectually: the Mountain of Truth in Ascona.[1]

ASCONA

At the end of the nineteenth century, intellectual Europe became preoccupied with the problem of its own unhappiness, malaise, or - to use Freud's word in *Civilisation and its Discontents* - 'Unbehagen'. The favourites of this rich and powerful civilisation - the economically and educationally privileged – felt themselves to be more unhappy than those less privileged. Those who seemed to feel the crisis most deeply were the Germans – meaning not only the inhabitants of Germany, but also German speakers all over Europe – who were moving faster than other peoples to grasp the glittering prizes of progress. Germany's cities and its industrial power had been growing for some time, and with them spread a sense of dismay and dislike of both industrialism and city life. In 1800, the population of what later became Germany stood at twenty-two million. In 1900, the figure was fifty-six million, and every second citizen lived away from the place of their birth – most of them in a city environment. By 1910, Germany contained as many big cities as all the rest of Europe.[2]

Max Weber spoke of an iron cage or framework which closed around a society when it entered the modern world. Sigmund Freud, in *Civilisation and its Discontents*, wrote that, 'it is impossible to overlook the extent to which civilisation is based upon a renunciation of instinct.'[3]

Many of the best European minds from 1900 onwards were devoted to understanding this problem and to 'solving' it. Both Freud and Weber were intellectually conservative, and their moral enthusiasms took second place to their loyalty to 'objectivity' and 'scientific neutrality'. But others were trying to solve the problem of civilisation and unhappiness more practically, emotionally and enthusiastically – by *living* a new life together, withdrawing from the cities and the professions and the 'objective' ways of thought, and by risking their own lives.

These people thought of Freud and Weber as enemies, and Weber and Freud thought of them as dangerous fools. But as we look back on that period – so like our own 1960s – we can see the two groups as complementary. Both must engage our interest, and perhaps compete for our loyalty.

Understanding the enthusiasts requires an extra effort on our part, for they have been largely consigned to the dustbin of intellectual history, and now look flimsy beside the serried volumes of Freud and Weber. It was a risk they knew they ran. But at the time it was different. In his 1880 pamphlet, *Spirit of Revolt*, Kropotkin wrote, 'There are periods of human society when revolution becomes an imperative necessity, when it proclaims itself as inevitable . . . The need for a new life becomes apparent . . . Weary of these wars, weary of the miseries which they cause, society rushes to seek a new organisation.'[4]

As Roger Baldwin noted about Kropotkin, this change was not merely political but included 'all social relations – marriage, education, the treatment of crime, the function of law, the basis of morality.'[5] Kropotkin was one of those who came to Ascona, a Swiss mountain village which became a centre of the counterculture in the period 1900–20.

The first intellectual immigrants into this area in 1900 settled on the top of a foothill of the Alps, called Monescia, which they renamed *Monte Verita*, the Mountain of Truth. There they stayed in the nature cure sanitarium, or in ramshackle cabins which they built with their own hands. (The sanitarium, run by Henri Oedenkoven and Ida Hofmann, gradually became the most conservative and commercial of Ascona institutions.) Visiting radicals often stayed in inns or furnished rooms in the village, or rented one of the houses, or slept in the open. As they walked the landscape, so totally unlike the industrialised cities of northern Europe, they came across many shrines to the Madonna, tended by the local people – a fact they were pleased to take as evidence of a pagan cult of Woman among these supposedly Christian peasants.

One way to approach this side of Ascona is through Gerhart Hauptmann's once-famous novel, *Der Ketzer von Soana* ('The Heretic of Soana'). This tells the story of a young priest of a mountain parish much like Ascona, who leaves Christ for Eros after succumbing to paganism in the form of a beautiful girl who has been brought up outside the Christian religion and civilisation. This novel was published in 1918 to great international success, selling 140,000 copies by 1925. It formed part of that literary propaganda for eroticism so prevalent after 1918, in which D.H. Lawrence played the largest part among English-language writers.

At the end of Hauptmann's story, the narrator meets for the first time the woman who seduced the priest. He is going down the mountain after hearing the latter's story, and she comes up towards him. He feels weak and small before her:

> There was no protection, no armour against the demands of that neck, those shoulders, and that breast, blessed and stirred by the breath of life. She climbed up and out of the depths of the world, past the wondering scribe – and she climbs and climbs into eternity as the one into whose merciless hands heaven and earth have been delivered.[6]

Such stories were written in all the languages of Europe between 1900 and 1920 and later, and many people joined the new centres of life because of them. However, that was not the only attraction. A complementary story, equally important to Asconans, was about the 'primal crime' committed by the patriarchal father/husband/master who dominated the new iron-clad society, especially in pre-1914 Germany. This story was myth rather than fiction and it existed in fragments. One was invented by Otto Gross, the most brilliant of the Asconans. He had a vision of a turning point in world history when a horde of ambitious half-apes burst out of a clump of bushes and flung themselves upon the naked and unsuspecting women who had till then, in matriarchal innocence, directed human life. They enslaved the women and took them as their wives – and with that event our history began.

Such a 'primal crime' is Asconan and not Freudian, because it accuses 'Man' so angrily. Gross and Ascona acknowledged the Oedipus complex, that most famous of Freudian ideas, but it was not in Ascona a matter of individual fantasy, but of history. When we put such stories together we have a program – an impeachment of Man, an enthronement of 'Magna Mater' – which was dear to all Asconans.

One of the few Englishmen who lived in Ascona in those years before 1914 was Harold Monro, who later ran the Poetry Bookshop in London for many years, a centre of modern poetry in England. During his summers in Ascona he worked on a long poem entitled 'Jehovah', in which he attacked the figure of God the Father. Monro went to visit the Whiteway commune in the Cotswolds, an English version of Ascona, which will be discussed later; and on one of Edward Carpenter's visits to Florence, Monro journeyed from Ascona to talk to him. These are all marks of the network of new life centres.

The idea of a sacred mountain has echoes in the stories of the Ten Commandments and the Sermon on the Mount in Biblical teaching. In our recent past, an American equivalent would be Big Sur in California, notable for its landscape and its association with the Esalen Institute and speculative orientalism. In the Joan Baez film of the 1960s, *Ceremony at Big Sur*, we see young people flocking towards an outdoor concert in the costumes of anarchism and protest, defying and provoking the communities through which they pass on their way, just like the *Naturmenschen* with their long hair, bare legs and sandals who flocked to Ascona between 1900 and 1920, to dance together to the sun. Memoirs of Ascona by writers such as Hermann Hesse and Emil Szittya, and the dancer Mary Wigman stress the 'pilgrimage' aspect of their approach to the place, walking through villages where the local people whispered and laughed behind the young hikers' backs.

WHITEWAY

The closest English equivalent to Ascona was perhaps Whiteway, a Tolstoyan agricultural colony near Stroud in the Cotswolds. It was less erotic, and a smaller-scale phenomenon in every sense, but was set up for the same reasons and had many of the same features. We notice recurrent Asconan themes of imprisonment, anti-militarism, nature cure and the simple life in the Whiteway colonists' talk and action. People went to join or visit the colony, to share those ideas or experiences or to put them into practice.

Whiteway was founded by a group of radicals based in the London surburb of Croydon. (D.H. Lawrence was a schoolteacher in Croydon and took an interest in such colonies in the years when it was functioning.) John C. Kenworthy, a disciple of Tolstoy, who visited Tolstoy in Russia and wrote about the visit, was pastor of the Croydon Brotherhood Church and editor of the Brotherhood Publishing Company. This church, founded in 1894, ran a store, a laundry and a dressmaking establishment before setting up its agricultural colony. 'Brotherhood' stood for 'Brotherhood of Man'; such churches were sometimes called 'Labour Churches'. They built their faith around the Social Gospel – the application of the Christian Gospel to issues of social justice. They were themselves a 'New Age' phenomenon, and from this Croydon matrix a few radicals took a giant step towards Whiteway's horizon of possibility, just as many Germans made their move from Munich to Ascona.

The English colonists made their big decision in 1898, just two years before the Asconans. (To be exact, they moved out of Croydon to Purleigh in 1897, and then, because of quarrels, away from there to Whiteway.) Three of the colonists officially bought the property, but they then burned the title deeds so that there should be no owning or owners. The original twelve, some of whom were Quakers, lived communally but also spontaneously. They shared even their clothes and took no vows, made no promises or pledges to each other. During their very first winter their money ran out and they lived on potatoes and parsnips.

However, though several left the colony, more came, with various intentions and from various countries. In 1900 there were twenty-four people, on forty-one acres. (W.H.G. Armytage gives an account of them in his *Heavens Below*.)[7] Let us take as an example Franz (or Francis) Sedlak, who later studied Hegel and wrote a book about him. Sedlak was born into a farming family in Moravia in 1873, four years before Otto Gross, one of the leading anarchists in Ascona. A rebellious boy, Sedlak contradicted his teacher's pious doctrines about priests and kings, denied his father's authority over him and, while away at school, was sent twopence to buy some rope to hang himself.

Sedlak was an intellectual from the start, attempting while young to devise a system of ideographic writing. He refused to work on the family farm and instead ran away from home to join the Foreign Legion. After a short time he deserted, was imprisoned, and returned home in time to be conscripted into the Austrian army.[8]

Sedlak soon came to have conscientious objections to obeying officers' orders. He refused to be a soldier, and was again jailed. (It is worth noting that armies are repugnant to anarchists because of their regimented discipline as well as because of their connection with violence. Places like Ascona and Whiteway were the opposite of military in both ways.) Sedlak studied the anarchist doctrines of Max Stirner, and as soon as he was free from the army, set out for England, where he had heard that an anarchist colony was operating in Newcastle-on-Tyne, headed by an Austrian (presumably Clousden Hill, founded in 1893 by a man called Klapper.) By the time Sedlak arrived, the colony had been turned into a private enterprise, in which he took work; but he soon set off for Russia, working as a stoker on board a steamship. Like Gandhi and Gross, he was a wanderer early in life.[9]

Also like Gandhi, Sedlak had heard about Tolstoy and his way of life before being inspired by Tolstoy's writings – although the Austrian military authorities assumed that Tolstoy's pacifist pamphlets had been at the source of Sedlak's recalcitrance. In Petersburg, in 1899, he realised that the great Russian was not far away, and he travelled to the provinces south of Moscow to visit him at his country estate, Yasnaya Polyana.

Sedlak kept a diary as he tramped and begged his way to Yasnaya Polyana. 'Well,' he wrote, 'I am about to see the most famous and original thinker of the dying century.' Arriving at dawn, penniless, he had breakfast with Tolstoy and told his life-story. The old man, having no money of his own, borrowed three roubles from the cook to get Sedlak back as far as Tula, asked him to write up his army experiences and told him about the English colonies set up by Tolstoyans at Purleigh and at Whiteway.

When Sedlak arrived at Purleigh, he discovered that it too had reverted to private ownership; but at Whiteway he finally found a welcome, and he stayed there till he died in 1935, living in a free union with Nellie Shaw, one of the original founders. Having begun as a Tolstoyan, he was later attracted to Theosophy, practised yoga and wrote a *Counterblast to Tolstoy*. Like many of these figures, his life was essentially experimental.

Like some of the Asconans (especially one Gusto Graeser) Sedlak was a vegetarian and practised nature cure. He is described as a figure of splendid manliness and perfect health by other colonists. (It is notable that these living icons were most often male.) *Mountain of Truth* (Green, 1986) contains a full-length portrait of Graeser, who slept in a cave, dressed in a toga and ate wayside fruits for much of his life. He also went barefoot, dressed in white cotton pants and shirts and wore his hair long. He was often photographed by strangers, and compared with paintings of Christ's Apostles.

Just as Sedlak and Kenworthy visited Tolstoy, and Harold Monro visited

Whiteway, a certain Dr Albert Skarvan – a Tolstoyan who was consulted by the Asconans when they designed their enterprise – visited both the Brotherhood Church in Croydon and Yasnaya Polyana. (Skarvan had been an army doctor, but resigned for reasons of conscience, and became a sponsor and protector to other men who refused military service.) Meanwhile, Gandhi visited Whiteway in 1909, and set up his own Tolstoy Farm in South Africa the following year.

GANDHI'S COLONIES

Mohandas Gandhi (1869–1948) was of course a world historical figure. Famous throughout India, he also set up two communes in South Africa and was official agent there for both the Vegetarian Society and the Esoteric Christian Union, the latter an offshoot of the Theosophical Society. Gandhi had originally travelled to Natal from his native province of Gujarat after training as a barrister in London and failing to find satisfactory employment in India. He felt falsified by the official cultural styles he had to imitate, and yet believed in the liberal rhetoric of the Empire, as did Ruskin. The best imperialists had a quasi-religious historical vision which could be compared with that of their more extreme opponents. The solution to this tension between east and west Gandhi found in the religious radicalism of 'New Age' institutions like the Theosophical Society.

His first major disciple was Henry Polak, a young Anglo-Jew who had come to Natal to work as a journalist. He was already a London 'New Ager', like Gandhi; an admirer of Ruskin and Tolstoy, a member of the South Place Ethical Society and ready to take the next step of living in a commune. The two men met at a vegetarian restaurant in Johannesburg, where Gandhi also met Albert West, a young working-class emigrant from England who became another of his loyal followers.

Gandhi took over a newspaper, *Indian Opinion*, of which Polak became the editor, and – inspired by Ruskin's *Unto This Last* – the two decided to publish it in an agricultural settlement called Phoenix outside Durban, where they could practise the simple life at the same time. Ruskin's book was a discussion of politically radical economics which had a great influence on most 'New Agers'. Later came Tolstoy Farm, where Gandhi offered shelter to the families of Indians jailed for their political activities.

In both places, the Indians built their own houses, did their own cooking and laundry, practised nature cure and so on. This was a protest against the Eastern as well as the Western 'iron cages', which trapped individuals in systems of control and limitation. The caste system, for instance, was one such prison. For obvious reasons, Gandhi stressed his opposition to the western examples, but he also broke all kinds of Hindu cultural regulations (for instance, he set a high value on physical labour). His followers, especially the women, found it hard to return to India from Africa because of the cultural restraints imposed upon them at home.

Of most immediate importance to Gandhi, however, were those 'New Age' freedoms that were anti-imperialist in their effects. He read the back-to-nature books written by both British and German enthusiasts. He followed the latters' directions for making mud-packs and recipes for wholemeal loaves. In religion, he tried to overcome the split between Muslims and Hindus and to build up their pride in being Indian, discussing great religious classics, like the *Qu'ran* and the *Bhagavad Gita*. But the moral authority in Phoenix and Tolstoy Farm clearly rested with Gandhi and not with any priest.

Millthorpe

In 1888, the same year that Gandhi came to London to study law, Edward Carpenter (1844–1929) published a book in praise of the simple and communal life that was to have a profound effect on the young Indian. This book, *Civilisation, its Cause and Cure*, was highly critical of Western civilisation and reinforced Gandhi's ideas.

Carpenter was a friend of George Bernard Shaw and of many of the Fabian Socialists though most disagreed with the book. Though born into the upper middle class and highly educated, Carpenter advocated poverty and followed Ruskin's ideas. He lived for some time at St George's Farm near Sheffield, a co-operative agricultural venture of the St George's Guild inspired by Ruskin. Later Carpenter bought himself a smallholding at Millthorpe, in Derbyshire, where he lived at first with a working-class family, and from 1890 on with his lover, George Merrill.

Carpenter shared Gandhi's admiration for Ruskin and Tolstoy. He could also be called a 'self-made Hindu': an Orientalist, he made a trip to Ceylon before settling at Millthorpe, and preferred the great religious classics of India to the Christianity in which he had been brought up. The connection between this love of the East and the 'simple life' is well illustrated by the sandals he habitually wore and made for his friends. The difference between sandals and bare feet on the one hand, and the traditional English leather boot on the other, was very significant. (His sexuality was also related to the East, since Carpenter – like E.M. Forster, and other writers after him – was physically attracted to oriental men.)

Free sexuality, and above all free homosexuality, was another part of Carpenter's teaching; a part with which Gandhi had no sympathy. Amongst Carpenter's popular titles was *Love's Coming of Age*. He was a poet in the style of Whitman, and worked many years on a long poem with the Whitmanesque title 'Towards Democracy'. It could be compared with Monro's 'Jehovah' poem, mentioned earlier. Carpenter constructed a crude shed in which he could sit to compose; the free open air was as important as the concept of freedom to his verse.

Carpenter was a popular speaker who often attracted an audience of as many as 2,000 to Sunday meetings at the Brotherhood church. He was also visited by a series of notables including Shaw and Henry Salt, whose pamphlets on vegetarianism converted Gandhi to the practice. (Strictly speaking, Gandhi practised vegetarianism before reading Salt, but the latter gave him a rationale.) Carpenter differed from Gandhi in his liberated erotic ideas and in the importance he placed on poetry. Indeed, one must go further and say that Millthorpe was not really a commune. But it was a centre of the new life between 1890–1910.

DITCHLING

Eric Gill (1882–1940) belonged to a later generation. His home at Ditchling in Suffolk certainly was a commune, though it was dominated by a single family, or more exactly by its patriarch. Although a writer like those discussed above, he was also a sculptor and woodcutter and practised a number of other visual arts – or, as he would prefer to put it, crafts. These 'New Age' leaders were all inspiring figures, but not all similar: one reason is that they were all eccentric in one way or another.[10]

At Ditchling, the role of religion in the commune was more prominent than at Millthorpe, where it took the form more of a diffused eroticism. Born into the Church of England, Gill was a convert to Roman Catholicism, and much of his work– for example, his Stations of the Cross in Westminister Cathedral – was Catholic and ecclesiastical. He had many admirers among the clergy, in particular the Dominican priest, Vincent McNabb. At the same time, Gill had read Nietzsche with enthusiasm, and, as with many Nietzscheans, much of his work was erotic in feeling. He admired D.H. Lawrence as a novelist, and his Catholicism was erotic. In the early years of the twentieth century in common with artists like Augustus John, Jacob Epstein, and Ambrose McEvoy, he saw Nietzsche as the source of a new religion, and he combined such ideas with his interpretation of Catholic/pagan traditions.

Gill was also strongly attracted to the ideas of the Hindu art historian Ananda Coomaraswamy, who lived in England until the outbreak of the First World War. Gill felt that he was applying traditional Hindu or Indian ideas in his own aesthetics, while in his *The Dance of Shiva*, Coomaraswamy wove Nietzschean ideas together with Hinduism. Coomaraswamy's wife

Ethel, later Ethel Mairet, a weaver and dyer, is said to have instructed Gandhi in spinning and weaving in England.

Ethel Mairet lived in an arts and crafts commune very like Ditchling, situated in Chipping Campden. Gill felt that in his later development he had moved beyond Arts and Crafts, to a whole revolution in the way of life of twentieth-century England. But we are bound to see a kinship between his craft work, Mairet's weavings, Bernard Leach's pots and Frank Brangwyn's engravings. Gill designed the masthead for A.F. Orage's journal *The New Age*, and a poster for the 'Back to the Land' movement.

In 1907 Gill bought a house in Ditchling village and in 1913 (the year of his religious conversion) moved to a farm on Ditchling Common, where he stayed until 1924. From there he and his extended family and apprentices moved to a settlement in Wales, and then to Piggot's farm near High Wycombe. In 1913 he described their project as follows: 'Their object was to own home and land and to produce for their own consumption such food as could be produced at home, for instance milk, butter, pigs, poultry and eggs, and to make such things as could be made at home.'[11] In his smock and stockings, Gill and his followers were as distinct from their neighbours as the Asconans were from theirs.

Community Farm

The writer and critic John Middleton Murry (1889–1957) had been attracted to the idea of farming, from his early years as a student at Oxford. Farming was linked in his mind with the idea of England, and so with a kind of mystical patriotism; and he had been interested in joining D.H. Lawrence in the commune project 'Rananim', which the latter tried from time to time to realise. The climactic moment in that scheme came in 1923, when Lawrence invited his friends to join him in New Mexico, but Murry refused.

After Lawrence died in 1930, however, Murry took to living in the country, and friends gathered round him at Larling and Langham. He said that what drew him to farming was 'the hunger for a religious basis, a suprapersonal allegiance in my life'.[12] But the move was also linked to Christian pacifism. Murry went to live in the Old Rectory at Larling in East Anglia in 1933, when he lost faith in the Independent Labour Party and began to take an interest in pacifism. He soon became director of the Peace Pledge Union (of which Gill was also a member at the time). 'I see in the pacifist movement the raw material of a new Christian church,' he wrote in *Peace News* in May 1940. 'The pacifist community is to me the analogue of the Christian community 1900 years ago.'

In 1935 Murry bought The Oaks, Langham, and established the Adelphi

Centre there as a venue for conferences deriving from ideas put forward in his journal, *The Adelphi*. The centre was run by a staff of a dozen men and women and included workshops (as at Ditchling) and a guest house. It was hoped that the journal might come to be printed there eventually, just as Gandhi's *Indian Opinion* was printed at Phoenix.

Murry's Community Farm of 180 acres was attached to the Adelphi Centre. A group of a dozen people worked on it, and it gradually developed into a successful agricultural concern. In the last decade of Murry's life he was quite a successful gentleman farmer. But he was always a promoter of 'new life' ideas.

The Adelphi Centre had been set up as a company, of which Murry was permanent chairman. The first Summer School was held there in 1936. George Orwell went to lecture there, as did Karl Polanyi, John Strachey and Herbert Read. Max Plowman, a very close friend and a Quaker, wrote *The Faith Called Pacifism*, and was General Secretary of the Peace Pledge Union. (The Pledge declared, 'I renounce war, and I will never support or sanction another.') Murry eventually succeeded Plowman in the post.

The two most important people to Murry in the first and more literary half of his career were Katherine Mansfield and D.H. Lawrence, both of whom took a strong interest in 'new life centres'. Mansfield spent her last months at G.I. Gurdjieff's experimental community, the 'Institute for the Harmonious Development of Man' at Fontainebleau, near Paris. Lawrence tried to organise his friends to join him in his 'Rananim' commune, to be located variously in Florida, New Mexico or Colombia. (In 1915 he described it as 'a little colony where there shall be no money but a sort of communism as far as necessaries of life go, and some real decency . . . [assuming] goodness in its members, instead of the assumption of badness'.)[13]

Murry had reservations about such enterprises, just as his friends had reservations about his own. But if one takes into account all Murry's publications, his teaching, his autobiographical writings, one surely has to acknowledge him as the central personality in the new cultural-aesthetic movement in England in the first half of this century. Murray may also be said to have sacrificed a very promising literary or scholarly career to this other work. Despite his preoccupation with his religious ideas, he wrote a number of excellent essays on, the example Wordsworth and Coleridge, and he was an enthusiastic appreciator of the very different personalities of D.H. Lawrence and T.S. Eliot. Even more strikingly, he was an enthusiastic admirer of Gandhi, who was ignored by both of these seminal literary modernists.

In 1938 Murry read Gandhi's book *Hind Swaraj* and described it in his journal as:

> a classic almost by the simple lucidity of its expression: and certainly an epoch-making little book by the profundity of its insight. A *great* little book, which I am very glad to have read, and shall read again. A masterpiece of religion and philosophy . . . There is room for a deeply interesting comparison of Rousseau and Gandhi.[14]

However, though Murry was read by quite a large non-scholarly public of spiritual seekers, as far as serious contemporary writers went he was considered the 'best-hated' man of his generation because of his self-identification with such a number of 'New Age' schemes, and his experimenting with his own emotions and relationships. He was excluded from the consensus of respect and was mocked and satirised by contemporaries including Aldous Huxley, Bertrand Russell and Leonard Woolf.[15]

The case of Murry therefore indicates the variety of 'new life centres' in his day in England, and also throws light on the half-hidden, half-hostile relations between countercultural projects and 'culture', as the latter constitutes itself in an age of consensus.

CONCLUSION

There are, then, patterns or waves of experimental thought and action connected with notions of a 'New Age' or 'new life' which recur throughout history. There are always connections between such experiments and the contemporary high culture of art, religion and philosophy – as was the case in the 1880–1920 period. In this chapter quite a few names have appeared which will be familiar to students of art and thought. But a real 'New Age' of the type in question is bound to be in revolt against the established forms of high culture. Consequently a revenge is taken by the latter in the consensus periods which occur between 'New Ages' – a revenge which often takes the form of satire on 'New Ages' and their proponents. In the realm of political action, also, the structure of a government or a party, or even the more fluid structure of a charismatic leadership, may be at odds with 'new life' freedoms, although there are partial exceptions to that rule, as we see in the case of Gandhi.

Academics (as readers of this essay are likely to be) are bound to pay special attention to those cases where 'new life' advocates have a demonstrable effect upon the large structures of established culture. But we should recognise and respect these other elements. We can best bring these things together by imagining an underground water system which, except in times of drought, always moves below the surface of high culture and professional propriety: a system that is out of our sight, and out of our sympathy much of the time, but that deserves to be studied because it is always necessary if the land is to be fertile.

Notes

1. In my *Mountain of Truth* (1986) and *Prophets of a New Age* (1992) I discuss these phenomena from a more broadly historical perspective
2. Linse (1983: 13).
3. Freud (1962 [orig. 1930]: 44).
4. Baldwin (1970: 35).
5. Ibid.: 33.
6. Hauptmann (1923: 184).
7. Armytage (1961).
8. Shaw (1935).
9. Shaw (1940).
10. MacCarthy (1989).
11. Ibid., 118.
12. Mairet (1958).
13. Boulton, ed. (1980).
14. Murry (1986: 184–5).
15. Green (1992: 175–6).

Bibliography

Armytage, W.H.G., 1961: *Heavens Below* (Toronto: University of Toronto Press).

Baldwin, R, ed., 1970: *Kropotkin's Revolutionary Pamphlets* (NY: Dover).

Boulton, James, ed., 1980: *The Letters of D.H. Lawrence*, vol. III (Cambridge: Cambridge University Press).

Freud, Sigmund, 1962 [orig. 1930]: *Civilisation and Its Discontents*, trans. R. Baldwin (NY: W.W. Norton).

Green, M., 1986: *The Mountain of Truth. The counterculture begins (Ascona, 1900–20)* (London: University Press of New England).

——1992: *Prophets of a New Age: the politics of hope from the eighteenth through the twenty-first centuries* (NY: Charles Scribner's Sons).

Hauptmann, Gerhardt, 1923: *The Heretic of Soana* (NY: B.W. Huelosch)

Linse, Ulrich, 1983: *Barfüssige Propheten* (Berlin: Siedler Verlag).

MacCarthy, Fiona, 1989: *Eric Gill* (London: Faber & Faber).

Mairet, Philip, 1958: *John Middleton Murry* (London: Longmans Green).

Murry, K.M., 1986: *Beloved Quixote* (London: Souvenir).

Shaw, Nellie, 1935: *Whiteway, a Colony on the Cotswolds* (London: C. W. Daniel).

——1940: *A Czech Philosopher on the Cotswolds* (London: C. W. Daniel).

4

Jung's Psychologising of Religion
Robert A. Segal

INTRODUCTION

In their desperation to find support for religion among its major theorists, scholars in religious studies often turn to the Swiss psychiatrist C.G. Jung (1875–1961). Clearly, Jung approves of religion, by which he means the institutionalised worship of God. For him, religion helps, not harms, adherents. He laments the decline of religion in the modern West and anxiously seeks a replacement for it. Surely, Jung, the son of a village parson, is 'pro-religion' and can be enlisted as a foil to the anti-religious diatribes of, above all, Marx and Freud.

To read Jung in so upbeat a way is in fact to misread him. Jung comes, if not to bury religion, not to praise it either. Rather, he comes to analyse it, which means to psychoanalyse it. No one, not even Freud, psychoanalyses – or, to use the broader term, psychologises – religion more relentlessly than Jung. For him, all religion – modern as well as primitive, living as well as dead, Western as well as Eastern – is a psychological enterprise in metaphysical guise. The origin, function and content of religion are wholly psychological.

Those who take Jung as the saviour of religion misconceive him. He not only explains but also evaluates religion entirely psychologically. Religion may deserve praise, but for its psychological, not its metaphysical, utility. Religion is the handmaiden of psychology. It serves to open adherents not to God but to the godlike side of their own personalities. To the extent that other activities, such as dreams and art, provide an *entrée* to the unconscious, Jung is prepared to propose them as alternatives to religion. At the same time Jung's stress on religion as the cultivation of the inner self accounts in part for his appeal to New Age practitioners.[1]

PSYCHOLOGY AND METAPHYSICS

Jung underscores his focus on the utility of religion by continually characterising himself as a mere psychologist rather than a philosopher. The truth of religion falls outside his professional purview:

> I approach psychological matters from a scientific and not from a philosophical standpoint. Inasmuch as religion has a very important psychological aspect, I deal with it from a purely empirical point of view, that is, I restrict myself to the observation of phenomena and I eschew any metaphysical or philosophical considerations . . . The psychologist, if he takes up a scientific attitude, has to disregard the claim of every creed to be the unique and eternal truth. He must keep his eye on the human side of the religious problem. (1969c: 2, 10)[2]

Jung regularly distinguishes his psychological use of the term 'God' from a metaphysical one: 'When I say "God" this is a psychic thing . . . This has nothing whatever to do with God *per se*' (1973: 487). Jung bristles at the characterisation of himself, especially by theologians, as a metaphysician – for example, the common labelling of him as a 'Gnostic'. Declares Jung: 'The designation of my "system" as "Gnostic" is an invention of my theological critics . . . I am not a philosopher, merely an empiricist' (1976d: 1642).[3]

Undeniably, Jung himself waxes metaphysical. He unabashedly professes belief in God. For example, he recounts that 'from the beginning' he had 'the conviction' that 'it was enjoined upon me to do what God wanted and not what I wanted. That gave me the strength to go my own way. Often I had the feeling that in all decisive matters I was no longer among men, but was alone with God' (1962: 48). Best known is Jung's answer to the question, posed by a BBC interviewer, whether he still believed in God: 'I *know*. I don't need to believe. I know' (1977: 428). Neither these statements nor others, however, are made on *psychological* grounds. Jung considers himself free to speculate on all topics, as he does most of all in *Memories, Dreams, Reflections*, but *not* as psychologist.

At the same time Jung refuses to refrain from psychologising the metaphysics of religion. His rigid, Kantian-like hiatus between the metaphysical and the non-metaphysical domains allows him to psychologise metaphysics without becoming metaphysical himself. Hence he objects as vigorously to theologians who deny him his psychological due as to those who mistake his psychology for metaphysics: 'Psychology has no room for judgments like "only religious" or "only philosophical," despite the fact that we too often hear the charge of something's being "only psychological" – especially from theologians' (1962: 350).

Jung finds most of his theological antagonists exasperating, not only because they mistake his psychological pronouncements for metaphysical ones but also because, as theologians, they focus on belief. For Jung, the heart of religion is not belief but experience – another respect in which his approach to religion appeals to New Age devotees. Thus Jung invokes Rudolf Otto's characterisation of religion as the encounter with an over-powering God:

> In speaking of religion I must make clear from the start what I mean by that term. Religion, as the Latin word denotes, is a careful and scrupulous observation of what Rudolf Otto aptly termed the *numinosum*, that is, a dynamic agency or effect not caused by an arbitrary act of will. On the contrary, it seizes and controls the human subject, who is always its victim rather than its creator. (1969c: 6)

Psychologised, the cause of this experience is not an external God but one's own unconscious, which has the same relationship to consciousness as, for the Lutheran Otto, God has to the believer. In insisting that religion is at heart experience, Jung denies that it is at heart creed: 'I want to make clear that by the term "religion" I do not mean a creed' (1969c: 9). For Jung, creed is secondary and indeed derivative: 'Creeds are codified and dogmatised forms of original religious experience' (1969c: 10). Experience shapes creed, not *vice versa*.

TRADITIONAL DIFFICULTIES FACING RELIGION

In its capacity to work psychologically, religion for Jung faces various problems, some traditional, some distinctively modern. Mainstream Christianity, especially in contrast to Gnosticism, has perennially failed to provide avenues to all parts of the unconscious. For example, by excluding Mary from the pantheon, it has blocked what would serve, and what in popular practice does serve, as a channel for the experience of the anima archetype – the feminine side of the male personality:

> Medieval iconology . . . evolved a quaternity symbol in its representations of the coronation of the Virgin and surreptitiously put it in place of the Trinity. The Assumption of the Blessed Virgin Mary, i.e., the taking up of Mary's soul into heaven *with her body*, is admitted as ecclesiastical doctrine but has not yet become dogma. (1969c: 251)

Similarly, the exclusion of Satan from the pantheon has closed off what would serve as a channel for the experience of the shadow archetype – the evil side of the human personality:

But the Christian definition of God as the *summum bonum* excludes the Evil One right from the start, despite the fact that in the Old Testament he was still one of the 'sons of God.' Hence the devil remained outside the Trinity as the 'ape of God' and in opposition to it . . . The devil is, undoubtedly, an awkward figure: he is the 'odd man out' in the Christian cosmos. That is why people would like to minimize his importance by euphemistic ridicule or by ignoring his existence altogether; or, better still, to lay the blame for him at man's door. (1969c: 252)[4]

Second, Jung faults mainstream Protestantism in particular for its failure to provide *safe* openings to the unconscious. By eliminating most sacra-ments and other rituals, Protestantism has left worshippers on their own, still able to encounter God and thereby the unconscious, but bereft of the guidance provided by fixed rituals and mediation by priests:

Protestantism, having pulled down so many walls carefully erected by the Church, immediately began to experience the disintegrating and schismatic effect of individual revelation. As soon as the dogmatic fence was broken down and the ritual lost its authority, man had to face his inner experience without the protection and guidance of dogma and ritual, which are the very quintessence of Christian as well as of pagan religious experience. Protestantism has, in the main, lost all the finer shades of traditional Christianity: the mass, confession, the greater part of the liturgy, and the vicarious function of priesthood. (1969c: 33)

Jung pointedly notes that the majority of his patients are Protestants and Jews rather than Catholics,[5] whose unconscious life 'has been channelled into the dogmatic archetypal ideas and flows along like a well-controlled stream in the inwardness of the Catholic psyche' (1968a: 21). For Jung, few persons harbour either the courage to undertake or the strength to with-stand a solitary encounter with the unconscious, even when the uncon-scious is experienced as God. Jung himself came close to being shattered by his confrontation with the unconscious following his break with Freud in 1912.

MODERN DIFFICULTIES FACING RELIGION

Jung faults Christianity generally, Catholicism no less than Protestantism, for its failure to reconcile itself with modern science. More precisely, Jung grants that religious *belief* is inherently incompatible with modern science. While belief, like the rest of religion, can be psychologised, the *acceptance* of belief requires the acceptance of it as true about the world, not merely as true about oneself.

To see the place of religion in Jung's scheme, it is helpful to note the various stages of psychological development into which he divides human-ity.[6] The key divide for him is between 'primitives' and ancients on the one hand, and moderns and contemporaries on the other. Primitives project themselves onto the external world in the form of gods and, more, identify themselves with those gods. Ancients also project themselves onto the world in the form of gods, but do not identify themselves with their gods. Ancients worship gods distinct from themselves.

Primitives and ancients alike interpret religion literally, so that it refers to the external world. Yet it still functions to connect them to their uncon-scious. It simply does so circuitously, via projection onto the outer world:

> All the mythologized processes of nature, such as summer and winter, the phases of the moon, the rainy seasons, and so forth, are in no sense allegories of these objective [i.e., external] occurrences; rather they are symbolic expressions of the inner, unconscious drama of the psyche which becomes accessible to man's consciousness by way of projection – that is, mirrored in the events of nature. (1968a: 7)

To encounter God is really to encounter oneself.

By contrast to both primitives and ancients, moderns and contempor-aries have largely withdrawn their projections from the world. They experience the world itself, unfiltered by their unconscious. That world is natural rather than supernatural, impersonal rather than personified. It is explained by science, not religion: 'Only in the following centuries, with the growth of natural science, was the projection withdrawn from matter and entirely abolished together with the psyche . . . Nobody, it is true, any longer endows matter with mythological properties' (1968d: 395).

Like primitives and ancients, moderns and contemporaries interpret religion literally, but then they must reject it in the name of science Moderns, who here part company with contemporaries, pride themselves on their rejection of religion, which they pit not only against science but also against their image of themselves as wholly rational, progressive, omniscient and omnipotent beings. They, not any gods, are the masters of their destiny. Nothing inner or outer lies outside their control. The notion of an unconscious is as anathema to them as the notion of God. In rejecting religion as irrational, they reject the best vehicle to date for encountering the unconscious. In similarly rejecting an unconscious as irrational, they see no need to find a psychological substitute for religion.[7]

The difference between moderns and contemporaries lies here: not in the rejection of religion, which they share, but in the necessity of a substitute, which moderns spurn and which contemporaries crave. Recognising the existence of an unconscious, contemporaries seek alternative, non-projective means of attending to it. They bemoan the loss of religion as a means, even while resolutely rejecting it as an explanation of the world. Moderns, scornful of the idea of an unconscious, see no psychological value in religion and unhesitatingly embrace science as its explanatory successor. Science for them does all that religion has done, and does it better.

The modern dismissal of the unconscious does not, however, eliminate it. Moderns still partly project their unconscious onto the world – for example, in continued deference to superstitions like not walking under a ladder. More important, all moderns still project themselves onto other human beings: 'Projection is now confined to personal and social relationships' (1968d: 395). Jung especially observes the projection of the shadow onto others:

> We are convinced that certain people have all the bad qualities we do not know in ourselves or that they practise all those vices which could, of course, never be our own. We must still be exceedingly careful not to project our own shadows too shamelessly; we are still swamped with projected illusions. (1969c: 140)

Yet as fully as moderns project their unconscious, to express it inadvertently is hardly to attend to it. To gain attention, the unconscious must now foist itself upon moderns in the form of neurosis:

> When in the Babylonian epic Gilgamesh's arrogance and hybris defy the gods, they create a man equal in strength to Gilgamesh in order to check the hero's unlawful ambition. The very same thing has happened to our patient: he is a thinker who has settled, or is always going to settle, the world by the power of his intellect and reason. His ambition has at least succeeded in forging his own personal fate. He has forced everything under the inexorable law of his reason, but somewhere nature escaped and came back with a vengeance . . . It was the worst blow that could be dealt to all his rational ideals and especially to his belief in the all-powerful human will . . . Being highly rationalistic and intellectual he had found that his attitude of mind and his philosophy forsook him completely in the face of his neurosis and its demoralizing forces. He found nothing in his whole Weltanschauung that would help him to gain sufficient control of himself. (1969c: 27, 51)

Jung is not faulting religion for losing moderns to science. As an explanation of the world, religion is incompatible with science, and moderns by definition accept science. Jung has no interest in sophisticated attempts to reconcile religious explanation with scientific explanation – for example, by placing God behind the scenes. Either God is capable of being experienced, or God is dead. A religion which removes God from the realm of human experience is no longer religion but, instead, philosophy.

Similarly, Jung is not faulting science for making atheists of moderns. Science is to be celebrated, not condemned, for its advances, and Jung sees the development of psychology as part of the scientific advance. He proudly deems himself a scientist of the mind. The triumph of science over religion poses a problem for religion, but the solution is not to reject science for religion. The solution is either to update religion or to replace it.

UPDATING RELIGION

For Jung, religion cannot be updated as an explanation of the world. Religion can be saved only by extracting the mythology from the rest of religion and then psychologising the mythology, by which he means the stories of the lives of gods and heroes. Jung does not try to extract ritual.

For Jung, mythology and religion have traditionally worked in tandem. Religion has preserved mythology, and mythology has sustained religion. Together with ritual, mythology has provided the best *entrée* to God. In contrast to belief, which gives only information, myth offers experience:

> The protean mythologem and the shimmering symbol express the processes of the psyche far more trenchantly and, in the end, far more clearly than the clearest concept; for the symbol not only conveys a visualization of the process but – and this is perhaps just as important – it also brings a re-experiencing of it. (1968c: 199)

Jung praises early Christianity for both adopting and adapting pagan myths: 'The fact that the myth [of the phoenix] was assimilated into Christianity by interpretation is proof, first of all, of the myth's vitality; but it also proves the vitality of Christianity, which was able to interpret and assimilate so many myths.' A religion that does not reinterpret its myths is dead. The 'spiritual vitality' of a religion 'depends on the continuity of myth, and this can be preserved only if each age translates the myth into its own language and makes it an essential content of its view of the world' (1970d: 474 n.297).

Unlike early Christianity, modern Christianity has failed to update its myths. That failure is a part of its overall failure to reinvigorate itself. Sometimes Jung argues that modern Christianity has gone astray by severing belief from experience and trying in vain to rely on sheer belief. Jung's objection here is twofold: that belief without experience is empty, and that the belief is often incompatible with modern scientific and historical knowledge. At other times Jung contends that modern Christianity has gone awry in trying to meet the challenge of modernity by turning belief into faith severed from knowledge. Jung's objection here is that even faith requires experience to sustain itself. As Jung sums up his criticisms of both options:

> The Churches stand for traditional and collective convictions which in the case of many of their adherents are no longer based on their own inner experience but on *unreflecting belief*, which is notoriously apt to disappear as soon as one begins thinking about it. The content of belief then comes into collision with knowledge, and it often turns out that the irrationality of the former is no match for the ratiocinations of the latter. Belief is no adequate substitute for inner experience, and where this is absent even a strong faith which came miraculously as a gift of grace may depart equally miraculously. (1970b: 521)

While these particular criticisms do not involve myth, at still other times Jung says that modern Christianity has erred in its attempt to update itself by *eliminating* myth. Jung is here referring to Rudolf Bultmann's 'demythologisation' of the New Testament (Bultmann 1953: 1–44). Jung's first objection is that the supposed incompatibility of myth with modern knowledge stems from a false, literal interpretation of myth: 'Theology [wrongly] rejects any tendency to take the assertions of its earliest records as written myths and, accordingly, to understand them symbolically' (1970b: 551). Jung's second objection is that myth is indispensable to experience and thereby to religion:

> Indeed, it is the theologians themselves who have recently made the attempt – no doubt as a concession to 'knowledge' – to 'demythologize' the object of their faith while drawing the line [between myth and religion] quite arbitrarily at the crucial points. But to the critical intellect it is only too obvious that myth is an integral component of all religions and therefore cannot be excluded from the assertions of faith without injuring them. (1970b: 551)

Here Christianity has sought to overcome the opposition between faith and modern knowledge by discarding belief at odds with knowledge. But in eliminating myth, it has eliminated experience as well.

At yet other times Jung maintains that modern Christianity has rightly turned to myth to resurrect itself but has still failed to reinterpret myth symbolically and thereby make it palatable to moderns:

> [R]eligions have long turned to myths for help . . . But you cannot, artificially and with an effort of will, believe the statements of myth if you have not

previously been gripped by them. If you are honest, you will doubt the truth of the myth because our present-day consciousness has no means of understanding it. Historical and scientific criteria do not lend themselves to a recognition of mythological truth; it can be grasped only by the intuitions of faith or by psychology. (1970e: 751)

Ironically, Bultmann, despite the misleading term 'demythologisation,' strives to do the same as Jung: not to eliminate myth from the New Testament but, on the contrary, to reinterpret myth symbolically in order to make it acceptable to moderns. And Bultmann, also like Jung, argues that the true meaning of the New Testament has always been symbolic, though for Bultmann, myth read symbolically describes the human condition rather than, as for Jung, the human mind.

By Christian mythology, Jung means the life of Christ. Read literally, the Gospels are incompatible with both history and science. But if, writes Jung, 'the statement that Christ rose from the dead is to be understood not literally but symbolically, then it is capable of various interpretations that do not conflict with knowledge and do not impair the meaning of the statement' (1970b: 521). Read psychologically, the life of Christ becomes a symbol of the archetypal journey of the hero from primordial unconsciousness (birth) to ego consciousness (adulthood) to return to the unconscious (crucifixion) to reemergence from it to form the self (resurrection). Understood symbolically, Christ serves as a model for Christians seeking to cultivate their relation to the self – an interpretation that tallies with that of New Age religiosity. Without denying the historicity of Christ, Jung maintains that Christ can be inspirational even as a mythical hero. Indeed, for Jung the prime appeal of Christ's life has always been mythical, which for Jung means psychological:

Christ lived a concrete, personal, and unique life which, in all essential features, had at the same time an archetypal character. This character can be recognized from the numerous connections of the biographical details with worldwide myth-motifs . . . The life of Christ is no exception in that not a few of the great figures of history have realized, more or less clearly, the archetype of the hero's life with its characteristic changes of fortune . . . Since the life of Christ is archetypal to a high degree, it represents to just that degree the life of the archetype. But since the archetype is the unconscious precondition of every human life, its life, when revealed, also reveals the hidden, unconscious ground-life of every individual. (1969c: 146)[8]

Jung contends, further, that the Gospels themselves present a combined mythical and historical figure: 'In the gospels themselves factual reports, legends, and myths are woven into a whole. This is precisely what constitutes the meaning of the gospels, and they would immediately lose their character of wholeness if one tried to separate the individual from the archetypal with a critical scalpel' (1969c: 146). Just like Bultmann, to whom he is in fact so close, Jung thus claims to be explicating the symbolic meaning intended by the Gospels all along. For both Jung and Bultmann, the obstacles that modernity poses to a literal rendition of Christ's life offer an opportunity to make clear for the first time the meaning intended from the outset.

REPLACING RELIGION

Jung never faults Christian mythology itself for its outdatedness, only its interpreters: 'Our myth has become mute, and gives no answers. The fault lies not in it as it is set down in the Scriptures, but solely in us, who have not developed it further, who, rather, have suppressed any such attempts' (1962: 332). Still, Jung recognises that religion has simply ceased to be an option for many, even if he is by no means assuming all present-day Westerners to be either moderns or contemporaries.[9] Jung's alternative solution to the incompatibility of religion and science is not to update the mythology but to replace it – by secular myths.

For Jung, secular myths take several forms. Minimally, artists recast traditional, religious myths in secular garb: 'Mythological motifs frequently appear, but clothed in modern dress; for instance, instead of the eagle of Zeus, or the great roc, there is an airplane; the fight with the dragon is a railway smash; the dragon-slaying hero is an operatic tenor; the Earth Mother is a stout lady selling vegetables; the Pluto who abducts Persephone is a reckless chauffeur, and so on' (1966: 152).

More significant for Jung has been the outright revival of traditional myth, of which his grandest example is the revival of the worship of Wotan in twentieth-century Germany: 'But what is more than curious – indeed, piquant to a degree – is that an ancient god of storm and frenzy, the long quiescent Wotan, should awake, like an extinct volcano, to new activity, in a civilised country that had long been supposed to have outgrown the Middle Ages' (1970a: 373). In parts of Germany, Wotan was taken as no mere literary metaphor but a real god 'out there,' worshipped with the slaughtering of sheep and other rituals. Here myth was lived out, not merely interpreted. To be sure, Wotan was not taken as a weather god, but he was considered the divine force behind Germany's destiny.

Still more significant for Jung has been the creation of new, distinctively secular myths, of which his best example is the belief in flying saucers. The belief is widespread. It arouses archetypal emotions of awe and fear. Flying saucers are invoked to explain events in the physical world. Above all, flying saucers, as a technologically advanced phenomenon, fit the present-day scientific self-image: 'It is characteristic of our time that the archetype . . . should now take the form of an object, a technological construction, in order to avoid the odiousness of mythological personification. Anything that looks technological goes down without difficulty with modern man' (1970c: 624).

For all Jung's insistence that the referent and in turn the function of myth are wholly inner, and for all his disdain for those who take the referent and the function of myth to be outer,[10] he himself revels in the outer as well as the inner function of myth. Psychologically, flying saucers, often depicted as round, symbolise the archetype of the self and thereby abet the attainment of that unified state. But flying saucers also symbolise gods, who are themselves typically associated with roundness:

> There is an old saying that 'God is a circle whose centre is everywhere and the circumference nowhere.' God, in his omniscience, omnipotence, and omnipresence, is a totality symbol *par excellence*, something round, complete, and perfect . . . On the antique level, therefore, the Ufos could easily be conceived as 'gods.' (1970c: 622)

Just as the archetype of the self unifies the opposing parts of the psyche, so flying saucers, sighted especially during the Cold War, served to inspire hope that God would soon come to earth and bring peace to a world threatened with nuclear war:

> The present world situation is calculated as never before to arouse expectations of a redeeming, supernatural event. If these expectations have not dared to show themselves in the open, this is simply because no one is deeply rooted enough in the tradition of earlier centuries to consider an intervention from heaven as a matter of course. We have indeed strayed far from the metaphysical certainties of the Middle Ages, but not so far that our historical and psychological background is empty of all metaphysical hope. (1970c: 623)

The myth of flying saucers thus serves to make humans feel at home in the outer world, not merely in the inner one.

In the case of primitives and ancients, both of whom personify the world through projection, Jung readily emphasises that myth functions outwardly:

> Primitive man is not much interested in objective explanations of the obvious, but he has an imperative need – or, rather, his unconscious psyche has an

irresistible urge – to assimilate all outer sense experiences to inner, psychic events. It is not enough for the primitive to see the sun rise and set; this external observation must at the same time be a psychic happening: the sun in its course must represent the fate of a god or hero who, in the last analysis, dwells nowhere except in the soul of man. (1968a: 7)

Personifying the external world gives it meaning and relevance. A personified world operates responsively, in accordance with the purposes of gods and the pleas of humans, rather than mechanically. To cite Jung's favourite example:

The Pueblo Indians believe that they are the sons of Father Sun, and this belief endows their life with a perspective (and a goal) that goes far beyond their limited existence . . . Their plight is infinitely more satisfactory than that of a man in our own civilization who knows that he is (and will remain) nothing more than an underdog with no inner meaning to his life. (1968e: 76)

Undeniably, most secular myths for Jung are non-projective. They presuppose the withdrawal of projections from the outer world, which is now experienced as impersonal and therefore meaningless: 'We have stripped all things of their mystery and numinosity; nothing is holy any longer' (1968e: 84). Most secular myths do not connect the inner world with the outer world, which remains the domain of science. Instead, they connect – better, reconnect – humans to the inner world.

Yet the characterisation of the external world as in fact meaningless really only holds for the earlier Jung. Once Jung, in collaboration with the physicist Wolfgang Pauli, develops the concept of synchronicity, the world for him regains its meaningfulness even without its personality. Indeed, that meaningfulness is now inherent in the world rather than imposed on it through projection: 'Synchronistic experiences serve our turn here. They point to a latent meaning which is independent of [our] consciousness' (1976a: 495). Meaningfulness for the later Jung stems not from the existence of God, or personality, in the world but from the symmetry between human beings and the world. Rather than alien and indifferent to humans, the world proves to be akin to them – not because gods respond to human wishes or because human wishes directly affect the world, but because human thoughts correspond to the nature of the world. As Jung writes of his favourite example of synchronicity, that of a resistant patient who was describing a dream about a golden scarab when a scarab beetle appeared, 'at the moment my patient was telling me her dream a real "scarab" tried to get into the room, as if it had understood that it must play its mythological role as a symbol of rebirth' (1976a: 541). Here the world seemingly responds to the patient's dream, but understood synchronistically, the world merely, if fortuitously, matches the patient's dream. It is the patient's conscious attitude that is 'out of sync' with the world.

With the concept of synchronicity, Jung restores to the world a meaningfulness that the withdrawal of projections still demanded by Jung removes.[11] Synchronicity is not itself myth. Synchronicity is the experience of the world as meaningful. Myth would be an account of that experience, but the pay-off would be less an explanation than connectedness to the world. Those secular myths which, like the myth of flying saucers, connect one to the world and not just to the mind, thereby accomplish more than either dreams or art, both of which function only inwardly. In the age of science, secular myth alone has the potential to duplicate the past psychological and existential feats of religion.

NOTES

1. On Jung's appeal to New Age practitioners, see Heelas (1996: 46–7); Hanegraaff (1996: 496–513).
2. All references to the Collected Works are to paragraph, not page, numbers.
3. In reply above all to the intellectually hapless Martin Buber, who confuses Gnosticism with atheism and who charges the 'Gnostic' Jung with reducing God to humanity, see Jung (1976c: 1499–1513). On Jung as a Gnostic see introduction in Segal (ed., 1992: 43–8).
4. On Jung's praise of Gnosticism for according places to the feminine and to evil, see Segal (1992: chs. 4 and 5).
5. See, for example, Jung (1976b: 370).
6. On these divisions see the introduction to Segal (ed., 1992: 11–19).
7. Jung castigates as well those who, while granting the existence of an unconscious, assume they can control it. The epitome for him of this psychological modernism is Freud. See, for example, Jung (1969c: 141).
8. Like a child in myth, Christ symbolises at once an archetype – the self – and the developing ego. On Christ as a symbol of the self, see Jung (1968b: 68–126). On Christ as a symbol of the ego in relation to the self, see Edinger (1973: ch. 5).
9. Jung's own position on Christianity is unclear. Some maintain that Jung seeks to replace dying Christianity with psychology: see esp. Hostie (1957); Philp (1958). Others contend that Jung seeks to resurrect Christianity through psychology: see esp. Schaer (1950); Cox (1959); White (1952); Stein (1985). Still others argue for a middle ground: see esp. Homans (1995).
10. On Jung's insistence that myth be analysed wholly psychologically, see Segal (1998: 3–7)
11. On synchronicity, see Jung (1969a, 1969b); Main (1997).

BIBLIOGRAPHY

Bultman, Rudolph, 1953 [1944]: 'New Testament and Mythology,' in *Kerygma and Myth*, ed. Hans-Werner Bartsch, tr. Reginald H. Fuller (London: SPCK).

Cox, David, 1959: *Jung and Saint Paul* (London: Longmans, Green; New York: Association Press).

Edinger, Edward F., 1973 [1972]: *Edgo and Archetype* (Baltimore: Penguin).

Hanegraaff, W., 1996: *New Age Religion and Western Culture* (Leiden: E.J. Brill).

Heelas, Paul, 1996: *The New Age Movement* (Oxford: Blackwell).

Homans, Peter, 1995 [1979]: *Jung in Context*, 2nd edn (Chicago: University of Chicago Press).

Hostie, Raymond, 1957 *Religion and the Psychology of Jung*, tr. G.R. Lamb (New York: Sheed and Ward).

Jung, C.G., 1962: *Memories, Dreams, Reflections*, recorded and ed. Aniela Jaffé, trs. Richard and Clara Winston (New York: Vintage Books).

—— 1966: 'Psychology and Literature,' in *The Spirit in Man, Art and Literature*, Collected Works, XV eds Sir Herbert Read *et al.*, trs R.F.C. Hull *et al.*, (Princeton, NJ: Princeton University Press).

—— 1968a [1959]: 'Archetypes of the Collective Unconscious,' in *The Archetypes and the Collective Unconscious*, Collected Works, IX, pt. 1, 2nd edn (Princeton, NJ: Princeton University Press).

—— 1968b [1959]: 'Christ, a Symbol of the Self,' in *Aion*, Collected Works, IX, pt. 2, 2nd edn (Princeton, NJ: Princeton University Press).

—— 1968c: 'Paracelsus as a Spiritual Phenomenon', in *Alchemical Studies*, Collected Works, XIII (Princeton, NJ: Princeton University Press).

—— 1968d: 'The Philosophical Tree,' in *Alchemical Studies*, Collected Works, XIII (Princeton, NJ: Princeton University Press).

—— 1968e [1964]: 'Approaching the Unconscious,' in Jung *et al.*, *Man and His Symbols* (New York: Dell Laurel Editions).

—— 1969a [1960]: 'Synchronicity: An Acausal Connecting Principle', in *The Structure and Dynamics of the Psyche*, Collected Works, VIII, 2nd edn (Princeton, NJ: Princeton University Press).

—— 1969b [1960]: 'On Synchronicity,' in *The Structure and Dynamics of the Psyche*, Collected Works, VIII, 2nd edn (Princeton, NJ: Princeton University Press).

—— 1969c [1958]: 'Psychology and Religion,' in *Psychology and Religion: West and East*, Collected Works XI, 2nd edn (Princeton, NJ: Princeton University Press).

—— 1970a [1964]: 'Wotan,' in *Civilization in Transition*, Collected Works, X, 2nd edn (Princeton, NJ: Princeton University Press).

—— 1970b [1964]: 'The Undiscovered Self,' in *Civilization in Transition*, Collected Works, X, 2nd edn (Princeton, NJ: Princeton University Press).

—— 1970c [1964]: 'Flying Saucers,' in *Civilisation in Tranzition*, Collected Works, X, 2nd edn (Princeton, NJ: Princeton University Press).

—— 1970d [1963]: 'Rex and Regina,' in *Mysterium Coniunctionis*, Collected Works, XIV, 2nd edn (Princeton, NJ: Princeton University Press).

—— 1970e [1963]: 'The Conjunction,' in *Mysterium Coniunctionis*, Collected Works, XIV, 2nd edn (Princeton, NJ: Princeton University Press).

—— 1973: *Letters*, eds Gerhard Adler and Aniela Jaffé, tr. R.F.C. Hull, I (Princeton, NJ: Princeton University Press).

—— 1976a: *Letters*, II (Princeton, NJ: Princeton University Press).

—— 1976b: 'The Tavistock Lectures' (*Analytical Psychology: Its Theory and Practice*), in *The Symbolic Life*, Collected Works, XVIII (Princeton, NJ: Princeton University Press).

—— 1976c: 'Religion and Psychology: A Reply to Martin Buber,' in *The Symbolic Life*, Collected Works, XVIII (Princeton, NJ: Princeton University Press).

—— 1976d: 'Jung and Religious Belief', in *The Symbolic Life*, Collected Works, XVIII (Princeton, NJ: Princeton University Press).

—— 1977: 'The "Face to Face" Interview,' in *C.G. Jung Speaking*, eds William McGuire and R.F.C. Hull (Princeton, NJ: Princeton University Press).

Main, Roderick, ed., 1997: *Jung on Synchronicity and the Paranormal* (London: Routledge).

Philip, Howard L., 1958: *Jung and the Problem of Evil* (London: Rockliff).

Schaer, Hans, 1950: *Religion and the Care of Souls in Jung's Psychology*, trs. R.F.C. Hull (New York: Pantheon).

Segal, Robert A., ed., 1992: *The Gnostic Jung* (Princeton, NJ: Princeton University Press; London: Routledge).

Segal, Robert A., ed., 1998: *Jung on Mythology* (Princeton, NJ: Princeton University Press; London: Routledge).

Stein, Murray, 1985: *Jung's Treatment of Christianity* (Chicago: Chiron).

White, Victor, 1952: *God and the Unconscious* (London: Collins).

Part 2: Places

More of the Same?
Christianity, Vernacular Religion
and Alternative Spirituality in Glastonbury

Marion Bowman

Throughout the centuries Glastonbury has been recognised as a sacred site of intense transformative energies. These energies are not the monopoly of any one belief system, but are available to all. In effect the island acts as a spiritual magnifying glass, amplifying the strength of both positive and negative energies, giving the individual a unique opportunity to accelerate the process of their own growth and awareness.[1]

Glastonbury is a small town (population c.8,000) in rural Somerset, in the southwest of England. Depending on whom you talk to, or what you read, it is also considered to be: the Isle of Avalon; the site of a great Druidic centre of learning; a significant prehistoric centre of Goddess worship; the 'cradle of English Christianity' visited by Joseph of Arimathea, and perhaps even Christ himself; the 'New Jerusalem'; a communication point for alien contact; the 'epicentre' of New Age in England; and the 'heart chakra' of planet earth. Glastonbury has been hailed as 'the fountainhead of three major religions: Wicca, Druidry and Christianity' (Shallcrass, 1995: 23), and, along with Findhorn and Iona, as one of Britain's three 'light centres' (see Monteith, Chapter 6). Numerous spiritual seekers (aligned and non-aligned) feel 'drawn' to Glastonbury (Bowman, 1993a).

If any site in Britain can provide an example of continuity and change in vernacular religion, or act as a microcosm of trends in alternative spirituality, Glastonbury must be a strong contender. Few places enjoy such high status among believers and spiritual seekers of so many different persuasions. Thousands visit Glastonbury for the Anglican and Catholic pilgrimages, for courses at the Isle of Avalon Foundation (which sees itself as the successor to the druidic university some claim existed there), for the vast array of healing on offer, for Goddess conferences, for ritual activity at various times on the eightfold calendar widely observed by pagans, and as individual pilgrims, spiritual seekers and tourists. While the Glastonbury Festival (at nearby Pilton) is primarily a contemporary music festival, it too has become an 'alternative' institution; in addition to the performance events, regular features of the festival have been The Healing Field site and the Sacred Space site, in which various forms of healing, spirituality and ritual experimentation have been promoted, practised and disseminated. Nor is Glastonbury's significance merely local or national. People come to Glastonbury not simply from Britain but from all over Europe, North America, Australia and elsewhere. Many more know of Glastonbury through myths (old and new), books, novels, articles, television features and assorted Glastonbury-related websites.

A review of religious activity in Glastonbury demonstrates the significance of folk or vernacular religion for many aspects of contemporary spirituality. In this chapter I shall first clarify what is meant by the terms 'folk' and 'vernacular' religion, then explore a number of trends in contemporary spirituality, demonstrating how these are exemplified in Glastonbury. I shall argue that the contemporary spiritual scene in Glastonbury in many respects feeds on vernacular religion, and that there exists in Glastonbury what might be described as 'alternative' Christianity. I want to show that in Glastonbury, vernacular religion has been instrumental in the development of alternative spirituality, and that Christianity, though frequently overlooked in the context of contemporary spirituality in Glastonbury, is a dynamic presence there, interacting with alternative spirituality. While the roots of much alternative spirituality in Glastonbury are in vernacular religion, however, many of the current fruits have grown from seeds sown in the late-nineteenth century and the early part of the twentieth century, and these will also be reviewed.

FOLK AND VERNACULAR RELIGION

Folk religion has been defined as 'the totality of all those views and practices of religion that exist among the people apart from and alongside the strictly theological and liturgical forms of the official religion' (Yoder, 1974: 14). Many of Glastonbury's myths and traditions fall into just such a category, and thus tend to be seen as the preserve of the folklorist rather than of the scholar of religion. However, such treatment perpetuates the idea that there is a 'pure' form of religion which matters (the official), and debased forms (such as folk and individual) which do not. In preference to the term 'folk religion', then, it is useful to employ the notion of vernacular religion. As Primiano argues (1995: 44):

> Vernacular religious theory involves an interdisciplinary approach to the study of the religious lives of individuals with special attention to the process of religious belief, the verbal, behavioral, and material expressions of religious belief, and the ultimate object of religious belief.

Rather than being a 'deviant' form of 'proper' religion, vernacular religion is 'religion' as it is played out on a day-to-day basis in the life of the individual. The neglect of the folk or vernacular element of religion has contributed to deficiencies in both academic accounts of religion and the popular understanding of it (see Introduction). In this chapter, I intend to show how in Glastonbury the study of 'vernacular' elements is essential for understanding not only traditional forms of religion but also 'alternative' spiritualities, including New Age and Paganism.

ALTERNATIVE SPIRITUALITY AND VERNACULAR SPIRITUALITY

'Alternative spirituality' in Glastonbury tends to be designated as such in implied contrast to Christianity. However, the folk/vernacular traditions of Christianity in Glastonbury exhibit an 'alternative' aspect of Christianity largely ignored by academia. In Glastonbury this alternative Christianity continues to flourish and has influenced many aspects of what is now regarded as alternative spirituality. It also interacts dynamically with developments in alternative spirituality. Consequently, when I refer to 'contemporary spirituality' in Glastonbury, I include both alternative spirituality and Christianity – and specifically vernacular Christianity – as part of the current spiritual scene.

NARRATIVE IN THE FORMATION OF VERNACULAR SPIRITUALITY

Religious Studies scholars employ 'myth' as a neutral term to describe a 'significant story', making no judgement as to its truth or falsehood. Significant stories of divine or human figures or events within a religious tradition have always been recognised as a vital element of religion *per se*. However, rather less attention has been paid to the narrative (i.e. story-telling) process itself as an ongoing, constantly evolving feature of religion. Of particular significance in vernacular religion, for example, is the 'belief story'. This is characterised by Gillian Bennett (1989: 291) as that class of informal stories which:

1. illustrate current community beliefs;
2. tell not only of personal experiences but also of those that have happened to other people;
3. are used to explore and validate the belief traditions of a given community by showing how experience matches expectations.

I have been told, for example, that the pedestrian crossing on Glastonbury High Street was built on a ley line to ensure that people benefit from its energies, whether or not they are aware of it. Unpacked, this utterance involves belief in ley lines, the locating of a particular ley line, the assumption that ley lines are beneficial on contact, and the confidence that someone in the Highways Department of the local council was sufficiently enlightened to position a pedestrian crossing in accordance with these insights.

Since personal experience narratives, corroborative legends and other stories underpinning popular perceptions are highly important in the establishment and maintenance of a belief system, knowledge of these stories is invaluable in accessing the world view of groups and individuals. Where there is no commonly recognised written canon, and where informal modes of transmission of belief predominate, belief stories should be seen as particularly significant. Such is the case with alternative spirituality. Narratives have always played an important part in establishing Glaston-bury as a Christian centre and they continue to underpin its character as a multivalent focus for alternative spirituality.

TRENDS IN CONTEMPORARY SPIRITUALITY

With the approach of the Millennium, there seem to have been a number of trends recurring in the contemporary spiritual scene, whether in more established forms of religion, in sectarian New Religious Movements or in non-aligned spirituality. Most of these trends can be documented to a greater or lesser extent in Glastonbury. They include the perceived importance of the personal spiritual quest; 'mix-and-match' spirituality; remythologising; healing; the pursuit of a 'Golden Age' and/or a form of 'Noble Savagery'; the revival of traditional customs; the search for hidden wisdom; perceptions of past lives, reincarnation and interconnectedness; and the importance of sacred landscapes, 'topophilia' and pilgrimage. Each of these is examined in more detail below.

THE PERSONAL QUEST

Although many people are currently operating outside established/con-ventional forms of religion (see Sutcliffe, Chapter 1, this by no means signals lack of belief. The extraordinary growth of 'Body, Mind, Spirit' sections in bookshops across Britain, for example, or the huge quantity of 'cyberspace spirituality' on the Internet, are among the indicators that many people are conducting their search for meaning outside (or in addition to) the more traditional forums. People putting together individual packages of belief can also draw on the many resources available through the 'spiritual service industry' which has arisen in Glastonbury and elsewhere (Bowman 1993a, 1994), providing everything from specialist literature, artefacts, courses, workshops, lectures and rituals to services such as Spirit Guide portraits and New Age Bed and Breakfast.

'MIX-AND-MATCH' SPIRITUALITY

While the stress on the individual spiritual quest and personal experience in contemporary spirituality has been much commented on, the 'customised' or 'mix-and-match' nature of much of what is now appearing, and the roles of intuition, personal experience and 'what works for you', are not new. There is a long tradition in vernacular religion of people incorporating diverse beliefs and practices into their version of whatever the notional offical religion might be – whether combining fairy belief with Presbyterianism (see Sanderson, 1976), reincarnation with Anglicanism or knocking the head off a statue of the Infant of Prague to guarantee good weather on a wedding day, under post-Vatican II Catholicism. Experience and belief in efficacy underpin personal belief and praxis, regardless of the tradition. However, in contemporary religion, the element of collage or *bricolage* is particularly pronounced, as people draw upon the great variety of religious and cultural traditions to which they now have access (see Introduction) and which have become 'commodified' in a variety of ways. Tradition-bending and -blending are very much the order of the day, as exemplified by the display in a Glastonbury shop of Bridget crosses and didgeridoos alongside 'dream catchers' specially charged with 'Glastonbury energies'.

REMYTHOLOGISING

A trend of considerable importance is 'remythologising'. The flurry of folkloric activity in the late nineteenth and early twentieth centuries, along with the attention paid to myth by Freud, Jung and such writers as Robert Graves, led to a renewed interest in and awareness of myth and legend which developed in a variety of ways throughout the century (see Segal, Chapter 4). Myths have been revisited and revived; myths have been acted out for ritual and therapeutic purposes (Leith, 1998); myths have been identified with (Rees, 1996); myths have been reinterpreted; myths have been created. There is now a storytelling revival akin to the folk music revival of the 1960s and 1970s (Heywood, 1998). Glastonbury, the focus of so much myth-making for so long, is naturally very much affected by this trend, both in terms of myths about Glastonbury's past and the effect of Glastonbury on individuals in the present (Bowman, 1993a; Dudley Edwards, 1999).

HEALING

Another significant trend in contemporary spirituality is the growing interest in healing and the concomitant growth in the variety of healing(s) on offer. Healing has traditionally been closely connected to vernacular religion, frequently involving the individual putting together a 'package' of complementary resources (prayers, charms, folk/traditional cures, conventional medicine) at times of need. It has also, of course, often been attributed to divine forces and associated with sacred sites. There are estimated to be over one hundred different forms of healing in and around Glastonbury, from aromatherapy and reflexology to crystal therapy, past-life regression and aura cleansing. Individuals can thus choose one form of healing or put together a combination particular to their needs and preferences.

THE GOLDEN AGE AND THE NOBLE SAVAGE

The notions of the Noble Savage or of some kind of 'Golden Age' are also increasingly influential (Bowman, 1995). In essence, there is a growing perception that in the past our ancestors (whether pagan or Christian) were more spiritual, more in touch with nature and had a deeper understanding and awareness of the sacred in everyday life. In Glastonbury, the recovery of a Golden Age and Noble Savagery takes three main forms:

1. Pursuit of the Celtic;
2. The 'revival' of customs;
3. Fascination with native peoples.

Celts

For many in the West, Celts (variously defined and imagined) have become role models for contemporary spirituality (Bowman, 1993b, 1996), and in Glastonbury this is reflected in a particular concern with Druidry, with observance of the 'eightfold calendar' and an interest in Celtic Christianity. The current interest in Brighid/Brigid/Bridget/Bride, as either a pagan Celtic goddess or a Celtic Christian saint (daughter of a Druid father and a Celtic Christian mother) epitomises such concerns. The Bridget Chapel at the rear of the 'Glastonbury Experience' complex, is 'deliberately kept free of specific symbology or artifacts' (*sic*), in order to make it 'welcoming to all, regardless of religious or spiritual affiliation' (Bridget Chapel leaflet). The custom (based largely on the Irish Catholic vernacular tradition) of making a 'Bride doll' at Imbolc (1 February, feast day of St Bridget) has been revived recently by those involved in Goddess spirituality in the town, and Bridget crosses are now among the artefacts on sale in Glastonbury shops. Meanwhile, there is a campaign to protect Bride's Mound, a site traditionally associated with St Bridget, and turn it into a 'sanctuary'.

There is also currently a sort of Christian 'euro-scepticism'. Many Christians see the Celtic church as purer, more spiritual, more in touch with nature and all other virtues valued at the present time. So the Celtic church is hailed as 'our native Christianity, before Roman Christianity imposed on us', and various means of 'recapturing' or 'reviving' the spirit of Celtic Christianity are sought (see Meek, 1992, 1996).

Revival of traditional customs

As assorted spiritual seekers try to recapture a Golden Age, there is much looking back in order to go forward. Many a claim is prefaced with 'tradition tells that . . .', though requests for evidence are often met with indifference verging on distaste. As one informant said dismissively, 'You mean, *observable* phenomena?' What Glastonbury was, is and might be is largely a matter of perception, and is as much to do with the people observing as the phenomena observed.

The White Spring at the foot of Glastonbury Tor, for instance, has become an ancient 'rag well' in recent years, and Derbyshire-style well-dressing (which involves the making of pictures on a bed of clay with flower petals) has been revived there. The person behind the well-dressing revival came to Glastonbury with the specific aim of establishing – or re-establish-ing – well-dressing as a national custom, believing the 'Christianised' Derbyshire form to be a survival of a once-widespread UK tradition.[2] He is interested in water conservation and ecological issues, and believes that if people learn to honour springs and think about water, they are more likely to use it sensibly and with respect. He claimed that Glastonbury is a cultural centre, and felt that if he could establish well-dressing here it could become a national custom again: 'If people see something at Glastonbury, they feel permitted to take it away.'

Native peoples

The concern with a Golden Age includes the idea that contemporary indigenous peoples elsewhere – such as native Americans and native Australians – have managed to sustain archaic forms of spirituality. The desire is to recapture that symbiosis between people and planet, to follow a spiritual path which incorporates the wisdom and praxis of the past and/or emulates existing native peoples. The growth of interest in shamanism as both spiritual path and healing technique, including Celtic shamanism (Matthews, 1991; Jones, 1994) and Druidic sweat lodges, is one example of this. A variety of native peoples, and people who claim to have worked with or been initiated by native peoples, have appeared as lecturers or workshop leaders over the years in Glastonbury.

HIDDEN WISDOM

There is a growing hunger for 'hidden' or secret knowledge of various sorts. This is being accessed through, for example, exploration of the Western Mystery traditions (see Greenwood, Chapter 8), and through 'channelled' wisdom which both imparts knowledge about the past, and advice for the present and future from diverse disembodied sources including historical figures, religious teachers, aliens, angels and ascended Masters. Glastonbury is considered a good receiving point for such wisdom. In the 1970s and 1980s communications were channelled from the 'Ramala Teachers' to the Ramala Centre in Glastonbury.[3] Participants in the Isle of Avalon Foundation's 'Avalonian Magic of Dion Fortune' workshop in 1998 were invited to 'form a living chalice into which the Company and Watchers of Avalon may choose to pour their wisdom and their vision' (workshop leaflet)[4].

Other forms of esoteric knowledge include gematria (sacred geometry) and numerology. John Michell, frequently described as a 'visionary', has been involved in alternative spirituality in Britain since the 1960s. He has written extensively and influentially on gematria in connection with Glastonbury, claiming that the ground plan of the Abbey coincides both with Stonehenge and the Holy City described in Revelation (Michell, 1992). I witnessed one shopkeeper in Glastonbury explaining to an assistant how she used numerological principles in pricing, raising or lowering prices slightly in order to avoid any inauspicious combinations of numbers.

PAST LIVES AND REINCARNATION

In alternative spirituality – as indeed among many who would self-identify as Christians (see Waterhouse, 1999) – it is increasingly commonplace to believe in reincarnation, and in the possibility of recalling past lives. Some people consider difficulties in this life to have been caused by events in a previous existence. Past-life regression as a healing technique is predicated on being able to deal with such problems by revisiting the past. One 'soul therapist' who operates in Glastonbury offers to take the client:

> back before the dawn of creation to connect with his/her soul essence. The soul then has unlimited energy and is naturally able to shed its conditioning. (publicity leaflet)

More positively, reincarnation for many is seen as spiritual progression; 'in every life a lesson' is a commonly quoted maxim in Glastonbury.

INTERCONNECTEDNESS

A trend of considerable importance in contemporary spirituality is the idea of interconnectedness between all life-forms, between humanity and nature, between the empirical world and unseen realms, between past, present and future. A number of the trends already outlined – renewed interest in myth, the search for hidden knowledge, the move to restore ancient beliefs and practices, 'channelling' wisdom from discarnate sources, past-life remembrances – all help to reinforce the notion of interconnectedness. This leads to people thinking more globally, indeed universally. As one of the UK's 'light centres' Glastonbury is not merely nationally significant but, as 'heart chakra' of planet earth, enjoys global significance (Samet, 1987).

SACRED LANDSCAPES AND TOPOPHILIA

At a time when geographical mobility is greater than ever before, Glastonbury furnishes powerful evidence of 'topophilia': the belief that certain locations are inherently powerful and exude a heightened sense of place. People consider all sorts of power (healing, revelatory, restorative, planetary) to be vested in locations such as Glastonbury, Iona and Stonehenge, and such sites are frequently the focus of myths, corroborative legends and

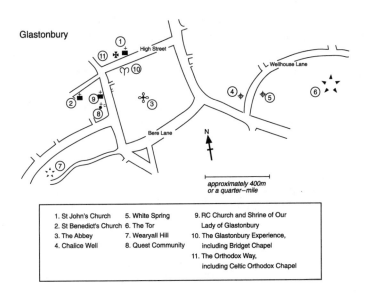

Fig 5.1: Glastonbury – significant sites

personal experience narratives. Moreover, in addition to clearly marked or constructed sacred space, there is a view that entire landscapes have been meaningfully moulded into symbolic shapes, such as the Glastonbury Zodiac (Maltwood, 1964; Caine, 1992). In addition to the Zodiac (which some consider to be the true 'round table' of Arthurian myth), some now discern a reclining Goddess figure in the landscape. Two different figures have recently been pointed out to me:[5] one whose womb is covered by the Lady Chapel of Glastonbury Abbey, and another whose belly is formed by Chalice Hill, with the red waters of Chalice Well as her menstrual flow. Some now see the outline of a swan encompassing the area of Glastonbury, claiming this to be a sign that it is under the special care of the Goddess Brighid.[6] All this is taking very literally the idea of sacred landscape – that landscape communicates its sacred character directly to those willing to see and understand.

PILGRIMAGE

Travelling with a purpose to sites considered more sacred or special than others plays a considerable part in the lives of diverse spiritual seekers. Pilgrimage is being developed by new groups, and rediscovered by more traditional adherents. Examples of the latter are the Baptists who flock to Iona or the Evangelicals who seek transformation in Toronto. Traditional (or what are perceived to be traditional) pilgrimages are being revived and new pilgrimages are being created. Journeying has long been associated with individual spiritual welfare and advancement. Frequently it is seen as part of a negotiation with the divine, often with an element of choice of location. Frequently, too, it takes place without the full approval or control of officialdom.

Glastonbury serves a variety of pilgrims – Christian, Pagan, New Age, Buddhist to name but a few – and hosts pilgrimages formal and informal, traditional and non-traditional, individual and group (Bowman, 1993a). It is a multivalent destination, an end-point and a location for spiritual journeying, with guides of your choice for the Glastonbury of your choice. The main object of Christian pilgrimage in Glastonbury is the Abbey, the focus one weekend each summer for an Anglican Pilgrimage on Saturday, and a Catholic Pilgrimage the next day. Gothic Image offers 'Mystical Tours' of Glastonbury, 'England's Jerusalem and gateway to the spirit realm, a place of natural enchantment' (tour leaflet). The 1997 Gatekeepers Trust 'Pilgrims Weekend' focused on the Glastonbury Zodiac, particularly 'wells on each of the Zodiacal signs and their use as spiritual gateways' (publicity leaflet). Naturally, a variety of shops and services exist to cater for the needs of this plethora of pilgrims.

As I have shown above, the current spiritual milieu in Glastonbury exemplifies a number of trends characteristic of late-twentieth-century religiosity. However, in order to contextualise what is happening in the much-publicised 'alternative' scene, and to understand how Christianity is both contributing to and participating in contemporary spirituality, I shall now turn to vernacular and 'alternative' Christianity in Glastonbury.

'ALTERNATIVE' CHRISTIANITY IN GLASTONBURY

SIGNIFICANT STORIES

Much of Glastonbury's success as a Christian centre has been built on vernacular religion. Local legend is an important feature of popular belief, since it roots matters of universal concern in one specific place; it localises the sacred. Glastonbury is awash with legend. (As one woman commented, 'There's a new myth created every day around Glastonbury.') Three sets of myths, concerning Joseph of Arimathea, Jesus and Arthur, have been particularly important to Glastonbury's Christian lore.

According to the first set of myths, Joseph of Arimathea, who provided a tomb for Jesus after the crucifixion, was sent by St Philip to spread Christianity to England. Landing with his companions at Glastonbury by boat, 'weary all' from their journey, Joseph is said to have thrust his staff into the ground on what is now known as Wearyall Hill, where it flourished to become the Glastonbury Thorn, which flowers both in Spring and around Christmas.[7] For many Glastonians, Wearyall Hill is *the* significant site, and the link with Joseph through the thorn is considered very precious. Joseph reputedly built a simple church dedicated to St Mary at Glastonbury, on the site where the Abbey later stood. Joseph is also said to have brought with him some sort of vessel, which became known as the 'Grail' (Carley, 1996). The vicar of St John's Church reports that visitors frequently come looking for Joseph's tomb, having read, or heard, that it lies in the church.[8] Early Welsh Calvinists played upon the idea that Joseph founded a primitive and pure Celtic church in Britain before the advent of missionaries from Rome, a claim which still resonates for many today.

The connection between Joseph, the Grail and Glastonbury is significant in relation to the second set, the Arthurian myths, in which the quest for the Grail forms an important motif. After his last battle, Arthur was said to have been taken for healing to the Isle of Avalon, which some identified with Glastonbury (Ashe, 1957; Carley, 1996); according to legend he 'rests' there still, waiting to reappear at some great hour of need. This legendary association seemed to be confirmed when, around 1190, it was announced that the bodies of King Arthur and Queen Guinevere had been found in the Abbey grounds, and they were reburied with great ceremony within the Abbey the following century. Although not strictly speaking religious relics, the remains of Arthur and his queen were a great draw for pilgrims, and the Abbey provided enduring 'proof' of the connection between Glastonbury, Arthur and Avalon in popular tradition.

The third set of myths concerns Jesus. One aspect of vernacular Christianity, 'the tales which derive from the Bible and its silences' (Utley, 1945: 1), has been and continues to be particularly significant for Glastonbury. One of the great silences of the New Testament surrounds what Jesus was doing between the age of twelve and thirty, and a variety of answers to this question have provided endless speculations and gap-filling in relation to Glastonbury. In a set of extrapolations from the Joseph of Arimathea myth, Joseph is said to have been a rich merchant who was accustomed to visiting the west of England in search of the tin and/or lead mined in the area, while Jesus is said to have been his nephew. What could be more natural, the logic runs, than for Joseph to have brought Jesus along on his business trips? This idea has been most famously and eloquently reflected in Blake's words:

> And did those feet in ancient times
> Walk upon England's mountains green?
> And was the Holy Lamb of God
> On England's pleasant pastures seen?

The idea that Jesus came to England, specifically to Glastonbury, has been a tremendously significant myth for English Christians, and is still an important draw for Christians today. As one Catholic priest said to me of the legends, 'It might have happened. I would like to believe it happened'. Some are less tentative on this point; typical of this genre is Kirsten Parsons who claims in *Reflections on Glastonbury*:

> It does seem reasonable to assume that Joseph of Arimathea took the boy Jesus with him on some of these trips, and that our Lord came to love the Isle of Avalon and its glorious setting. So He undoubtedly came one day and decided to stay, spending the remainder of His time before commencing His ministry in Galilee. (1965: 6)

The speculation continues. There is the British Israelite prediction that Christ will appear in Glastonbury at the time of the Second Coming. There is the belief that Jesus came to Britain, to Glastonbury in particular, seeking instruction at the great Druidic teaching centre believed by some to have existed there. Similarly, in an updated version of the tradition, some now talk of Christ coming to Glastonbury 'to walk along the ley lines' (*The Guardian*, 9 June 86, p. 10).

CHRISTIAN CUSTOM

Each December, at the Anglican parish church of St John the Baptist, Glastonbury, there is a 'thorn-cutting ceremony' at which sprays of flowers from the Holy Thorn in the church grounds are cut in the presence of the Mayor, members of the town council, children from the Church of England primary school and other Glastonians. These sprays are then sent to the Queen and the Queen Mother. The ceremony provides the occasion for the retelling of the Holy Thorn legend, highlighting the significance of its flowering around the time of the two major Christian festivals of Christmas and Easter, and the singing by the schoolchildren of 'The Holy Thorn' song.[9] This is very much a local custom and attracts few outsiders.

In St John's, Glastonbury, a free leaflet entitled 'The Glastonbury Thorn' outlines 'The Facts, The Legends and The Meaning'. Under the heading of 'botanical information', the leaflet explains that the Thorn 'can only be grown by grafting it into a native Hawthorn'. Under 'Meaning', the leaflet goes on:

> Each generation of seekers after Truth has been grafted into the family of the Church, made part of the Body of Christ, and shares His love.

However, probably most apposite for Glastonbury is this comment at the end of the 'Legends' section:

> REMEMBER –The importance of a legend is not whether it can be proved, but whether it helps us find the truth.

Nevertheless, while many Christians are attracted to Glastonbury precisely because of the vernacular traditions, it has been claimed that some are deeply uncomfortable with such aspects:

> the 'liberal establishment' in the churches finds the Christian traditions of Glastonbury (i.e. St Joseph of Arimathea; the visit of Our Lord, etc.) acutely embarassing, and as part of the 'lunatic fringe.' (Ives, 1998)

While St John's plays an important part in preserving and presenting tradition, however, it is worth noting that many members of the church have experienced 'God's Blessing' (the term now used in preference to the 'Toronto Blessing'). For some this has led not only to a sense of healing and renewal, but a feeling of increased confidence in relation to 'alternative' groups. The vicar who thought that his ministry would be with 'New Agers' has found himself 'midwife to a Christian revival'. Both traditional and more experiential forms of worship are available to the congregation of St John's, and people from other churches attend the services, where the Blessing continues to be offered and received.

CELTIC CONNECTIONS

Christianity in Glastonbury has long played on its Celtic connections. The Abbey claimed links with a variety of Celtic saints, including St Columba, St David, St Bridget and St Patrick; one abbot insisted that St Patrick was buried there! For some, the Celtic link supports the druidic connection, implying a smooth transition from the old religion to the new, in which the Celtic church both gained esoteric knowledge and remained closer to 'native' religion. The Abbey shop sells an array of Celtic and Arthurian merchandise, as well as jewellery made from Holy Thorn leaves.

The Celtic Orthodox Church

Glastonbury is also home to a branch of the Celtic Orthodox Church, which sees itself as successor to, and draws inspiration from, the Celtic Church in Glastonbury and the saints of Britain.[10] Its mission is to 'restore' orthodoxy to the British Isles. Prominent on Glastonbury High Street now is 'The Orthodox Way', premises of the Celtic Orthodox Church, containing a shop, a library and the Chapel of the Mother of God and the Saints of Glastonbury. (There is also a little Glastonbury Thorn in the back garden.) The Orthodox priest is deliberately 'high profile' in his manner of dress; a very obvious symbol of the presence of Christianity, and specifically Orthodoxy, in Glastonbury. Some of his regular worshippers maintain their denominational allegiances elsewhere, but are attracted by and welcomed to the Orthodox liturgy. The Orthodox priest offers tours of Glastonbury and takes part in the Anglican Pilgrimage procession. It is now his 'tradition' to bless the waters of Chalice Well at Epiphany.

Ecumenical Christianity

In 1993 an ecumenical group, The Quest Community, was founded 'specifically to work among the many and varied visitors to Glastonbury' (Quest leaflet). This group took its inspiration from the Iona Community (see Chapter 6) and draws 'inspiration from the Celtic tradition, whilst holding on to what is good in our own varied church backgrounds' (*Glastonbury Thorn*, 4, Winter 1996-7: 8).[11] Quest's core community members have crosses made from Glastonbury Thorn, a symbol of 'Christian witness taking root by settling' (*Glastonbury Thorn*, 4, Winter 1996–7: 1), and come from a variety of denominational backgrounds.[12] In 1996 the community took part in the Beltane Well-Dressing at Chalice Well and the White Spring, having been invited to give Christian blessings at each site. A Celtic blessing was considered appropriate for the occasion. In a variation of the rag well motif, the Quest Community has a 'prayer curtain' or 'prayer hanging', onto which people were invited to tie wool, symbolising their prayer. The hanging was a gift, embroidered at the top with the words 'In my Father's House there are many rooms' and at the bottom 'Blessed Be', 'a greeting which is meaningful to both Christian and Pagan' (*Glastonbury Thorn*, 4, Winter, 1996–7: 4). With their shared respect for the Celtic past, such interactions and 'cross-creativity' provide examples of the ways in which Glastonbury functions as a melting-pot for belief and praxis.

PAGAN–CHRISTIAN–PAGAN BORROWING

Pagans are borrowing from Christians, Christians from Pagans. It may be a truism that Christianity 'christianised' aspects of pre-existing pagan practice, but in the effort to reassert Paganism there is now conscious borrowing and adaptation from Christian practice. In Glastonbury the custom of tying rags to certain trees and honouring wells persisted in the vernacular Christian tradition; although it is now most obvious at the largely pagan White Spring, this is a recent development.

There are those in Glastonbury who are self-consciously 'bridge-building', and in some quarters both sides appear to be willing to learn from each other. One minister in the United Reformed Church claimed that working with 'alternatives' in Glastonbury had taught her to appreciate the value of meditation, candles and flowers. A Catholic priest responded to this by saying that he was saddened by the impoverished understanding of Christianity which seemed so prevalent nowadays, and that people were looking outside Christianity for the very spiritual fulfilment and practice it traditionally contained. However, the fact remains that it was through interaction with the 'alternative' community, not with the Catholic church, that such insights had come.

Much of Glastonbury's drawing power as a Christian site might be described as 'alternative'. It is a colourful, creative contrast to the pared-down version often presented as normative in academic accounts of Christianity, and it relies on a long history of vernacular religious myth-making and custom. In keeping with contemporary trends, some Christians are exercising a degree of 'mix-and-match' *within* Christianity which goes beyond denominational choice, attending the services of other Christian traditions, experiencing healing, experimenting with Celtic Christianity and interacting with other groups in the town. Christians are keeping Glastonbury customs and legends alive, adding to the store of myth with personal experience narratives and corroborative legends.[13]

In many accounts of contemporary spirituality in Glastonbury, Christianity seems either to be absent or to be presented as an endangered species. However, as we have seen, it is as vibrant, responsive and innovative as the other strands of spirituality in the town.

PRECURSORS OF CURRENT TRENDS

Many would argue that much of what is happening in Glastonbury now was set in motion a long time ago by aliens, Druids, Jesus, Celtic Christians, Arthur or ascended masters, to name but a few contenders. However, as other authors in this volume (Green, Tingay) indicate, interesting parallels can be drawn between the present situation and characters, ideas and events at the end of the nineteenth and the beginning of the twentieth century.

In the theories and writings of Dr John Arthur Goodchild (1851–1914), for example, we find speculation on Glastonbury's Celtic connections, the assumption of a smooth transition between Druidry and the Celtic church, and a belief in the survival of an ancient Irish cult venerating the female aspect of the Deity which became attached to the figure of Bride (see Benham, 1993). Goodchild also discerned in the landscape of Glastonbury the ancient 'Salmon of St Bride', a monument he considered equal in importance to Stonehenge. It is worth noting that a number of people involved with the last *fin de siècle* Celtic revival had Glastonbury connections, including Goodchild, William Sharp (*aka* Fiona Macleod), and the artist John Duncan (Benham, 1993).

Meanwhile, in addition to bringing gematric and numerological principles to his excavations of Glastonbury Abbey, Frederick Bligh Bond (1864–1945) also claimed to have received instruction, through the medium of automatic writing, from a former Glastonbury monk named 'Johannes'. Bond, in the preface to his book *The Company of Avalon* (1924), speaks of:

> the Company of Avalon, a group of souls who are impregnated with the devotional ideal which was translated into architectural symbol by the Benedictine brethren of old time. These, the 'Elect of Avalon', combine as a united spiritual force in an effort which is really one of response to those of us who, of our own volition, have attuned ourselves to their 'vibrations'. (Benham, 1993: 206)

There has also been an important Theosophical connection with Glastonbury. The early meetings of the Bath Lodge reveal Goodchild speaking on 'The Teaching of Fiona Macleod' (July, 1906), Frederick Bligh Bond on 'Symbolism in Architecture' (November, 1907) and 'Some Psychic Happenings' (December, 1908), and Wellesley Tudor Pole on 'Colour and Number Symbolism' (July, 1906).[14] These and other topics – 'The Druids: Their Beliefs and Customs', 'The Mystery of Ra', 'The Brotherhood of the Future' – would not be out of place on the current programme of the Isle of Avalon Foundation. Dion Fortune's involvement in the Christian Mystic Lodge which was interpreting Christianity in terms of Theosophy, and *vice-versa*, (Benham, 1993: 255) should also not be overlooked.

It is clear that in these decades there was also a variety of pilgrimage activity, with small groups and individuals such as Goodchild, Bligh Bond, the Tudor Poles and Alice Buckton[15] following their own pilgrimage routes within Glastonbury, incorporating rituals such as tying white rags on hawthorn trees or meditating at significant spots. One might see the universalism of contemporary Glastonbury prefigured in Alice Buckton's flyleaf dedication to *Eager Heart* (1904): 'Inscribed to all who see and worship the One in the Many' (Benham, 1993: 150). What is interesting, as Benham points out, is that all of the above-mentioned, however idiosyncratic their beliefs and practices, considered themselves Christians or in their own way honoured Christianity.

These examples indicate that much of what we have seen in Glastonbury in the latter decades of the twentieth century has not in fact been quite as new or revolutionary as may at first sight appear. There has been continuity as well as change.

GLASTONBURY AND THE 'NEW AGE'

Glastonbury has been hailed by the media as 'epicentre of the New Age in England'. That epithet might seem deserved in terms of its crystal shops, bookshops, Archangel Michael's Soul Therapy Centre offering 'tools for personal and planetary transformation', its 'client cult' activities such as the many workshops and lectures and the courses offered at the Isle of Avalon Foundation. However, 'New Age' is a notoriously contested term (see Introduction) which has frequently been used as shorthand for 'alternative'. In Glastonbury, as we have seen, much of what has latterly been dubbed 'New Age' is an extension and public expression of what existed in the vernacular tradition and in the religious experimentation of earlier periods.

Nevertheless, some are actively anticipating a New Age – 'a new culture, an emerging, sacred reality that's going to change everything in our world' – and feel that Glastonbury will have an important part to play in it. As one man said of Glastonbury's legendary Arthurian connection: 'The whole idea that [Arthur] lies here sleeping and will rise again, some people interpret that as meaning he'll rise again to lead us into a New Age.' However, one could argue that in Glastonbury even the notion of a 'New Age' is nothing new. According to tradition, Austin Ringwode, last of the Glastonbury monks, made the deathbed prophecy that 'The Abbey will one day be repaired and rebuilt for the like [sic] worship which has ceased; and then peace and plenty will for a long time abound' (Ashe, 1957: 362). A member of RILKO (Research into Lost Knowledge Organisation), who regards Glastonbury as the 'New Jerusalem', stressed to me the importance of 'rebuilding the Temple' at Glastonbury, to restore not only the spiritual well-being of the nation but 'Britain's greatness'.[16]

The most ambitious project proposed at present, and one very much in keeping with the 'global' status Glastonbury now claims, is the plan by the Isle of Avalon Foundation for the building of a universal Sanctuary in Glastonbury:

> We hold a vision to build and maintain a great Sanctuary in Glastonbury, ancient Isle of Avalon, dedicated to the divine essence within all spiritual paths. Our aim is to create a sacred space of prayer, peace, meditation and healing in the centre of Glastonbury where pilgrims of all faiths and spiritual beliefs can meet and celebrate together. We believe this is a wholly unique venture on the planet now, which will progress religious and spiritual ideas and structures in ways which we cannot yet imagine . . . Drawing on the traditions of the past and present, it will be a seed of spiritual regeneration for the third millennium. (www.glastonbury.co.uk/ioaf/sanctuary.html)

CONCLUSION

While in no way underplaying the differences in outlook and tensions which undoubtedly exist within Glastonbury, there is a sense in which the 'alternative' is not quite so threatening or alien as it might seem, and the polarisation between alternative spirituality and Christianity is not as extreme as might be assumed. Despite occasional flashpoints, Glastonbury seems to deal well with pluralism. One Christian minister commented that people in Glastonbury tend to ask 'What is *your* truth?', rather than 'What is *the* truth?' He found that if he talked about 'my truth' rather than 'Truth' in dialogue with those in the 'alternative' community, there could be meaningful exchanges.

As befits an environment where the avoidance of an 'either/or' attitude is prevalent, there is an acceptance in Glastonbury that one revelation may shed light on another, that following one way need not negate another, that ideas and practices from one tradition might transfer to another and that existing beliefs and praxis can be enhanced by new revelations or developments. Such insights are implicit in both vernacular religion and contemporary spirituality.

Within the Christian and alternative communities in Glastonbury, there is a spectrum of beliefs and practices. Myths are being made and recycled, customs are being created, and there is a seeming abundance of spiritual experience. There are undoubtedly similarities between alternative spirituality and features of the vernacular religion which has always existed alongside what the academy regards as 'official' religion. The dynamism, creativity and versatility of both vernacular religion and alternative spirituality are amply displayed in Glastonbury. The challenge for scholars is to recognise, value and study them as legitimate, coherent aspects of religion *per se*.

NOTES

1. This quotation is taken from the 1995 Isle of Avalon Foundation Tour brochure.
2. Since 1985, a group from St John's, Frome (a small town near Glastonbury), has been dressing and blessing a well in the centre of the town each Spring. According to the local paper, 'Frome is one of the few towns in the country to continue the religious tradition known as well-dressing.' In 1998 'Hydrangea, chrysanthemum and carnation petals were used . . . along with dried bread, toast and cornflakes for the face and hands of Jesus.'
3. The Ramala Teachers were described as 'belonging to a Spiritual Hierarchy, on a higher plane of existence, responsible for helping humanity through this time of crisis' (Introduction, *The Wisdom of Ramala*, 1986). The communications were received in the Ramala Centre's Sanctuary of the Holy Grail.
4. The Isle of Avalon Foundation, formerly known as the University of Avalon, was founded in 1991 with 'the vision of creating a recognised University of the Spirit in Avalon' (1994 Prospectus).
5. When I asked one Druid what he thought about the Glastonbury Zodiac, he opined that it was 'fanciful'. He then explained that what the landscape really revealed was a huge reclining Goddess figure, one breast of which is the Tor.
6. The same outline viewed from a different perspective has been identified as male genitalia with an erect penis.
7. In a variant of this legend, the tree is said to have grown from a thorn of the Cross of Thorns brought to Britain by Joseph of Arimathea.
8. Parsons (1965: 12) makes the definite, but wholly inaccurate, assertion that:
    Joseph died 27th of July AD 82. His sarcophagus can be seen in St John's Church, Glastonbury. The epitaph on his grave (in latin) translates: 'I came to the Britons after I buried CHRIST. I taught – I rest.'

9.   The Holy Thorn

There is a very special tree
We call the Holy Thorn,
That flowers in December,
The month that Christ was born.

We're told this very special tree
Grew from a staff of thorn,
Brought by a man called Joseph
From the land where Christ was born.

It now is our tradition
To send a sprig of thorn,
To greet Her Gracious Majesty
On the day that Christ was born.

10. Originally part of the British Orthodox Church, which in 1994 became a diocese of the Coptic Orthodox Patriarchate of Alexandria, Glastonbury and some other BOC churches 'broke away' in 1997 to become the Celtic Orthodox Church.

11. A St John's Church member, commenting on Quest's interest in the Celtic Church, said, 'We have renewal, we don't need revival.'

12. The members include Quakers, Methodists and Anglicans. The latter tend to be connected with St Benedict's rather than St John's.

13. In The Orthodox Way, for example, the relationship of the contemporary Celtic Orthodox Church to the historical Celtic Church is expressed visually in icons of Celtic and British saints painted in Orthodox style. One such icon, 'Our Lady of Glastonbury surrounded by Celtic Saints', was purchased in 1997 by an American Orthodox couple who donated it to the 'Celtic Saints Corner' of their church in Atlanta, Georgia. Visitors to the Glastonbury shop are now shown a letter from this couple describing how, between late December 1997 and early January 1998, a sweet fragrance was smelt around the flowering sprig of Glastonbury Thorn in Mary's right hand and the Christ Child's feet. This was interpreted in Atlanta as a sign of the rightness of that church moving back to the 'Old Calendar'. This is reminiscent of an incident at the time of the shift from the Julian to the Gregorian Calendar in 1752, when the timing of the Christmas flowering of the thorn in Glastonbury was popularly regarded as proof of the invalidity of the new dating system (Vickery, 1979; Bowman, forthcoming).

14. I am indebted to Kevin Tingay for information on the Bath lodge of the Theosophical Society. See Monteith (Chapter 6) for further information on Wellesley Tudor Pole and his connection with Iona.

15. Alice Buckton (1867–1944), radical educator, poet and playwright, lived at Chalice Well in Glastonbury for thirty years. She founded the Guild of Glastonbury and Street Festival Players who in 1914 performed Buckton's play The Coming of Bride, a dramatised biography of the saint which culminated in Bride's arrival in the Glastonbury area and her foretelling of the coming of King Arthur, the Round Table and the Quest for the Holy Grail (Benham, 1993: 143–69).

16. Somewhat less ambitiously, the Celtic Orthodox priest has proposed that the Abbey grounds be restored as a religious site of permanent pilgrimage, 'an "ecumenical" centre, supported by Churches Together in England', with daily liturgical worship and a permanent altar with canopy (Ives, 1998).

BIBLIOGRAPHY

Ashe, Geoffrey, 1957: *King Arthur's Avalon: The Story of Glastonbury* (London: Collins).

Benham, Patrick, 1993: *The Avalonians* (Glastonbury: Gothic Image Publications).

Bennett, Gillian, 1989: ' "Belief Stories": The Forgotten Genre,' *Western Folklore*, 48/4: 289–311.

Bowman, M., 1993a: 'Drawn to Glastonbury', in Ian Reader and Tony Walter, eds, *Pilgrimage in Popular Culture* (Basingstoke and London: Macmillan), pp. 29–62.

—— 1993b: 'Reinventing the Celts,' *Religion* 23: 147–56.

—— 1994: 'The Commodification of the Celt: New Age/Neo-Pagan Consumerism,' in Teri Brewer, ed, *The Marketing of Tradition* (London: Hisarlik Press), pp. 143–52.

—— 1995: 'The Noble Savage and the Global Village: Cultural Evolution in New Age and Neo-Pagan Thought,' *Journal of Contemporary Religion* 10/2: 139–49.

—— 1996: 'Cardiac Celts: Images of the Celts in Contemporary British Paganism,' in *Paganism Today*, Graham Harvey and Charlotte Hardman, eds (London: Thorsons, 1996), pp. 242–51.

—— forthcoming: 'Faith, Fashion and Folk Religion in Glastonbury: Joseph of Arimathea's Legendary Luggage,' in Anders Gustavsson and Maria Santa Vieira Montez, eds, *Folk Religion – Continuity and Change: Proceedings of the Second Symposium of the SIEF Commission of Folk Religion*.

Caine, Mary, 1992: 'The Glastonbury Giants or Zodiac: An Arthurian Reflection' in Anthony Roberts, ed, *Glastonbury: Ancient Avalon, New Jerusalem* (London, Sydney, etc: Rider), pp. 43–72.

Carley, James P., 1996: *Glastonbury Abbey: The Holy House at the head of the Moors Adventurous* (Glastonbury: Gothic Image Publications).

Dudley Edwards, Leila: 1999: *Modern Expressions of a Traditional Festival: Contemporary Paganism and Halloween*, unpublished PhD Thesis, University of Sheffield.

Heywood, Simon, 1998: *The New Storytelling*, Papyrus No. 1 (London: Daylight Press/Society for Storytelling).

Ives, John, 1998: *Glastonbury: 'Museum Park' or 'Place of Pilgrimage'?*, unpublished discussion paper.

Jones, Leslie, 1994: 'The Emergence of the Druid as Celtic Shaman' in Teri Brewer, ed, *The Marketing of Tradition* (London: Hisarlik Press), pp. 131–42.

Leith, Dick, 1998: *Fairytales and Therapy*, Papyrus No. 2 (London: Daylight Press/Society for Storytelling).

Major, Albany F., 1911: Correspondence, *Folklore* 22: 495–6.

Maltwood, K.E., 1964: *A Guide to Glastonbury's Temple of the Stars: Their Giant Effigies Described from Air Views, Maps, and from 'The High History of the Holy Grail'* (London: James Clarke & Co).

Matthews, John, 1991: *The Celtic Shaman: A Handbook* (Shaftesbury: Element Books).

Meek, Donald, 1992: 'Modern Celtic Christianity: The Contemporary "Revival" and its Roots', *Scottish Bulletin of Evangelical Theology* 10: 6–31.

Meek, Donald, 1996: 'Modern Celtic Christianity' in Terence Brown, ed, *Studia Imagologica: Amsterdam Studies on Cultural Identity* 8: 143–57.

Michell, John, 1992: 'Glastonbury – Jerusalem. Paradise on Earth: A Revelation Examined' in Anthony Roberts, ed, *Glastonbury: Ancient Avalon, New Jerusalem* (London, Sydney, etc: Rider), pp. 169–77.

Parsons, Kirsten, 1965: *Reflections on Glastonbury* (London: Covenant Publishing Co. Ltd).

Primiano, Leonard, 1995: 'Vernacular Religion and the Search for Method in Religious Folklife', *Western Folklore* 54: 37–56.

Rees, Kenneth, 1996: 'The Tangled Skein: The Role of Myth in Paganism' in Graham Harvey and Charlotte Hardman, eds, *Paganism Today* (London: Thorsons), pp. 16–31.

Samet, Rosalie, 1987: 'Harmonic Convergence', *Kindred Spirit* 1(1).

Sanderson, Stewart, ed., 1976: *The Secret Common-Wealth & A Short Treatise of Charms and Spels (sic) by Robert Kirk* (Cambridge: D.S. Brewer Ltd for The Folklore Society).

Shallcrass, Philip, 1995: *A Druid Directory* (British Druid Order).

The Wisdom of Ramala, 1986: (Saffron Walden: The C.W. Daniel Company Limited).

Utley, Francis Lee, 1945: 'The Bible of the Folk,' *California Folklore Quarterly* 4 (1): 1–17.

Vickery, A.R., 1979: *Holy Thorn of Glastonbury*, West Country Folkore No. 12.

Waterhouse, Helen, 1999: 'Reincarnation Belief in Britain: New Age Orientation or Mainstream Option?', *Journal of Contemporary Religion*, 14 (1): 97–110.

Yoder, Don, 1974: 'Toward a Definition of Folk Religion', *Western Folklore* 33/1: 2–15.

6

Iona and Healing: A Discourse Analysis
W. Graham Monteith

INTRODUCTION

In this chapter, the island of Iona will first be characterised as a social construct of Christians and other groups involved in diverse 'pilgrimages' to and settlements on the island in the period 1928–1996. Second, examples are given of how specific groups focused on Iona have initiated and sustained an interest in both Christian healing and what might be classed as 'New Age' healing, developing in the process a fragmented discourse of healing and wholeness.

Iona is a tiny island at the tip of the Ross of Mull in the Inner Hebrides. For most visitors, travelling there involves a long journey to Oban on the Scottish west coast, then a ferry to Mull, and then another ferry from Fionnaphort to the island. Although by today's standards transport is relatively simple, the island's remoteness still gives the impression of isolation, solitude and tranquillity. This has led to the romanticisation of the site and of its religious significance.

IONA AND THE IONA COMMUNITY

When George MacLeod (1895–1991), a distinguished Church of Scotland minister, founded the Iona Community in 1938, he did so for urban activists within the Church, not as a community of contemplatives. This has meant, in essence, that the activities in the island's Abbey – which the Iona Community restored over a period of years – were aimed at the mainland and that the concept of a 'pilgrimage site' remains alien to most Iona Community members and other visitors who, unlike the thousands of daily tourists in high summer, stay for more than just a few hours. The Iona Community finds it hard to live with the erroneous expectations of visitors who tend to prefer the contemplative mode (Golliher, 1989: 79ff.). Later it will be shown how one Iona Community member is addressing the tension between activism and contemplation and has described the link in terms of healing.

Apart from the Border Abbeys and the Roman Catholic grotto at Carfin in Lanarkshire, the Scottish pilgrimage site with most claim to authenticity is St Ninian's settlement at Whithorn in Galloway, which was established in 397 CE, one hundred and sixty-six years before St Columba arrived on Iona from Ireland (Hill, 1997). All these sites have some claim to healing, but only Carfin has any ongoing concern with healing. Iona, on the other hand, was the only site to fall outside the control of a church hierarchy and, whilst the others were kept under control, the privately owned[1] ruins of Iona were the target of various projects in the 1920s.[2] The acquisition by George McLeod of a lease of Iona Abbey from the Iona Cathedral Trustees and the founding by him of the Iona Community, allowed the radical development of a theology of which 'divine healing' was part. This in turn, along with the increasing fame of the island, encouraged its adoption by other groups and interests.[3]

The Iona Community is not a church or an institution which demands rigid conformity. Rather, it offers an open-ended milieu in which individuals may develop an attitude towards 'wholeness'. It has a 'Rule' which is currently under review, although healing and wholeness are not directly referred to in its text: it calls for a degree of spirituality, openness to a communal lifestyle and a political commitment which has usually been to the Left. Over the years, the membership of around 200 has lost its clerical majority, and many of those who have entered recently come from a medical background. Each member is expected to work out his or her commitment practically, normally in a project involving social change.

'Wholeness' currently appears as a topic for morning prayer on the twentieth day of each month, while the fifth day concerns 'the Church's ministry of Healing'. There is also a weekly service of 'Divine Healing' focusing upon healing and 'wholeness', when there is the opportunity to go forward for the laying-on of hands. George MacLeod had instituted prayers of intercession for the sick and wounded at the beginning of the Second World War, when demands for prayers arrived on Iona with a great urgency. After the war, the laying-on of hands was tentatively and carefully introduced and largely confined to the clergy. The service of Divine Healing has continued weekly to the present day, but has become open to almost anyone showing a genuine interest in leading the service. It has always been maintained that Divine Healing is a gift of God to all and not to a few 'healers'.

The 'history' of the island and its many ruins provides character and ambience. The reconstructed buildings of today are in fact closer to the monastery's medieval architecture than to the early Celtic settlement. There is a story about the training of visitor guides which is known to all who have an intimate knowledge of Iona: at the beginning of each season, they gather to decide where MacBeth is buried this year. This anecdote in particular is symptomatic of certain attitudes towards history which McArthur (1995) suggests have been characteristic of the Iona Community. She argues that many of the island's historical sites are artefacts of a mythical history. For instance, she suggests that 'the hermit's cell' may in fact not be the remains of such, but a structure built for milking cows during the 1890s (ibid.: 15). In general she claims that the Iona Cathedral Trustees have at various times over the years offended the native islanders over their strictures and changes to historical traditions, for the sake of archaeological and architectural probity. This has probably accelerated due to the recent Celtic revival.

The concept of conflicting ideas within a site of pilgrimage is fundamental to any understanding of Iona as a social construct. Eade and Sallnow (eds, 1991) examine the variety of discourses which may arise from the vested interests of those engaged in a pilgrimage site. They argue that, contrary to the model of Durkheim which stresses the community and solidarity of pilgrimages, and the alternative model of pilgrimage sites as being a place for the restoration of individuality, pilgrimage sites become the sum total of the different discourses represented. They assert that it is the conflicting realities of the contributions of different interests which make up the richness of the site. On Iona we can identify various discourses both within the setting of the Iona Community and beyond, which make up the type of model suggested by Eade and Sallnow (ibid.: 15). An introductory list of these discourses can be briefly sketched: within the Iona Community there might be 'Divine Healing',[4] peace issues, ecological discourse and spirituality; whereas within the peripheral 'New Age' community there might be leyline discourse, healing and energy/cosmological discourse. I will only deal in this chapter with Divine Healing in the Iona Community, which is in fact an activity focused not only on Iona but conducted internationally by the Iona Prayer Circle; and with energy (psi) healing[5] and other systems which involve cosmological discourse in 'New Age' parlance, whose advocates have over the years attached themselves to the island.

Reader (1993) maintains that sites produce different meanings that are:

a) individualistic;
b) multifarious;
c) arise from some common feature on to which all pilgrims can latch.

Miracles or healings are often the foundation of such meanings, particularly in the past but even in the present day. I contend that the concentration on Divine Healing by the Iona Community has created a meaning that goes beyond the original intention of the Community's founder, George MacLeod, and has allowed other groups to develop their concerns for healing and wholeness in connection with Iona, including tourists and 'New Age'-minded visitors. Evidence for this assertion may be found in leaflets published by other bodies with establishments on Iona, as well as by Jones's (1994: 152) assertion that the Iona Community is famous for its search for 'wholeness'. In fact, all of the Community's interests were founded on an incarnational theology stressing social justice, and MacLeod himself became interested in nuclear disarmament and economics.

A social construct is most easily identified by comparison with a potentially similar situation which has not so developed. Thus Iona might be compared with Whithorn in southwest Scotland. St Ninian came to Whithorn in 397 CE after studying in Rome and visiting St Martin of Tours in France (Patterson, 1991; O'Riordain, 1997). Ninian's aim was to convert the Britons of Galloway and further afield. Thus he brought Christianity to mainland Scotland more than a century-and-a-half before St Columba settled on Iona in 563 CE. Nevertheless, Columba has always overshadowed Ninian and Whithorn has been bypassed by the glamour of Iona. A factor in Iona's supremacy has been the classic biography of St Columba by Adomnan, which glamorised his relationship to Celtic and Druidical practices and gave the modern impression that Celtic theology accommodated the worship of nature characteristic of the Celts and Druids (Sharpe, 1995). Adomnan's biography also sought to establish the healing powers of Columba by illustrating his supremacy over the myths of Celtic culture. The motive for this is generally regarded as political: the establishment of Columba as a figure of strength. By contrast the biographer of Ninian, Aelred of Rievaulx, was commissioned to write an academic biography (Squire, 1969: 111*ff.*), dwelling on Ninian's alleged miracles (Hill 1997: 19*ff.*) but without the political and personal intensity of Adomnan. Adomnan tried to link Columba's miracles to Celtic and Druidic practices for political reasons, but Aelred felt no such impulse.

Other voices: Anthroposophy, spiritual healing, 'New Age'

In addition, the cult of Iona stems from a much more eclectic base than that of Whithorn. Iona became popular as a tourist resort for the rich in the very late 1800s when holidays on the Clyde coast became affordable by the masses from Glasgow (MacArthur, 1991). The displaced class of visitors and holiday-makers moved to the West Highlands and some reached Iona, which developed rapidly in terms of accommodation. Some were inspired by the privately owned ruins of the Abbey and Nunnery on the island. By the 1920s and 1930s these included not only members of the clergy, but rich philanthropists. Many engaged in the fashionable pursuits of psychic research and the archaeology of sacred sites such as Glastonbury. The peculiar intermingling of mainstream Christianity with Anthroposophical and psychic interests established a climate which was to become dominant in the 1960s.

In founding the Iona Community, George MacLeod forged close links with Sir David Russell, who was a millionaire mill-owner in Fife, and shared with him a love of Iona. In 1929 Russell had established the Iona Fellowship, which organised retreats on the island for divinity students (Macintyre, 1994: 109*ff.*). However, despite being an elder of the Church of Scotland, Russell showed considerable interest in Theosophy and Anthroposophy.[6] He was also greatly influenced by Wellesley Tudor Pole, with whom he corresponded almost every day. Having discovered psychic and healing powers during the First World War, Tudor Pole developed a mediumship which led him into many areas of mysticism. Tudor Pole recounts his experiences in a book entitled *The Great War* (Macintyre, 1994: 124) including a search in Istanbul for hidden treasures associated with Glastonbury (ibid.; Benham, 1993). In his many negotiations over the rebuilding of Iona Abbey, George MacLeod subsequently learned of Tudor Pole's beliefs and the healing powers he had exercised.

In the early days of *The Coracle*, the journal of the Iona Community, there appeared three articles by Karl König under the overall title of 'Integration'. These articles represented a manifestation of Anthroposophy within the annals of the Iona Community and they were evidently invited by George MacLeod who also liked to use the term 'integration'. From the first article, it became clear that both men used 'integration' and 'wholeness' interchangeably to cover everything from housing to personal well-being. 'Integration' was in 1939 the nearest term to 'wholeness' in the vocabulary of George MacLeod and it is reasonable to assume that it came from König. König's second article was entitled 'Integration in Medicine'; the third dealt with agriculture. MacLeod greatly admired König's work in Aberdeenshire, where he had founded the Camphill Community for profoundly disabled children, run on Anthroposophical principles. MacLeod was not convinced by Anthroposophy but admired its radicalism in the face of the Church's perceived inertia (Ferguson, 1990).

MacLeod wrote fifteen theses on Divine Healing that were never published, but in which he stressed that healing comes from many sources and was not confined either to the medical profession or the Church (Monteith 1997: 90ff.). To emphasise this point, he entered into correspondence in the 1950s with a Mr L.E. Eeman of Baker Street, London. The correspondence began with an approach by the latter to the then Archbishop of Canterbury's Commission on Spiritual Healing, in which Eeman attempted to gain support for scientific research in NHS hospitals into the laying-on of hands. Eeman, a healer for thirty-six years, wanted to confine his research to casualty patients who were bruised, in the hope that the 'healing touch would remove the discolouration'.[7] MacLeod subsequently read one of Eeman's books, *Co-operative Healing: The Curative Properties of Human Radiations*, and became so convinced of 'Odic forces' (a term proposed in the mid-nineteenth century by Baron von Reichenbach to denote electrical and electromagnetic forces within the body [Kahili King, 1992: 38]), that he used the term several times in lectures.

This correspondence coincided with Sir David Russell's decision in 1951 to set up the 'Fundamental Research Centre' in London to investigate 'new energy forms' in the treatment of cancer. Various other kinds of treatment were developed and were no doubt discussed with George MacLeod on many occasions, as he and Russell corresponded frequently during these years about the Iona Community. Russell's friend Tudor Pole was also working in the field of psychic healing at the time. He wrote of George MacLeod: 'In my opinion . . . [he] is on very shaky ground when he says he cannot find any authority in the New Testament for the idea that healers in this world can be helped by those who have passed on, or by others in the Unseen World' (cited in Macintyre, 1994: 246). Russell was very interested in faith healing and presumably this too was part of ongoing correspondence both with George MacLeod and Tudor Pole.

A little later, in the mid-1960s the Columba Hotel on Iona was bought by a certain John Walters who undertook to facilitate the Iona Community by gearing meals and accommodation to the Abbey's programme. The Iona Community actively encouraged Walters to set up the Columba Hotel, but the goodwill between the two parties faded slightly in the 1970s when the Wrekin Trust, a 'New Age' body, began to run separate conferences in the hotel inspired and led by Sir George Trevelyan.

Whilst the Iona Community was wooing John Walters, another 'New Age' activist, Peter Caddy of the Findhorn community in Moray, northeast Scotland, contacted Walters to offer to work in the hotel for a summer to help establish a link between the newly-formed Findhorn group and Iona. This link was important to Caddy's wife Eileen, whose psychic 'guidance' was quite adamant when it came to the island. She thought that both Peter and she should run the Columba Hotel, thus ensuring that most of the accommodation on the island was available to 'New Age' sympathisers. It would also allow them to develop other strategies such as demonstrating that the island could be self-sufficient in vegetables and other produce (Caddy, 1996: 253).

Why were Peter and Eileen Caddy so interested in linking Iona and Findhorn? Eileen Caddy believed strongly in a sacred triangle of Iona, Findhorn and Glastonbury, as is illustrated by her 'guidance' to Peter before his first pilgrimage to Iona to meet John Walters:

> It is a linking up with a very strong Centre of Light. This is a triangle, Glastonbury, Iona, Findhorn. You may not see the significance of this now, but you will do in the days to come. Peter is to be open to every contact, and there will be several very important ones. They will be drawn to him. My blessings are on this journey. Many important events will spring from it. (Caddy, 1996: 238)

Later still, in the 1980s, an American couple spent some time on the island. Concluding that the island lacked a quiet retreat centre, Lindley and Gerry Fosbroke bought the former Free Church manse, which they renamed 'Duncraig', and set up the Cornerstone Foundation to provide retreat facilities, mainly for burned-out ministers and others – particularly Americans – desiring a quiet time. They called the house 'Christian', and the Cornerstone Foundation still stresses this. Thus was introduced yet another type of search for healing and wholeness, this time as a reaction against the activities of the Columba Hotel and also the perceived frenetic lifestyle of the Iona Community. The Church of Scotland minister on Iona at the time, Harry Miller, was against the activities of those associated with the Columba Hotel and vehemently attacked its encouragement of Spiritualism, but he was also highly critical of what he regarded as the superficial preaching and teaching of the Iona Community. He was, therefore, sympathetic to the aims of the Cornerstone Foundation.

The examples of the Columba Hotel and Duncraig, then, illustrate the tensions both between Christian and 'New Age' parties, and even within and between different Christian groups, as to the appropriate way to use the restorative qualities of Iona.

Discourses encapsulated: the MacManaway family

To recapitulate, four distinct areas of discourse in relation to Iona and healing have been identified: tourism; Divine Healing, 'New Age' approaches and the island's harnessing to various mainland projects. Major

Bruce MacManaway and his family illustrate all four and thus bring into focus the conflicting discourses which arise on and through the island. First, in relation to tourism the MacManaway family had access to scarce accommodation since they owned a house on the island; second, Bruce MacManaway's religious background often conflicted with the Iona Community's practice of Divine Healing; third, he brought his 'New Age' interests to bear upon the Columba Hotel, being greatly involved in a series of conferences hosted there in the 1970s and 1980s; and last, the chief locus for his family's work was in fact not on Iona, but an alternative healing centre in rural Fife, one of the first of its kind in the UK.

MacManaway was the grandson of the Bishop of Clogher in Eire, and the son of an army officer. His mother was interested in Spiritualism but kept her concerns to herself for fear of upsetting the family. MacManaway served as an officer in the Second World War, discovering his gift of healing when he treated wounded soldiers after medical supplies ran out. In a lecture in Cheltenham delivered on Armistice Day, 1972, at an event run by two 'New Age' bodies, Universal World Harmony and the Wrekin Trust, he recounts the following:

> At the age of twenty I found myself with a company to look after in France, and in the ensuing three week battle, which culminated in Dunkirk, medical supplies ran out, doctors were not available, and inevitably many people got hurt. I then found a tremendous impulse, to get my hands on my own wounded. This I did, with very extraordinary results, and according to doctors to whom we subsequently managed to get our wounded, it had saved their lives both from shock and from their wounds.[8]

The Second World War as a formative experience for healers has been a recurrent story in my researches (Monteith, 1997) and it is no less so in the case of MacManaway, who often illustrated talks with incidents from his war experiences. However, he never lost his Anglican background and repeatedly either castigates the church for its intransigence or builds his own doctrine to justify his particular understanding of Jesus as a psychic healer. For example, in his book *Healing: the Energy that can Restore Health* (MacManaway and Turcan, 1983), he expresses resentment that many clergy fail to acknowledge the healing skills of the laity and insist that any laying-on of hands must be undertaken by those ordained by the Church. MacManaway stressed that Jesus bestowed his gifts of healing on ordinary people, the laity. According to him, all healing gifts come from God and are interspersed throughout the population; furthermore, they may become available to many more after training in meditation, relaxation and heightened awareness of the 'Odic Forces' present both within the world of the living and of those who have 'passed on'.

MacManaway develops a theory of wholeness that is based on an understanding of Capra's (1975) view of the atom as a form of vibrating energy that permeates the whole universe, and which we may tap into, with heightened awareness of our unity with nature. In common with a number of Capra's disciples, MacManaway does not do justice to this thesis (which is more about the nature of dualism than about energy); nonetheless, Capra's assumed emphasis on energy, and mankind's potential to harness and use it as a source of power does provide MacManaway with a basis for a popular explanation of the talents of healers.

MacManaway begins by equating wholeness with being in touch with nature:

> If we define healing not merely as curing symptoms but as making and becoming more whole, of bringing out the full potential, then we can include all life forms, and even the earth itself in the category of things worthy of our attention. (MacManaway and Turcan, 1983: 39)

The ability to heal depends upon becoming 'tuned in' to the energy which flows throughout nature, which at a microscopic level can be felt in the 'tingling' experienced during the laying-on of hands during healing[9] or in psychic experience of those who have 'passed on' (ibid.: 41). MacManaway's true interest, then, lies in the paranormal, mediumship and Spiritualism, and in later chapters of his book he again tries to legitimise such activity by quoting Church of England reports on the subject.[10] A chapter devoted to dowsing is fairly conventional and might even be accepted by Ian Cowie,[11] currently the Iona Community's most eminent healer, but then MacManaway writes of dowsing by proxy (ibid.: 67), which is certainly beyond Cowie's credulity.

At first sight, Bruce MacManaway appears to be a gifted healer who accepts that healing is of God, and gives praise for his gifts. But he acknowledges his indebtedness to spiritual healers such as Harry Edwards and to the Wrekin Trust, and thus never strays far from Spiritualism, 'New Age' and the general conviction that there are cosmic energies into which we can all tune and thus become much more complete people. MacManaway's spouse still teaches meditation and yoga at Westbank Natural Health Centre, which was established in 1959 in Strathmiglo in the farmlands of Fife, and Wallis (1992) has recounted how he attended a course there involving the laying-on of hands for healing. MacManaway's sons are likewise involved in alternative therapy. Patrick, for example, trained as an orthodox physician but now works mainly in geomancy, or 'psychic cleaning', and in the study of sacred sites. He maintains that sacred sites such as Iona tend to occur on ley lines that cause a heightened awareness of spirituality.

Conclusion

Current interest in Iona as a site of pilgrimage and healing is characterised by plurality which allows many different belief systems to coexist in a pick-and-mix fashion under many different kinds of authority. This can leave many people confused and searching for understanding, including visitors to Iona trekking across Mull without any clear conception of the cultural history of Iona. Indeed, some members of the Iona Community now seriously question the role and continued presence of the Community on the island. Much of the radical theology of the Iona Community is quite inaccessible to the average visitor. Despite this, the publishing arm of the Community continues to attempt to produce accessible literature. Church of Scotland minister and former Abbey warden Kathy Galloway (1991) has written of healing as an attraction to many who arrive on the island feeling incomplete. Along with others, she maintains that the healing available on Iona partly meets a need to alleviate guilt (ibid.: 6). This is no special pleading on her part but represents a conviction that people still seek healing and wholeness in the ritual of the Iona Community and are comfortable with its overtly Christian emphasis.

In 1996 the then Warden of the Abbey, Peter Millar, suggested that it was the task of the Iona Community to interpret the purpose of the ongoing work of the Abbey and Community to the visitors who, consciously or not, lived in a postmodern age of immediacy and religious pick-and-mix.[12] In subsequent correspondence he has addressed the question of how postmodernism relates to healing. He argues that people in a postmodern age are more inclined to seek a 'direct' experience of God and may invest their search in a quest for healing, which can be made without reference to an overall authority (such as in the past has often split Christian congregations). He writes:

> I also believe that we are discovering (or rather rediscovering) the power of prayer in healing. This is partly because the modern mind, in my opinion, wants a direct experience of the divine rather than some mediated experience. Within post-modernism there is this search for the transcendent; we cannot live in a world denuded of transcendence. I think also that healing is seen to be important in many lives because of a greater recognition of evil/darkness/threatening powers. Many people want to be 'healed' and what they mean is taken out of their 'inner darkness' which they feel powerfully.[13]

The above quotation appears to connect the major strands which have built Iona as a modern Scottish site of spiritual pilgrimage. First, there is tourism, with its immediacy and transiency; second, the Iona Community, with a presence on the island for sixty years, and theologies which have appealed to the fringes of Christianity as well as the mainstream; and third, 'New Age' groups, which have been attracted by the cult of Iona and have developed their own interests in the realm of healing, wholeness and 'direct experience' in an existing setting of religious tolerance.

Hence in Iona, today, there has developed an accommodation between the various groups discussed above; and in several instances a mature mutual acceptance. A common repudiation of nuclear weapons and the current interest in the 'Celtic revival' offers the foundation on which people may retreat to find wholeness and its concomitant, healing. The cult of Iona has never faded but has been enhanced, for instance, by the recent burial on the island of the former Labour Party leader, John Smith. The magic which people claim to find on the island finds its expression most deeply in the weekly healing service and laying-on of hands at the Abbey. In the brevity of the service with its lack of emphasis on the miraculous, the meanings and discourses of many find a common meeting point and purpose.

NOTES

1. By the Duke of Argyll, who entrusted them to Iona Cathedral in 1899.
2. One such was advocated by Clare Vyner who wanted to establish an 'Undenominational Social Service' training centre on Iona which would offer a training in 'health and hygiene, agriculture, fishing and gardening, weaving, etc.' There would also be theological training and the students would return to the mainland in a missionary capacity based on Quaker principles (McIntyre, 1994: 193*ff.*).
3. The Iona Community became formally associated with the Church of Scotland in 1951, since when it has reported each year to the Church's General Assembly, the highest Court within the Church of Scotland's presbyterian system of government. On the history of the Iona Community and the life of George MacLeod, see Ferguson (1988, 1990).
4. A term used by George MacLeod which was not actually favoured by some official bodies, such as the Archbishops' Commission of the Church of England, which commenced work in 1953, or certain charismatic Christians today.
5. Cf. Benor (1994: 211):
   Healing has many names, reflecting the 'blind man and the elephant' phenomenon of multiple observers' reports from varied perspectives. My preference in scientific discussions is the term '*psi* healing', where the Greek letter is used in parapsychology to denote the range of phenomena.
6. See Tingay (Chapter 2).
7. Eeman, L.E., letter to various hospitals *re*: Commission on Spiritual Healing, in the

George MacLeod and Iona Community Papers preserved in the National Library of Scotland (NLS), Edinburgh: Acc. 9084/337.

8. MacManaway, B., 'Evidence for Survival', unpublished typescript delivered at Cheltenham Town Hall, Armistice Day, 1972, p. 2.

9. Cf. the description of healing energies in Hedges, and Beckford (Chapter 10).

10. For instance, *The Church of England and Spiritualism*, Psychic Press (no date), cited in MacManaway & Turcan (1983: 91).

11. Significantly, Cowie attended a primary school run on Anthroposophical lines, and another member of his family farmed on these principles in Moray. Cowie's daughter – whom he describes as 'very New Age' – currently works in a Steiner school. See NLS papers (*op. cit.*): Acc. 11569.

12. Millar, P.W., 'A Reflection on our Ministry on Iona', unpublished paper delivered on the island during Community Week, 1996.

13. Millar, P.W., correspondence, 7 August 1996. NLS papers: Acc. 11569.

Bibliography

Benham, P., 1993: *The Avalonians* (Glastonbury: Gothic Image).

Benor, D.J., 1994: *Healing Research – Holistic Energy Medicine and Spirituality* (Munich: Helix; first published 1987 as *The Psi of Relief*).

Caddy, P., 1996: *In Perfect Timing: Memoirs of a Man for the New Millennium* (Forres: Findhorn Press).

Capra, F., 1975: *The Tao of Physics* (London: Wildwood House).

Eade, J., and Sallnow, M.J. (eds), 1991: *Contesting the Sacred: the Anthropology of Christian Pilgrimage* (London: Routledge).

Ferguson, R., 1988: *Chasing the Wild Goose* (London: Fount).

—— 1990: *George MacLeod* (Glasgow: Collins).

Galloway, K.: 'Transfigured by Ceremony', *The Coracle*, Winter 1991, p. 6, reprinted in: *Getting Personal – Sermons and Meditations* (London: SPCK 1995).

Golliher, J.M., 1989: 'Pilgrimage as Quest and Protest on the Isle of Iona', unpublished PhD thesis, State University of New York at Buffalo.

Hill, P., 1997: *Whithorn and St Ninian – the Excavation of a Monastic Town* (Stroud: Sutton).

Jones, N., 1994: *Power of Raven, Wisdom of Serpent – Celtic Women's Spirituality* (Edinburgh: Floris Books).

Kahili King, S., 1992: *Earth Energies* (Illinois: Quest Books).

MacArthur, E.M., 1991: *Iona through Travellers' Eyes* (Iona: New Iona Press).

—— 1995: *Columba's Island – Iona from Past to Present* (Edinburgh: Edinburgh University Press).

Macintyre, L., 1994: *Sir David Russell: A Biography* (Edinburgh: Canongate).

MacManaway, B., and Turcan, J., 1983: *Healing: the Energy that can Restore Health* (Wellingborough: Thorsons).

Monteith, W.G., 1997: 'Paths to Wholeness: An Investigation in terms of Discourse Analysis of "Divine Healing" in the Iona Community and Associated Activities on Iona', unpublished PhD thesis, University of Edinburgh.

O'Riordain, J.J., 1997: *A Pilgrim in Celtic Scotland* (Blackrock: Columba).

Patterson, A.R.M., 1991: *Whithorn, Iona and Lindisfarne – A Celtic Saga* (Edinburgh: St Andrew Press).

Reader, I., 1993: 'Conclusions', in Reader, I., and Walter, T., eds, *Pilgrimage in Popular Culture* (London: Macmillan).

Sharpe, R., 1995: *Adomnan of Iona – the Life of St Columba* (London: Penguin Classics).

Squire, A., 1969: *Aelred of Rievaulx: A Study* (London: SPCK).

Wallis, R., 1992: 'Encounter with Healing', *Journal of Alternative and Complementary Medicine*, April, 1992.

Alternative Spirituality in Europe: Amsterdam, Aups and Bath

Michael York

As the Millennium has approached, bringing with it both explicit and implicit apocalyptic tensions, new forms of alternative religion and spirituality have proliferated throughout the Western world. These range from identifiable New Religious Movements (NRMs) to more amorphous religiosities such as Human Potential, 'New Age', Neo-paganism and Goddess spirituality. Compared to traditional church and sect sociological forms, these last are 'diffused religions' – a concept I used (York, 1995) when examining the 'New Age' and Neo-pagan movements in the late 1980s, and which develops from Colin Campbell's concept of the *cultic milieu* (Campbell, 1972), Geoffrey Nelson's understanding of the *cult movement* (Nelson, 1968), Rodney Stark and William Sims Bainbridge's delineation of the *audience cult*, *client cult* and *cult movement* (Stark and Bainbridge, 1985), and Roy Wallis's work on the *social movement* (Wallis, 1979). In an institutional context, diffusion takes place from multiple centres rather than from any single, unitary locus. Within the contemporary world of alternative spirituality, such centres as Sedona and Esalen in the United States, Glastonbury in England and Findhorn in Scotland continue to emerge as nuclei to which people are drawn and from which ideas are disseminated. These places are linked through various channels of connection: travelling speakers and workshop facilitators, as well as the contemporary seeker and religious supermarket consumer (York, 1994; Sutcliffe, 1997).

The network of alternative spirituality draws both from its more established and 'traditional' centres and from its countless local manifestations. Each locality in some sense becomes yet another centre or focus for the repeated exclamation, 'It's happening here!' This chapter explores non-mainstream religiosities in three different European localities: Amsterdam, the official capital of the Netherlands; the Provençal village of Aups, along with French Provence more generally; and the Georgian city of Bath in England.

Since Amsterdam is recognised as the successor to San Francisco in the early 1970s as the centre of the counterculture, the presence of alternative forms of spirituality is greater here than it is in either Bath or Provence as a whole. The major focus in this chapter, therefore, is on the city of Amsterdam (population one million), which presents a much larger and richer field of study than either Bath, with its smaller number of residents, or Provence, with its diffused rural life. Nevertheless, both these more marginal communities have been penetrated in the current expansion of alternative spirituality developing from Western metropolitan centres, and they are examined in this respect.

AMSTERDAM, CENTRE OF THE COUNTERCULTURE

Both the 'New Age' and Neo-pagan movements owe a large part of their origins to the counterculture which emerged in San Francisco in the late 1960s (York, 1997). This was the period of the 'flower-child' or 'hippy', whose paean to the Age of Aquarius found expression in the musical *Hair* of that time. In the 1960s, society became polarised between establishment 'straights' and anti-establishment 'freaks', but by its culmination in the late 1960s/early 1970s, hippy culture had become infiltrated by underworld drug barons, and centres such as Haight-Ashbury, once the womb of the counterculture, were lit up by the harsh glare of surveillance lamps and police cameras. As the Vietnam war continued under the Nixon administration, the extended 'Summer of Love' ended in 1970 with the Charles Manson murders and the National Guard's slaying of students at Kent State University. In the subsequent exodus from California, the centre of the counterculture shifted from San Francisco to Amsterdam.

Between 1970 and 1974, the capital of the Netherlands acquired the colour formerly associated with California's 'City by the Bay'. The central park of Amsterdam became a veritable scene from *The Arabian Nights*, with an exotic tented encampment and a raucous bazaar of magicians, shamans, belly-dancers, snake-charmers, sages and crazies of all kinds – a colourful and mysterious wonderland to be seen through the thick haze of burning incense, *chillum* smoke and Amstel fog. Communes proliferated throughout the Netherlands, but especially in Amsterdam, as they once had in California and San Francisco. Vegetarian and macrobiotic restaurants developed, and alternative centres – quasi-independent and quasi-state sponsored – such as the Kosmos Centrum, the Melkweg and the Paradisio, became social meeting places for the vagabond counter-culture. These were combination discos, coffee houses, theatre centres and workshop venues. With liberal laws and lax police enforcement,

Holland seemed, to the 'hippy refugee' from America and elsewhere, the perfect haven.

Being an eminently pragmatic people, the Dutch tolerated this transnational influx, much as they tolerated their own youthful 'drop-outs'. Communes, in both privately owned and so-called 'cracked' (illegally occupied) houses, were not opposed, as long as the individuals involved paid the proper taxes and utility charges. In this way, the Dutch successfully reincorporated a wide range of marginal lifestyles into the mainstream: in the Netherlands, nobody escapes the plethora of integrating bureaucracy.

Nevertheless, though the countercultural scene changed radically and had largely disappeared in Amsterdam by the late 1970s, its legacy survived. Renowned for the freedom it has traditionally accorded to gays and prostitutes, Amsterdam has functioned *vis-à-vis* Europe in much the same way as San Francisco in North America. And just as the counterculture has come of age elsewhere, it has similarly matured in Holland.

The more anti-establishment element within the counterculture has emerged today in the various expressions of contemporary paganism. By contrast, the element of the former counterculture which has come to terms with the 'establishment' or even re-merged with it is essentially what we now understand as 'New Age'. The foremost manifestations of 'New Age' appear, in descending order, in the USA, the UK and the Netherlands, whilst the foremost manifestations of Neo-paganism appear, again in descending order, in the UK, the USA and the Netherlands – these three countries forming the primary nexus of exchange. Both movements continue also to grow in other European countries (e.g. Germany, France and Italy) and in non-European countries such as Canada, Australia and New Zealand. As the traditional haven for freedom and nonconformity and as the legendary post-Haight-Ashbury centre, Amsterdam is the major networking venue for both the New Age and Neo-pagan movements.

The city of Amsterdam dates back to 977 CE when a charter was first granted allowing the levying of tolls on those wishing to ford the Amstel River, where two small islands had originally formed a natural crossingpoint. By extending the islands, damming the river and redirecting the waters through an elaborate series of sluices and canals, Amsterdam – 'the dam on the Amstel' – came into being. A strong Catholic presence gave way in the sixteenth-century Reformation to Calvinism in the form of the Dutch Reformed Church. In the seventeenth century, Amsterdam emerged as one of the foremost mercantile centres of the world and the foundations for its growth and wealth were established. With the rise of rationalism in the eighteenth and nineteenth centuries, and inheriting Calvinism's world-affirming adaptability, Amsterdam became one of the leading centres in the twentieth century for liberal and secular thought.

In the Netherlands at present, church membership is the lowest of all Western European countries. As Janssen (1997: 2) explains, whilst secularisation is strongest in predominantly Protestant European countries, and although in the whole of Europe, Protestants score consistently lower on religious indices, ironically 'in the Netherlands it is the . . . Catholics who show lower scores: they go to church less, are less interested in religion, pray less, pay less and so on.' Nevertheless, Janssen finds that most Dutch people are neither atheist nor fundamentalist, but rather retain a 'private, insecure, non-specific and abstract' religious identity. In fact, when measured not by church membership, but by 'attendance, prayer and the salience of religion in one's life', Dutch youth score highly in spirituality.[1]

During the 1960s the Netherlands, which Janssen (1997: 3) recognises as 'a plural country by name and definition', became further pluralised through secularisation, individualisation and the emergence of New Religious Movements. In his survey of Dutch youth, Janssen was able to classify 16 per cent as 'New Age-minded' on the basis of their non-affiliation to a church and their participation in various activities such as Tarot, Yoga, astrology and Buddhism. This figure compares with 39 per cent who still belonged to a church, former members of a church who still prayed (18 per cent), 'doubters' who never belonged to a church but still prayed (9 per cent) and non-believers who lacked any religious involvement whatsoever (18 per cent). 'On several items,' Janssen reports:

> the New Age youngsters score higher than both the orthodox and the non-believers. They are more interested in art and literature, in experiencing beauty, and place greater weight on personal development. They are more interested in Oriental wisdom and believe more strongly in reincarnation. Politically they are left-wing oriented, and they are more revolutionary in their political opinions and actions. Furthermore, they report more psychological problems than do the other groups. (1997: 3)

With regard to prayer, nearly two-thirds of the entire Dutch population claimed to pray. But whilst older people prayed to God, younger people tended not to pray. 'When we look for common concepts that the young use to describe God, we first find that God is more often described as an activity than as a being. In 32 per cent of the definitions they say "God is"; in 75 per cent of their texts they say "God does".' (Janssen, 1997: 7)[2] This is reminiscent of what Margo Adler finds among American Neo-pagans: the emphasis is less on belief than on practice (1986; *vide* York, 1995: 102).

In fact, in the case of much contemporary alternative spirituality, belief is incidental. With its liberal, humanistic and secular traditions, the Netherlands has stripped away traditional support for official, institutional religions of belief. Amsterdam is at the forefront of this tendency. It is also in the vanguard of non-official spiritual developments consisting in an experiential and experimental approach to religion.[3]

The current centre for alternative spirituality in Amsterdam is the Oibibio, a large canal building facing the Centraal Station. This building has been expensively renovated and is now known locally as a colossal folly, understood to be perpetually on the verge of bankruptcy. Nevertheless, it serves as the New Age centre for Amsterdam – replete with large gathering areas, workshop rooms, lecture theatres, banqueting rooms, concerts, a Japanese teahouse, a sauna with various bathing, tanning and massage facilities, a café/restaurant, a bookshop, statue and crystal shop, a warehouse specialising in children's items, clothes, household decorations, paper goods, alternative medicines and cosmetics: in short, all the amenities necessary to function as a social and spiritual nexus for the contemporary Dutch seeker.

The New Age spirituality promoted by the Oibibio can clearly be detected in the list of the top ten books promoted in its Spring 1997 programme. This included two works by Deepak Chopra, as well as one each by Paulo Coelho and Barbara Marciniak. The list also included James Redfield's *The Celestine Prophecy*. With a focus on the business world, Oibibio also offered in this same programme training in the transformation of organisations from linear hierarchies to networks, storytelling management, team management, 'Beethoven voor Business', self-direction, 'Photoreading and Mindmapping', empowerment, meditation for managers, spiritual leadership ('*Spiritueel Leiderschap*'), exterior strength through inner power ('*Ondernemingsraad: uterlijke macht door innerlichke kracht*'), stress relief, sabbatical programmes, personal leadership using dolphin strategies, and 'I Vision'.[4]

Among the more affordable workshops and courses, the Oibibio programme included under the heading 'The Basics', oriental belly dance, trance dance and contemplation training based on 'the spontaneous play of being'. Under the heading of 'Movement', aikido, yoga aerobics and meditation were on offer. Three different tarot trainings were listed under the section entitled 'oracles'. 'Personal growth' included 'Sabbatical-Day', '*Vrouwen en Spiritualiteit*' ('Women and Spirituality'), 'Touch for Health', and, relating to Redfield's book mentioned above, '*De Celestijnse Boodschap*' ('The Celestine Message'). For its 'shamanism' offering, Oibibio presented a study day on 'ritual around the medicine wheel'.[5] Most courses and workshops were given in Dutch, but some teachers from the international New Age circuit were American and British, and English was therefore also used as a *lingua franca*, such as when an American came to channel White Eagle, 'the spirit master from the White Brotherhood'.

In its 1997 celebration of the Buddhist festival of Wesak, the Oibibio presented a programme of ritual, reading and meditation. Those familiar with the Wesak celebrations held at St James's, Piccadilly, in London, would recognise a basic similarity between the Dutch format and that offered by the British-based Alternatives Programme (York, 1995: 230–1, 234–5). Besides Wesak, in the Spring of 1997, Great Master Chen Xiaowang gave a T'ai Chi demonstration, Lama Karta spoke on the power and meaning of Buddhist mantras, and Bert van Riel gave a talk on feeling and understanding as the only means for survival in the year 2000. The Oibibio also holds a swing music dance evening on the first Saturday of each month.

Whilst the Oibibio is by no means the only centre or venue for workshops or alternative spirituality gatherings, it illustrates both the nature of current religious experimentation and innovation as well as its transnational or international scope. The Oibibio is thus exemplary of the diffused New Age religiosity currently to be found in Amsterdam.

The New Age is a loose confederation of Neo-pagan practices, psychotherapy, psychophysical body work and gnostic–theosophical orientations. Much of the emphasis upon human potential grew out of the Gestalt school of psychotherapy,[6] represented in Amsterdam by the therapy collective Spetéra,[7] which describes itself as 'a collective for consciousness, contact and spirituality.'[8] In addition to Gestalt, Spetéra offers therapy, workshops and schooling in the methodologies of Psychomotor, Enlightenment Intensive, Biodynamics and Biorelease as well as individual Taoist massage and guiding as 'Sacred Intimates'. Besides its *ad hoc* venues, Spetéra sponsors regular monthly gatherings. Interest has also developed in the connection between the emotions and sexuality. 'Man Fire Feast' and 'Female Fire Feast' are workshops organised for separate single-sex groups, in which participants learn to give and receive Taoist erotic massage. For men, this is followed by 'My Heart's Desire', a workshop in further erotic massage and sex magic – that is, the generation of erotic energy through genital massage. 'The last two days [of the workshop] . . . focus on sex magic or using the erotic energy we generate as creative force.'[9] To allow participants to contact 'the magician and artist within your body', the workshop employs erotic rituals claimed to be based on Tantric, Taoist and Native American traditions.[10]

In a third centre, the 'Stichting Performing Inside Out', a more gnostic leaning is to be discerned. An outgrowth of William Pennell Rock's nonprofit organisation, Origins (USA), the foundation is described as 'dedicated to returning the healing power of vital energy, myth and ritual to contemporary performing arts'.[11] Rock explains his basic workshop as Gestalt, archetypal psychodrama. A former instructor with Oscar Ichazo's Arica Institute in New York and California and the Jungian Institute in Zurich, Rock is a co-founder of the Center for Transpersonal and Expressive Arts Therapies in Los Angeles. His innovation is to combine the Human Potential Movement with experimental theatre.

Rock's workshop, as well as the theatrical performance which develops from it, is called 'Love Story' and is based on the Hindu *Ramayana* epic archetypes of the hero (Ráma), heroine (Sita), monster (Ravana) and nature spirit (Hanuman). As improvisational performance, the approach is called 'entheotic' or 'oracular',[12] with participants being encouraged to identify with each of the epic archetypes. The Stichting Performing Inside Out also sponsored a weekend workshop called 'A Hero's Journey' at the beginning of May in 1997. Other workshops span two weekends and are designed for people with work commitments during the week.

The Oibibio, Spetéra and Stichting Performing Inside Out are three of the plethora of centres for alternative spirituality in Amsterdam. The city also boasts an array of New Age shops to cater to the diverse needs of the New Age consumer. Typical is 'Himalaya'[13] which offers books (indigenous and imports), videos, New Age music, posters, incense, jewellery, aroma lamps, games, pendants, crystal balls, Bach remedies, ionisers, art cards, tarot cards, etheric oils, gems (and remedies), Ayurvedic medicines, massage oils, pyramids, Buddha figures, a large collection of Tibetan clothes and cymbals, and so forth. There are also many popular Dutch periodicals which focus on alternative spirituality and related consumer goods: *Bres, Visioen, Para-Astro, Prana, Paravisie, Koörddanser, Onkruid, Jonas* and *Ode*. Furthermore, entheogenic *ayahuasca* use is increasingly becoming a central feature in Amsterdam, as it is in the more urban expressions of New Age elsewhere.

Linked to New Age but often distinguished from it is the alternative spiritual tradition understood by practitioners and sociologists as Neopaganism. In Amsterdam, Wiccan covens have emerged, and the city is a familiar destination for contemporary pagan teachers such as Marian Green or Vivianne Crowley (York, 1995: 117–22, 151–4). Green, for example, has been visiting and working in Amsterdam since 1987: she now gives several weekend workshops each year, and a week-long summer school. These courses are usually for groups of a dozen people or less and are designed essentially for beginners who wish to learn the basic arts of Western magic. 'The Dutch are very open,' Green said during a December 1997 interview, 'and long for a Western connection.' She sees interest in magic as a progressive development from the Indonesian influence established in the country's imperial past. Her concentration on people new to the alternative spirituality tradition stems from her conviction that the initial contact must be made correctly: 'It infuses you for life – if not in your next incarnation.' Green sees alternative spirituality as a living and growing experience for many people – and a liberation from orthodox faiths.

As with New Age generally, publishing is an important means of disseminating pagan ideas. Several of Green's books have been translated into Dutch. On the other hand, the *Wiccan Rede* is an English and Dutch language quarterly, published in Zeist, which serves the pagan community in both the Netherlands and (chiefly Flemish-speaking) Belgium. Another Wiccan/pagan organisation that serves both Belgium and Holland is Greencraft, which publishes its own magazine four times a year.

AUPS, PROVENÇAL VILLAGE

Provence in the South of France, between the Rhône valley and the present-day French–Italian border, has since prehistoric times been a crossroads of large-scale ethnic immigration. The most recent occurred in the 1920s when numerous Italian families settled throughout the area. As a result, roughly half the family names in the village of Aups are Italian. Demographically, Aups is about one-half Roman Catholic and one-half Communist. When I first moved to the Midi (the vernacular name for the South of France) in the early 1970s, the local *Var-Matin* newspaper ran a series of articles investigating the claim that half of the population of the *département* of Var was *étrangé*. In the final article, the paper did indeed determine that fifty percent of the people who lived in the Var were foreigners, but concluded that as long as everyone lived harmoniously together, it did not matter.

The cosmopolitan flavour of Provence is virtually as rich as that more usually found in urban communities, and yet the Midi remains essentially a rural area. When I first settled in the village of Aups, the town claimed a residency of 1,500. Today, that figure is around 1,800, but during the summer months, with the influx of tourists and vacationers (chiefly Parisian) who maintain a holiday residence in or near to the town, the population more than doubles. It is this combination of a multicultural population and a distinctively rural environment that gives the Midi its unique character.

When I first came to live in Aups, a vendor would pass through the village once every four or five years offering small, ornamental stones for sale. In those days, even the purchase of fresh milk was difficult unless one went direct to the local farmers. In the past two decades all that has changed. The town now has supermarkets and is fully integrated into the French commercial mainstream. In the 1990s, not only can local residents purchase packaged milk and butter distributed through national franchises, but there is also a choice of crystals, amber, lapis luzuli and other stones from up to ten different merchants who come to the weekly *marché* on Wednesdays and Saturdays during the summer months.

The village of Aups was reputedly the capital of a Celto-Ligurian tribe known as the *Oxigii*. When the area became the *Provincia Romana*, or the first imperial province of the Roman Empire beyond Italy, Julius Caesar is reputed to have said, 'I would rather be first in Aups than second in Rome.' The village derives its name from the dative plural *Alpibus*, signifying '[way] to the Alps'. Indeed, behind the Plain d'ûchane on which the town is situated, it is possible to catch one's first glimpse of the Alps from the southwest.

Provence has had a long connection with practitioners of alternative or spiritual healing. These are variously designated as *guérisseurs* ('curers'), *rebouteurs* ('bone-setters') or *magnétiseurs* ('magnetic healers'). Usually, this indigenous practice has taken the form of a 'laying-on of hands'. 'Magnetic' curers, however, are not sanctioned by the state and can neither advertise nor charge for their services. They are instead known locally and by word of mouth. Payment is optional and is left to the discretion of the client, as a donation. But even allopathic medicine is not averse to treatments that would elsewhere be considered alternative or even suspect. Perhaps as many as half the registered doctors of the medical profession in Provence include Chinese acupuncture and acupressure, if not homeopathic treatments, among their services.

The combination of heritage and contemporary cosmopolitanism has fostered a burgeoning New Age spirituality in the Midi which shows remarkable affinities to the patterns already seen in Amsterdam and elsewhere – for example, in London, Glastonbury, New York, Los Angeles, San Francisco or even in such smaller American communities as Naples, Florida, or Providence, Rhode Island. A survey of rural France affirms the global dissemination of New Age programmes and concepts and the possibility that New Age religiosity is today to be found throughout the Western world.

The obvious centres in Provence include both Marseille and Aix-en-Provence as well as the Côte d'Azur (St Tropez, Cannes and Nice). For instance, in April 1997 *L'Association* ‹‹*L'isthme*›› sponsored its second programme on Sufism at various venues in Avignon, Montpellier, Marseille and Aix-en-Provence.[14] In most of the more urban centres of Provence, one

can find courses in the practice of yoga. In Marseille, there is a]
d'Étude et de Méditation Bouddhique.[15] In Aix, both l'Ateli
Psycho-Corporelle, l'Éspace MANUEL and le Centre CO
between them host courses in yoga and relaxation, la Méthode ..
morphopsychologie and la sophrologie[16], as well as individual consultations tot
Chinese massage, le Tarot psychologique, palm reading and les Remèdes
Floraux du Dr Bach.[17] During May 1997 in the town of Gordes, not far
from Aix, a three-weekend course was conducted for trainers on Califor-
nian massage, Shiatsu and Korean relaxation, attended by twenty-five
people.

In the more immediate environs of Aups, workshops are held in T'ai Chi
and other forms of dance, in yoga and in medicinal therapies. Through local
interviews I learned that the most popular stage (workshop) at present is that
of story-telling. A relatively new development, this has been rapidly
spreading through Provence in 1997 and may represent an emerging
interest to re-connect with the earlier contador traditions. The return to
the tradition of the contes follows in the wake of the growing Provençal
interest in the 1990s in both crystals and American Indian philosophy. In
Aups, according to local informants, and, judging from newspapers,
television and national booklists, in France in general, both the terms
'New Age' and 'Nouvelle Age' are becoming more widely used. Again, local
informants explain that, throughout the Midi, the wearing of crystals has
become a means of mutual recognition for those with New Age interests.
The social changes which appear to be occurring as a result of the growing
pursuit of New Age spirituality are attributed to an increase of communication between the genders, more equal sharing of activities among
(chiefly younger) couples, and a greater ambiguity following the decline
of traditionally defined gender roles.

The expatriate étranger community has also brought with it additional
esoteric elements ranging from Osho sannyasins to American Indian
spiritualists and the Gurdjieff teachings.[18] Albeit on a smaller scale, the
same massage, body work and personal growth techniques are to be found
here or in the surrounding area as in the more urban conglomerations of the
western world.

BATH, GEORGIAN CITY

Between the Provençal village of Aups and the capital city of Amsterdam,
we have the Georgian city of Bath, England. Bath has a population of
roughly 85,000, but contains a diversity of religious expression which is
surprising for a city of its size. According to records held by the Bath

Archive for Contemporary Religious Affairs (BACRA), the city's religious communities include Seventh Day Adventists, Baptists, Anglicans, Roman Catholics, Quakers, Spiritualists, Moslems, Buddhists, Mormons, Methodists, Orthodox, Pentecostals, Salvation Army, Non-denominational Protestants, Christian Scientists and Unitarians.[19] There are also noteworthy New Age and Neo-pagan communities, as evidenced by the city's metaphysical bookshops – the oldest being 'Arcania', established in the late 1980s – and by the influence of individual activists such as Marian Green.

Bath traces its origins to Bladud, an exiled son of the king of the Britons, whose leprosy was cured by bathing in the hot springs for which the city has subsequently become famous. Bladud reputedly returned to the springs *circa* 880 BCE and, in gratitude for his healing, erected the first bath and temple. According to local legend, he also established a perpetual flame such as we find today in Banaras or Baudinath. In honour of this, a candle is now kept continually burning at the local Cross Bath. Bladud is also credited with having established the first university in Britain, possibly connected to the nearby stone circle of Stanton Drew, which, after Stonehenge and Avebury, is the third largest in Britain. In time, under the Romans, the tutelary deity of the springs, Sulis, was identified with the goddess Minerva, and a huge temple and bathing facility complex was erected corresponding in size and location with what later became the medieval walled city.

In the early eighteenth century, the city began its evolution into the sophisticated Georgian showplace of today. Employing esoteric Masonic principles,[20] the architect John Wood the Elder (1704–54) and his son, John Wood the Younger (1728–1801), constructed many of the city's most famous buildings and squares. The King's Circus (1754–69) was modelled on the dimensions of Stonehenge, whilst the number of houses surrounding the Circus corresponds to the number of stones at Stanton Drew, which, John Wood the Elder believed, had been the heart of all British Druidism.

With its architectural legacy and tradition of 'sacred' springs, Bath is currently being spoken of as a nascent pilgrimage centre. There is talk in the local metaphysical bookshops, at the Cross Bath, during Druidic moots and throughout the occult network in general, of the city being poised to become once again the place of pilgrimage it was in its pre-Roman, Roman and Georgian past. At present, in the New Age and contemporary pagan circuit, the nearby town of Glastonbury remains pre-eminent (Bowman, Chapter 5; also Bowman, 1993a and b), but virtually all the personal and spiritual growth techniques to be found in Glastonbury are also to be found in Bath: astrology seminars, holistic massage, Bach flower therapy, polarity bodywork, acupuncture, reflexology, aromatherapy, homeopathy, chiropody, on-site massage (OSM), overtone chanting, kinesiology, storytelling, sacred song and dance, iris diagnostics, shiatsu, reiki, Chinese medicine, chakra energising, drumming, rebirthing, neuro linguistic programming, sweat lodge, Transformation Game, craniosacral therapy, visualisation, non-stylised movement healing, yoga – and so forth.

Although various Wiccan-orientated ceremonial circles have been organised for the equinoxes, solstices and Celtic quarter festivals, the stronger influence in Bath is Druidic, stemming from a vernacular earth-centred folk-orientation that might be termed 'geo-pagan'. In 1995 Bath resident and leader of the Secular Order of Druids, Tim Sebastian, laid claim to the 'ancient druidic chair of Caer Badon' (that is, of Bath as the alleged site of King Arthur's last battle). According to Sebastian (whom locals in his pub refer to as 'Archie Druid'), Bath has been reestablished as a Druid centre and is the first to be honoured with a bardic, druidic and ovatean chair (Bowman, 1998).

Perhaps the most prominent metaphysical centre in Bath is 'Arcania' – formerly known as 'Arcania New Age Centre'. Arcania's proprietor since 1995 is Richard Howard, who came to Bath via Glastonbury from London. During a December 1997 interview, Howard explained that the bookshop has existed as a beacon across the British southwest for those interested in alternative spirituality and, as such, has created an audience which today gives it a solid (i.e. 'spiritually reputable') foundation. However, on the business level, any bookshop must deal with the problem of small profit margins which 'do not equate' with extremely high rents and rates. Howard has developed a cynical response to the high degree of charlatanism which he perceives throughout the spiritual scene, with its increasingly materialistic and profit-motivated emphasis: namely, the plethora of people who claim healing powers or a privileged spiritual vision. In an effort to infuse 'integrity' into the *cultic milieu* and his own services, Howard and his staff invoke 'the spirit of Arcania' each morning before the shop opens and pay their thanks to the establishment's spirit at the end of the day before enveloping the premises in 'a protective bubble' for the night. This ritual 'dialogue' solicits a future for Arcania through what Howard terms 'integrity', which he explains as the 'recognition to give back to the spirit equal to what has been received' – although he admits that having to keep to the commitment can be a 'pain in the ass'.

Howard recognises the 'massive potential' of Bath and sees the proposed reopening of the spas as a means of augmenting spiritual energy in the city and attracting more like-minded people. Howard himself was drawn to Bath by its cosmopolitan nature, and sees Arcania as providing an 'open doorway for everybody', in contrast to Glastonbury, where, in his perception, access to information concerning spiritual matters was available only to those already involved with a particular elitist path. Though Howard himself admits to having been a 'member' of the Glastonbury 'spiritual club' he did not like its exclusiveness. Preferring the greater openness he finds in Bath, he says, 'People are becoming more accepting – even excited – by the fact that Arcania is truly different – a unique experience within the city.'

A former resident of the city itself, now resident within the 'Bath Triangle' (consisting of Bath, Bristol and Glastonbury), Marian Green divides her time between this area and Amsterdam. Publisher of *Quest* magazine since 1970 and founder of the networking/contact-making association the Green Circle, she has also organised the esoteric Quest Annual Conference since 1968.[21] Green is a pioneer in British pagan spirituality, operating within what she terms the 'Western Mystery Tradition'. A purveyor of 'Magic for the Aquarian Age', she also runs postal workshops through 'The Invisible College'. As she explains, 'A lot of the New Age may lead to dead ends rather than to a new spiritual direction. But at least it can awaken people to the options.'

Like Howard, Green talks enthusiastically about the reopening of the spas in Bath but claims the spiritual consequences will depend largely on how they are used, and for what ends. Recognising the area as an ancient place of pilgrimage, she argues that if the spas are used as religious sites and not just for recreation, the reopening will be positive. During my interview with her in December 1997, she explained that the spiritual aura of the place is 'tidal', but that, when the town is left to itself and not packed with summer tourists, one can sense the 'old energies'. Consequently, Green takes small groups of people around the baths early in the morning, in order for them to experience a more natural feeling. The sanctuary of Sulis Minerva is, according to Green, 'the oldest named shrine in Britain'. Cross Bath 'guardian' Margaret Marian Stewart makes the same claim.

At the time of writing, the dominant issue in the world of alternative spirituality in Bath is the proposed reopening of the spas, which have been closed since 1979. New Age and geo-pagan sentiment, expressed throughout the local alternative spirituality network, tends to see this as a further opportunity to promote the reawakening of Bath as a spiritual centre – a view which has general public support. The local council intends to incorporate the city's Cross Bath, Hot Bath and Beau Street Bath as a three-component facility. The council argues that only by including all three centres can the Bath Spa Project be an economically viable package. However, earlier in 1991, the Council had granted the independent Springs Foundation the right to maintain the Cross Bath and open it for public sightseeing. In practice, this chartered organisation operates the Cross Bath as a low-key but ostensible pagan sanctuary. But with the advent of the

Bath Spa Project which aims to re-open all three centres as bathing facilities, the Springs Foundation – which might be termed a pagan 'front organisation' – is now reluctant to relinquish control of the Sulis sanctuary. In this way, the Bathonian sacred geography issue has links with other geo-pagan political concerns, such as the road protest movement, or the environmental issues espoused by the 'eco-magickal' organisation, Dragon. Whilst geo-paganism entails a more individualistic and spontaneous response, as opposed to the organised and formal ceremonial response to nature and the supernatural which is characteristic of Wicca, Druidry, Asatru and other forms of Neo-paganism, the parameters of the Cross Bath as a sacred place present a potentially divisive political issue.

CONCLUSION

In this chapter, I have portrayed alternative forms of spirituality in three different European communities. Amsterdam is of course the largest and, correspondingly, the most expressive of the full range of contemporary non-mainstream religiosity. But even such a relatively remote community as the Provençal village of Aups reveals the presence of numerous elements deriving from the same *cultic milieu*. Whilst the numbers involved with new forms of religiosity remain hard to identify precisely, we can at least recognise the ubiquity and growth of the diffuse religious consumer supermarket which demonstrates an increasingly vital presence in both urban Holland and rural southern France. These areas are witness to the spiritual ferment which is either a product of, or concomitant with, the decline of traditionally western forms of religion and the growth of secularisation as the acceptable form of public life. Change occurs against a background of ubiquitous experimentation and innovation with regard to spiritual practice – one which eschews dogma, conformity and belief and emphasises both individual autonomy and direct experience.

Like Dutch Amsterdam and French Provence, the English city of Bath is a cosmopolitan environment. More of a town than Amsterdam yet more of a city than Aups, Bath nevertheless reveals the same plethora of New Age or New Age-type spiritualities as is found on the European continent, let alone in North America. In terms of alternative forms of spirituality, Bath benefits both from its own indigenous heritage and from its axial location between London and Glastonbury. Being the more urban conglomeration, Amsterdam has always been ahead of Bath in terms of spiritual change, but even the English town reveals a notable conformity to such quasi-spiritual growth as, for instance, that of vegetarianism (Twigg, 1979 and Hamilton *et al.*, 1995). Vegetarian fare was available in the Dutch capital as early as the late 1960s, while in Bath in the 1990s virtually every restaurant includes one or more vegetarian or even vegan dishes on its menu. In Aups, by contrast, the occasional health food shop or even vegetarian restaurant has been established, but these have remained essentially ephemeral, usually lasting only a few years. Whereas both the Netherlands and Britain are more open to direct influences from the USA, France is dependent on its imported innovative ideas arriving first through French Canada. Consequently, awareness of, and demand for, vegetarian food has been slow to develop in France – although there are now signs of influences beginning to arrive via Quebec. Bulletin boards in natural foods shops and metaphysical bookstores in both Amsterdam and Bath serve as information resources allowing interested consumers to locate goods, services and workshops on offer in the New Age market. In a village like Aups, on the other hand, the occasional poster is to be seen attached to a tree or even in the window of the main café on the town square.

An analytical look at the communities of Amsterdam, Aups and Bath indicates the newer kinds of development which, if not transforming, are augmenting the range of western spiritual expression. All three locales reveal a remarkable similarity in the specific types of psychophysical, human potential and other non-traditional spiritual alternatives which are available. Whilst each of the three retains local differences conditioned by indigenous settings, historic legacies and ethnic divergences, the general conformities support the current sociological theories of globalism which suggest the growing dissemination of a Western religious consumer market.[22]

NOTES

1. Of sixteen countries, Dutch youth rank third, after Ireland and Italy, in spirituality in terms of 'attendance, prayer and the salience of religion in one's life'. Whilst only 39 per cent of Dutch youth admit to church membership, 82 per cent claim to pray at least on some occasions (Janssen, 1997: 5). Janssen found that the young prayed primarily when facing problems or as part of meditational practice, and for psychological effect.
2. Janssen found that when asked to define God, only 32 per cent said 'He is'. He found this reduced to 25 per cent in written sources. In other words, three-fourths of textual references to God said that 'God does'.
3. For a further profile on Dutch spirituality based on data collected in the mid-1970s, see Thung (1985).
4. *Oibibio: Programma overzicht* (April–July, 1997). Dr A. Kamphuis' three-day dolphin strategy training cost fl 2950 (£900) plus VAT; Karin Aartsen's two-day vision training charged fl 1950 (£600) plus VAT.
5. Fl 115; £35, including lunch.
6. The Gestalt school of psychotherapy pioneered by Fritz Perls rose to prominence at the Esalen Institute in California and in Perls' own headquarters near Victoria, Canada, in

the 1960s. Among the many spin-offs of Gestalt beside transpersonal psychology, there is the Body Electric School of Massage founded by Joseph Kramer. In Amsterdam, Kramer's work finds chief expression via Spetéra.

7. Spetéra developed as a cooperative venture from the Kristallijn Gestalt Opleidingen, a school for Gestalt therapists founded by Hans Koch in 1985.

8. 'My Heart's Desire' promotional letter from Hans Koch.

9. 'My Heart's Desire: a workshop in erotic massage and sex magic,' Therapeutenkollektief Spetéra brochure.

10. The venue is De Roos on the Vondelstraat, and in 1997 the full four-day workshop cost fl 600 (£185).

11. Playbill for the performance of 'The 2 in 1: A Saga of All That Is Incomplete', the Odeon Theater, November 1996.

12. The performers are led to 'discover and strengthen their own individual process towards wholeness and harmony. This consists of discovering the essential active (*yang*) and receptive (*yin*) capacities of the self, freeing them from the inner saboteur who uses their energy in its drive towards disharmony, and reuniting them in balance under the Nature Spirit's guidance.' See reference in preceding note.

13. Himalaya (New Age winkel).

14. The organisational base for *L'association* ‹*L'isthme*› is La Colonne, Route de Sérignan, 84100 Orange. The Association also maintains chapters in Paris.

15. The Centre d'Étude et de Méditation Bouddhique is to be found in Marseille. The centre also maintains Le Refuge.

16. *Sophrologie* was founded by Alfonso Caycedo, a medical doctor, to treat symptoms such as stress, fatigue, anxiety, depression, insomnia, poor memory and so forth. The term derives from the Greek roots for 'health, harmony' (*sos*), 'brain' (*phren*) and 'study, science' (*logos*). It seeks to encourage the individual to employ the means to live positively and optimally to resist the many negativities of life. As part of its agenda to develop self-creativity, it endeavours to assist individuals faced with ordeals such as exams, sporting contests or childbirth. The goal of *sophrologie* is to attain a consistent 'therapeutic level'.

17. L'Atelier d'Évolution Psycho-Corporelle and L'Espace MANUEL are based in Aix-en-Provence. Le Centre CO-NAISSANCE is based in Aix-les-Platanes.

18. Peter Eliot, a resident of the nearby town of Carcès, has hosted one- or two-year workshop courses in Aups for students of the Gurdjieff teachings.

19. See also Bowman (1994: 32–7).

20. *Vide* Bowman, 1994, 1998; Mowl and Earnshaw, 1988.

21. The 31st Annual Quest Conference was held in March 1998 in south Bristol.

22. For globalism theory, see Robertson (1992), Beyer (1994) and Simpson (1997).

BIBLIOGRAPHY

Adler, Margo, 1986: *Drawing Down the Moon: Witches, Druids, Goddess-Worshippers, and Other Pagans in America Today* (Boston: Beacon Press).

Beyer, Peter, 1994: *Religion and Globalization* (London: Sage Publications).

Bowman, Marion, 1993a: 'Drawn to Glastonbury' in Ian Reader & Tony Walter, eds, *Pilgrimage in Popular Culture* (Basingstoke: Macmillan).

—— 1993b: 'Reinventing the Celts', *Religion* 23: 147–56.

—— 1994: 'Religion in Bath', *Religion Today* 9.3: 32–7.

—— 1998: 'Belief, Legend and Perceptions of the Sacred in Contemporary Bath', *Folklore* 109: 25–31.

Campbell, Colin B., 1972: 'The Cult, Cultic Milieu and Secularization,' in Michael Hill, ed., *A Sociological Yearbook of Religion in Britain* 5 (London: SCM Press), pp. 119–36.

Hamilton, Malcolm, *et al.*, 1995: 'Eat, Drink and Be Saved: the Spiritual Significance of Alternative Diets', *Social Compass* 42.4: 497–511.

Janssen, Jacques, 1997: 'The Abstract Image of God: the Case of the Dutch Youth', paper presented to 'Nuovi Movimenti Religiosi, Sette e Sacro Alternativo nei Giovani Europei', 13th International Conference, Trento, 3 October 1997.

Mowl, Tim, and Earnshaw, Brian, 1988: *John Wood, Architect of Obsession* (Bath: Millstream Books).

Nelson, Geoffrey K., 1968: 'The Concept of Cult,' *The Sociological Review* 16: 351–62.

Robertson, Roland, 1992: *Globalization: Social Theory and Global Culture* (London: Sage Publications).

Simpson, John H., 1997: 'The Sacred in the Global System: Three Theses,' in Folker Schmidt, ed., *Methodische Probleme der empirischen Erziehungswissenschaft: Festschrift für Hans Merkens (zum 60sten)* (Baltmannsweiler: Schneider-Verlag, Höhengehren).

Stark, Rodney, and Bainbridge, William Sims, 1985: *The Future of Religion: Secularization, Revival and Cult Formation* (Berkeley: University of California Press).

Sutcliffe, Steven, 1997: 'Seekers, Networks and "New Age" ', *Scottish Journal of Religious Studies* 15.2: 97–114.

Thung, Mady A., 1985: *Exploring the New Religious Consciousness: An Investigation of Religious Change by a Dutch Working Group* (Amsterdam: Free University Press).

Twigg, Julia, 1979: 'Food for Thought: Purity and Vegetarianism', *Religion* 9 (Spring): 13–35.

Wallis, Roy, 1979: *Salvation and Protest: Studies of Social and Religious Movements* (London: Frances Pinter; New York: St Martin's Press).

York, Michael, 1994: 'New Age in Britain', *Religion Today* 9.3: 14–22.

—— 1995: *The Emerging Network: A Sociology of the New Age and Neo-pagan Movements* (Lanham, Maryland: Rowman and Littlefield).

—— 1997: 'New Age and the Late Twentieth Century', *Journal of Contemporary Religion* 12/3: 401–19.

Part 3: Practices

8

Gender and Power in Magical Practices

Susan Greenwood

*'As above, so below'. Upon earth we see the reflection of the play
of the heavenly principles in the actions of men and women.*
(Dion Fortune, 1987: 129)

INTRODUCTION

In this chapter I examine how power is gendered in magical practices: how
power relationships are worked out through notions of femininity and
masculinity in high magic (sometimes called 'ceremonial magic' or 'western
mysteries') and contemporary witchcraft, or Wicca. High magic and Wicca
are often termed a form of Paganism.[1] However, this is problematic because
'Paganism' is a rather vague umbrella term for a group of magical practices
which are often seen to pre-date Christianity. The word 'pagan' is derived
from Latin *pagus* meaning 'rural', 'from the countryside', and has often been
used to designate the 'other' from Christianity (Jones & Pennick, 1995: 1).
Contemporary self-designated Pagans use the term broadly as 'one who
honours nature'. A contemporary definition of Paganism is as 'a Nature-
venerating religion which endeavours to set human life in harmony with
the great cycles embodied in the rhythms of the seasons' (Jones & Pennick,
1995: 2). A study of history shows that, rather than being based on an
indigenous nature religion, many current magical practices stem from the
revival of magic in the Hermeticism[2] of the Renaissance and more recently
in the nineteenth-century magical organisation, the Hermetic Order of the
Golden Dawn. Magical practices by their very nature – their association
with 'the occult', with secrecy, the mysterious, and with the realm that lies
beyond the range of ordinary knowledge – have a certain *frisson*: an
excitement induced by contact with what are seen to be otherworldly
powers. My focus in this paper is on how this contact is gendered: how
certain conceptions of femininity and masculinity are constituted through

magical practice and how women are seen to gain power through this gendering.

Modern magical practices are diverse and include many groups ranging from Druidism to anarchistic Chaos Magick[3]; they do not form a systematic body of beliefs although they may be described as a western form of shamanism.[4] Traditionally, a shaman is a person who, in a state of trance, journeys to spiritual otherworlds on behalf of a community for knowledge or healing. The anthropologist Michael Harner has defined a shaman as 'a man or woman who enters an altered state of consciousness – at will – to contact and utilize an ordinarily hidden reality in order to acquire knowledge and power . . .' (1990: 20). The emphasis is on bringing about an altered state of consciousness. In its western form, shamanism has been interpreted broadly to mean any magico-religious practice involving trance or altered states of consciousness. Contemporary magicians[5] employ ritual techniques aimed at changing consciousness which involve trance experiences of another realm of reality which is often called the 'otherworld'. Ritual provides a channel of communication by which the powers of the otherworld (often expressed as deities or animals or a combination of both, as in the Egyptian pantheon) are mediated by the magician by the use of the magical will – the direction of the mind and emotions to a particular magical objective. The communication with otherworldly beings – which might involve the magician embodying[6] the deity – is seen to be the source of all the magician's power. Thus, magicians work with esoteric rather than exoteric knowledge: their practices are shaped by a direct communication with otherworldly beings. This imbues them with an aura of mystery, setting them apart from the ordinary world, and implies occult power as a mastery of unseen forces.

The practice of magic is essentially about obtaining power, and I shall examine how this power is gendered. As Sherry Ortner (1974) has noted, women are culturally conceived as being closer to nature than men, and in magical practices femininity is also associated with the magical otherworld and intuition, while masculinity is connected to rationality, patriarchy and the wider non-magical culture. Magical ritual is the space where the ordinary consciousness – the rationality – of mainstream culture is reversed. In its explicit glorification of 'unreason' and femininity, the current practice of magic may be viewed as a romantic reaction to the Enlightenment emphasis on reason and its association with masculinity (Seidler, 1989). This gender polarity places women in a uniquely powerful position, because the female body and femininity are valued as a source of power. This is particularly clearly shown in Wicca. Gender roles in many magical practices have been strongly influenced by Dion Fortune, a one-time member of the

Hermetic Order of the Golden Dawn, and I shall discuss the influence of her work on high magic and Wicca. Before turning to an examination of gender roles I shall look at high magic and witchcraft in more detail to argue that modern witchcraft is not a pre-Christian Pagan tradition but a development of the Hermetic tradition.

THE HIGH MAGIC – WITCHCRAFT CONTINUUM

High magic or ceremonial magic developed from the Renaissance and is based on the Hermeticism of Renaissance magi such as Marsilio Ficino (1433–99), Pico Della Mirandola (1463–94) and Giordano Bruno (1548–1600). These magi derived influence from a body of philosophical and astrological writings, called the *Corpus Hermeticum*, dealing with sympathetic magic and with drawing down the powers of the stars, which they believed to be the work of an Egyptian priest Hermes Trismegistus. However, according to the historian Frances Yates, the *Corpus Hermeticum* was not ancient Egyptian but probably Greek in origin[7] and was written in the second to third centuries AD (Yates, 1991).

Ficino, who was a physician and priest, developed a system of 'natural magic' which concerned the drawing down of the natural powers of the cosmos. Ficino's theory of magic was based on the guiding of spirit from the stars using the natural sympathies, or knowledge of energies running through nature, by which one thing could be drawn to another[8] – a process which the Victorian theoretical anthropologist Sir James Frazer termed 'sympathetic magic' ([1921] 1993).

Pico was influenced by Ficino's natural magic but, in a bid to increase its power, incorporated the Jewish mystical Kabbalah (sometimes spelt 'Qabalah' or 'Cabala') to tap higher powers of angels and archangels in a form of esoteric Christianity. Pico's magical work laid the foundation for contemporary esoteric Christian high magic.

By contrast, Bruno sought to take magic back to what he saw as its purer pagan source in Egypt. Bruno's practical magic consisted of drawing spirits and demons, also through the use of the Kabbalah. In contrast to Pico, who wanted to work solely with angelic forces, Bruno actively wanted to unlock the inner power of demonic forces. The essence of Bruno's magic was the discovery of the human divine nature through a magical communication with nature; it focused on the glorification of Man, who was believed to have divine origins and divine powers.[9]

Contemporary high magic has its roots in the nineteenth-century revival of occultism which led to the formation of the magical society, the Hermetic

Order of the Golden Dawn. There are two clear strands of magical philosophy emerging from the Golden Dawn which draw directly from the Renaissance magical workings of Pico and Bruno. The first strand is based on a Christian interpretation and involves the use of what magicians see as higher angelic beings and an emphasis on the light and the celestial. Christian-influenced high magic mythology is based on the mastery of the 'lower self' and baser nature through the Kabbalistic 'Tree of Life' glyph (see Figure 8.1) in the spiritual pursuit of true identity in the Light of the Ultimate Being. This is commonly explained by reference to the Judeo-Christian 'Fall' – the separation of humanity from godhead which created the need for human nature to be redeemed. At the beginning of the twentieth century Dion Fortune was the leading magician associated with this tradition.

The second strand is a direct rebellion against Christianity. It follows Bruno's return to Egyptian religion and is represented today by Aleister Crowley's Nietzschean glorification of the self. Crowley's magick, which also made use of the Kabbalah but focused more explicitly on sex magic, was based on 'liberating energy' to develop the divine self – human nature being seen as inherently divine. Aleister Crowley took sexuality, specifically female sexuality, as a central organising principle of his 'magick', as demonstrated by his spelling of the word' with a 'k' to denote the emphasis on *Koth*, 'the hollow one', meaning 'female genitalia' (deriving from *kteis*, the Greek word for 'genitals'). Crowley was involved in two magical orders, the Argenteum Astrum and the Ordo Templi Orientis, which utilised sexual techniques for 'establishing a gate in space through which the extraterrestrial or cosmic energies may enter in and manifest on earth' (Grant, 1976: 136)[10] and his work was closely identified with eastern forms of Tantra. In particular, Crowley's Gnostic Mass, a reversal of the Christian Catholic mass,[11] is centred on the veneration of woman as priestess of the gods and 'Queen of Space'. This ritual formed the basis of Wicca, a new conception and practice of witchcraft formulated by Gerald Gardner, who claimed that it was a form of an ancient mystery cult ([1954]1988). Gardner used a high magic framework to construct a nature religion. Thus, contemporary witchcraft or Wicca is not an unbroken tradition springing from the pagan folk practices and spell-making of the peasantry, as many modern witches would have it: it is a development of Bruno's magical anthropocentrism, based on the view that human nature is essentially divine.

Current practice of Wicca is largely centred on the creation of rituals conducted in a circle marked by correspondences with nature, both in the external environment and within the individual witch. East represents light and intellect, south represents fire and the witch's will, west represents water and emotions, while north is symbolic of earth and the human body. Witches celebrate eight solar rituals which mark the turning of the year and are linked to a mythological cycle of the Goddess and her son/lover. There are four Greater Sabbats: Candlemas (2 February), May Eve (30 April), Lammas (1 August), and Samhain (31 October). The Lesser Sabbats are the Midsummer and Midwinter Solstices and the Spring and Autumn Equinoxes. Witches also perform magical work such as spell-making or healing based on a lunar pattern of either full or dark moon workings. Thus witchcraft is a practice which connects the individual to the rhythms of the sun and moon: for witches, internal nature is a reflection of the wider cosmological forces.

THE POWER OF THE OTHERWORLD

A central Wiccan rite concerns the 'Drawing Down the Moon' invocation, during which the High Priest invokes and draws down the energy of the goddess into the High Priestess. Vivianne Crowley,[12] a Wiccan High Priestess, describes invocation as:

> a process by which the Goddess or God will temporarily incarnate in the body of a selected worshipper – a priestess if the deity is the Goddess, a priest if the deity is the God. Both Goddess and God may be invoked in the rites, but traditionally only the Goddess speaks what is known as a *charge*. A charge is a ritual utterance that conveys a message from the deity to the worshipper. (1993: 133, emphasis in original)

Geoffrey Samuel indicates that it is possible that this central element of Wiccan practice may derive from Indian Tantra (Samuel, 1998).[13] The embodiment of deity and the assumption of the status and power of deity is the basis of magical power in high magic and Wicca. Both practices are founded on the notion of spiritual transformation. This was also a central part of the Greek Mysteries, the purpose of which was to bring initiates into contact with otherworldly powers (D'Alviella, 1981: 33–6). I have argued elsewhere that invocation of the Goddess gives the Wiccan High Priestess a particularly privileged and powerful position in the coven and that this may be contrasted with the feminist democratic interpretation of witchcraft.[14] The purpose of ritual is to provide the space for the magician to contact and embody the powers of the cosmos (represented by various deities) using the magical will. I have also suggested that the magical will is gendered (see Greenwood, 1996b).

Thus, all contemporary magical practices involve a notion of communication with an otherworld which is distinct from the world of ordinary reality. This communication is conducted when the magician is in a state of trance; the otherworld is experienced when the magician is in an altered state of consciousness.

The philosopher Lévy-Bruhl (1966) was the first to point out that human beings had two co-existing mentalities (what we would call two forms of consciousness): rational–logical and mystical. The anthropologist Stanley Tambiah (1991) developed Lévy-Bruhl's ideas by proposing that it is possible to distinguish two orientations to the cosmos – two orderings of reality that women and men everywhere are capable of experiencing. The first is causality which emphasises atomistic individualism and distance and is represented by the categories, rules and methods of positivistic science and discursive mathematico-logical reason; the second is participation, an orientation to the world which places that person in the world fully as a totality, and where action is often expressed through myth and ritual. These two orientations to the cosmos correspond to what Michael Harner (1990) terms 'Ordinary State of Consciousness' (OSC) – which accords with causality – and a 'Shamanic State of Consciousness' (SCC) – which parallels with participation. It is through SSC that magicians contact the otherworld. Samuel identifies shamanism specifically with alternate states of consciousness and defines it as:

> the regulation and transformation of human life and human society through the use (or purported use) of alternate states of consciousness by means of which specialist practitioners are held to communicate with a mode of reality alternative to, and more fundamental than, the world of everyday experience. (Samuel, 1993: 8)

Samuel points out that shamanism has been defined in a restrictive and typological fashion by the emphasis on either the element of shamanic flight or that of spirit possession. He argues for an alternative approach that concentrates on common techniques of transformations of consciousness and what they mean for the functioning of human societies (Samuel, 1997: 326–7). In the context of this paper, magical ritual may be seen as a theatrical space where magicians utilise a shamanic altered state of consciousness to develop a connection with the 'power source' of the otherworld; it is a space in which boundaries can be negotiated between the microcosm of the self (and how it is gendered) and the forces of the macrocosm (the totality).

GENDERED POWER: THE INFLUENCE OF DION FORTUNE

Man should not for ever be potent, but should lie latent in the arms of Persephone, surrendering himself. Then she who was dark and cold as outer space before the creative Word, is made queen of the underworld, crowned by his surrender, and her kisses become potent upon his lips. (Dion Fortune, 1987: 132–3)

The influence of Dion Fortune on both high magic and Wicca is clear. Her notions of masculine/feminine polarity (influenced by Jungian psychology – see Fortune [1935]1987: 100) have shaped contemporary magical practices. Magicians' gendered relationships with the otherworld are remarkably similar in both high magic and Wicca. However, magicians often stereotype the differences between these two practices: it is widely believed that high magic adopts a more formal and intellectual (and therefore more masculine) approach. By contrast, Wicca is said to be more practical and celebratory of nature (and associated with femininity).[15] We can see in Wicca, therefore, the most developed notions of femininity and of feminine power, and I shall return to an analysis of this. But firstly I turn to an examination of Dion Fortune's ideas. I start with her influential work *The Mystical Qabalah*, originally published in 1935, which was formative in my own high magic training.

When I was a student high magician during fieldwork, I learnt the attributes of the various sephiroth (or spheres) of the Kabbalistic 'Tree of Life' glyph (see Figure 8.1). I was taught that the sephirah Chokmah represents wisdom and the great primary male force. It is concerned with all masculinity, the father, and father-figures such as employers, authority and the state. The sephirah Binah represents understanding and is associated with form, restriction and limitation; it comprises all that is latent or passive – it is the 'social unit' in which the force of action has to work. Binah is the Great Mother, representing death and rebirth but also the home as the domain of the feminine side of life. The aim of learning the Kabbalah is to internalise the attributes of each sephirah of the 'Tree of Life' glyph, and so although the sephiroth of Chokmah and Binah are gendered in their association with notions of masculinity and femininity, the high magician must work towards balancing all the attributes of all the sephiroth within the self, leading to a form of spiritual androgyny. As my magical supervisor pointed out: 'On the inner, we are neither male or female – we just are.' When I questioned her about the gender of God, she said:

'If you want to worship God in the female aspect, that's fine, but remember that male and female forces are equal – neither is superior or inferior and the Universe has to have both to be balanced both on the macrocosm and the microcosm.'

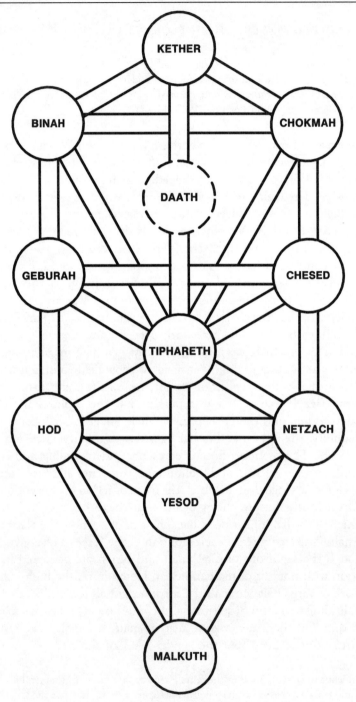

Fig 8.1: The Kabbalistic 'Tree of Life' glyph

Thus the emphasis is on balance: balance equals wholeness. The high magician works on becoming whole, aligning the microcosm (the self) with the macrocosm (the cosmos) and thereby helping humanity to evolve spiritually. As my magical supervisor commented: 'When we are whole (or well on the way to being) we alter the whole of our race and in turn, the Universe'.

Dion Fortune's main influence is on the dynamic nature of polarity: she was the first magician to incorporate Jungian psychology into magical ideas and to interpret it in such a way as to give women magical power. For Fortune, the sephirah Binah is associated with form and restriction, but this does not mean that femininity is viewed solely as passive: the relationship between the two aspects of polarity is active and dynamic and women are seen to be passive on the outer planes but active on the inner:

> In the outer, he is the male, the lord, the giver of life. But in the inner he taketh life at her hands as she bendeth over him, he kneeling. Therefore should he worship the Great Goddess, for without Her he hath no life, and every woman is Her priestess. In the face of every woman let him look for the features of the goddess, watching her phases through the flow and return of the tides to which his soul answereth; awaiting her call, as he needs must, aching in his barrenness. (Fortune, 1987: 132)

In her magical novel *The Sea Priestess*, Fortune tells of Wilfred Maxwell, a feeble asthmatic, who is taught the secrets of magic by Morgan Le Fay, the Sea Priestess. Fortune uses the medium of the novel to convey what she sees as essential magical lore, explaining how that which is 'dynamic in the outer planes is latent in the inner planes' (1989: 160). The Sea Priestess is an initiate of the 'higher mysteries' and was herself taught by the Priest of the Moon that manifesting Life had two modes or aspects – the active, dynamic and stimulating and the latent and passive which 'receives the stimulus and reacts to it.' The Priest of the Moon showed her how the two modes 'changed places one with another in an endless dance, giving and receiving: accumulating force and discharging it; never still, never stabilized, ever in a state of flux and reflux as shown by the moon and the sea and the tides of life . . .' (ibid.: 159). In turn, the Sea Priestess taught Wilfred that 'in every being there are two aspects, the positive and the negative; the dynamic and the receptive; the male and the female' (ibid.: 16).

Thus, there is gender equality in the inner magical spiritual domain, but this may be expressed using gender polarity on the outer planes and in the performance of ritual, as the following high magic ritual 'The Summer Greeting Rite' shows.[16] This ritual demonstrates the close connection between high magic and Wicca and the cross-over of ideas between the two: it is enacted around a central cauldron (a symbol of femininity borrowed from Wiccan ritual) and focuses on the Lady and Lord as sacred couple. The Lady summons the feminine powers of earth and water (rivers, streams and lakes), while the Lord summons the powers of air and fire which are identified with masculinity:

> LADY: I am She who is the summer's breath, who holds the balance of the year.
> I am She who is in the brooks set free from winter's snare.
> I am She that in dappled shade of full leafed tree will whisper:
> Come to me!
> I am She in whose care all things have their time and place.
> I am She who replaces madcap maid with loving woman's face.
> I am She who calls to man and beast, bow before the power of love.
> Come to me!
> I am She whose warm breath feeds the earth and turns the fields to gold.
> I am She who is the core of every fairy tale that's told.
> I am She without whose love the life of men would wither all away.
> Come to me!

Compare the role of the Lord:

> LORD: Look on me without terror, for I am strength.
> Lean on me without restraint, for I will hold thee.
> Know me for what I have always been, the Life Force of the Land.
> My Horns are the symbols of that Force, as is my upraised phallus.
> Do not turn from me in shame, but glory in my manhood
> For it but reflects your own.
> Hear my voice in the October wind and the Winter's silent snow.
> Feel my power in the surge of Spring and Summer's bounty.
> Weep not when I am cut down, for I will rise again.

Note that Binah, the Great Mother represented by Nature, is receptive ('Come to me!'), and that Chokmah, the masculine force symbolised by the phallus, represents strength and 'the Life Force of the Land'. If we now turn to contemporary Wicca we shall see a similar gender polarity.

WICCA AND THE EMPHASIS ON FEMININITY

Contemporary Wicca is practised in small groups called covens and attaches great importance to the aspect of family. According to Frederic Lamond,[17] an initiate of Gerald Gardner's original coven, Wicca is a family which is based on gender polarity but with a 'special emphasis on femininity'. Wicca is unique among magical practices in that the head of a coven is usually a High Priestess. When a witch reaches the Third Degree, the highest level of initiation, she may 'hive off' to form her own coven. Polarity is essential to the way that witchcraft is worked. Lamond points out that all is divided into male and female; that perpetuation requires the union of both genders, and that this is the basis of the nature of the powers: the primal mother and father brought earth and all its creatures into existence. This polarity is portrayed by the High Priestess and the High Priest in the highest Wiccan sacrament of the 'Sacred Marriage' or 'Great Rite', which aims to channel what are seen as the essential male and female sexual polarity of High Priest and High Priestess into the cosmos in such a manner as to transcend duality. Vivianne Crowley describes the Great Rite as a 'sacred marriage' in terms of Jungian psychology and in the tradition of Dion Fortune:

> On the physical level it takes place with a priest or priestess; on the psychological level it takes place with the animus or anima; on the metaphysical level it takes place with the Goddess or the God. On the psychological level, the anima and animus can be considered as our initiators into the world of the True Self. (1989: 227)

Here the polaric forces of masculinity and femininity are seen as having physical, psychological and metaphysical elements which must be united in order to achieve a harmonious balance and effect the spiritual transformation of the true self. Masculine and feminine roles are also demonstrated on the mundane level. It is usually considered preferable to enter a Wiccan coven as a couple; some people do gain entry singly, but this is perhaps less easy for a man.[18] On first entering the coven the neophyte witch is sponsored by a teacher of the opposite sex, and in this way the teachings of Wicca are passed on from female to male, and vice-versa. In addition, Wiccan rituals that I attended were explicitly ordered by gender. Before the ritual, women and men occupied clearly demarcated zones – spaces set aside where the ritual could be discussed beforehand, where men and women could rehearse the lines of the sacred drama, where they could get changed and talk generally about the ritual and also about 'family' relationships.

The Wiccan ritual is based on explicit gender division and gender roles: the Wiccan priest is very masculine – he will often call in the powers of the otherworld in a deep and commanding voice, using male imagery such as bulls and rams. The priestess is feminine, and this polarity is expressed in a manner similar to the high magic 'Summer Greeting Rite' already described. Both practices demonstrate the need for strong gender identity as a prerequisite for working polaric magic, and I have spoken to high magicians and Wiccans who believe that homosexuals cannot work magic because they do not generate the required energy. However, it is interesting to note that the magical robes worn in some rituals make both male and female magicians appear androgynous.

THE USE OF MAGICAL POWER

Magical power is based on secret knowledge, and magicians identify themselves through their connection with the otherworld. Magical ritual is a theatrical space where social power relationships are reversed: the otherworld is where women as representatives of the Goddess are powerful *vis-à-vis* men. As already noted, Fortune suggested that women, following dominant notions of femininity, were outwardly passive in the ordinary world, but dynamic on the inner planes of the otherworld (Fortune, 1989). This means that in Wicca men have to give up their social power and surrender it to women. The High Priestess is the leader of the coven and the High Priest her partner. According to Vivianne Crowley, the rationale for this is derived from a ritual, *The Legend of the Goddess*, which is enacted as a mystery play during the initiation ceremony for High Priestesses. In the play, the Priestess enacts the role of the Goddess and undertakes a 'heroic quest' where she confronts the force of death, represented as male (Crowley, 1993: 135). This stems from Gardner's *The Myth of the Goddess*, which he called 'the central idea of the cult', in which the goddess journeyed to the nether lands to the realm of death: 'Such was her beauty that Death himself knelt and kissed her feet . . .' (Gardner, [1954]1988). This has been interpreted by the Wiccans Janet and Stewart Farrar as: 'Such was her beauty, that Death himself laid down his sword and crown at her feet' (Farrar, 1984: 29, quoted in Crowley, 1993: 135). Crowley notes that in Wicca the sword and the crown are seen as symbols of power and legitimate authority, and are given by the God to the Goddess. According to Crowley, this 'recognizes the underlying reality of male-female relations: the greater physical strength of the male'. The woman can only rule because the man permits her to do so and 'in Wicca, he does' (1993: 135).

Gendered ritual contact with the otherworld does in some circumstances empower women. I have argued elsewhere that witchcraft (Wiccan and feminist versions) is concerned with the empowerment of the self and aims to (re)define selfhood (Greenwood, 1998; 2000); I have also suggested that Wicca is a specifically female model of power (Greenwood, 1996b; 2000). Male Wiccans enact a role where they give up their social power to a woman as representative of the Goddess. In Tantric practices women are worshipped as manifestations of goddesses, but according to Elizabeth Puttick in her study of women in new religions, the main debate is whether the woman in a Tantric relationship is primarily a sex object for the man's enlightenment or whether she is an equal partner (1997: 56). Puttick concludes that such practices do appear to have worked for women's as well as men's spiritual enlightenment in the past, but argues that success depends on high discipline and equality (1997: 58). It seems reasonable to suggest that there is potential for spiritual transformation based on a genuine equality, but that there is also the potential for abuse of power by magicians of either gender. Some male Wiccans may experience the loss of control as sexually stimulating: as an indulgence in the forbidden as a form of eroticism, or a transgression of the social world in the tradition of de Sade (Airaksinen, 1995) – a response which does not challenge institutions of masculine power in mainstream society. The practice of Wicca does not challenge social or political convention and thus largely supports the gender status quo of feminine subordination in the ordinary world. In this respect it differs from feminist versions of witchcraft which do not work in gender-stereotyped ways and which allegedly practise magic to transform what they regard as the patriarchal social structures of ordinary reality (see Greenwood, 1996a). Wicca works on notions of femininity based on traditional feminine stereotypes of intuition, feeling, relating and nurturing, but ultimately women's legitimate power and authority is given to them only when men choose to surrender it. As Puttick notes, this seems to undermine the basis of female power by defining its conditions as social and as a 'precarious authority granted by men, which can therefore be abrogated by men' (Puttick, 1997: 217).

The promise of occult power is one reason why many people are attracted to magical practices. Magical power has two aspects: as an energy or force brought through as deity from the otherworld; and as a form of this-worldly identity and status. Some tentative work is emerging that associates magical practices with people who have suffered abuse. The practice of Wicca may involve using magical rituals to work out childhood feelings of powerlessness, thereby improving participants' self-conception and this-worldly identity. Shelley Rabinovitch, in research conducted for an MA thesis, has noted the high incidence of abuse among those engaged in Paganism in North America.[19] She found that many people involved in witchcraft came from abused or severely dysfunctional backgrounds, with either alcholic parents, a history of drug dependency, or physical, sexual or emotional abuse (1992). Drawing on Rabinovitch's work, Sian Reid argues that magic is a metaphor for expressing and manipulating the meaning context of life: by using spells, witches heal themselves from their personal histories of trauma. She claims that magical practices confer certain psychological benefits to survivors of abuse. Abuse leaves its victims feeling powerless, but by engaging in meditation, visualisation, rituals and roleplay which confer power and control as self-knowledge it is possible for victims to re-integrate parts of the personality to alter consciousness and work towards change. Reid argues that magic is born out of the inner strength of 'traversing darkness' and that it gives a positive value to pain as a part of individual growth (1996: 160–3).

Although there are no accurate figures, my impression is that many women involved in magical practices in London had also experienced some form of similar trauma. One High Priestess that I knew had suffered from sexual and physical abuse as a child and used her power in her coven as a means of redressing her intense childhood feelings of powerlessness. In such cases – which may be unrepresentative of Wicca as a whole but nevertheless cannot be ignored – the ritual may convert these feelings of powerlessness to experiences of empowerment. Everyday coven interactions may also de-monstrate this power relationship. This particular High Priestess routinely humiliated her High Priest and another male member of the coven who shared their house. On one occasion they both knelt down in front of her to be reprimanded for not doing the necessary cleaning of the floor before the ritual. It appeared to me at the time that both men enjoyed this perfor-mance (cf McClintock, 1993) and that there were elements of sadomaso-chism (S/M)[20] in the relationship. The connections between Paganism and S/M have been explored in the American Pagan magazine *Green Egg*.[21] In an article on the subject, Dossie Easton and Catherine Liszt argue that S/M is 'consensual power exchange' and that S/M fantasies can come from areas deep within childhood memory and experience. A characteristic of S/M is the exploration of the psyche as an 'adventure in the forbidden': an investigation of the Jungian shadow, the realm containing all that is excluded from awareness in the pursuit of transformation. They point out that 'when we add ritual to our S/M, performing it with spiritual intention, we can travel deeper yet . . . beyond the personal unconscious mind and into universal consciousness, or spiritual awareness' (1997: 18). In this context, magical ritual may be a cathartic space of transformation of the social realm; a negotiated space where feminine and masculine gender roles are enacted as a theatrical play to work out deep-seated psychological issues in the name of goddesses and gods. In short, magical ritual may be a place where social relationships of power from the ordinary world are negotiated and transgressed.

CONCLUSION

In this paper I have shown how a study of history reveals an underlying Hermetic framework to contemporary western magical practices and highlighted the problems of using terms such as 'Paganism' with its association with pre-Christian indigenous nature religion. I have argued that contemporary magical practices are based on Hermeticism and that the gender roles employed in both high magic and contemporary Wicca are largely shaped by the work of Dion Fortune. Fortune's conception of gender polarity gives female magicians, as representatives of the goddess, power in the ritual space of contact with the otherworld. The question remains whether this feminine power, exemplified by the Wiccan High Priestess as a queen crowned by masculine surrender in a ritual context also empowers women in the ordinary world of mainstream culture.

NOTES

1. Some practitioners of magic (usually of the Nordic traditions) prefer to call themselves 'Heathen', which is the north European equivalent (Harvey, 1996).
2. All contemporary magical practices form a complex mixture of religious ontologies broadly termed the Hermetic tradition.
3. There is some debate as to whether Chaos Magicians are Pagans because Chaos Magicians reject all 'belief systems'. I have spoken with some Chaos Magicians who do identify as Pagan.
4. The word 'shaman' comes from the language of a small Tungus-speaking group of hunters and reindeer-herders in Siberia (the Evenk, Even, Nanay, Orochi and Udegey). The term was adopted by Russian scholars and means 'the ecstatic one'. In 1951 the historian of religion Mircea Eliade published *Shamanism* in which he used Siberian practices as classic cases of what he suggested were techniques employed by tribal peoples all through time and all over the world. As a result, the terms 'shaman' and 'shamanism' have since become generalised (Hutton, 1993: 10).
5. I use the term 'magicians' in preference to 'Pagans' as a more specific name which relates to the actual practice of magic rather than its associations or belief.
6. I prefer the term 'embodying' to 'possession', as the latter suggests a negative Christian interpretation of being possessed by demons.
7. The early Greek philosophers made no distinction between body and soul or the physical and the spiritual, and a sense of wholeness was the most typical feature of their world view (Kitto [1951] 1968).
8. During the Renaissance it was commonly believed that astrological signs ruled the body and that different bodily temperaments were related to the planets.
9. Bruno was influenced by Henry Cornelius Agrippa's survey of Renaissance magic, *De Occulta Philosophia* (1533).
10. Crowley left little in written form on sexual magick. The topic was taken up by his student Kenneth Grant (Shual, 1995).
11. However, Katon Shual argues that for Aleister Crowley the 'quintessence of the divine

was phallic', suggesting that Crowley's 'veneration' of woman as priestess was for masculine ends (1995: 28).

12. No relation to Aleister Crowley.

13. Samuel notes that Tantric Buddhism had its origins in India. It was practised in the fourth to eighth centuries CE by small initiatory cult groups. The central ritual was conducted in a nocturnal circle (*ganacakra*), often in a cremation ground, and included the ritual use of sexuality, possession, dancing and singing (Samuel, 1998).

14. Feminist witchcraft, which developed from the 1960s 'second wave' feminist movement, is specifically opposed to gender polarity and is supposedly more egalitarian (Greenwood, 1996a, 1998).

15. It must be born in mind, however, that magicians often practise both high magic and witchcraft and any typology built on difference is essentially a heuristic tool.

16. This ritual comes from the Servants of the Light (SOL) school of occult science.

17. At a *Talking Stick* Magical Conference held at Conway Hall, Holborn, London on the 12 February 1994.

18. This is due to the fact that many men may be attracted to Wicca for the 'wrong reasons' i.e. the sexual attraction of working with 'skyclad' (naked) women.

19. At the *Nature Religion Today* conference held at the Lake District campus of Lancaster University 9–13 April 1996. Rabinovich noted that most abuse was carried out in the nuclear family and that the frequency of abuse among her informants was so high that she had to modify her questions: only 1 out of 40 persons interviewed did *not* undergo trauma.

20. The sexologist Richard von Krafft-Ebing coined the terms 'sadism' and 'masochism' in 1885 as medicalised psychopathologies of the flesh. Sadism was defined as an innate desire to humiliate, hurt, wound or destroy to create sexual pleasure. By contrast, masochism was the passive enjoyment of pain or humiliation (McClintock, 1993: 208–10).

21. Thanks to Tobie Glenny for bringing my attention to this edition.

ACKNOWLEDGEMENTS

I would like to thank Annie Keeley, Liz Puttick and Geoffrey Samuel for helpful discussions. Any errors of interpretation are my own. This work has been funded by the University of London Central Research Fund and the Economic and Social Research Council.

BIBLIOGRAPHY

Airaksinen, A., 1995: *The Philosophy of the Marquis De Sade* (London: Routledge).

Crowley, V., 1989: *Wicca: the Old Religion in the New Age* (London: Aquarian).

—— 1993: 'Women and Power in Modern Paganism' in Elizabeth Puttick & Peter Clarke, eds, *Women as Teachers and Disciples in Traditional and New Religions* (Lampeter: The Edwin Mellen Press).

D'Alviella, G., 1981: *The Mysteries of Eleusis* (Northampton: Aquarian).

Easton, D. & Liszt, C., 1997: 'Sex, Spirit & S/M' in *Green Egg*, May-June 1997, 29. 119: 16–19.

Eliade, M., [1951], 1989: *Shamanism: Archaic techniques of ecstasy* (London: Arkana).

Fortune, D., [1935], 1987: *The Mystical Qabalah* (London: Aquarian).

—— 1987: *Applied Magic* (Northampton: Aquarian).

—— 1989: *The Sea Priestess*. (Northampton: Aquarian).

Frazer, J., [1921], 1993: *The Golden Bough* (Hertfordshire: Wordsworth).

Gardner, G., [1954], 1988: *Witchcraft Today* (New York: Magickal Childe).

Grant, K., 1976: *Cults of the Shadow* (New York: Samuel Weiser).

Greenwood, S., 1996a: 'Feminist Witchcraft: a transformatory politics' in Nickie Charles & Felicia Hughes–Freeland, eds, *Practising Feminism* (London: Routledge).

—— 1996b: 'The magical will, gender and power in magical practices' in Harvey, G., and Hardman, C., eds, *Paganism Today* (London: Thorsons).

—— 1998: 'The Nature Goddess: Sexual Identities and Power in Contemporary Witchcraft' in Pearson, J., Roberts, R., and Samuel, G., eds, *Nature Religion Today: Paganism in the Modern World* (Edinburgh: Edinburgh University Press).

—— 2000: *Magic, Witchcraft and The Other World: An Anthropology* (Oxford: Berg).

Harner, M., 1990: *The Way of the Shaman* (San Francisco: Harper).

Harvey, G., 1996: 'Heathenism: a North European Pagan Tradition' in Harvey, G., & Hardman, C., eds, *Paganism Today* (London: Thorsons).

Hutton, R., 1993: *The Shamans of Siberia* (Somerset: The Isle of Avalon Press).

Jones, P., & Pennick, N., 1995: *A History of Pagan Europe* (London: Routledge).

Kitto, H., [1951], 1968: *The Greeks* (Harmondsworth: Penguin).

Lévy-Bruhl, L. [1910], 1966: *How Natives Think*, tr., Lillian Clare (New York: Washington Square Press).

McClintock, A., 1993: ' "Maid to Order": commercial S/M and gender power' in Gibson, Pamela Church, and Gibson, Roma, eds, *Dirty Looks: women, pornography and power* (London: British Film Institute).

Ortner, S., 1974: 'Is Female to Male as Nature is to Culture' in Rosaldo, M., Lamphere, L., eds, *Woman, Culture and Society* (Stanford: Stanford University Press).

Puttick, E., 1997: *Women in New Religions: in search of community, sexuality and spiritual power* (Hampshire: Macmillan).

Rabinovitch, S., 1992: 'An' Ye Harm None, Do What Ye Will': Neo-pagans and witches in Canada', unpublished M.A. thesis, Department of Sociology, New York University.

Reid, S., 1996: 'As I Do Will, So Mote It Be: magic as metaphor in neo-pagan witchcraft' in Lewis, James, R., ed, *Magical Religion and Modern Witchcraft* (Albany: State University of New York Press).

Samuel, G., 1993: *Civilized Shamans: Buddhism in Tibetan societies* (Washington: Smithsonian).

—— 1997: 'Some Reflections on the Vajrayana and its Shamanic Origins' in *Les Habitants du Toit du Monde* (Nanterre: Société d'ethnologie).

—— 1998: 'Paganism and Tibetan Buddhism: Contemporary Western Religions and the Question of Nature' in Pearson, J., Roberts, R., and Samuel, G., eds,

Nature Religion Today: Paganism in the modern world (Edinburgh: Edinburgh University Press).

Seidler, V., 1989: *Rediscovering Masculinity: Reason, Language and Sexuality* (London: Routledge).

Shual, K., 1995: *Sexual Magick* (Oxford: Mandrake).

Tambiah, S., 1991: *Magic, Science, Religion, and the Scope of Rationality* (Cambridge: Cambridge University Press).

Yates, F., 1991: *Giordano Bruno and the Hermetic Tradition* (Chicago: University of Chicago Press).

9

Boggarts and Books:
Towards an Appreciation of Pagan Spirituality
Graham Harvey

INTRODUCTION

Paganism is a religion centrally concerned with celebrating Nature. Pagans are people who are listening to the living, speaking Earth (Harvey, 1997: 16). Whether the first, more systematic, phrase is preferable to the second, more mythopoeic one is probably a matter of taste or emphasis. There are many different sorts of Pagan (e.g. Druids, Witches and Heathens) and all celebrate Nature in one way or another. Few offer systematic definitions of their religion or of 'Nature', and they are rarely dogmatic about how to celebrate. The more mythopoeic phrase helpfully suggests an attitude diffused throughout life, rather than implying that this religion (or any other) is a discrete set of ceremonies or beliefs. Actual celebrations of Nature are not the entirety of Paganism, but are manifestations of a way of life. Pagans do not obsessively consider the environment in everything they do: while they are likely to use biodegradable washing-up liquid, they are unlikely to treat washing-up as an opportunity to indulge in invocations of deities, ancestors and elementals. Even during ceremonies, the focus of attention may not be on 'celebrating Nature' but on rites of passage, welcoming new members of the group or healing. This chapter presents a series of vignettes of typical Pagan activities and engagements with the world.

An adequate portrayal of Pagan interests (and a rounded picture of what Pagans consider Paganism to be) requires examination not only of the ceremonies but also of the rest of life. Although the festivities described here draw attention (sometimes in passing) to concerns that are lived out in 'ordinary life', a fuller exploration of Paganism should resist the temptation only to observe strange ceremonies. Similarly, the idea that Paganism can be studied only from books or the Internet should be dismissed.

SAMHAIN IN THE GREENWOOD

It is nearly midnight and about twenty warmly-dressed people are sitting or lying around a fire. They are in the depths of a wood some distance from a village, twelve miles or so from a British city. This is a celebration of the beginning of winter. To be precise, this sitting or lying by the fire is the celebration. This is not merely an interlude between ceremonies. What is significant to these people is just being here, by the fire, in the wood, on this night, with these friends. If you face the fire your front is warm and your back chilled. This is winter's beginning.

Hollowed pumpkin and turnip lanterns hang from nearby trees, another is sitting on a chair-like mossy rock. People have been cooking potatoes in the fire, and brought other food and drink with them, some for themselves and some to share. Currently it is fairly quiet as people gaze into the fire, doze off, share a drink or reach for another potato. Most have been here since they finished work, some have been here most of the day and others will arrive as soon as the village pub shuts. Some will stay the night, others will leave soon to sleep in warm beds at home.

The assertion that this sitting around the fire is itself the celebration of winter is tested by a question: 'When are we going to do something?'. Some of the company consider ritual to be a necessary part of the celebration, or even the entirety of it. Sitting round a fire may be fun, but something more is required. Those who have been celebrating here regularly for several years think it is sufficient, but the gathering has grown, partly by invitation, partly by rumour and the accretion of friends. A conversation ensues in which no one objects to a ceremony, but some do not want to join anything elaborate. It is agreed that those who want to will move a short distance from the fire and form their circle at midnight, which seems an apt time to honour the cold and dark. But first there is time for those who have been here before to talk about the place.

This is a wood that is enjoyed by many people from the area, not only Pagans. It is a mixed, semi-natural wood, a remnant of an old working wood, now going wild. Most people find it a peaceful place to be, especially sitting by a spring which bubbles up in a small pool not far from the fire site. Although there is a small conifer plantation on one side of the wood, most of the trees are native and have grown in Britain since the end of the last ice age. There are several distinct areas within the wood, from old hazel coppice, to a rocky area near where the stream has cut round a craggy outcrop, a stand of birch and a boggy area of alder and willow. The fire itself burns in a clearing by the largest oaks in the wood. Just up the bank, tall beeches whisper with every breeze and sound like waves breaking when the wind blows strongly. There are hares, foxes, badger, otter and deer in the wood. Occasionally salmon make it up the stream. Owls, herons, pigeon and rooks are among the many birds here. But the wood has other inhabitants too. British folk traditions speak of them as elves, dwarves, boggarts and so on – and collectively as the faery folk. But it is often traditional only to use circumlocutions like 'Them'.

At this point in the orientation to the wood and its inhabitants, in case things are getting overly serious, a spontaneous outburst of spooky noises is made by some of the group. Melodramatic witchy cackles and screeches resound for a while. Uncannily enough, the noise helps the latecomers, just now arriving from the pub, find their way to join in the fun. Samhain coincides with Hallowe'en: both festivals may be key times for honouring the ancestors, the dead, and Death itself, but this is often achieved with humour, games, fun and mischief (Edwards, 1996; Hutton, 1991, 1996). Cold spaghetti in a bag is 'the entrails of the dead', peeled grapes are their eyes. It is too cold in the wood for anyone to want to duck for apples but an attempt is made to hang apples in a nearby tree so people can try to bite them without using hands.

When things calm down again, someone wants to know more about 'Them'. The Victorians almost persuaded us that 'fairies' are diminutive and cute. Tolkien permitted a grander, more noble vision of proud and powerful if elusive inhabitants of the twilight and fringes of the world, but his elves are not at home in human-centred Middle Earth. They are not, in the end, the elves of earlier tradition, native to their forests and fringe lands. They are not the tricksters and kidnappers of Irish folklore, of Thomas the Rhymer and Tam Lin or the hidden, arrow-firing human foes of Scandinavian and Anglo-Saxon tradition. In this wood, and other reaches of the Greenwood, strange things happen: well-known paths become maze-like labyrinths, conjunctions of bough and branch reveal and hide watchers. You have only to go to the spring on this night to see that candles cast light like bonfires and incense billows like mist. Although this year it was the 'spooky' noises that drew latecomers deeper into the wood, in previous years flutes have been heard and followed to a fireside where no flute or flautist could be seen. And some have seen 'Them' dance. While the thought of this is enchanting and seems to validate Pagan traditions, a sense of unease tinges the story-telling here. The presence of faeries may not be a safe thing, 'They' may just be real and 'They' may just be here. Happily, someone is able to quote from Terry Pratchett on the subject:

Elves are wonderful. They provoke wonder. Elves are marvellous. They cause marvels . . . Elves are terrific. They beget terror . . . No-one ever said elves are *nice*. Elves are *bad*. (Pratchett, 1993: 169–70)

A round of favourite quotations from this prolific writer of comic fantasy ensues. Many (though not all) Pagans enjoy Pratchett's style and humour, and also think they recognise a Pagan world in his imagined 'Discworld'. Some might even recognise themselves or their fellow Pagans in its inhabitants. The company returns to the pleasure of the evening (although now some have a word for the feeling that there are unseen participants in the revelry). It should be noted, in passing, that 'badness' in this context does not mean 'evil' but 'trickster': one who does antisocial and dangerous things which sometimes harm but may benefit others.

Conversation and storytelling continue, sometimes about the 'themes' of the festival (death, winter, conclusions), sometimes about folklore and ideas from other cultures about 'invisible beings'. It also emerges that the 'sitting by the fire is the celebration' interpretation is somewhat disingenuous: the collecting of firewood and the building and lighting of the fire in this particular place in the wood were themselves ritualised. The wood was asked for permission and help in finding firewood and a brief explanation of the purpose of the fire (the celebration of winter) was given. Offerings were made in several places: candles and incense were lit by the spring, strands of wool tied in several significant trees, cake was scattered and beer poured at the roots of a particular tree. In previous years the fire site had been elsewhere in the wood, much nearer its boundary with fields. This year those gathering wood shared a feeling of being invited to celebrate in a new place to which they felt directed (in some low-key, non-apocalyptic sense). While building the fire they 'cast a circle' around it, greeting the directions and associated elements, and placed protective symbols around it. One of the wood-gatherers has developed a tradition of collecting twigs from native British trees into a 'protective bundle', built around a central 'rowan and red thread' and re-encoding Robert Graves's poetic mythology (Graves, 1948). No-one articulated what 'protection' was required for, although the later evocation (but not invocation) of 'Them' might offer part of an answer. The presence of the dead is clearly not feared but welcomed and explicitly invited. A mild concern was expressed that some who would join the celebration might be afraid (of the dead, of the night, of 'Them'?) and that their fear might be disturbing.

It was my observation of this event and this conversation as a participant that led me to suggest that Paganism is less a 'spiritual path' than a 'spiritual sitting among the trees' (Harvey, 1993: 91; 1997: 224). This should not be taken too seriously; it is intended simply to highlight the fact that the significant activity in similar Pagan events is a sense of being at home within the ecology of the Earth. Being 'at home' requires a journey towards celebration of the reality of what exists, the physical body and earth.

The 'journey' is further illustrated by the fact that those who participated in this ceremony included people from fairly organised or initiatory 'paths' (Heathenism, Druidry, Ritual Magick and Wicca) as well as a majority of 'simply Pagans'. This 'ad hoc' grouping (Luhrmann, 1989) indicates not a lack of identity, but a more fluid and nature-centred movement that draws on all available 'paths' in a thoroughly postmodern way – and probably includes the majority of Pagans.

This particular evening did eventually include a midnight ritual led by Druids who, despite common perceptions even among Pagans, do not only celebrate 'in the eye of the sun', i.e. in daylight and in public. However, this section concludes by noting that although Druids and others share a concern with celebrating Nature, the 'sitting by the fire' type of Pagans generally devote less energy to contemplating themselves and their personal growth than Pagans of more initiatory paths. There is no great divorce here, simply a question of emphasis. Wicca is a nature religion concerned with personal growth or self-understanding (Crowley, 1989, 1996), while 'fireside' Pagans primarily focus on celebrating Nature with little reference to Jungian archetypes or the individual's 'true self'. So it was clear to some of those present that the point of describing the wood and its inhabitants was more than merely scene-setting. Our hosts and companions were being introduced to those of us who were otherwise merely casual visitors. In this event, winter was being celebrated not only by human people sitting around a fire, but also by the wood which provided the firewood (not only metaphorically) and by all the other personal beings in that community/environment. Trees, hedgehogs, owls, bats, fish, insects, rocks, breezes, 'Them', the dead, elementals and a host of other people (human and other-than-human) were engaged in a single festive encounter.

CIRCLES IN AVEBURY

To mention Druids is to conjure up images of bearded men in white robes processing into ancient stone circles. The archetype is sometimes more than stereotype and is sometimes manifest in reality: there *are* bearded male Druids and some do celebrate in ancestral sacred sites. However, they are rarely alone: Druids today come in both genders and all ages, and they do not only celebrate at Stonehenge at midsummer sunrise but at night elsewhere too (as noted above) – and some of their celebrations are far less organised than the word 'procession' implies. However, rather than directly challenge the stereotype, this vignette accompanies a regular Druid gathering at Avebury in Wiltshire.

By around noon on the Saturday nearest any given festival in the annual cycle of eight celebrated by the majority of Pagans,[1] people will start gathering together within the ancient circles (bank, ditch and several rings of standing stones) at Avebury, in Wiltshire. They come from various Druid Orders and many wear some sort of costume. For some, a simple white robe is sufficient; others wear blue or green tabards to indicate that they are Bards or Ovates. Some wear more elaborate costumes, indicating their affinity for particular animals or their understanding of themselves as reincarnations of historical (or mythic?) characters such as Arthur. The Druids are not alone; Pagans from other traditions regularly join them and play significant roles in the gathering, but there are also Buddhists, Christians, Baha'is and others among the participants.

Rarely will a ceremony begin by noon, even when the ritual asserts that the 'sun is at its zenith'. Time among nature-respecting traditions rarely follows the decree of watches, so 'Druid Time' and 'Pagan Time' are comparable to 'Powwow Time' among First Nation North Americans. The ceremony will begin when the Chosen Chief has finished his pint, or when a respected participant eventually arrives, or when a media interview is finished. A low level of impatience with these dignitaries is typical and various attempts are sometimes made to move things on. At other times, nothing discernible and no-one in particular is evident in marking the transition between gathering and ceremony. A procession of sorts begins.

A female Druid leads some of the party on the 'Goddess path' around the perimeter of the ancient circles, anti-clockwise or, more appropriately, counter-sunrise. This happens to be the shortest and least strenuous route from the usual gathering places to the usual focal point of the celebration in either the northern or southern inner circle. The longer 'God path' follows three-quarters of the outer circle, climbing and descending the steep banks at several places. These distances and difficulties, rather than gender, seem to determine whether people, other than the leaders, follow the God or Goddess path. Both parties meet by the two large stones at Avebury's eastern ceremonial entrance.

The representative of the Goddess or the Guardian of the Place sits in a niche within one of these stones. She is greeted respectfully by the company who also request permission to enter the circle for the festivities. So far, she has always been happy to welcome the celebrants. A few years ago some of the group spontaneously formed an arch with staffs beneath which everyone else entered the outer stone circle. This has now become traditional and the staffs are occasionally joined by wands or didjeridus.

Sometimes (depending on which Order's Chiefs are leading the event) the party stops en route to the inner circle to bless marriages and children at the remains of a 'ring stone'. The majority of the stones at Avebury were assaulted by Puritan Christians determined that something so obviously 'devilish' should not survive. Some stones were broken up for building roads and homes, and others were pushed into deep pits. Earlier this century, many of the stones were re-erected or their locations marked by a concrete bollard. The ring stone is said to have been a holed stone like one that survives in Cornwall. The blessings here are usually brief and formulaic, rather than individually crafted ceremonies, but are nonetheless enjoyed by many couples and families. Under other leadership, such blessings are made within the specific celebration of the season conducted within the remains of either of the inner circles. Sometimes elaborate marriage ceremonies are performed at Avebury, but they too are usually part of the regular round of seasonal festivals.

Druid celebrations typically begin like other Pagan events with the forming of a circle and the greeting of the four quarters. Some Druids do this by the recitation of elemental and totemic associations: north is 'the great bear of the starry heavens and the deep and fruitful earth'; south is 'the great stag in the heat of the chase and the inner fire of the sun'; west is 'the salmon of wisdom dwelling within the pool'; and east is 'the hawk of dawn soaring in the clear pure air'. Others simply face each direction and bid it or its 'spirits' welcome.

After a brief speech announcing the purpose of the gathering (i.e. naming the festival and the season it celebrates), everyone is invited to join in the chanting of Awen, 'flowing spirit' or inspiration. Although this is a common tradition among contemporary Druid Orders (some consider it equivalent to the Hindu 'Aum'), there is no universal agreement on how it should be done, some chanting it as written, others chanting the sounds 'A I O', but always in one long unbroken breath. The sound reverberates as it is repeated three times. Those who have never chanted it before will have caught on and joined in by the third round. Now all in the circle are participants, no longer mere observers. The chant enchants; it is not only a symbol of inspiration, it is an experience of it, as it flows around the circle and outwards, changing things.

Now that everyone has found their voice, they are invited to contribute songs, stories, poems or anything they wish to the celebration. For a while, people take turns to step into the circle and perform with greater or lesser skill. Some are clearly more popular than others, but this is not a competition and is supposed to encourage greater attunement to inspiration and celebration of the Earth. Many of the contributions evolve from understandings of traditional stories or from experiences in direct action confronting road, quarry and housing developments. After a while, the group is invited to participate in 'the Druid Prayer':

> Grant, O Goddess, thy protection; and in protection, strength; and in strength, understanding; and in understanding, knowledge; and in knowledge, the knowledge of justice; and in the knowledge of justice, the love of it; and in the love of it, the love of all existences; and in the love of all existences, the love of Goddess and all Goodness.[2]

This, of course, loses all but the Druids who have done it before – and even they stumble, unsure whether to say 'Goddess' or 'God and Goddess' or 'Goddesses and Gods' or some other version. (Its eighteenth-century author, the Welsh revivalist/folklorist, Iolo Morganwg, wrote 'God'). Not that anyone objects to any particular version; Paganism is rarely fundamentalist even about understandings of, or invocations to, divine beings.

If marriages and other blessings did not happen earlier, they may happen at this point. Otherwise, seasonal food or drink may be shared (mead horns, wassail bowls and loaves of bread are common). The ritual draws towards an end with the threefold repetition of the vow:

> We swear by peace and love to stand, heart to heart and hand in hand,
> Mark, O Spirit and hear us now, confirming this our sacred vow.[3]

Finally, the directions are bid 'hail and farewell' and the circle is declared 'open' – that is, the ritual is over and we return to the pub, restaurant or home. Some wander among the stones communing with themselves, their friends, the place and its inhabitants, spirits and energies. There are those who are certain that what makes some celebrations 'work' is the presence and blessing of the ancestors who built these sacred circles. Others celebrate the almost palpable sense of awareness in the place itself which imbues all that happens here with significance. Perhaps there is even wisdom to be gained here: a complete stranger happily announced, 'These moles know a thing or two' as he strolled by. Understandings and appreciations of Avebury are fluid and relaxed, and the place has rarely witnessed the animosities evident around Stonehenge. There is an openness and freedom here that is still matched by the lack of fences, ticket offices and security guards. Those who engage in struggles for land-rights elsewhere usually visit Avebury in a lighter frame of mind and spirit.

Vikings get married

Obsession with the Celts is almost ubiquitous (not only among Pagans) in the West (cf Bowman, 1993, 1996), but some people actively celebrate their Anglo-Saxon and Norse ancestry. A marriage between leading members of one Heathen group explicitly links the honouring of ancestors with ensuring the continuity of the lineage.

The location is a popular beauty and picnic spot near another northern British city. To the bride and groom it is significant, both because their Viking ancestors settled near here and because they are involved in its environmental protection and enhancement. Neither of these reasons is less significant than the other, and both are stressed in speeches welcoming guests. The ceremony begins with a procession from the car park to a central rock outcrop. The couple's group lead the way, with family and invited guests following. Like other religionists, Pagans of all traditions dress up for ceremonies (robes, jewellery and symbolic blades are commonplace), but this group's distinctiveness is evident in their regalia. Thor's Hammer (*Mjölnir*) pendants are common among Heathen groups – even those whose affinity with Odin might lead them to wear his *Walknot* symbol of three interlocked triangles – but this group displays their self-understanding in more elaborate ways. The clothes they wear for ceremonies would make any re-enactment society envious. In fact, some members of the group do re-enact tenth-century Norse-settlement life, but their festive costume and equipment is of a considerably better quality than that used in mock-battles. Wool tunics, linen shirts, leather belts and boots, jewellery, swords and axes, banners and mead horns all declare this to be a proud, warrior tradition strongly supported by expert craft-workers. For example, the groom wears a precise replica of the Sutton Hoo helmet and among his gifts to his bride is a fine copy of a Danish brooch.

Arriving at the marriage site, the quarters are greeted. A hammer is held aloft and the directions are named in a way that adds different nuances to this typical Pagan engagement with the world. Alongside wider under-standings of the elemental associations of the directions 'north', 'east', 'south' and 'west' are the names of four dwarves who hold up the sky. So, while the greeting of the quarters is always a summary of Pagan cosmology, the Heathen version addresses issues of security, strength, mutuality among the world's inhabitants and the animation of seemingly abstract forces. Deities are honoured by poetic invocations and, as the occasion is a marriage, those most associated with ancestry and love predominate. Thor, Sif, Freyr and Freyja are named several times: their presence and inspiration are requested and their powers are drawn upon.

The actual wedding ceremony draws on traditional Norse understandings. Ancestry, kin and family rather than romance are central in the ceremony – although romance is far from absent. The continuity of the family line and differentiation of the roles of husband and wife are stressed on the authority of 'ancestors', 'tradition' and 'nature'. Similar understandings are prevalent among other nature-centred indigenous religions, but provoke frequent debate among Pagans and their observers. However, the ceremony itself is not a time for debate but for affirmations, especially between the couple. They make vows of commitment to one another and to their kin (ancestors, friends and descendants), validating them on significant symbols such as hammer, sword and, of course, rings. Finally, the bride's hair is plaited by the groom as a sign of his care for her and of their mutual entwining.

A horn full of mead is shared by the couple and also offered to the deities by pouring in a hollow on the rock. It is then passed around family and friends. Further feasting takes place after the ceremonies, in a pub reception. Nothing would have attracted particular attention to this if it had not been for the costumes of the wedding party and the fact that some are carrying swords. The more 'secular' or embodied aspects of rites of passage and calendar festivals require little change in order to be incorporated into Pagan ceremonies, or perhaps, in order for the essential elements of such celebrations of life in this world to be retrieved. Concurrently, Pagan ceremonies, like polytheistic deities, send us back into the world with a renewed sense of the value of our ordinary human lives (Harvey, 1997: 168–9; Green, 1989).

RE-SOURCING PAGANISM

Pagans do not spend all their lives, or all the significant moments of their lives, out of doors. Many Pagan activities take place indoors. Not all elements of the celebration of Nature require contact with the mud and matter of the other-than-human environment. The inspirations and validating experiences of Pagans are not solely 'natural', nor do they consist exclusively of encounters with the Greenwood and its inhabitants or immersion in woodlands and wildernesses. The development of Paganism in this century has involved considerable study of anthropology, history, folklore, herbalism, philosophy, archaeology and other disciplines. As individuals and in groups, Pagans draw on a wide range of (re)sources in the evolution of their world view. This is rarely if ever deliberately planned: like most other religions, Paganism does not have an agenda requiring continuous codification. The fact is more straightforwardly that Pagans are influenced by what they read, hear and experience – and that they tend to be well-read in areas that have a bearing on nature, ancestry, cosmology and spirituality. This final vignette of contemporary Pagan engagements with the world visits the home of a woman who facilitates a Matriarchal Studies group. This is a purely local group of like-minded women who share an affinity with Goddess traditions, feminist spirituality and a Pagan understanding of life. There are larger networks and journals which are important to some of the group members, but belonging to this group does not exclude other affiliations and identities. The group meets in this house as near as possible to each full-moon evening.

There is nothing exceptional about the house, which was built as a council house, now privately owned. Its small gardens do not contain strange herbs like Belladonna or Aconite. There is no besom broomstick just inside the front door – this woman is 'not that kind of witch', although she knows witches who do grow herbs and display broomsticks. She dislikes the stereotype, but only mildly, and celebrates the connection it represents with those persecuted as witches in the past. In fact, she rarely calls herself a witch, but does use some of the symbolism and techniques employed by those who are, conversely, happy to identify themselves with 'the Craft' or 'Wicca'. A major difference between this woman's Paganism and that of the Craft is that she sees no need for male symbolism, participation, deities or stereotypes. When challenged that this is unbalanced, she quietly points out that it is the imposition of men and male symbolism, deities, stereotypes and activities which is dominating and unbalanced. By devoting her energies to women and their well-being she considers herself to be making a small start towards redressing the imbalance of patriarchy. It has been quite difficult for me to gain her trust sufficiently to be invited to meet her in her own home. There is certainly no possibility of my participating in any event she organises, although I know about half of the women in this group. They are not secretive about their activities, although they doubt I will under-stand or value everything they say or do, but they have no intention or desire for male participation in their discussions or celebrations. This lack of interest in men does not extend to all their relationships – many are happy in heterosexual relationships – nor to the books they study. It is these books and their study that I am interested in discussing with the group's facilitator.

There are books in most rooms in the house, alongside notes in files and on loose sheets of paper. Some are academic books: predominantly history, archaeology, classical literature and folklore. Books about local history, geography and (ancestral) sacred places are also common. There are many books about Goddesses from different cultures and times, and others that bring them together so that people can honour 'the Goddess'. There are 'how to' books with guidance on rituals, calendars and political and cultural empowerment. Plenty of novels and other works of 'fiction' are scattered among the shelves; some seem well used. Most of the books here could be found in other Pagan homes, although perhaps not in such profusion. Although there is a clear focus on Goddesses and the Goddess, this is not unique to feminist women's groups or Matriarchal study groups. For example, Elinor Gadon's *The Once and Future Goddess* (1990) and Starhawk's *The Spiral Dance* (1989) are popular among many Pagans (including the less male-dominated forms of Heathenism). Starhawk's *Truth or Dare* (1990) and Merlin Stone's *When God was a Woman* (1976) are not quite as common, requiring a degree of activism or feminism beyond some other Pagan books. Meanwhile, Terry Pratchett's *Wyrd Sisters* (1988) is probably the most commonly cited of a series in which many Pagans enjoy recognising 'their sort of people'. It is not accompanied in this house by many other 'fantasy' books: Tolkien, for example, is conspicuously absent – my host asserts that Tolkien contributes little of value to feminists.

These are all sources of significance to the Study Group. Intrigued as I am to make sure that I have not missed some central text that explains the interests and activities of this significant branch of Paganism, I want to know how the group makes use of these books. What kind of authority do they have? Are they consulted to confirm existing understandings or to develop new ones?

In their monthly meetings the group discusses a chosen issue or theme. Sometimes these are treated as a series – for example, 'Celtic Goddesses and Saints' or 'African Goddesses'. One of the group will volunteer to read everything she can find (often borrowed from the facilitator) and report back to the group. The facilitator clearly intends the group to use this discussion as a means of 'consciousness-raising' or 'self-empowerment'. These are not simply discussions of ancient history or interesting cultures. They are about finding better ways of understanding the world and better ways of living. They are intended to counter patriarchy, to move towards its end. Various members of the group also belong to movements engaging in direct action of one sort or another, and all are encouraged to consider the rooting of ideas in lifestyles. As is common in the Goddess Spirituality movement, there is no dogmatism about whether Goddesses exist 'out there' in their own right, 'within the human heart' as empowering archetypes, 'between women as that which happens when women meet', or as 'personifications of the natural processes of life, death and rebirth'. Nor is this a dogmatic system in which 'the Goddess' is 'one or many' (see Christ, 1979, and Long, 1994). All these views (and others) are held by members of the group, but rarely cause conflict.

The books provide resources for imagining and re-imagining, inventing or re-inventing oneself and one's place and time. Authority derives from the experience of being women, and the experiences of women in a (late) patriarchal culture. The books that are valued here are those which disseminate ideas and resources, inspire action rather than passivity and are enabling, not belittling. Finally, there seems to be an openness towards new possibilities. While there is certainly a standard (feminism) by which any proposed resource must be judged, the group invites change and searches for alternatives to the way they and others live in the world today.

Vignettes are not snapshots

These four vignettes are illustrative of significant Pagan themes and engagements. They are neither exhaustive nor complete. Nor are all their ramifications made explicit here; that is left to a continuing dialogue between Pagans and those who study them. Finally, it should be noted that, although the vignettes draw on actual events and encounters, they are also all (to one degree or another) composite images. They are not snapshots of single events, but attempts to convey the life of a variety of ways of being Pagan. Only by doing a little violence to the particular embodiment of selected events can I hope to have avoided stealing the soul of Pagan engagements with life.

Notes

1. Harvey (1997).
2. Oral tradition, Harvey (1997).
3. Ibid.

Bibliography

Bowman, Marion, 1993: 'Reinventing the Celts', *Religion* 23: 147–56.
—— 1996: 'Cardiac Celts: Images of the Celts in Paganism', in Harvey, G., and Hardman, C., eds, *Paganism Today* (London: Thorsons), pp. 242–51.
Christ, Carol, 1979: 'Why Women Need the Goddess: Phenomenological, Psychological and Political Reflections' in Christ, C., and Plaskow, J., eds, *Womanspirit Rising* (New York: Harper & Row) pp. 273–87.
Crowley, Vivianne, 1989: *Wicca: the Old Religion in the New Age* (London: Aquarian).
—— 1996: 'Wicca as Modern Day Mystery Religion' in Harvey, G., and Hardman, C., eds, *Paganism Today*, pp. 81–93.
Edwards, Leila, 1996: 'Tradition and Ritual: Halloween and Contemporary Paganism' in Harvey, G., and Hardman, C., eds, *Paganism Today*, pp. 224–41.

Gadon, Elinor W., 1990: *The Once and Future Goddess* (London: Aquarian).

Graves, Robert, 1948: *The White Goddess* (London: Faber and Faber).

Green, Deirdre, 1989: 'Towards a Reappraisal of Polytheism' in Davies, G., ed., *Polytheistic Systems* (Edinburgh: Edinburgh University Press), pp. 3–11.

Harvey, Graham, 1993: 'Gods and Hedgehogs in the Greenwood' in Flood, G., ed., *Mapping Invisible Worlds* (Edinburgh: Edinburgh University Press), pp. 89–93.

—— 1997: *Listening People, Speaking Earth: Contemporary Paganism* (London: Hurst & Co; Adelaide: Wakefield Press). Also published by New York University Press as *Contemporary Paganism*.

Harvey, Graham, and Hardman, Charlotte, eds, 1996: *Paganism Today* (London: Thorsons).

Hutton, Ronald, 1991: *The Pagan Religions of the Ancient British Isles* (London: Blackwell).

—— 1996: *The Stations of the Sun: a History of the Ritual Year in Britain* (Oxford: Oxford University Press).

Luhrmann, Tanya M., 1989: *Persuasions of the Witch's Craft: Ritual Magic in Contemporary England* (Oxford: Blackwell).

Long, Asphodel, 1994: 'The Goddess Movement in Britain Today', *Feminist Theology* 5: 11–39.

Pratchett, Terry, 1988: *Wyrd Sisters* (London: Gollancz).

—— 1993: *Lords and Ladies* (London: Gollancz).

Starhawk, 1989: *The Spiral Dance* (San Francisco: Harper & Row).

—— 1990: *Truth or Dare* (New York: Harper & Row).

Stone, Merlin, 1976: *When God was a Woman* (New York: Harcourt Brace Jovanovich).

Holism, Healing and the New Age
Ellie Hedges and James A. Beckford

INTRODUCTION

The main aim of this chapter is to show that theoretical and empirical research on aspects of the healing activity which is associated with the New Age has called in question many widely held assumptions. Our argument will be in two parts. The first will suggest that commentators have tended mistakenly to portray alternative healing or complementary therapy as an excessively individualistic activity. The second will draw on empirical findings to argue that some currently fashionable notions of the body as a site of cultural confusion, change and conflict do not help fully to explain the processes whereby so-called New Age healers acquire their skills, but that notions of 'flow' and 'tuning in' are relatively more helpful. Our contribution will therefore be theoretical and empirical.

We place particular emphasis on the combination of theoretical and empirical analysis for the simple reason that the literature on healing, bodies and the New Age is rich in speculation and conceptual debate but relatively poor in empirical reports of healing activity. In fact, the disparity between the ambitious sweep of theoretical generalisations and the meagre supply of reliable observations is astonishing. There seems to be no limit to the extent to which social scientists are prepared to go in allegedly charting massive historical changes of consciousness, identity and imagery in relation to human bodies and healing. Yet there seems to be little appetite for careful observation and collection of reliable information about the actual patterns of belief and practice. This chapter is therefore offered as a contribution towards a theoretically informed, but critical, understanding of how at least one particular group of New Age healers were equipped for their work.

Part of the distinctiveness of our work also lies in the fact that we deliberately studied people who had chosen to try to heal *other people's bodies*. Starting from a position of scepticism about many of the claims made about the individualism and narcissism allegedly inherent in New Age or alternative therapies, we wanted to show that some of these therapies really depended upon forms of sociality and ideas which were collective and holistic. Our evidence about the healers' concern for 'whole persons', including their physical bodies, is incompatible with much of the literature about the New Age which is narrowly focused on individuals' images of their own bodies and ailments.

NEW AGE

The term 'New Age' is notoriously slippery. It seems to us that attempts to legislate for its use by drawing sharp boundaries around the concept are likely to be self-defeating. This is because virtually every conceptualisation emphasises the family resemblance among the New Age's many manifestations. In other words, very few people who use the term intend it to be applied in a narrowly restrictive fashion (but see York, 1997). On the contrary, the intention is usually to draw attention to the simultaneous 'flow' of variegated sentiments, beliefs, experiences and practices in different but compatible directions. In so far as coherence is sensed among these 'flows' it inheres less in a small number of fixed, shared characteristics and more in a hopeful expectation that they will be, or can be, reconciled in a well-ordered life. The search for logical consistency between them, or for empirical proofs of their effectiveness, misses the point that their effects are ideally to be experienced in the course of trying to live by them. This is partly why the notion of human *potential* looms large in most accounts of New Age phenomena. Another way of putting this point is to say that New Age beliefs and practices are an anticipation of a hoped-for state of affairs which is conditional upon people living their lives in the present as if a New Age had already dawned. This requires faith or, at least, a radical suspension of doubt, even if only for a brief period of time.

What is the family resemblance which indicates that the sentiments, beliefs, experiences and practices that flow around the New Age are indeed connected to each other? None of the common features that we shall list here is indispensable; and there is no minimal number of features required to warrant the designation of anything as 'New Age'. The phenomena are both broad and diffuse, but they usually include currents of:

1. *hope* that the seeds of a significant improvement in the quality of human life have already been sown and are ready for cultivation by individual human beings who have the required combination of knowledge, trust, diligence and patience to give expression to their 'authentic' selves, instead of merely conforming with routines and roles;

2. *criticism* of aspects of the prevailing modes of living in advanced industrial societies as being materialistic, shallow, unreflective and unfulfilling to the point where the natural human potential for creativity, compassion and play is stifled. There is also criticism of religious and ethical systems which arouse feelings of guilt for infractions of supposedly absolute obligations, rules or standards;

3. *openness* to fresh ideas about the interconnectedness of all life forms and the value of taking personal responsibility for living one's life in ways which anticipate, and accord with, a better ordered and more fulfilling world where authentic selves can realise higher values. An experimental and pragmatic attitude to new ideas, experiences and practices is common among New Agers;

4. *appreciation* of the merits of seeking to minimise human disruption, corruption and exploitation of the natural world conceived as complex systems of normally harmonious and self-equilibrating forces, as symbolised in some pre-modern belief systems.

We have deliberately chosen highly general terms in which to frame the family resemblance among the richly diverse tributaries of thought, experience and feeling which flow into and around the New Age. In practice, of course, there is a bewildering variety of ways of translating them into personal outlooks, shared practices and even social organisations. Some 'translations' require strongly individualistic, self-directed and self-centred thought and action, while others give pride of place to selfless, altruistic submission to the communal will. In fact, Paul Heelas (1996: 215) attributes the vitality of the New Age to the *tension* 'between autonomous, expressive personhood and that which derives from without'. The challenge for the New Age is therefore 'to find ways of ensuring that it minimizes the trivialized and self-indulgent whilst at the same time not becoming too traditionalized or hierarchically authoritative' (214). Whilst this formulation is helpful in drawing attention to the extremes of thought found in the New Age, we shall argue that it is misleading to portray the New Age in sharply dichotomous terms. Our claim is that some unexpected combinations of self-centred and selfless practices can coexist in the New Age and that the distinction between inner and outer sources of authority is not always clear. In short, the choice facing would-be New Agers is not one of trivial self-indulgence versus selfless submission to nature or community. Our interpretation of the process whereby one particular type of New Age 'holistic' healer is recruited and trained will show just how complex and subtle the texture of New Age spirituality and healing practice can be.

In order to prepare the way for our interpretation of holistic healing, however, we need to clear up some of the confusion that has crept into some influential commentaries on the societal roots of 'alternative therapies' and so-called self-religions.

SELF-RELIGION, HOLISM AND HIGH MODERNITY

Firstly, the term 'self-religion' (Heelas, 1991, 1992, 1996) is entirely appropriate for the many new and alternative forms of spirituality and religion which encourage practitioners to draw inspiration and guidance from within their own minds and bodies rather than from external texts, traditions or human authorities. 'Personal authenticity', 'inner truth' or 'higher self' are characteristic goals of this inward turn. It can lead in some cases to ego-dominated, assertive outlooks which favour narrow self-interest and material prosperity or social power. But the New Age can produce many other outcomes which turn on transpersonal psychologies constituting the 'true self' as naturally social, compassionate and attuned to the rhythms of the natural world. In these cases the search for the 'true self' means escape from ego domination. It also promises a sense of de-alienation or re-identification with others, such that self-actualisation requires working with others to restore the social and natural harmonies and sense of wholeness that have supposedly been subverted by centuries of dominance and exploitation of humans and the material world.[1] The true self is not therefore an island or an atom: it is only one part of a much larger whole. To borrow from Charles Taylor's analysis of 'the modern identity', the search is for 'new languages of personal resonance' or fresh ways of bringing 'crucial human goods alive for us again' (Taylor, 1989: 513). This means trying to abandon utilitarian outlooks and habits which give priority to the rewards that individuals gain from being instrumentally rational. It also involves commitment to values of benevolence and justice having deep roots in human cultures.

Secondly, we see evidence of this search for sources of moral commitment (and of the break with the idea of the 'disengaged subject') in many forms of holism. The *holistic* notion of self, as we shall show later, is integral to New Age healing ideologies and practices (Beckford, 1984, 1985). But some commentators on the New Age have failed to appreciate the full significance of holistic notions of the self. For example, they impose a premature closure on 'holism' and its cognates by applying them exclusively to individuals, viewed in isolation. Thus, Coward (1989) frames 'the whole person' in terms which isolate him or her from other people and from social or natural environments. Holism allegedly 'suggests the possibility of integration, of feeling that all parts of ourselves belong to the same essential person' thereby implying that 'the whole person can be found and that when it is, the *individual* will be healed' (Coward, 1989: 68, emphasis added). In her opinion, 'holistic' is entirely a 'quality of personal attention and care' which 'appears to give an individual an unparalleled sense of participating in his or her own well-being'. At the centre of this sense of well-being is supposedly 'the kernel of a whole person' (ibid.). While this very attenuated version of holism may be characteristic of some New Age healing philosophies, it is by no means universal. In fact, it is incompatible with the first principle of holism as promulgated by the British Holistic Medical Association – that holism means 'responding to a person as a whole *within the environment*, seeing that person as mind, body and spirit' (BHMA leaflet, quoted in Sharma, 1992: 110, emphasis added). The image that Coward deploys of a 'kernel' of wholeness lying inside individuals is an entirely inappropriate way of representing holistic relations between human beings and their environments. It is merely an image of 'integration' at the level of the individual as an isolated entity, whereas holism also conceives of humans as being ideally in relations of mutuality with their environment. From a truly holistic point of view, individuals could experience wholeness (or integration) only if they also felt in harmony with other people and their physical surroundings. Coward's preoccupation with the idea of an 'inner core' is therefore misplaced as far as the New Age healing practices that we shall analyse below are concerned. It is also at odds with her own acknowledgement that 'a small minority' of holistic healing practitioners stressed 'the links between individual and environment' and that 'many people within the alternative therapies movement are concerned in active ways with anti-nuclear and ecological politics' (Coward, 1989: 204–5).

By contrast, others such as Michael York (1995, 1997) and William Bloom (1987, 1991) stress the potential of some, though not necessarily all, New Age healers to emancipate humans from the limitations of conventional spirituality and to give them the novel opportunity to select and combine spiritual ideas and practices from the whole gamut of possibilities. Thus, York (1995: 38) cites with approval the view of *Sunday Times* journalist, Katie Saunders, that 'the movement is a revival of Sixties mores and a revolt against the hedonism and "selfish bingeing" of the 1980s – a "hanging loose" but without a "dropping out".' The point at which all the diverse streams of New Age spirituality converge, according to York (1995: 39, emphasis added), is the vision of 'a radical mystical transformation on both the personal *and collective levels*'. An even clearer construal of the holism inherent in New Age 'visions' is the claim that 'the New Age is always ultimately directed toward the communal, that is, toward something greater or more inclusive than merely the self or that reification of the self which is termed the "Self"' (York, 1997: 414–15).

Thirdly, outright rejection or ridicule of ideas about the New Age and holism is relatively rare among the informed specialists in the social sciences or religious studies, but a number of 'social critics' have reproached these ideas for a wide range of reasons. The broad lines of criticism directed against New Age ideas in general and ideas of self-fulfilment or the realisation of human potential in particular are too well known to need exposition here. We shall merely record that they have been dismissed for being, among other things, 'psychobabble' (Rosen, 1978), 'subjective expressivism' (Taylor, 1989), 'self-absorption' (Schur, 1976), 'the shrinking of America' (Zilbergeld, 1983), and 'narcissism' (Lasch, 1979).

These dated assessments of the New Age are much less interesting than more recent attempts to locate some of the same phenomena in the context of very broad characterisations of present-day social change. We therefore need to review briefly two particular commentaries on the condition of 'high modernity' or 'postmodernity' which have indirect implications for the cultural significance of the human body and its 'maintenance' but which still do not do full justice to the meaning of New Age healing.

In the first place, Anthony Giddens is critical of Lasch's idea that concern with the state of one's health is necessarily a sign of narcissism. Instead, Giddens regards the construction of the self as a 'reflexive project' which is made necessary by the erosion of traditions and community in late modernity. The resources for this project include the popularised versions of expert knowledge which, in itself, draws increasingly on experience from all parts of the world. Awareness of risks and of the limits of expert systems is apparently just as important as awareness of therapies, drugs and regimes with the capacity to protect or to heal. Giddens therefore explains the reappearance of belief in fate as a response to the awareness of what he calls 'low-probability high-consequence risks'. By this, he means the calamities which are unlikely to strike but which are nevertheless worrying because we have no experience of what they may entail; which are remote but, we suspect, potentially catastrophic. Giddens does not include holistic healing among the 'adaptive' responses to these risks. Instead, he regards all forms of therapy with a degree of ambivalence: they may promote 'dependence and passivity' but they can also permit 'engagement and reappropriation' (Giddens, 1991: 180). In fact, he virtually confines 'therapy' in high modernity to psychotherapy, psychoanalysis, self-help and counselling. This allows him to construe therapy solely as a form of 'self-mastery' which allegedly acts as a substitute for morality. By contrast, 'new forms of religion and spirituality' represent 'a return of the repressed' for Giddens (1991: 207) and apparently have no place in either emancipatory politics or life politics. Accordingly, the human body is represented as a site of choice, control and experimentation on which the interaction between person and planet can be observed and modified. The pressing problems of the natural environment, new technologies of biological reproduction, and globalisation are therefore taken into consideration in life politics mainly in so far as they have an impact on the 'reflexive project of the self'. We believe, however, that the philosophies and practices of holistic healing can represent a much less individualistic, psychologistic or moralistic response to high modernity than can be captured in Giddens's notion of therapy. In particular, they cut across the sharp distinctions that he seeks to make (Giddens, 1994) between tradition and expertise (or guardians and experts). Holistic healing actually represents a fascinating re-mix of tradition, expertise and modernity.

In the second place, the attempt made by Philip Mellor and Chris Shilling (1997) to move beyond what they regard as the excessively cognitive and psychological approach of Anthony Giddens offers two promising ways forward. Their work not only takes uncompromising account of the 'embodied' nature of human experience, but it also insists on re-establishing links between historically changing forms of embodiment and changing forms of human sociability and community. This approach augurs well, therefore, for a sensitive analysis of New Age healing, but Mellor and Shilling's very conceptualisation of the 'baroque modern body' places so much emphasis on 'carnality' and 'sensual experiences' that, ironically, the specificity of much New Age healing is obliterated. If it is true that 'banal associations may dominate the formal institutions of contemporary society, but they cannot contain the human body in its entirety' (Mellor & Shilling, 1997: 173), carnality or sensuality may indeed come to serve as the basis for new forms of partial sociality, i.e., 'sensual solidarities'. They are groupings 'based on the feelings, emotions and the effervescence which can derive from *being with others*' (Mellor & Shilling, 1997: 174, emphasis original), at least temporarily, in the form of, for example, charismatic religious assemblies, initiation rituals or crowds of spectators at soccer matches. They are all allegedly manifestations of the sacred because they bind people together – for good or evil – and remind them of the sacred totality of life.

Like Giddens, Mellor and Shilling limit their discussion of 'therapy' to psychoanalysis and psychotherapy, thereby making it easy to characterise it as a form of banal association on the grounds that it involves nothing but talk.[2] They claim that '[a]s with all banal associations, the fleshy body is relegated to a position beneath information and talk' in conventional therapy (Mellor & Shilling, 1997: 183). Exorcism and fear of satanic activities, by contrast, supposedly give rise to sensual solidarities because they depend upon beliefs about the danger of evil invading and inhabiting human bodies. But the sharp opposition that Mellor and Shilling make between 'banal' therapy and 'sensual' exorcism misses the point that we wish to make, namely, that some forms of holistic healing are distinctly sensual and embodied whilst *also* thriving within relatively banal forms of association. In short, the fact that banal associations and sensual solidarities can be combined in advanced industrial societies is not necessarily a symptom of societal schizophrenia but might actually be a search for wholeness understood in bodily, cognitive, emotional and spiritual terms.

To sum up our conceptual argument before introducing empirical evidence, we believe that the conceptual distinctions between (a) tradition and expert systems, and (b) banal associations and sensual solidarity are exaggerated caricatures. In reality, some of the most interesting developments in religion and healing confound these dualities by drawing creatively on their opposed poles. The material from our case study will show that creative compromises[3] between tradition and expertise, no less than between banality and sensuality, are characteristic of some New Age healing practices, philosophies and organisations.

How New Age healers acquire their skills

Discussions of the New Age have emphasised the importance of courses, workshops and seminars addressing self-development and self-therapeutic approaches (Bowman, 1999; Heelas, 1992; Van Hove, 1999). Participants may attend these for self-healing and then perhaps progress to become practitioners in what Bowman has termed 'the healing industry' associated with the 'spiritual marketplace' (1999: 188). Our observations here, however, concern the experiences of a group of nurses whose development as healers occurred as an unintended consequence of their practice of aromatherapy and 'holistic massage'.

Although only eight nurses, all females, were included in the study, they were part of a larger group who were receiving tuition to diploma level in aromatherapy and 'holistic massage' from a local nursing sister.[4] While several of the members of this group had experienced periods of personal crisis which, in New Age terms, might be seen as indicating a need for some form of healing for themselves, the ethic of care that dominated their nursing practice provided a vehicle for incorporating self-development within their professional development. Such experiences had enhanced their capacity and willingness to empathise with the sufferings of others. The often fervently expressed desire to do something for those patients whom conventional medicine could not help exemplifies this. There was, then, a relationship between working on their own well-being and that of their patients, but their sense of professional identity countered the supposedly individualistic and narcissistic tendencies widely attributed to the New Age.

The importance of their professional identity as nurses could mean that the term 'New Age' as a description of this group is both secondary to their main identity and inappropriate. The difficulties encountered in using the term have already been made clear. Taking Rose's (1998) finding that the majority of New Age participants are female, aged between 35 and 54, and middle-class, the nurses in our study could be said to meet the first set of criteria. In addition, Rose's study showed that women were much more likely than men to be interested in healing. Whether our respondents would have described themselves as New Agers is doubtful, however. Studies such as that by Van Hove (1999) suggest a reluctance to identify oneself within such a category. Indeed, some of our respondents with more limited conceptions of the holistic basis of healing were decidely unsettled by phenomena such as channelling which have been characterised as typically New Age (Riordan, 1992).

However, certain members of this group had, through practising massage and aromatherapy, found themselves upon a path of self-development consonant with typically New Age concerns. This path incorporated, to varying degrees, those qualities that we identified earlier with the New Age, but especially an appreciation of what is often described as an 'holistic' world view. The tensions between self-centred and selfless practices, and between inner and outer sources of authority, which we have argued are inherent in the New Age, were felt particularly strongly by members of this group, because of the conflicting demands of their personal lives (with their own priorities and sense of personal development) and their professional practice (where professional development was demanded but also bounded by a healthcare system whose culture was rapidly being colonised by managerialism). It is not surprising then to discover that the diverse beliefs and practices of the New Age were translated by different members of the group in characteristically varied ways.

Central to the experiences to be recounted here is the importance of what has been described as the Human Energy Field (HEF) (Brennan, 1988). This consists of 'primary subtle energetic fields that underlie and contribute to the functional expression of the physical body', and that are harmonised through energy work with universal natural energies (Gerber, 1988). The presence of the HEF is experienced in several ways, for example as tingling, or pulsating, but heat is the most common sensation experienced by both healers and their clients (Benor, 1992). Nurses in this study reported that their patients had remarked upon the warmth of nurses' hands when they were giving a massage. They also reported localised sensations of tingling or pulsating in the part of the body requiring attention when the nurse paused and held her hands over that area during a massage. Nurse respondents also experienced heat and sometimes found the flow of what they described as healing energy so intense that the palms of their hands became almost painful.

The significance of the HEF here is, firstly, its partial acceptance (through the practice of particular therapies) within the arena of conventional medicine, albeit within specific institutional circumstances (for example some hospices) whose ethos is sufficiently receptive to make this possible. Secondly, there is its role in providing sensual experiences in the context of a healing intent, which depend upon and reinforce the construction of shared experience and which may produce experiences similar to those described by Luckmann as transcendental (Luckmann, 1990). He describes such experiences in their most minimal form as no more than 'suspicions of another reality' (1990: 129). On a more complex level, there can be intermediate and great transcendences which, Luckmann argues, are universal, socially constructed and can be systematised and institutionalised. Although the scope of the transcendent in modern societies is shrinking, and becoming privatised in the modern sacred cosmos through such themes as self-realisation, he suggests that this 'does not mean a loss of the "sacred" ' (1990: 138). Instead, there is a 'powerful "elective affinity" between the structural privatisation of individual life and the "sacralisation" of subjectivity that is celebrated in much of modern consciousness' (Luckmann, 1990: 135). There is a sense, then, in which transcendent experiences may act for some individuals as openings to what they regard as the sacred in modern life.

Luckmann suggests that these experiences are intersubjectively articulated, for example through re-telling, to become part of collective memories. What we shall be arguing here is that they are also constructed intersubjectively through the shared experience of the HEF, and that this occurs through the healing activities described below, which combine rationalised and bureaucratised healthcare with therapeutic practices which access the HEF. Our nurses were involved in activities which cut across the distinction between 'banal associations' and 'sensual solidarities' (Mellor & Shilling, 1997).

HOLISM AND HEALING

We have already characterised the New Age representation of the 'true self' as naturally social, compassionate and attuned to the rhythms of the natural world, working on self-actualisation through interaction with others and directed at the restoration of a sense of wholeness. We have also argued that holistic notions of the self operate on a continuum which moves between the 'kernel' of wholeness within an individual and relations of mutuality between individuals and their environment. Both these notions of the self are discernible in the accounts of our respondents, not necessarily because they were familiar with the tenets of the New Age but rather because these tenets appeared to have an affinity with some aspects of their professional ethic of care.

While the notion of holism inherent in much New Age thinking has been criticised for its individualising tendencies, it is also possible to argue that its universalising tendencies foster a sense of compassion for others, rather than individualistic self-improvement. Our respondents adopted an holistic approach to healing in various ways. Their perceptions of holism were threefold in nature, reflecting the different levels of holistic philosophy identified by Power through her content analysis of 'holistic health' materials in the 1980s: the 'whole body', the 'whole person', and 'the integrity of creation' (Power, 1991; see also Hedges, 1997).

The first category, the 'whole body', focused to a large extent on the physical, seeing approved forms of health behaviour (e.g. diet, exercise) as the chief means of dealing with symptoms. Only minimal therapeutic intervention by the practitioner was required, sufficient to stimulate the body's own self-healing force. The category of 'whole person' perceived illness as occurring on the emotional, mental and spiritual levels as well as the physical. Self-help techniques and individual responsibility were necessary to effect real improvements. The third category of 'the integrity of creation' envisaged widespread social renewal brought about by intentional changes in personal consciousness. (This belief is, of course, central to the New Age.) Sources of healing energy were threefold, and were attributed to the love and energies within oneself as a giver; to whichever divine source of energies one might believe in; and to the universe, which was seen as providing extraordinary energies.

It was those respondents who focused on the third level, the integrity of creation, who demonstrated most confidently their familiarity with the HEF, and were receptive to associated ideas such as the language of chakras and auras. Regardless of whether these respondents identified themselves as New Agers, their interaction with the HEF enabled them to express their compassion more effectively than might otherwise have been possible. So profound was this engagement that they found themselves acknowledging a new identity for themselves as healers and an unexpectedly strong sense of their own spiritual development. Some examples of how they prepared for and gave a treatment session help to demonstrate this process.

'I WAS JUST MASSAGING A BODY,
BUT I KNOW IT'S NOT JUST THAT ANY MORE'

While several of the respondents were preoccupied with holistic philosophy, its emphasis on stress as the cause of illness and the educative and counselling aspects of their role as nurses which derived from this philosophy, several other respondents almost completely ignored these issues. This was because of their experiences when giving massage and aromatherapy. This was predominantly a shared experience, both in the sense that the nurse giving the massage anticipated the patient's needs and responses during the interaction, but also because what happened was an exploration of a sensual experience which was new to both of them.

One nurse commented upon the effects of her contact with the HEF as she felt a stronger flow of energy passing through her hands as she became more practised. Whilst she included a request to God to help her in healing as part of her preparations for giving a massage, the resulting energy flow was so powerful that she felt unable to control or make full use of it. Indeed, it made the palms of her hands feel most uncomfortable, and she sensed that the condition was 'getting worse' as the energy intensified from one massage session to the next. In her own words:

> 'I usually try [to] what I call, centre myself, ask for help from God, before I start, in his name, you know . . . "Please help me, send healing to this person", and then I usually put my hands on the person so that we can communicate in a way before we start the procedure, so that I invade her privacy slowly. And you ask them to breathe, so that you almost synchronise yourself with that person. And then as I start to massage I feel this energy. These last four weeks it's got worse, and I've started to make a log now, of what the woman says to me, because she's noticed this energy too. And she'll tell me that I do stop at times over the places where she's got problem areas, and she will feel a pulsating from my hands . . . but I'm not aware that I'm doing it . . . and it can go on for a while afterwards, get quite uncomfortable. I don't know how to stop it. I need it, I call for it and it comes, then I feel it's such a waste, then.'

The process of massaging produced not only the sensation of a flow of energy for patient and nurse, but also reports from patients (and nurses who had been massaged) of bright flashes of colours:

> 'They're beautiful . . . even if you open your eyes, you can still see them. I've seen red, lilac, silver, gold, but oh, they're beautiful colours, really bright, almost fluorescent. Pink, I've seen . . . not always as a complete field, though, just flashes that float.'

These 'healing colours', as the nurses called them, had also been seen as purple, amethyst, gold and turquoise.

The impact of a treatment on patients could be quite profound. One nurse described her patient's response thus:

> 'She says she goes right inside herself, she says it's an incredible feeling, I can't tell you, I can't put it into words . . . She'll say she goes all pins and needles, and the area [I'm resting my hands over] starts to pulsate, and she'll say "I feel as if I've had a boost".'

The benefits of aromatherapy and massage were seen in stark contrast to the organisational environment in which they were offered. Thus the patients benefited from knowing that they were going to have someone else's undivided attention for longer than would normally have been possible on the ward:

> 'If you go to a place of quietness with a "Please do not disturb" sign on the door, they know you're going to give them total care. You're there, well, you've got to make them feel you've got all the time in the world. You may have a mental note that this can't take more than an hour and a half, but they don't know that, and they're the most important thing that you've got . . .'

> 'Total commitment to that person without being disturbed . . . that's very important and you cannot get that on the ward.'

The success of a treatment depended on preventing distractions and on evoking the appropriate atmosphere through a ritualistic lighting of candles and burner, dimming of lights and the playing of New Age music. Giving a treatment could, however, have negative effects in that respondents reported taking on their patients' symptoms after the massage; preventive measures to 'cleanse your aura' included meditation, taking Bach flower remedies, drinking a glass of cold water and washing of hands in cold water. While these precautions might be disregarded when in a hurry (thereby leaving only the nurse herself open to ill effects), other preparations to 'set the scene' were rarely neglected.

In answer to the question of whether aromatherapy provided the patient with something unique, one nurse answered:

> 'Well I think it probably does . . . You can comfort someone by talking to them, or by putting your arm round them or holding their hand, but that isn't prolonged, is it? But if you're massaging someone, there's even more of a closeness there, and everything is, well, everything else is blocked out . . . you know, totally.'

The same nurse talked about how her patients had reported greater heat from her hands as she had become better practised:

> 'People do say your hands have gone very hot . . . and that was something I hadn't experienced or knew about and it's like, sort of the energy in your hands . . . To start with, as far as I knew and was concerned, I was just [very deliberately enunciating the words] *massaging a body*, but I *know it's not just that any more*, and I *can feel that it isn't that any more.*'

Comments such as these, seen in the context of their respective interviews, illustrated respondents' perceptions of an enhanced function for the techniques of aromatherapy and massage. Using such techniques, they were no longer operating at the most immediate level of the 'whole body' or even the 'whole person'. Whatever they might achieve was on a level which transcended everyday experience and provided a gateway to universal energies of a divine origin. The shared experience of the HEF reinforced this. What these nurses considered themselves to be facilitating was the process of 'healing'.

SHARING INNER TIME: MAKING HEALING TOGETHER

Healing within the New Age is understood, Albanese (1992) suggests, as a 'work of reconciliation'. Its holistic ethos means that this form of healing 'emphasises a forgiveness that dissolves physical disease, emotional hurt, and the collective distress of society and nature. Healing in this sense is different from curing. To experience healing may or may not be the same as effecting a physiological change' (Albanese, 1992: 78).

Similarly, efficacy is not seen as the main consideration of healing rituals by Neitz and Spickard (1990). They draw our attention to the fact that healing rituals can be judged effective even when there is no immediate evidence of success. They attribute such occurrences to a shared participation in a 'vivid present' (1990: 31) which, they suggest, is fundamental to an understanding of the religious experiences underlying other elements of religion such as beliefs, symbols and meaning systems. Such ideas further illuminate the social, as distinct from the individualistic, nature of healing discussed in this chapter.

Learning to work with the HEF involves more than the acquisition of a formulaic technique in Giddens's sense of traditional knowledge. Rather, it appears to involve two components: 'flow' and 'tuning in'. Neitz and Spickard (1990) show how these may be combined in order to account for religious experience, citing firstly Csikszentmihalyi's definition of 'flow':

> Flow denotes the holistic sensation present when we act with total involvement . . . It is the kind of state in which action follows upon action according to an internal logic which seems to need no conscious intervention on our part. We experience it as a unified flowing from one moment to the next, in which we feel in control of our actions, and in which there is little distinction between self and environment; between stimulus and response; or between past, present and future. (Csikszentmihalyi, 1975, quoted in Neitz and Spickard, 1990: 20)

Certain activities are more likely than others to precipitate flow experiences. Whether one is rock-climbing, playing chess, composing music or meditating, three structural characteristics prevail: 'selflessness, limited sensory input and the match between the challenge of a task and one's ability to complete it' (Neitz and Spickard, 1990: 20). By 'selflessness', Csikszentmihalyi means that one is no longer conscious of the separateness of self from one's surroundings. The self becomes relatively superfluous. Interpersonal negotiation is less important than the willingness and ability to lose oneself in the activity, even when others may be involved (for example, in some sort of ritual). The intense concentration selectively reduces one's sensory stimuli, so that the only focus is those sensations associated with the activity itself. Flow occurs in the space between one's apprehension of the task as difficult but realisable, and its achievement. In particular, extraordinary experiences are likely to result, which language is, on the whole, felt to be inadequate to describe.

While Csikszentmihalyi suggests that religious rituals can demonstrate flow, Neitz and Spickard are cautious about accounting for religious experience in these terms alone. Although it is possible to argue that flow emerges from structured activities which have to be learned, and that the type of experiences produced by flow are not, therefore, entirely private, Neitz and Spickard argue that a sociology of religious experience also needs to take account of the notion of 'otherness', in particular in terms of the tuning-in relationship discussed by Schutz.

Schutz's exploration of how people make music together as a mutual tuning-in relationship is relevant to healing because both processes articulate meaning independent of 'talk'. Rather than relying on interpretation of a semantic system, Schutz suggests that communication is effected by the sharing of inner time, through the process of *durée* (a term borrowed from Bergson):

> Two series of events in inner time, belonging to the stream of consciousness of the beholder, are lived through in simultaneity . . . [T]his sharing of the other's flux of experiences in inner time, this living through a vivid present in common,

constitutes what we call . . . the mutual tuning-in relationship, the experience of "We", which is at the foundation of all possible communication. (Schutz, 1951: 173, quoted in Neitz and Spickard, 1990: 28)

Such experience is closer, Schutz suggests, to the meaning of religious participation than the rehearsal of beliefs alone. In order for it to work, certain conditions are necessary such as a general knowledge of religious culture. In addition, the experience is eminently social, in that sociality depends on 'the possibility of living together simultaneously in specific dimensions of time' (Schutz, 1951, in Neitz and Spickard, 1990: 28). Even individuals separated in outer time and space can achieve this shared experience; as Neitz and Spickard point out, it does not take much extension of this idea to talk of feeling that one has tuned-in to nature as an inspiration for religious experience, or, in the case discussed here, tuned-in to the universe's abundant energy flow. Applied to a particular healing ritual, all present would become, in effect, 'healers' and all are 'healed' as they share a 'vivid present' (Neitz and Spickard, 1990: 31).

CONCLUSION

In this chapter, we have suggested that the 'healing' activities described here cut across the banal associations characteristic of rationalised and bureaucratised healthcare and the sensual solidarities evoked by the experiences of healing. In particular, we have argued that the process of holistic healing incorporates experiences which are common to spheres of meaningful human interaction such as religion and aesthetic apprecia- tion. Rather than encouraging the individualism for which holism is so often criticised, this process provides opportunities for the expression of values such as love and compassion, albeit within the ambit of a profes- sionalised ethic of nursing care. Through a mutual tuning-in relationship between healer and patient, as well as between healer and patient and the source of healing energies, there is a blurring of the boundaries between selves which, as an inter-subjective construction of transcendence, may bind people together. For some individuals this would also have sacred significance. The nature of the interaction, structured as it was in terms of shared time between patient and nurse through the mutual experiencing of the Human Energy Field, meant that these experiences were incontro- vertibly social.

NOTES

1. We are referring to what Charles Taylor (1989: 495) has called 'the disengaged and instrumental modes of thought and action which have steadily increased their hold on modern life'.
2. 'Conventional therapy depends on choice, involves an attempt to reconstruct the self through discourse, requires a decision to enter into a contract which can be revoked at any time, and is directed towards reconciliation and reform rather than transcendence.' Mellor & Shilling (1997: 183).
3. In the positive, French sense of *compromis*, not in the negative sense of 'compromission'.
4. The study was conducted in 1992 in the English East Midlands by the first-named author and was initially concerned with the integration of complementary therapies into nursing practice. Eight nurses were interviewed in depth, using semi-structured interviews which allowed respondents to develop autobiographical narratives as part of their response. Additional interviews were conducted with a Roman Catholic nun who, as a nurse tutor, taught the nurses holistic massage and aromatherapy, and with a local consultant in palliative care who facilitated the use of these therapies in the hospice where he worked. Analysis of the data from these interviews was with reference to grounded theory (Glaser and Strauss, 1967). The data used in this chapter draw on the interviews with the nurses only.

BIBLIOGRAPHY

Albanese, Catherine L., 1992: 'The Magical Staff: Quantum Healing in the New Age', in Lewis, J.R., & Melton, J.G., eds, *Perspectives on the New Age* (Albany: State University of New York Press), pp. 66–84.

Beckford, James A., 1984: 'Holistic imagery and ethics in new religious and healing movements', *Social Compass* 31 (2–3): 259–72.

Beckford, James A., 1985: 'The World Images of New Religious and Healing Movements' in Jones, R.K., ed., *Sickness and Sectarianism* (Aldershot: Gower).

Benor, Daniel J., 1992: *Healing Research: Holistic Energy Medicine and Spirituality*, Vol. 1 Research in Healing (Deddington: Helix).

Bloom, William, ed., 1991: *The New Age. An Anthology of Essential Writings* (London: Rider).

Bloom, William, 1987: *Meditation in a Changing World* (Glastonbury: Gothic Image).

Bowman, Marion, 1999: 'Healing in the Spiritual Marketplace: Consumers, Courses and Credentialism', *Social Compass* 46/2: 181–9.

Brennan, Barbara, 1988: *Hands of Light: A Guide to Healing through the Human Energy Field* (New York: Bantam).

Coward, Rosalind, 1989: *The Whole Truth. The Myth of Alternative Health* (London: Faber and Faber).

Csikszentmihalyi, M., 1975: 'Play and Intrinsic Rewards', *Journal of Humanistic Psychology* 15: 41–63.

Gerber, Richard, 1988: *Vibrational Medicine: New Choices for Healing Ourselves* (Santa Fe: Bear).

Giddens, Anthony, 1990: *The Consequences of Modernity* (Cambridge: Polity Press).
—— 1991: *Modernity and Self-Identity* (Cambridge: Polity Press).
—— 1994: 'Living in a Post-traditional Society', in Beck, U., Giddens, A., & Lash, S., eds, *Reflexive Modernization* (Cambridge: Polity Press), pp. 56–109.
Glaser, B.G., and Strauss, A.L., 1967: *The Discovery of Grounded Theory* (Chicago: Aldine).
Hedges, Ellie, 1997: 'Holism, Healthism and the Embodied Practice of Healing', unpublished paper delivered at the ISSR Conference, Toulouse.
Heelas, Paul, 1991: 'Cults for Capitalism? Self-religions, Magic and the Empowerment of Business', in Gee, P., & Fulton, J., eds, *Religion and Power. Decline and Growth* (London: BSA Sociology of Religion Study Group).
—— 1992: 'The Sacralization of the Self and New Age Capitalism' in Abercrombie, N., & Warde, A., eds, *Social Change in Contemporary Britain* (Oxford: Polity).
—— 1996: 'De-traditionalisation of Religion and Self: the New Age and Post-modernity' in Flanagan, K., and Jupp, P., eds, *Postmodernity, Sociology and Religion* (London: Macmillan).
Luckmann, Thomas, 1990: 'Shrinking Transcendence, Expanding Religion?', *Sociological Analysis* 50 (2): 127–38.
Mellor, Philip, and Shilling, Chris, 1997: *Re-Forming the Body. Religion, Community and Modernity* (London: Sage).
Neitz, Mary Jo and Spickard, James V., 1990: 'Steps Towards a Sociology of Religious Experience: The Theories of Mihaly Csikszentmihalyi and Alfred Schutz', *Sociological Analysis* 51 (1) : 15–33.
Power, Richenda, 1991: 'The Whole Idea of Medicine: A Critical Evaluation of the Emergence of "Holistic Medicine" in Britain in the Early 1980s', unpublished PhD thesis, London: Polytechnic of the South Bank.
Riordan, Suzanne 1992: 'Channelling: A New Revelation?' in Lewis, J.R., and Melton, J.G., eds, *Perspectives on the New Age* (Albany: State University of New York Press), pp. 105–26.
Rose, Stuart, 1998: 'An Examination of the New Age Movement: Who is Involved and What Constitutes its Spirituality', *Journal of Contemporary Religion* 13 (1) : 5 – 22.
Rosen, R.D., 1975: *Psychobabble* (New York: Atheneum).
Schur, Edwin., 1976: *The Awareness Trap: Self-Absorption Instead of Social Change* (New York: Quadrangle Books).
Schutz, A., 1951: 'Making Music Together: a Study in Social Relationship' in Brodersen, A., ed., *Collected Papers II: Studies in Social Theory* (The Hague: Martinus Nijhoff).
Sharma, Ursula, 1992: *Complementary Medicine Today. Practitioners and Patients* (London: Routledge).
Taylor, Charles, 1989: *Sources of the Self. The Making of the Modern Identity* (Cambridge: Cambridge University Press).
Van Hove, Hildegard, 1999: 'L'émergence d'un "marché spiriuel" ', *Social Compass* 46/2: 161–72.

York, Michael, 1995: *The Emerging Network. A Sociology of the New Age and Neo-Pagan Movements* (Lanham, MD: Rowman & Littlefield).

—— 1997: 'New Age and the Late Twentieth Century', *Journal of Contemporary Religion* 12 (3): 401–18.

Zilbergeld, B., 1983: *The Shrinking of America. Myths of Psychological Change* (Boston: Little, Brown).

11

An Analysis of the Festival
for Mind–Body–Spirit, London

Malcolm Hamilton

INTRODUCTION

If New Age can be characterised as to some extent an audience cult[1] then
the Festival for Mind–Body–Spirit held annually in London is one of the
main sources of the dissemination of its ideas. As with the UFO convention
described by Stark and Bainbridge (1985), visitors to the Festival for Mind–
Body–Spirit listen to lectures, attend workshops, watch performances and
demonstrations, pick up literature and leaflets and purchase commodities
and services from exhibitors. They accept many, all or none of the ideas
presented to them as they see fit and are 'interested in' and often willing to
try out any new idea, therapy or technique to be found in the general milieu
of the alternative sub-culture. The Festival might be described as the annual
convention of New Age in Britain. But New Age is not simply an audience
cult. Although it comprises a number of them, it also embraces many client
cults and other groups and movements which belong to neither of these
types. It is perhaps best described, as Michael York (1995) argues, following
Gerlach and Hine (Gerlach and Hine, 1970; Hine 1977), as a segmentary,
polycephalous, integrated network (SPIN).[2] The Festival for Mind–Body–
Spirit reflects this in the astonishing diversity it brings together annually
under one roof. In 1997 the Festival offered 97 exhibitors, 32 lectures, 47
workshops and 108 stage events and demonstrations from inversion therapy
to the Aetherius Society, from Kirlian photography to belly dancing.
Comparison with an eastern bazaar is irresistible and there is always an
air of 1960s experimental exuberance about it.

BACKGROUND AND HISTORY

Started in 1977 by Graham Wilson,[3] the Festival[4] took place originally at
Olympia, West Kensington in London, where it remained for six years.
That the first Festival filled this enormous exhibition centre is revealing. As

a result of undergoing out-of-body experiences during his champion cross-country runs, Wilson had for some years been exploring the world of the psychic and paranormal and had become involved in the alternative scene. It was a world that was, however, largely esoteric and underground, and one that was closed to most people. Information about it was hard to come by. Wilson wanted to introduce it to a wider public. The familiar venue of Olympia, more usually associated with the Ideal Home Exhibition and the Motor Show, would seem well chosen for this purpose, except that its size and its choice expressed tremendous faith in the growing appeal of alternativism. It was a confidence that was not, at least initially, misplaced. The first Festival attracted some sixty thousand visitors over its five days. By the third Festival in 1979 a peak of eighty-eight thousand visitors was reached.

During the Eighties, however, attendance figures of this kind could not be sustained. At this time there was, Wilson explains, a decline in interest in things spiritual and alternative and greater interest in more material pursuits and in making money. Attendance at the last Festival at Olympia in 1982 had fallen to twenty thousand, for which the venue was clearly too big and too expensive. In 1983 the Festival moved to the smaller Royal Horticultural Halls near Victoria. This had an additional advantage in that it was better suited to the provision of lectures and workshops in smaller meeting rooms for which there had been a growing demand. It also allowed the organisers to exercise closer control over the character of the exhibitors so as to ensure the Festival retained a broad appeal. In 1979 Wilson took the Festival to New York and later to Los Angeles and San Francisco and eventually to Australia. The US Festivals were later replaced by Whole Life Expos as an independent operation. Similar independent festivals based upon the London event later sprung up in many other parts of the world.

Wilson's experience in the USA led to ideas which enhanced the character of the Festival for Mind–Body–Spirit. In the States, psychic fairs[5] were popular but these were virtually unknown in the UK. Wilson felt that there would be considerable interest in Britain for similar events and in 1980 launched the Psychics and Mystics Fair as a regional event, eventually running eight annually. Also in 1980 he started the London Natural Health Clinic at his headquarters at Arnica House, Notting Hill Gate, northwest London.[6]

Attendances at the main Festival at the Royal Horticultural Halls began to grow again during the later 1980s, eventually reaching fifty thousand. Wilson's experience has been that there is a marked growth in interest in the alternative scene during periods of recession. Such was the demand that the duration of the Festival was extended to ten full days, and by 1996, a second Festival was launched, in September at Alexander Palace in North

London. Meanwhile the burgeoning interest in all forms of alternative and complementary medicine and healing techniques saw the establishment by Wilson of the Healing Arts Festival in 1988.[7]

The Festival for Mind–Body–Spirit has, in many respects, been the centre of, and the inspiration for, a worldwide network of similar and related New Age events, especially in the English-speaking world where New Age is largely based. It is truly international in itself with a large proportion of exhibitors and practitioners coming from the USA, Australia and elsewhere. In this way it has acted as a focus for New Age, both in the sense of bringing this diverse world together and in disseminating its message very widely.

DEVELOPMENTS

Over the years a number of significant changes can be observed in the character of the Festival. One which Wilson cites as being perhaps the most noticeable and significant is that in terms of those attending it has shifted New Age ideas and concerns from the esoteric fringe to an almost mainstream position. On the other hand, when something becomes too mainstream it tends to drop out of the Festival. The Body Shop was a feature of early Festivals but its success meant that it no longer had the alternative edge that made it appropriate for the Festival or the Festival useful to it.[8] Some of the environmental groups, prominent in the early years, also found more appropriate and often more political channels for their energies. It is important, Graham Wilson feels, that the Festival does not become *too* mainstream. Part of the appeal of the Festival, and one might add of the alternative scene generally, is precisely that it is alternative and not established, and it is important to preserve a balance in bringing the esoteric to a wider mainstream audience and clientèle.

Perhaps even more important than the shift towards the mainstream has been that from what I shall term a 'conversion' to a 'consumption' orientation. In the early years of the Festival there was a greater emphasis on putting a message across, on disseminating an idea or a philosophy and upon influencing and converting visitors to a way of thinking. Prominent at early Festivals, for example, were groups such as the Rajneeshees. This gave way in the 1980s to an emphasis upon the sale of products and services. As Graham Wilson puts it, in the past visitors looked more to gurus for personal growth, whereas now they seek to enhance it by the application of various techniques and therapies.

Another noticeable change that has occurred has been a decline in prominence of groups and organisations concerned with more universal questions such as the environment in favour of rather more self-oriented concerns relating to personal and inner growth and development. Greenpeace and Friends of the Earth were regular exhibitors in the early years. The sixth Festival in 1981 specially featured Friends of the Earth at the tenth anniversary of their foundation. A thirty-five-foot inflatable Planet Earth was suspended from the roof in the centre of the hall. In 1982 the theme of the Festival was Peace and Greater Planetary Awareness. It was at this Festival that alternative and complementary medicine was introduced for the first time at the Festival's Holistic Health Centre. By 1984 the theme of the Festival had become Healthy Living. Alongside conservation and the environment, the programme introduction for that year emphasised alternative medicine, natural living, herbs, aromatics, skin and body care, spirituality, human potential and psychic sciences.

The commercialisation of the Festival which accompanied the increased emphasis upon the more self-oriented and bodily concerns of health and personal growth perhaps reflects the general ethos of the 1980s. However, it is also in many ways stimulated by an inherent logic embedded within New Age or certain aspects of it and particularly those concerned with healing, body work and personal well-being, growth and development. The commodification and marketisation of these aspects of New Age is homologous with its diffuse and fragmentary nature, individualism, relativism and eclecticism. Characteristic of it is the absence of binding doctrines, of any overall organisation and of any overall leadership. This has implications both for the way disseminators of New Age ideas and practices operate and the way in which devotees relate to them. Disseminators become practitioners and devotees become clientèle.

MARKETISATION

Practitioners can best support themselves as professional disseminators of New Age thought and practice through the market system. They readily make the transition from disseminating a message to selling a commodity or service. The New Age had its roots in the hippie culture of the 1960s, but when members of the hippie generation found themselves having to settle into the business of making a living and supporting a family, some turned to retailing in the spiritual marketplace as a means of livelihood.[9] Others became craftsmen and women selling their products directly to the consumer. Yet others fashioned less tangible 'products' concerned with care of mind, body and spirit. This in turn admirably fitted the needs of consumers who were not interested in religion of the traditional kind which tended to demand exclusive commitment. The countercultural generation wanted to retain the freedom to experiment and thrived in an ethos of eclecticism and variety. New Age appealed to those who were not interested in substantial commitment of time or dramatic changes in their pattern of life of the kind demanded by some of the New Religious Movements such as the Unification Church or ISKCON. As New Age moved more towards the mainstream the cult and the commune gave way to counselling and colour therapy. Such activities can be readily slotted into normal lifestyles and are compatible with following a regular profession or occupation. The spiritual life becomes a leisure and consumption activity. Thus, followers of New Age are not members of a religion or religious organisation, but are participants in a variety of client and audience cults and in a cultic milieu (Campbell, 1972) in which they 'pick and mix' their own individual and personal combination of elements which they can change to suit and as they themselves change and develop. This in turn reinforces the impetus towards commodification as practitioners find their customer base more fluid, less deferential towards spiritual authority and leadership and more likely to transfer their allegiance elsewhere. This decline of deference towards experts and the process of detraditionalisation (Heelas, 1996)[10] is, of course, often considered to be a general development in contemporary societies, but it has particular consequences for religious and quasi-religious life, which has traditionally been based upon either prophetic or priestly charismatic leadership (Weber, 1965). In the contemporary religious world, characterised as it is to a considerable degree by epistemological individualism (Wallis, 1984) of which New Age is the most striking example, it is increasingly difficult for disseminators of spiritual truths to operate except through the commodification of what they have to offer. With no binding doctrine and no organisation there is no membership and therefore no source of income for the support of leaders. The Festival for Mind–Body–Spirit does, of course, lend itself particularly to such commodification processes, but they are in any case characteristic of the way much of the New Age/alternative milieu has developed.

This is a much more specific point about New Age than one that is often made about it, namely that it exemplifies the religious pluralism of modern society, its epistemological individualism (Wallis, 1984), detraditionalisation (Heelas, 1994, 1996) or the spiritual circus (Lyon, 1993). In these and other analyses, the echo of Berger's original 'market and marketplace' metaphor (1973) is indeed very prominent, but it is the aspects of variety, choice and consumer sovereignty that are stressed[11] rather than the delivery of commodities and services through a market mediated through monetary exchange. Lyon, for instance, points out that the New Age has 'much to do with a market place – shopping mall or circus – of religious and quasi-religious elements focused on self and on choice' (p. 117). These analyses tend to conflate a number of different things. Religious pluralism, despite being dubbed the 'religious supermarket', does not in itself imply commodification. It refers to a wide range of choice between religious alternatives. These could all involve a process of conversion or joining a bounded sect, cult, denomination or church financially supported by donations, tithes or gifts and the direct input of voluntary labour on the part of its members, rather than by the sale and purchase of anything. Secondly, there is the aspect of *bricolage* (Van Hove, 1999) or 'pick-and-mix' in which components from possibly diverse sources are put together by the individual to comprise a personally satisfying conglomeration which may be unique to them but also changeable at will. Neither does this necessarily involve commodification of the elements. Finally, true commodification involves the selling and buying of spiritual commodities and services in a market system in which money is the medium of exchange and where what is offered and its price are determined by the conditions of supply and demand. It is the latter which has not received sufficient emphasis in the literature, and which the Festival for Mind–Body–Spirit is so well adapted to provide. However, in doing so it only reflects, as argued above, broader developments in the world of alternative and New Age spirituality and holism. Graham Wilson's company, New Life Promotions, which promotes the Mind-Body-Festival, is also, for example, involved in mounting regular tours for some of the regular workshop-providers in the Festival. In some senses, then, the Festival is a trade show for holistic and alternative therapies and techniques for healing and spiritual development. As with any trade show, it is a forum enabling practitioners to find out what the competition are doing as well as to promote their own products.

Competition tends to promote product development and the capture of a distinct market niche. The spiritual supermarket is no exception and the Festival tends to reflect the movements of fashion in the world of alternativism. Graham Wilson considers that the continuing success of the Festival requires the addition of new things which will attract interest, and that this can be quite difficult. Fashions that have been noticeable in the past have included Aromatherapy, colour therapy, crystals and more recently Reiki. New products have to attract customers, and many fall by the wayside if there is insufficient money in them. Turnover of exhibitors and workshop leaders is very high (see Table 11.1). For example, only nine exhibitors in 1997 had also participated ten years earlier.

Table 11.1: *Turnover of Exhibitors, Lecturers and Workshop Organisers, 1987–1997*

	1987	1992	1997
No. of exhibitors	83	98	97
No. remaining from 1987	–	23	9
No. remaining from 1992	–	–	21
No. of lecturers and workshop organisers	40	42	53
No. remaining from 1987	–	8	2
No. remaining from 1992	–	–	8

Of course, a number of exhibitors find that their efforts are best placed elsewhere rather than in mounting exhibitions at such events. This would include the Body Shop, Greenpeace and so on, as noted above, but most of those who have disappeared over the years have probably done so as a result of changing fashions, loss of interest and economic unviability. Among workshop providers only two of the forty who had attended in 1987 did so in 1997, namely the mass healer Mathew Manning, and Dr Richard Lawrence, executive secretary of the Aetherius Society.[12]

The Festival is, then, to some extent a testing ground for new products and services. For some exhibitors it is their main source of income – or certainly used to be. They could earn, according to Wilson, as much, or almost as much, during the Festival as they could during the rest of the year put together. This may still be true for some. There is, as a consequence, considerable competition to be included in the Festival. Whereas once exhibitors had to be coaxed to participate, now the organisers can be selective in who they choose and in Wilson's opinion, there is considerable kudos in being chosen. The Festival has been and remains to some extent crucial in supporting in a very material way an alternative subculture.

PLAUSIBILITY STRUCTURES

The Festival is probably crucial in supporting the subculture in another way also. It provides a central pillar of the plausibility structure of the alternative and New Age subculture. In gathering together such a large number of like-minded people – exhibitors, practitioners and visitors – most of whom probably have little contact with others similarly committed to alternativism, the Festival creates a strong sense of the force and significance of the alternative world view. As Campbell (1972) says of the cultic milieu, it 'is kept alive by the magazines, periodicals, books, pamphlets, lectures, demonstrations and informal meetings through which its beliefs and practices are discussed and disseminated' (p. 123). The Festival is one of the most important of such meetings and it has always attempted to project a sense of a growing, spreading and developing movement. The close juxtaposition of exhibitors who, in isolation, would appear perhaps to be offering something quite bizarre and deviant, lends to all of them a collective authority and credibility which they might never otherwise enjoy. A visitor who is well disposed to aromatherapy or Shiatsu may well be prepared to take inversion therapy or even the Aetherius Society and by extension the whole alternative scene more seriously for the fact they appear as part of this large and well-supported event. As Campbell puts it, 'the individuals who "enter" the cultic milieu at any one point frequently travel rapidly through a wide variety of movements and beliefs and by so doing constitute yet another unifying force within the milieu' (1972: 123). If, as Hanegraaff (1996: 17) argues, the New Age is the cultic milieu become conscious of itself in a particular phase of its historical development, then such gatherings as the Festival for Mind–Body–Spirit are at the centre of the process by which it becomes self-aware and a movement. If, as Hanegraaff points out (ibid.: 19), the elements and components of the New Age movement are linked not by similarity but by contiguity, then the Festival for Mind–Body–Spirit is in a very literal sense a physical manifestation of that contiguity.

For the more committed devotee, the intensive workshops provide the strongest form of reinforcement of their world view. These were first introduced in 1984 and have become a central feature of the Festival, reflecting a demand for more in-depth and participatory involvement on the part of visitors. Attendance at the workshops came to outstrip attendance at lectures. In the early Nineties, double (two-hour) workshops were introduced to meet this growing demand for more intense participation. In 1997, of the 47 workshops on offer, no fewer than eight were led by Denise Linn, of which two were double. Her workshops were devoted to past-life regression and the miraculous healing power of the mind. Descended from a Cherokee grandmother, she is the biggest draw of the Festival and also runs one-day workshops in London, her advertising presenting the typical eclecticism of New Age healing, stating that she has served apprenticeships with a Japanese Zen master, a Hawaiian kahuna, a Pueblo Indian medicine man, Aborigine elders, a Maori Tohunga and an Apache Indian shaman. With two double workshops and a mass-healing event, Mathew Manning was the next most active workshop director, in 1997 celebrating twenty years of involvement with the Festival.

SURVEY DATA

This move towards more intensive participation may reflect the deepening involvement of a significant section of visitors in alternative and holistic healing and therapy over the years. A small-scale survey carried out by the author at the Festival in 1990[13] revealed that 47.3 per cent of visitors sampled had attended previous Festivals, 13.4 had attended twice before, 11.4 per cent had attended three times previously and 18.7 per cent had visited it more than three times; 40.3 per cent had previously visited similar types of event elsewhere.

Visitors were asked about their use of alternative and complementary therapies; about their involvement in sects, cults and New Religious Movements and in human potential groups and activities; about their readership of human potential, New Age and health magazines; and about their support for environmental concerns.[14] Table 11.2 summarises the data.

Table 11.2: Involvement in Alternative Activities by Sex and Age
(% of Festival sample)

	Women	Men	16–25	26–35	36–45	46–55	56+
Use of therapies	89	76	78	80	88	92	89
Health magazines	65	49	39	55	72	70	69
Human potential groups	51	39	35	44	56	56	40
Human potential magazines	71	63	57	65	72	78	77
Sects and Cults	14	24	4	20	17	20	34
Green	65	59	64	62	66	60	51

As might be expected, the figures are high, the highest being for use of therapies. Women generally score more highly than men. With the exception of support for Green movements, involvement tends to rise with age at least up to the 46–55 age group (and further in the case of sects and cults), after which it tends to falls off somewhat. The figures show a fairly high degree of immersion in the New Age subculture and a considerable overlap between this and related concerns such as environmentalism, vegetarianism, animal rights and so on. This and the growing demand for intensive workshops perhaps indicates that, although appropriated as a commodity and slotted into lifestyles in relatively undemanding ways, the consumption of New Age products and services is nevertheless based upon something more than fickle seeking for spiritual entertainment, novelty and exoticism. As Swatos (1983) suggests, 'even as the new religious sensibility is fed commodities . . . one must concede that something is there, to which the market responds . . .' (p. 334).

CONCLUSION

That there *is* something there perhaps receives strongest testimony in the conviction expressed by Graham Wilson (based upon numerous personal reports to him from visitors to the Festival) that the Festival for Mind-Body-Spirit can change – and has changed – many people's lives. It may do this in a very general way, by drawing them into a new world, giving them a new direction in life or giving them the confidence and encouragement to change their jobs, careers and lifestyle. More specifically, it may lead them to establish personal contacts which facilitate such change, to become a practitioner of a form of alternative therapy or to set up a New Age business of their own. The effects that the event can have are not sufficiently appreciated, according to Graham Wilson. Indeed, when not being put down as a seductive con, the Festival is often seen and portrayed somewhat unseriously as offering a rather light-hearted romp through an amusing assemblage of engaging and congenial weirdness. In some senses it might be said to be for many just that – an opportunity for playful indulgence in dreams and fantasies, in a romantic make-believe world. As Luhrmann (1989: 336) puts it, speaking of the present day practitioner of witchcraft and magic, 'he plays at magic and understands the play as serious'. Put differently, however, is this not to say at the same time that the Festival provides a means of transcending the apparent meaninglessness and arbitrariness of ordinary existence? For a great many attendees, the Festival offers a potent concentration of practical and effective solutions to real and otherwise intractable problems of mind, of body or of spirit, or of mind-body–spirit, for which the normal medical and traditional religious means of addressing have, in their own experience at least, been manifestly less than adequate.

NOTES

1. The audience cult is characterised by Stark and Bainbridge (1985) as diffuse and unorganised and one in which membership, if it can be called that, remains for the most part a consumer activity. 'Members' seldom if ever gather together physically in a given place but consume cult ideas and information through magazines, books, newsletters, and other media outlets. Today one would probably add the Internet to this list.

2. Gerlach and Hine (1970) developed this concept to describe the very fragmented and diffuse movements they were studying such as Black Power and Pentecostalism. Movements of this kind are characterised by a multiplicity of groups with no overall organisation and no single person or body to speak for the movement as a whole or to take authoritative decisions. There is often only loose organisation within many of the groups, considerable competition between them, fluidity with respect to the formation, fission and disintegration of groups and varying understandings of the goals and aims of the movement. Most participant groups have limited knowledge of the other participant groups or the extent of the movement and only partial knowledge of the extent of their own 'membership' or following. Followers are attached to the groups with varying degrees of commitment and involvement. The segmented fragments of the SPIN are

linked by what York (1995: 326) calls an 'unbounded reticulation' manifested through a number of features. There is, for example, considerable overlap of membership of many groups; there are many personal ties of kinship, friendship and personal contact between the members of particular groups; there is liaison and communication between the leaderships of various groups and exchange of information between them; there are travelling evangelists and spokespersons who move extensively between the groups, and large gatherings and demonstrations at which many groups are represented; finally, there is sharing of a core set of beliefs or ideology disseminated through a whole variety of means and outlets.

3. I am grateful to Graham Wilson for most of the following information, which was obtained through personal interview with him on 18 November 1997 at Arnica House, and for his comments on the first draft of this article. I am also grateful to him for providing me with a number of back programmes and videos made of past Festivals from which much additional information has been drawn. Also, I have drawn upon observations made on many personal visits to the Festival over the years almost from its inception.

4. It was originally entitled the 'Festival for Mind and Body' becoming the 'Festival for Mind–Body–Spirit' in 1979.

5. Gatherings of various types of alternative healers and practitioners, astrologers and diviners, experts in the Tarot, counsellors and meditation guides, etc.

6. This was, according to Wilson, the first comprehensive alternative therapy clinic of its kind in Britain, bringing together a variety of alternative and complementary forms of healing and types of practitioner. Wilson saw a market advantage in making available to customers a range of services in one location which had previously only been available from scattered specialist outlets.

7. The Healing Arts Festival, while in many respects very like the Mind-Body-Spirit Festival, emphasises more specifically 'natural', holistic, alternative and complementary healing defined in the broadest sense. 'Healing' here includes the pursuit of inner peace, happiness and joy as much as it does the alleviation or removal of physical symptoms. There is the same mixture of exhibitors, lectures, workshops and performances as at the Mind-Body-Spirit Festival.

8. Although Anita Roddick, founder of the Body Shop, was at the time of writing booked to give a lecture for the first time at the Festival.

9. Jorgensen and Jorgensen (1982) found much the same thing in their study of occult practitioners in a large city in the Western USA, where the sale of occult services seemed to be a strategic adaptation to survival in the larger society which does not detract from the fact that these practices are located within 'quite complex theosophies wherein magic is secondary to enlightenment or salvation' (p. 377). Campbell (1972) also suggests that it is the substantial commercial substructure of the cultic milieu which enables it to survive.

10. This is defined by Heelas (1994: 103) as the process whereby there is an 'internalisation of authority' (Bellah, 1991: 223) and in which traditional external loci of authority which cannot be ignored without feelings of guilt and sinfulness become centred within the individual whose own wishes, desires, ambitions, beliefs and judgements become pre-eminent.

11. See also Wilson (1976).

12. This snapshot approach, taking Festivals five years apart, may, of course, miss some regular participants but gives a good indication, nevertheless, of the degree of turnover.

A notable figure who has been missed by this procedure should be mentioned, namely Sir George Trevelyan, who opened the first Festival and continued to do so for many years thereafter as well as being a regular lecturer at the Festival. Also a regular contributor to the Festival was Peter Caddy, founder of the Findhorn Community.

13. The project was funded by the Nuffield Foundation, to whom thanks is due. A brief questionnaire was administered to 402 visitors and participants during the whole course of the Festival in 1990. Of these, 252 were female and 148 male and in two cases the sex of the respondent was not recorded. Two hundred and thirty one were single, 100 married, 62 divorced or separated and 9 widowed. Seventy-four were under 26, 147 between 26 and 35, 95 between 36 and 45, 50 between 46 and 55, 35 over 55 and in one case the respondent's age was not recorded. The respondents were interviewed mainly around the steps leading up to the performance area and, while the sample was not random, it was probably as representative as it could have been. The questionnaire was actually concerned with the dietary practices of visitors to the Festival in connection with a study of wholefood, health food and organically produced food consumers. Striking is the extent to which the sample showed distinctive dietary practices. Almost 74 per cent were following unorthodox diets. Fully 60 per cent of the sample were vegetarians of one kind or another, a figure massively greater than the proportion of vegetarians in the general population (between 3 and 6 per cent). Those following whole, health or organic (WHO) diets comprised around 45 per cent of the sample. Of these, a high proportion, about 70 per cent, were also vegetarian. Conversely, of vegetarians, about 52 per cent reported that they followed WHO diets. Significantly, catering at the Festival has always been vegetarian and organic. At Olympia the Festival was, for this reason, uniquely granted autonomy in providing the catering. On vegetarianism and alternative/spiritual values, see Twigg (1979, 1983) and Hamilton (1993, 1995).

14. Respondents were given a range of therapies, magazines, etc., listed on a card and asked if they had used, been involved in, read, etc., any of them. The figures are for any level of use or involvement, i.e. one or more positive responses for each type of item.

BIBLIOGRAPHY

Bellah, R., 1991: *Beyond Belief* (Oxford: University of California Press).

Berger, P., 1973: *The Social Reality of Religion* (Harmondsworth: Penguin).

Campbell, C. B., 1972: 'The Cult, the Cultic Milieu and Secularisation' in Michael Hill, ed., *A Sociological Yearbook of Religion in Britain* (London: SCM Press).

Gerlach, L., and Hine, V., 1970: *People, Power and Change: Movements of Social Transformation* (Indianapolis: Bobbs Merrill).

Hamilton, M. B., 1993: 'Whole foods and health foods: beliefs and attitudes', *Appetite* 20, 3: 223–8.

Hamilton, M. B., Waddington, P. A. J., Gregory, S., and Walker, A., 1995: 'Eat, Drink and be Saved: the spiritual significance of alternative diets', *Social Compass* 42, 4: 497–511.

Hanegraaff, W., 1996: *New Age Religion and Western Culture: Esotericism in the Mirror of Secular Thought* (Leiden: E. J. Brill).

Heelas, P., 1994: 'The Limits of Consumption and the Post-Modern "Religion" of the New Age' in Keat, R., Whiteley, N., and Abercrombie, N., eds, *The Authority of the Consumer* (London: Routledge).

——1996: *The New Age Movement* (Oxford: Blackwell).

Hine, V., 1977: 'The Basic Paradigm of a future Socio-cultural system' in *World Issues*, April/May (Centre for the Study of Democratic Institutions).

Jorgensen, D. L. and Jorgensen, L., 1982: 'Social Meanings of the Occult', *Sociological Quarterly* 23: 373–89.

Luhrmann, T., 1989: *Persuasions of the Witches Craft: Ritual Magic and Witchcraft in Present Day England* (Oxford: Blackwell).

Lyon, D., 1993: 'A Bit of a Circus: Notes on Postmodernity and New Age', *Religion* 23, 2: 117–26.

Stark, R., and Bainbridge, W. S., 1985: *The Future of Religion* (Berkeley: University of California Press).

Swatos, W. H., 1983: 'Enchantment and Disenchantment in Modernity: The significance of "religion" as a sociological category', *Sociological Analysis* 44: 321–37.

Twigg, J. 1979: 'Food for Thought: Purity and Vegetarianism', *Religion* 9: 13–35.

——1983: 'Vegetarianism and the Meaning of Meat' in Murcott, A., ed., *The Sociology of Food and Eating* (Aldershot: Gower).

Van Hove, H., 1999: 'L'émergence d'un "marché spirituel"', *Social Compass* 46, 2: 161–72.

Wallis, R., 1984: *The Elementary Forms of the New Religious Life* (London: Routledge).

Weber, M., 1965: *The Sociology of Religion* (London: Methuen).

Wilson, B., 1976: *Contemporary Transformations of Religion* (London: Oxford University Press).

York, M., 1995: *The Emerging Network: A Sociology of the New Age and Neo-Pagan Movements* (London: Rowman and Littlefield).

12

Personal Development:
the Spiritualisation and Secularisation
of the Human Potential Movement
Elizabeth Puttick

INTRODUCTION

The Human Potential Movement (HPM) was one of the most significant and influential movements of the counterculture of the sixties and seventies. It originated as an experimental rebellion against mainstream psychology and organised religion. Its explorations and advances trailblazed the now widespread interest shown by mainstream society in personal development, the quality of relationships, emotional literacy, human values in the workplace and the replacement of 'hard' political causes with 'softer' issues such as environmentalism. Its values have pervaded our outlook to the point where even philosophy may be interpreted in terms of the philosopher's emotional problems, as with a recent biography of Bertrand Russell.[1] The bestselling success of *Emotional Intelligence* by Daniel Goleman (1996), as well as a plethora of popular self-help books, highlight the growing acceptance of these values. The magnitude of the shift may be gauged by comparison with the following quotation from a speech by the Conservative MP Nicholas Soames, grandson of Winston Churchill, which epitomises traditional British attitudes towards personal development:

> This terrible counselling thing has grown up in Britain. Whatever you do wrong it's somebody else's fault, or your mother hit you. I think that's all balls. It's ghastly political correctness. People need to pull themselves together. I'm not a great believer in blubbing in your tent. I do get melancholy now and again, but you go to bed, sleep well and wake up pawing the ground like a horse in the morning.[2]

Whilst such reactionary views may raise a laugh, they also contributed to the crushing Conservative defeat in the 1997 general election. The landslide Labour victory highlighted a shift of values in which 'caring', 'compassion', 'cooperation' and 'feeling' are paramount. There seems to have been a fundamental transformation of the British people: from a stiff-upper-lipped race keeping feelings firmly under lock and key apart from a discreet tear at weddings (but not funerals), to an emotionally expressive people self-disclosing in public, print and on television. The change was most dramatically illustrated a few months later in the public displays of emotion following the death of Diana, Princess of Wales, and indeed during her life the princess had both expressed and provoked many such displays. Soames was one of the princess's most vociferous critics, describing her as 'mentally unstable' and a 'loose cannon'.[3] Whatever the truth of their respective positions, emotionally-centred values are now in the ascendancy. These changes have not taken place overnight but have been building up from the grass roots for over thirty years.

My argument here is that the phenomenal growth and success of the HPM has been in two opposite directions: spiritualisation and secularisation. On the one hand, the process of integration between psychology and spirituality that began in the 1970s has continued to inspire and provide tools for new developments in psychospirituality. On the other hand, the biggest growth area for psychospirituality has been in business, education, even politics and the armed forces. Although these are quite different strands, one of the most interesting developments is the ever-closer association between the traditionally opposed worlds of religion and business, with both areas taking on each other's values and methods – though not always smoothly or successfully.

The HPM has expanded from margin to mainstream, and become quasi-institutionalised in representative councils and associations such as the Association of Humanistic Psychology (AHP) and hundreds of training organisations; also, less formally, in management training programmes, teacher training, and academic courses.[4] This exemplifies what Weber termed the 'routinisation of charisma'. It also illustrates an important principle of social change that I have described elsewhere (Puttick, 1997a), and will summarise here.

Mainstream society may be seen as a relatively static, stable conglomeration of individuals, groups and institutions that throws up more dynamic, deviant groups on its margins. This margin covers all fields, including politics, science, health, gender, the arts, and religion, and it has a significant role: it may also be the leading edge, whose experiments help create the future. New Religious Movements (NRMs) are examples of marginal groups that have an impact and influence on society beyond the numbers of people involved. Their members have chosen their status actively and consciously. This is partly why social marginality has been discredited as a conversion theory.[5] Particularly in the counterculture, marginality could be a voluntary status, and was celebrated by hippies and others who proudly bore the label of 'freak'. Osho, who as Bhagwan Shree Rajneesh was leader of the most fashionable NRM of the 1970s, elevated marginality into superior status:

> The people who have gathered around me are all misfits in the rotten society. Any intelligent person is bound to be a misfit in a society which is dead, out of date, superstitious, based on belief systems. Only retarded people can be the fit ones . . . All the great names in the history of man were just misfits in their society. To be a misfit is a tremendously valuable quality. (Osho, 1985: 413)

It has been widely noted that NRMs flourish during periods of rapid social change, arising as vehicles of protest, rebellion and challenge. They are responses to change but also agents of transformation. They function as laboratories experimenting with new ideas and practices, often in sealed-off communities, isolated from the norms, conventions and restrictions of society. The more successful experiments are taken up – usually in a more diluted, digestible form – by mainstream society.

The HPM is sometimes seen as a NRM, though this is an overextension of the classification. Firstly, 'Human Potential Movement' is an umbrella term, not always recognised or used by its practitioners, who sometimes used 'growth movement' or no label at all. They have always consisted of loose congeries of individuals, centres and schools of thought, some of whom saw themselves in alliance as the vanguard of a new wave of consciousness, while others disagreed fiercely with each other. Secondly, its origins were secular, providing an alternative, sometimes an adversary, to religion. Its more spiritually-oriented practitioners tended to become Buddhists or join a NRM, in particular the Osho movement. However, on the whole there is enough correspondence among their ideas, values and methods to constitute a cultural movement, best chronicled by John Rowan (1976).

THE ORIGINS OF THE HUMAN POTENTIAL MOVEMENT

The 1960s marked the beginning of a period of rapid social change, and an explosion of rebellious creativity. It also included a millennial dimension aimed at a transformation of the world and of consciousness, which has been termed a 'paradigm shift'.[6] The causes of the shift are complex and multidimensional and can be traced back at least as far as the eighteenth-century Romantic movement. However, the 1960s counterculture seemed both at the time and in retrospect to mark a turning point. This was partly because it followed a period of particularly staid conservatism in the 1950s; partly because, rather than remaining a fringe subculture, it grew to have enormous impact on all aspects of society: politics, social and political activism, the arts, literature, fashion, health, gender, sexuality, and spirituality.[7]

The counterculture arose partly as a rebellion against the materialism and 'technocracy' of the postwar climate. Furthermore, the militarisation of two world wars had encouraged a rigidity and repression that Wilhelm Reich (1968), a radical progenitor of the HPM, called 'character armour', and which he identified as the cause of neurosis, many psychosomatic disorders and sociopolitical problems, including fascism. In this austere climate the Roman virtues of discipline, duty, gravity, firmness, tenacity, hard work and frugality restrained the 'softer' virtues and the spontaneous expression of affection. So the children of the postwar period grew up economically privileged but emotionally and spiritually deprived. A small but influential minority rejected their parents' goals of wealth, success and status in favour of the search for meaning and fulfilment.

The HPM may be seen as the psychospiritual wing of the counterculture. It was largely an outgrowth of humanistic psychology, which was developed by Maslow (1970) as a 'third force' in response to the limitations of psychoanalysis and behaviourism. In contrast, Maslow developed a more optimistic, holistic theory based on mental health rather than pathology, with an emphasis on choice and values, best explicated in his 'hierarchy of needs'.[8] His main contribution was his concept of the 'self-actualised' human being: one who is fully alive and responsive; who has solved the basic survival needs and psychological problems, and is therefore capable of ecstatic 'peak experiences', including mysticism. Maslow thus paved the way for the later spiritualisation of psychotherapy, although the HPM was originally more secular in its aims.

Maslow's theories and methods were adapted and developed into a number of major schools of humanistic psychology and psychotherapy, in particular Carl Rogers's (1980) person-centred counselling, Fritz Perls's gestalt therapy, Eric Berne's Transactional Analysis (TA), and Will Schutz's encounter groups. Their common approach was the exploration of the realms of feelings and relationships, a taboo area in British society at the time. The result was the demystification and destigmatisation of therapy, which was now seen as a path for 'normal neurotics' to explore the full range of human potential. In the 1960s, these techniques were further developed by countercultural 'growth centres', of which the largest and best known is Esalen, founded in California in 1962. Despite some criticisms of the ethics and effectiveness of psychotherapy (Masson, 1989; Hillman & Ventura, 1992), it has grown enormously. In Britain in the 1990s there were over 300 different kinds of counselling and psychotherapy available, over 500 training organisations, tens of thousands of practitioners, and over one hundred thousand clients. In these circumstances it is perhaps not surprising that British culture is undergoing a shift towards 'softer', more 'feminine', emotionally-based values.

THE SPIRITUALISATION OF THE HPM

Despite the tremendous creativity and experimentation in the HPM, it hit a barrier around the early 1970s.[9] There was a widespread feeling that the full potential implied in self-actualisation had not been realised: self-improvement had indeed happened, but not radical transformation. One psychotherapist summarised the mood of the time: 'By now I'd been doing groups for two years very intensively, and I began to feel there was something more. All this looking inside and emoting all these feelings, behind that was something deeper, but I had no idea how to reach it.'[10] Many seekers shared this frustration, which stemmed partly from a limited understanding of the inner quest.

Even within psychology this confusion was apparent, as expressed by a psychologist of religion: 'Self-love is perhaps the most crippling of the cravings from which the person on the contemplative path needs to be liberated' (Thouless, 1971: 123). The antipathy may spring partly from a perceived contradiction between the therapeutic goal of self-actualisation and the Christian ideal of service and sacrifice. It exemplifies a widespread misunderstanding of the nature and purpose of personal development, echoed by social commentators such as Wolfe (1976), Schur (1976) and Lasch (1978), who satirised or castigated the movement for its narcissistic self-indulgence and lack of social conscience. This dualistic dichotomising of self-development and service is emphasised by labelling groups and traditions that incorporate personal development as 'self religions' or 'self-spirituality' (Heelas, 1996), ignoring their own emphasis on the importance of love and service. Just as the two 'wings' of Buddhism (itself a 'self religion' by this definition) are wisdom and compassion, so the basis of humanistic psychology is the understanding that insight, self-love and love for others are inextricably linked and mutually enhancing. This ideological shift is well summarised in a section entitled 'The self-love of the counsellor' taken from the standard textbook for person-centred counsellor training:

The world is full of helpers whose activity is a desperate strategy to avoid confronting themselves. This self-evasion is sometimes mistaken for selflessness and can receive reinforcement from a misguided understanding of the Christian tradition where the concepts of selfishness and self-love have often become hopelessly confused. According to this misunderstanding one's own needs must always be subordinated to the needs of the other and it is considered unhealthy even to reflect unduly on one's own state of being. Once such a way of thinking is allied to a common distrust of introspection, the scene is well set for the kind of helping which is permeated by a dogged sense of martyrdom and further damages the self-respect of the person being helped. For the person-centred counsellor the ability to love herself is, in fact, the cornerstone for her therapeutic practice, and in its absence the usefulness of the helping relationship will be grossly impaired. It is impossible to offer a client acceptance, empathy and genuineness at the deepest level if such responses are withheld from the self. (Mearns & Thorne, 1988: 23)

Yet misidentification of spirituality as self-sacrifice persists, as demonstrated by the following recent book review in a national newspaper. It should be remembered that, at the time of writing, self-development books filled the bestseller lists, while Christian theology was a minority specialist genre.

Wander into the 'spiritual uplift' section (or whatever it's called) of a modern bookshop and amuse yourself at the ridiculous attempts contemporary authors make to help you convince yourself that you are wonderful. Compare with à Kempis: 'The highest and most profitable form of study is to understand one's inmost nature and despise it.' This is why *The Imitation of Christ* has been in print for 500 years, and *I'm OK, You're OK* won't be.[11]

Those who looked deeper perceived HPM ideology as a rebellion against the arid intellectualism of Western philosophy and theology and the aggressive destructiveness of scientific materialism. Turning inwards was partly the result of a widespread disillusion with politics in the aftermath of the Vietnam war and the failure of idealistic political movements to change the world. The ranks of those espousing alternative spirituality today have been swelled by numerous ex-socialists and communists following the fall of the 'Iron Curtain' in the late 1980s. Science had disenchanted and desacralized the world, nature, and the self. On the other hand, the Judaeo-Christian tradition was perceived as either arid, hypocritical, apathetic (particularly Anglicanism) or damaging. Furthermore, Christianity had mainly treated the psyche as a 'forbidden zone', and possessed only a very limited methodology for personal development.

THE INFLUENCE OF EASTERN SPIRITUALITY
ON WESTERN PSYCHOTHERAPY

The appeal of Eastern mysticism to the counterculture has been well documented.[12] Although it may be traced back to the nineteenth century or even earlier, most of its influence on the HPM has been via psychology. Psychologists from Jung onwards have claimed a natural correlation between psychology and Buddhist philosophy. Jung had been very interested in Eastern mysticism and symbolism, though his interpretations have been criticised by both Indians and Westerners.[13] Fromm (1950) and Maslow (1943) made theoretical connections between psychoanalysis and Zen Buddhism, but until the 1970s psychotherapy and meditation were largely perceived as different, mutually exclusive paths. Fitzgerald (1986: 286) argues that it was Alan Watts 'who constructed the intellectual bridge between the therapists and Bhagwan Shree Rajneesh' by interpreting the Eastern mystical traditions as being closer to psychotherapy than to philosophy or religion. He thus influenced many people to travel to India to discover meditation.

The 'Beat Zen' of Allen Ginsberg and other Beat poets in the 1950s and early 1960s had popularised Buddhism in the counterculture, while the Indian gurus of the sixties and seventies offered a praxis of meditation and mysticism. Transcendental Meditation (TM), for example, was an adaptation of these techniques designed for busy Westerners, who could slot it into their daily routine without renouncing material comforts or retiring to a monastery. Other Indian NRMs popular in the West in the early 1970s were ISKCON, the Divine Light Mission (later 'Elan Vital') and Muktananda's Siddha Yoga.

The problem with the teachings of the Indian gurus was that they had no organic connection with Western spiritual and cultural traditions. Psychology had made theoretical connections, but it was within the practical, experiential approach of psychotherapy that a living synthesis between Eastern spirituality and Western psychotherapy was created. Therapists of the HPM were utilising meditation as an adjunct to 'personal growth' and experimenting with it in their groups, particularly at Esalen. One of the first growth centres in Britain was Quaesitor, founded in London in 1970 by Paul and Patricia Lowe. At first their main focus was on psychotherapy, but soon they and their clients began to meditate, and a natural integration started.[14] Clare Soloway (formerly Patricia Lowe) described the process in an interview:

> There isn't a point where therapy ends and transformation begins; it's a continuation. We were laying the groundwork for that at that time. We were

involved with meditation, because it's a process of self-awareness. We were continuously looking for the new, always looking for the next person who would come, and who could shine a light from that angle. We were on the path of searching very consciously. So there wasn't a time when anything began, we were already in that process of finding ourselves very consciously.

In 1972 the Lowes went to India to meet an Indian guru, Bhagwan Shree Rajneesh (later known as Osho), and became initiated as *sannyasins* (disciples). Osho's first Western disciples were drawn from hippies and seekers travelling around India, but the Lowes inspired other key HPM therapists to join. His following then grew very fast from their clientele. Wallis summarises the phenomenon: 'Rajneesh's tantrism overlapped extensively with the principal ideological elements of the Human Potential Movement, but offered something far more, a path to Enlightenment' (1986: 197). By the mid-1970s the Osho movement had become one of the most fashionable and fastest growing NRMs in the West (Puttick, 1997a).

Much of the popularity of the Osho movement was derived from its praxis, based on Osho's own meditations which were themselves partly derived from powerfully cathartic Reichian technique.[15] The rationale for his departure from silent Buddhist sitting meditations such as *vipassana*, was that the former were devised at a time when life and the human mind were much simpler. The complexity and stress of contemporary life, with its frenzied activity and emotional repression, make it hard for Westerners to sit in meditation for long periods. As one Buddhist convert expressed it: 'I've been sitting *zazen* for years and I still don't like it particularly. It makes me mad. I shake, sometimes very violently' (Needleman, 1977: 48). This was a problem described by some of my own respondents who had previously been Buddhists, which was resolved by Osho's 'Dynamic Meditation': an active meditation featuring breathing, but in a chaotic rather than the controlled way typical of Eastern meditations. As breath is perceived to be the bridge between body and soul, so these meditations became a significant bridge between East and West. Osho's HPM therapists greatly expanded his methodology into an innovative programme of psychospiritual development, beginning with body-based, cathartic methods and progressing through encounter-style groups to the more subtle Buddhist meditations:

When Western people come to me, I put them into the groups. That is good for them. They should start with what is easier for them. Then by and by, slowly I change. First they go into cathartic groups like encounter, primal therapy, and then I start putting them into intensive enlightenment, then vipassana. Vipassana is a witnessing. From encounter to vipassana there is a great synthesis. When you move from encounter to vipassana, you are moving from West to East. (Osho, 1977: 170)

In the 1970s the Osho movement was almost alone in its attempt to integrate the techniques of psychotherapy and meditation into a new psychospirituality. Other Eastern traditions and Eastern-based NRMs in the West tended to ignore or disparage psychotherapy, especially in Britain where a deep-seated distrust of psychology has combined with a belief in meditation as a 'higher' path. The Friends of the Western Buddhist Order (FWBO) in particular has been hostile towards the HPM. Subhuti (1988: 33) condemned attraction to Buddhism as therapy on the grounds of its encouragement of 'egocentric self-involvement', proclaiming that 'Buddhism had to be distinguished from therapy'. Yet personal development is seen as fundamental to Buddhism as a spiritual path in the West. Although the ultimate goal of *nirvana* is attained through the extinction of the idea of self (*anatta*), paradoxically the praxis of meditation and other techniques involves a process of self-knowledge and insight that effectively extends the methods of the HPM into spiritual growth.

In America, homeland of the HPM, the two movements – Eastern spirituality and Western psychotherapy – were seen as compatible and mutually enriching. Indeed, the HPM 'gave Buddhists a new language for expressing human problems', introducing key terms such as 'growth', 'openness', and even 'peak experience' as a synonym for *nirvana* in Buddhist terminology (Prebish, 1978: 165). The Buddhist psychologist Jack Kornfield (1989) is probably the best known advocate of this synthesis, arguing that repressed emotions, psychic woundedness and 'unfinished business' can obstruct progress in meditation. This more positive attitude towards the benefits of psychotherapy is now pervading British Buddhism also, and even the FWBO is beginning to recommend it under certain circumstances.

Self-development in Shamanism and Paganism

The main criticism made by philosophers and theologians such as Jacob Needleman (1977) and Harvey Cox (1979) about the 'turn East' was that Eastern traditions were inherently alien to Westerners, who should return to their 'roots' – which they assumed to be the Judaeo-Christian tradition. There are several problems with this essentialist position in a pluralist, multifaith, multicultural society, including the claim of many participants to feel more 'at home' in these movements than in their religion of birth. Nevertheless, in the 1990s there has been a return, not to organised religions, but to 'earth traditions': interpretations of living tribal traditions such as Shamanism, and reconstructions of European Paganism such as Wicca and Druidry.

Political activism has been partly replaced by environmentalism, which has fuelled the growing appeal of nature religions in the West in the 1980s and 1990s. While ecology has been the main influence on the beliefs and values of these movements, their magical praxis and language have been strongly influenced by Jungian psychology and the HPM. These have also influenced the shift away from an emphasis on political power towards personal development in magical ritual. Reciprocally, some shamanic healing techniques have been taken up by psychotherapists, although shamans interpret spirits and the 'non-ordinary reality' in which they are encountered as ontologically more 'real' than the material world, representing the true nature of existence and the cause of events. Psychologists, on the other hand, tend to interpret these experiences as elements of the personal psyche or archetypes. 'Soul retrieval' presents the most significant challenge:

> The ancient practice of soul retrieval and modern psychology potentially have much to offer each other. By restoring lost soul parts, the shaman can give the psychotherapist a whole patient with whom to do psychological work, thus making possible faster and deeper results. (Ingerman, 1991: 40)

In the past, one of the key differences between the New Age and Paganism has been their attitude towards money. While the HPM and New Age have generally been enthusiastically entrepreneurial, Pagans have tended to prefer simple living, 'downshifting' and right livelihood as being more environmentally-friendly. However, Heelas (1996: 90) argues that 'many work and business activities fall into an indeterminate zone where one really does not know whether what is going on is primarily Gaean or primarily commercial'. While the majority of Pagans probably still endorse the former philosophy, there appears to be a more positive attitude towards money as 'energy' with creative potential in some circles. Susan Greenwood argues that 'the magical vision of the development of the self motivated by spirit begs comparison with Weber's conception of the Protestant ethic as a motivational structure of action which is well-suited to capitalism' (1995: 47). There is an increase in workshops and the sale of magical tools to create business success, and 'wealth magic' is an accepted practice for chaos magicians. Such practices link them with New Age prosperity consciousness, which has both influenced and been influenced by business and management training.

HUMAN POTENTIAL VALUES IN THE WORKPLACE

Training, and especially management training, is one of the fastest-growing service industries, extending throughout the public and private sectors into business, the professions and education. Most training is basically technical in character, dealing with issues of day-to-day competency in the workplace, but, increasingly, personnel and management training is probing into the areas of attitudes and feelings known as the 'affective domain'. Educationalists and trainers have long regarded this as the most difficult and contentious form of training, but also know that it can have the greatest rewards in bringing about changes beneficial to the individual and the company (Armstrong, 1991).

These processes have a twofold provenance. They were originally developed in Japanese and American companies, sometimes resulting in spectacular increases in productivity and profitability. Amway, a pyramid selling company, is one of the most dramatic American examples of this philosophy in action – and has been criticised as a cult practising 'mind control' (Bromley, 1991). In Britain, so far such practices are mainly found in companies that are part of multinational corporations, but they are on the increase. On the other hand, some of the ideas and techniques may be traced to the HPM, beginning with Kurt Lewin's T-groups (training groups), developed at MIT (Massachusetts Institute of Technology) in the 1940s (Armstrong, 1991). Despite some criticisms, this approach has been highly influential on management training and has developed into various other methods including sensitivity training, interpersonal skills development and group dynamics. Another major influence has been Eric Berne's Transactional Analysis (TA), and most trainers include TA 'games' in their repertoire. Other important methods and tools imported from the HPM are workshops, roleplay, group exercises, feedback and stress management.

Contemporary organisational restructuring processes often have two levels: financial/practical and ideological – although they tend to be presented jointly to participants as primarily a business model to increase productivity and/or profitability. The ideological aspects are increasingly being rationalised as attempts to agree shared workplace values, including the value of personal and corporate financial growth. (As such, they may be seen as the 1990s face of mercantile idealism and the protestant ethic, repackaged for the contemporary world as the 'Gospel of Prosperity' [Bromley, 1991]).

Despite the HPM's emphasis on personal development extending into spiritual growth, it has usually been largely pro-business and entrepreneurial. For example, many of its practitioners have amassed large personal fortunes and founded successful commercial organisations. This is also often the case with some of the NRMs who become involved in business consultancy and management training, particularly those fitting into the 'world-affirming' category (Wallis, 1984). Some NRMs are directly involved in the workplace as training consultants, either through individual members or the group as a whole, of which the best known is the Forum (formerly *est*; Rupert, 1992). Others include Scientology's subsidiaries WISE and Sterling Management, Programmes Ltd, MSIA's Insight Seminars (whose founder has written a number of self-help bestsellers; John-Roger & McWilliams 1992), Lifespring, and Silva (1993; see Heelas 1999 for an extensive list). Most of these groups were founded for personal development, but often their clientele was drawn from the sales and business world – as were some of their founders, including Werner Erhard (*est*) and John Hanley (Lifespring). This was also the case with neuro linguistic programming (NLP), which achieved respectability via this route (O'Connor & Prior, 1995). Many people who have undergone Werner Erhard's *est* training and other similar trainings have gone on to become business and training consultants.

Most of these trainings do not focus on spirituality directly, even when originating from NRMs, though the values may be implicit. One of the books that best exemplifies the trend is a recent bestseller in the lucrative self-help/business genre, *The Seven Habits of Highly Effective People* by Stephen Covey (1992). It carries seven pages of endorsements by top personal development and business celebrities, from the premier self-help guru M. Scott Peck, to business gurus Tom Peters and Rosabeth Moss Kanter, to chief executive officers of multinational corporations. Yet although he writes mainly about success and self-improvement in professional life, Covey (1992: 319) ends with a personal inspiration note that epitomises HPM spirituality: 'I believe that as human beings, we cannot perfect ourselves. To the degree to which we align ourselves with correct principles, divine endowments will be released within our nature enabling us to fulfill the measure of our creation'. The 'god within' has been secularised – and personal power made divine.

BUSINESS AND SPIRITUALITY

The combination of spirituality and business is one of the most interesting aspects of the apparent secularisation of the HPM. It is most dramatically expressed by the futurist (and former TM leader) Peter Russell: 'My aim is to get all IBM's managers to experience themselves as God' (Heelas, 1999: 51; see also Evans & Russell, 1990). Hundreds of Japanese companies have implemented corporate meditation programmes through the Maharishi Corporate Development International, which has several multinational corporations as clients, as does the Osho movement's Centre for Consciousness in Organizations.

Within the broader New Age there are also many examples of this mutual influence between the spiritual and secular realms. London venues such as the Mind–Body–Spirit Festival, Neal's Yard on the fringes of Covent Garden, and Alternatives at St. James's, Piccadilly, regularly put on talks on prosperity consciousness. Alternatives is moving even further in that direction, with the money workshops of its co-founder William Bloom (1996) and current director Nick Williams and his colleague Steve Nunn. Magazines such as *Human Potential* and *Caduceus* have recently devoted whole issues to the theme. The Scottish New Age community of Findhorn has been interested in these issues for many years, and in 1997 organised an international conference on 'Business for Life'.

Just as HPM-influenced NRMs, New Age groups and individual trainers are affecting business philosophy, so there is a reciprocal trend of business leaders themselves becoming interested in spirituality, and inculcating these values into their organisations. Richard Barrett (1995), an executive of the World Bank, is also founder of the World Bank's Spiritual Unfoldment Society, whose members discuss personal development, meditation and reincarnation. He believes that spirituality can improve the bottom line of companies and even the health of national economies. Most business gurus are American, but the well known British management thinker Charles Handy's (1997) recent book is almost a spiritual self-help manual. Anita Roddick's Body Shops have transformed our attitudes to beauty care; previously seen as epitomising self-indulgent vanity, The Body Shop is now compatible with environmental ethics and Roddick has founded a business school espousing her vision, with spirituality on the syllabus.

Controversies and dangers

As indicated, the ideology of the HPM, and to some extent also of New Age and spiritual ideas, has been quite easily grafted onto the more evangelical business philosophies of the past fifteen years. The aims of each are in some respects consonant but in others opposed, which is causing some confusion and controversy. Some of the confusion is linguistic in origin: terms such as 'empowerment' and 'personal development' have quite different meanings and associations in the counterculture and the enterprise culture. Furthermore, it is sometimes unclear whether the training industry is selling a product or an ideology. More controversially, some of the more confrontational techniques formerly used in Mind Dynamics, Synanon and *est*

(Rupert, 1992) have been provoking criticism in some training programmes. In America some people have successfully sued these organisations and their employers for psychological damage.

Another dimension to this is the relatively high failure rate of many programmes of corporate culture. It has long been recognised that changing culture in a company is very difficult, and in desperation, senior managers are resorting to ever more radical programmes. It should also be noted that the business training market, and the company restructuring market, are both intensely competitive, with numerous consultants jostling for patronage in this very profitable arena. As a result there is a tendency for consultants to try to present their unique process as the most innovative, radical, and hard-hitting option. Psychological and spiritual techniques are seen as 'grist to the mill', to be exploited in the service of corporate change.

These problems were graphically exemplified in a business restructuring programme in which I participated at a multinational publishing corporation, which was later researched by Robin Puttick (Puttick, 1995). It was introduced into the company with no induction preparation or explanation, so that most participants were confused and alienated. The title was 'Vision and Values', but, rather than being created organically from within, the values were imposed top-down without consultation by a management who were perceived as not fully endorsing them. There was no attempt to encourage 'ownership' by staff, which created much resentment and resistance. The staff felt most of the values were either self-evident or contradictory: although the majority were 'soft', they were implanted with 'hard' techniques, and the main thrust of the programme was financial and commercial. There was also no encouragement or time for the reflection that is fundamental to training purportedly based on 'action learning'.[16] As a result, very few people experienced the promised increases in empowerment or personal development. The consultants were sacked after about a year (and an alleged cost of several million dollars) and replaced by another firm.

Whether business, personal development and spirituality can combine as easily and smoothly as some of these experiments would like has yet to be seen. As with NRMs, the combination seems to work most effectively in organisations led by a strong charismatic leader with a clear vision, such as Anita Roddick, although there have been allegations that The Body Shop's business practice does not always live up to its ideals. On the other hand, failure is almost guaranteed when spiritually-oriented restructuring programmes are adopted by organisations whose chief executives do not share or practise these values.

Out of this mass of diverse and sometimes conflicting evidence, one can perhaps discern two trends where business and spiritual ideologies combine effectively. Firstly, the so called 'Gospel of Prosperity' (Bromley, 1991) and its New Age variation 'prosperity consciousness' (Heelas, 1999) support capitalism, sharing its self-centred aggressive expansionism. Secondly, and conversely, the Buddhist and Pagan ethic of recycling and 'right livelihood' correlates with the 'new economics' of sustainable development, based on the work of E.F. Schumacher, author of *Small is Beautiful*, whose writings have been promoted by various organisations and initiatives such as The Other Economic Summit (TOES), the New Economics Foundation, and the Intermediate Technology Development Group. Consumerism is still rampant in the 1990s, but as the public and policy-makers become more aware of the limits of growth, the ethic of consumption may be replaced by one of personal development and ecospirituality.[17] There is a growing grassroots trend towards these values, exemplified by the numbers choosing to reject the rat-race and the corporate treadmill in favour of 'downshifting' (Ghazi & Jones, 1997).

In the meantime, the Findhorn community is not planning a follow-up to its Business for Life conference. The organiser informed me: 'Unless the world of business accepts a spiritual reality behind its *modus operandi*, I believe we have no chance of shifting the consciousness of humanity into the Aquarian age.' Hence it is yet to be seen whether the ancient duality between world and spirit will prevail, perhaps even deepen, or whether a more holistic synthesis between these values – the secular and the spiritual – will emerge on a global scale.

NOTES

1. *Bertrand Russell: The Spirit of Solitude* by Ray Monk (London: Cape, 1996).
2. Interview with Lynda Lee-Potter, *Daily Mail*, 25.5.96.
3. Soames's remarks were made on television following the 1994 'Panorama' television documentary comprising a frankly self-revealing interview with the Princess of Wales.
4. Most corporate management training programmes, particularly personnel training, and university business schools that I have heard of or come across, display clear influences.
5. Sociology and psychology have tended in the past to explain the appeal of NRMs in terms of social marginality or deprivation, but research on more recent movements has tended to find that people join movements that directly affirm their personal values, e.g. Wallis (1979); Stark & Bainbridge (1985).
6. The term was invented by the historian and philosopher of science Thomas Kuhn in 1962, and popularised by various New Age writers, particularly Marilyn Ferguson (1989). 'New Paradigm' is also sometimes used by the more intellectual wing of this movement in distinction from what they see as the 'flakier' New Age end.

7. See Campbell (1999); Hutton (1998), for the influence of Romanticism, respectively on the New Age and Paganism. For more detailed accounts of the counterculture see Roszak (1968); Bellah (1970); Wuthnow (1976); Glock & Bellah (1976); Mullan (1983); Ferguson (1989).

8. I have argued elsewhere (Puttick, 1997b) that Maslow's hierarchy of needs can be adapted and applied to religion, particularly NRMs, to explain spiritual choice. Needs and values are the key factors determining why people join an NRM and which movement they choose.

9. Peter Berger (1974: 186) saw this as an inherent problem of modern social life: 'The paradox of techniques . . . applied to the attainment of nonfunctional relations with other people points to the inherent difficulty of the de-modernizing impulse: one wants to be sensitive to others in the manner of a poet, and one is trained for what purports to be such sensitivity in situations that are planned and manipulated in ready-made packages.'

10. This and all following unattributed quotations are taken from interviews with members of the Osho movement that I conducted as part of my doctoral research in 1991–3.

11. Review by Nicholas Lezard in the *Guardian* 9.2.96.

12. See for example Bellah (1970); Wuthnow (1976); Glock & Bellah (1976); Needleman (1977); Cox (1979); Ellwood (1979); Tipton (1982).

13. Koestler (1960) has noted that Jung has no following in India and is disliked for his perceived misinterpretations of Indian religion and philosophy. Jones (1979) shows how they were based on unqualified, unproven assumptions of correlations between Western psychology and Eastern religion.

14. The appeal of meditation was partly an outcome of mystical experiences induced by psychotropic drugs, partly a direct interest in Indian and other Asian mystical traditions as more and more proto-seekers travelled to these countries. See Puttick (1997), for a fuller discussion.

15. Wilhelm Reich was the most significant pioneer in body-based psychotherapy, partly for his discovery of the fundamental role of the breath in breaking down 'character armour'. He believed that 'the inhibition of respiration was *the* physiological mechanism of the suppression and repression of emotion, and consquently *the basic mechanism of the neurosis* in general' (Reich, 1968: 297). Reichian theory was the main influence on Osho's Dynamic meditation and other active meditations, and a key element in Rajneesh therapy.

16. 'Action learning' is generally considered the most effective management training programme with its emphasis on initiating change through real, work-based experiences and problems, and its focus on personal learning, reflection, analysis, and team-building. The most widely used book on the subject is *Action Learning* by Krystyna Weinstein (London: HarperCollins, 1995).

17. Ecospirituality, *aka* deep ecology, is a widely used term referring to the spiritual wing of the environmental movement. It is often used by Pagans and members of other nature religions, as well as non-affiliated spiritual seekers.

BIBLIOGRAPHY

Armstrong, M., 1991: *A Handbook of Personnel Management Practice*, 4th edn (London: Kogan Page).

Barrett, Richard, 1995: *A Guide to Liberating Your Soul* (Alexandria, VA: Unfoldment).

Bellah, Robert, 1970: *Beyond Belief* (New York: Harper & Row).

Berger, Peter & Kellner, Hansfried, 1974: *The Homeless Mind* (Harmondsworth: Penguin).

Bloom, William, 1996: *Money, Heart and Mind* (London: Viking/Penguin).

Bromley, David, 1991: 'Quasi-religious Corporations', unpublished paper presented at the conference on 'Religion and the Resurgence of Capitalism', University of Lancaster, July 1991.

Campbell, Colin, 1999: 'The Easternization of the West', in Wilson, B., ed., *New Religious Movements: Challenge and Response* (London: Routledge), pp. 35–48.

Claxton, Guy, 1981: *Wholly Human* (London: RKP).

Covey, Stephen, 1992: *The Seven Habits of Highly Successful People* (London: Simon & Schuster).

Cox, Harvey, 1979: *Turning East* (London: Allen Lane).

Ellwood, Robert, 1979: *Alternative Altars* (Chicago: University of Chicago Press).

Evans, Roger & Russell, Peter, 1989: *The Creative Manager* (London: Unwin).

Ferguson, Marilyn, 1989: *The Aquarian Conspiracy* (London: Paladin).

Fitzgerald, Frances, 1986: *Cities on a Hill* (New York: Simon & Schuster).

Fromm, Erich, 1950: *Psychoanalysis and Religion* (New Haven: Yale University Press).

Ghazi, Polly & Jones, Judy, 1997: *Getting a Life: the Downshifter's Guide to Happier, Simpler Living* (London: Hodder & Stoughton).

Glock, Charles & Bellah, Robert, 1976: *The New Religious Consciousness* (Berkeley: University of California Press).

Goleman, Daniel, 1996: *Emotional Intelligence* (London: Bloomsbury).

Greenwood, Susan, 1995: 'Wake the Flame Inside Us: Magic, healing and the enterprise culture in contemporary Britain', *Etnofoor* 8 (1): 47–62.

Handy, Charles, 1997: *The Hungry Spirit* (London: Hutchinson).

Heelas, Paul, 1996: *The New Age Movement* (Oxford: Blackwell).

—— 1999: 'Prosperity and the New Age Movement', in Wilson, B., ed., *New Religious Movements: Challenge and Response* (London: Routledge), pp. 51–77.

Hillman, James & Ventura, Michael, 1992: *We've had 100 Years of Psychotherapy and the World's Getting Worse* (San Francisco: HarperSanFrancisco).

Hutton, Ronald, 1998: 'The Discovery of the Modern Goddess', in Pearson, J., Roberts, R. & Samuel, G., eds, *Nature Religion Today* (Edinburgh: Edinburgh University Press).

Ingerman, Sandra, 1991: *Soul Retrieval* (San Francisco: HarperSanFrancisco).

John-Roger & McWilliams, Peter, 1992: *Do It!* (London: Thorsons).

Jones, R. H., 1979: 'Jung and Eastern religious traditions', *Religion* 9(2): 141–56.

Koestler, Arthur, 1960: *The Lotus and the Robot* (London: Hutchinson).

Kornfield, Jack, 1989: 'Even the Best Meditators Have Wounds to Heal,' *Yoga Journal*.

Lasch, Christopher, 1978: *The Culture of Narcissism* (New York: W. Norton).

Maslow, Abraham, 1943: 'A Theory of Human Motivation', *Psychological Review* 50: 370–96.

Maslow, Abraham, 1970: *Religions, Values and Peak Experiences* (Harmondsworth: Penguin).

Masson, Jeffrey, 1989: *Against Therapy* (London: Fontana).

Mearns, Dave and Thorne, Brian, 1988: *Person-centred Counselling in Action* (London: Sage).

Mullan, Bob, 1983: *Life as Laughter* (London: Routledge).

Murphy, Michael, 1993: *The Future of the Body* (Los Angeles: Tarcher).

Needleman, Jacob, 1977: *The New Religions*, second edn, (New York: Doubleday).

O'Connor, Joseph & Prior, Robin, 1995: *Successful Selling with NLP* (London: Thorsons).

Osho, 1977: *The Tantra Vision*, vol. 1 (Poona: Rajneesh Foundation).

Osho, 1985: *From the False to the True* (Cologne: Rebel Press).

Prebish, Charles, 1978: 'Reflections on the transmission of Buddhism to America', in Needleman, J. & Baker, G. (eds), *Understanding the New Religions* (New York: Seabury), pp. 153–72.

Puttick, Elizabeth, 1997a: *Women in New Religions* (London: Macmillan).

—— (1997b): 'A New Typology of Religion Based on Needs and Values', *Journal of Beliefs and Values* 18(2): 133–45.

Puttick, Robin, 1995: 'Vision and Values: A programme of corporate transformation in a book publishing house', unpublished M.Ed thesis, University of Sheffield.

Reich, Wilhelm, 1968: *The Function of the Orgasm* (London: Granada).

Rogers, Carl, 1980: *A Way of Being* (Boston: Houghton Mifflin).

Roszak, Theodore, 1968: *The Making of a Counter Culture* (London: Faber).

Rowan, John, 1976: *Ordinary Ecstasy* (London: RKP).

Rupert, Glenn, 1992: 'Employing the New Age: Training Seminars', in Lewis, J. & Gordon Melton, J. (eds), *Perspectives on the New Age* (New York: SUNY Press) pp. 127–35.

Schur, Edwin, 1976: *The Awareness Trap* (New York: Quadrangle).

Silva, J., 1993: *The Silva Mind Control Method* (London: HarperCollins).

Stark, Rodney & Bainbridge, William, 1985: *The Future of Religion* (Berkeley: University of California Press).

Subhuti, 1988: *Buddhism for Today* (Glasgow: Windhorse Publications).

Thouless, Robert, 1971 *An Introduction to the Psychology of Religion* (Cambridge: Cambridge University Press).

Tipton, Steven, 1982: *Getting Saved from the Sixties* (Berkeley: University of California Press).

Wallis, Roy, 1979: *Salvation and Protest: Studies of Social and Religious Movements* (London: Pinter).

—— 1984: *The Elementary Forms of the New Religious Life* (London: Routledge).

—— 1986: 'Religion as fun?' in Wallis, R. & Bruce, S., eds, *Sociological Theory, Religion and Collective Action* (Belfast: Queen's University Press).

Wolfe, Tom, 1976: 'The Me Decade and the Third Great Awakening', in *Mauve Gloves and Madmen* (New York: Farrar, Straus & Giroux).

Wuthnow, Robert, 1976: *The Consciousness Reformation* (Berkeley: University of California Press).

13

The New Age and Secularisation
Steve Bruce

INTRODUCTION

The purpose of this essay is to locate New Age spirituality in the general context of changes in the nature of religious belief and behaviour in modern societies (by which I mean specifically the industrial democracies of western and northern Europe, North America and Australia and New Zealand), and to consider its likely impact.

I will begin with some quotations which exemplify the start and finish of the process of social mutation which has brought us to the New Age. All concern the nature of truth and authority and the social relationships that are associated with divergent attitudes to the status of what the speaker takes to be the divine truth. The first is from Bishop Augustine of Hippo:

> There is an unjust persecution which the ungodly operate against the Church of Christ; and a just persecution which the Churches of Christ make use of towards the ungodly . . . The Church persecutes out of love, the ungodly out of cruelty. (cited in Kamen, 1967: 14)

As a dissenter from the orthodoxy of his time one might have expected the sixteenth-century reformer Martin Luther to take a more charitable view of diversity, but he heavily constrained his claims for freedom of conscience which, he argued: 'cannot be absolute freedom because no one can be free from the obligations of truth' (Kamen, 1967: 30).

My third quotation is from a statement written by Tissington Tatlow for the British Student Christian Movement (SCM) in 1910. For a decade, Tatlow, a young evangelical episcopalian, had been working to extend the student movement's support beyond its original evangelical base. He and other activists had frequently been challenged on the doctrinal soundness of the endeavour by suspicious Church of England bishops. The following statement of the 'interdenominational' position (consciously contrasted with an 'un-denominational' position) became the foundation of the 1910 World Missionary Conference in Edinburgh and was the credo on which the entire ecumenical movement was to develop. Tatlow described the SCM as follows:

> The Student Christian Movement is interdenominational in that while it unites persons of different religious denominations in a single organisation for certain definite aims and activities, it recognises their allegiance to any of the various Christian Bodies into which the Body of Christ is divided. It believes that loyalty to their own denomination is the first duty of Christian students and welcomes them into the fellowship of the Movement as those whose privilege it is to bring into it, as their contribution, all that they as members of their own religious body have discovered or will discover of Christian truth. (Tatlow, 1933: 400)

The statement cleverly avoided determining just which bodies were 'Christian' and thus allowed the gradual expansion of what would be accepted as being in some sense valid. What it also contained was the first hint of relativism. At the heart of Tatlow's draft was the notion that in the dark cloud of apparent contradiction could be found the silver lining of fundamental unity. Where previously, in what was known as 'un-denominational' work, co-operation required that differences be tactfully overlooked, now they were to be celebrated while the law of non-contradiction was suspended. Where the Bishop of Hippo would persecute those who differed with him, the bishops of the major Christian churches that formed the ecumenical movement would eventually endorse everything from high Catholicism through the evangelicalism of the Salvation Army to the pantheism of American native religion.

The fourth quotation comes from Sir George Trevelyan, doyen of British New Age spirituality, who concluded one account of his beliefs with the words: 'This is what things look like to me. If it doesn't seem like that to you, you don't have to accept what I say. Only accept what rings true to your own Inner Self' (in Greer, 1995: 159).

A VOCABULARY AND TRAJECTORY

In order that we have a consistent set of terms in which to discuss changes in religion, I want to introduce a typology developed by Roy Wallis.

Wallis believes that most of the important differences in how people organise their religious lives can be identified if we look at just two questions: (a) Does the religion see itself as having a unique grasp of salvational knowledge? (b) Is the religion seen by others as respectable or deviant?

Table 13.1: A Typology of Ideological Organisations

Internal Conception	External Conception	
	Respectable	**Deviant**
Uniquely Legitimate	Church	Sect
Pluralistically Legitimate	Denomination	Cult

Source: Wallis (1976: 13)

Members of the Exclusive Brethren believe that their organisation offers the only way to God. Hence they try to persuade people to join their uniquely legitimate organisation. The Christian Church of the Middle Ages took a similar view. But there is considerable difference in the popularity, acceptability and prestige of the Christian Church in the Middle Ages and the Exclusive Brethren: the former was a 'church' while the latter is a 'sect'.

What unites the denomination and the cult is that they do not claim a unique possession of the truth. They think they have something valuable to offer, but they recognise many other organisations as being every bit as valid. They think of themselves in the terms of Tatlow's interdenominational basis for the ecumenical movement. Similarly, the vast majority of purveyors of cultic wisdom and esoteric practice do not claim the monogamous commitment of their followers. Indeed, the relationship between purveyor and consumer is so loose that terms such as 'member', 'adherent' and 'follower' are usually inappropriate in the cultic milieu. Cults see themselves as simply one of many guides on the single but very broad road to enlightenment.

Again, what separates them is 'external conception': the extent to which they have succeeded in establishing themselves in their society. Denominations are a respectable part of our social and cultural landscape; cults are not.

The point of introducing these distinctions is to offer a very simple way of describing the major changes in the religious climate of the western world so that we can understand why New Age spirituality takes the form that it does, why it has become popular now and why its cultural consequences are likely to be constrained. We can observe the possibility and popularity of the four forms of religion in different sorts of society. I am not suggesting that sects were unknown prior to the Reformation, and that denominations and cults were unknown prior to the last quarter of the nineteenth century. Even within the massive consensus of the Holy Roman Empire one had Christian humanists (such as Erasmus) who searched for common values to unite the range of religious expression they confronted. However, I am suggesting that there is a crucial difference in the number, size and popularity of the exemplars of the various forms. Church is characteristic of the pre-modern world church; church and sect of the early modern; sect and denomination of the modern; and the cult is characteristic of the late modern period.

The key to the shift between these four forms is *modernisation*, by which I mean the historically and geographically specific package of major social, political and economic changes that came with economic growth, urbanisation and industrialisation in western Europe, and the form of consciousness associated with those changes (see Berger, Berger and Kellner, 1974). I am not at this point making any universal claims or offering observations about societies that have more recently been affected by some of those changes. The extent to which the patterns may be repeated will depend on the extent to which new circumstances match the old. Naturally, what follows can only be the briefest of sketches (but see Wilson, 1982, and Bruce, 1996).

FROM CHURCH TO DENOMINATION

Modernisation makes the church form of religion impossible. The church requires either cultural homogeneity or an elite sufficiently powerful to disregard diversity. Societies expand to encompass ever larger numbers of religious, ethnic and linguistic groups, and improved communication brings increased knowledge of that diversity. Modernisation also undermines the hierarchical and rigid social structures which permit the maintenance of monocultures. What at first sight might appear to be two countervailing tendencies combine to encourage and legitimate diversity.

First, as Durkheim notes in his distinction between mechanical and organic solidarity, the increased division of labour and growth of economies creates ever greater social diversity and social distance (Durkheim, 1964). The feudal estate and closed village became the town and the city. The medieval old town of Edinburgh, where people of very different 'stations' lived on different floors of the same tenement and threw their excrement into the same street, was superseded by the New Town, inhabited by the bourgeoisie and their servants, separated from the trades and the factories. Increasingly, differing social circumstances created increasingly divergent cultures, which in turn created religious diversity. Different social groups re-worked the dominant religious tradition in ways that made sense from their position in the world.

At the same time, as Gellner in his theory of nationalism persuasively argues, modernisation produced a basic egalitarianism (Gellner, 1983). A division of labour need not undermine a hierarchical society (the caste system of India is profoundly hierarchical and the castes are defined by their occupations) but economic development also brought change and the expectation of further change. And it brought occupational mobility. People no longer followed the traditional family pattern of employment. Occupational mobility made it hard for people to internalise visions of themselves that suppose permanent inferiority. People cannot simultaneously strive to improve themselves and their class position while thinking of themselves as fixed in a station or a degree or a caste in an unchanging hierarchical world. Modern societies are thus inherently egalitarian.

Economic expansion increased contact with strangers. Profound inequalities of status are tolerable and can work well when the ranking system is well known and widely accepted as legitimate. Soldiers can move from one regiment to another and still know their place because there is a uniform ranking system and rank is displayed through the wearing of uniform. Economic innovation and expansion mean constant change in the nature of occupations and increased mobility, both of which in their different ways mean that we have trouble placing people. There is no way of ensuring that we know whether we are superior or subordinate to this or that new person.

The separation of work and home, of the public and the private, further makes for equality. 'Serf' and 'peasant' were not job descriptions; they were all-enveloping social, legal and political statuses. One cannot be a serf during working hours and an autonomous individual for the evening and at weekends. A temporary work-role is not a full identity and though work-roles may be ranked in a hierarchy, they can no longer structure the whole world view. In the absence of a shared belief system which would sanction inequality and subjection (and the decline of religion usually removes that), egalitarianism becomes the default position.

The precondition of employability, dignity, full moral citizenship and an acceptable social identity is a certain level of education, which must include literacy – and literacy in a single language common throughout the economy. Once this was recognised, socialisation became standardised and placed in the hands of a central agency which was not a family, clan or guild but a society-wide education system. It required a single cultural and linguistic medium through which people could be instructed.

Gellner is, of course, not saying that in modern societies everyone is equal. His point is that the profound and fixed division of rights one finds in traditional and feudal societies is incompatible with economic development. Modernisation and the development of the capitalist economy require the end of the old world.

The fundamental egalitarianism that came with modernisation meant that, at the political level, the costs of coercing religious conformity were no longer acceptable: the state was no longer willing to accept the price in social conflict, and it adopted a position of neutrality on the competing claims of various religious bodies. In some settings, the neutrality was explicit (as in the United States Constitution); in others, it was implicit (as in the 'fudge' by which the established Churches of England and Scotland were left with notional advantages over their competitors but no real privileges). At the level of individual consciousness, it made it ever more difficult (though, of course, still possible) to dismiss religious views which were at odds with one's own as being of entirely no account.

FROM SECT TO DENOMINATION

In some countries, where the Lutheran influence predominated, the religious upheavals of the Reformation were largely contained within the church form. In others, religious dissent, accelerated by the social changes of the early modern period, created a profusion of sects, most of which initially tried to establish themselves as 'the church'. It was only after failing to achieve power, either through becoming the majority religion or effecting a minority coup, that many of them discovered the principle of toleration and evolved into denominations (Bruce and Wright, 1995).

At the same time as external relations with other religious organisations and with the state were giving the sect good reason to moderate its claims, there were a variety of internal pressures in the same direction, which are summarised in the well-known Niebuhr thesis (1962). For millenarian sects, the failure of the world to end is one problem that must be faced. For almost all sects the status of the children of sect members calls into question the initial hard demarcation between the saved and the unregenerate. It was hard for sectarians to suppose that their children, who had been raised in the faith, were the same as the children of outsiders. Gradually the strict membership tests were relaxed. Survival for any length of time brought assets (buildings, publishing houses and capital) which required to be managed. The creation of a bureaucratic structure in turn brought officials whose interests were to varying degrees at odds with the original radical impetus of the sect. The asceticism of the sect often resulted in upward social mobility. Even if there was no independent 'Protestant ethic' effect, most sects endured in circumstances of general economic growth. Increasing prosperity meant that the sacrifices inherent in asceticism grew proportionately ever larger. When coupled with the lower levels of commitment found among those generations which had inherited their sectarianism rather than acquired it through choice, the result was a gradual relaxation of Puritanism and a gradual accommodation to the ways of the world.

There is nothing inevitable about this; Wilson (1990, 1993) explores a variety of ways in which certain sects have avoided the erosion of their initial radical sectarianism. To give just one example, the moderating effects of increased prosperity can be blunted if, as is the case with the Seventh Day Adventists, that prosperity is channelled and controlled by the sect itself and can thus serve as a device for maintaining commitment (Bull and Lockhart, 1989). But we cannot look at the sect's deployment of commitment mechanisms in isolation from the sect's surrounding environment. The sectarian form of religion is demanding and disruptive because it challenges other belief systems and modes of behaviour (religious and secular). To the extent that a nation-state or a society is prepared to allow its people social space in which to create their own subcultures, the sect form can prosper (as one sees with fundamentalism in America). However, the distance between a sect's beliefs and those of most people in the modern world is so great that few outsiders will be attracted and its success will depend on socialising its children in the faith.

That the sectarian form of religion is demanding of its members and requires a social structure loose enough to allow effective subcultures means that its influence in the modern world is limited. The fact that the mass media frequently print or broadcast scare stories about the growth of fundamentalism (often inspired by a failure to appreciate that Iran is very unlike Britain or America) does not disprove this. It is evidence of the failure of commentators to appreciate that the numerical decline of the denominational form of religion leaves the sectarians as an ever greater part of the ever smaller number of believers.

THE CULTIC MILIEU OF THE NEW AGE

Thus far in what must be a massively simplified view of the history of religion in the West, we have seen the church form faced first with competition from the sect and then both churches and sects tending to become denominations. But where does the cult come into this account? First with the New Religious Movements of the 1960s and 1970s and then with the New Age of the 1980s, we have seen a flowering of alternative religions. Some, such as Transcendental Meditation and Rajneeshism, are re-workings for the western mind of traditional eastern religions; others, Scientology for example, are spiritualised versions of lay psychotherapies. In comparison with the popularity of the Christian denominations and sects, the cultic form of religion remains very much the minority case. However, it is, I would argue, emblematic. Other contributions to this volume discuss various New Age beliefs and therapies in detail. What I aim to do here is sketch the major themes of the milieu (Heelas, 1996).

First, there is the belief that the self is divine. Christianity always assumed a division between God the Creator and the people he created. More than that, it assumed that people were basically bad. They only became good by subjecting themselves to God's will and God's commandments. Religion was about controlling the self and shaping it into a valuable object. The New Age does not espouse that division of God and his creation. Instead it supposes that we have within us the essence of holiness. The human self is essentially good. If it is bad, that is a result of our environment and circumstances. The aim of many New Age belief systems and therapies is to strip away the accumulated residues of our bad experiences and free our human potential. The point of the spiritual journey is to free the God within, to get in touch with our true centre.

Second, New Agers are holistic. They have borrowed from Hinduism and Buddhism the idea that everything – ourselves, the material world, the supernatural world – is really just one single essence. This gives many New Agers a keen interest in, and a new slant on, environmentalism. We should protect the material world from ruthless exploitation, not just for our own future good, but also because the planet is a spiritual being. Hence many New Agers are vegetarians and many are interested in holistic approaches to physical and psychological 'healing'.

Third, as the Trevelyan quotation at the start illustrates, in the New Age there is no authority higher than the individual self. Of course we can learn by reading books and listening to great teachers, but the final arbiter of truth is the individual. If something works for you, then that is the truth. Personal utility is the final test.

This in turn brings in the fourth characteristic: eclecticism. As we differ in class, in gender, in age, in regional background, in culture, we will all have different notions of what works for us. The New Age milieu offers an enormous cafeteria of cultural products from which consumers can select. A simple way of illustrating the range of what is on offer is to consider the subjects covered in a very popular series of books called 'The Elements of . . .' The nouns that follow that opening phrase include: Alchemy, Astronomy, Buddhism, Christian Symbolism, Creation Myth, Crystal Healing, Dreamwork, Earth Mysteries, Feng Shui, Herbalism, Human Potential, Meditation, Mysticism, Natural Magic, Pendulum Dowsing, Prophecy, Psychosynthesis, Shamanism, Sufism, Taoism, Aborigine Tradition, Chakras, Goddess Myths, the Grail Tradition, Qabalah, Visualisation and Zen.

Even many of the new religious movements of the 1970s such as Scientology and Transcendental Meditation, whose cadres privately believe that they have the truth and everyone else is plain wrong, have been forced by market pressures to accept the eclecticism of the New Age milieu. Instead of recruiting loyal followers, they market their services to people who will take some courses, attend some events, and then move on to some other revelation or therapy. It is worth adding that, unlike the movement of conservative Protestants within sects, New Age sampling is not usually driven by dissatisfaction. People are as likely to move on because they feel they have acquired the benefits of this particular practice or insight as because they feel let down. Or to put it another way, consumers maximise benefits by compositing elements into their own best fit, rather than by searching for the one perfect match.

Eclecticism requires an appropriate epistemology. In practice, New Agers are relativists. Many simply sample a range of ideologies and therapies without noticing incompatible assumptions and truth-claims. If forced to attend to paradoxes they can assert Trevelyan's credo and find a philosophical reconciliation in the perennialist notion of a 'fundamental' unity behind apparent diversity.

A final central feature of New Age spirituality is its focus of attention or manifest purpose. All the major world religions have claimed that if we follow their teachings we will be happier and healthier people, but those therapeutic benefits have generally been secondary or latent. The medieval Christian followed the instructions of the Church because that is what God required. While one hoped for a good life, it was always possible that God's inscrutable providence destined otherwise. In this scheme of things, suffering was accepted and could be given spiritual significance. In much New Age spirituality, therapy is the manifest, not the latent function. Insights and practices are marketed as ways to feel better, to get the better job, to improve your marriage.

CHANGES IN THE CHURCHES

My reason for supposing that the New Age is sociologically significant is that many of the characteristics just listed can be found in a minor key in the mainstream churches. The twentieth century has seen an increasingly positive evaluation of the human self and a corresponding decline in the notion of God the all-powerful creator. The idea that most people are going to hell has completely disappeared. Indeed, hell itself has vanished from all but the smallest and most conservative Protestant sects. The modern Christian self may not yet be divine but it is a pretty splendid thing.

Modern Christians are reluctant to accept authority; they no longer do what their churches tell them to do. British Catholics may admire the Pope but they do not follow his instructions on abortion, contraception or divorce. The therapeutic emphasis on benefits in this world is increasingly evident in all the churches.

These changes are not specific to Britain. In a general summary of the religious life of Americans, Wade Clark Roof said: 'The religious stance today is more internal than external, more individual than institutional, more experiential than cerebral, more private than public' (Roof, 1996: 153). Hammond makes the same point when he talks of a 'shift in the meaning of the church from that of a collective–expressive agency to that of an individual–expressive agency' (Hammond, 1992: 169). Writing about religion in the West generally, Wilson said: 'Despite the persistence of external church structures, the privatization of religion and the demand for contemporary this-worldly salvation can be seen powerfully in Charismatic renewal, in the house church movement, and in the new concern with healing and the enhancement of personal competence' (Wilson, 1988: 204).

That one finds resonances of the dominant assumptions of the New Age in the Christian churches, which one might have supposed to be relatively resistant to such ideological innovation, suggests that the New Age is not an accident. There is something about the cultic form of religion that makes it particularly well suited to late capitalism.

SOCIAL FUNCTIONS OF THE NEW AGE

One of the major virtues of the epistemology of the New Age is that it solves the problem of cultural pluralism. If everyone believes the same thing and sees the world the same way, then it is possible for a society to believe that there is one God, one truth, one way of being in the world. However, when that single culture fragments into a whole series of competing visions, you have the possibility of endless argument and conflict. One resolution is to change the basic idea of knowledge so that we become relativists. We suppose that there is no longer one single truth, one single way to God but a whole variety of equally good ways. We shift in effect to a perennialist view of reality which supposes that behind all the apparent diversity there is a single essence.

Relativism also accords well with our increasing self-assertiveness in that it allows a thoroughly democratic attitude to knowledge. We can picture the 'new science' and 'new medicine' of the New Age as the third stage in a progressive rejection of authority. Once culture was defined by experts. Now we accept the freedom of personal taste: 'I may not know much about art but I know what I like'. In the late 1960s claims for personal autonomy moved to a second stage of matters of personal behaviour: 'I may not know much about ethics and morals but I know what I like to do and claim my right to do it'. In the third stage we now find the same attitude applied to areas of expert knowledge: 'I may not know much about the nervous system but I know what I like to believe in and I believe in chakras and Shiatsu massage and acupuncture'.

But such individualism would bring social conflict if it was framed within the traditional notion that there is one true version of reality. The solution is relativism. Though the term 'hermeneutic' is still foreign to most people, the general notion that different sorts of people will see the world in different ways has become deeply embedded in our culture. As a sign of just how far we have moved from the confidence in our ability, by rational inspection, to discover the truth, let me quote from the essay of a good final year sociology student who concluded a discussion of the problems of source bias by saying: 'In an ideal world there would always be a balance of sources to present everyone's view'. She did not write: 'In an ideal world we would research our way past bias to the truth'. The best we can hope for now is equality of opportunity to assert our preferences.

There is no space here to fully explain the rise of relativism but I suspect that our increasing unwillingness to accept the authority of professionals and experts is part of a general decline, not in class differences, but in the deference that used to accompany them. In the early 1960s sociologists used to distinguish professions from other occupations by accepting at face value the claim made by professionals that they were motivated not by a desire for money and power but by a commitment to serve fundamental social values. Professional autonomy (including the power to maintain lucrative closed shops) was defended as essential to preserving some social good (such as justice or health). Sociologists are now much more sceptical. More to the point, so is the general public, which readily assumes that people are self-interested and finds altruism implausible. The assumption that most of us have motives baser than the ones we assert is accompanied by an implicit epistemological premise. People's perceptions will be influenced by their backgrounds. Hence objective or authoritative descriptions of the world are not possible; hence there can only be partial understandings.

Claims to professional expertise have also been undermined by the growth of the natural sciences. When scientific knowledge was not extensive and relatively undifferentiated, social respect for those who carried it was common. The 'professor', the man in the white coat who saved the planet from space invaders in those early 1950s science fiction films, was just a 'scientist'. Now biology, physics and chemistry are subdivided into hundreds of highly specialised fields. The number of practitioners has vastly expanded and their social status has been reduced. What is now done by scientists is too esoteric for us to understand, let alone admire, while those who do it are too numerous and too ordinary to command respect.

The mass media have played an important part in devaluing the status of science. As has become very obvious in the reporting of such health scares as the BSE story or the outbreak of *E. coli* food poisoning, journalists are simply not equipped to evaluate competing positions and so reporting very easily slips into the conventional confrontational mode of aiming for balance rather than accuracy.

A further explanation for the decline in deference to experts is the increased level of education of the general population. In 1900 there were 25,000 people in full-time higher education in Great Britain (Halsey, 1972: 206). In 1991 there were 400,000, in itself a doubling of the number for 1970 (Church, 1994: 47). Whether the expansion of higher education means that we are really better educated than our grandparents is neither here nor there. What is important is that more of us are at least superficially closer in status to the experts than was previously the case.

These observations deserve to be explored further, but it is enough to note here that the high place accorded to the self in the New Age fits well with the class background of most New Agers. The principal denizens of the New Age milieu are graduates. Or the point can be reversed. We can ask why it is that the unemployed and the poorly paid, who would most benefit from increased mastery over their fate, are least likely to be interested in New Age techniques for empowerment. One might suppose the costs of many programmes would be prohibitive until one compares them to the costs of smoking, drinking alcohol, taking drugs, or attending major football matches. A more fruitful line of explanation is to be found in ideas about self-confidence and cultural capital. A basic requirement for an active interest in 'new science' or 'new medicine' is the belief that one is intellectually on a par with the experts in the old science and old medicine.

A final point to be made here is that the assumptions of the New Age fit well with a society which is short on authority and long on consumer rights. In the free market for consumer durables, the autonomous individual maximises his or her returns by exercising free choice. In the free market for ideas, the individual New Ager maximises his or her returns by exercising free choice and synthesising his or her best combination of preferences.

IMPACT

New Age spirituality may be better suited to late capitalism than more traditional forms of religion, but this does not guarantee that it will sweep all before it. In any consideration of the New Age we need to begin with a realistic assessment of its popularity. At first sight the growth of the New Age is impressive. The first Festival of Mind–Body–Spirit in 1977 was a one-day event; the 1993 version lasted ten days. In most bookshops the occult is now given more space than Christian titles. Popular magazines carry articles on Feng Shui, spiritual healing and Shiatsu. New Age publishers proliferate and, a good sign of the strength of the market, most of the major commercial publishers now have a 'Mind–Body–Spirit' imprint.

It would be easy to take all this endeavour as proof that interest in the supernatural is a constant; that we have mistaken for secularisation what is merely a change in the mode of expression of that interest. It would be easy but wrong.

First, we need to get the numbers in proportion. Thousands of people attend the Festival of Mind–Body–Spirit, but then it is an annual showcase taking place in the nation's capital. Numbers resident at the Findhorn Community, Britain's oldest New Age centre, rarely exceed two hundred and many of them come from continental Europe and the United States (Riddell, 1990: 132). Barker (1989) estimates the membership of some of the best known new religions in the hundreds. Those organisations which, rather than recruit followers, offer specific training can claim much larger numbers of people as having demonstrated an interest in, or fully acquired, their product. *est* claims to have had 8,000 'graduates' during its time in Britain. A similar number may have gone through the Forum, *est*'s successor. The same again may have been trained by Exegesis and by the Rajneesh Foundation and so on (Barker, 1989: 151). On Barker's informed estimates, the totals involved at some point in all such organisations cannot exceed 100,000 people over 25 years.

Such figures can be viewed in two comparative contexts. In 1985 the Christian denominations and sects in Britain could claim 7 million members (Bruce, 1995: 31–42). Furthermore the decline in the main religious traditions leaves ever larger numbers of people free to experiment; free because they are personally not tied to an older form and because the older forms can no longer effectively stigmatise cultic alternatives as 'deviant'. Even leaving out the very old and very young, there must be at least twenty-five million people in the UK who have no connection with any mainstream religious organisation (Brierley, 1997). The Methodist figures are typical of the major denominations. In 1947 there were 743,000 Methodists in Britain. In 1995 there were 380,000. Even the most generous estimates of the New Age are unlikely to have the new spiritual seekers filling the space left by the decline of just one denomination. Over the course of the twentieth century, the proportion of the adult population in church membership has declined from about 30 per cent to under 10 per cent (Bruce, 1995: 31–42). The proportion of those who display any interest in New Religious Movements or New Age spirituality is very small in comparison.

In assessing the New Age we need to think not only about numbers but also about the nature of commitment. We should appreciate the very limited investment that most people make in the New Age. It oversimplifies, of course, but we can think of influence as a choice between range and depth: the least demanding activities are the most popular. For the vast majority of people interested in the New Age milieu, participation is shallow. They read a book or two and attend a few meetings. They do not become committed adherents to particular cults; they do not regularly engage in time-consuming rituals or therapies; they do not radically alter their lives.

Even for the small numbers of people who are deeply committed to various forms of new religion or new psychology, the impact may be limited. Or to be more precise, the changes that result from such involvement may be largely perceptual and rhetorical. For all the talk about transformation and empowerment, many New Age revelations and therapies (especially those closest to the secular Human Potential Movement) are intended to make people better at what they already do; *est* courses will not turn the stock trader into a community activist; they will make him a more effective and happier stock trader. In Zen Buddhism the secular man peels potatoes, the religious man thinks of God while peeling the potatoes, but the truly enlightened man just peels the potatoes. The point of this paradox is that, for the Buddhist, the last stage of seeking detachment from the world is to become detached even from the search for detachment. Final liberation means liberation even from the spiritual quest. Much New Age thinking waters down this principle so that the ascetic period of monastic discipline is neglected and what is advertised as personal transformation is actually the acquiring of a new vocabulary to describe one's pre-existing attitudes. At its most banal, it is simply the adoption of Dr Pangloss's insistence that everything is for the best in this best of all possible worlds. What is advertised as a way of taking control of one's destiny turns out to be more a way of accepting one's fate.

This should not be scorned. There is doubtless much to be said for accepting one's self and circumstances. However, transformations of the personality that do not much change behaviour and have no impact on the performance of social roles should not be confused with those that do. The Methodist movement profoundly changed those people who joined it and they in turn profoundly changed the wider society. The same could be said of very few parts of the New Age.

The individualism of the New Age acts as a major constraint on its influence. Major changes in Christian culture such as the Reformation or the rise of Methodism were effective because the new persona was supported and disciplined by a believing community, typically the sect. The new psychology was supported by a new social order. Individualistic epistemologies make such cohesion impossible. There is not enough detailed agreement on substance to create a cultural movement with momentum.

The final constraint is the lack of ideological weight. Because they are not embedded in large organisations or sustained by a long history (in the UK at least), many elements of the New Age are vulnerable to being co-opted by the cultural mainstream and trivialised by the mass media. The growth in the number of television channels and the supplements to our daily newspapers has created a need for cheap, lightweight product. What better for our narcissistic culture than alternative medicine (so much easier to understand than the conventional kind), human potential psychology and eastern spirituality? To its expert practitioners, Chinese geomancy is a powerful tool for divination. To the editor of a Sunday paper's 'lifestyle' section, Feng Shui is a new angle on decorating and furniture arranging. To the major supermarkets, aromatherapy is just a new word for bubble bath.

CONCLUSION

New Agers are fond of seeing themselves as being both 'alternative' and representing the future. My analysis suggests they are neither. While some elements of the New Age are tangentially radical, its fundamental principles are those of modern capitalism. Insofar as it is popular, it is so because its individualistic epistemology, consumerist ethos and therapeutic focus resonate with the rest of our culture. The New Age is important not for the changes it will bring but for the changes it epitomises.

The greatest of those can be seen if we return to the Wallis typology of ideological collectivities. Wallis distinguishes the denomination and the cult in terms of their respectability and deviance. But the idea of deviance presupposes a consensus. Obviously Methodism is still better thought of than spiritualism, theosophy or Wicca, but it is equally obvious that the distinction is being eroded. The decline of value consensus which is exemplified in the individualism and consumerism in the New Age means the distinction between the denomination and the cult will also decline. Rather than see the New Age as an antidote to secularisation, it makes more sense to see it as a style and form of religion well-suited to the secular world.

BIBLIOGRAPHY

Barker, Eileen, 1989: *New Religious Movements: a Practical Introduction* (London: HMSO Books).

Berger, Peter L., Berger, Brigitte, and Kellner, Hansfried, 1974: *The Homeless Mind* (Harmondsworth: Penguin).

Brierley, Peter, 1997: *Religious Trends* (London: Christian Research).

Bruce, Steve, 1995: *Religion in Modern Britain* (Oxford: Oxford University Press).

—— 1996: *Religion in the Modern World: from Cathedrals to Cults* (Oxford: Oxford University Press).

Bruce, Steve, and Wright, Chris, 1995: 'Law, Religious Toleration and Social Change', *Journal of Church and State* 37: 103–20.

Bull, Malcolm, and Lockhart, Keith, 1989: *Seeking a Sanctuary: Seventh Day Adventism and the American Dream* (New York: Harper and Row).

Church, Jenny, 1994: *Social Trends 1994 Edition* (London: HMSO).

Durkheim, Emile, 1964: *The Division of Labor in Society* (New York: Free Press).

Gellner, Ernest, 1983: *Nations and Nationalism* (Oxford: Basil Blackwell).

—— 1991: *Plough, Sword and Book: the Structure of Human History* (London: Paladin).

Greer, Paul, 1995: 'The Aquarian Confusion: Conflicting Theologies of the New Age', *Journal of Contemporary Religion* 10: 151–66.

Halsey, A. H., 1972: *Trends in British Society Since 1900* (London: Macmillan).

Hammond, Phillip E., 1992: *Religion and Personal Autonomy* (Columbia, SC: University of South Carolina Press).

Heelas, Paul, 1996: *The New Age Movement* (Oxford: Basil Blackwell).

Kamen, Henry, 1967: *The Rise of Toleration* (London: Weidenfeld and Nicolson).

Niebuhr, H. Richard, 1962: *The Social Sources of Denominationalism* (New York: Meridian).

Riddell, Carol, 1990 *The Findhorn Community: Creating a Human Identity for the 21st Century* (Forres: Findhorn Press).

Roof, Wade Clark, 1996: 'God is in the Details: reflections on religion's public presence in the United States in the mid-1990s', *Sociology of Religion* 57: 149–62.

Tatlow, Tissington, 1933: *The Story of the Student Christian Movement* (London: SCM Press).

Till, Barry, 1977: *The Churches' Search for Unity* (Harmondsworth: Penguin).

Wallis, Roy, 1976: *The Road to Total Freedom: a Sociological Analysis of Scientology* (London: Heinemann).

Weber, Max, 1976: *The Protestant Ethic and the Spirit of Capitalism* (London: George Allen and Unwin).

Wilson, Bryan, 1982: *Religion in Sociological Perspective* (Oxford: Oxford University Press).

—— 1988: 'The Functions of Religion: a Re-appraisal', *Religion* 18: 199–216.

—— 1990: 'How Sects Evolve: Issues and Inferences' in his *The Social Dimensions of Sectarianism: Sects and New Religious Movements in Contemporary Society* (Oxford: Oxford University Press).

—— 1993: 'The Persistence of Sects', *Diskus* 1: 1–12.

Expressive Spirituality and Humanistic Expressivism: Sources of Significance Beyond Church and Chapel

Paul Heelas

We all know the great polarization that has split the religious life of our times, affecting everyone except Christians of convenience and people with absolutely no religious sense at all: the split between Christianity and a religion which repudiates any historical content, whether it be undogmatic monotheism, or pantheism, or a purely spiritual condition not entailing any specific beliefs.

(Georg Simmel, 1976: 258–9 [orig. 1917])

The other world, which religion located in a transcendental reality, is now introjected within human consciousness itself. (Peter Berger, 1965: 41)

For is He not all but that which has power to feel 'I am I'?

(Tennyson, 'The Higher Pantheism')

INTRODUCTION

One of the great challenges facing social science is to determine the extent to which traditional cultural formations, providing order and significance, have collapsed, disintegrated, fragmented or otherwise lost their plausibility. For example, was Marx correct in supposing that the development of capitalism has eroded long-standing authoritative orders, including religion, to the extent that 'All that is solid melts into air'? And an even greater challenge, perhaps, is to ascertain whether people find 'new' sources of significance for their lives when traditional, long-standing formations do in fact lose their hold, rather than simply engaging in hedonistic consumption and bland relativism.

Reflecting on the situation in Britain, virtually all commentators – whether academic or from the public world – agree that traditional, institutionalised religion, the religion of church and chapel, is in decline. But what is happening elsewhere, beyond the territories of church and chapel? Is disenchantment as widespread as cultural theorists, in particular, like to claim? Having introduced what is taking place elsewhere in the 'religious' culture, the point is made that many more people are 'involved' – albeit to varying degrees – than those who continue to go to church and chapel (or mosque and temple) on a regular basis. Urgency is thus lent to the task of engaging in further exploration. Does Christianity, the historically dominant tradition in Britain, still provide the key influence? Alternatively, what is to be made of Thomas Luckmann's (1970) claim that 'a new religion is in the making', indeed, has now 'come to occupy a dominant position in the sacred cosmos' (ibid., 40: 107)?

BEYOND CHURCH AND CHAPEL

Some thirty-five years ago, Thomas Luckmann wrote that the 'sociology of religion is exclusively concerned with church-oriented religiosity' (1970: 22 [orig. 1963]). Today, there is a much greater awareness of what lies beyond church and chapel: namely, those beliefs which are religious, spiritual, supernatural, paranormal or supra-empirical in that they transgress what the secular frame of reference takes to be 'obviously' factual, rational, reasonable, sensible, and convincing, and which are not readily demonstrable to the public in general.

More specifically, but without aiming to be comprehensive or unduly systematic, such beliefs include: orthodox, theistic Christianity (Islam, etc.), associated with private Bible study or prayer (for example); less conventional and/or attenuated forms of traditional teachings; 'alternative' (and cognate) spiritualities, envisaging the ultimate as integral to the person and/ or the natural order as a whole; magical or occult powers, found in connection with astrology, card-reading, palmistry, clairvoyance, mediumship, parapsychology and many superstitions; out-of-the ordinary phenomena such as Atlantis, ley lines, crop circles, Mayan mysteries, angels, alien life-forms, the mysterious happenings of 'X-file' culture; out-of-the-ordinary or uncanny experiences, taken to be of religious, spiritual or supernatural significance; and the relatively inchoate – for example, the belief that 'there must be something more, a "Higher Power", out there' or intimations of the Shakespearean 'There are more things in Heaven and Earth . . . than were ever dreamt of in your philosophy' variety.[1]

NUMERICAL SIGNIFICANCE

Is 'religion' (relatively broadly conceived) beyond church and chapel in decline, or does it show signs of sustainability, even vitality? It is simply not possible, in the present context, to address the evidence pertaining to all kinds of beliefs. Neither is it possible to explore the significance of beliefs for the lives of adherents. Instead, our aim is limited to drawing on a few claims and indices to argue that very considerable numbers of people are involved.

Among others, the case has been made by David Martin and Grace Davie. Martin (1969), writes, 'Whatever we are, we are *not* a secular society, particularly if by that omnibus adjective we mean an increasing approximation of average thinking to the norms of natural and social science' (p.107). He continues, 'There is a luxuriant theological undergrowth which provides the working core of belief more often than is realized' (p.108), concluding, 'our society remains deeply imbued with every type of superstition and metaphysic' (p.113). Turning to Davie (1994a), the claim is that 'some sort of religiosity persists despite the obvious drop in [institutionalised] practice. The sacred does not disappear – indeed, in many ways it is becoming more rather than less prevalent in contemporary society' (p.43).

In some contrast, however, Steve Bruce (1996: 273) argues that '. . . in so far as we can measure any aspect of religious interest, belief or action and can compare 1995 with 1895, the only description for the change between the two points is "decline" '. Explicitly addressing Davie, his argument runs 'Davie (1994a) sees . . . [latent or implicit religion] as a compensating alternative [with regard to the decline of institutionalised religion]. Given that such measures of latent religiosity as are available show the same decline as those of involvement in formal religion (starting from a higher point but heading in the same direction), it seems more plausible to view them as evidence not of a compensating alternative, but of a residue'.

What is to be made of these contrasting assessments? First, it can be argued that religion beyond church and chapel is a growth area relative to what has been taking place within the traditional, institutionalised frame of reference in the UK. Dwelling on developments since the Second World War, institutionalised religion might indeed be argued to have shown very considerable decline: from some 40 per cent of the adult population attending church in England and Wales in 1950, to some 10 per cent in 1990 (Bruce, 1995: 40). But during roughly the same period, belief in '. . . a personal God' and '. . . some sort of spiritual or vital Force which controls life' only declined from 84 (in 1947) to 79 per cent (in 1987) in Britain (see Bruce, 1996: 270). Clearly, this strongly suggests that religious belief, showing only a small decline (or dip?), is considerably more durable than church attendance. Furthermore, and taking into account the fact that the 84 per cent of 'believers' of 1947 presumably includes the (approximately) 40 per cent attending church, it appears that 44 per cent then believed without attending (84 minus 40 per cent), the equivalent figure for the late 1980s being 69 per cent (79 minus 10 per cent). By this way of reckoning the matter, in other words, religious belief beyond church and chapel has become progressively more significant relative to numbers going to the traditional institutions.

Second, it is also possible to draw on statistics to argue that the numbers of those who have some kind of 'religion' without being involved in institutionalised worship has actually been increasing. The argument, in this regard, runs as follows. Again citing figures provided by Bruce (1996: 270), 10 per cent in Britain were atheists in 1991, 14 per cent being agnostics (totalling 24 per cent). Assuming, as is perhaps reasonable, that figures for 1950 were half this, 5 per cent were then atheists, 7 per cent agnostics (totalling 12 per cent). Then think of the decline in church attendance in England and Wales – from 40 per cent (1950) to 10 per cent (1990), it will be recalled. With all these figures in mind, it seems that more people (30 per cent) have left church and chapel than have rejected religion or become agnostic (12 per cent). And this entails that those who are (somehow) religious without attending church or chapel have been increasing in number.

To emphasise a crucial point: it would be misleading in the extreme to conclude that everything going on beyond the frame of institutionalised worship is of great 'religious' (or spiritual, paranormal, etc.) significance. It is highly likely that much is trivial or tucked away for occasional or nominal use. But the fact remains that *many* more people are (somehow) 'religious' without going to church on anything approaching a regular basis than are attendees. One set of figures indicates that the difference is between some 70 per cent (for those believers in a personal God and a spiritual/vital Force who are not attendees) and 10 per cent (for regular attendees). In short, there is much to commend Luckmann's claim concerning 'the replacement of the institutional specialisation of religion by a new *social* [that is, beyond church and chapel] form of religion' (1970: 90–1; my emphasis).

TWO SOURCES OF SIGNIFICANCE: CHRISTIANITY AND EXPRESSIVE SPIRITUALITY

But what exactly is going on within this 'social' form? What happens to 'orthodox' beliefs when they cease to be taught, sustained and regulated by institutionalised participation? Are they being challenged by other sources of significance? Given the (apparent) variety of things taking place beyond church and chapel, and given the (relative) paucity of (tricky) research, it is far from easy to provide satisfactory answers. What seems pretty clear, however, is that inquiry should focus on two 'sources of significance' – Christianity (by virtue of its traditional role) and expressive spirituality (by virtue of the fact that it provides the most clearly and comprehensively formulated alternative to what Christianity has to offer).

Given the historical importance of Christianity, it is hardly surprising that in 1987 37 per cent of the British population claimed belief in 'a personal God' (Bruce, 1996: 270). With only something in the order of 10 per cent of the population being regular church attendees, the majority of such believers clearly do not 'belong' to the institutionalised order of traditional religion. In the absence of evidence to the contrary, however, it seems safe to say that their 'personal God' bears witness to the continuing influence of the Christian, theistic tradition.

It would be rash indeed to deny that Christianity continues to provide resources drawn upon by those who – in the main – do without regular, collective involvement. There are those (especially the elderly) who follow the Bible without going to church; there are those who turn to the Christian God (and perhaps the church) during periods of crisis; there are all those who use the church for life-cycle rituals; there are those who draw on Christian teaching to articulate their ethical commitments, perhaps in educational settings. However, the role that Christianity continues to play should not be overestimated.

According to Grace Davie, 'If belief persists, though increasingly detached from its institutional moorings, it begins inevitably to drift away from anything which might be called orthodoxy' (cited in The Mission Theological Advisory Group, 1996: 2). Beliefs remain (relatively) orthodox when people receive institutionalised instruction. But when beliefs are no longer 'policed' by 'official' institutions, those who have stopped going to church, or who only attend rarely, forget the details. Furthermore, 'believers' beyond church and chapel (and indeed within) are open to all sorts of different 'religious' messages: articles about film stars and Buddhism in Hello magazine, popular books on Shamanism, The X Files, Mystic Meg, perhaps other religions if they are at school, for example. True, Christian messages are also received through the culture (newspapers, Songs of Praise, etc.). But this takes place together with all the other – 'alternative' – communications: communications which open up the options and which can therefore facilitate the process of 'drifting' from more 'official' doctrines.

As for evidence of the weakening hold of Christianity, a crucial consideration is that belief in 'some sort of spirit or vital force which controls life' has now become more important than the (more clearly Christian-influenced) belief in 'a personal God'. Again drawing on figures provided by Bruce (1996: 270), 39 per cent of the British population believed in the former in 1947, 42 per cent in 1987, the respective figures for the latter being 45 per cent and 37. Given that belief in 'some sort of spirit or vital force which controls life' would appear to deviate, in significant regards, from Christian 'orthodoxy', it is reasonable to suppose that the belief is (typically) informed by 'alternative' cultural influences which do not belong to Christianity *per se*.

Further evidence is provided by Davie's (1994a: 56) claim that 'latent or nominal Anglicanism persists as the most common form of English religiosity'. This, surely, is tantamount to saying that 'the most common form of English religiosity' is remarkably insignificant. Take the word 'nominal', defined in the dictionary as 'something that is . . . supposed to have a particular identity or status, but in reality does not have so' (an illustration being, 'Dad, nominally a Methodist, entered churches only for weddings and funerals'). Nominal Anglicanism, that is to say, involves people paying lip service to religion, communal engagement – when indeed it takes place – being of little or no religious significance.

The waning exercise of policed, (supposedly) clear-cut Christian instruction due to declining institutionalised involvement, together with the influence of the apparently increasing number of 'alternative' messages found in the culture as a whole, strongly suggests that Christianity is losing its hold in the territories beyond church and chapel. So it comes as no surprise to find that much of what remains of Christianity would appear to be 'latent' or weak; and that there is also evidence of 'drifting', as from belief in 'a personal God' to belief in a 'spirit or vital force'. Indeed, Davie (1994a: 76) goes so far as to say that 'drifting of belief is, probably, a greater challenge to the churches of the late twentieth century than the supposedly secular nature of the society' (see also ibid.: 43, 122).[2]

And so to our main concern. Could it be the case that Christianity is in the process of being replaced by *another* primary 'source of significance'? Indeed, as Thomas Luckmann and Colin Campbell (for example) have argued, could it be the case that Christianity is *no longer* the primary source?

Claiming that the 'the span of transcendence is shrinking', Luckmann (1990: 138) goes on to state that 'modern religious themes such as "self-realisation", personal autonomy, and self-expression *have become dominant*' (my emphasis; see also Luckmann, 1970: 107). And in similar fashion, Campbell writes that 'an Eastern theodicy . . . has now *replaced* the dominant Western version. What this means in practice is that the concept of a transcendent God has been replaced by an immanent conception of the divine' (personal communication; my emphasis).

Accordingly, attention is now directed to exploring the significance of what I here call 'expressive spirituality'. This is the spirituality which has to do with that which lies 'within' rather than that which lies over-and-above the self or whatever the world might have to offer. This is the spirituality which is integral to what it is to be truly oneself; which is integral to the natural order as a whole. This is the spirituality which serves as the font of wisdom and judgement, rejecting authoritative sources emanating from some transcendent, tradition-articulated, source. This is the spirituality which informs ('expressive') authenticity, creativity, love, vitality. This is the spirituality which interconnects.

It is terribly easy, of course, to provide example after example of expressive spirituality in action. Whether teachings and activities be couched by reference to the East, the pagan, the therapeutic, the mystical, the gendered, even by way of sport, dance, voice training (together with fusions of such renderings), the basic message is the same: seek liberation from the contaminating effects of society and culture; seek genuine experience; seek to express all that one truly is as a spiritual being; and – for many – seek to experience and nurture all that is embedded within nature, beyond the reach of the artificial, the power games of the lower self, the destructive implementations of the technological.

But has expressive spirituality become dominant? I think not. Consider, in this regard, Bruce's forceful argument concerning the (relative) insignificance of New Age spirituality (and the 1970s New Religious Movements):

> Given the millions who have been lost to the church and, given the decline in the power of the Christian churches to stigmatise alternatives, the number of people who have shown any interest in alternative religions is minute, the commitment of most is slight, the most popular products are those which are most secular, and most are consumed by people as a slight flavouring to their mundane lives. (Bruce, 1996: 273)

Bruce, it might immediately be objected, overstates the case for insignificance. Alternative and complementary healing, for example, is widely utilised, very often encourages people to make contact with the spiritual realm, and – given what is often at stake, namely being healed – is surely more than a consumer item for many of those involved. However, the fact remains that it would be rash in the extreme to maintain that expressive spirituality has become the 'dominant' source of significance within religion today. Places like Totnes, Glastonbury and Findhorn are the exception; in the great majority of population centres – from Barrow-in-Furness to Worthing to south London – expressive spirituality is decidedly marginal.

'HUMANISTIC EXPRESSIVISM'

But I still think it can be argued that a formidable rival to Christianity is abroad in the culture, a rival which is playing a major role in weakening the hold of Christianity beyond church and chapel.

The matter can be approached by considering Luckmann's 'invisible religion' thesis. A key claim, which almost certainly owes a great deal to Arnold Gehlen (1980 [orig. 1949]), himself quite probably influenced by the many writings on religion by Georg Simmel, concerns the turn to the self as the primary source of significance. On the one hand, as Luckmann (1970: 115–16) puts it, '. . . the functional rationality [of primary social institutions] is not part of a system that could be of "ultimate" significance to the individuals in the society'. On the other, the corollary of this 'dehumanization' of the mainstream order (ibid.: 116) is that '. . . "ultimate" significance is found by the typical individual in the "private sphere" – and thus in his "private" biography' (ibid.: 109). What really matters, in other words, now belongs to one's *own, personal* experiences. 'The individual', we read, 'who is to find a source of "ultimate" significance in the subjective dimension of his biography embarks upon a process of self-realization and self-expression . . .' (ibid.: 110); or again, 'Religious themes originate in experiences in the "private sphere". They rest primarily on emotions and sentiments . . .' (ibid.: 104). Family life, friendships and sexual relations are called into play as sources of ultimacy. So are those 'secondary institutions' operating at a more organised, cultural level:

> These institutions attempt to articulate the themes arising in the 'private sphere' and retransmit the packaged results to potential consumers. Syndicated advice columns, 'inspirational' literature ranging from tracts on positive thinking to *Playboy* magazine, *Reader's Digest* versions of popular psychology, the lyrics of popular hits, and so forth, articulate what are, in effect, elements of 'ultimate' significance. (ibid.: 104)

In all cases, however, the aim is the same: to acquire a sense of ultimate identity by way of what 'private life' has to offer.

As will be apparent, 'the modern sacred cosmos', which, for Luckmann, serves to sanctify 'subjective "autonomy"' (ibid.: 116), contains a great deal: the *Reader's Digest* on popular psychology, for example; even wife-swapping (ibid.: 106). Containing so much, Luckmann's 'sacred cosmos' would indeed appear to add up to a formidable rival to Christianity; indeed, it could well have become 'dominant'. But, as has often been pointed out, it surely contains too much. Informed by his definition of religion as that which involves 'the transcendence of biological nature by the human organism' (ibid.: 49), his 'sacred cosmos' suffers from being implausibly inclusive, ending up as more or less synomous with all those cultural vehicles which address personal life, if not the cultural realm *per se*.

Luckmann's claim (it will be recalled), that 'modern religious themes such as "self-realization", personal autonomy, and self-expression have become dominant', is not helped by his inclusivistic theory-cum-definition of religion. However, it is possible to reformulate his thesis concerning the religious significance of the turn to the 'subjectivities' of the self so as to stand on more solid ground.

What *can* be religious – or partially so – about this turn, I suggest, is best conceived in terms of the fact that the way people talk about themselves and each other is – at least on occasion – associated with concepts and discourses which do not obviously belong to the secular frame of reference. Their ways of talking about 'inner' states of affairs, that is to say, at least on occasion transcend what the secular – defined as *knowledge derived from the application of reason to publicly demonstrable states of affairs* – has to offer.

The anthropological study of human anthropology, of indigenous psychology, of how people understand their nature, has barely got off the ground in contemporary Britain. However, one strongly suspects that very few would accept that they are merely bodies and brains; merely, if they know of behaviourism, a series of stimuli-responses. Conversely, one strongly suspects that the great majority would insist on their own (somehow irreducible) ability to act (not simply react), make decisions and judgements, exercise choice, free will and conscience, be creative, be faithful, trusting or suspicious out of their own volition. The (implied) ontology of this *sui generis* 'I' is far from being obviously secular. Discourses, we might say, not infrequently imply *inner agency*; the existence of an – ultimately mysterious – *entity*-cum-*process*, namely consciousness. Standing over the world of material causality, being irreducible to bodies and brains, in effect it functions as something *super*natural; better, 'superempirical'. It comes as no surprise to find it reported that some 60 per cent believe in the notion of 'soul' (see Davie, 1994b: 58).

For the most part, however, people do not believe in *themselves* as a crucial and explicitly *religious* source of significance, serving as a religious alternative to Christianity beyond church and chapel (or, for that matter, to institutionalised Christianity itself). Rather than dwelling on the capacities of the autonomous, inner self *per se*, most people, most of the time (except, perhaps, when experiencing the loneliness and reflexivities of an existential crisis), envisage their capacities in relational fashion. Acting in terms of frames of reference which, so to speak, take the self out of itself, modes of self-understanding or identity – so the argument continues – are (predominantly) informed by (predominantly) secular frames of reference: the calculations required to make ends meet; the activities required to be a successful producer or consumer; the efforts required to be healthy and fit. And in such contexts, whatever might be taken to be 'religious' – or supra-secular – about the capacities of the self *per se* fades out of view.

Nevertheless, there remains a discourse of *self*-understanding which clearly does point to an – ontologically-speaking – religious source of significance. We enter the realm of what shall here be called 'humanistic expressivism', namely that expressivism of 'authenticity' where the inner self is seen as the key and irreducible locus of identity awareness; as the primary site of *being* and *purposive action*.

As Robert Bellah and associates argue in *Habits of the Heart* (1985), as well as catering for the 'utilitarian' mode of selfhood, culture also services the 'expressive'. Whereas the former comes into prominence when people think of themselves in terms of the means and ends of capitalistic culture, expressivist beliefs and values have to do with a 'richer', more 'profound' rendering of what it is to be a person. Drawing on Charles Taylor's *The Ethics of Authenticity* (1991), the rendering is seen as 'part of the massive subjective turn of modern culture', a turn which involves 'a new form of inwardness, in which we come to think of ourselves as beings with inner depths' (p.26). Crucially, '. . . the *source* we have to connect to is deep in us' (ibid.: 260; my emphasis). The 'principle', as he writes, is that:

> everyone has a right to develop their own form of life, grounded on their own sense of what is really important or of value. People are called upon to be true to themselves and to seek their own self-fulfilment. What this consists of, each must, in the last instance, determine for him- or herself. No one else can or should try to dictate its contents. (ibid.: 14)

Values come from within; 'Morality', as Taylor puts it, 'has, in a sense, a voice within' (ibid.: 26); freedom is 'self-determining' (ibid.: 27); 'Being true to myself means being true to my own originality'; (ibid.: 29); 'Revelation comes through expression' (ibid.: 61). And as another illustration, here is a powerful passage from Edward Shils:

> There is a belief, corresponding to a feeling, that within each human being there is an individuality, lying in potentiality, which seeks an occasion for realization but is held in the toils of the rules, beliefs, and roles which society imposes. In a more popular, or vulgar, recent form, the concern to 'establish one's identity', 'to discover oneself', or 'to find out who one really is' has come to be regarded as a first obligation of the individual. Some writers on undergraduate education in the

United States say that a college is a place where young people can 'find out who they really are'. They suggest that the real state of the self is very different from the acquired baggage which institutions like families, schools, and universities impose. To be 'true to oneself' means, they imply, discovering what is contained in the uncontaminated self, the self which has been freed from the encumbrance of accumulated knowledge, norms, and ideals handed down by previous generations. (Shils, 1981: 10–11)

In contrast to the utilitarian mode, then, being oneself is taken to involve much more than merely satisfying desires generated (or enhanced) by producer and consumer culture; more generally, being oneself is taken to involve liberation from all social and cultural 'impositions'. We are in the realm of self-exploration, self-fulfilment and self-expression: all to do with an inner *source*; a fount of 'authenticity' and 'wholeness'. And so to a key point. *Both substantively and functionally, this source belongs to the religious order of things.* True, expressivist discourse generally takes a 'humanistic' rather than an explicitly religious form: the language of the 'true' or 'natural' self, not of the 'soul' or 'spirit'. But this should not blind us to the implied religious ontology and capacities. One should be true to *oneself*, trust one's *sui generis* authenticity, have faith in one's *own* 'intuition' or in what 'feels right', rather than simply relying on reason or tradition; one should trust what *is* integral to oneself, one's *own experience*, rather than depending on what the establishment might happen to dictate. And this is to *be* informed by (ultimately) irreducible and inexplicable consciousness-cum-agency: of a kind which clearly has characteristics which do not belong to secular (rationalistic, constructivistic, etc.) accounts of the nature (biological or socialised) and operation (calculative, hedonistic, or tradition-informed) of the person.

As we saw earlier, expressive spirituality – which, it should now be apparent, provides an explicitly or 'radically' spiritual rendering of 'humanistic' expressivism – is not especially significant. But the same cannot be said of expressive authenticity. Themes to do with 'being ourselves', 'finding ourselves', 'expressing ourselves', 'developing ourselves' and 'fulfilling ourselves', all premised on there being an inner *source* (to use Charles Taylor's useful term again), run through countless lives, personal relationships, publications, therapies and counselling practices, management trainings, environmentalist activities, feminism and women's movements, educational practices of the child-centred variety, and so on.

Furthermore, humanistic – or naturalistic – expressivism is a growing force in western cultures, including Britain, as can be illustrated with figures from the leading researcher in the area, Ronald Yankelovich (1990: 91). Of Yankelovich's sample of those born between 1906 and 1915, only 6 per cent hold 'postmaterialist' – that is, expressivist – values. This percentage increases progressively as one moves towards those born between 1956 and 1965, the figure for this last cohort being 15 per cent.[3]

CONCLUSION

We have been looking at three main sources of religious significance in contemporary Britain. One, sustained in collective settings by institutionalised, traditional religion, is in (overall) decline. Another, Christian-influenced religion found beyond church and chapel and sustained by memory and cultural transmissions (books, the media), is also – it appears – diminishing in influence. But with regard to the third, involving faith in the self, the human, the natural, what it is to be alive – there are distinct signs of vitality.[4]

Dwelling on the third, we have seen that the self as a source of significance is thought of in three main ways. The source is least articulated among those who, whilst refusing to accept that they are merely brains and bodies, are too firmly locked into modes of identity provision (including the utilitarian, and, for some, transcendent Christianity) to have had reason to dwell and elaborate on what the self provides *per se*. The source receives a more fully articulated rendering among those who – at least on occasion – adopt the discourses of humanistic expressivism. And it is most fully articulated among those – again, at least on occasion – who have entered the territory of expressive spirituality.

Of these three degrees of articulation, the 'religious' significance of the first is too insubstantial, too occasional, too obscured by (predominantly) secular modes of identity provision, to serve as a serious *religious* rival to Christianity. And the third is (currently) too insignificant, with regard to numbers involved, to amount to much of a threat. Bearing in mind its cultural significance, however, humanistic expressivism serves as a formidable rival. Indeed, there is little doubt that it has played an important role in weakening the influence of Christianity, both with regard to church attendance and with regard to belief in the Christian God beyond church and chapel.

Virtually by definition, humanistic expressivists stay away from church and chapel, and, in the realms 'beyond', reject theistic beliefs. And if they should want to move beyond their quest for 'authenticity' to find something yet deeper or more profound, their faith in what their 'autonomous' selfhood or 'personal' *life* has to offer, combined with their distrust of the dictates and judgements of tradition, means that they are highly likely to turn to expressive spirituality as a source. In sum, the greater the enculturation of humanistic expressivism, the greater the threat to church attendance *and* the hold of theism beyond church and chapel.[5]

What of the future? Together with the historical point that expressivism is more important today than, say, at the beginning of this century, a whole range of theoretical considerations – primarily to do with the development of capitalism and humanism – means that it is highly likely that the self, as a source of significance, will continue to grow in importance. Writing some ninety years ago, Georg Simmel (1976: 251 [orig. 1909]) argued that 'The subjectivism of modern personal life is merely the expression of [the fact that] the vast, intricate, sophisticated culture of things, of institutions, of objectified ideas robs the individual of any consistent inner relationship to culture as a whole, and casts him back again on his own resources'. Whether it be for the reasons given by Simmel, or due to other factors to do with detraditionalisation and pluralism (for example), there is little doubt that the turn to the subjectivities of the self is one of the key features of the time in which we live. And as Simmel acutely observed, when people *have* to rely on their own resources to make sense of their lives, what he called 'spiritual reality' is likely to thrive. It is when people are left to themselves, dwell on themselves and what they have to offer, that we find ' the change to the religious shaping of life itself, and to the spiritual reality that, in philosophical terms, one could call the self-consciousness of the metaphysical significance of our existence – the change by which all otherworldly yearning and dedication, bliss and rejection, justice and mercy, are no longer found in the lofty heights above life, as it were, but in the depths within it' (1997: 18–19 [orig. 1918]).

Those who have been thrown back upon themselves, who find themselves left with themselves (albeit with other 'selves'), whose selves have come into ultimate prominence, are therefore faced with the sheer necessity of making sense of life 'of' and 'from' themselves. Being highly self-conscious or reflexive about deriving the meaning of life by way of self-exploration, such people are those most likely to feel that there is something of ultimate and *sui generis* ontology and value about themselves (including Buberian I–Thou relationships); something irreducible with regard to the public world of hard materiality; something which in the last resort has such depth (when can one stop exploring?) and source-significance as to remain mysterious, wonderful, full of what really counts. Citing Simmel again, ' this emotional reality – which we can only call *life* – makes itself increasingly felt in its formless strength as the true meaning or value of our existence' (1997: 24 [orig. 1918]). And, as he continues, 'This tendency [to experiencing 'life'] seems to have increased as culture has evolved' (ibid.). The more the self engages with itself, the more 'it' in and of 'itself' is experienced as the source of *being*; and directs those concerned accordingly.

Given the turn to the subjectivities of the self, more and more people (it appears) are likely to favour beliefs and practices – whether to do with 'authenticity' or 'spirituality' – which emphasise *immanence*: which point to that which is part and parcel of personal life; which point to that which serves to enrich identity, agency, and relationships; which serve to inform what it is to be *alive* in the *experiences* of the here and now. Religion within church and chapel will be affected (there already being clear signs of this happening); and in the realms 'beyond', Luckmann's 'modern religious themes' of 'self-realisation, personal autonomy, and self-expression' will surely appeal to those who, whilst not being content with atheism or agnosticism, hold values – especially of the self *itself*, the freedom to *be* oneself, the *authority* of the self – which are not exactly catered for by traditional, theistic, religion emphasising the transcendent authority of God and the limitations of the human condition.[6]

Thomas Jefferson declared 'I am a sect myself'; Thomas Paine, that 'My mind is my church' (cited in Bellah *et al.*, 1985: 233). More recently, Stanley Spencer has thought of his artistic vision in terms of 'the Church of Me' (cited by The Mission Theological Group, 1996: 20); and an unnamed respondent, also cited by the Theological Group, states 'life is our God' (ibid.: 78). If the argument of this chapter is valid, Luckmann's 'new social form of religion' has a promising future: a future where the self (together with intimate relationships) is the primary site for the *life* of authenticity-cum-spirituality; indeed, where the self (or the lives of selves together) serves as an '*institution*', a source of significance taken to provide truth, judgement, identity, the essentials of what it is to *be*.

Two closing observations. The first concerns moving beyond the 'New Age': not the 'movement', but the term. I have not used it in this chapter (except once in scare quotes). However useful it might have been to describe a form of spirituality, when deployed as it often is to make negative evaluations the term now does more harm than good. In certain quarters, that is to say, it has come to be used polemically, to dismiss certain beliefs and practices as (supposedly) inauthentic, trivial, superficial, consumeristic. And it is not as though the term is necessary. 'Expressive spirituality' is relatively neutral in usage and therefore serves perfectly well to designate all those teachings and practices which dwell on inner spirituality, including the natural order as a whole.

The second observation concerns a more problematic issue. In the main, the preceding discussion of the fate of sources of significance – institutio-nalised Christianity, 'popular' Christianity beyond church and chapel, expressive spirituality (beyond traditional religious institutions) and human-istic expressivism (also beyond the traditional) – has rested on the assumption that these are distinct sources, and that people only become involved with one or another. It can readily be objected that this ignores the complexities of life on the ground. That such sources are not distinct, it might well be pointed out, is clearly seen in the fact (for example) that institutionalised Christianity not infrequently contains a strong spiritually expressivist dimension ('creation spirituality', among other things), as well as humanistic expressivism (as with liberal forms of teaching). Furthermore, as has often been claimed, rather than being content with any one form of religion, very considerable numbers are now 'religious individualists' (to use Roof and Gesch's term [1995: 72]), and 'seekers' (Roof, 1993), functioning as *bricoleurs* and seekers to draw on an (apparently) diverse range of religious 'resources' – beliefs, values and practices – as and when occasion demands.[7]

If indeed, on the side of 'provision', sources of significance are all mixed up, and if indeed, on the side of 'usage', *bricolage* is the order of the day, my attempt to contribute to the thesis that 'Self-immanence' is on the road to replacing (Christian) theism as the primary source of (significant) significance is clearly doomed to failure. In defence, all I can say here is that however fashionably 'postmodern' it might be to claim that (deconstructive) freedom is the order of the day, as when religious individualists serve to undermine the exclusivistic authority of any particular tradition by 'mixing' it with others, much strongly suggests that at least some boundaries – that is, source-informed differentiations – remain operative. Rather than 'religions of choice' running wild, 'polarisation' – to use Simmel's term from the quotation with which we began – has far from disappeared with the advent of some (supposed) postmodern condition. Of particular note, expressivists either avoid theistic, transcendental Christianity, or – if they should draw on it – 'experience' tradition in ways which accord with their own source of significance. *Expressivists* do not become *theists*. Belonging to a rival camp, their challenge to theistic 'orthodoxy' is firmly on the agenda for the future.

PERSONAL ENDNOTE

What on earth 'am I'? For those, like myself, who are not content with answers provided by the institutional order, the search within for responses to existential questions is unlikely to be associated with atheism (surveys suggest that only some 10 per cent of the adult British population are atheists). I am an optimistic humanist because my own experience of 'life' makes it much harder for me to believe in atheism than to hope that 'life' really is as mysterious and supra-empirical as it appears.

ACKNOWLEDGEMENTS

I would like to thank Steve Bruce and Linda Woodhead for illuminating discussions on studying the territories beyond church and chapel.

NOTES

1. In addition various combinations of these beliefs may be held, sometimes in coherent or integrated fashion, sometimes not.

2. A recent, graphic illustration of the weak hold which Christianity exercises within the culture is provided by a *Daily Telegraph* survey in which only 15 per cent gave the correct answer to the question, 'Could you tell me what event the forthcoming Millennium in the year 2000 commemorates?' (*The Daily Telegraph*, 14.3.98).

3. Since writing this chapter, I learnt about Sylvia Collins' survey of 1,090 young people, aged 13 to 16 years. Her findings provide further evidence of the importance of expressivism, and indeed – and to my relief! – support much of what I have been trying to argue. Whereas 'Only a minority of young people actually invest faith in Christianity and derive some sort of ontological security from it', much suggests that 'Faith would seem to be, in Luckmann's terms, "invisible" . . . For most of the young people it is organised around family, close friends and the reflexive self. These were the referents which formed the immanent faith structure which gave the young people existential meaning, hope and purpose'. In sum, Collins finds that, 'In accordance with the nature of immanent faith, the majority of young people do not refer to an absolute transcendent authority when forming moral opinions, but rather adopt a morality based on the principles of autonomy and authenticity, relativism and tolerance' (unpublished report, based on Collins, 1997). Anna King's (1996) exploration of 'spirituality', during which she draws on Margaret Chatterjee's phrase, 'the search for the trans-empirical' (p. 347), also provides support for what I have been arguing.

4. Having provided an extremely useful survey of material pertaining to religion/spirituality both within and without church and chapel, John Wolffe (1993: 341) concludes that 'it could be that a characteristic feature of twenty-first-century religion will be a change in the position of Christianity from the normative expression of religion in Britain to a position of prominence but not necessarily of dominance within a much more varied range of religious options'.

5. Roof and Gesch (1995), for example, provide evidence of this threat. 'Individual–expressive views of the church' (p. 74), among a sample of the baby-boom generation in the States, are associated with those who 'have dropped out of organised religion' (p. 68), turning instead to the more 'spiritual' (p. 72). See also Roof (1993).

6. On the turn to (expressivist) self within the church, see for example Hunter (1987: 64–71).

7. See, for example, Roof and Gesch (1995: 72–3) on those (expressivistic) 'religious individualists in the States who 'combine Judaeo-Christian beliefs with reincarnation, astrology, and other "New Age" beliefs and practices such as communicating with the dead, exploring psychic powers, and meditating'. Luckmann (1970: 80–1) provides a useful discussion of 'individual religiosity', now with regard to the '"official" model of religion'. More generally, Lyotard (1984: 66) writes that 'the temporary contract is in practice supplanting permanent institutions'.

Bibliography

Bellah, Robert, Madson, Richard, Sullivan, William, Swidler, Ann, and Tipton, Steven, 1985: *Habits of the Heart. Individualism and Commitment in American Life* (Berkeley, Los Angeles, London: University of California Press).

Berger, Peter, 1965: 'Towards a Sociological Understanding of Psychoanalysis', *Social Research* 32/1: 26–41.

Bruce, Steve, 1995: *Religion in Modern Britain* (Oxford, New York: Oxford University Press).

—— 1996: 'Religion in Britain at the Close of the 20th Century: A challenge to the silver lining perspective', *Journal of Contemporary Religion* 11 (3): 261–75.

Collins, Sylvia, 1997: *Young People's Faith in Late Modernity* (Unpublished PhD, University of Surrey).

Davie, Grace, 1994a: *Religion in Britain Since 1945. Believing Without Belonging* (Oxford: Blackwell).

—— 1994b: 'Unity in Diversity: Religion and Modernity in Western Europe', in Fulton, J., and Gee, P., eds, *Religion in Contemporary Europe* (Lewiston, Queenston; Lampeter: Edwin Mellen), pp. 52–65.

Gehlen, Arnold, 1980, [orig. 1949]: *Man in the Age of Technology* (New York: Columbia University Press).

Hunter, James Davidson, 1987: *Evangelicalism. The Coming Generation* (Chicago and London: The University of Chicago Press).

King, Anna, 1996: 'Spirituality: Transformation and Metamorphosis', *Religion* 26 (4): 343–51.

Luckmann, Thomas, 1970, [orig. 1963]: *The Invisible Religion. The Problem of Religion in Modern Society* (New York: Macmillan; London: Collier-Macmillan).

—— 1990: 'Shrinking Transcendence, Expanding Religion?', *Sociological Analysis* 50 (2): 127–38.

Lyotard, Jean-Francois, 1986: *The Postmodern Condition: A Report on Knowledge* (Manchester: Manchester University Press).

Martin, David, 1969: *The Religious and the Secular. Studies in Secularization* (London: Routledge & Kegan Paul).

Mission Theological Advisory Group, The, 1996: *The Search for Faith and the Witness of the Church. An Exploration by The Mission Theological Advisory Group* (London: Church House Publishing).

Roof, Wade Clark, 1993: *A Generation of Seekers. The Spiritual Journeys of the Baby Boom Generation* (San Francisco: HarperSanFrancisco).

Roof, Wade Clark and Lyn Gesch, 1995: 'Boomers and the Culture of Choice. Changing patterns of work, family, and religion', in Ammerman, N., and Roof, W.C., eds, *Work, Family and Religion in Contemporary Society* (New York and London: Routledge), pp. 61–80.

Shils, Edward, 1981: *Tradition* (London: Faber & Faber).

Simmel, Georg, [orig. 1909], 'The Future of Our Culture', in Lawrence, P.A., 1976: *Georg Simmel. Sociologist and European* (Middlesex: Thomas Nelson), pp. 250–2.

—— [orig. 1918]: 'The Problem of Religion Today', in Georg Simmel 1997, *Essays on Religion* (New Haven and London: Yale University Press), pp. 7–19.

—— [orig. 1917]: 'The Crisis of Culture', in Lawrence, P.A., 1976: *Georg Simmel. Sociologist and European* (Middlesex: Thomas Nelson), pp. 253–266.

Taylor, Charles, 1991: *The Ethics of Authenticity* (London: Harvard University Press).

Wolffe, John, 1993: 'The Religions of the Silent Majority', in Parsons, G., ed., *The Growth of Religious Diversity. Britain from 1945, Vol.1: Traditions* (London: Routledge and the Open University), pp. 305–46.

Yankelovich, Daniel, 1990: *Culture Shift in Advanced Industrial Society* (Princeton: Princeton University Press).

Notes on Contributors

James A. Beckford is Professor of Sociology at Warwick University. His many publications include *Cult Controversies: the Societal Response to New Religious Movements* (1985), *Religion and Advanced Industrial Society* (1989), and (with Sophie Gilliat) *Religion in Prison: Equal Rites in a Multi-Faith Society?* (1998). He is also editor of *New Religious Movements and Rapid Social Change* (1986) and co-editor of *Secularization, Rationalism, and Sectarianism* (1993). His current research concerns religious diversity, chaplaincies, and the relationship between religion and politics.

Marion Bowman is Senior Lecturer in the Study of Religions and Programme Director of the MA in Contemporary Religions at Bath Spa University College. She has written extensively on vernacular religion, Celtic spirituality, pilgrimage and Glastonbury. She is a former Honorary Secretary of the Folklore Society.

Steve Bruce is Professor of Sociology at Aberdeen University. He is the author of thirteen books on the sociology of religion, religion and politics and terrorism, including *God Save Ulster: the Religion and Politics of Paisleyism* (1986), *The Rise and Fall of the New Christian Right: Conservative Protestant Politics in America 1978–1988* (1988), *Pray TV: Televangelism in America* (1990), *The Red Hand: Loyalist Paramilitaries in Northern Ireland* (1992), and *Religion in the Modern World: From Cathedrals to Cults* (1996).

Martin Green is a writer and cultural critic who has recently focused upon the 'New Age' qualities of new literary-cultural movements. He has written some thirty books, including *Children of the Sun: a Narrative of Decadence in England after 1918* (1977), *Tolstoy and Gandhi, Men of Peace* (1983), *Mountain of Truth: the Counterculture Begins, Ascona 1900–1920* (1986), and *Prophets of* *a New Age* (1992). Before retirement he taught at Tufts University, Massachusetts.

Susan Greenwood lectures in Gender Studies at the University of Kent at Canterbury and has conducted anthropological fieldwork among magicians in London over several years. Her research interests include magical philosophies and feminist politics and her publications include 'The British Occult Subculture: Beyond Good and Evil?' in *Magical Religion and Modern Witchcraft* (ed. J.R. Lewis, 1996). She has recently taught an undergraduate course on Shamanic Consciousness at Sussex University.

Malcolm Hamilton is Senior Lecturer and Head of the Department of Sociology at the University of Reading. His publications include *The Sociology of Religion: Theoretical and Comparative Perspectives* (1995), *The Charismatic Movement: Sociological and Participant Perspectives* (1997), and *Sociology and the World's Religions* (1998). His research interests include quasi-religion and new spirituality, and the sociology of food and diet, especially vegetarianism.

Graham Harvey is Senior Lecturer in Religious Studies at King Alfred's College of Higher Education, Winchester. His most recent book is *Listening People, Speaking Earth: Contemporary Paganism* (1997). Although best known for his interest in Paganism he has also written about Judaism (*The True Israel*, Brill, 1996). He has also edited *Indigenous Religions: a Companion* (Cassell, 1999), an international project introducing the majority of the world's religions.

Ellie Hedges is Senior Lecturer at University College, Worcester. She is particularly interested in the relationship between religion, spirituality and health, and is researching a PhD on contemporary healing groups with special reference to holistic medicine and New Age and Neo-Pagan ideas.

Paul Heelas is Professor of Religion and Modernity in the Department of Religious Studies at Lancaster University. His earlier work concentrated on indigenous psychologies in premodern ethnographic settings. More recently he has researched selfhood in the contemporary West. His books include *The New Age Movement: The Celebration of the Self and the Sacralization of Modernity* (1996), *Detraditionalization: Critical Reflections on Authority and Identity* (1996; coedited with S. Lash and P. Morris), and the edited volume *Religion, Modernity and Postmodernity* (1998).

W. Graham Monteith was a Minister in the Church of Scotland before retiring on health grounds. He has studied sociology, sociology of religion, and divinity at the Universities of York and Edinburgh, and at the Université Catholique de Louvain. He gained his PhD at New College, Edinburgh, in 1997, and now works there as an Honorary Associate Secretary of the Student Christian Movement in Scotland. His writings include *Disability: Faith and Acceptance*.

Elizabeth Puttick completed a PhD in the sociology of religion at King's College, London. She is a literary agent and teaches in London on holistic spirituality at the City University, and on women in religion at the American College of Liberal Arts. Her latest book is *Women in New Religions: In Search of Community, Sexuality and Spiritual Power* (1997), and her current research interests include shamanism, and exploring connections between Eastern, Western and tribal/earth-based/animistic spirituality.

Robert A. Segal is Professor in Theory of Religion in the Department of Religious Studies at Lancaster University, and European editor of *Religion*. He is the author of *The Poimandres as Myth* (1986), *Joseph Campbell: An Introduction* (1987; revised, 1997), and *Theorizing About Myth* (1999). He is also editor of *The Gnostic Jung* (1992), *The Allure of Gnosticism* (1995), *Jung on Mythology* (1998), and *The Myth and Ritual Theory* (1998).

Steven Sutcliffe is an independent writer and researcher who has taught in Religious Studies at Stirling University and the Open University, where he completed a PhD in 1998 on the history and ethnography of 'New Age' in Britain. He has published articles on 'New Age', alternative spirituality, the Findhorn Community, and method and theory in the study of religions, in several international journals.

Kevin Tingay is Rector of Bradford-on-Tone in Somerset and Inter-Faith Advisor in the Diocese of Bath and Wells. He has a particular interest in alternative spiritual traditions and is currently researching a doctoral thesis at Bath Spa University College on the nature and impact of the Theosophical movement.

Michael York is a Research Fellow at Bath Spa University College, where he also teaches sociology of religion and co-coordinates the New Age and Pagan Studies programme. He is the author of *The Emerging*

Network: A Sociology of the New Age and Neo-Pagan Movements (1995) and *The Divine Versus the Asurian: An Interpretation of Indo-European Cult and Myth* (1996). His current interest is the religious dimensions of imaginal consciousness.

Index

Catching the Bug

Dedication
To Ian Wallace

Title: Catching the Bug
Subtitle: A Sound Approach guide to the birds of Poole Harbour

Text: Mark Constantine, Nick Hopper & The Sound Approach

Artwork: Killian Mullarney
Sounds: Magnus Robb, Mark Constantine, Arnoud B van den Berg, Killian Mullarney, Dick Forsman, Pim Wolf & Peter Nuyten
Sonagrams: Magnus Robb & Cecilia Bosman
Maps: Cecilia Bosman
Photographs: Nick Hopper, Arnoud B van den Berg, René Pop, Killian Mullarney, Mike Coleman, Kevin Lane, Claire Lodge, Richard Skins, Cecilia Bosman, James Lidster, Graham Armstrong, Richard Crease, David Larcombe, Iain H Leach, Steve Trewhella & others

Sound editing: Magnus Robb
Photo editing and lithography: René Pop
Text editing: Magnus Robb & Arnoud B van den Berg
Graphic designers: Anneke Boekhoudt, Cecilia Bosman & Mientje Petrus

The Sound Approach: Arnoud B van den Berg, Mark Constantine & Magnus Robb

Published by The Sound Approach, 12 Market Street, Poole Dorset BH15 1NF, UK © 2012
Printed by Tienkamp, Groningen, Netherlands

ISBN: 978-90-810933-0-9
NUR-code: 435

Cover and CD labels: Hobby and European Nightjar (*Killian Mullarney*)

You can order this book by phone: +44(0)1202-641004 or online: www.soundapproach.co.uk

Catching the Bug

A Sound Approach guide to the birds of Poole Harbour

MARK CONSTANTINE, NICK HOPPER & THE SOUND APPROACH

Contents

Species guide to the accompanying CDs

See the main text for details such as location, date, age, sex, background species and catalogue number.

CD1-01 **Common Wood Pigeon** *Columba palumbus*
CD1-02 **Stock Dove** *Columba oenas*
CD1-03 **Eurasian Collared Dove** *Streptopelia decaocto*
CD1-04 **Common Nightingale** *Luscinia megarhynchos*
CD1-05 **Common Nightingale** *Luscinia megarhynchos*
CD1-06 **Dark-bellied Brent Goose** *Branta bernicla*
CD1-07 **Coal Tit** *Periparus ater*
CD1-08 **'Soundscape'**: Canada Goose *Branta canadensis*, Common Pheasant *Phasianus colchicus*, Water Rail *Rallus aquaticus*, Common Wood Pigeon *Columba palumbus*, Common Cuckoo *Cuculus canorus*, Eurasian Wren *Troglodytes troglodytes*, Common Blackbird *Turdus merula*, Song Thrush *T philomelos*, Eurasian Reed Warbler *Acrocephalus scirpaceus*, Common Whitethroat *Sylvia communis*, European Blue Tit *Cyanistes caeruleus*, Common Chaffinch *Fringilla coelebs* and European Goldfinch *Carduelis carduelis*
CD1-09 **Dartford Warbler** *Sylvia undata dartfordiensis*
CD1-10 **Dartford Warbler** *Sylvia undata dartfordiensis*
CD1-12 **Common Whitethroat** *Sylvia communis*
CD1-13 **Dartford Warbler** *Sylvia undata dartfordiensis*
CD1-14 **Dartford Warbler** *Sylvia undata undata*
CD1-15 **Dartford Warbler** *Sylvia undata undata*
CD1-16 **Dartford Warbler** *Sylvia undata dartfordiensis*
CD1-17 **Dartford Warbler** *Sylvia undata dartfordiensis*
CD1-18 **Dartford Warbler** *Sylvia undata dartfordiensis*
CD1-19 **European Stonechat** *Saxicola rubicola*
CD1-20 **Dartford Warbler** *Sylvia undata dartfordiensis*
CD1-21 **Sardinian Warbler** *Sylvia melanocephala*
CD1-22 **Dartford Warbler** *Sylvia undata undata*
CD1-23 **Dartford Warbler** *Sylvia undata dartfordiensis*
CD1-24 **Dartford Warbler** *Sylvia undata undata*
CD1-25 **Dartford Warbler** *Sylvia undata undata*
CD1-26 **Dartford Warbler** *Sylvia undata undata*
CD1-27 **Great Cormorant** *Phalacrocorax carbo*
CD1-28 **Atlantic Great Cormorant** *Phalacrocorax carbo carbo*

CD1-29 **Continental Great Cormorant** *Phalacrocorax carbo sinensis*
CD1-30 **Atlantic Great Cormorant** *Phalacrocorax carbo carbo*
CD1-31 **Continental Great Cormorant** *Phalacrocorax carbo sinensis*
CD1-32 **Little Egret** *Egretta garzetta*
CD1-33 **Little Egret** *Egretta garzetta*
CD1-34 **Cabot's Tern** *Sterna acuflavida*
CD1-35 **Sandwich Tern** *Sterna sandvicensis*
CD1-36 **Song Thrush** *Turdus philomelos*
CD1-37 **Mistle Thrush** *Turdus viscivorus*
CD1-38 **European Robin** *Erithacus rubecula*
CD1-39 **Yellow-legged Gull** *Larus michahellis*
CD1-40 **Herring Gull** *Larus argentatus*
CD1-41 **Lesser Black-backed Gull** *Larus fuscus*
CD1-42 **Ring-billed Gull** *Larus delawarensis*
CD1-43 **Long-billed Dowitcher** *Limnodromus scolopaceus*
CD1-44 **Black-headed Gull** *Chroicocephalus ridibundus*
CD1-45 **Mediterranean Gull** *Larus melanocephalus*
CD1-46 **Mediterranean Gull** *Larus melanocephalus*
CD1-47 **Mediterranean Gull** *Larus melanocephalus*
CD1-48 **European Nightjar** *Caprimulgus europaeus*
CD1-49 **European Nightjar** *Caprimulgus europaeus*
CD1-50 **European Nightjar** *Caprimulgus europaeus*
CD1-51 **European Nightjar** *Caprimulgus europaeus*
CD1-52 **European Nightjar** *Caprimulgus europaeus*
CD1-53 **European Nightjar** *Caprimulgus europaeus*
CD1-54 **European Nightjar** *Caprimulgus europaeus*
CD1-55 **European Nightjar** *Caprimulgus europaeus*
CD1-56 **Redwing** *Turdus iliacus*
CD1-57 **Common Starling** *Sturnus vulgaris*
CD1-58 **Ring Ouzel** *Turdus torquatus*
CD1-59 **Common Blackbird** *Turdus merula*
CD1-60 **Song Thrush** *Turdus philomelos*
CD1-61 **Ring Ouzel** *Turdus torquatus*
CD1-62 **Common Chaffinch** *Fringilla coelebs*
CD1-63 **Common Chaffinch** *Fringilla coelebs*
CD1-64 **Common Chaffinch** *Fringilla coelebs*
CD1-65 **Brambling** *Fringilla montifringilla*

CD2-41	**Common Firecrest** *Rugulus ignicapilla*
CD2-42	**Siberian Chiffchaff** *Phylloscopus collybita tristis*
CD2-43a	0:00 - 0:17 **Siberian Chiffchaff** *Phylloscopus collybita tristis*
CD2-43b	0:18 - 0:34 **Siberian Chiffchaff** *Phylloscopus collybita tristis*
CD2-43c	0:35 - 0:53 **Siberian Chiffchaff** *Phylloscopus collybita tristis*
CD2-44	**Anatolian Common Chiffchaff** *Phylloscopus collybita brevirostris*
CD2-45	**Caucasian Common Chiffchaff** *Phylloscopus collybita caucasicus*
CD2-46	**Siberian Chiffchaff** *Phylloscopus collybita tristis*
CD2-47a	0:00 - 0:22 **Siberian Chiffchaff** *Phylloscopus collybita tristis*
CD2-47b	0:22 - 0:46 **Siberian Chiffchaff** *Phylloscopus collybita tristis*
CD2-48	**Siberian Chiffchaff** *Phylloscopus collybita tristis*
CD2-49	**Siberian Chiffchaff** *Phylloscopus collybita tristis*
CD2-50	**Siberian Chiffchaff** *Phylloscopus collybita tristis*
CD2-51	**Siberian Chiffchaff** *Phylloscopus collybita tristis*
CD2-52	**Siberian Chiffchaff** *Phylloscopus collybita tristis*
CD2-53	**Siberian Chiffchaff** *Phylloscopus collybita tristis*
CD2-54	**Eurasian Curlew** *Numenius arquata*
CD2-55	**Eurasian Curlew** *Numenius arquata*
CD2-56	**Eurasian Whimbrel** *Numenius phaeopus*
CD2-57	**Common Greenshank** *Tringa nebularia*
CD2-58	**Common Greenshank** *Tringa nebularia*
CD2-59	**Common Redshank** *Tringa totanus*
CD2-60	**Spotted Redshank** *Tringa erythropus*
CD2-61	**Common Sandpiper** *Actitis hypoleucos*
CD2-62	**Wood Sandpiper** *Tringa glareola*
CD2-63	**Green Sandpiper** *Tringa ochropus*
CD2-64	**Common Moorhen** *Gallinula chloropus*
CD2-65	**Eurasian Coot** *Fulica atra*
CD2-66	**Water Rail** *Rallus aquaticus*
CD2-67	**European Otter** *Lutra lutra*
CD2-68	**Eurasian Bittern** *Botaurus stellaris*
CD2-69	**Woodlark** *Lullula arborea*
CD2-70	**Woodlark** *Lullula arborea*
CD2-71	**Woodlark** *Lullula arborea*
CD2-72	**Woodlark** *Lullula arborea*
CD2-73	**Woodlark** *Lullula arborea*
CD2-74	**Woodlark** *Lullula arborea*
CD2-75	**Woodlark** *Lullula arborea*
CD2-76	**Woodlark** *Lullula arborea*
CD2-77	**Woodlark** *Lullula arborea*
CD2-78	**Rook** *Corvus frugilegus*
CD2-79	**Carrion Crow** *Corvus corone*
CD2-80	**Western Jackdaw** *Corvus monedula*
CD2-81a	0:00 - 0:21 **Common Greenshank** *Tringa nebularia*
CD2-81b	0:22 - 0:42 **Osprey** *Pandion haliaetus*
CD2-81c	0:43 - 0:58 **Lesser Spotted Woodpecker** *Dendrocopos minor*
CD2-81d	0:59 - 1:53 **Eurasian Hobby** *Falco subbuteo*
CD2-81e	1:54 - 2:14 **White-tailed Eagle** *Haliaeetus albicilla*
CD2-81f	2:16 - 2:31 **Eurasian Wryneck** *Jynx torquilla*
CD2-81g	2:32 - 3:10 **Common Kestrel** *Falco tinnunculus*
CD2-81h	3:11 - 3:20 **Green Woodpecker** *Picus viridis*
CD2-81i	3:21 - 3:52 **Eurasian Hobby** *Falco subbuteo*
CD2-81j	3:53 - 4:14 **Peregrine Falcon** *Falco peregrinus*
CD2-82	**Eurasian Hobby** *Falco subbuteo*
CD2-83	**Eurasian Wryneck** *Jynx torquilla*
CD2-84	**Eurasian Hobby** *Falco subbuteo*
CD2-85	**Common Kestrel** *Falco tinnunculus*
CD2-86	**Eurasian Hobby** *Falco subbuteo*
CD2-87	**Eurasian Hobby** *Falco subbuteo*
CD2-88	**Eurasian Hobby** *Falco subbuteo*
CD2-89	**'Reedbed Cuckoo'** *Cuculus canorus* and **Eurasian Reed Warbler** *Acrocephalus scirpaceus*
CD2-90	**'Forest Cuckoo'** *Cuculus canorus*
CD2-91	**Eurasian Bullfinch** *Pyrrhula pyrrhula*
CD2-92	**Common Snipe** *Gallinago gallinago*
CD2-93	**Eurasian Woodcock** *Scolopax rusticola*
CD2-94	**Eurasian Woodcock** *Scolopax rusticola*
CD2-95	**Eurasian Woodcock** *Scolopax rusticola*
CD2-96	**Eurasian Woodcock** *Scolopax rusticola*
CD2-97	**Jack Snipe** *Lymnocryptes minimus*
CD2-98	**Jack Snipe** *Lymnocryptes minimus* and **Common Snipe** *Gallinago gallinago*

Acknowledgements

The Sound Approach are Arnoud van den Berg, Magnus Robb, Killian Mullarney, Dick Forsman, René Pop and me, Mark Constantine. While the book is written in the first person it is a concentrated mix of the thoughts and opinions of us all. However, any mistakes are all mine.

For this book we enlisted Nick Hopper, who apart from writing and taking many of the photos, also conducted a series of new studies of waterbirds, gulls and corvids especially for our book. The Sound Approach would like to thank Claire, for keeping him sane during the process.

Gilbert White included his friends' letters in *The natural history and antiquities of Selborne* (White 1789); I'm sure he reproduced their words faithfully. We have made our own interpretations of our birders' actions, conversations and emails, and even sprinkled them with a little folklore. Nick and I would like to thank all the bird pub visitors mentioned in the book and ask for forgiveness for the liberties taken, but would point out that we were constantly encouraged by Shaun Robson, who gave his support, collected the photographs of birders for publication and even allowed us to publish stories about him even when there was only a grain of truth remaining. Shaun is also the benign dictator of *Out & About*, a Dorset-based internet group that grew from a small, local bird newsline. We've borrowed freely from the opinions and debates expressed in that forum and would like to thank all the contributors. We thank Mo Constantine who read or had

read to her endless drafts, and accompanied Mark throughout the stories told and the writing process.

The Sound Approach would like to single out Ian Alexander who, besides giving us an environmental master class, explained the various agencies and government initiatives. Where we've used his opinions we have quoted him. Hamish Murray advised on the management of nature reserves and especially the sounds birds make when migrating. Dave Chown, Neil Gartshore and James Lidster all assisted Nick in our surveys; James also acted as an enthusiastic guide and kindly helped us with the gull chapter. Andy Musgrove kindly listened to and commented on our criticisms of WeBS. Furthermore, we thank Pete Miles of Dorset Oysters who advised on the clams and crabs of the harbor sea bed. Neil Johnson and Chris Thain helped with the history and geography of Brownsea Island. We thank Cecilia Bosman who through the years assisted Arnoud on most of his travels, and materialised this book with Anneke Boekhoudt from Lampenistenpers, Amsterdam, and Mientje Petrus from Em-space, Amstelveen. Spencer Burge, Matt Fairhall, Kerry Fletcher and Paul Moreton assisted in various ways.

The Sound Approach would also like to thank Eloisa Matheu of Alosa, who supplied recordings that helped to clarify the geographical variation of Dartford Warbler sounds across Iberia; STRIX, Carlos and Cláudia Cruz and Paulo Monteiro for help with logistics in Portugal; and Pim Wolf who provided accommodation and good company for many a migration recording session in Zeeland, the Netherlands, and also allowed us to use recordings of a first-winter Siberian Chiffchaff making sounds we have not recorded ourselves. Peter Nuyten also supplied a sound recording, and we appreciate all the help he has given with our equipment. Eugene Archer gave invaluable assistance when Magnus and Killian went to study Dartford Warblers in France, Vasil Ananian directed Magnus and René to the best sites for chiffchaffs in Armenia and Brian Cresswell kindly shared his knowledge of European Nightjar sounds. We are grateful to all the people who assisted Arnoud to record sounds of Siberian Chiffchaffs in Siberia, especially Sergey Gashkov from Tomsk State University. We thank José Luis Copete, Pierre-André Crochet, Łukasz Ławicki, Richard Millington and Ricardo Gutiérrez for timely responses to questions on cormorants' distribution, and Klas Strandberg from Telinga microphones for his continuous support.

The recordings are stereo, digital and were recorded where possible using a SASS or stereo ambient sampling system that gives the listener the impression of being present at the scene. For this reason, they are best listened to on headphones. Rather than use words where we wished to interpret the sounds, we used sonagrams, which we made using Raven Pro 1.3. Sonagrams are just graphic interpretations of sound. They are best approached in the same way you would look at a stocks and shares graph. Just as the shares' rise or fall is shown by the rise and fall of a line on a graph, on sonagrams the higher or lower the trace appears above the baseline, the higher or lower pitched it sounds. And in both cases the horizontal axis represents time. Just as the success or failure

of stocks is tracked over time from left to right, in sonagrams the duration of a sound is represented by the horizontal span of a trace.

If you are unfamiliar with sonagrams, start with these three simple songs (**CD1-01** to **CD1-03**). Listen to the recordings and follow the notes on the page.

CD1-01 **Common Wood Pigeon** *Columba palumbus* Middlebere, Poole Harbour, Dorset, England, 06:00, 25 April 2005. Song of two different individuals. Background: Canada Goose *Branta canadensis*, Common Shelduck *Tadorna tadorna*, Common Teal *Anas crecca*, Eurasian Collared Dove *Streptopelia decaocto*, Pied Wagtail *Motacilla yarrellii*, Eurasian Wren *Troglodytes troglodytes*, Dunnock *Prunella modularis*, Common Blackbird *Turdus merula*, Song Thrush *T philomelos*, Eurasian Blackcap *Sylvia atricapilla*, Carrion Crow *Corvus corone*, Common Chaffinch *Fringilla coelebs* and European Greenfinch *Chloris chloris*. 05.005.MC.04630.21

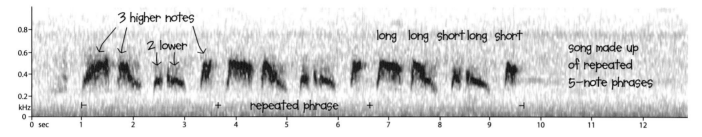

CD1-02 **Stock Dove** *Columba oenas* Arne, Poole Harbour, Dorset, England, 07:30, 10 March 2007. Song of two different individuals. Background: Black-headed Gull *Chroicocephalus ridibundus*, European Robin *Erithacus rubecula*, Song Thrush *Turdus philomelos*, Goldcrest *Regulus regulus*, European Blue Tit *Cyanistes caeruleus* and Western Jackdaw *Corvus monedula*. 07.001.MC.11115.02

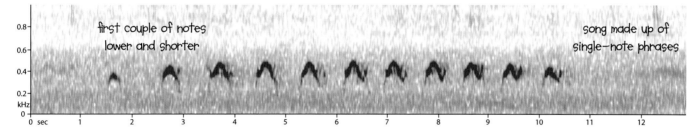

CD1-03 **Eurasian Collared Dove** *Streptopelia decaocto* Middlebere, Poole Harbour, Dorset, England, 05:45, 25 April 2005. Song. Background: Common Wood Pigeon *Columba palumbus*, Eurasian Wren *Troglodytes troglodytes*, Common Blackbird *Turdus merula*, Eurasian Blackcap *Sylvia atricapilla*, Great Tit *Parus major*, Common Chaffinch *Fringilla coelebs* and European Greenfinch *Chloris chloris*. 05.005.MC.03330.02

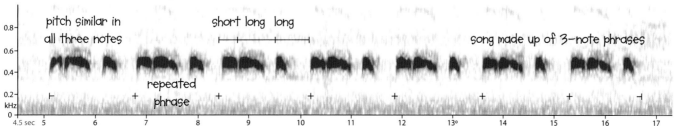

15

Introduction: Tuesday night 9pm

Mo and I were planning our wedding when, on Thursday 8 March 1973, the windows of her London office were blown in. The IRA had bombed the Old Bailey. Our honeymoon was already booked for the Dingle Peninsula on the west coast of Ireland. Wanting isolation amongst nature we had rented a middle terrace country cottage on Ventry Strand. Come June, we escaped the strains of London and took our very first flight, arriving in Cork.

Old Bailey, London, 8 March 1973 *(Corbis images)*

Our honeymoon cottage was set amongst the dry stone walls where *Ryan's Daughter* had been filmed a couple of years before. Dingle, a twice-weekly bus ride away, had a long history of hospitality and most of the shops were licensed to sell alcohol. The language spoken in the bar in Ventry when we were there was Gaelic and as the Oscar-winning film had a republican theme, I asked the barman if there was still IRA activity in the area.

"Do you know who your neighbour is?" the barman asked quietly.
"No", I replied.
"Seán Mac Stíofáin."
I looked suitably ignorant.
"The chief of staff of the Provisional IRA. He's just come off hunger strike and he's recuperating in the cottage next to yours."

I spent the first night of our honeymoon being sick into a bucket, not with fear you understand, but 'because I ate the crab'. Sitting with Mo amongst the dunes the next day watching Mac Stíofáin and his family negotiate a walk across the incoming waters on the strand, we were suddenly distracted by Gannets fishing behind them, plunging from 100 m deep into the surf. Exhausted by city life, we decided to move out of London when we got back.

Birders at The Blue Boar pub, Poole, Dorset, 24 August 2010 *(Arnoud B van den Berg)*. Clockwise from left: Stephen Smith, Kevin Lane, Shaun Robson, Magnus Robb, Killian Mullarney, Mark Constantine, Ian Lewis, Ewan Brodie and Margaret Lewis.

The parish of Poole lies in the eastern corner of the county of Dorset in England, where people are blessed with long lives, low crime rates and the mildest weather on the British mainland. We settled there. As we explored the area, it wasn't as we had imagined. It seemed that every aspect of nature was under threat. Gamekeepers, commercial egg-collectors and shooters were devastating bird numbers. Heathland was disappearing under new roads, housing estates and conifer plantations. Local chemical works processes were leaking into Holes Bay, assisting in the corrosion of old prams and supermarket trolleys. When BP discovered the biggest onshore oilfield in Western Europe under Poole Harbour in December 1973, Mo and I joined the local group of Friends of the Earth (FoE) to see what could be done.

Run by Jenny Ottaway and Martin Price, there were 10 active FoE members and we each had a responsibility for one aspect of the environment. We would have liked to be responsible for wildlife but the slightly eccentric birder Charles Flynn held that portfolio, (as president of the student union, Charles had worn his long blonde hair in the style of General Custer but under a top hat). We got transport and as Mo and I cycled everywhere on a metallic pink tandem, we occupied ourselves with designing cycle routes. At meetings, Charles talked flamboyantly of Hen Harriers, Hobbies and Woodlarks while we listened in awe, never having seen or heard any of them.

We were in the era of *The Good Life* and Richard Mabey's *Food for Free* (1972) and we were into plants. Cycling along hedgerows, we picked Dog Rose petals to make into jam, and elderflowers for fritters. Along with close friends Jeff and Geri Osment who had also moved to London and back, we tried self-sufficiency,

being granted an allotment for growing vegetables. So while Charlie boy was watching Hobbies, the nearest we were getting to any birds was collecting poo from local racing pigeon fanciers' lofts. We needed this fiercely alkaline additive to balance the pH of the allotment's soil, which was highly acidic due to its location on the edge of one of Britain's finest lowland habitats, Canford Heath. A major battleground for Poole FoE, it was fast becoming the largest private housing estate in Britain. Mo and I would cycle across the remaining heath, avoiding gangs of bored youths and scrambling motorbikes, looking for what Charles had told us were the last couple of pairs of Woodlarks in the county. We did eventually see them, and we also struggled to see the bird so closely linked to heathland, Dartford Warbler.

Inspired by our new portfolio and upset by the environmental impact of cars and road building, I had chosen not to drive, so for our next holiday we cycled from Poole to the Brecon Beacons, staying at the Tyn-y-Caeau youth hostel. The warden Eric Bartlett's hostel garden was full of Pied Flycatchers, and he pointed them out to us from a shady seat. I think they were our first looks. Eric must have liked us because he took us to visit a farmer's wife who had a couple of deserted cygnets on her pond. I remember him telling her, "I hear the Reed Buntings are breeding again this year." How intriguing. I couldn't hear much. What sort of sound were they making? On the way back he suddenly hit the brakes and put the car into reverse to show us a Tawny Owl sitting in a bush on the side of the road.

What wonderful birds! I was star-struck with Eric's skill. I wrote in the diary, "he's editor of Breconshire Birds, a National park warden, a member of the mountain rescue team and it looks as if he's writing a book as well."

Silver Fern, bright blue bugs and Cuckoo Flower all dropped out of our notebooks and were replaced with Whinchats and Common Redstarts. In two hours, Eric Bartlett had inspired Mo and me to become birders.

Once home, I wanted to know more about the local birds. On Sunday nights I would contact three birders to find out what they had seen over the weekend. The first, Martin Cade, now warden of Portland Bird Observatory, was young, devoted and very cool. He watched Radipole and Lodmoor in Weymouth. What made Martin especially cool (apart from his general demeanour and the girls liking his legs in shorts) was his record at rarity finding. In one year, 20 British Birds rarities had been recorded in Dorset and he had found and identified 10 of them. During one of our Sunday night conversations, I asked him how many days a year he got out into the field. We worked out that he hadn't missed a day's birding in Dorset for two and a half years.

Then I'd call Dave Smith at the other end of the county. A fitness instructor by profession, Dave birded like a boxer and saw knockout birds. When I tried to see them, they melted into frustratingly sweet mysteries. I soon realised that he was pushing all his senses to their limits, and if I was combative when it came to bird finding, he was formidable. Hengistbury Head and Stanpit in Christchurch where Dave watched had been part of Hampshire until a boundary reorganisation, and sometimes when he had found something that none of the rest of us saw, we would wish they still were.

My third phone call of a Sunday night was to Hamish Murray, the warden of Durlston. This was a new headland reserve near Swanage, just over an hour's cycle ride away. Hamish and his wife Barbara became our friends, and Mo and I spent most of our birding time at Durlston.

As I became more interested in birds, it was no use keeping a British life list. Without a car, twitching for me would have to be a local affair. I started keeping a list of the birds I had seen at Durlston. Then through the '80s I competed with my three top local birders to see the most species in Dorset each year. Success came from finding your own birds on your own patch, but Poole Harbour couldn't really compete with Christchurch harbour, Portland and Weymouth, or Durlston. Hamish would joke derisively that I should write a book called *Birds of Baiter* At least Baiter, an area of reclaimed land a short walk from the town centre, was accessible while the rest of the harbour was vast. 100 square miles of mud and water, surrounded by private country estates and large quiet conifer forests and heaths.

There were a few local naturalists who would get together in an observation hut on Studland heath. Studland was an easy cycle from our new house in Rossmore Road, and on Sunday mornings we would visit the heath and find the warden Rees Cox and his group of volunteers drinking tea from flasks and eating cake. Elizabeth Ollivant, Peter Hawkins and Stephen Guy all helped Rees keep an eye out for fires, adders, and the odd nudist from their eyrie overlooking Little Sea. One stalwart, Len Howell, would arrive each weekend from Southampton to erect bird hides here and at nearby Brand's Bay. It was good to catch up on what everyone had seen, but despite being good naturalists, they were not really birders, so bird news within the harbour remained frustratingly scarce.

Then things changed. Dave Collins (1986) published *Waders and wildfowl of Poole Harbour* for BP, a survey designed to assess bird populations and their distribution in the harbour in the light of possible oil pollution. (Nick has spent two years replicating Dave's groundbreaking survey for this book, but more of that later.)

In 1987, a group of us formed the new Dorset Bird Club. Soft-spoken biologist and bird report editor George Green became the chairman and member 001. This created a vacancy for a new report editor, and Martin Cade took the job. We wanted the new county bird reports to have twice the number of pages as the old ones, and as Martin had helped Dave Collins with his BP survey so he was able to provide new Poole material. The new report was funded by donations from the core members, and through sponsored bird races.

Then came the introduction of birdlines, premium rate telephone numbers with news about birds seen over the past few days. Birdline Southwest washed away the need for local networks and created the feeling that information was a right rather than a privilege. The lines were very lucrative and the organisers were treated as if they were pornographers, with this expensive 'birders' porn' tempting birdwatchers to give up more worthwhile work like surveys and conservation to become twitchers.

Nick was at university and sharing a flat and phone bill with a friend. He remembers one morning picking up the phone to make a call and finding to his horror that the birdline was still going from the night before. Some birders would visit friends and call birdline from their phone, while pretending to be making a more innocent call.

All this created tensions where friendships had existed before, and now I didn't make the Sunday evening calls but rather phoned 'the line', although I seldom had news to call in and very few birders were bothering with Poole Harbour. Then I met Robin Ward who was surveying Redshank numbers from the as yet unopened Holes Bay road in preparation for a new Poole town bridge. I can't remember where we met, but it was his idea to start a 'bird pub'.

The Crown Hotel pub, Poole, Dorset, 17 April 2012 (*Richard Skins*)

The Antelope pub, Poole, Dorset, 17 April 2012 (*Richard Skins*)

The Blue Boar pub, Poole, Dorset, 17 April 2012 (*Richard Skins*)

We started in The Crown in Market Street, five minutes from my office, and over the years we moved several times ending up at our present home at The Blue Boar. Over time we slowly recruited the other locals who populate this book.

Ian Lewis was one of the first. Ian is a worldwide twitcher and bird club member 007. I asked him recently what number of birds he had seen and got this typical reply. "Assuming your book won't be published before the end of July when I get back from New Guinea, you can use the figure of 7150 (Clements 2007)." An 'A' ringer and retired virologist, Ian is very well read, acting as the Wikipedia at the pub. You know, not always accurate but no one else knows enough to argue.

Bob Gifford was next. He had a hidden agenda for coming to the pub. He wanted to learn how to be a bird ringer from Ian. Having been interested in birds as a little boy in the '60s, Bob and his egg-collecting big brother would sneak past the Upton House keepers cottage in search of snakes, mice and birds' eggs. Bob remembers as his biggest crime stealing a Herring Gull's egg from the tree nests on Brownsea and smuggling it home in a Weetabix box.

Faced with Bob's request, Ian suggested that they would first ring Blue Tits, notoriously vicious in the hand and dull enough to put off an uncommitted student. But fortune smiled on Bob. Ian belonged to the Stour Ringing Group, and they were involved in ringing and radio tracking Nightjars. So as luck would have it, Bob's first bird in the hand was a beautiful Nightjar. He was hooked, and in time became secretary of the group.

The next pub regular was Bob's friend Nick Hull, a military fireman. Nick was brought up on Wool Manor Farm where his dad was a tenant pig farmer. Rough shooting Mallard and Teal around the farm, he loved birds and worried about misidentifying them and shooting the wrong ones. "What if I had shot a Goldeneye?" he explained down the pub. Flocks of wintering Bewick's Swans would fly in to roost on the pond outside his window on winter nights, and their sounds kept a young Nick awake with excitement. When he was 16, his grandparents paid for membership of the RSPB, and he was soon cycling to Arne to attend guided walks on Grip Heath with the warden, looking for Dartford Warblers.

Nick and Bob added a lot to the volume of the heated discussions at the pub, although they both calmed down with the arrival of Jackie. She had met Nick at her first local RSPB meeting, and was soon running the local young ornithologists group with him. There is no formality to the pub, no officers or agendas. We used to take a subject each and discuss it. Jackie would bring in cuttings of birds that presented identification challenges, such as Long-eared Owl and Short-eared Owl in flight, so we could discuss features and share our knowledge.

Robin then met Stephen Smith and encouraged him to come. I recognised him from Friends of the Earth. Stephen, an environmentally angst-ridden German teacher, paid his first visit to the pub on Wednesday 3 August 1988 when we were puzzling over a large influx of Yellow-legged Gulls into the harbour.

Stephen was the local WeBS co-ordinator, and during the following weeks brought with him a good map of Poole Harbour, showing all the important feeding and roosting areas for waders. He suggested we decided on a proper recording area. His map was a good basis to start from, though the area was later expanded to include under-watched Ballard Down and Corfe Mullen tip. We still don't completely agree on the boundary for the area, but in this book's maps you can see the version that I've used for this book.

In October 1991, Shaun Robson arrived at the pub, around the time Robin went off to study ecology. Drinking with a trading standards officer has its up side: from then on we always got a full pint. As time passed we all noticed Shaun getting more assertive and wondered if he had been on a course. Whatever the reason, he did gain confidence and created pub calm and order where often there had been chaos. He also changed the meetings to Tuesday night 9pm.

By then we were meeting in The Antelope and would bring in bird feathers and road kills to quiz each other. I became quite expert at identifying which feather matched which feather tract, and it helped us learn more about moult and identification. When Nick Hull came back from holiday and brought in a plastic sack full of Black Vulture feathers, the publican encouraged us to move by turning the music up every time we came in. More positively, Nick had compiled the all time list of birds of the Isle of Purbeck, based on H G Alexander (1969), and a systematic catalogue of the birds of Purbeck (Austen 1885). Inspired by this I had a go at working out an all time Poole Harbour list.

By now there were quite a few regulars, and a bird diary was kept at the pub. Inevitably, there were heated debates, many fuelled by copious amounts of Speckled Hen. One of the hottest, which still carries on today, concerned which areas should or should not be a part of the recording area. The biggest sticking point at the time was Ewan Brodie's garden. A veteran of the harbour, Ewan worked nights at the local pie factory. His garden hosted some of the most reliable Bramblings in Dorset, essential for any good winter bird list. It was decided that all our gardens would be included, to encourage us to contribute observations from Poole as well as the harbour and local headlands.

One of Rees Cox's recruits, Ewan had been birding locally since the age of 10, when he and another local lad Roger Howell used to watch birds together after Sunday School. Looking at birds and often not knowing what they were, they still managed to identify Smew, Little Owl, Grasshopper Warbler and Bearded Reedling, and had heard Nightingale in Bluebell Woods, all by the age of 13. (It's much harder to find a Nightingale in Poole Harbour nowadays, but you can hear recent echoes of former times in **CD1-04** and **CD1-05**.) Roger later went to a different school and lost touch with Ewan and birds. 23 years later Roger started birding again when a mutual friend, Phil Greaves (Fireman Phil), told him that he and I were hoping to see a Great Northern Diver. Roger gently broke the sad news to Phil that "You don't get Great Northern Divers in Poole Harbour," but we all went anyway. We did see one and it got Roger birding again and coming down to the pub.

Now we had moved to a quieter pub, I could bring in bird sound recordings to use for quizzes. In 1993, we also started a competition to find who could see the most bird species in Poole Harbour in a year. For the annual prize, we framed a Little Egret feather found under the first Poole Harbour egret roost. Nigel Symes was good at all these competitions. One night he got every one of the British tern sounds right, and in the first year he won the egret feather, seeing 167 species in Poole Harbour. Nigel was one of an increasing number of professional conservationists now working in the area. He was in charge of the RSPB's heathland team. Their job was to restore heathland by removing scrub and maintaining the age and health of the heather. Amazingly, Dartford Warblers have been in Poole Harbour for more than 7,000 years, and Nigel's job was to recreate a heathland more typical of several hundred years ago when they were at their peak.

This book is in part the conversations of the birders in the pub and in the field over 20 years, and at a wedding reception in 2009. The first part will go on to explore the history of Poole, and the chances of Dartford Warbler being the first English endemic.

Common Nightingale *Luscinia megarhynchos* near Corfe Castle, Dorset, England, 19:11, 4 May 2010. One of two males that sang at the same spot. In the second half of the recording, you can hear a few quiet *tuc* calls. Background: European Robin *Erithacus rubecula*, Common Blackbird *Turdus merula* and Lesser Whitethroat *Sylvia curruca*. 100504.MC.193301.01

CD1-04

Common Nightingale *Luscinia megarhynchos* near Corfe Castle, Dorset, England, 19:11, 4 May 2010. One of the two males sings to the accompaniment of church bells. Background: Eurasian Wren *Troglodytes troglodytes*, Common Blackbird *Turdus merula*, Song Thrush *T philomelos*, Eurasian Blackcap *Sylvia atricapilla* and Common Chaffinch *Fringilla coelebs*. 100504.MC.191100.02

CD1-05

Chapter 1: And did those feet in ancient times

The next wave of folk who came to the pub started with local lad James Lidster, who Mo and I met while birding. He told us he had a forklift license, so despite him being a birder and potentially unreliable, he came to work with us. A great rarity finder, he pinned down the first twitchable Icterine Warbler on Ballard. I was delighted, and was sitting there trying to sketch it when Nick Hopper wandered up and looked over my shoulder. He cheekily asked me which bird I was drawing. It was 9 September 1997, a Tuesday, which says a lot about both of us. Nick had just moved to Poole, having run up too many unpaid parking tickets in Bath, and I invited him down to the pub. James had a close birding friend called Ian Stanley who had also moved into the area, and this completed the trio. They shared a flat together on Poole High Street.

When Nick was little, his mum took him to church a couple of times and he tried Sunday school once but didn't like it. As a boy, I was primarily educated at a Church of England school and sang in the church choir twice on Sundays. He seems to have a better grasp on prehistory than I do. Had I been asked down the pub, "what is the age of the earth?" the first answer that popped into my head would have been, "about 6,000 years plus seven days". This is a creationist view that was subtly introduced to churchgoers of my age, and could be worth a spin if it weren't for Ian Lewis's Wikipedian superpowers. He could point out, and has, that the current scientific consensus on the age of the earth seems to be around 4.5 billion years. I can remember him explaining how 'climate change' was a constant reality with the temperatures varying from Arctic to Mediterranean, and that before the current worries about warming we thought we were heading into an ice age.

I must also admit to thinking that the ice age was just that, a period of time when everything was ice (and by everything I mean Poole Harbour). Now I realise that you have to go back around 640 million years to find our area completely covered in ice.

Anyway, I'm not a creationist in this religious debate. I also believe that Poole's climate has constantly changed. I find it a bit harder to believe that scientists can calculate accurately something as complex as man's influence on the earth's weather, or that politicians can co-operate enough to control it, but that's another subject. Climate scientists often seem to have little in common with meteorologists, and in many ways they seem closer to archeologists. For example, they use compilations of 26,000 years of tree ring history to work out the ancient changes in the weather. They also take deep samples of soil deposits, analysing the grains of pollen to reconstruct the dominant vegetation and likely temperatures stretching back thousands of years into the past.

We can also learn much about the ancient climate from bird bones, fossilised insects, and teeth from a variety of creatures,

White Stork *Ciconia ciconia*, Wareham Water Meadows, Dorset, 2 October 2010 (*Mike Coleman*). 'From a period with a warm climate, c 45,000 years ago, the remains of, eg, White Stork were found north of Poole.'

all of which can be identified and carbon dated. Take the crocodiles. They became extinct in Poole Harbour 100 million years ago. We know that crocs were out there, because when you search Poole Harbour mud you can still find their teeth.

For more recent time scales, the picture is less muddy and to imagine birding in Poole in the last 100,000 years we recommend *Birds and Climate Change* (1995) where John Burton, a modern Sherlock Holmes, describes the amazing changes to Britain's birdlife over the millennia. When we read Burton's book alongside *The History of British Birds* by Yalden & Albarella (2009), the amazing list of birds for Poole Harbour makes Nick and me hyperventilate.

Evidently, 65,000 years ago Willow Grouse and Little Bustard would have been here. Their remains were found just west of us at Tornewton cave in Devon. Some 45,000 years ago, the climate became far warmer. Poole's acid soil isn't perfect for preserving tiny skeletons, and the nearest discovered remains from this period were further north, where there were White Stork, Alpine Swift and Crag Martin.

Between 22,000 and 17,000 years ago came another spell of cooling temperatures. This was the 'Last Glacial Maximum', which saw an ice sheet extend southwards to within 500 km of Poole. Massive amounts of seawater were 'locked up' in the ice caps, lowering sea levels by an estimated 127 m. At this time, Britain was a part of a large continental land mass and the area that is now Poole Harbour was just a floodplain with a river running through it, a tributary to another more distant river. Not only the harbour, but also the English Channel and much of the North Sea were dry land.

Our local patch, like all of southern Britain, had become a semi-polar desert, uninhabited by man and home to birds and beasts you would now associate with the far north. Arctic Fox, Woolly Mammoth and Collared Lemming remains dated to this period have been found in nearby counties. Presumably, Rock Ptarmigan, Gyrfalcon, Snowy Owl and Snow Bunting would have been around, and some northern waders would have bred in the area.

The continuing cold pushed deciduous woodland, its birds and mammals (including mankind) further and further southwards, concentrating them into ever shrinking areas that eventually became a few isolated pockets. These pockets or 'refugia' included the Iberian Peninsula, the Balkans and Ukraine. During this period of isolation, the birds in each 'refugium' essentially formed 'island populations', following their own independent evolutionary course. When the climate eventually warmed up, as the bird populations spread from their separate refugia and reunited, they were often no longer compatible. Over the course of several glacial cycles, this led to new species being formed.

By 13,000 years ago, the last ice age was fast losing its grip and the ice sheet was retreating back northward, taking its Arctic conditions with it. Poole Harbour was now no longer a semi-polar desert, but at least partly covered in forest, with scattered lakes and bogs, a landscape akin to today's Finland and with birdlife to match. Nick loves the list of rare birds that would have been hanging around the area, with Nutcrackers occupying his garden up Nutcrack Lane, and other gems like Willow Grouse, Hazel Hen, Hawk Owl and Tengmalm's Owl nearby.

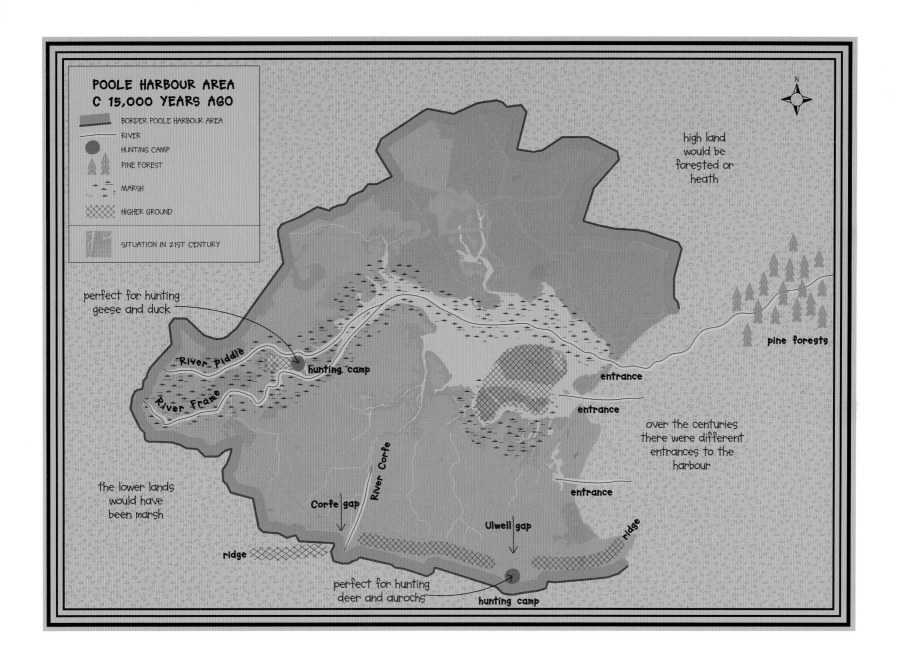

POOLE HARBOUR AREA
C 15,000 YEARS AGO

BORDER POOLE HARBOUR AREA
RIVER
HUNTING CAMP
PINE FOREST
MARSH
HIGHER GROUND

SITUATION IN 21ST CENTURY

high land
would be
forested or
heath

pine forests

perfect for hunting
geese and duck

River Piddle

River Frome

hunting camp

entrance

entrance

over the centuries
there were different
entrances to the
harbour

the lower lands
would have
been marsh

River Corfe

Corfe gap

Ulwell gap

entrance

ridge

ridge

perfect for hunting
deer and aurochs

hunting camp

Humans also spread north after the last ice age. There was a population explosion, and Britain was repopulated with hunters. Stephen Oppenheimer specialises in a new branch of science called phylogeography, or whose ancestors came from where, and when. In *The Origins of the British* (2006), he describes his research into our genes. He suggests that my south coast ancestors were most likely Paleolithic hunter-gatherers who had been successfully killing mammoths in the treeless steppe tundra of what is now Ukraine. Since there was no English Channel, they could have walked in a straight line all the way. In practice they preferred to move along watercourses, hunting and fishing like ancient strandlopers. Nick's Somerset ancestors most probably came up the Atlantic coast from a human refugium in the Basque country, along with those who settled in Wales and Ireland. Nick loves the sea, and both his granddad and great granddad were in the navy, so he feels at home with this idea. Oppenheimer also suggests that despite repeated invasions, the genes of these early arrivals typically still predominate close to where they settled.

Lillian Ladle and her fellow archeologists ran one of Britain's longest running amateur digs near Wareham. At Bestwall between the rivers Frome and Piddle, they found the remains of one of the early settlers' camps, dating from around 11,000 years ago. The semi-nomadic hunters had dug holes through to the gravel and worked the flint nodules into sharp stone tools and arrowheads. They made the most of the fishing, collected shellfish, and hunted Red-breasted Mergansers, Great Bitterns, Great Crested Grebes, Little Grebes and Common Cranes (Ladle & Woodward 2009).

Over the next few thousand years, things got drier and temperatures continued to increase until they peaked at between 9,000-7,000 years ago. Strawberry Tree, Spotted Slug, European Bee-eater, Eurasian Hoopoe and Dartford Warbler appeared with this Mediterranean climate. Around the time, the gradual melting of the ice had raised sea levels to the point that the land connection between Britain and France disappeared. Then about 8,000 years ago, a huge undersea landslide off the Norwegian coast caused a massive tsunami. This almost certainly contributed to the disappearance of low-lying Doggerland, the last remaining dry land in the southern North Sea (Weninger et al 2008). Britain became an island, and Poole was now on the coast.

The shallow dish of the Stour and Piddle flood plain formed a huge harbour, the silt forming deep and treacherous mud flats between the hilltops, which were now islands poking out of the water. Over time, the surrounding ridge of hills gradually eroded away, leaving the chalk stacks called Old Harry and his wife, a gap that is Poole Bay, and 24 km east of Old Harry, the corresponding chalk stacks of The Needles on the newly formed Isle of Wight. The soft sandy cliffs along the new seashore soon crumbled and deposited tons of sand, and over the next 7,000 years this formed the beaches and harbour mouth. This is how Poole Harbour was formed, the largest and shallowest natural harbour in Europe.

Climate change concerns more than just temperature and is really about the changes in weather patterns created by the relative distribution of sea and land, ice packs and deserts. Now that Britain was surrounded by water, its weather became more anticyclonic. All this disrupted the birds' habits. It also stranded the Dartford Warbler.

Dartfords would have bred in the bush undergrowth on the edge of pines or in scrub along the harbour shores. There were no open heaths yet according to soil deposits. Pollen samples taken at the Bestwall dig showed how at first junipers were common, then birch arrived and was succeeded in turn by pine, oak and elm as the climate became warmer, while lime and alders grew along the wetter meadows. This creates a glorious picture of bird-filled forests with very few people, and Dartfords singing along the margins.

Starting around 5,000 years ago, our ancestors felled the forests to farm the crops that began to account for half the pollen samples in the deposits. Evidently, 3,500 years ago the land was divided into fields where barley, wheat and beans were cultivated and sheep and cattle kept. Red Kites, Ravens, Carrion Crows, Jackdaws and Starlings would have thrived as they learnt to exploit our husbandry. Most of the soil outside the richer river valleys was soon exhausted, and it was this environmental catastrophe that left us with Poole's heathland.

Poole Harbour 2,000 years ago would have been more like an estuary than today, with three entrances to the harbour: one south of Pilot's Point and a second in the middle near today's entrance. A third recently discovered entrance is now deep under Panorama Road, a couple of hundred yards before it reaches the chain ferry, where the North Channel flowed out into Poole Bay (Dyer & Darvill 2010).

An archeological dig on and around Green Island was televised on Channel 4's *Time Team* (Taylor 2004). It found evidence of a thriving trade and most exciting for us, in amongst the pots and amphoras, the remains of a White-tailed Eagle. Around 2,200 years ago, the area nearby would have had an industrial feel with shale working, iron working, clay mining and pottery production, and salt production centred on Ower. Cross-channel boats would have been moored to a substantial dock between Ower and Green Island. The archeologists also discovered that pigs were slaughtered, butchered and salted, so maybe this attracted the eagle. The leftovers would certainly have fed hundreds of large gulls.

In fact salt production was to become a major feature around the southern shores of the harbour for some time to come. The warm climate was ideal, and saltpans were soon popping up all over the place. There were around 50-100 acres at Arne alone with many more in Brand's Bay and at least 32 pans in Studland Bay. One can assume it was a typical Mediterranean scene with breeding Red-crested Pochards, Black-winged Stilts, Kentish and Little Ringed Plovers, and Black Terns. Although the climate did subsequently cool, salt production was able to be maintained for the next thousand years by heating the water with shale.

The best addition to our ancient bird list has to be the Dalmatian Pelican. With a colony only 80 km away on the Somerset Levels, I think we can assume a few young birds would have investigated the fishing here.

Little Sea was
formed by the
drifting sands

the stone ridge
of South Haven
looked like this
in the 16th
century

blown sand built
up and by 1721
it was looking
like this

by 1886 the
sand had formed
Little Sea

in the north of England ice has created th
landscape; in Poole, shifting sands hav
opened and closed the saltmarshes from th
sea, and they form the channels and marshe
of which birds take advantag

SHIFTING SANDS

the last breeding
Common Ringed Plovers were blown-up
by the bomb disposal unit here

over the last decade, the
beach has narrowed and the
wader roost has moved to
Brownsea lagoon

Poole's first written bird record was made by the area's first birder. He was literally a saint, St Aldhelm (639-709), and he wrote of more familiar birds like Wood Pigeon, Swallow, Nightingale and Chaffinch (Prendergast & Boys 1983). During his lifetime, better weather prevailed again. This was the start of the medieval warm period that lasted until 1250. Summer temperatures rose to around 1-2°C higher than today, bringing back the warmth-loving birds, and in AD 998 we suspect that birds such as Quail, Eagle Owl, Hoopoe and Golden Oriole were in Poole Harbour.

From a bird's point of view, people weren't such an issue in the 10th century as there were so few. Poole had a couple of fisherman's cottages. Wareham had a population of a few hundred tending fields of garlic, with a handful of people at Studland, Ower, Goathorn, Arne and Hamworthy. Brownsea was owned by the church until 1539, and seldom had more than a hermit or two living there. Ravens were common, and referring to the year 1635, Denis Bond wrote in his chronicle "A Raven bred som tym before Christ dyd this yeare in Corfe Castell" (Cooper 2004). The fortress was rendered useless by Parliamentarian explosives in 1646, but Ravens still breed in its ruins today.

Around this time, major geographical changes were unfolding in the Studland area. Longshore drift was shifting sand along the beach and slowly closing the harbour mouth. By 1700, the drifting sand had formed dunes, which managed to cut off the open sea behind Pilot's Point entirely, isolating Little Sea and making it one of the most recent naturally formed lakes in England.

By 1750, most of Dorset and all of the areas surrounding Poole Harbour were heathland. Only the river valleys and the harbour shores were more fertile. A person living on the edge of Wareham then would be heating their home with peat, while on the edges of the heath the scrubby trees, the heather and gorse had to provide him with fodder, fuel and building materials. This management stopped trees encroaching and kept the gorse in perfect condition. It would have been ideal for the Dartford Warblers, whose population must have peaked around this time.

Poole was built by fishermen and merchants. Their focus was the sea, especially the newly discovered cod fishing at the Grand Banks off Newfoundland, Canada. They built the port and their business by taking salt and other provisions to Newfoundland, where over time many of them settled. Poole had more ships trading with North America than any other English port, and while the men were busy sailing the seas, the birds flourished.

By 1820, the golden age of the Newfoundland trade had ended, prices for cod had halved and bankruptcies and ruin followed. The Napoleonic wars were over, and although smuggling was still profitable, it didn't pay as well as it had. The weather had become far colder and the men of Poole who had hardly been home for 200 years had to look to Poole Harbour's natural resources for an income, starting with water birds.

Shell Bay, Studland, Dorset, 25 November 2009 (*Nick Hopper*). Looking north-west. 'Shifting sands: God forming Shell Bay on a Saturday.'

Chapter 2: Neptune's poultry yard...

One December night in 1998, Shaun suggested that we should list the different species of birds that we got on our Christmas cards and see who got the most. In the odd insecure moment I have counted my Christmas cards, but this competition created another perspective completely. We all started to be strategic. In an assorted box of RSPB cards, there are a few garden scenes with a Chaffinch, Blackbird, Wren etc. There are also many with one Robin on a spade, or a Barn Owl. Those judged more popular were only sent Robins, while garden scenes full of birds at a table were saved for those who had fewer friends.

CD1-06   **Dark-bellied Brent Goose** *Branta bernicla* Texel, Noord-Holland, Netherlands, 30 March 2002. A few *rrrot* calls at the start, then a growing murmur before the flock of about 100 takes off and heads out over a sea dyke towards tidal mudflats. Background: Pied Avocet *Recurvirostra avosetta*. 02.012.MR.12950.02

Dark-bellied Brent Goose *Branta bernicla*, juvenile, Bramble Bush Bay, Studland, Dorset, 16 March 2010 (*Nick Hopper*). 'The last brent?'

It became obvious that not many geese are featured on Christmas cards, at best a Greylag with a line inside about Christmas coming and the goose getting fat. Apart from Brent Geese **(CD-06)**, and the ubiquitous introduced Canada Goose, you don't get many geese using Poole Harbour either, unless it is very cold. Snow and ice elsewhere is usually what brings them to our part of the country. With one exception, the only place you get snow in Poole in December is on Christmas cards. This Dickensian Christmas is also an illustration of climate change, and the prolonged period of cooler weather that was coming to an end during Dickens' lifetime. In 1814 when Dickens was born, we were in the middle of this 'little ice age'. Consequently,

there were Brent Geese in their thousands feeding on eelgrass inside Poole Harbour.

One night in the pub, the conversation turned to wintering Red-breasted Mergansers. For as long as we could all remember there had been a dawn movement of up to 300 birds into the harbour. We would often see them in pairs or loose groups, flying higher than the stream of cormorants, shags and the odd sea duck that accompanied them. Counting was easy if you stood at the harbour mouth, a method first used by veteran,

Wildfowlers at Brand's Bay, Studland, Dorset, 19 November 2011 (*Nick Hopper*)

duffle-coated Dr Godfrey, who would tuck himself into the shelter of the Sandbanks Hotel wall. At dusk you could count them out again.

Anyway, the commuting had now stopped. What was the reason? Assuming that they were roosting somewhere fairly close out to sea, we worried that the ferry might be disturbing their roost. Or had they been taking advantage of night fishing? Was climate change affecting their movements, or was it a combination of these things? The conjecture went on for years. Now, having researched this book, I wonder if the answer was simpler. Wildfowling.

Birds have been hunted in Poole Harbour for 11,000 years, and not just for human consumption. In 1762 Benjamin Lester, a local fishing fleet owner, could still pay an old man to knock down 300 Puffins a day with poles, to provide bait for his fishermen (Dyer & Darvill 2010). Today, Puffins in Poole are rarer than crocodile teeth.

By the time of Dickens, Poole's transatlantic trade had declined. The men were back on dry land and struggling to find ways to put food on the table. If they were a good shot they could pot a goose for Christmas dinner. If they were a very good shot they could earn a living. Fowlers at the top of their game could earn the equivalent of £370 for a day and a night's work. They worked areas where we now count the ducks, like Shotover Moor and Shotover Creek in between Fitzworth and Ower.

Colonel Hawker was a famous local wildfowler. In his diary (1893), he explains that by 1830 Poole Harbour was *the* place to come and shoot wildfowl. It had gunners' punts lined up along the beach "in rows and rows" and was "one of the best grounds for wildfowl in the kingdom".

These punts are still called Poole canoes. They had a shallow draught (had they been completely flat-bottomed, they would have been awkward to row and likely to throw you out when you took a shot), and had grooves in the hull so that they could be pulled off the cloying harbour mud. The fowlers often had a dog on board. A favourite was the big black fluffy 'Newfoundland' mastiff, a formidably strong swimmer. According to Wikipedia they even have webbed feet.

You needed skill to earn that money, but it didn't take long for someone to come up with a gun that needed less skill and increased the catch. Called a punt gun, it could shoot up to 12,000 pellets in a single shot, while a normal shoulder shotgun fired 200. Swivel-mounted on the boat, the punt gun was prone to misfiring, occasionally taking the bottom out of a boat or knocking the shooter into the water.

Colonel Hawker described how one night he found himself staying with a band of Poole smugglers in the hostel on the end of South Haven. Leaving them to their trade, he got out before dawn into Brand's Bay, rowing through the frosty moonlit night up one of the many creeks. To be successful with the punt gun, he had to be downwind of the ducks that he could hear, and see outlined in the half-light. He tried his best not to flush a Curlew, knowing its raucous call would spook all the other birds. Then as he got within three or four gunshots of the birds, he lay down and pushed along with a setting pole. Now being in the perfect position, he let loose and took out 50 wildfowl in one shot.

Not that he got to bring all 50 birds home: "Should you have been successful, you will, if at night, generally *hear* your cripples beating on the mud, *before you can* sufficiently recover your eyes, from being dazzled by the fire, to see them. Your man then puts on his mud boards, taking the setting pole to support him, and assists the dog in collecting the killed and wounded; taking care to secure *first* the *outside* birds, lest they should escape to a creek... The *gunner* generally calculates on bringing home the half only of what he shoots" (Hawker 1859).

I suggest that to avoid being shot, Red-breasted Mergansers developed the habit of roosting out at sea until it was light enough to work out just where the wildfowlers were. So it wasn't that something was disturbing them now, but rather the opposite, and it had taken them 140 years to feel secure enough to return to their former habits. Apart from the odd one or two that still roost at sea, the majority have since been found to roost just to the west of Brownsea Island along with Great Crested and Black-necked Grebes, Goldeneye, and the odd Great Northern Diver.

Commercial wildfowling didn't stop completely in Poole until the sale of wild geese was banned in the '60s. Wildfowling still goes on today but not to the same degree. In my early years birding the harbour, it wasn't unusual to see injured birds. I remember being particularly upset by seeing a Razorbill crippled in this way. Despite the carnage, wildfowling brought people closer to nature and most of the early interest in birds came from hunting them to eat.

This mix is beautifully illustrated in the memoir *Longshoreman* by Benjamin Pond (2009). Known affectionately as 'Lord Goathorn', he was a supertramp living on Studland heath from 1914. He describes digging ragworm at Redhorn rocks to use as bait to catch flounders, which he would fry over a pinecone fire. He drank the water from Brand's Ford and lived in a clay workers' hut at Newton. He bartered his fish, rented out his boat, smuggled, and beach-combed. Most importantly, he had a Poole Harbour life list, recording "240 kinds of birds around the harbour".

When I told Shaun this he panicked and counted his list. As usual with this game, it brought out his competitive side. "I bet he counted male and female Hen Harriers as separate species". Maybe he did, but he probably didn't know the difference between many of the birds we identify today like Marsh and Willow Tit, and certainly couldn't have identified a Ring-billed Gull. Shaun's list, when based on the BOU list rather than the more generous taxonomy used in this book, is 248 and Ian Lewis's is 249, so they both get into Ben Pond's Poole Harbour 240 club. Pond has a few 'blockers' though, having found "a Black Grouse nest with six eggs", no doubt to the sound of the Corn Crakes that were still breeding on Newton heath at the time.

Another bird on Pond's list that is no longer around is Red-billed Chough. Studland, as its name suggests, was originally a place where horses were kept, and choughs used to feed there, flicking over the horse dung in search of insects and flakes of undigested food. There were a lot of horses then, used for pulling anything from a plough to a hearse. And a lot of horses produce a lot of dung! Roughly 12 kilos per horse per day. At that time in Britain there was a horse for every 21 people. Around the harbour, this meant 1,156 horses producing nearly 14,000 kilos of dung a day, and goodness knows how many flies

Studland heath, Dorset, 2 September 2010 (*Nick Hopper*). Seen from the viewpoint.

this attracted. In the 1900s tractors began to replace the horse and were in widespread use by 1927 when the final choughs disappeared from Ballard.

Shooting had by now descended into a 'sport', and a contemporary of Pond, C J Cornisch (1895), describes sailing into Poole on 1 August, the first day of shooting: "bare-legged fisherman were standing on one or two shingle-banks just left by the tide, firing at flocks of ring-dotterels [Ringed Plovers] which were shifting about the harbour."

At that time on the Sandbanks side there were only 12 small houses, although the tourists that would flush the breeding plovers from the Sandbanks beaches were already crossing the harbour mouth on Scott's Ferry to sunbathe, sometimes naked, on the Studland side.

It can never have been much fun for Ringed Plovers trying to nest on Poole Harbour's beaches. Pond describes one three-day sand storm burying a bungalow up to the eaves, the sand coming from a high dune to the rear. It took him four days to dig it out. With the 'sand banks' moving enough to cover a house, the scraped plovers' nests can hardly have remained unscathed. According to Pond, one November storm widened the harbour mouth by 13 m, which must have surprised at least one pair of returning Ringed Plovers the next spring. On the other hand, the drifting sands also widened the beach further along, with the high water mark advancing 10 m in some years, right up until 1960.

Despite the widening of the beach, by 1963 Ringed Plovers were down to two pairs on Studland, which according to the Bird Report "successfully raised young despite the presence of holiday makers". A more spectacular end for the plovers was this: "three birds blown up by the Bomb Disposal Unit along Studland beach on the 29th Oct 1976. Another three were found dead and one concussed the next day" (Morrison 1991), after a missile had been exploded near Pilot's Point. During the

Second World War, Studland beach was used for rehearsing the Normandy landings, and although over 84,000 missiles and 200 unexploded bombs were later removed from the beach, the odd one or two were inevitably left behind. By 1981 the Ringed Plovers had lost the battle, and the only pair left breeding in the harbour was in Holes Bay. When a new road was built there, this pair also disappeared.

Another species followed by Pond was Black-headed Gull. It is thought that the colony on Little Sea started when the lake was first formed. Back then, Little Sea was twice the size it is now, and full of gulls. "2,500 pairs of Black-headed Gulls had nested there, the nests being so close together that a small triangular depression existed between every three nests; each nest contained three eggs, or at least it should do. But the birds squabbled among themselves so much that odd eggs rolled out of some of the nests into the triangular depressions. I never had to rob a nest, as I could always fill a basket of eggs by collecting those which had rolled out of the nest instead."

As with all good things, Pond's supply of free eggs finally came to an end. "It was now 1925, which saw the coming of a new road that was built across the heath from South Haven Point to Studland… Part of this road passed the north end of Littlesea Lake and the noise of the passing cars caused the gulls to desert the area."

Chapter 3: Marooned

Sometimes on pub night I've suggested that it would be interesting to know more about what is going on under the water. This has never been greeted with much enthusiasm. I've also tried chatting to the fisherman to try and find out which fish like to hang out where. Not that they are keen to part with their secrets. Botanists are more forthcoming, but they mostly want to talk about *Spartina,* whether it's decreasing and by how much. Botanist John Mansell-Playdell found the first small clump of what was then an unusual cord grass at Ower on 17 July 1899. It was *S* x *townsendi*, a hybrid between a local cord grass and an American immigrant, and he thought it may have arrived, like other alien plants, on the bottom of transatlantic boats (Humphreys & May 2005). It was a botanical rarity until August 1907 when it appeared in "hundreds of spots". The roots were able to attract and hold together the silt, and by 1924, nearly a third of the harbour's intertidal areas were covered in this short green grass. It was great for breeding Redshank, but it also provided firmer ground for the hunters and their dogs.

One strictly underwater plant was the eelgrass *Zostera*, which formed meadows grazed by Brent Geese and Wigeon. While *Spartina* was changing the appearance of the harbour, the eelgrass was dying out. By 1925 it had almost completely disappeared, not just locally but throughout the whole of the North Atlantic. A parasitic microorganism was thought to be responsible. The combination of shooting and the disappearing eelgrass decimated the Brent Geese and by the '60s, Alan Bromby of Brownsea Island could write that he was only counting "up to four Brent Geese in the harbour during January and ten there on 27th December" (Bromby 1963). By 1966, they were no longer regular visitors, only being recorded in twos and threes on odd occasions (Dixon 1966).

Many other birds were considered a nuisance or just fair game. Crows were routinely poisoned, and the local Ravens that had been at Corfe for centuries finally vanished. Rooks were barely tolerated, and their young were taken annually. Even Barn Owls were shot and stuffed, as were any scarce or rare birds. Thomas Hardy made numerous references to Dorset bird-catchers snaring and selling wild Goldfinches, Bullfinches and Yellowhammers. Bird feathers in hats, and bird skins as clothes were routine.

I would have hated seeing all this carnage and capture, and I despise the argument that landowners will only look after the wildlife on their land if it has a commercial purpose. The RSPB was in its infancy, having been started as *The Plumage League* by Emily Williamson and a group of ladies as an anti-plume hunting activist group. In 1927, Mary Bonham-Christie, a radical pioneer who hated cruelty to animals, bought Brownsea Island. Wanting absolutely no human interference at all, she proceeded to evict all the islanders. The island's population that had stood at 270 in 1881 was down to just five in 1961.

Peregrine Falcon *Falco peregrinus*, Old Harry Rocks, Ballard Down, Dorset, 17 November 2009 (*Nick Hopper*). 'This species was the most obvious victim of organochlorides in the '60s.'

alien conifers marched
across the heath
between 1948 and 1950

oil discovered December 1973

Brownsea Isl

POOLE

1950: Enid Blyton
having a round of
golf, where once
there was heath

Marsh Harrier eggs
thinned due to
DDT, breeding
stops in 1963

on 25 January
a collision involvin
oil tanker oiled
Great Northern Di

North

THE SCENE BY THE SIXTIES

winter of 1962/63
Dartford Warbler was
exterminated

Popular English children's writer Enid Blyton immortalised Bonham-Christie's Brownsea for children, when she called it 'Keep-Away Island' (Blyton 1962). Even the scouts, whose founder Baden Powell had organised their first camp on Brownsea in 1907, were banned. Bonham-Christie is reported to have said of them, "I many times stopped them ill treating without cause older people's dogs and cats, stealing the eggs from the nests of birds and killing with a catapult birds in trees" (Moore 2003). (Mo was in the guides in the '60s, and can remember the girls' outrage at seeing boy scouts catapulting birds.)

Unsurprisingly, Bonham-Christie's actions created resentment, and when the last family was finally evicted a fire was started that raged across the island for three days. This was bad news for the several pairs of Dartford Warblers on the island, although changes in pesticide use in Dorset gave them more serious problems. Chemical fertilisers and pesticides were replacing the tons of horse dung, and this enabled heath to be 'improved' to create Studland golf course, for example, which was owned by Enid Blyton and her husband, and Greenlands farm below it.

I was at school while this was going on. Enid Blyton's books were frowned upon there, while Shakespeare was encouraged. I remember auditioning for The National Youth Theatre by reading the scene in Macbeth where the forest of Birnam marched on Dunsinane. Something similar happened here when fertilisers enabled foresters to plant conifers across our heathland. Between 1948 and 1950, pines advanced across 5000 acres of heath all around the golf course, covering an area from Corfe Castle to Goathorn and only stopping at Greenlands farm. The concept of forest renewal was also taught at our school, although the birdsong-filled Scots Pines, oaks, elms, limes and alders our forefathers had been removed were now being replaced by silent rows of Corsican Pines. While some birds like Siskin, Coal Tit (**CD1-07**) and the various vocal types of crossbill increased, on the whole you visited a commercial pine forest for silence. By the '60s, two thirds of Dorset's heathland had gone. Dartford Warblers were now in serious decline.

Coal Tit *Periparus ater* Rempstone, Poole Harbour, Dorset, England, 10:11, 30 March 2008. Song of two rival males in a Corsican Pine plantation, with very high rattling calls heard frequently in the second half of the recording. Background: Common Chaffinch *Fringilla coelebs*. 080330.MR.101100.01

CD1-07

At that time all the estates around the harbour employed gamekeepers, so birds of prey were routinely snared or poisoned and hung nearby to show diligence. Egg collecting was a popular hobby, and in the '50s the heaths were a favourite destination for amateur birdwatchers searching out nests and taking home an egg or two. Ilay Cooper's *Purbeck revealed* (2004) contains his memories of birds and birding in the harbour. Children were far more active then, and he tells a tragic story about himself and a friend clambering, aged 14, over the cliffs a little short of Ballard Point. He and Keith MacDonald used to go out along the cliffs looking for gulls' eggs or simply birdwatching. On one expedition when Keith had climbed down at the highest stretch of cliff, "The large piece of rock which he was gripping gave way and he fell to his death."

Fortunately, not all children's adventures ended this way. In 1943, the children from Bryanston School Natural History Society recorded three sightings of a female or juvenile Marsh Harrier at Swineham. At the time, there had only been three

Rempstone heath and Enid Blyton golf course, Dorset, 24 August 2004 (*René Pop*). Looking north from Studland heath viewpoint.

records in the past 40 years. Three years later a male was seen carrying reeds, and in 1949 the first signs of breeding were observed at Keysworth. By 1954, five pairs were breeding in the harbour at Little Sea, Keysworth, Middlebere, The Moors and on 'Keep-Away Island'. Up to 22 adults and 12 young were seen that year. Sadly, by 1963 breeding had stopped. It was thought that human intrusion, egg collecting, shooting, and flooding of nest sites caused a decline from which the birds never recovered, then fragile eggs caused by the toxic pesticide DDT dealt the final blow.

Cooper (2004) describes another catastrophe that happened on 25 January 1961, when there was a collision at the harbour entrance during gale force winds. The harbour was full of birds when two ships collided… "one carrying red paint the other carrying blue paint. Apparently, all the seamen were marooned," commented Nick while helping with the text. He was finding all this doom and gloom a little depressing. If you also think the story is a little too Shakespeare and not at all Enid Blyton don't worry. There are only a couple more pages to go before it cheers up.

Sadly, then, it wasn't colourful paint but a mass of crude oil that was spilled, and the shore was littered with oiled birds, dead and dying. "We caught what we could," writes Cooper. "In our warm kitchen my mother tolerated two guillemots, two black-necked grebes, a great northern diver and a little purple sandpiper. Part of an organised survey, we patrolled the shore, marking each dead beak with red nail polish to avoid double counting." The whole of the area south of Brownsea Island was covered in oil, as were 300 birds of 32 different species. Worst were 10 dead and eight oiled Great Northern Divers.

Then came the worst winter weather for 223 years. 8 cm of snow fell on 26 December 1962, with a further 23 cm three days later, this time accompanied by northeast gales. These blizzards piled snow into 2-3 m deep drifts, and in some exposed places it was 6 m deep. The thaw was a long time coming. January and February were dominated by heavy frosts, allowing the snow to remain intact for a further 70 days, with most lasting until 6 March.

"Bitterns and Woodcock were reported dead or dying in an emaciated state and in areas close to houses where they would not normally be seen. Black-tailed Godwit and Redshank seem to have suffered the heaviest losses… Victims of the freeze up include many Shelducks", wrote county recorder J C Follett (1963).

H G Alexander (1974) takes up the tale. "The most extraordinary assemblage of waders was found by Trev Haysom and myself on the three-mile-long sandy beach to the north of Studland on 7th February. The frost had gone so deeply into the sea that masses of razors and other shell-fish from the shallow seas had been frozen and thrown up dead all along the beach. This had attracted crowds of gulls and waders. The gulls we reckoned at approximately 5000; the waders at 2000." In the Bird report for 1963: "Goldcrest complete or almost complete absence … Wren drastically reduced in all areas…Stonechat numbers considerably reduced." Dartford Warblers were thought to be down to four pairs for the whole of Dorset.

These were desperate times. DDT had been replaced by a new range of chemicals: organochlorides like dieldrin, aldrin and heptachlor. They were very effective at eliminating fungi from grain, moths from cloth, and scourge from sheep. Unfortunately they drained from the fields into the watercourses and up the food chain to fish and eels. In this way they also killed otters and herons. Pigeons and pheasants that ate the grain were also poisoned, along with the foxes that predated them. Among the most obvious victims were the local Peregrines. I remember reading in 1973 of a leading local environmentalist and broadcaster Kenneth Allsopp, who died of a drug overdose after writing for the Sunday Times on the loss of the last breeding Peregrines in Dorset.

Chemical manufacture in Britain had its beginnings in Poole, with alum and copperas for ink being produced at Evening Hill. Now it had moved into the centre of town, on the edge of the harbour. I had a conversation with the man who was responsible for maintaining the pumping equipment at this local chemical works. He told me that in the '60s, the hydrochloric acid would corrode the pipe work and hundreds of gallons would regularly leak into Holes Bay. Years later, the chemical works blew up on a pub night and 2,500 people were evacuated. A passing van shot into the air, traffic lights melted, the blast blew a man off his bike and I could see chemical drums hurtling through the air. Anglers three miles out to sea were splattered. We postponed the pub to the following week, and the chemical works moved inland.

Back in April 1961, Mary Bonham-Christie died aged 98, and things looked bleak. Shooting syndicates prepared to buy Brownsea Island, while her son applied for permission to build 400 houses there.

Poole's birds needed protection. Thankfully help was at hand, and although many conservationists helped to save the day, three clear heroes emerged.

One of them was birder Helen Brotherton. In 1961 she became the secretary of the appeal to save Brownsea. Arguing in favour of its qualities as a nature reserve, she was part of a small team who defeated the housing suggestion and persuaded the nation to take Brownsea in lieu of Bonham-Carter's death duties, giving it to the National Trust. Helen also helped start the Dorset Naturalists' Trust, which took over the management of the lagoon and a third of the Island. When Arne came up for sale, Brotherton alerted the RSPB, liaising and encouraging them into buying the peninsula and setting up the first Dorset RSPB reserve in 1966.

The second was renowned amateur conchologist Captain Cyril Diver, who was also clerk to the financial committee of the House of Commons. In both roles, he had a reputation for being thorough and coping with a lot of detail. Diver made two painstaking ecological surveys of Studland during the '30s. He wrote a detailed paper that led to the creation of The Nature Conservancy (Diver 1947), and then he became its first director general.

The third was Ralph Bankes, who inherited the Bankes estate and in the tradition of eccentric landowners, lived in just three rooms of Kingston Lacey, the family's stately home. His son John Bankes lived even less ostentatiously in Fulham. The estate was vast at over 8,000 acres, and included 12 working farms, Corfe Castle, all of Studland, the Ballard peninsula, the harbour shore at Middlebere and the Purbeck Hills, in other words many of the best birding sites. In 1954, Diver and Bankes made Hartland Moor one of the first National Nature Reserves, starting a series of reserves and alliances that were to encircle the harbour. They then went on to create what was described at the time as Britain's second largest reserve out of Studland peninsula, which Diver's own intimately detailed studies had certainly shown had some of the highest biodiversity in Britain. Ralph Bankes became ill, and his son John seemed poorly qualified to run the estate, so in 1981 Ralph bequeathed it all to the National Trust. It was a massive gift. John Bankes died in 1996 and lies in Studland churchyard.

In 1981 Holton Heath was added to the protective ring around the harbour, when Diver made it a National Nature Reserve. All these reserves form a substantial area of habitat managed for wildlife. Today this combination of heath and wetland

James Lidster, in hide at Middlebere Farm, Middlebere channel, Poole Harbour, Dorset, 24 August 2004 (*Rene Pop*)

makes Poole Harbour the most important natural area in the county, and happily it also ranks as one of the most successfully conserved areas in Britain. The birds have never had it so good, at least not in the last 150 years, and the birding has got so much better. In **CD1-08**, you can hear a typical scene at one of our favourites among the places protected by the likes of Bankes, Brotherton and Diver.

CD1-08   **Middlebere at dawn**, Poole Harbour, Dorset, England, 04:54, 14 May 2010. Canada Goose *Branta canadensis*, Common Pheasant *Phasianus colchicus*, Water Rail *Rallus aquaticus*, Common Wood Pigeon *Columba palumbus*, Common Cuckoo *Cuculus canorus*, Eurasian Wren *Troglodytes troglodytes*, Common Blackbird *Turdus merula*, Song Thrush *T philomelos*, Eurasian Reed Warbler *Acrocephalus scirpaceus*, Common Whitethroat *Sylvia communis*, European Blue Tit *Cyanistes caeruleus*, Common Chaffinch *Fringilla coelebs* and European Goldfinch *Carduelis carduelis*. 100514.MC.045400.01

If you have been wondering what a conchologist does, Captain Diver was really keen on snails, well, snails and taxonomy. He made a study of the snails in the trenches while on active service in the First World War and on his return was considered an authority on the importance of fossil records for geneticists. He was also an expert on sinistrality, the way snails with left handed whorls on the shell cannot mate with those with right handed whorls. Had he been alive today he would have known that this difference has come down to a single gene and is the basis for much of modern taxonomy.

Dartford Warbler

weak flight, whirring wings

nominate *una*
(C & E Iberia, S Fran
W Mediterranean islands & It
is more uniformly slate-grey ab
than *dartfordie*.
(S England, W France, NW Ibe

undata

grey

characteristic shape with long, cocked tail giving distinctive silhouette

brownish

males, summer

dartfordier

warm brown

first-winter males average a little brighter than females

juvenile's shape and demeanour as adult but darker-eyed, giving 'kinder' expression to face

undata juv

juvenile *undata* typically greyish above and below

first-winter male *dartfordiensis* (October)

dartfordiensis juv

juvenile *dartfordiensis* typically brownish above, washed light apricot-buff below

juvenile's tail slightly shorter, wing feathers fresher than in adult summer

female, spring *dartfordiensis*

saturated vinous red in male, often looks very dark

male, spring *dartfordiensis*

Chapter 4: If that's a Bibby's Warbler I'll eat my hat

After researching the first chapters I asked the fellows down the pub the big question. Why isn't the English Dartford Warbler a species? We've been able to see how Dartford Warblers arrived in what is now Poole Harbour between 9,000 and 7,000 years ago as a warming climate pushed the ice back. Perhaps they came up the Atlantic coast with Nick's ancestors from a refuge in Spain or Portugal. As his ancestors cleared the trees, the Dartford Warblers exploited the resulting heathland.

Then came the formation of the English Channel, effectively stranding these non-migratory birds. On their isolated northern outpost, they became exposed to a fluctuating climate, facing some serious challenges during the colder spells. However, right up until the 1900s there was no shortage of habitat. Maps from around 1750, show that the Poole area was covered in heathland, and in the warmer periods the population would have reached a peak. It must also have been these same large amounts of suitable habitat that enabled them to survive the cold periods.

Bournemouth and Poole expanded, and modern pesticides and fertilizers enabled the local heath to be 'improved' into farmland, commercial forests and golf courses. By 1960, two thirds of our heathland had gone. The depleted Dartford population struggled to survive. After the seriously cold winter of 1962/63, there were thought to be just four pairs for the whole of Dorset, all on the fringes of Poole Harbour.

It is generally accepted that there are three subspecies of Dartford Warbler. *Dartfordiensis* is the one we have in England, the largest group, *undata* is found in the rest of southwest Europe, from about halfway down through France, and the third, *toni*, is found in North Africa. However, in a recent monograph on the *Sylvia* warblers (Shirihai et al 2001), a detailed analysis of Dartford Warbler skins from museums throughout Europe struggled to establish exactly where the ranges of the three subspecies of Dartford Warbler began and finished.

Dartford Warbler is closely related to Balearic Warbler and slightly more distantly related to Marmora's Warbler. The common ancestor of all three split from Spectacled Warbler just over five million years ago, around the time when the waters of the Mediterranean returned after a long period of drought, creating many of the islands familiar to us today (Voelker & Light 2011). The details have yet to be worked out, but it seems likely that Dartford, Balearic and Marmora's subsequently evolved on separate islands in the western Mediterranean, and Balearic and Marmora's have remained isolated there until today.

In most field guides, Dartford Warblers are illustrated with a slate-grey back, but if you glance across at Killian's plate you'll notice that *dartfordiensis* has a brown back. This makes it even easier to separate from male Marmora's and Balearic Warblers, which like *undata* have grey backs. Juvenile *dartfordiensis* are also distinctive when compared with *undata*.

Killian sketched *dartfordiensis* on Hartland Moor, where Colin Bibby made his series of classic studies that set him on the path to become the head of conservation science for the RSPB, and later head of BirdLife International's research team. Killian avidly read Bibby's papers on Dartford Warbler, having developed a particular interest in the species following his discovery of the third record for Ireland when he was 14 years of age.

Colin Bibby was 20 when he started his study of Dartford Warbler ecology (1977). The work, for which he gained a PhD, looked carefully at the status and habitat needs of the species, translating the results into a plan for its conservation. He showed that Poole Harbour's Dartford Warblers were dependent on dry, open heathland with mature gorse, and needed the right management to thrive. It was 1968 and there were 31 pairs. Not many, but 50% more than in 1967. It was Bibby who pointed to Stonechats associating with Dartford Warblers. He believed that the Dartfords took advantage of the Stonechats' vigilance.

Colin Bibby died in 2004, and his obituary in the Daily Telegraph mentioned his reputation for being brusque. "Once, during a study of merlins (small, normally ground-nesting falcons), a team member telephoned to report finding a nest in a tree. Bibby replied: 'If that's a merlin's nest, I'll eat my hat.' After seeing for himself that at least one pair had indeed built a nest in a tree, he joined the team for a meal, and a hat was brought to him on a silver salver. He promptly bit off a chunk, chewed and swallowed it."

Bibby found that Dartfords don't go far in their lives. He followed this up with a study starting in September 1974, again at Hartland, where he colour-ringed adults and metal-ringed

Breeding ranges of Atlantic Dartford Warbler ('Bibby's Warbler') *Sylvia undata dartfordiensis* (red), Mediterranean *S u undata* (green) and North African *S u toni* (purple) (after Gabriel Gargallo in Shirihai et al 2001). In shaded areas, it is unclear which of two taxa occurs. It should be stressed that this map is a rough sketch and that, in most coloured areas, the species has a patchy distribution, not being widespread but occurring locally in certain habitats and in numbers that vary from year to year.

young for two years. He discovered that once paired, the adults will be faithful to the breeding site through snow and fire, and it is the young males that venture further afield. Most often they turn up along the coast in Kent and Sussex, rather than risking a sea crossing. Adults only move a few metres from a favoured gorse bush, and this may explain why their numbers get hammered each bad winter.

So *dartfordiensis* doesn't travel far, and has at times been reduced in numbers to a mere handful of birds. This is the classic mechanism for the evolution of an endemic species. Killian jokingly called it 'Bibby's Warbler'. Meanwhile I had *Greensleeves* playing in my head as I thought about the Holy Grail: a real English endemic…. 'English Warbler'.

However, there is a problem with our new English 'endemic'. There are quite a lot in France. Distribution maps vary, and it is difficult to know where *dartfordiensis* stops and *undata* begins, but Arnoud investigated and it seems that *dartfordiensis* is the western, maritime race, going right down the Atlantic coast. Curious, Magnus and Killian visited Eugene Archer, a birder friend living in Nantes on the west coast, to find out whether the Dartfords there sounded the same as in Dorset. They found the brown-backed *dartfordiensis* occupying small patches of habitat much the same as in Dorset (only now they were in the company of Melodious Warblers and Cirl Buntings). Next, Magnus and Killian flew down to Portugal, taking a road trip from Cabo da Roca on the west coast to Monfragüe in central Spain. They found no *dartfordiensis*, but watched and sound recorded obvious *undata* in the company of Sardinian Warblers, Spectacled Warblers and Griffon Vultures.

Back home, Magnus was able to analyse sonagrams from a large number recordings of both *dartfordiensis* and *undata*. He found some interesting differences. The main call of Dartford Warbler is a low, descending *churr,* typically a single note, or a two-note call with the second shorter and slightly lower than the first. Much less commonly, three or four-note versions can be heard. The calls vary in pitch, length, number of notes and how frequently they are repeated, depending how excited the bird is.

Dartford Warbler *Sylvia undata dartfordiensis*, male (at back) and female (pair), Pornic, Loire-Atlantique, France, 28 May 2011 (*Killian Mullarney*)

Dartford Warbler *Sylvia undata undata*, juvenile, Monfragüe, Extremadura, Spain, 2 June 2011 (*Killian Mullarney*)

Dartford Warbler *Sylvia undata undata*, juvenile, Monfragüe, Extremadura, Spain, 2 June 2011 (*Killian Mullarney*)

Dartford Warbler *Sylvia undata undata*, juvenile, Sintra, Portugal, 30 May 2011 (*Killian Mullarney*)

Dartford Warbler *Sylvia undata undata*, juvenile, Sintra, Portugal, 30 May 2011 (*Killian Mullarney*)

Comparing calls of *dartfordiensis* and *undata*, Magnus limited himself to males in their second calendar-year or older, to make sure any differences he found were not a matter of sex or age. This left him with 13 recordings of *dartfordiensis* from Dorset and western France, and 34 of *undata* calls from Iberia, southern France and Corsica. The result was that male *dartfordiensis* calls average lower-pitched and slightly longer, with a more gradual descent in pitch and a slightly more 'grainy' timbre. Listen to

Dartford Warbler *Sylvia undata dartfordiensis*, juvenile, Donges, Loire-Atlantique, France, 29 May 2011 (*Killian Mullarney*)

CD1-09   **Dartford Warbler** *Sylvia undata dartfordiensis* Pilot's Point, Poole Harbour, Dorset, England, 12 May 2002. Calls of a male. Background: Meadow Pipit *Anthus pratensis*, Eurasian Wren *Troglodytes troglodytes*, Dunnock *Prunella modularis* and Common Linnet *Linaria cannabina*. 02.010.MC.11800.32

these two examples from the UK (**CD1-09**) and France (**CD1-10**), and compare them with calls of *undata* from Portugal (**CD1-11**). Male *undata* calls average slightly higher pitched and shorter, with a steeper descent in pitch and a less grainy timbre. The latter two characteristics give them a somewhat more whining

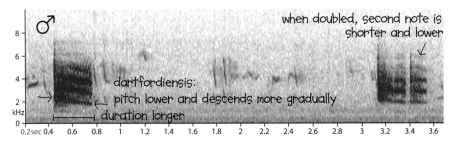

CD1-10   **Dartford Warbler** *Sylvia undata dartfordiensis* Donges, Loire-Atlantique, France, 11:40, 29 May 2011. Calls of a male. Background: Eurasian Skylark *Alauda arvensis* and Barn Swallow *Hirundo rustica*. 110529.MR.114022.01

Dartford Warbler *Sylvia undata undata* Sintra Cascais Natural Park, Lisboa, Portugal,   **CD1-11**
10:51, 30 May 2011. Calls of a male. Background: European Stonechat *Saxicola rubicola*, Sardinian Warbler *Sylvia melanocephala*. 110530.MR.105134.00

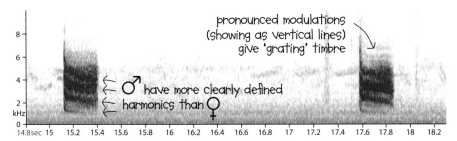

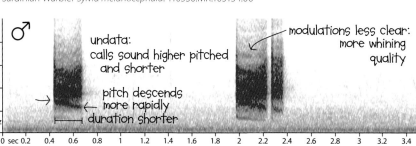

quality. The differences are subtle, and *dartfordiensis* can sound more like *undata* when excited.

A more basic problem is to tell Dartford Warbler from Common Whitethroat calls. Listen to the whitethroat in **CD1-12** and see if you can hear what sets it apart from Dartford. The most helpful difference is the level pitch, not descending as in Dartford, and another important difference is that whitethroat calls are never doubled in the way that Dartford calls often are. Calls of *undata* are less whitethroat-like, being higher pitched and purer, so less likely to be confused.

Dartford Warbler *Sylvia undata undata*, female, probably second calendar-year, Monfragüe, Extremadura, Spain, 2 June 2011 (*Killian Mullarney*). Recorded on CD1-14.

Common Whitethroat *Sylvia communis* Cabo Espichel, Lisboa, Portugal, 08:02, 13 September 2009. Calls of an autumn migrant. Background: wing sound of a Peregrine *Falco peregrinus* stopping at a pigeon, yellow wagtail *Motacilla*, Common Nightingale *Luscinia megarhynchos* and House Sparrow *Passer domesticus*. 090913.MR.080242.10   **CD1-12**

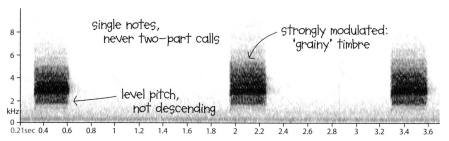

Dartford Warbler *Sylvia undata dartfordiensis* Pilot's Point, Poole Harbour, Dorset, England, 12 May 2002. Calls of a female. Background: Meadow Pipit *Anthus pratensis*, Dunnock *Prunella modularis*, Common Blackbird *Turdus merula* and Common Chaffinch *Fringilla coelebs*. 02.010.MC.10640.03   **CD1-13**

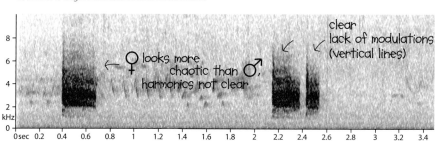

Dartford Warbler *Sylvia undata undata* Monfragüe, Extremadura, Spain, 13:47, 2 June 2011. Calls of a female. The weaker calls in the background are probably a juvenile. 110602.MR.134722.02   **CD1-14**

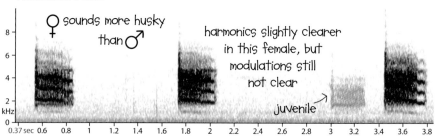

We were curious to know whether we could tell calls of males and females apart. When Magnus compared calls of both sexes in three *undata* pairs, along with a pair of *dartfordiensis*, it soon became clear that an often-quoted difference in pitch between males and females (V C Lewis in Cramp et al 1992) is unreliable. The only consistent but very subtle difference he found was that males had a clearer voice while the females were more husky or hoarse-sounding. Listen to female *dartfordiensis* (**CD1-13**) and *undata* (**CD1-14**) and see if you agree.

Adult Dartford Warblers also have some other important call types besides contact calls. We already mentioned that they vary the number of notes in a call according to how excited they are. Well, when they are really alarmed, eg, by the presence of humans or potential predators near their brood, you start to hear short but rather loud rattles interspersed with the usual calls. Typically, the final note of a normal two-note or three-note call is replaced by a rattle, which can be the length of the replaced note, or up to a second long (**CD1-15**). Occasionally the first note is omitted altogether, so you just hear a series of short, loud rattles.

Alarm rattles are typically heard at the height of the breeding season, but another, much quieter and generally shorter, twittering *trrrt... trrrt...* can be heard at any time of year. This can be heard in a variety of contexts, typically from rather excited but not especially alarmed birds, and is often given during short flights. In **CD1-16**, both members of a pair are giving them. Magnus and Killian also heard these calls from a male repeatedly making short flights, trying to persuade his brood to follow him away from the human intruders.

CD1-15   **Dartford Warbler** *Sylvia undata undata* Rosmaninhal, Beira-Baixa, Portugal, 08:28, 31 May 2011. Rattling alarm calls of a male near nestling or fledglings. Background: Eurasian Hoopoe *Upupa epops*, Thekla Lark *Galerida theklae*, song of another male Dartford Warbler, and Corn Bunting *Emberiza calandra*. 110531.MR.082848.01

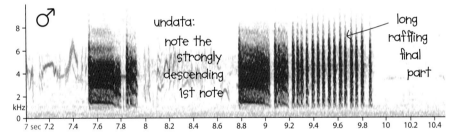

CD1-16   **Dartford Warbler** *Sylvia undata dartfordiensis* Soldier's Road, Poole Harbour, Dorset, England, 17:00, 5 January 2006. Twittering calls of a pair at dusk, responding to song of a neighbouring male (not heard). Background: European Robin *Erithacus rubecula* and Common Blackbird *Turdus merula*. 05.032.MR.11027.12

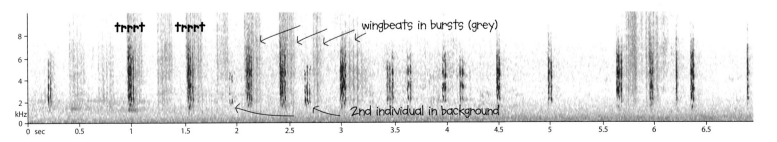

When following families of Dartford Warblers during the summer, it can be difficult to tell who is who. Some calls of juveniles can be similar to adults. However, when they are begging for food, juveniles use some quiet calls that give away their age. In **CD1-17**, listen to the long, low, churring notes, followed by higher-pitched, whining notes. It is the frequent alternation of these two types of sound that readily identifies a juvenile.

The song of Dartford Warbler, both *dartfordiensis* and *undata*, is very fast with many notes squeezed into a short song that is surprisingly low-pitched for a bird of Dartford's small size. Here is a typical example of *dartfordiensis*, recorded in Poole Harbour (**CD1-18**).

CD1-17 **Dartford Warbler** *Sylvia undata dartfordiensis* Ham Common, Poole Harbour, Dorset, England, 1 September 2002. Calls of a juvenile begging for food from an adult female, which calls twice at 0:20. Background: European Robin *Erithacus rubecula* and Common Linnet *Linaria cannabina*. 02.040.MR.02517.02

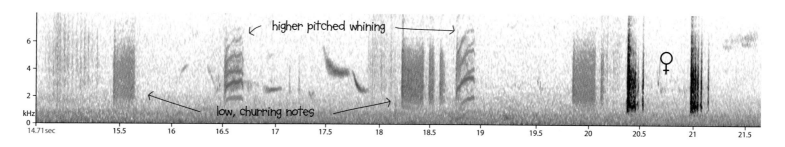

CD1-18 **Dartford Warbler** *Sylvia undata dartfordiensis*, Middlebere, Poole Harbour, Dorset, England, 12 May 2002. Song of a male. Background: Mediterranean Gull *Larus melanocephalus*, Eurasian Wren *Troglodytes troglodytes*, Common Blackbird *Turdus merula*, Common Chaffinch *Fringilla coelebs*, European Greenfinch *Chloris chloris*, Common Linnet *Linaria cannabina* and Yellowhammer *Emberiza citrinella*. 02.010.MC.04030.02

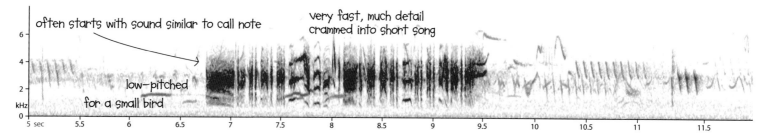

European Stonechat *Saxicola rubicola*, Kennemerduinen, Noord-Holland, Netherlands, 07:46, 20 March 2011. Song of a male. Background: Greylag Goose *Anser anser*, Great Spotted Woodpecker *Dendrocopos major*, Dunnock *Prunella modularis*, Carrion Crow *Corvus corone*, European Greenfinch *Chloris chloris* and Common Reed Bunting *Emberiza schoeniclus*. 110320.AB.074632.02

Dartford Warbler *Sylvia undata dartfordiensis* Pornic, Loire-Atlantique, France, 11:40, 28 May 2011. Song of a male, recorded from less than 2 m distance. Background: Melodious Warbler *Hippolais polyglotta*. 110528.MR.110700.11

Stonechat song can sound superficially like Dartford Warbler but is higher-pitched, more whistled, less hurried, and typically sounds a bit slurred. Stonechat also has shorter songs than Dartford. Have a listen to this Stonechat recorded in the dunes along the Dutch coast (**CD1-19**), followed by another example of Dartford Warbler, this time a *dartfordiensis* from western France (**CD1-20**).

In southern Europe, other small *Sylvia* warblers add to the challenge of identifying Dartford Warbler song. For example, the range of *undata* is almost exactly the part of Dartford's European range that overlaps with Sardinian Warbler. The two can often be found together, and at times their songs can be difficult to distinguish. Sardinian usually has a drier, more staccato quality, sings slightly less hurriedly and with clearer articulation, and nearly always starts the song with a high-pitched, fairly pure-sounding whistle, which seems to be optional in Dartford. Here is a typical example of Sardinian Warbler song from Portugal (**CD1-21**).

CD1-21   **Sardinian Warbler** *Sylvia melanocephala* Castelo Branco, Beira Baixa, Portugal, 08:29, 13 May 2009. Song of a male. Background: Common Wood Pigeon *Columba palumbus*, European Turtle Dove *Streptopelia turtur*, Great Tit *Parus major* and Cirl Bunting *Emberiza cirlus*. 090531.MR.082928.01

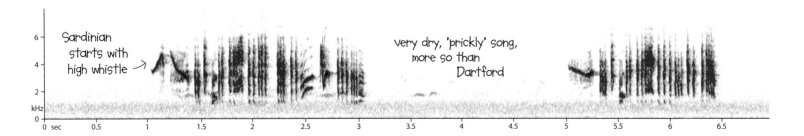

Undata can sometimes sound rather like Sardinian Warbler, and may even adopt rattles of Sardinian Warbler in its songs. So one way to tell *undata* songs from *dartfordiensis* may be to listen for similarities to, or borrowings from, Sardinian Warbler. For example, *undata* may have a slightly more generous scattering of high-pitched notes and rattles in the song. **CD1-22** is an example of *undata* song, recorded at Monfragüe in central Spain, at a location where both species occur in good numbers.

Like several other *Sylvia* warblers, Dartford has a specialised songflight that it uses in moments of higher excitement. The strophes delivered during these flights tend to be longer than in perched song. Greater length can be achieved by including many repetitions (near or exact) of short fragments. The *dartfordiensis* in the next recording (**CD1-23**) gives a songflight 38 seconds into the recording, which lasts for 5.5 seconds. Typical song lengths when perched are in the order of 2-3 seconds, though much shorter songs in flight can also sometimes be heard.

CD1-22   **Dartford Warbler** *Sylvia undata undata* Monfragüe, Extremadura, Spain, 11:08, 2 June 2011. Song of a male. Background: Common Swift *Apus apus* and Spectacled Warbler *Sylvia conspicillata*. 110602.MR.110832.11

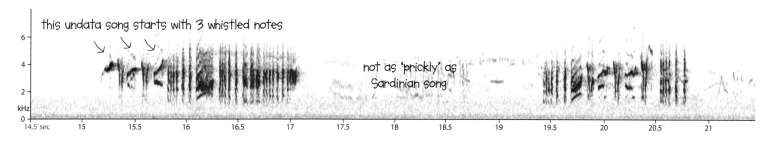

CD1-23   **Dartford Warbler** *Sylvia undata dartfordiensis* Glebelands, Poole Harbour, Dorset, England, 09:48, 4 April 2008. Song of a male, with the long final strophe being delivered in flight. Background: Common Pheasant *Phasianus colchicus*, Eurasian Skylark *Alauda arvensis*, Eurasian Blackcap *Sylvia atricapilla*, Common Chiffchaff *Phylloscopus collybita* and Carrion Crow *Corvus corone*. 080404.MR.094808.31

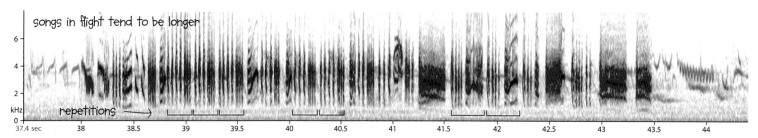

Dartford Warbler *Sylvia undata undata*, male, Sintra, Portugal, 30 May 2011 (*Killian Mullarney*). Recorded on CD1-11 and CD1-24.

Now listen to the *undata* in **CD1-24**, which performs a 4 second songflight, with more whistles than its English counterpart.

Dartford Warbler *Sylvia undata undata* Sintra Cascais Natural Park, Lisboa, Portugal, 12:42, 30 May 2011. Songflight of a male. 110530.MR.124254.21 **CD1-24**

Dartford Warbler *Sylvia undata undata*, male, Sintra, Portugal, 30 May 2011 (*Killian Mullarney*). Recorded on CD1-11 and CD1-24.

Dartford Warbler is a species that sings through most of the year, and it is common to hear song in late summer and autumn. At this time, many of the singers are young of the year. In **CD1-25**, a first-winter in mid-September in Portugal, you can hear a slow transition from a very quiet, hesitant and indistinct subsong to a more confident plastic song. Typically for plastic song, there

CD1-25 **Dartford Warbler** *Sylvia undata undata* Cabo Espichel, Lisboa, Portugal, 09:43, 19 September 2008. Song of a first-winter male, slowly changing from hesitant subsong to more confident plastic song. Background: Sardinian Warbler *Sylvia melanocephala* and European Greenfinch *Chloris chloris*. 080919.MR.094322.32

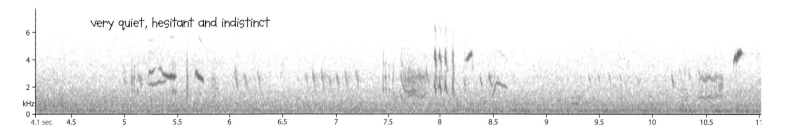

are many imitations, here including very brief fragments of Barn Swallow *Hirundo rustica*, Eurasian Wren *Troglodytes troglodytes*, and two species that can also be heard in the background: Sardinian Warbler and European Greenfinch *Chloris chloris*. Now listen to another recording of a first-winter in Portugal, made in mid-October (**CD1-26**). It contains several imitations of Meadow Pipits *Anthus pratensis*, which arrive in Portugal around the beginning of that month.

Despite having lost any hope of an English endemic, I still find it an amazing story, these maritime *dartfordiensis* apparently having stayed close enough to the sea to cling to life despite hard winters and heath fires in the summer. The plumage and sound differences between them and *undata* certainly merit further investigation. And should *dartfordiensis* ever be split, it would be nice to think that a future researcher might honour Colin Bibby. It would be a tragedy to call it Nantes Warbler.

Dartford Warbler *Sylvia undata dartfordiensis*, male, Arne, Poole, Dorset, 9 May 2009 (*David Larcombe*)

CD1-26   **Dartford Warbler** *Sylvia undata undata* Sagres, Algarve, Portugal, 09:27, 16 October 2009. Plastic song of a first-winter male with rather short, hesitant strophes. Background: Song Thrush *Turdus philomelos*, Sardinian Warbler *Sylvia melanocephala*, Great Tit *Parus major* and European Greenfinch *Chloris chloris*. 091016.MR.092742.01

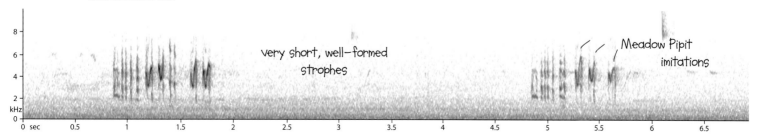

Chapter 5: Where was I?

I'm not a great traveller. Birding for me is not about new experiences but rather layering one observation on another. I do travel, although having another full time job, a large part of my holidays is spent writing. A major disadvantage of travelling is that someone (or worse, everyone) may see something good in Poole while I'm away. This obsession has been described before and the usual name for it, 'twitching', conjures up for me an image of hordes of nervous lemmings, without a thought in their head except for seeing a rare bird. However, a bird doesn't have to be rare to knock me right off course.

Without wishing to be unkind to sufferers of the real thing, the phenomenon is best described as 'bird Tourette's'. For example, I was giving a talk in the lounge of the Haven Hotel, which has huge picture windows that look across the harbour mouth. While addressing a large group of work colleagues about something important, I involuntarily jerked my head round toward the window and cried, "cormorants". 200 delegates looked at me astounded. I apologised, but from then on struggled to regain my train of thought. Cormorants? Having got past the initial stages of separating them from shags, I do find them fascinating, but I'll come back to them later. Hamish Murray summed things up, pointing out that when you come out of a meeting you've forgotten the content in minutes, but see a good bird and you remember it for the rest of your life.

I blame my condition on Martin Cade, who started it all off by analysing where Dorset rarities had been found from 1983 to 1992. In the 1993 bird report, he wrote; "With its large concentrations of, for example, wildfowl and waders, Poole Harbour could be expected to attract its share of rarities. However this volume of common birds, and the sheer size of the site, seem to make rarity detection difficult, such that the Harbour and its environs attracted just 6% of the county's rare bird total." It was just a modest three-page article showing how great Portland was (41%) and how Weymouth (17%) and Christchurch (17%) accounted for most of the other rarities. 6%! We had been weighed and found wanting.

To become an official British rarity, a birder's find has to be vetted by the 'Rarities Committee', which was set up by British Birds magazine in 1959. If you think you've seen a rare bird you can send a written description, drawing, photo and/or recording to the committee. Then 10 men decide whether they believe you to have seen and correctly identified your bird. They are like food critics. If they endorse your sighting, you are a five star Michelin birder but if they reject it you are doomed to months of introspection as you imagine them thinking of you as overenthusiastic, incompetent, a braggart or worse a liar. At present in Britain we have an excellent committee and great chairman, but the system has its flaws.

Common Kingfisher *Alcedo atthis*, Little Sea, Studland, Dorset, 24 August 2010 (*Arnoud B van den Berg*). View from a hide where more than 30 years before a Pied-billed Grebe *Podilymbus podiceps* turned up.

American Robin *Turdus migratorius* (*Killian Mullarney*)

Horace Alexander is an example of that. A life-long dedicated birder, he lived to be 100. He was also one of the first members of the Rarities Committee and had a good go at finding rarities in Poole Harbour.

Alexander was a Quaker, and his church sent him to India, where he spent a fair bit of his long life advising Gandhi, even introducing the concept of birdwatching to him. When India gained independence, he returned home to Swanage and liked to visit Poole Harbour. Birding with friend Martin Cutler on 17 January 1961, he describes "walking along the path from Holton Heath railway station towards Poole Harbour when … a bird settled on the telegraph wire, beyond an impassable thicket of gorse. It seemed to be a small thrush, which might have been a Song Thrush, only that it had a very distinct pale wing-bar; and this showed on both wings. It soon flew down and disappeared into the scrub. As it did so, I noticed white edges to the outer tail feathers, as in Mistle Thrush. But this was no Mistle Thrush; it was much too small, and the colour of its upper back and wings was too warm a brown: the lower back was paler" (Alexander 1974). Was there any such bird? Well in the end he found there was, namely the female Siberian Thrush.

Siberian Thrush is a mega-rarity, and Alexander's credentials were spotless. He advised Gandhi on ethics, and his birding skills were well regarded. For reasons unknown to us, however, Siberian Thrush is not on the Poole Harbour list, nor is it listed as rejected. Who's to say whether Horace made a genuine error, let his imagination run away with him, or was in fact correct with his identification? We all struggle with the thought that in the past a bird was accepted or rejected on the birder's credentials.

At this stage I should explain I have tried to get help for my Poole Harbour bird obsession. I talked things through with my doctor. She thought it was healthy for a man to have a passionate interest (although now I think about it, she did encourage me to visit a therapist). It is true that many birders live long lives.

Whether he was right or not, it's these stories that fuel my passion. In *The Sound Approach to birding* (2006), I joked about being buried in Studland churchyard with this memorial engraved on the gravestone: "Here lies Mark Constantine. He found a Siberian Thrush in this churchyard." What I didn't write was that at a party, after a few beers, I mentioned this to Ian Stanley and we agreed that other birders would probably piss on it. So maybe it's not such a great idea.

Trev Haysom is guaranteed a memorial in Studland churchyard. A stonemason and sculptor, he carved the man-sized stone cross on the green outside the church. I first met Trev as I nervously lowered myself down St Aldhelm's crumbling cliff to go seawatching, using a metal cable and clutching frantically at the sea lettuce. He bounded past me, binoculars bouncing of his chest, with a cheery "Good morning," and I joined him on the rocks some time later. His memorial? He found the American Robin in Poole Harbour, a great rarity and one that did enter the record books.

Returning from a Purbeck Natural History field trip on 15 January 1966, on a bleak midwinter day with a little snow on the ground, he found it foraging along the edge of the saltmarsh on Redhorn Point in Brand's Bay. Later it moved to a more sedate residence in Miss M Crosby's Canford Cliffs garden, where at one magical moment it shared the same bush as a Waxwing.

We did not have many rarities in the past, but there were some lovely birds. On 8 June 1967, Studland warden Bunny Teagle and his wife were with Bryan Pickess, driving from Arne to Corfe. Pulling over the hill past Slepe, they spotted a Roller sitting on a telegraph wire, right opposite Maranoa farm. Bryan swore in his

Woodchat Shrike *Lanius senator senator* (*Killian Mullarney*)

excitement and Mrs Teagle, who had no sympathy for any kind of bird Tourette's, gave him a good telling off.

The rarity status of different birds has changed over the years. Woodchat Shrike was a national rarity when, on 31 May 1975,

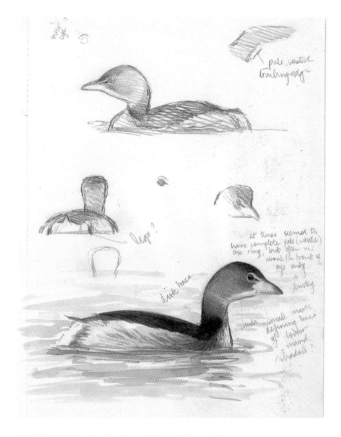

Pied-billed Grebe *Podilymbus podiceps* (*Killian Mullarney*)

place to watch Teal and sometimes Kingfishers, only this time it was a Pied-billed Grebe that came out of the reeds. Mo and I did see this one. Over several visits we watched it displaying, calling, and catching sticklebacks. It stayed till 28 April, moulting into summer plumage. Iain moved to Poole, and continued to find rarities, many of which stayed around long enough for us all to enjoy. He seldom misidentified a good bird and was always keen to share it, making sure everyone knew it was there.

For birders, the number of rare birds they've seen or better found is the currency of birding, and if you have found a lot of good birds you are a millionaire. Taking this metaphor a little further, just as those that say "It's not the money it's the principle" really mean "it's the money", so those birders that say "I'm not really interested in rare birds myself" should always be included in any rarity ringaround. In the past, however, many birds didn't hang around long enough for the finders to get to a telephone. Take for instance the Common Nighthawk.

I'm not sure who was waiting for who outside the toilets at the base of Ballard, but at 11:00 on 23 October 1983, Kate Massey, husband Mike and friend Margaret Howard watched a Common Nighthawk high over the trees and then over them. They wrote: "The bird flew rapidly into view, it twisted and turned as it flew. Its wings were long with pointed tips and noticeable patches of white on underside and top. The head was small, the tail was short with a small fork" (Green 1983).

I didn't even hear about the nighthawk. The problem wasn't just the lack of information, but the speed at which it moved. With no birdlines, mobile phones, internet or pagers, the nighthawk information would only arrive weeks later.

the Godfreys found an adult male sitting on a wire at Wytch. Now it has even turned up at Lytchett, and only needs a few brief notes sent to the local rarity committee.

Iain Prophet was a serial rarity finder. He snared his first really rare Poole bird when down from Bristol on 10 February 1980, visiting the tiny triangular hide at Studland around teatime. It's a nice

At Pilot's Point at 13:45 on 26 November 1983, David Bryer-Ash saw a Little Swift as it flew low over the dunes. As he ran to the payphone, he met a YOC group led by Nigel Spring, most of whom were able to spot it as it attempted to feed in poor weather. By 15:20, several locals had seen it. I was blissfully unaware, entertaining my mother-in-law for lunch until around 16:00 when it was nearly dark. The next day I joined a scene unprecedented since the D-Day rehearsals. Over a thousand birders were searching for it. Keen Dorset lister Keith Vinicombe wrote: "It seems likely that this year's individual succumbed after an appalling afternoon of cold, wet weather. The large turn-out of would-be observers the following day soon degenerated into the inevitable 'social event' and only the discovery of an exceedingly confiding female Lapland Bunting *Calcarius lapponicus* prevented an early adjournment to the cafes and pubs of nearby Poole" (Rogers & the Rarities Committee 1984). I saw the bunting, a good second prize.

Sharing birds had its drawbacks. Take Stephen Morrison's experience. Quiet and awkward, he started coming to Studland as a boy, soon developing into a persevering birder. On the afternoon of 1 May 1987, he found Poole Harbour's first Alpine Swift feeding over Godlingston Heath. He told Ewan Brodie who, unable to go, phoned Ian and Janet Lewis. They drove to Studland and walked the heath towards the Agglestone, finding the swift shortly before it headed over to Christchurch harbour. One of the rewards for finding a national rarity is seeing your name in British Birds magazine. It prints the names of the first three to send in a written report, in alphabetic order. When Stephen received the eagerly anticipated issue with the rarity report for 1987, he was dismayed to find Ian and Janet Lewis's names first, making it look for all the world as if they had found it.

Sabine's Gulls *Xema sabini* with Common Tern *Sterna hirundo* (*Killian Mullarney*)

Only two weeks after the swift, on 13 May, Stephen made another memorable find at the same location: a beautiful male

Pectoral Sandpiper *Calidris melanotos*, juvenile (*Killian Mullarney*)

Red-footed Falcon. On 24 May Mo, out birding with Rowena Bird, saw it again sitting on a flagpole on one of the greens on Studland golf course. Guy Dutson had also submitted the Red-footed Falcon. We would joke afterwards that all this turned Stephen to the dark side, and after that he would only contact birders whose name followed his alphabetically.

Guy Dutson birded the harbour with Paul Harvey when they were kids, before going on to find fame elsewhere, Paul as warden of Fair Isle and Guy in Papua New Guinea. Asked about his childhood memories recently at a visit to the pub, Guy reminisced about Sabine's Gulls in flocks on the south side of the harbour, ink-black Spotted Redshanks on Lytchett Pool,

Twite in Ian's kitchen and still regular, and Smew on the ice in the Wareham Channel. Matching his memories to the official record, "a flock of Sabine's Gulls" could be in 1987 when two birds were together off Fitzworth on 5 September, ink-black Spotted Redshanks still turn up on Lytchett Pool, but Twite is really rare and the harbour's second record was three in 1983 in Lytchett Bay, one of which did find its way into Ian's kitchen to be ringed.

One of the main reasons Robin Ward started the bird pub was to pass on news of rarities, and we were quickly rewarded when he himself found an adult female Wilson's Phalarope in Holes Bay on 20 June 1988. Mo and I got great views.

If Martin is to blame for my obsession, Graham Armstrong was responsible for starting Shaun's when he flushed a subadult Purple Heron from the back of Lytchett Bay Pool on 8 April 1992. Graham followed it into the far fields where it settled, then phoned out the news. Shaun, who had never visited Lytchett before, soon arrived and immediately fell in love with the place. He could see potential he felt others had overlooked. That autumn he visited Lytchett Bay every day after work for six weeks, but the next rarity there wasn't his.

Shaun didn't even get a call when Ewan found a lovely Pectoral Sandpiper there on 11 September 1992. Trying to avoid embarrassing episodes of bird Tourette's at the office, Shaun had asked Ewan not to call him at work. That evening, instead of going straight to Lytchett Bay he had decided to play squash first, dropping in for a pint afterwards and finally arriving at the bay at around 18:30. On reaching the gate he noticed a neatly folded and tied note addressed "To Shaun". He opened the note, "Pectoral Sandpiper on the pool all afternoon, we have all seen it but I couldn't ring you, Ewan". Frantically, he scanned the pool but it wasn't there. Then he started to run up and down the lane, looking for gaps in the hedge to get different angles on the pool but, it was all in vain. By now it was low tide, and the bird had moved on, perhaps to join another seen on a flash pond at Swineham from 20 to 22 September. The latter was found by Stephen Morrison and shared only with the alphabetically appropriate Peter Williams.

People communicate well when they like each other, and the bird pub created friendships. It really started to come together for us all when Stephen Smith found an immature male Lesser Scaup at Hatch Pond on the evening of the 28 November 1992. Not getting good views in the failing light but very clearly seeing a scaup with strange vermiculations on its flanks, he discussed the bird at the pub with Shaun and me. Shaun rediscovered it on 4 December, and the following day, helped by phone calls to Killian and other friends, we were all able to help confirm its identity and also check that it had no leg rings. When we were content with its identification, we circulated the news, and the bird was enjoyed by 50 birders.

It felt good to identify what was then a first for Dorset and a fifth for Britain. Lesser Scaup was the last rare bird found in the period that Martin analysed, but it was the beginning of a great new chapter for the harbour when we would explore every nook and cranny to see what was hiding there.

Chapter 6: Paradise regained

Had I blurted out "Cormorants", as I did at work, in the middle of reading to my fellow pupils at school, I would have been given a detention. It wasn't unusual to find me in detention after class. The teacher would set appropriate extra work. "Right, Constantine, I want 200 lines starting with 'I find cormorants fascinating because…'"

So I start writing my lines. "I find cormorants fascinating, because in *Paradise Lost* John Milton described Satan sitting 'like a Cormorant' in the tree of life, looking down on paradise…" Perfect! That's how I see them,- perched on a post or dead tree, drying their wings in the sun and watching generation after generation of Poole folk going about their business. The bait draggers and clam boats, marines from the Special Boat Service, conscious of their image, speeding out from Hamworthy or floating down into Studland Bay on parachutes, lifeboat men on an exercise, searching for a dummy body, oyster seeders scattering the young oysters on Poole Harbour's bed then hauling up the full grown catch to become dinners on Valentine's day, busy, busy oilmen going to and fro, while peacocks fly into the trees to roost on Brownsea, and yachties head out to the Isle of Wight for lunch. They all pass a cormorant or two and some recognise them and some don't, but very few realise how fascinating they are.

For a start there isn't just one type of cormorant in Poole Harbour but two, maybe even three. They bring into question the idea of subspecies, and as a consequence they challenge birders, scientists and conservationists to question the status quo. As I'm only on imaginary detention, I feel free to return to the present and Google the term 'subspecies'. I read, "Note that the distinction between a species and a subspecies depends *only* on the likelihood that in the absence of external barriers the two populations would merge back into a single, genetically unified population. It has nothing to do with 'how different' the two groups appear to be to the human observer" (Wikipedia, 22 September 2011).

That certainly describes 'our' cormorants. Sorting through these inky black, coal black seabirds is a real art. First separating the Shags from the cormorants, then looking again for the far heavier Atlantic Great Cormorants *Phalacrocorax carbo carbo* which are the only type breeding in Dorset. They nest on the sea cliffs at Ballard and are declining a little more each year.

Continental Great Cormorants *P c sinensis* breed on the mainland of Europe in trees. They are highly migratory and happily feed inland on rivers, ponds and canals. The scientific name *sinensis* suggests that their roots could be China where many cormorants were (and some still are) kept as slaves to assist in the fishing industry. The technique is fairly simple. You starve your tame bird for a day, then tie a string around its neck and

Continental Great Cormorant *Phalacrocorax carbo sinensis*, Amsterdamse Waterleidingduinen, Zandvoort, Noord-Holland, Netherlands, 27 April 2012 (*Arnoud B van den Berg*). At same nesting tree as where CD1-31 was recorded. Though not as extensively white on the head as most breeding *sinensis* at the peak of courtship activity this bird, which was attending a nest with eggs or hatchlings, showed more extensive white than most others present at the time at this site. In *sinensis*, the white patch on the cheek/throat is about the same width as the gular skin in front of it; in *carbo*, the white patch is considerably wider.

take it fishing. Each time it catches a fish you steal it. At the end of the day you have a bucket full of fish and feed a few to your slave. In the 16th century, cormorants were brought into France and especially England, and fishing with them had become a fashionable sport amongst the aristocracy by the 18th century (Olburs 2008).

Nobody can tell for sure whether *sinensis* cormorants were released into Poole Harbour in the 16th century, but we do know from a study in the Baltic where large numbers of *sinensis* breed today that the skeletal remains of cormorants that were there during earlier times are the size of *carbo*. "Precisely when… *sinensis* immigrated into the Baltic is unknown, but it must have occurred sometime between 1500 and 1800 AD" (Ericson & Carrasquilla 1997).

It would be fun, just for the duration of my detention, to assume that having discovered the best fishing cormorant known to man we brought it into Europe, which then escaped into the wild and has been pushing nominate *carbo* further west ever since. However, genetic evidence suggests that there was a refuge of European *sinensis* in the Danube basin during the last ice age, and the Chinese birds are distinguishable from European ones, having an even greater gular angle than 'our' *sinensis*. So, whatever role the slave cormorants from China may have had, there had already been *sinensis* in Europe for thousands of years.

In 1966, John Ash recorded three continental birds flying into Poole Harbour on 13 February. But they had probably been sneaking around in the harbour way before that, because Britain's first documented record of *sinensis* was taken 11 miles up the road at Christchurch in 1873.

Continental Great Cormorants seem to have increased in the harbour over the last 10 years, mirroring a similar increase across the whole of eastern and southern England. Whether this is just due to increased awareness is difficult to say. Whenever one of us makes an effort, we can identify a few continental birds, and they have been seen in the Wareham Channel, sitting in groups on the Keysworth shore, on Hatch Pond, in Poole Park and perched on Poole Quay breakwater, among other places. However, we have not found any breeding yet.

Various studies have shown that in some inland tree colonies in England and France, both *carbo* and *sinensis* are present (eg, Goostrey et al 1998, Winney et al 2001). Just how much hybridisation is going on is unclear, with different genetic analyses giving different results. So our Wikipedian distinction between subspecies and species is difficult to apply. Whatever may be going on, *carbo* and *sinensis* do represent clearly separate lineages with a long history of separation, largely in different habitats. If any mixing is going on now in Britain and France, it is taking place in the tree-nesting colonies and not on cliffs, which *sinensis* appear to avoid (Marion & le Gentil 2006). So, we can assume that our Dorset cliff-nesters are clear examples of *carbo*.

Curiously, *'carbo'* from northern Norway do not appear to be closely related to *carbo* from elsewhere, despite their similarity in size and habitat. It has been suggested that they are more

Atlantic Great Cormorant *Phalacrocorax carbo carbo*, Rosslare, Wexford, Ireland, 18 February 2012 (*Killian Mullarney*). The bristle-like white filoplumes on the top and sides of the head and the prominent white thigh patch are features of courtship plumage. Acquired in late winter/early spring, they will have largely disappeared in most birds by late spring.

closely related to Japanese Cormorant *P capillatus*, and may have colonised from the Pacific via the Northeast Passage (Marion & le Gentil 2006). Might these birds also visit Poole Harbour in the winter?

We didn't really understand how many of our cormorants were migrants until one long summer's day at Brownsea lagoon, when Jim and Stan identified large numbers of juvenile *sinensis*. They were using a new technique pioneered by Per Alström, which involved noting the size and angle of the yellow gape. Time passed, then one day Nick had a go at photographing a series of random cormorants scattered about the harbour. When he got out his protractor he found that over 50% of these birds could be identified as *sinensis*.

Now intrigued, the rest of the Sound Approach team followed up, with Killian making a trip to Brownsea on 7 February 2011. Back in Wexford, Ireland, where Killian lives, all the cormorants are *carbo*. On Brownsea, he found that of the cormorants roosting in the lagoon, at least 80 were *carbo* while over 100 were clearly *sinensis*. Another 235 or so were hidden behind them and could not be seen well enough for identification.

We then turned our attention to their sounds. I've only recently noticed cormorant vocalisations. Lars Svensson too, apparently. In the *Collins bird guide* (Mullarney et al 2009), he only describes "Various deep, guttural calls at colony", but there is far more

to them than that. Now I realise they are very noisy, their calls filling Brownsea lagoon every night (**CD1-27**). They sound so distinctive to me now, but suppose I mistook them for gulls or ducks in the past.

Great Cormorant *Phalacrocorax carbo* Brownsea lagoon, Poole Harbour, Dorset, England, 18:35, 11 September 2011. In this recording of birds arriving at a large roost, both *carbo* and *sinensis* were present. Background: Canada Goose *Branta canadensis*, Greenshank *Tringa nebularia* and Sandwich Tern *Sterna sandvicensis*. 110911.MC.183554.02

So we asked ourselves, are there any vocal differences between *carbo* and *sinensis*? The most serious attempts to understand cormorant vocal behaviour were published without accompanying recordings or sonagrams (Kortland 1938, 1995, van Tets 1965). So by necessity, their descriptions of the different call categories are phonetic or as we call it, 'birdie talk'. Among the sounds heard most often from cormorants are loud, rolled 'r's. Have a listen to these rolled 'r' calls of *carbo*, recorded

CD1-28 **Atlantic Great Cormorant** *Phalacrocorax carbo carbo* Carnsore Point, Wexford, Ireland, 23 August 2002. Raucous calls and slow rolled 'r' call of a successful attacker in a 'perch dispute'. Background: Common Tern *Sterna hirundo*, Roseate Tern *S dougallii*, Pied Wagtail *Motacilla yarrellii* and Grey Seal *Halichoerus grypus*. 02.039.MR.03951.22

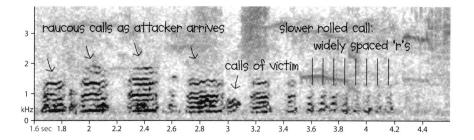

accidentally after the breeding season in Ireland (**CD1-28**), while trying for Roseate Terns.

In this case, one adult was displacing another from a post, a ritualised behaviour described by Kortland (1938). The attacker arrives giving a series of raucous calls with its plumage somewhat puffed out, its neck in an S-shape, and with the hyoid bone sticking out in its throat. Then when it has successfully expelled the other, it gives a couple of triumphant rolled calls in an erect posture with a thick neck and its bill pointing slightly downwards.

In most of our cormorant recordings, especially those in large roosts and breeding colonies, it is much harder to know what was going on. You can often hear calls very similar to those heard in 'perch disputes'. Other situations where calls with a rolled 'r' sound can be heard are summarised in BWP (Cramp & Simmons 1977). It can be hard to be sure whether you are hearing a *rrrrr* (pre-flight/pre-hop call), *rooor* (post-landing call), *r-r-r-r-r* (given during 'gape display') or *rrrrr* (associated with rubbing and entwining of necks). This is the trouble with 'birdie talk' descriptions, lacking sonagrams.

At the risk of mixing up similar-sounding calls associated with different behaviours, Magnus checked and compared the quality of the rolled 'r' in our *carbo* and *sinensis* recordings and found that in *sinensis* it seemed to sound faster on average. Listen to these *sinensis* at a post-breeding roost in Bulgaria (**CD1-29**) and see if you agree that they sound slightly different from the *carbo* you just heard. Magnus then analysed sonagrams of 20 rolled calls of *carbo* from Ireland and 29 of *sinensis* from Bulgaria and the Netherlands, recorded both in breeding and non-breeding contexts. In order to complete the first four rolls of a rolled 'r' call, *carbo* took an average of 12% longer than *sinensis*, or in other words *carbo* roll their 'r's more slowly.

CD1-29 **Continental Great Cormorant** *Phalacrocorax carbo sinensis* Burgas lake, Burgas, Bulgaria, 09:19, 20 September 2007. Cormorants arguing over perches at a roost as new birds arrive. Rolled 'r' calls of several individuals can be heard. Background: Yellow-legged Gull *Larus michahellis* and European Robin *Erithacus rubecula*. 070920. MR.091907.01

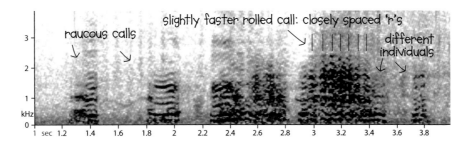

Listen to another recording of *carbo* (**CD1-30**). These Irish breeders were nervous, because Killian was rather close to their colony. At 00:05, a rolled 'r' call can be heard from a presumed female, and despite the anxiety, it still sounds marginally slower than average calls of *sinensis*. This may be related to the larger size of *carbo*, and perhaps other physical differences. After all, if their gular patches differ, why not the anatomy of their throats?

CD1-30   **Atlantic Great Cormorant** *Phalacrocorax carbo carbo* Saltee Islands, Wexford, Ireland, 12:05, 10 April 2011. Two adults on different nests: a male slightly to the left and a presumed female slightly closer in the centre, calling in response to Killian's movements. The presumed female gives a rolled 'r' call at 00:05. Background: Eurasian Wren *Troglodytes troglodytes*, Black-legged Kittiwake *Rissa tridactyla* and large gull *Larus*. 110410.KM.120550.02

Now listen to another recording of *sinensis*, this time from a large colony in the Netherlands (**CD1-31**). In this recording, you can hear various calls with a rolled 'r' quality, perhaps associated with a wider range of behaviours and displays than in a post-breeding roost. Again the 'r's seem to be rolled a little faster than in *carbo*. Whether the small vocal difference between *carbo* and *sinensis* still stands when calls of known sex and from a narrowly defined behavioural context are compared will have to wait for a more thorough study. In the meantime, we should start scrutinising their behaviour more closely.

CD1-31   **Continental Great Cormorant** *Phalacrocorax carbo sinensis* Amsterdamse Waterleidingduinen, Zandvoort, Noord-Holland, Netherlands, 19:56, 11 May 2011. Sounds of a colony, including a variety of adult calls with a rolled 'r' sound, and high-pitched whistled begging calls of nestlings. Ignore the loud calls of a Grey Heron *Ardea cinerea* from 1:00 in the recording. Background: Common Chiffchaff *Phylloscopus collybita* and Willow Warbler *P trochilus*. 110511.AB.195608.01

It's only recently that cormorants have gained some protection in the UK. Trev Haysom's father would take friends along the Ballard cliffs to shoot them. "The cormorants, nesting here and feeding in Poole Harbour were shot as rivals by fishermen who claimed a government bounty." On one occasion the birds got off lightly when "one careless man shot through the bottom boards" (Cooper 2004).

Fishermen also caught cormorants and shags by applying glue to suitable perches and returning later to cut off their tails to collect a bounty. Persecution is still going on, here and there, throughout Europe. As a recent example, in an isolated Mediterranean colony of *carbo* on the island of Sardinia, up to 1000 were being killed each winter in the '90s, until by 2002 they were all gone. It was much the same in the Netherlands where numbers of *sinensis* were kept to 500 pairs per colony according a quota system, until the creation of the IJsselmeer from the Zuiderzee in the '30s distanced the cormorants' breeding colonies from their feeding grounds, and the bird got into difficulties. The collapse in breeding numbers was reversed in the '70s when they started to nest in newly created polders. Cormorants started to be noticed on Brownsea lagoon in 1971 when the warden wrote, "suddenly 100 birds started to roost on the seawall or within the lagoon especially in late summer" (Wise 1981). Perhaps this was the start of the most recent influx of *sinensis* into Poole Harbour.

For years we counted cormorants flying to and from a roost somewhere out in Poole Bay and thought we were getting all the birds of the harbour. However, the Brownsea roost and a third roost on Long Island or Arne beach weren't counted at the same time. On the morning of 2 November 2009, Nick and

Approximate breeding ranges of Atlantic Great Cormorant *Phalacrocorax carbo carbo* (green) and Continental Great Cormorant *P c sinensis* (red). Continental *sinensis* is so adventurous that we can soon see the colours on this map changing, and indeed in Britain the breeding numbers are on the increase. On the other hand, in recent years, also a handful pairs of Atlantic *carbo* have been found in Continental *sinensis* colonies along continental North Sea coasts, such as in the Netherlands. Atlantic *carbo* also breeds along the coasts of north-western France but it is unclear how far south and inland it occurs.

I counted 689 heading across the harbour to fish, with others flying inland over our heads at our eyrie at Constitution Hill. This was a new county record and puts Poole among the top five sites in Britain.

This is not all good news. Fishermen still hate cormorants and the current British Fisheries Minister Richard Benyon MP is a fisherman. He recently announced a review of the current licensing regime for cormorant controls, whereby Poole fishermen will be able to take matters into their own hands to protect their local fish stocks. So, while still discussing speciation, we could see Atlantic Great Cormorants heading for extinction as a breeding bird as efforts to control cormorant numbers, though ill informed and ill judged, get the go-ahead from the government's Department for Environment, Food and Rural Affairs (DEFRA).

Paradise lost and then regained fits my view of these birds in Poole Harbour. It would be so sad to see paradise lost again as the last local breeding Atlantic Great Cormorants are exterminated, hanging dead from the channel posts, waiting for fishermen to cut off their tails for a bounty.

ATLANTIC GREAT CORMORANT
carbo

adult winter

males are larger than females with a heavier bill and more muscular neck, but reliable sexing difficult if not seen as pair

slender billed Great Cormorants (probably always young females) resemble Shag; note different head shape, Great Cormorant's brighter and more extensive yellow gular pouch and Shag's yellowish bill colour in winter

juvenile
(pale)

peaked forehead

juvenile
(intermediate)

carbo nests colonially, usually on coastal cliffs

Shag
(adult winter)

most juvenile *carbo* are extensively white on underparts, often including breast and foreneck (top)

considerable variation in extent of white on underparts of juveniles, darkest birds closely resembling older birds; however, in juvenile, scapulars, tertials and wing coverts are always narrower and more pointed than in subsequent plumages and when fresh juveniles have fine pale tips to greater coverts

patchy plumage with mixture of old, faded and new fresh feathers

courtship dress acquired around late winter/early spring (on average later in *carbo* than in *sinensis*); white on head and thigh disappears as breeding progresses

juvenile
(dark)

subadult

adult winter

adult
courtship

ONTINENTAL GREAT CORMORANT
sinensis

(and comparisons with Atlantic *carbo*)

typically *sinensis* fish collectively, forming dense rafts and diving in synchrony

subtley shorter-necked and less massive than *carbo*; at times, slightly quicker wingbeats reminiscent of Glossy Ibis !

Atlantic *carbo* courtship dress

length and density of white filoplumes increase with age, but *carbo* averages less white than *sinensis* (below)

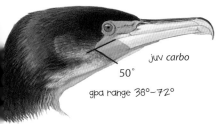

juv *carbo*

50°

gpa range 38°–72°

st reliable difference between *carbo* (above)
d *sinensis* (right) in all plumages is the
-called 'gular pouch angle' (gpa) highlighted
e in red;
 more acute in *carbo*

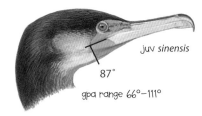

juv *sinensis*

87°

gpa range 66°–111°

comparatively slender bill indicative of female;
males have a slightly heavier bill with a less concave culmen

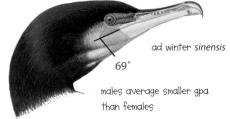

ad winter *sinensis*

69°

males average smaller gpa than females

identification can be tricky when gpa is around 70° overlap zone; comparison with more distinctive individuals directly alongside may be helpful !

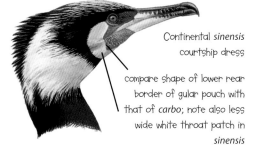

Continental *sinensis* courtship dress

compare shape of lower rear border of gular pouch with that of *carbo*; note also less wide white throat patch in *sinensis*

venile
le)

as in *carbo*, juv *sinensis* ranges from almost entirely white below to almost all dark

juvenile (dark)

Double-crested Cormorant resembles *sinensis*; yellow extending onto bill is diagnostic

Double-crested Cormorant

adult male winter

starts to lose white on head and 'thigh patch' at onset of incubation

both sexes acquire courtship dress

breeding colonies usually located in trees on inland lakes; *carbo* prefers rock outcrops on offshore islands

Chapter 7: The return of the natives

Neil Hagger didn't have a comfortable relationship with the police. Handsome, his face slightly scarred from a car accident, he looked roguish. We spent several summers in the early '80s driving through the night together, surveying owls in Poole Harbour.

The prize amongst the shadowy copses with hooting Tawny Owls was the secretive Long-eared Owl. I had previously found Long-eared a few miles out of Dorchester, and had read of birders in Norfolk finding nests by listening for the young's far carrying calls. In Poole Harbour, Long-eared Owls had bred at Arne and Studland between the wars but seemed to have become really rare. Or had they? Perhaps if Neil and I systematically worked the harbour on warm, windless summer nights, we could find them.

Two men driving around in the middle of the night, pulling up and standing listening near isolated copses and cottages regularly attracted the police. 'Birdwatching' really wasn't an adequate excuse in the dark, and Neil was usually antagonistic and occasionally sarcastic. I tried to encourage a calmer approach. "Just wind down your window, explain what we are doing and ask the officer how you can help", I would suggest.

Long-eared Owls like to use old crow nests, particularly in lines of conifers, and the British Gas oil gathering station at Wytch looked promising. One moonlit night, Neil decided he wanted to photograph the bright lights of the site through the evergreens. I was busy so he took his friend, Mark 'the gas fitter'. Driving up the private oil roads, he parked the car, opened the boot and got out his tripod and camera. Suddenly a Land Rover with lights at full beam had him in its glare. It pulled up and out jumped two security guards who demanded to know what he was up to. Neil gave a typically sardonic answer about working for British Gas, waved his tripod and said that if they came any closer he would zap them with his super ray gun. Surprisingly, they drove off. Neil took the pictures and was driving back through Corfe when three police patrol cars swooped. He wound down the window ready to explain, but they wrenched open the door, pulled him out of the car, slapped his hands on the roof and spread his legs. With no apparent sense of irony they then asked, "Right, which one of you has the super ray gun."

Neil had his film confiscated and we never found nesting Long-eared Owls, but I did get a taste for birding on the western shores of the harbour. On 29 August 1993 after a pre-work search for Aquatic Warblers at Swineham, I was relaxing on the train back to Poole. On reaching Holton Heath, I noticed a cloud of gulls that had just been put up in the channel. My heartbeat quickened because this usually meant a raptor. Frantically searching through the melee, I found the culprit. It was an Osprey. Phones had just been installed on trains so I experimented with a call to Hamish, and as I continued to London he rushed down to the Holton shore and saw it. Osprey

Eurasian Spoonbills *Platalea leucorodia* and Pied Avocets *Recurvirostra avocetta*, Brownsea Island, Dorset, 4 October 2009 (*Claire Lodge*). Looking towards Poole.

must have bred in the harbour for 2,000 to 3,000 years, and there are records of breeding birds nearby on the Isle of Wight until 1557. Around that time fishermen and gamekeepers began to see them as competition. With their huge nests and habit of roosting out in the open, killing them was easy. Only in Scotland did breeding Osprey hang on right through to 1908.

If you would like to see an Osprey fishing, go to Ham Common, the urban nature reserve just south of Rockley Caravan Park, in the early morning (around 08:30) in August or September. If you look southwest with the sun behind you up this beautiful broad stretch of water, you will see two small islands and beyond them the church tower of Lady St Mary at Wareham. Suddenly in the distance the gulls will fly up. You'll scope the flock and find an Osprey fishing, just as I saw one from the train.

After the National Trust built a hide at Middlebere Farm, we discovered Ospreys roosting in the bare trees on the south side of Arne. Knowing the roost, we could watch the birds leaving in the morning to patrol the edge of the Holton shore and elsewhere in the harbour. Strangely, they often flew very high in the sky.

When in Poole Harbour, Ospreys eat Thin-lipped Grey Mullet. Weighing around a kilo, the mullet appear in the harbour in May. As the waters warm up they develop a habit of lying near the surface of the water as if sunbathing, making them an easy catch. The mullet normally disappear in November, and the fishermen at first thought they moved to warmer seas followed by the Osprey, but a few shoals have been found hibernating locally in deep water out of reach. You won't find an Osprey in the harbour after this time.

Curious, I asked Dick Forsman how Ospreys see fish from so high up. "They can't see fish from that high, so they are probably defending a territory." He explained that females leave their young with the males at the breeding grounds, then come to sites like Poole Harbour to claim the fishing rights. The males and juveniles then join the females in late August. Intrigued, I began sexing and aging Poole's summer Ospreys and confirmed that the early birds did all look like females. Whenever I have seen three together, they have always turned out to be two adults and a juvenile.

I wondered where the harbour's Ospreys were breeding. Ospreys first reappeared in Scotland in the mid-'50s, and by 1966 there were at least three pairs. We had only three records in the 60 years before 1966. Then a bird arrived in Poole Harbour on 17 August that year, staying until 3 September. We have enjoyed Ospreys in late summer and early autumn most years since. I think that Poole Harbour is a favoured fishing site for Scottish Osprey families feeding up before migration. We can be sure that Scottish Ospreys pass through, because Roy Dennis radio-tagged one (SO6) that flew straight through Poole Harbour on 19 August 1999, then again on 2 April the following year.

Ospreys may soon be spending much more time in the harbour. Seven nest platforms have recently been erected at various sites along the Wareham Channel, some complete with their own polystyrene birds. It is hoped that these will be enough to entice future birds down to stop and breed.

At one time, egg collectors were a reserve warden's main preoccupation, and the thought of protecting an Osprey nest would have been a nightmare. Some of Poole Harbour's wardens have been put to the test before. Take Tony Wise, the first warden of Brownsea Island Nature Reserve.

On 10 July 1982, Tony wasn't happy. I can't remember how I got to see what was then a very rare Little Egret, sitting in a tree on Brownsea's West Lake one Saturday morning, but I do remember that Mo came with me on the Sunday and I returned with George Green on the Monday. By then it was sitting out with the Grey Herons, giving great views, as was a Hobby nearby. By the following Saturday it had become a bit of a focus for visiting birders. With a Squacco Heron in Weymouth, two Spoonbills at Brownsea and the Little Egret staked out, there was a chance of four 'herons' in a day.

Little Egret *Egretta garzetta*, adult, Bramble Bush Bay, Studland, Dorset, 15 March 2010 (*Nick Hopper*)

Being members of the Dorset Naturalists' Trust, George, Mo and I were allowed access to the reserve, as were Ian and Janet Lewis and Paul Harvey. When Tony found four other twitchers hidden in his freshly creosoted hide, he was livid and demanded that the 'trespassers' join the trust. Three did but one refused, so Tony attempted to 'arrest' him. "It was brilliant", said Ian, "with Tony banging his walking stick on the ground as he attempted a citizen's arrest, demanding Paul Harvey act as a witness, which was awkward for him because he was friends with the fellows concerned."

Little Egrets would not remain rare for much longer. The first large influx occurred in 1990, when 14 visited the harbour. By 1995 our coordinated roost count at Brownsea, Little Sea and Arne had recorded up to 84 birds.

A few of these looked very young with obviously shorter wings, and it was difficult to comprehend how they could be flying across the Channel. Surely they must be breeding locally. Everyone was now on the lookout for the first British breeding pair. I remember in August 1996 watching egrets at Seymers on the northwest end of Brownsea, with an adult sitting in the trees watching as a juvenile tried to fish, mantling its wings to create a shaded hunting area, and stabbing repeatedly.

On 18 October 1997, I was really shocked when the Guardian announced that Little Egret had bred for the first time in Britain, with two pairs raising three young on Brownsea in 1996. Had I been watching the first British parent and fledgling Little Egret to breed in Britain for 500 years?

Later, I had a little moan about being kept in the dark. Kevin Cook told me that he was amazed I hadn't heard them. He had a point, and a little further down you will hear why I should have noticed. Still, it could have been worse. While ringing at Lytchett one night, Ian Alexander's fellow ringers secretly put a white plastic heron between the nets. It worked a treat as they watched Ian creep along on his belly in the dark and throw a sack over it. Within four years, 46 pairs were breeding in the tall pines at Brownsea.

By now it seemed that the roost opposite Len's triangular hide at Little Sea held most of the harbour's post-breeding Little Egrets. It still does. Arriving each evening up to two hours before dusk, the birds fly in over the Studland ferry road. Some feed around the roost, while others sit on the top like sentinels (**CD1-32**). Numbers peaked at 197 on 14 October 2001.

Little Egret *Egretta garzetta*. Little Sea, Poole Harbour, Dorset, England, 21:13, 26 August 2010. Calls at a roost as newcomers arrive. Background: Common Blackbird *Turdus merula*. 100826.AB.211300.12

CD1-32

Brownsea heronry was established in the early 1800s but deserted when the island's human population peaked and all the trees were felled to make way for farmland. The heronry moved to the Arne peninsula until wartime training disturbed it and it returned to Brownsea. The wonderfully eccentric Bonham-Christie wouldn't let anyone on to count the birds, but in 1961 she met her match, when a frustrated Angela Hughes flew over the island in a small plane and counted between 30 and 40 white-spattered Grey Heron nests. Not that it would have been any easier from the ground. Grey Herons nest high

Little Egrets *Egretta garzetta*, Little Sea, Studland, Dorset, 23 August 2010 (*Arnoud B van den Berg*). Arriving at roost in evening (CD1-32).

in the pines from early March through to July, so any sort of systematised count is very difficult.

Once the Dorset Naturalists' Trust took charge of the heronry, it remained protected from disturbance, and only John Follett was allowed in to do the census. When Grey Heron numbers peaked in 1971 with 131 pairs, Brownsea was Britain's second largest heronry. Sadly, it would never make it to the number one spot, and within 40 years there were no breeding herons or egrets on the island at all.

The reason? Ravens, or more specifically a young pair of Ravens that took up residence on the island. Being themselves rare birds in Dorset, Ravens were protected and as a result were starting to flourish around the harbour. The young pair on Brownsea, however, were to become notorious, after nesting in the Castle grounds. Imagine everyone's horror when they started feeding their young with Little Egret chicks. They pushed the Egrets and Grey Herons off the island, and the island's heronry became abandoned. In 2012, Grey Herons have returned to breed again on Brownsea.

Things do seem to go in cycles, and it was Arne that picked up the baton, with the Grey Heron colony, now including Little Egrets, re-establishing itself on the peninsula. With permission, Nick and I recorded there last summer and were treated to some amazing gargling calls (**CD1-33**). Over the past three years the colony has remained stable with around 20 pairs of Grey Herons and 20-25 pairs of Little Egrets.

CD1-33   **Little Egret** *Egretta garzetta* Arne heronry, Poole Harbour, Dorset, England, 05:00, 3 June 2011. Loud calls of an adult arriving at the colony, followed by cackling of another adult, and harsh calls of nestlings. Background: Common Chiffchaff *Phylloscopus collybita*. 100603.MC.043200.01

In the past, if you wanted to see a Spoonbill there might be one or two birds about, perhaps an adult and a juvenile at the entrance to Middlebere, or along the southern shores of the Wareham Channel, roosting in Arne Bay or most regularly Brownsea on the lagoon. That was the situation for 70 years.

Little Egret *Egretta garzetta*, chick on nest, Arne, Poole Harbour, Dorset, 13 June 2010 (*Nick Hopper*)

Numbers started creeping up from 2003 onwards, then suddenly in October 2007, as if word had got around that it was safe to come back, there were 26! I had a phone call at home and rushed upstairs to where I could see across to the lagoon 4 km away, to count the white ellipse-shaped blobs through my telescope. A 27th bird was present at Middlebere at the same time.

Mo is more observant than I am, and while returning in a queue of cars along the Wareham by-pass in summer 1985 she saw a yellow-billed egret feeding with cattle. Thinking that Little Egrets don't have yellow bills, she mentioned it to me and we rushed back but couldn't relocate it. It would have been Poole Harbour's first Cattle Egret, but that milestone had to wait until one was found by Nigel Symes at Ower on 26 August 1996. This one was only seen in the summer, so we were initially surprised to read in the bird report that it had been roosting with the Little Egrets until 29 December on Little Sea (observed by Stephen Morrison).

Poole's younger generation of birders had to wait until 30 July 2001 to unblock this species on their lists, when one was found by Eddie Thorpe and identified by Langton Steve Smith at Middlebere. A pattern seems to be emerging here. One or two scouts are followed by a small invasive force, then breeding. An unprecedented UK invasion started when Shaun was doing his rounds at Lytchett Bay in November 2007, and four Cattle Egrets flew over him. More followed, with three on the Wareham Moors, one joining the cattle at Upton Country Park, and another bird at East Holme. That year, Cattle Egrets went on to breed in Somerset. From then on Cattle Egrets have become annual in the harbour.

As all herons continue to recover from persecution, there are plenty more to come. In France, breeding Purple Herons have increased by 46% in a decade, while breeding pairs of Squacco Heron and Cattle Egrets have doubled. Great White Egrets only arrived in France in 1994, and now have 180 nests in 18 colonies (Marion 2009). What next for Poole Harbour?

Chapter 8: If that's a Cabot's Tern I'll eat my...

It's a miracle that Nick and I have actually finished writing this book together, and if it weren't for Magnus acting as a buffer and editor, I would have either killed him or he me. From my point of view it's not just the book, it's also the birds. Take last month. Mo and I rented the cottage on Brownsea. It cost us over a thousand pounds for a week, but I argued it looked perfect for a rarity. There was a full moon, we were in September, and a hurricane had just left North America. We took up residence on the Thursday night, but knowing that we would have to go to a meeting on Monday and Tuesday, I called Nick and asked if he would like to come over and bird the days we couldn't do. In fact he came a couple of days early with Claire. We had a lovely time, drinking wine and watching the birds. Then the minute I was gone, he found the harbour's first Buff-breasted Sandpiper, which stayed for only two hours. Fortunately Nick had also gone by the time I got back!

It was lovely staying there though. Huge numbers of birds use the lagoon in a day. One night I went out, and there were over 4,000 gulls roosting up against the wall. On that day, I reckoned that at least 9,000 birds were using the lagoon. One of the most interesting was a group of 24 Arctic Terns driven in for a few days. They are uncommon in Poole.

When the Dorset Wildlife Trust took over the reserve at Brownsea, one of the aims was to encourage terns to breed.

The first tern islands were finished in 1963, and within a decade Sandwich Terns had a go at nesting. The single nest in 1972 was deserted. Then in 1973, 23 pairs produced 25 young. In what was to become a familiar pattern, the following year nesting attempts failed when a local Sparrowhawk made regular visits. Since then, the population has become nationally important with around 230 pairs.

Sandwich Terns migrate south to winter off West Africa and beyond. The odd bird occasionally stays, but most have usually gone by the beginning of November. Nick specialises in finding those that hang round. I first learnt this when he was driving on a January bird race and suggested calling in to see if a Sandwich Tern was about. We were rather short of time, and I then made one of my most vulgar and regrettable comments. "If there is a Sandwich Tern here Nick I'll eat my own shit." We pulled into the car park and there on the mud, right in front of us, was one.

In 2009, in mid-November, a couple of weeks after apparently seeing the last ones off, there was a long spell of bad weather and Nick found 10 new Sandwich Terns in the harbour. Given the run of southwesterly depressions, he was hoping that one of them could have been blown across the Atlantic and would turn out to be Cabot's Tern *Sterna acuflavida* (**CD1-34**), a recent split from Sandwich Tern (**CD1-35**), but still regarded as a subspecies at that time.

Sandwich Tern *Sterna sandvicensis* (showing characteristics of Cabot's Tern *S acuflavida*), Baiter, Poole, Dorset, 30 November 2009 (*Nick Hopper*)

To identify Cabot's Tern, you have to sort out the age and stage of moult. One of the diagnostic features of adult birds is thin white edges to the primaries that end short of the tip, compared with the much thicker edges of Sandwich Terns that continue to the tip. Nick found one showing these diagnostic features, but then when he remembered that immature Sandwich Terns also show this, he realised he needed to take a closer look.

Some time later, after several more visits he then found another candidate that was definitely an adult. This bird looked very interesting as it still had all its old primaries. According to BWP, all Sandwich Terns by the end of November should have completed or at least be well into their wing moult, whereas Cabot's Terns do not complete their moult until early spring. It was certainly at the correct stage of moult for Cabot's.

Cabot's Tern *Sterna acuflavida* San Padre Island, Texas, USA, 26 April 1999. Two cuts of advertising calls, passing overhead. Background: Least Tern *Sternula antillarum*, Caspian Tern *Hydroprogne caspia*, Royal Tern *Sterna maxima* and Laughing Gull *Larus atricapilla*. Btlg02.MC.01925.31

CD1-34

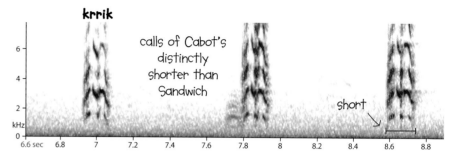

Cabot's Terns *Sterna acuflavida*, adults and first-winters, Dominical, Costa Rica, 12 January 2001 (*René Pop*)

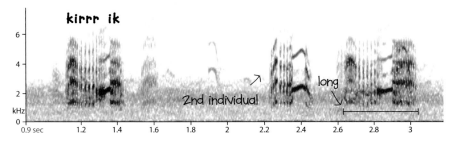

CD1-35 **Sandwich Tern** *Sterna sandvicensis* Griend, Friesland, Netherlands, 18:00, 15 April 2006. Advertising calls and 'barking' calls of several adults passing close overhead. Background: Eurasian Oystercatcher *Haematopus ostralegus* and Black-headed Gull *Chroicocephalus ridibundus.* 06.005.MR.20000.01

The head pattern was reasonable but the bill just didn't look the right shape no matter what angle he tried looking at it. Have a look at the photo and see what you think. Before you make your decision however look at the picture taken by René of Cabot's in Costa Rica. After what happened last time with Nick and Sandwich Terns, this time I won't be commenting!

We've had a few rare terns on Brownsea. There have been a couple of fleeting visits by Caspian Tern, and an adult White-winged Tern was found on the lagoon by Alan Bromby the National Trust warden and Helen Brotherton on 15 June 1964. This species must surely be due for a return visit. Much less rare but frustratingly difficult to catch up with is Black Tern. Once every blue moon or so, they suddenly arrive in great numbers. Imagine the scene on 18 August 1952, when 1,000 Black Terns arrived on the beach in Studland Bay, accompanied by up to 3,000 other terns. On 24 August 1977, another flock of 130 arrived on Brownsea after heavy rain. Two days later, most had moved on.

Each year there is one prize bird to search for: Roseate Tern. For at least 50 years, there has usually been a pair or two hidden in among the Sandwich Terns in spring and summer. They are indisputably beautiful with their pink-flushed breasts and long tail streamers, and essential for all the birders' year lists. They display most years, but the only firm evidence of breeding was in 1985, when one pair nested and subsequently deserted, and again very recently in 2010. Our birds may be wanderers from Irish breeding colonies, as an adult in 2003 had been ringed there.

Whether you see a rare tern or not, one of the best bird experiences you can have is sitting in the MacDonald hide in mid-summer and being surrounded by breeding terns. You can almost reach out and touch the Common Terns, also beneficiaries of the tern islands. They first bred in the harbour in 1951 and could hardly wait for the islands to be finished in 1963, when eight pairs bred. This grew to 90 pairs by 1970. Numbers continued to rise, and in 1990 the Brownsea breeding colony reached 130 pairs. By 1997 it was classified as nationally important. During the last 10 years, we have had anything from 180 to 246 pairs, raising 100 to 150 young.

This success is still precarious, and creating safe refuges for terns is like growing lettuces. Recently roosting cormorants have been treading on their eggs, and everything likes a nice tern egg or fledgling. Fortunately there are no foxes on Brownsea, which really helps. In the '60s and '70s it was the Herring Gulls that gave the most trouble, and to help protect the terns, the gulls were controlled by pricking their eggs. Which brings us to another puzzle. What is Britains rarest breeding bird, and breeding as it does on Brownsea lagoon, why is it in danger?

Chapter 9: 'appiness

Simon Emmerson is a birder and musician and over the past few years, he and I have been involved in making music for an English spa. It's a broad, multicultural, British sort of Englishness, which draws on everything from sea shanties to The Clash. Being birders, we like to pop in a bit of bird sound. This means that people of Paris or Tokyo may find themselves being massaged to the sound of a Song Thrush, with Corfe Castle church bells in the background (**CD1-36**), or a Mistle Thrush singing at dawn from Slepe Copse (**CD1-37**).

CD1-36   **Song Thrush** *Turdus philomelos* Purbeck Hills near Corfe Castle, Dorset, England, 09:00, 1 June 2008. Song of a male, accompanied by church bells. Background: Common Wood Pigeon *Columba palumbus*, Eurasian Wren *Troglodytes troglodytes*, Dunnock *Prunella modularis*, Common Chiffchaff *Phylloscopus collybita* and Common Chaffinch *Fringilla coelebs*. 08.013.MC.04405.32

CD1-37   **Mistle Thrush** *Turdus viscivorus* Slepe Copse, Poole Harbour, Dorset, England, 05:46, 3 May 2010. Song. Background: Mallard *Anas platyrhynchos*, Eurasian Wren *Troglodytes troglodytes*, European Robin *Erithacus rubecula*, Common Redstart *Phoenicurus phoenicurus*, Common Blackbird *Turdus merula*, Eurasian Blackcap *Sylvia atricapilla*, Common Chiffchaff *Phylloscopus collybita*, Goldcrest *Regulus regulus*, Common Treecreeper *Certhia familiaris*, European Blue Tit *Cyanistes caeruleus*, Great Tit *Parus major*, Long-tailed Tit *Aegithalos caudatus*, Western Jackdaw *Corvus monedula*, Carrion Crow *Corvus corone*, Common Chaffinch *Fringilla coelebs* and Eurasian Siskin *Spinus spinus*. 100503.MC.054600.01

It is interesting to consider which birds are very British… How about Rooks, and perhaps Tawny Owl, if only because they can be found in the background of every BBC TV whudunnit? I tried recording a melancholic Robin singing on Thomas

Hardy's grave in Stinsford churchyard (**CD1-38**), but Simon hasn't used that one yet.

CD1-38   **European Robin** *Erithacus rubecula* Stinsford church, Dorchester, Dorset, England, 09:32, 22 March 2009. Song while perched on Thomas Hardy's grave. Background: Dunnock *Prunella modularis*, Mistle Thrush *Turdus viscivorus*, European Blue Tit *Cyanistes caeruleus*, Great Tit *Parus major*, Common Chaffinch *Fringilla coelebs* and European Greenfinch *Chloris chloris*. 090322.MC.093200.12

For me Herring Gull is a must, accompanying *By the Sleepy Lagoon* as it introduces *Desert Island Discs* on BBC radio 4 (or the Home Service as my mum still calls it). The theme music has been used for nearly 70 years, but it wouldn't be the same without the 'sea gulls'. In each episode, a celebrity imagines being marooned on a desert island, and has to select some music, a book and a luxury they would like to have with them. In the '70s, the presenter Roy Plomley misunderstood Brigitte Bardot's strong French accent when she declared her chosen luxury to be "a peenis". Plomley, a little taken aback, said: "Most interesting and why, precisely, may I ask?" "Well," explained Bardot, "it's what the world needs most – 'appiness." Which brings me very neatly to James, who is never happier than when he can hear gulls. Preferably thousands of them as they circle a rubbish tip.

His favourite venue was Beacon Hill landfill, where he would peer through the chain link fence like a fan at the stage door.

Slepe Copse, Poole Harbour, Dorset, 23 August 2004 (*René Pop*). CD1-37 was recorded here.

Never popular with birders' spouses, a fascination with dumps is almost normal for birders. Yvie, James's girlfriend at the time, did get to share her boyfriend's strange obsession when on the first anniversary of their relationship in February 2000 they found an Iceland Gull.

Birding with Yvie had got him noticed, and although he was alone on his next visit, the site manager came over and asked him what he was up to? James sheepishly explained his 'problem'. Would he like to come in? James was confused. Normally site managers throw you off; they don't invite you in. Delighted, he explained his surprise and the chap said, "we are going to be here for 25 years and not many people like that idea. Those that do we welcome with open arms."

James started to visit regularly, very regularly. At first he borrowed a hard-hat and high visibility jacket, but soon he had his own. During February, March and April, the three most productive months for gull watchers, he became friends with the staff and other tip regulars, leaving his parents puzzled when skip lorry drivers honked and waved as they passed him driving round the town. His gull watching was going well too, notching up another Iceland and an adult Ring-billed Gull.

Gull identification is a fast moving game, and you have to be on the ball to keep up with the latest developments. James worked hard, and this paid off when on 11 April 2001 he found and identified a vagrant Kumlien's Gull, the subtly different North American version of Iceland Gull. Graham Armstrong, Andy Farr

Smithsonian (American Herring) Gull *Larus smithsonianus*, Corfe Mullen tip, Beacon Hill, Dorset, 11 March 2002 (*Graham Armstrong*)

Birders at the Corfe Mullen tip, Beacon Hill landfill site, Dorset, 5 and 9 March 2002 (*James Lidster*)

and Iain Prophet got there in a tick, and were ceremoniously lent hard hats and jackets before being signed in to what was becoming one of the most select rarity sites in the area.

James was back again next year for the start of the 2002 season, kicking off with an adult Ring-billed Gull in February. On 4 March, James arrived for 'work' as usual at 09:00 and was confronted by over 8,000 gulls. In the next two and a half hours he systematically worked his way through them. Reaching an end, he was about to take a break when he noticed "an obvious two toned bill on a 1st winter herring gull". Although not unusual in itself, he then noticed how uniform its underparts were, and that it had a large section of retained juvenile rear scapulars, all looking superbly fresh. Surely it was an American Herring Gull (also known as Smithsonian Gull).

Being wary of the many pitfalls, he was just pondering over the high degree of variation that existed within *argenteus* when suddenly the whole lot took to the air. The commotion was due to the arrival of a Red Kite, normally a joyous event but not right at this moment. He started to panic. What if his gull disappeared? Could he claim it on these views? Should he put it out? Having briefly seen the tail pattern as it went into the air he decided he had seen enough and put the news out.

After more than an hour's anxious wait, the kite eventually moved on. The birds resettled and to his relief James quickly relocated the American Herring Gull and was able to satisfy himself completely with the identification. Only Nick and Brett Spencer managed to get there before the tip closed, and when the bird didn't show the next day it looked like it was going to be a real Dorset blocker for the lucky three. Thankfully for the rest of us, it did come back the day after that, settling into a routine and becoming the first twitchable mainland English bird, staying until 6 May.

Over 300 of us were welcomed at Beacon Hill. Everyone, including all the locals, was signed in and given safety wear. We all stood in lines in amongst the rubbish, looking like a scene from Star Wars, hats glinting in the sunlight as we peered down our scopes. We bought the site employees a *Collins bird guide* and a pair of binoculars.

James then completed a hat trick of 'live' Dorset firsts (Kumlien's Gull had previously been found dead) when he found and photographed a Caspian Gull on 19 February 2003. Unfortunately this bird didn't hang around.

Caspian Gull *Larus cachinnans*, Corfe Mullen tip, Beacon Hill, Dorset, February 2003 (*James Lidster*)

Chapter 10: Lady Muck

Then it all went wrong. It started with the arrival of a new site manager who brought with him new guidelines. First the watching of gulls inside the tip was discouraged. Then the gulls themselves were discouraged. The officers at the Environment agency had decided that gulls were vermin and a threat to public health. Blokes with large guns and falcons were brought in, and the gulls were forced to leave.

I had been enjoying the run of rare gulls so, frustrated by this turn of events, I looked around for someone to blame. Who was in charge, I wondered? I googled the CEO of the Environment Agency and there she was, Baroness Young of Old Scone. I realised that I had met her. She had been Chief Executive of the RSPB and had shaken my hand at the Bird Fair. I couldn't wait to get down the pub for a rant.

There were three candidates for Britain's rarest successful breeding birds in 2007, the most recent year compiled by Britain's Rare Breeding Birds Panel. A pair of Green Sandpipers that reared three young in an old Wood Pigeons' nest in the Scottish highlands, a pair of Fieldfares that managed to produce three young in Derbyshire, and a pure pair of Yellow-legged Gulls that discreetly fledged two young in Poole Harbour.

Graham Armstrong identified the harbour's first Yellow-legged Gull in Poole Park in February 1982. He saw the first one on the roof of the Kerry Foods pie factory in 1988 after searching unsuccessfully for the Wilson's Phalarope nearby in Holes Bay. In the early '90s a few *michahellis*, as they were affectionately called then, began to appear here regularly in the late summer, but it was James and Stan who really put Kerry Foods on the birding map.

They usually counted together but fell out temporarily (Nick suggested that it was over a girl), and were soon visiting separately. This lead to a series of Dorset record counts, each one just a bit higher than the last, as they tried to outdo each other. By August 1999, over 200 birds were regularly being counted.

The northerly dispersal of these continental breeding birds in late summer is now an annual event, but numbers have leveled off in recent times. In **CD1-39**, you can hear a juvenile that Magnus recorded in late August, along the coast at Lodmoor. They used to feed at the pie factory, but now just use it as a pre-roost gathering site, seemingly content to stand around on the rooftops, leaving the regular delivery of pies for other gulls to squabble over. More recently we have discovered that they roost off of the end of Swineham in the Wareham Channel. Both sites now share top spot with around 100 birds each at the peak of the season.

Yellow-legged Gull *Larus michahellis* Lodmoor, Dorset, England, 10:29, 22 August 2006. Very coarse calls of a juvenile. Background: Common Moorhen *Gallinula chloropus*, Eurasian Coot *Fulica atra*, juvenile large gull *Larus* and Common House Martin *Delichon urbicum*. 060822.MR.102932.31   **CD1-39**

Black-headed Gulls *Chroicocephalus ridibundus*, Brownsea lagoon, Dorset, 6 June 2009 (*Claire Lodge*)

With echoes of Little Egret, Brownsea became the site where Britain's first pair of Yellow-legged Gulls decided to settle. They have bred every year since 1995, and are still the only pure pair ever to have bred in Britain. And that is what fuelled my pub rant: 'Barbara Young, previous CEO of the RSPB makes the life of Britain's rarest breeding bird a misery.' When I suggested this down the pub the others shook their heads. They knew that for many people gulls are vermin.

Yellow-legged Gull *Larus michahellis*, adult with chick, Brownsea lagoon, Dorset, 13 June 2009 (*Nick Hopper*)

"Gulls don't have the same rights as other birds", someone said. I was indignant; "When it comes to conservation, there shouldn't be a difference between one species and another." I argued that the Environment Agency should have leeway to look after Britain's rarest breeding bird when it joins the flocks at Poole's landfill sites. "But do they join them?" asked Graham. I argued that there had been 40 records at the tip over the years. "Not many when you think of the numbers of birds in the harbour, Mark." He had a point.

So the Baroness and her henchman weren't really villains? If I wasn't able to fit them up with the harassment of Britain's rarest breeding gull, they still have a case to answer. James moving to the Netherlands for a start, and they stopped Herring Gulls feeding at tips. Now there's a bird that really is in trouble.

In the '40s, Herring Gulls were at a bit of a low, but with the help of new bird protection legislation they were soon back on the increase. The real catalyst however was the introduction of The Clean Air Act in 1956, which banned the burning of rubbish. Together with our increasing willingness to throw food away (currently running at 350 kilos of waste food per person per year), it created an inexhaustible supply of food for the gulls at rubbish tips, which they were quick to exploit.

Things started going wrong on a local level when in 1965 Herring Gulls nesting on Brownsea lagoon had their eggs destroyed to help the terns. Traditionally a cliff-nesting bird, Herring Gulls normally just make scrape nests lined with weeds. On Brownsea, however, the largest number nested in the trees on Caroline Cliffs, the southern high ground behind Brownsea Castle. Here, in what was surely the world's only tree nesting colony of the species, nests were woven with sticks and lined with moss. At its peak in 1971, there were 930 pairs.

By 1981, Tony Wise could still describe them as "the most numerous breeding bird on Brownsea", despite the fact that the colony had now nearly halved in number to around 500 pairs. In fact, Herring Gull populations were crashing everywhere, and within a further seven years the colony was down to 100 birds. Nowadays it has gone completely, and there are none breeding on the island.

Maybe the decline in nesting wasn't just to do with the egg pricking. Traditional cliff-nesting Herring Gull numbers also show a markedly downward trend, halving from 1993 to 2009. Nobody is really sure what is causing the decline. Perhaps the decline in the number of fishing boats has had an influence. Some say that the ecology of our coastal environment is irreparably changing. In 1990, Herring Gulls started nesting on the roofs in Poole Old Town (**CD1-40**). Working there with them is a delight in my opinion. Whatever the cause, these birds are abandoning the cliffs for the urban lifestyle in order to survive, causing much consternation amongst us their new hosts.

CD1-40   **Herring Gull** *Larus argentatus* Poole Old Town centre, Dorset, England, 07:20, 29 March 2009. A wave of long calls of locally breeding adults. Background: Eurasian Collared Dove *Streptopelia decaocto* and Pied Wagtail *Motacilla yarrellii*. 090329.MC.072000.01

Herring Gulls are now in such decline that they have joined Dartford Warbler and Nightjar on the Red List of species most in need of conservation. Despite this, the Environment Agency's real boss, The Department of Environment, Food and Rural Affairs, still issues general licenses that allow Herring Gulls to be killed and their eggs and nests legally destroyed. Perhaps the RSPB should make amends for Baroness Young's deeds and feature Herring Gull in their *Aren't Birds Brilliant* campaign.

Another gull nesting on Poole's rooftops, although in smaller numbers, is Lesser Black-backed Gull (**CD1-41**). They are something of an enigma in Poole Harbour. If you walk around Poole Harbour on an average spring or autumn day you would do well to see more than 10 birds, but if you hung around the Wareham Channel on the same evening you could count over 2,000. That's because for most Lesser Black-backs, Poole Harbour is basically a Travelodge. Both migrants and wintering birds spend the day somewhere else, then as the light begins to fail they come to spend the night in Poole Harbour. Many don't arrive until it is nearly dark, and many more turn up when we can't even see them. Then at daybreak they are off again, not even stopping to pick up breakfast.

Lesser Black-backed Gull *Larus fuscus* Poole Old Town centre, Dorset, England,   CD1-41
07:05, 29 March 2009. Long calls of a pair at the same time. 090329.MC.070500.02

When there is an evening low tide or particularly bad weather, the gulls arrive earlier for a wash and brush up. This is when most of the harbour's high counts are obtained at Lytchett Bay, which has fresh running water and is ideally placed between Corfe Mullen tip (still used as a pre-roost site after the hawkers have left) and the main Wareham Channel roosts. In 2007, our harbour gull survey included a co-ordinated harbour roost count, which produced a total of 4,850 birds. Some came in very late and were difficult to identify, but the majority were thought to be Herring Gull.

Best species of the 2007 co-ordinated count award went to Dave Chown for his Ring-billed Gull off of Swineham Point. Historically, however, Lytchett Bay is the best place to look for Ring-billed. Shaun found the harbour's first there on 18 April 1996. Since then, there have been a further 11 records in the harbour, seven of which have been at Lytchett, including three in a year. Unfortunately, much of Lytchett is strictly private, so we really enjoyed the most recent 'pond jumper', a very confiding first-year Ring-billed at Poole Park in February 2011, where it could be seen by birders coming to visit our latest Long-billed Dowitcher. We didn't manage to sound record the

Ring-billed, but in case you wonder how they sound, here is a recording of adults in New Jersey (**CD1-42**). Magnus did record the dowitcher, which considering it was so tame proved to be more difficult than you might imagine (**CD1-43**).

Ring-billed Gull *Larus delawarensis* Stone Harbour, Cape May County, New Jersey, USA, 18:30, 25 September 2004. Long calls of adults. Background: Caspian Tern *Hydroprogne caspia* and Roseate Tern *Sterna dougallii*. 04.009.KM.01310.01 CD1-42

Long-billed Dowitcher *Limnodromus scolopaceus* Poole Park, Dorset, England, 16:30, 3 February 2011. Calls of a first-winter, standing on the mud. Background: Canada Goose *Branta canadensis* and Common Kingfisher *Alcedo atthis*. 110203.MR.163000.22 CD1-43

Ring-billed Gull *Larus delawarensis*, first-winter, Poole Park, Poole, Dorset, 17 February 2011 (*Nick Hopper*)

Long-billed Dowitcher *Limnodromus scolopaceus*, first-winter, Poole Park, Poole, Dorset, 14 February 2011 (*Nick Hopper*). CD1-43.

The gull count also produced around 21,000 roosting Black-headed Gulls, many of these also having spent their day inland. Nick worked out their daily itineraries by attempting to follow them to and from the roost by car, which proved a little hazardous at times. The furthest birds north were found at Fifehead Magdalen, a little village on the River Stour and an 86 km round trip for the few birds that made it this far. Birds that followed the River Piddle were found as far as Piddlehinton, a 60 km round trip from the Poole roost. Interestingly, these birds actually ended up a lot nearer to the Weymouth Bay roost but chose to remain loyal to the more distant Poole one. Not all birds were quite so adventurous, however. For some their daily trip involved visiting Poole Park where they patiently loafed, waiting for the breakfast to be served at 10:00, when the gates open and the public arrive with bags of stale bread.

If Ben Pond were to come back and look for breeding Black-headed gulls, he would be impressed by their continual adaptation. After being driven from Little Sea, they were pushed from pillar to post by fires, forestation, and most recently commercial egg collecting, which almost finished them off. He would also be glad of the happy ending. Today the colony at Holton Heath islands is nearly 9,000 strong, representing around 5% of the British breeding population. They are being helped in no small part by their continental cousin the Mediterranean Gull, whose discovery on the islands ensured their long-term protection. Fortunately for both species, the islands are not easily visited, so I recorded these Black-headed on the shore at Holton Lee during Lushfest, where they like to socialise (**CD1-44**).

Ewan Brodie found the first Mediterranean Gull in the harbour as it bathed on Little Sea in the afternoon of 20 April 1976. In May the following year Keith Godfrey found a breeding pair on Brownsea. They attempted to breed but without success. Still, this got everybody's pulses racing. In 1986 Dave Collins, while doing his survey in the harbour, discovered a pair of summer plumage birds frequenting the Holton Heath islands, and realised that they must be breeding among the Black-headed Gulls.

At the time, gulls' eggs were being collected by local fishermen under license, but Mediterranean Gull was a Schedule 1 bird and could not be disturbed. The locals had a good thing going selling the eggs off as Quails' eggs, and they were not going to give up that easily, but despite their protestations, the egg collecting licenses were revoked in 1990, by which time there were six pairs of Mediterranean Gulls on the islands.

The egg collectors were peeved and carried out nocturnal raids, so the RSPB had to coordinate watches, helped by us volunteers and Dorset Police's Marine Section. As John Day wrote, however, this was not enough. "Unfortunately the surveillance of the colonies has not prevented many of the eggs laid in early April from illegally being taken in some years. When culprits have been caught, they have been prosecuted. Even court cases and publicity did not stop the whole colony being totally collected out between early April and the 20th April 1996" (Pickess & Underhill-Day 2002).

CD1-44   **Black-headed Gull** *Chroicocephalus ridibundus* Holton Lee, Poole Harbour, Dorset, England, 09:45, 9 April 2004. Calls of adults socialising about 1 km from their breeding colony. Background: Common Redshank *Tringa totanus*, Icelandic Black-tailed Godwit *Limosa limosa islandica*, Eurasian Skylark *Alauda arvensis*, Dunnock *Prunella modularis*, Common Chaffinch *Fringilla coelebs* and European Greenfinch *Chloris chloris*. 04.005. MC.01200.21

Mediterranean Gulls *Larus melanocephalus*, adults in summer plumage, Brownsea lagoon, Dorset, 6 June 2009 (*Nick Hopper*)

Numbers have since increased dramatically, with an RSPB survey in early May 2008 conservatively counting 87 Mediterranean Gull nests. As expected, there was also evidence of a few nests being washed away by the flood tide. Adult summer Mediterranean Gull is a very handsome bird. If you haven't seen one you are in for a treat. Brownsea lagoon in April is the best place for close views. Here the rather vocal summer plumaged adults, often already in pairs, can be seen practicing their courtship techniques before they move onto the breeding islands. But they can be seen at many other places in the harbour

as well. The two in **CD1-45** were passing the rookery at Ower Quay on their way towards Studland Bay. Listen to the distinctive low-high-low inflection of their call note. Although they do have other sounds in their repertoire, this is the one that nearly always alerts us to their presence, so it is a very useful call to learn.

Mediterranean Gull *Larus melanocephalus* Ower Quay, Poole Harbour, Dorset, England, 10:00, 18 April 2010. Typical calls of two adults on their way to Little Sea. Background: Barn Swallow *Hirundo rustica*, European Robin *Erithacus rubecula*, Rook *Corvus frugilegus*, European Blue Tit *Cyanistes caeruleus* and Common Chaffinch *Fringilla coelebs*. 100418.MC.100000.02

CD1-45

Baiter is another favourite pre-breeding haunt. Late afternoons are best here, when birds gather on the shoreline before going to roost. Up to 40 adult birds have been counted here recently, providing a real treat as I cycle past on the way home from work. Post-breeding sees birds heading back to a traditional wintering area at Studland Bay. From as early as June, failed breeders arrive to join up with the few immature birds that have spent all summer here. Later, numbers are supplemented by the year's juveniles, many bearing foreign leg rings, having already crossed the channel. In **CD1-46**, you can hear how juvenile Mediterranean Gulls sound in early autumn. A good time to hear them is when they are feeding on flying ants, as was the case when Magnus made this recording in Bulgaria.

Mediterranean Gull *Larus melanocephalus* Durankulak lake, Dobrich, Bulgaria, 09:40, 17 September 2007. A large flock, almost all juveniles, feeding on flying ants. Background: Black-headed Gull *Chroicocephalus ridibundus*, Eurasian Penduline Tit *Remiz pendulinus* and Bearded Reedling *Panurus biarmicus*. 070917.MR.094028.00 **CD1-46**

Nick has been keeping his eye out for ringed birds here for the past few years, recording birds from France, Belgium, the Netherlands and Germany. Sending in bird ring sightings doesn't always guarantee a reply, so he was pleasantly surprised

Mediterranean Gull *Larus melanocephalus*, chick, colour ringed (AAEE), Pionierinsel Lühe, Landkreis Stade, Niedersachsen, Germany, 17 June 2006 (*Simon Hinrichs*). This German chick was photographed as an adult by Nick at Studland Bay on 9 October 2009.

Mediterranean Gull *Larus melanocephalus*, adult, ringed in Germany (AAEE), Studland Bay, Dorset, 9 October 2009 (*Nick Hopper*)

to receive a rather excited email from some Germans who had ringed one of the Studland birds as a pullus, even sending him a photo of 'their' bird as a youngster.

Pim Wolf, a dedicated birder and ringer from Zeeland in the southwest of the Netherlands, also had reason to be excited on 28 August 2008. After a morning being shown the delights of Poole Harbour by Nick and Magnus, they all stopped off at Studland's South Beach café for some refreshments. While getting through their pasties and hot chocolate, they found three Belgian-ringed birds, one of which Pim himself had ringed as a chick.

As winter progresses some birds move on, but good numbers can still be seen here. They like to feed on the invertebrates in the seaweed. This normally just involves a bit of pecking. Sometimes if the prey jumps, the bird may have to leap and catch it in mid-air. If the weather is bad, they scavenge among the flotsam and jetsam in the bay. Even really rough weather with gale force winds will not deter them from feeding among the large breakers, at a time when most other gulls are keeping their heads down. **CD1-47** was recorded in early January in Portugal, and may well involve birds that have passed through Poole Harbour. Research has shown that Portugal is the main wintering area for Mediterranean Gulls from northern Europe (Poot & Flamant 2006).

Returning to James Lidster, before moving to the Netherlands, he did achieve one last ambition. While he was surveying the gulls off of the Holton Heath islands for this book in the late afternoon of 17 January 2008, he realised that there were so many birds coming in that he just couldn't keep up and so abandoned the count. He decided to settle for just scanning through the many Common Gulls to search for something interesting, perhaps a Ring-billed Gull. Then in the failing light he came across a small, dark-mantled gull. He had to do a double take, not quite able to believe what he was looking at. After some panic then a moment's composure he had a proper look. It was obviously small with a diminutive, all-dark bill and he could make out white eye-crescents. He was watching a Franklin's Gull.

Further panic ensued as he tried to phone everyone, while at the same time taking a photo with the same phone in the failing light. Nick jumped in his car and drove for all he was worth, through Wareham up through Sandford and along the heavily pot-holed road down to Holton Lee. Nick ran from the car, adrenalin pumping through his system, and after a rather desperate sprint up the fields, across the bridge and through the bramble strewn path, he scrambled frantically down the bank to the shoreline. He reached James's scope gasping for breath and shoved his eye to the eyepiece, just in time. As for Mo and I, we got there a little too late to see it. We tried a couple more times, but no luck. It's on Nick's list and I know he saw it, but sometimes I'm not so sure he has the same confidence in me…

CD1-47   **Mediterranean Gull** *Larus melanocephalus* Foz de Lizandro, Lisboa, Portugal, 12:58, 10 January 2011. Calls of first-winters and adults bathing and displaying aggressively. For much of the non-breeding season, the best-known call of adults (CD1-45) is rarely heard, and you are more likely to hear harsh calls associated with feeding and aggression. From late winter onwards, the smoother calls return. Background: Eurasian Wren *Troglodytes troglodytes*. 110110.MR.125850.32

Chapter 11: Blinded by adrenalin

It's early November, 08:40 in the morning, and overcast. We're seawatching. I'm perched on my stool looking through my scope. Graham Armstrong is sitting on one side, Mo on the other.

I pick up what at first appears to be a tiny falcon, compact and flying purposefully about five metres above the waves, range 200 to 300 metres and moving west across the bay. Graham gets onto it and says, "It's a petrel."

Mo sees it as well. I increase my concentration. It has no head markings and looks all-dark. This is not like any petrel I've ever seen here, neither British Storm Petrel nor Leach's Storm Petrel. Its flight is more direct and the wind doesn't seem to affect it. I watch it for what seems like an eternity, hoping for the blinding light of recognition...

In reality the whole episode must have lasted just 3 or 4 minutes as it flew towards Studland before continuing over the waves and out of sight. Adrenalin crashed through my system, and as I sat crumpled on my tiny stool I must have looked awful. My nerves weren't robust enough for an all-dark petrel. Graham looked away. Mo said, "If someone else saw you like this they would get you to hospital. Come on, I'll take you home."

Branksome Chine is to blame. You can sit there for days on end watching nothing but the sea. If you are lucky you have company.

Over the years I have discussed how to ripen avocados in a paper bag with Iain Prophet, the Beano with Killian, and the standards of cleanliness at the nearby public toilets with Shaun. Pulse rates are somewhere close to an iguana's when suddenly there's a good bird and everyone experiences a level of excitement that would put an astronaut's constitution under strain.

It was Graham who invented Branksome as *the* local seawatching site. He also made Leach's Storm Petrel the bird we all wanted to see. During a gale on Christmas Eve 1989, he saw 30 of them off Branksome. At the time he lived a short walk from the chine, so when he got home he phoned Roger and Ewan, who rushed down there seeing somewhere between 40 and 50 Leach's in an hour. That inspired the rest of us.

Branksome lies half way between the harbour mouth and Bournemouth pier, at the bottom of orange sandy cliffs, and it has facilities. A car park, some toilets, a café, and beach huts, the porches of which offer us shelter in all but direct southerly gales. There is also the lady who picks up dog poo but doesn't have a dog, the spartan swimming sisters who first thing every morning go for a swim in horrid conditions, and the cyclist passing in a red frogman's outfit complete with flippers and mask. On the way down the path we have seen a lady in her pyjamas cutting a hedge with a pair of scissors. That's because at the top of the cliff is St Anne's Hospital, "serving the needs of people with severe and enduring mental illness".

Seawatching, from left to right Nick Hopper, Killian Mullarney and Mark Constantine, Branksome Chine, Poole, Dorset, 25 August 2010 (*Arnoud B van den Berg*)

Nick hates seawatching here. It's right on the promenade, with locals and tourists constantly passing. Some stare quizzically and others come over. "What are you all looking at?" is the usual question. "Nothing," is the honest reply, so they nod, smile and walk on. Seawatching is like that. I had a call from Barbara, Hamish's wife, during one seawatching season. She said, "I'm very worried about Hamish's mental health. For days now he's been standing on the edge of a cliff wearing three pairs of trousers in the most appalling conditions." I told her that was quite normal and not to worry.

There isn't any other easy place to go seawatching from Poole Harbour. On dry days you can be up on Ballard Down squinting into the sunlight miles above the sea, trying to tick a Glaucous

Seawatching point at Middle Beach car park, looking towards Old Harry, Dorset, 23 August 2004 (*René Pop*)

Gull off Swanage. Nick prefers the National Trust car park at Middle Beach, overlooking Studland Bay. "Its better for shearwaters," which can be dots from Branksome. Balearics can glide through here, and on one July evening he counted 93 Manx Shearwaters pass close by in just over 30 minutes, a harbour record. Writing this, I started to think of the cost so I phoned Nick.

"What about the car park fees when you watch from Middle Beach?"

"It's free if you are in the National Trust."

"Are you in the National Trust?" I find myself innocently saying as the penny drops.

"Well, I was..." and we start to giggle.

One morning, I was watching with Shaun at Branksome, while Nick was sitting by his car up on Middle Beach, no doubt keeping one eye out for the National Trust parking attendant. It was fairly quiet until we picked up a Pomarine Skua slowly making its way west, occasionally dropping onto the water. I rang Nick and asked if he could see it. "No," was the reply, "I can't see that far into the bay. But no bother, it has to come out this way." While Nick was patiently waiting, it lifted up off the sea and began circling to gain height. Then it turned north and flew inland, straight over Poole town. To add insult to injury, Shaun swears that it flew right over Nick's former house.

Pomarine Skuas are actually quite well known for crossing over land. On 26 May 2002, a very similar thing happened. Stan was seawatching off Branksome when he saw six 'Poms' moving slowly west. They also spent some time on the sea, allowing Nick and James just enough time to get there from home and see them head inland over Studland, before being lost very high over the Purbeck ridge.

During strong easterlies, all sorts of birds can completely miss out Durlston and Purbeck, sneaking through the harbour mouth and the southern half of the harbour, then generally nipping out through Middlebere. Over the years this has created a series of seabird records in weird places. More noteworthy ones include a Fulmar west over Stoborough and another found grounded on a pavement in Wareham after a heavy hailstorm. Occasionally a stray Gannet also heads up the Middlebere channel and across to Gad cliff and the sea, and there have been several records of Sabine's Gull in the southern parts of the harbour.

The most celebrated case was on 31 August 1998, a bird race day with very strong easterlies. At 8:15, Jackie and Mo were at the main hide overlooking Little Sea when they were surprised to see a skua flying across Godlingston. I was cycling nearby with my son Jack when it flew directly over my head. I tried to memorise some features as it went over. Straining my neck and not looking where I was going, I soon ended up in a heap on the path. After I had picked myself up, I rang Killian. I described the barred underparts and remembered seeing a pale nape. He immediately suggested juvenile Long-tailed Skua.

About four hours later, Shaun and Roger were standing at Hartland Moor when Roger shouted, "Skua!" They then watched in amazement as a pale-morph Long-tailed Skua flew out of the Middlebere channel and across the heath, right in front of them.

I must admit to being rather glad Nick likes seawatching at Middle Beach as he can turn up some good birds lingering in the bay. On 30 October 2007 after a quiet seawatch, he had just started his survey of the bay when he came across "two fat-headed scoters with pale face patches". He immediately thought Surf Scoters, but because of their distance and lack of any nape patches he needed to rule out odd-looking juvenile Velvet Scoters. These niggles soon disappeared when the birds began to drift in, confirming the head and bill shape and revealing the strongly capped appearance of juvenile Surf Scoter. Mo and I were there in a jiff and enjoyed close views of two great birds.

James Lidster, Graham, Mo and I finally caught up with Leach's Storm Petrel after 12 years of drought at Branksome on 2 February 2002, when a lovely close Leach's was seen by all of us. Shaun had been packing for a holiday when he got the call, and rushed down. He was soon sniping way to the west and was rewarded when he picked up another distant Leach's heading towards us. Eventually it made its way slowly past an awestruck line of us, giving perfect views. Shaun whooped and even Nick, who had just arrived, gave a little cheer.

With the internet and flexible work schedules, it is now easier to experience a wreck of Leach's Storm Petrel. While working on this book, Magnus and I were having our elevenses and reading our emails when I read that Roger Howell had just seen five Leach's off Mudeford quay near Christchurch. At 12:00, we heard that Cliff Rogers had seen 20 in half an hour at Abbotsbury. We went to Branksome for lunch. When we arrived, two Great Skuas were close in harassing the passing Kittiwakes, then Magnus saw the first Leach's at what must have been 13:00. In the next hour and a half, we saw 10 Leach's struggling against a strong south-westerly gale and even some hailstones. Nick (still trying to avoid Branksome) was photographing another two birds

Little Auk *Alle alle*, Brownsea, Poole, Dorset, 13 November 2007 (*Kevin Lane*)

hanging around the harbour mouth. By late afternoon all the Leach's had gone, and there were none the next day.

You don't need bad weather to watch Poole's seabirds. Most summers, a company of Gannets fishes off Sandbanks. Fulmars breed secretly up on the cliffs at Ballard among the Shags and cormorants. We don't have any nesting auks, although Razorbill and Guillemot can normally be found in the bay and up to Poole Quay outside of the breeding season. Puffin is rare, really rare. None of us has ever seen one in the harbour. Little Auk is far easier to see.

Little Auks occur most years in November and while waiting for one to pass Branksome, Mo and I had a conversation with bachelor Graham about his dog. I think we had just watched a flock of scoters flying past when he told us of his problem. He said that as he lived with his parents, they normally looked after his dog when he went on trips across the globe looking at seabirds. Since his mum had died, his father had remarried and the new stepmother was less obliging. His dog had been given to a new home.

Graham Armstrong and Marie Hobby, Poole, Dorset, August 1998 (*Anonymous*)

During the course of that month he updated us on the state of affairs. Between watching the Fulmars glide by and identifying small parties of Arctic Terns, he explained that he was now buying his dad's house while his dad was moving into his new wife's home. This still left Graham with a problem. He wanted to get a new dog but now that he was living alone, who would look after it when he was away? I suggested that he found someone to look after the house, keep it clean and look after his dog when he was away.

Seawatching is very seasonal. We watch in spring in the hope of seeing Pomarine Skua and then look for a variety of species during the autumn windy season from late August to November. So it was in the spring six months later when I was able to ask him, "Did you get another dog?" "No", he told me. "Couldn't you find someone to help with the house?" "Yes," he blushed. "Her name's Marie and she's moved in. I don't think I'm going to be bothering about getting a dog". I met Marie sometime later and then again in a crowd at the Bird Fair. I was surprised to feel my bottom pinched and turned to find that she was the culprit, beaming alongside Graham.

Marie encouraged Graham to go to musicals. So now while we are waiting for something good to pass we can compare the relative merits of Les Miserables and Miss Saigon. That's when we are not thinking of the dark-rumped petrel, and how Nick pointed out that one of the last strange 'petrels' at sea in Dorset turned out to be a Nightjar.

Chapter 12: Nearer to God than Godlingston

Folklore, mystery and strange country names don't help when getting to grips with nightjars. Stories of 'goatsuckers' living in the 'twilight zone' make them seem much larger in the imagination than they are in real life. An adult European Nightjar seen perched on a post at close range is exquisite. Its body is only the size of a Starling, but its wings cloak the body and deceive the eye.

We have loads of nightjars breeding on the heaths of Poole Harbour. Nick has surveyed them, and points out that walking around on your own in the pitch darkness on an unfamiliar large heath, with a distinct lack of footpaths and numerous treacherous bogs interspersed with high tussocks, can be quite a challenge physically and mentally, particularly if you hear unfamiliar noises and have just watched *An American werewolf in London*. Despite the werewolves, Nick found a lot more birds than he had expected: 46 males on Studland and Godlingston Heath alone.

The way we find the males is by listening for their churring song. Males churr from early May onwards, and this is usually the first indication that they have returned from Africa. When churring, they are always perched, usually on a snag, a fencepost, or on top of a tree. They like to choose strategic spots like clearings, where the sound will resonate off the surrounding forest. It grows from almost nothing. When it has your full attention it starts making pendulum-like swings between two pitches. For several minutes, it envelops and hypnotises you. Then the nightjar suddenly stops, often while clapping its wings together and flying off. You wake up with a start. **CD1-48** was recorded at Studland at 03:26 in the morning, along the path that the nudists use to get to the beach.

CD1-48   **European Nightjar** *Caprimulgus europaeus* Studland, Dorset, England, 03:26, 16 June 2010. Churring song of an adult male, with wingclaps when it flies off at the end. Background: Common Teal *Anas crecca*, Herring Gull *Larus argentatus* and Common Reed Bunting *Emberiza schoeniclus*. 100616.MC.022600.01

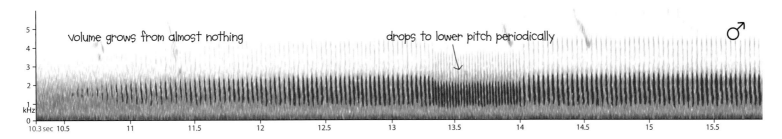

European Nightjar *Caprimulgus europaeus*, Belarus, 12 May 2003 (*René Pop*)

When moving to a different songpost, the churring ends with a sound like a propellor engine winding down. For about five seconds, a series of wingclaps alternate with whistling notes, which gradually morph into a low whirring sound and peter out. In **CD1-49** you can hear churring of a male nightjar that ends this way. It was recorded in Morocco, where Arnoud spent a night recording nightjars in open cork oak forest under a full moon, just beyond the stables of one of the king's palaces.

Although most people associate nightjars with dusk, they are actually more active during the last hours of the night. By this time, feeding has stopped and they can concentrate on defending their territory, reminding everyone else where their boundaries are before going off to sleep. This is when most vigorous interactions between males seem to occur, as they chase each other around with plenty of *co-ick* calls and surprisingly loud wing-clapping. It is quite a vigorous display, and it often carries on well into the first light of dawn, when we

are able to see them. Then before we know it, all is quiet and daylight is upon us.

We could have chosen an example of *co-ick* calls from dawn, but **CD1-50** was recorded at 02:00. We chose this recording because we suspect that it includes calls and wingclaps of both sexes. It was recorded in the same Moroccan territory, 15 minutes after the last recording. By now all the king's horses and dogs had woken up, but it was still too dark to see the nightjars. So the sexing of these birds is provisional, based on the female's weaker calls and wingbeats. The male calls and claps his wings three times, with the female following suit. According to our interpretation, all subsequent calls are given by the male.

Being alone in the dead of night with a nightjar 'butterflying' around your head is a magical experience. Sometimes their dancing seems particularly animated, as if they are being jerked on a piece of string. This is more pronounced in windy

CD1-49   **European Nightjar** *Caprimulgus europaeus* Dar Es Salam, Rabat, Morocco, 01:45, 22 June 2010. *Co-ick* calls, then churring song, which has a special ending with whistled notes and loud wingclaps, typically used when moving to a different songpost. Background: Maghreb Tawny Owl *Strix aluco mauritanica*. 100622.AB.014500.01

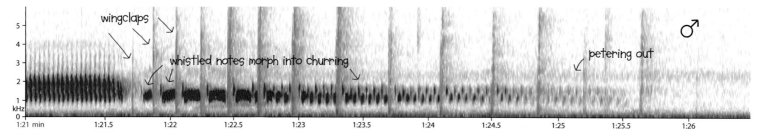

conditions, when the small effort used for forward movement is counteracted by the wind, and the bird ends up flickering on the spot. If you walk a footpath through the Godlingston Heath on a midsummer's night, you may experience this several times as you pass through different territories. The nightjar, usually a female, warns its family of your presence with *kuk* calls (**CD1-51**).

Surprisingly, while having so many in Poole Harbour does make it easy to see them, it seems that studying family behaviour is easier when there is only one pair. A few years ago, Killian was treated to the rare event of a single pair of nightjars breeding near his home in Ireland, where on average there are less than five breeding records a year. By observing carefully over a series of days, he managed to make some fascinating recordings. Fortunately, the nest was visible from an elevated point some distance away, allowing Killian to gain some idea how far the pair had progressed with their breeding attempt. By the time he recorded **CD1-52**, the young were about two and a half weeks

CD1-50 **European Nightjar** *Caprimulgus europaeus* Dar Es Salam, Rabat, Morocco, 02:04, 22 June 2010. *Co-ick* calls of a presumed pair. First, a call and three wingbeats of presumed male, then the same sequence from the presumed female, with all subsequent calls being from the male. Background: distant domestic dogs and horses. 100622.AB.020400.11

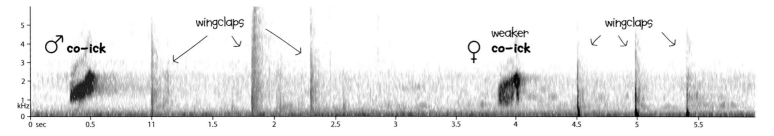

CD1-51 **European Nightjar** *Caprimulgus europaeus* Leusderheide, Utrecht, Netherlands, 22:59, 6 July 2004. *Kuk* calls of an alarmed female while circling and hovering over the intruding recordist with slow wingbeats. 04.021.AB.20043.11

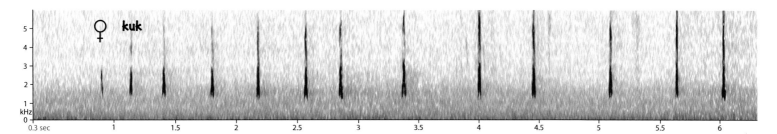

old. In this recording, you can hear *kuk* calls of the male, whose white wing-flashes and tail corners Killian managed to see by the light of a crescent moon.

As in so many bird species, juvenile nightjars have one call type that serves mainly to reveal their location, and another that they use while actually being fed. In **CD1-53** you can hear both, with some calls of juvenile humans in the background. The adult male arrives with food after 01:30 with a rapid series of *kuk* calls, after which the juvenile's calls gradually change to a much harsher and more rapidly repeated wheezing.

The biggest surprise was when Killian managed to record a churring female (**CD1-54**). This is a rarely heard sound, and we are not aware of any other published recording. It took place on the same day as the last two recordings. At one point the female churred quietly in the foreground while the male churred in the distance. When Killian returned two days later, the female had moved to another nest nearby to start a second brood, which proved to be unsuccessful.

The final recording in our nightjar selection is one that you are unlikely to hear unless you are a ringer holding one in your hand. A gargling hiss is used as a last resort threat call when a nightjar senses that it is in very grave danger. It is delivered with the bill wide open, revealing the enormous size of the gape. Adding to the snake-like impression, the nightjar writhes and squirms as it gives this call. The one in **CD1-55** was recorded at a ringing station in Kazakhstan where nightjars of three subspecies were being caught. *C e sarudnyi* is the subspecies that breeds over much of Central Asia.

CD1-52   **European Nightjar** *Caprimulgus europaeus* Ballyvalloo, Wexford, Ireland, 23:00, 10 July 2005. *Kuk* calls of a male accompanying juveniles, whose calls can be heard in the background. 05.002.KM.14747.11

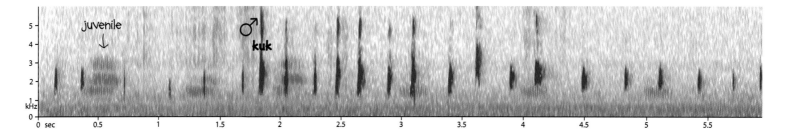

CD1-53 **European Nightjar** *Caprimulgus europaeus* Ballyvalloo, Wexford, Ireland, 22:50, 10 July 2005. Two call types of a juvenile: first a buzzing call that serves to reveal its location, then a hissing call while being fed by an adult male. The adult gives rapidly repeated *kuk* calls. Background: children playing. 05.002.KM.14008.02

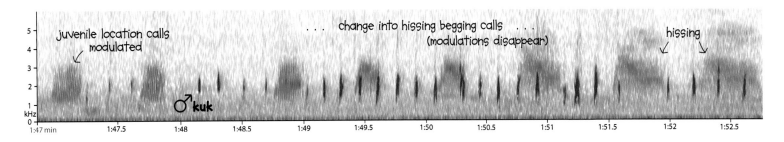

CD1-54 **European Nightjar** *Caprimulgus europaeus* Ballyvalloo, Wexford, Ireland, 22:00, 10 July 2005. Weak churring song of female, with *co-ick* calls of male in background. Background: Common Blackbird *Turdus merula*. 05.002.KM.05905.23

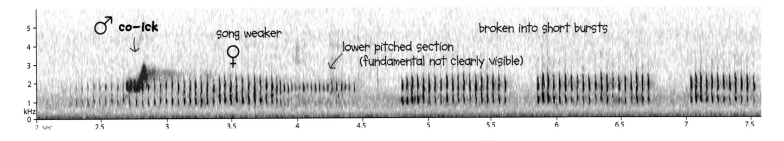

CD1-55 **European Nightjar** *Caprimulgus europaeus sarudnyi* Chokpak Station, Zhambyl, Kazakhstan, 13 May 2000. Weird hissing calls given in the hand while captive for ringing purposes. Background: Eastern Nightingale *Luscinia megarhynchos golzii* and Red-headed Bunting *Emberiza bruniceps*. 00.027.MR.04408.01

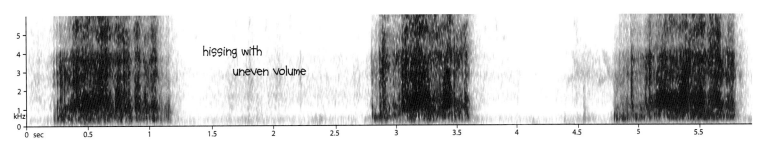

Chapter 13: The glory of migration

From the minute dawn broke, a constant stream of Song Thrushes flew past us, heading north. Within half an hour, several thousand had flown through. Not high overhead but low and often at eye level, in sizeable flocks of 30 to 50 birds, flying over the bushes and out over the dunes, then circling overhead before heading off north-west, high over Brownsea lagoon towards Poole.

Mo and I were perched up on the dunes behind the National Trust toilets at Studland. It was 16 October 2005, and birder and butterfly man Tom Brereton had co-ordinated a group of birders to count visible migration through Dorset. The idea was for Mo and I to see how many birds flew past in a two-hour period. I used my Telinga parabolic microphone to help make the high-pitched calls more audible, and to separate the short, less obvious Song Thrush calls from the longer, more obvious Redwing sounds. We kept counting for four hours, and by the end had seen 6,205 Song Thrushes and 2,896 Redwings. With 4 Ring Ouzels, 6 Blackbirds and 43 Fieldfares, it was to become one of the best thrush days on record in southern England.

As the thrush passage slowed a little, the first of 3,000 finches started coming through, in groups of 20 to 30, including 927 Linnets, 812 Chaffinches, 452 Siskins and 345 Greenfinches, all in the course of the morning. Accompanying them were eight different Sparrowhawks; adult males, and both young and adult females. A total of 48 Eurasian Jays made their way through the bushes, seemingly nervous to fly over the water, circling up and then returning over our heads, before hesitantly setting off over Brownsea.

Adding variety were two Crossbills, five Bramblings, a Woodlark, 11 Skylarks, two Redpolls, a Bullfinch, 35 Meadow Pipits, 92 White/Pied Wagtails, two Grey Wagtails, 54 Barn Swallows, 12 House Martins, 118 Starlings mixed in with the Redwings, and a record 34 Reed Buntings. The strange thing is that these migrants were all flying north, not the obvious direction for birds heading to the continent, and in some cases Africa.

The Song Thrush count was an excellent record. Some 1,100 passed Durlston on 30 October 1989, which had previously been the largest single day passage recorded either for Dorset or as far as I can tell, for Britain. In the Netherlands, where large numbers of migrating Song Thrushes are seen annually, the largest recorded passage has been over 30,000 in a day. Watching thrushes and other birds migrate in this way is well organised over there, and for several years now, counts from a large number of migration watchpoints have been collated in a database at www.trektellen.nl (Trektellen).

Common Starlings *Sturnus vulgaris*, Sterte Esplanade, Poole, Dorset, at dusk, 11 January 2011 (*Richard Crease/Bournemouth Echo*). 'A starling roost so spectacular it intruded into people's lives, they could not drive, they brought children to watch... such was the noise that teachers could not teach. People could only stand and stare.' Starlings migrate into southern England in cold weather from northern Europe. Recorded in CD1-57.

Song Thrush *Turdus philomelos*, on migration, Texel, Noord-Holland, Netherlands, 29 September 2010 (*René Pop*)

Recently, this system has been expanded to a number of other European countries including Britain. Some keen migration watchers here have entered their older data. So, looking on this site we can see that in October 2005, watchers from Scotland and northern England recorded very little migration of Song Thrushes. However, in the week leading up to our British record, Dutch coastal watchers saw huge numbers with a peak of over 30,000. By 16 October, Dutch sites were back to reporting them in low numbers.

The Migration Atlas (Wernham et al 2002) sums up ringing data collected by the BTO. Reading their summary on Song Thrushes ringed in autumn in Britain and controlled in spring enables us to make an educated guess that 'ours' were from the Nordic countries and had flown in overnight from Holland. So that's probably where they came from, but where were they going?

Nowhere. At least not for a little while, they had just arrived at their destination. That morning the weather had delayed and concentrated them, and we had witnessed the ensuing spectacle. Ringing records suggest that Song Thrushes are consistent in their habits, and slowly move west across southwest Britain and Ireland during the winter (Alerstam 1990, Wernham et al 2002).

The count of 2,896 Redwings was another record for the harbour, although we know that large numbers pass unseen high overhead during migration. Unlike the Song Thrushes that regularly winter in our area, the Redwings' destination appears to be a lottery.

Leaving Norway, Sweden and Finland, they decide which direction to fly more or less on take off, depending on the wind. If they find a tail wind that takes them east, they end up wintering around the Black Sea. If it blows them our way they winter in the west of England, Ireland and France and down the Atlantic seaboard as far as Morocco.

Migration from Scandinavia normally starts just after a depression has passed. The Redwings sense that the time has come to move, and tens of thousands lift off from a huge area around 40 minutes after sunset. They call to each other as they climb upward at a rate of 75 m per minute while searching for a good tail wind (**CD1-56**). In the dark, the individual Redwings listen to each other's calls and gauge the speed of the birds above and below them, joining them if they are moving faster. This concentrates their numbers, but they don't fly in dense flocks and can be 50 m apart even on a busy night (Alerstam 1990). Sometimes we can hear these passing birds' calls as we make our way to the pub, and we dream of seeing them in their thousands, passing overhead the next morning.

Redwing *Turdus iliacus* Fair Isle, Shetland, Scotland, 18:30, 17 October 2005. A mass exodus of migrants at dusk, on a windy autumn day. Background: European Golden Plover *Pluvialis apricaria*. 05.027.MR.02400.02 **CD1-56**

Once on the go, those coming our way travel fast. Recently, birds likely to include Redwings were recorded flying over the Netherlands at 100 km/h by radar. A few nights later, birds were detected arriving directly from Norway at an average speed of 90 km/h (Hans van Gasteren pers comm).

Wind directions vary at different heights above the ground, and by comparing them we can learn something about the bigger picture. Watch a column of smoke rising from a factory chimney and you will see a kink at the point where it reaches the crosswind. If you are watching birds in the morning from a headland on a windy day, try the following method of weather forecasting. Find an exposed spot and stand with your back to the wind. Look up and watch the direction of the clouds. You may be surprised to see them scudding from your left to your right. If this is the case, you need to get under cover as the weather is deteriorating. If on the other hand the clouds are passing from right to left, the weather is improving (Watts 1968).

Watching visible migration or 'vismig' started innocently enough when in the summer of 1998 I took Mo out for a romantic dinner and after a few glasses of wine, I asked her if she had ever seen the glory of finch migration. Graciously, with tears of laughter in her eyes, she replied, "No I haven't. That would be lovely." I explained how on breezy October days, I had watched the steady passage of flocks of finches and wagtails passing the coast at Durlston. I started to wonder where I could take Mo inside the harbour to see the same.

When I got home I took my maps out. I explained earlier about my maps marked up with rarities. Now I drew the potential flight line of finches as they might follow the coast flying into the harbour, having left Durlston and Swanage Bay, and came up with a line that passed across the ridge at the top of Ballard and down to the east of Glebelands, then over Studland village. If I was right, the flight line would pass somewhere around the trig point.

In a northeasterly wind on 4 October 1998, Mo and I went to investigate straight after dawn. There it was, the glory of finch migration, mixed in with the last of the thrushes finding cover after flying through the night. It seemed fantastically busy, with thrushes dropping out of the sky and making their way down into the village: 25 Blackbirds, 22 Redwings, five Mistle Thrushes, three Song Thrushes and thrilling as always, three Ring Ouzels. Then groups of finches were all around us: Chaffinches, a Brambling, Greenfinches, Goldfinches, Siskins and Linnets. After an hour or so, the final tally was over a thousand birds and also included Skylarks, Meadow Pipits, Tree Pipits, Pied Wagtails, a Yellow Wagtail, Sand Martins, House Martins and Barn Swallows. All streaming down the fields towards Poole Bay. Mo thought it was lovely.

Finches are far more predictable than the thrushes. Take Chaffinches for example. Having passed down through Denmark,

Germany and Holland every October, at least 30,000 will make landfall on the Dorset coast. In easterlies, some of these birds will fly high and cross the c 180 km from the Low Countries to Norfolk, having flown at around 40 km/h for several hours each morning. But with westerly winds 'our' Chaffinches will fly low and continue along the French coast to Cap Gris-Nez or beyond to approach Dorset from the south.

Migrating birds suffer the same problems as a marching army. Napoleon for example, well known for putting his men far ahead of his supply lines, relied on finding local provisions and billets for the men. Having a division of 20,000 men to look after, the quartermasters would have to spread them over a large area (Chandler 1995). Our army of Chaffinches has the same problems, having reached the coast and finding their fat reserves running low, they then make their way inland looking for food and shelter. Some will settle in Dorset for the winter, but there are far more of them than the local area can support, so most have to keep moving on, many continuing northwest to Wales and across the sea to Ireland.

Chaffinches, Goldfinches and other day-migrating birds tend to have less reliable food sources than the night migrants, because of big annual fluctuations in the size of seed crops. Southeast Dorset is unusual among migration sites for its large numbers of Goldfinches, with up to 35,000 passing through Durlston in most Octobers. Unlike the Chaffinches, the Goldfinches are British birds that will winter to the south and west. By migrating during the day, they can find local food and connect with Goldfinches that have been around longer. This way they can follow these birds to a safe roost. The next morning they again follow the more purposeful Goldfinches to rich local feeding sites.

European Goldfinches *Carduelis carduelis* and other passerines on migration, Ballard Down, Dorset, 12 October 2010 (*Nick Hopper*)

Shaun's garden is well stocked each evening with niger seed. Like roast pig is to Napoleon's old guard, so niger is to Goldfinches. However at Shaun's there's no such thing as a free lunch and he catches the visiting Goldfinches, rings them and sets them free. Most of us watching our local garden birds would imagine that they are the same fellows each day. Shaun has caught around 50 birds and hasn't retrapped any. More food disappears when he is at work during peak visible migration days than quiet ones. Shaun calls it the Napoleon Index.

Large roosts are common for most birds. Staying together through the night reduces predation and as we've seen, enables

1000s of Wood Pigeons pass from
Evening Hill high to the west
in early November

migrants concentrate
by the narrowing of the
South Haven peninsula

some migrants like
Siskin roost in the
alders and willows
on the edge of
Little Sea

wagtails and
Skylarks
will cross the
bay in NE winds

BROWNSEA ISLAND WITH
POOLE IN THE BACKGROUND

BOURNEMOUTH

PILOT'S POINT

STUDLAND VILLAGE

when wind is
northwest, most
migrants pass high
overhead Brownsea
lagoon

North

THE MIGRANTS' PATHS

in late October 1000
of finches and thrushes
pass over here towards
Studland village

visitors to get to know the best feeding sites. Two of the species that use communal roosts are great ambassadors for birds. Pied Wagtails in Poole move their winter roosts around, sharing the spectacle among schoolchildren at Poole Grammar School, senior citizens at the nursing home and Christmas shoppers at Falklands Square in the town centre. Even more noticeable are the starling roosts.

In 2010, Pete Miles stood on Poole High School's playground with his sons, watching 50,000 Starlings. The flock filled the sky, one moment looking like a swarm of bees, the next a shimmer of herring foming a bait ball high over their heads. Splitting into fragments, the swarm streamed over the school buildings, across the railway line and poured into the conifers lining it. As if there were some hidden signal, a blizzard of 10,000 birds vanished, each finding its perch in a split second. The birds immediately started to murmur to each other. "A wonder like that… and us just looking makes you think," said Pete.

They certainly make a lot of people think, with crowds gathering as they would to watch a firework display. Car drivers, queueing to get out of town in the evening rush hour, are thrilled by the sight of the wheeling flocks. We went there ourselves in early 2011 and recorded the spectacle. Magnus has edited out the worst of the traffic, but otherwise this is just how they sound if you are close enough to the roost when they come in (**CD1-57**).

CD1-57   **Common Starling** *Sturnus vulgaris* Poole High School, Dorset, England, 16:52, 9 January 2011. A flock of around 10,000 starlings coming to roost. At first you can hear a faint whisper of wings and the occasional low call, followed by a much louder fluttering of wings as they land, then a swelling tide of bickering as they compete for the best perches. Background: Common Blackbird *Turdus merula* and Eurasian Magpie *Pica pica*. 110109.MC.165200.33

There is one other bird that we see in huge flocks. Wood Pigeons. At Christchurch in late October, migration watchers were getting big numbers of Wood Pigeons. They must, I reasoned, be passing through the harbour too, but where? They didn't seem to be flying over the harbour mouth. Mo and I started to look across Canford Heath to the north of the conurbation on suitable mornings, and at Corfe Castle. Then we had a verandah built at the top of the house and thought that this would be a great place to monitor pigeon flocks.

Come 1 November 2006, Mo and I were stationed at our new lookout. Just after dawn, a few aimless flocks of Wood Pigeons were milling round over the town. After a while they started to fly a little more purposefully, and we could see them join a much larger flock really high in the sky (around 300 m) over Brownsea. These birds flew a little way west, then turned and headed over the ridge towards the coast. Scanning back at the same height, we found another flock, and another. I had arranged with James and Graham to watch from South Haven, so that we could co-ordinate our efforts. They could see the same heavy passage of Wood Pigeons, but far higher than we normally looked, with a number of large flocks of over a thousand, and some lines of birds stretching across very long distance. James counted about 30,000 in total.

Then at 08:45 a Little Bunting announced itself to James and Graham with its distinctive call as it flew over the harbour entrance. That put paid to the counting of Wood Pigeons at South Haven for the morning, and was something of a shock to Mo and I up in our distant eyrie. We had counted 41,505 Wood

Pigeons. Another 14,100 the next day and 6,000 the day after that added up to 61,605 migrating over the three days. Would we have swapped all these Wood Pigeon flocks for one flyover Little Bunting? Of course!

It didn't put us off though, and in 2007 we were back up on the verandah again, managing 41,200 on 31 October, together with over 1,000 Stock Doves. This smaller species benefits considerably in speed and energy by moving within the Wood Pigeon flocks. Some 900 Jackdaws flying west beneath the 'Woodies' may also have been taking advantage of the mass movement in the same way.

The Wood Pigeons did help me solve one final puzzle. Why do so many migrating birds we see on the south coast fly into the wind, often going a different way each day? One particular morning, the morning before Bonfire night, Wood Pigeons were struggling. As is often the case when the nation plans its bonfire parties and little boys are looking forward to fireworks, the weather wasn't perfect. There was a strong westsouthwest wind and heavy rain showers. You wouldn't expect to see the Wood Pigeons on such a morning, because they normally move on clear calm days with no cloud. In fact Nick was lying in his bed, exhausted from chasing Firecrests around Studland the day before, so my 08:00 phone call wasn't really welcome.

"The Wood Pigeons are moving, Nick."

"Really? In this weather? I'm knackered. Claire has got the day off." A good excuse that translates as, "I'm not allowed out. Let me know how it's going."

20 minutes later I called again, "Hi Nick, I'm watching a flock of a thousand, they really are moving." I was worried it looked like a record day, and I explained to him that I had a date at 10:00, taking 80 school kids out on the bird boat. I entreated, but it was no use.

Nick was doing a corvid study for this book, so unrelentingly I called again at 08:30. "Jackdaws are moving. I've just seen 372. You really must come." Suspecting he was being tricked out of bed, Nick exploded, "Can you guarantee me Jackdaws?"

No, I couldn't guarantee the Jackdaws. I wasn't even sure I could identify them at such a distance. They sneak past looking like Wood Pigeons in bright light, but smaller with a different size and flight. They don't rise up like the Woodies, but prefer skimming the tops of the trees at Brownsea. So they are hard to do, Nick hardly believed my count. Still, he'd never believe me if I couldn't get him over here to look. I added my count to Trektellen and Nick called. We apologised to each other, admitting the frustration of trying to be in the right place at the right time, watching the right thing, especially day after day.

That evening, I posted the Wood Pigeon numbers on our local web group, 'Out and About'. I read of sites further west getting flocks of 1,000 Wood Pigeons, and the descriptions were like my own. "Long lines of birds stretching hundreds of metres." The Woodies seemed to have gone as far west as Dawlish Warren, 103 km as the Wood Pigeon flies. I started thinking about that same old question: why do so many of the migrating birds we see in the harbour fly into the wind no matter which direction it takes them? The Napoleon theory doesn't really help with Wood Pigeons.

At first I imagined that all these Wood Pigeons were continental birds coming from Holland, until Magnus explained that Wood Pigeons don't migrate along the coast of Holland or Belgium but follow the border with Germany. I then pursued the idea that they were Norwegian birds coming down through Scotland, where the British co-ordinator of Trektellen, Clive McKay, had been counting many passing along the east coast. A phone conversation with him soon corrected that. The birds Clive sees are doing local movements, and none of the traditional Scottish migrant islands or North Sea oilrigs see any Wood Pigeon flocks in the autumn.

By a process of elimination we can deduce that they must be British birds moving south to join huge numbers from elsewhere, to winter in Spanish oak forests. Awkwardly, however, there are so few European recoveries of British-ringed birds that we can't prove this theory.

Let's assume that they roost in the millions of pines throughout the New Forest, then in early November when the temperatures drop about half an hour after dawn, they rise up and up, clearly wanting to migrate. Flying so high in the sky first thing in the morning, on a good clear day they should be able to see across the English Channel. More importantly, this test flight allows them to check the direction of the cross winds for something suitable.

On 7 November 2010, a local fishermen saw large pigeon flocks flying over his boat. Hardly surprising, because on that morning Mo and I hit a huge jackpot, counting 161,257 woodies moving across Poole Harbour in just a few hours. (I should mention that the numbers were counted more carefully at the beginning and end of the count, hence the 257, while they were estimated with practiced accuracy when in full flow.)

Suddenly it all came together when I remembered my last trip to Scilly, flying in a tiny plane out of Newquay. It was a squally day, and to make the ride as comfortable as possible the pilot was navigating around the obvious squalls. I realised that the Wood Pigeons on this day were doing something similar. That's what they were looking for, the right spot to cross the channel. It's not the distance across water that matters most. It's the wind speed and direction, and the lack of rain. When truly migrating, the birds will go like the clappers, but they have to find the right spot in the weather system to cross water or risk drowning.

The principle that enables you to stand with the wind to your back, determining whether the weather is going to deteriorate or improve by watching the overhead clouds, works because the wind blows out of high pressure, and in towards low pressure. Perhaps it would be more appropriate to say it slips off the high pressure.

I realised then that all migrating land birds use this strategy when crossing the channel from the south of England during unpredictable weather, and that this was another reason why we often saw birds flying into the wind. Whether it intends to cross or forage locally, any finch, swallow, lark or in this case Wood Pigeon flying into the wind will always be flying towards better weather. Those that choose a different course may well perish.

Not even this theory got Nick out of bed. At that time he still didn't approve of too much focus on migrating common birds. He preferred rarities.

Chapter 14: A flock of birds forever in flight

When Nick first heard that many of the local birders had stopped searching the bushes for rarities in October to watch birds migrating, he was disgusted. I can't remember what he said, but it was probably unprintable even for me. It wasn't that he thought visible migration was uninteresting, but rather a matter of priorities. He also wondered about the accuracy of the call identification. "I'm going to line you all up on a hill, and as the birds fly over I'm going to check what each of you thinks they are." He had a point. We learn how to identify these passing birds through experience, but the only test is standing by other birders and seeing if you shout out the same bird at the same time. Nick gave me my exam on 12 October 2010.

Lying in wait for the glory, we tucked ourselves in sheltered bramble bushes just out of the northeast wind, high on Ballard Down. Nick had his camera ready, and I deployed the SASS to record calls. Almost immediately we spotted two Ring Ouzels, alerted by their calls (**CD1-58**). For me, this sound is typical.

CD1-58   **Ring Ouzel** *Turdus torquatus* Ballard Down, Dorset, England, 07:25, 12 October 2009. Tongue-tutting sound normally transcribed as *tock*, in series sounding rather like winding clockwork. In this ambient recording, the bird splutters to get the notes out fast enough. When it gets excited (often with little provocation), the pitch does not rise markedly as in Common Blackbird. Background: Meadow Pipit *Anthus pratensis*, European Robin *Erithacus rubecula*, Common Blackbird *T merula*, European Goldfinch *Carduelis carduelis* and Eurasian Siskin *Spinus spinus*. 091012.MC.072501.22

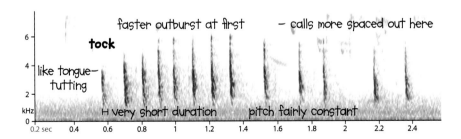

Old Harry and Ballard Down, Dorset, showing the view a spring migrant would have, 10 August 2008 (*Nick Hopper*). 'You can see swallows and Skylarks over the water here.'

Ring Ouzel *Turdus torquatus*, Ballard Down, at migration watchpoint, Dorset, 12 October 2009 (*Nick Hopper*). CD1-58

In autumn, Ring Ouzels hiding in gorse bushes give themselves away with this sound. You can hear the equivalent calls of Blackbird and Song Thrush in **CD1-59** and **CD1-60**.

CD1-59   **Common Blackbird** *Turdus merula* Bica de Cana, Madeira, Portugal, 3 April 2002. *Tock* calls escalating smoothly into dramatic higher-pitched outbursts. This was at dusk in a conifer plantation with a high density of the species. Background: European Robin *Erithacus rubecula*. 02.013.MR.12515.31

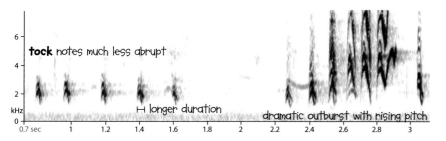

The first Sound Approach CD was a freebie of flight calls for Dutch Birding subscribers called *Out of the blue* (van den Berg et al 2003). At the time, Magnus taught me a sound I had been missing. This is the Ring Ouzel's basic flight call (**CD1-61**). Nick and I heard one of the birds using this as it continued its journey. Since *Out of the blue*, Magnus spent an autumn living in Poole, and many of the migration recordings in this chapter were made by the two of us locally.

Chaffinches were flying north along a narrow front, maybe 100 m across. The line drifted a little as they flew into the wind. Finding local migration corridors is a fieldcraft exam in itself. This one happened to be half way along a high ridge, and we could have missed it, had the wind been from another direction. The best weather to hear the glory of migration on Ballard is when the wind is northeasterly.

CD1-60   **Song Thrush** *Turdus philomelos* IJmuiden, Noord-Holland, Netherlands, 17 October 2001. *Tock* notes are very similar to those of Ring Ouzel, but deeper-sounding and not quite so abrupt. In Song Thrush they tend to be combined with much powerful, explosive *tix!* notes (heard here after 10 seconds) and the marked and sudden contrast between these sounds is something to listen for. Background: European Robin *Erithacus rubecula*, Dunnock *Prunella modularis* and Common Chaffinch *Fringilla coelebs*. 01.041.MR.13919.32

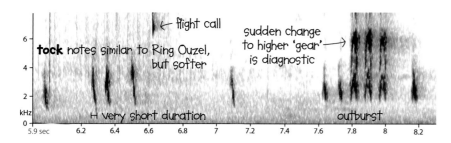

Ring Ouzel *Turdus torquatus* Breskens, Zeeland, Netherlands, 08:48, 13 April 2007. A flock of 12 passing a migration watchpoint on spring migration. Background: Common Shelduck *Tadorna tadorna*, displaying male Marsh Harrier *Circus aeruginosus*, Meadow Pipit *Anthus pratensis*, Great Tit *Parus major* and Common Reed Bunting *Emberiza schoeniclus*. 070413.MR.084048.21   **CD1-61**

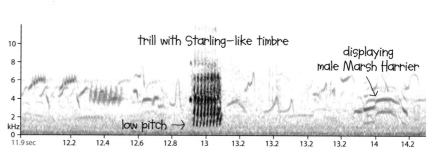

These migration corridors are three dimensional with birds like swallows and wagtails happy to fly low over Swanage Bay, while the layers of migration can reach unseen up to 4 km high, depending on weather conditions.

On this typical autumn morning, Scandinavia's Blackbirds were arriving for winter, literally tumbling out of the sky from great heights before disappearing into cover. Joining the flocks of finches flying into the wind, they headed up to our ridge from where Hamish was counting on Long Meadow. They gained height over Swanage Bay to skim just over our heads on top of Ballard Down, before descending over the fields to Studland village and on past Little Sea to South Haven.

There must be hundreds of these migration corridors. It wasn't until 2005 that Hamish discovered the magic of Long Meadow. Having walked across it thousands of times, he had been blissfully unaware of its true potential over 27 years of intensive Durlston birding. At present, it has to be one of the finest migratory corridors in Britain. We can scope it from where we are sitting. Running north-south for 300 m and up to 70 m wide, it has woodland along one side and a double running hedge bordering a quiet access road along the other.

The finches and buntings flying past on migration have a couple of predictable types of call. In Chaffinches the same calls are heard overhead from females, males and first-winters. One call type is described in the *Collins bird guide* as *yupp*. Here is an example of it from a Chaffinch that was recorded on a day when the migration was southbound. It had already passed over Ballard and was heading across Long Meadow (**CD1-62**).

Common Chaffinch *Fringilla coelebs* Durlston, Dorset, England, 08:30, 9 October 2008. Flight calls of a single individual passing at close range. Background: European Robin *Erithacus rubecula*, European Blue Tit *Cyanistes caeruleus* and European Goldfinch *Carduelis carduelis*. 081009.MR.083000.21   **CD1-62**

Common Chaffinch *Fringilla coelebs* Ballard Down, Dorset, England, 08:19, 12 October 2009. *Fink* calls of a female that paused during migration. Later, after finding a friend, it took off again with *yupp* calls. Background: European Robin *Erithacus rubecula*. 091012.MC.081916.22   **CD1-63**

The other Chaffinch call heard on migration flights, more noticeably though actually less frequently, is described as *fink*. It is more powerful than the flight call, and more strongly associated with perched Chaffinches. Here is a solitary female that has paused to perch on a bramble and is calling while looking skywards, presumably to try to attract another Chaffinch (**CD1-63**). Now listen to another female Chaffinch mixing the two calls as she flies north past us (**CD1-64**).

Common Chaffinch *Fringilla coelebs* Ballard Down, Dorset, England, 07:50, 12 October 2009. *Yupp* and *fink* calls of a solitary female passing on autumn migration. Background: Pied Wagtail *Motacilla yarrellii*, Long-tailed Tit *Aegithalos caudatus*, Great Tit *Parus major* and European Goldfinch *Carduelis carduelis*. 091012.MC.075006.12   **CD1-64**

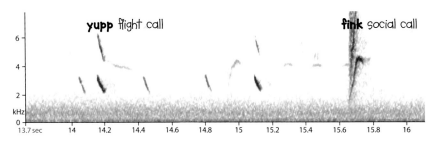

Using the example of migrating Chaffinches and Bramblings, we can illustrate a basic guideline that helps in identifying a range of other species. Single migrants often use different call types than birds migrating in groups. The more common the migrant, the more likely that they will be giving 'flight calls' as the flocks pass. These are often not very striking calls, and en masse they may at first sound like anonymous chattering. Many of the following examples feature single birds giving flight calls, but this is to help you learn them. Chaffinch and Brambling seldom use flight calls while perched, but in other species they may signal an intention to fly. In the *Collins bird guide*, Lars Svensson suggests *yupp* for Chaffinch and *yeck* for Brambling.

Fortunately for us, the scarcer the migrant the more likely it is to be alone and using different, far-carrying calls in the hope of attracting friends of the same species. For convenience, let's call these 'social calls'. These are designed to stand out from the general background of hundreds of other finches migrating together using their flight calls. On the breeding grounds, the same sounds are often repeated from prominent perches, and in most finches and buntings you hear them routinely all year round. Sometimes given when a bird is in danger from a predator, they may seem to be used as alarm calls, but in fact the idea is to attract reinforcements to help with mobbing. In different species, these calls have been given different names. In crossbills for example, they are usually called 'excitement calls'.

Back on Ballard a little later in the morning, and a single Brambling was passing by. You can hear its flight calls and one distinctive social call in **CD1-65**. It is mainly the social calls that alert us to Bramblings passing, but to count them, it is better to listen for flight calls. In years where there are a lot of Bramblings, they can sneak past high on southerly winds in poor light and in mixed flocks. If they don't use their social calls, we risk misidentifying them as Chaffinches. Here are some Bramblings

CD1-65   **Brambling** *Fringilla montifringilla* Ballard Down, Dorset, England, 08:15, 12 October 2009. Single migrant passing in autumn, giving flight calls and a single social call. Background: Eurasian Skylark *Alauda arvensis*, Dunnock *Prunella modularis*, Common Chaffinch *Fringilla coelebs* and Eurasian Siskin *Spinus spinus*. 091012.MC.081536.23

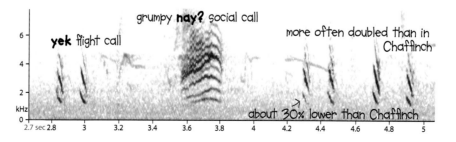

that Magnus recorded at migration watchpoint de Nolledijk in the Netherlands (**CD1-66**). On this occasion, they passed by without giving any social calls.

CD1-66   **Brambling** *Fringilla montifringilla* de Nolledijk, Zeeland, Netherlands, 08:28, 1 October 2007. Flight calls during autumn migration, possibly all from a single individual. Background: Meadow Pipit *Anthus pratensis* and Common Chaffinch *Fringilla coelebs*. 071001.MR.082858.12

Another bird that I tend to identify mainly by its social call is Siskin. This is how I like my Siskins (**CD1-67**): all alone and giving plenty of descending piercing whistles. What you normally get can be heard from a little flock passing Nick and me that Monday morning on Ballard (**CD1-68**). First a few high frequency descending whistles which make you look round for Siskin, then as the birds get closer, surge after surge of six or seven flight calls that are superficially like muted Goldfinch flight calls.

CD1-67   **Eurasian Siskin** *Spinus spinus* IJmuiden, Noord-Holland, Netherlands, 09:01, 18 November 2007. Social calls of a solitary migrant passing on autumn migration. Background: Fieldfare *Turdus pilaris* and European Blue Tit *Cyanistes caeruleus*. 071118.MR.090101.12

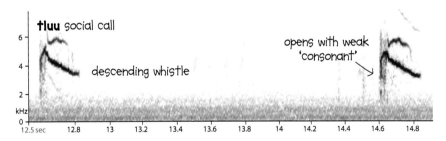

CD1-68   **Eurasian Siskin** *Spinus spinus* Ballard Down, Dorset, England, 07:33, 12 October 2009. Social and flight calls of a flock passing on autumn migration. Background: Long-tailed Tit *Aegithalos caudatus*. 091012.MC.073353.22

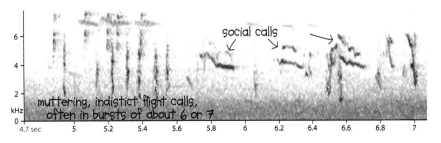

Here is a flock of Goldfinches from Durlston. One individual has been left a little behind and is rushing to catch up. These twittering flight calls are musical, and seem easy to recognise on that quality alone. The pitch bounces up and down, creating a sparkling effect **(CD1-69)**. Siskins seem to mutter indistinctly by comparison. Flocks of Goldfinches are something of a speciality on the British south coast, andw this massive Goldfinch migration would be glorious even without anything else. Here is a larger flock heading towards the harbour from Durlston **(CD1-70)**. In Goldfinch and the next species Linnet, we have not noticed much difference between the calls uttered by single migrants and those within migrating flocks.

CD1-69   **European Goldfinch** *Carduelis carduelis* Durlston, Dorset, England, 08:15, 29 September 2008. Large flock of about 50 migrating. Towards the end, individual flight calls can be heard clearly from a straggler passing closer than the others. Background: Eurasian Siskin *Spinus spinus*. 080929.MR.081538.12

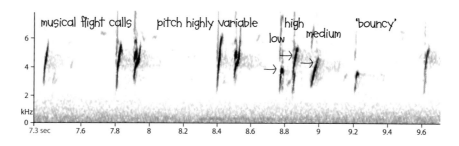

CD1-70   **European Goldfinch** *Carduelis carduelis* Durlston, Dorset, England, 09:23, 2 October 2008. A flock of 12 passing on autumn migration. Background: Eurasian Wren *Troglodytes troglodytes*, Western Jackdaw *Corvus monedula* and Common Chaffinch *Fringilla coelebs*. 081002.MR.092342.01

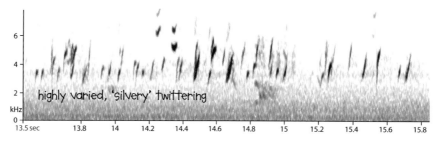

CD1-71 **Common Linnet** *Linaria cannabina* Durlston, Dorset, England, 08:07, 29 September 2008. Flight calls of a single migrant passing in autumn. Background: White/Pied Wagtail *Motacilla alba / yarrellii*, European Robin *Erithacus rubecula* and European Goldfinch *Carduelis carduelis*. 080929.MR.080706.12

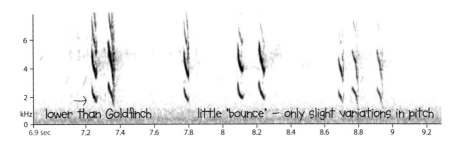

Linnets have a duller plumage and duller flight calls (**CD1-71**). A tight flock of Linnets sounds a little like a flock of Goldfinches, but their twittering averages lower-pitched, and has far less

range between the higher and lower notes. They often deliver their flight calls in pairs, mixed in with singles and triplets. Migrating Siskin, Goldfinch and Linnet can occasionally throw in bits of song, and call types other than flight calls. Here is an example of Linnets singing a little as they pass by on migration (**CD1-72**). Juveniles have a different call (**CD1-73**), which can occasionally be heard in migrating flocks early in the autumn.

CD1-72 **Common Linnet** *Linaria cannabina* IJmuiden, Noord-Holland, Netherlands, 08:37, 10 September 2006. Flight calls and fragments of song from two migrants passing on autumn. Background: gull *Larus* and Meadow Pipit *Anthus pratensis*. 060910.MR.83746.01

CD1-73 **Common Linnet** *Linaria cannabina* Kennemerduinen, Noord-Holland, Netherlands, 13:48, 1 July 2009. Flight calls of adults, with calls of an accompanying juvenile. 090701.AB.134831.31

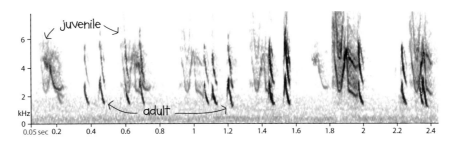

Lesser Redpolls migrating are fun to learn and identify. They have distinctive harsh but not deep *che che che* flight calls, delivered in rapid-fire bursts of two or three notes, interspersed with the occasional social call. The combination sounds like a steady repeated flat *dot-dot dot-dot dash* of morse code. This lone Lesser Redpoll flying over Long Meadow gave no social calls (**CD1-74**), but now listen to a single migrant in the dunes at IJmuiden in Holland, and you can hear the typical *pyuee* (**CD1-75**). A little like a cat's meow, it resembles the Siskin's whistled social call but always has a question-like rise in pitch.

The flight calls of Greenfinch, the last of Dorset's commoner finches, are one of the more familiar sounds on migration along the south coast of England (**CD1-76**), although we no longer hear them as often as we used to. Delivered in rapid-fire bursts

faster than Linnet calls, faster even than Lesser Redpoll flight calls, they can almost sound like a trill. Greenfinches have a social call too, but interestingly, autumn migrants don't seem to use it in flight. Juvenile Greenfinches can be mistaken for crossbills, but generally give an almost continuous series of identical calls (**CD1-77**).

European Greenfinch *Chloris chloris* Breskens, Zeeland, Netherlands, 09:40, 23 March 2006. A single individual migrating with flight calls. Background: Mallard *Anas platyrhynchos*, Common Chaffinch *Fringilla coelebs* and Common Linnet *Linaria cannabina*. 06.002.MR.11940.22   CD1-76

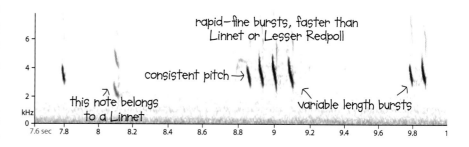

CD1-74   **Lesser Redpoll** *Acanthis cabaret* Durlston, Dorset, England, 08:13, 9 October 2008. Flight calls of a single migrant passing in a mixed autumn finch flock. Background: European Robin *Erithacus rubecula*, Goldcrest *Regulus regulus*, Common Chaffinch *Fringilla coelebs* and Eurasian Siskin *Spinus spinus*. 081009.MR.081354.02

CD1-75   **Lesser Redpoll** *Acanthis cabaret* IJmuiden, Noord-Holland, Netherlands, 9 November 2003. Social calls and flight calls of at least two autumn migrants. Background: Eurasian Wren *Troglodytes troglodytes*, European Robin *Erithacus rubecula*, Goldcrest *Regulus regulus* and Eurasian Magpie *Pica pica*. 03.039.MR.01740.02

European Greenfinch *Chloris chloris* Vlieland, Friesland, Netherlands, 13 October 2001. Begging calls of a young bird still accompanied by its parents. Background: Common Chaffinch *Fringilla coelebs*. 01.040.MR.03703.10   CD1-77

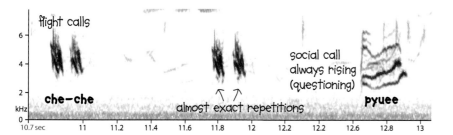

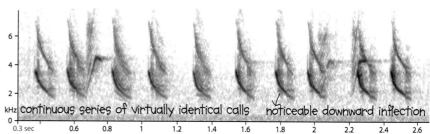

Crossbills come in various vocal types, and in *The Sound Approach to birding* (2006) we explained how Parrot and Scottish Crossbill, widely regarded as species, just happen to be two of the best known. Neither type has occurred in Poole Harbour, but we do receive visits from other vocal types, which we believe are no less, or more, worthy of species status. Once learnt, crossbill vocal types are far easier to separate than some other closely related migrants, such as Rock Pipit and Water Pipit.

Many birders know when they are hearing a crossbill, but only the attentive know which vocal type. As a group, they have powerful, incisive, metallic-sounding flight calls. Glip Crossbills are *the* common crossbill from Finland to Poole (cf Lindholm 2011). Here you can hear a flock of 11 passing Nick and me. Nick suspects that I am not taking my exam very seriously (**CD1-78**).

It turned out to be a record day for Glip Crossbills with 212, and a further 451 passing during two subsequent visits that week (**CD1-79**).

Glip Crossbill *Loxia curvirostris* type C and Birders *Homo sapiens* Ballard Down, Dorset, England, 09:00, 12 October 2009. Flight calls of a small flock of eight crossbills passing at close range, then Nick catches Mark daydreaming. Background: Meadow Pipit *Anthus pratensis*, European Robin *Erithacus rubecula* and Common Chaffinch *Fringilla coelebs*. 091012.MC.090030.22 — CD1-78

Bullfinches migrate past regularly and give themselves away with social calls. The migrant in **CD1-80** was resting between flights. Bullfinches also have an insignificant-sounding, soft *bit* flight call that is mainly used as a precursor to flight, although attentive listeners may occasionally hear it from passing birds too, in between the more noticeable social calls.

CD1-79 **Glip Crossbill** *Loxia curvirostris* type C Ballard Down, Dorset, England, 08:34, 12 October 2009. Flight calls of a flock of seven migrating at close range. Background: Meadow Pipit *Anthus pratensis*, Dunnock *Prunella modularis* and Common Raven *Corvus corax*. 091012.MC.083422.03

CD1-80 **Eurasian Bullfinch** *Pyrrhula pyrrhula* Ballard Down, Dorset, England, 08:45, 12 October 2009. Social calls of a solitary male, paused during migration. Background: Meadow Pipit *Anthus pratensis*, Eurasian Wren *Troglodytes troglodytes* and Common Chaffinch *Fringilla coelebs*. 091012.MC.084556.23

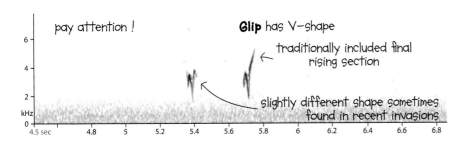

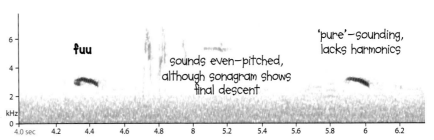

One of the most sought after migrants for my Poole Harbour list used to be Hawfinch. I had a blind spot, although it really wasn't so much a blind spot as a deaf spot. I'm not very good on anything that sounds vaguely like a Robin. As this recording illustrates (**CD1-81**), the Hawfinch's social and flight calls are both fairly Robin-like and quite unlike any of the other finches. The highly distinctive social call is much lower-pitched than the flight call, a stony *fwit* that is often doubled. However, this is not the usual migration call. Instead it is a very high-pitched, lisping flight call that should alert you to Hawfinches more often. I eventually saw one migrating as I was waiting for the ferry at North Haven, on 30 October 2005. The ferry chains drowned any finer sounds, so hearing one as it passes overhead is a treat still to come.

Twite tend to migrate from late October to early November and being hardy birds, most winter further northeast, stopping anywhere from the Thames estuary northwards. They are extremely rare in Poole Harbour, although the

Hawfinch *Coccothraustes coccothraustes* Ankarudden, Södermansland, Sweden, 19 November 2004. Flight and social calls of a migrant flying past the recordist. Background: Mealy Redpoll *Acanthis flammea* and Northern Bullfinch *Pyrrhula pyrrhula pyrrhula*. 04.044.MR.00146.02 **CD1-81**

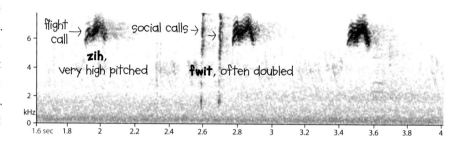

occasional bird must be overlooked. So we assume our Twite will be travelling alone and are listening out for its extremely distinctive social call, a nasal, rising *keet* (**CD1-82**). Twite flight calls are like Linnet notes delivered in the style of a redpoll. They show almost no variation in pitch, so they sound rather flat by comparison with Linnets. None of us has managed the

CD1-82 **Twite** *Linaria flavirostris* IJmuiden, Noord-Holland, Netherlands, 10 November 2003. Social calls of a passing migrant, with a few flight calls towards the end. Background: Lesser Black-backed Gull *Larus fuscus* and Eurasian Wren *Troglodytes troglodytes*. 03.039.MR.03636.14

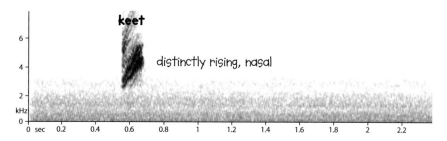

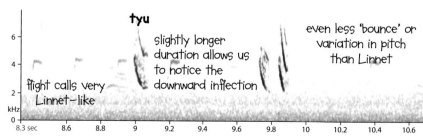

equally rare Serin yet on migration through Poole (**CD1-83**), though Durlston has managed four autumn migrants. Serins have a high-pitched jangle with the sparkling quality of a Goldfinch, but delivered as a rattle-like burst of identical notes.

Snow Bunting's flight calls are more musical than Serin's, their lower pitch creating a more rippling effect. Experienced observers have been known to confuse the two. Fortunately, Snow Bunting has a highly distinctive social call that typically alternates with its flight calls (**CD1-84**). Lapland Bunting's flight calls are also a rapid succession of about 3 or 4 notes, delivered at a similar speed to Serin and Snow Bunting. In Lapland, each note is a hard staccato *tic*, and the combination of several results in a rattle (**CD1-85**). It has a social call similar to Snow Bunting, but contrasting so strongly with its rattle that a single migrant passing overhead can create the illusion of two entirely different species.

None of the buntings are common migrants in Poole, so many of these recordings were collected by Magnus as he stood in the dunes of IJmuiden on the Dutch coast. Nick is very proud of a Lapland Bunting he managed to record flying over his Stoborough house in the dark, not least because he was lying in bed at the time. He had put his microphone on the roof and connected it to a very long cable, which he runs to his machine and earphones in the bedroom.

In October and early November, Reed Buntings shoot past South Haven daily in ones and twos, but in IJmuiden there may be up to 100 in a morning. Reed Bunting has a very odd, low-pitched and nasal-sounding flight call quite unlike anything else

European Serin *Serinus serinus* Cabo Espichel, Lisboa, Portugal, 08:18, 10 November 2009. Flight calls of a passing migrant. Background: European Robin *Erithacus rubecula*, Common Chaffinch *Fringilla coelebs* and Eurasian Siskin *Spinus spinus*. 091110.MR.081800.01 **CD1-83**

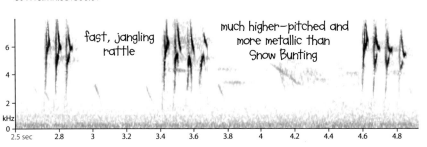

Snow Bunting *Plectrophenax nivalis* IJmuiden, Noord-Holland, Netherlands, 6 November 2003. Flight and social calls of a flock. Background: Common Chaffinch *Fringilla coelebs*. 03.038.MR.14103.33 **CD1-84**

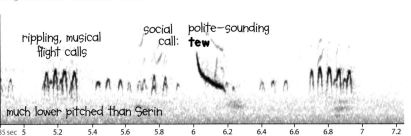

Lapland Bunting *Calcarius lapponicus* IJmuiden, Noord-Holland, Netherlands, 29 September 2002. Flight and social calls of a foraging migrant, one of a group of three. Background: Meadow Pipit *Anthus pratensis*. 02.042.MR.12048.02 **CD1-85**

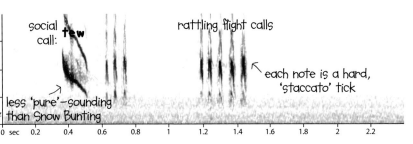

(**CD1-86**). This is probably an adaptation to living in reedbeds, where rustling reeds could easily obscure shorter and higher-pitched flight calls on windy days.

The social calls of Reed, Lapland and Snow Bunting are all short descending whistles. Reed Bunting's social call is much higher pitched and purer-sounding than the other two (**CD1-87**). Lapland and Snow Bunting's social calls are very similar and easily confused, but Lapland has some lower-pitched, shorter and more nasal variants that are missing in Snow Bunting.

Corn Buntings on migration flights only use their flight call: an electric, fairly low-pitched click described in the *Collins bird guide* as bt… bt… (CD1-88). They are surprisingly rare here on migration, and only the occasional one or two pass over South Haven towards the end of October. Yellowhammers breed locally but are only occasionally seen as passing migrants. Their flight calls are dry ticking notes, given singly or in twos or threes,

CD1-86 **Common Reed Bunting** *Emberiza schoeniclus* IJmuiden, Noord-Holland, Netherlands, 08:37, 17 October 2006. Flight calls of a solitary passing migrant, with a single social call towards the end. Background: Meadow Pipit *Anthus pratensis*, Dunnock *Prunella modularis*, Song Thrush *Turdus philomelos* and Common Starling *Sturnus vulgaris*. 061017.MR.83742.22

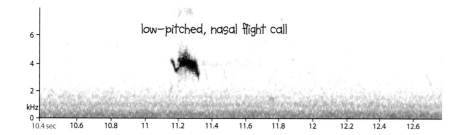

Common Reed Bunting *Emberiza schoeniclus* de Nolledijk, Zeeland, Netherlands, 08:52, 8 November 2005. Social calls of a solitary passing migrant. Background: Eurasian Wren *Troglodytes troglodytes* and Great Tit *Parus major*. 05.028.MR.15222.01 **CD1-87**

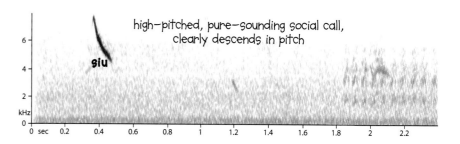

Corn Bunting *Emberiza calandra* Cabo Espichel, Lisboa, Portugal, 08:25, 18 September 2008. Flight calls as one passes by. Background: Crested Lark *Galerida cristata*, Northern Wheatear *Oenanthe oenanthe* and Spotless Starling *Sturnus unicolor*. 080918. MR.082556.22 **CD1-88**

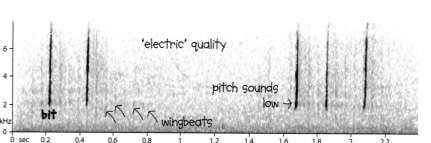

in which case the first note is higher than any that follow (CD1-89). Yellowhammer's social call is a dry buzzing sound (CD1-90), very different from the whistled social calls of Reed, Lapland and Snow.

CD1-89 **Yellowhammer** *Emberiza citrinella* de Nolledijk, Zeeland, Netherlands, 09:21, 3 November 2006. Single and two-note variants of flight call from a migrant passing at close range. Background: European Robin *Erithacus rubecula*, Redwing *Turdus iliacus*, Brambling *Fringilla montifringilla* and Chaffinch *F coelebs*. 061103.MR.92135.12

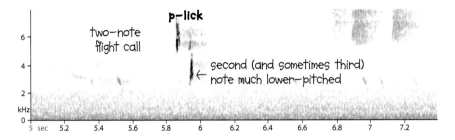

Ortolans are probably overlooked in Poole Harbour. Nick heard one calling when walking at the top of Glebelands, close to the track. He followed the call to the hedge thinking that since he was in Poole Harbour it really couldn't be one. The call moved and then an Ortolan popped its head up. He was really chuffed. There it was right in front of him, a first for Poole Harbour. The call Nick heard was a repeated single note something like this (**CD1-91**). Ortolans on migration use similar flight calls, but usually showing much more variation in pitch (**CD1-92**). The calls are typically single notes spaced well apart, plucked from different strings of the same instrument.

CD1-90 **Yellowhammer** *Emberiza citrinella* Helgoland, Schleswig-Holstein, Germany, 08:39, 13 October 2007. Flight and social calls of a passing migrant. Background: Meadow Pipit *Anthus pratensis*, Eurasian Wren *Troglodytes troglodytes*, Redwing *Turdus iliacus*, Brambling *Fringilla montifringilla*, Chaffinch *F coelebs* and Common Reed Bunting *Emberiza schoeniclus*. 071013.MR.083930.32

Ortolan Bunting *Emberiza hortulana* IJmuiden, Noord-Holland, Netherlands, 17 September 2003. Several calls of a first-winter male when flushed and flying a short distance. Background: Meadow Pipit *Anthus pratensis*, Rock Pipit *A petrosus* and Eurasian Magpie *Pica pica*. 03.035.MR.12155.01 **CD1-91**

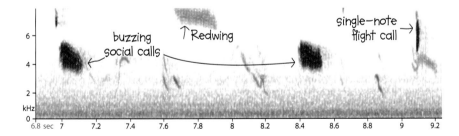

Ortolan Bunting *Emberiza hortulana* IJmuiden, Noord-Holland, Netherlands, 09:46, 10 September 2006. One migrating along the Dutch coast. Roy Slaterus who was birding a kilometer further north at the time heard this Ortolan migrating, and rang through enabling Magnus to point his parabola in the right direction and get this unusually long recording. Background: Meadow Pipit *Anthus pratensis*, yellow wagtail *Motacilla*, Dunnock *Prunella modularis* and Common Reed Bunting *Emberiza schoeniclus*. 060910.MR.94605.11 **CD1-92**

If you are struggling to hear these fine calls, it's probably your speakers. Things will improve if you use headphones.

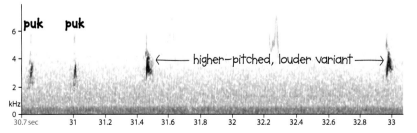

Magnus recorded this Little Bunting migrating through IJmuiden (**CD1-93**) when he was still learning his flight calls. I was quite sceptical when he claimed it, but now I believe him. We've had just the one record here in Poole, the bird that flew past Graham and James at South Haven. Superficially, the *tic* call sounds like a Robin, but when they combine the flight call with a *chup* that is probably the social call, we can only confuse them with Yellowhammer.

CD1-93   **Little Bunting** *Emberiza pusilla* IJmuiden, Noord-Holland, Netherlands, 12 October 2001. One migrating in a flock of Common Chaffinches. Background: Herring Gull *Larus argentatus*, Meadow Pipit *Anthus pratensis* and Common Chaffinch *Fringilla coelebs*. 01.041.MR.00228.11

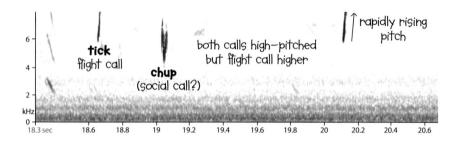

Leaving behind finches and buntings and their penchant for social and flight calls, the other big group of passing birds is the pipits and wagtails. As with all lessons, things get a little tougher the further you get into the course. Imagine you are attending a wedding in a rural Dorset church, and that the organist is hard of hearing. The bride and her father have arrived and are waiting to walk up the aisle, accompanied by strains of *Hear comes the bride*. The organist is blissfully unaware, and various people including the groom are trying unsuccessfully to attract his attention. *Pssst… pssih… ist ist ist… spibz… viisst… psit…*

This descriptive 'birdie talk' is from the *Collins bird guide*'s descriptions of various pipit and wagtail sounds. It prepares you for flight calls of Meadow Pipit, Rock Pipit and Water Pipit, which can all overlap. Meadow Pipit's *ist ist ist* is extremely varied in pitch and delivery, but these calls are among the easier to identify as every note is short and rises in pitch (**CD2-01**). The calls in this recording have been brought into close focus by the recording equipment. You can hear the way variations grade into one another, with the sounds varying in length, pitch and intensity. The next recording is more representative of the real experience, with varied calls coming from several directions, and other species trying to confuse the issue (**CD2-02**). Meadow Pipit is the most common pipit through the harbour, with 100 passing Ballard Down on a reasonable day and a record 372 on 7 October 2009.

Meadow Pipit *Anthus pratensis* IJmuiden, Noord-Holland, Netherlands, 09:18, 12 September 2002. Variable flight calls of a passing migrant. Background: gulls Laridae. 02.027.AB.02937.03   **CD2-01**

Meadow Pipit *Anthus pratensis* Durlston, Dorset, England, 08:57, 8 October 2008. More relaxed-sounding calls of a small flock migrating. Background: European Robin *Erithacus rubecula* and Common Linnet *Linaria cannabina*. 081008.MR.085700.22   **CD2-02**

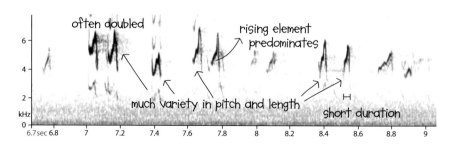

Now listen to *viisst* calls of a Rock Pipit, this time recorded on Tory Island in Ireland (**CD2-03**). Compared to Meadow Pipit flight calls these are higher-pitched, longer and shriller.

CD2-03   **Rock Pipit** *Anthus petrosus* Tory Island, Donegal, Ireland, 12:01, 18 March 2008. High-pitched flight calls while socializing on a rocky Atlantic beach. Background: Eurasian Oystercatcher *Haematopus ostralegus*. 080318.MR.120147.02

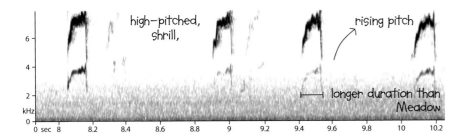

If you look at the sonagram you can see that Water Pipit is similar to Rock Pipit but lower-pitched and coarser (**CD2-04**). These examples illustrate distinctive variants of their calls, and this is how we'd like to hear them all the time, but unfortunately they can sound extremely similar. Both Rock and Water Pipit can

CD2-04   **Water Pipit** *Anthus spinoletta* Tacumshin, Wexford, Ireland, 20 November 2005. Typical flight calls from a wintering individual, circling over a shallow lake. Background: Black-headed Gull *Chroicocephalus ridibundus*, Eurasian Wren *Troglodytes troglodytes* and Dunnock *Prunella modularis*. 05.004.KM.00914.02

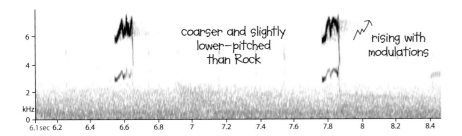

sometimes even sound very Meadow Pipit-like when migrating in groups. Rock Pipit is occasionally recorded migrating in Poole but not Water Pipit. Both overwinter along the bays and edges of the harbour.

Tree Pipit is a far easier bird to identify when flying over on migration. The pitch sounds even or slightly descending, and not rising as in the last three species. There is some variation, especially in length and intensity, most obvious when Tree Pipits migrate in small groups. This first example is of just two individuals migrating in Bulgaria, one after the other, making the detail easier to hear (**CD2-05**). They are using flight calls and a very short *sip* note, which may be equivalent to the social calls of finches and buntings. This example is followed by one from Durlston, showing the greater variety of calls heard in a flock (**CD2-06**). The high pitch and sibilance makes it difficult for some people to hear them.

Tree Pipit *Anthus trivialis* Atanasovo lake, Burgas, Bulgaria, 15:53, 22 September 2007.   CD2-05
One migrating, using both strong, full-length flight calls and two very short *sip* calls. Background: Crested Lark *Galerida cristata* and Common Starling *Sturnus vulgaris*. 070922.MR.155333.22

Tree Pipit *Anthus trivialis* Durlston, Dorset, England, 07:48, 8 September 2008. Strong,   CD2-06
full-length calls and shorter, more conversational calls from a flock of six migrating. Background: Green Woodpecker *Picus viridis*, Common House Martin *Delichon urbicum*, European Robin *Erithacus rubecula* and Eurasian Jay *Garrulus glandarius*. 080908.MR.074842.12

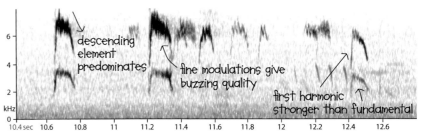

Arguably, the flight call of Richard's Pipit is the strongest and most attention grabbing of any pipit (**CD2-07**). You normally hear them when they're still a long way off, and you can look forward to watching a big pipit bounding your way. Tawny Pipits have flight calls with a very different, chirruping quality, something like a cross between a sparrow and a Pied Wagtail (**CD2-08**).

White and Pied Wagtails both migrate through Poole, and their flight calls are not really separable. I don't know where I learnt that their calls are a 'disyllabic' *chis-ick*, but like a good boy, when they fly past that's what I hear. When I listen to our recordings, I realise that in reality migrants frequently give monosyllabic and trisyllabic calls too. Magnus points out that the *chis-ick* is

CD2-07   **Richard's Pipit** *Anthus richardi* Cabo Espichel, Lisboa, Portugal, 07:41, 20 October 2010. Flight calls of a passing migrant that flew in a wide semi-circle around the recordist. Background: Eurasian Whimbrel *Numenius phaeopus*, Yellow-legged Gull *Larus michahellis*, White Wagtail *Motacilla alba*, Zitting Cisticola *Cisticola juncidis*, Sardinian Warbler *Sylvia melanocephala*, Carrion Crow *Corvus corone*, European Greenfinch *Chloris chloris*, Common Linnet *Linaria cannabina* and Cirl Bunting *Emberiza cirlus*. 101020.MR.074132.22

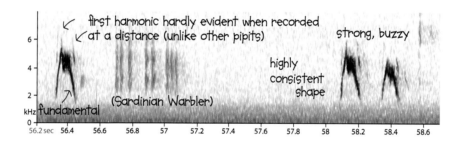

CD2-08   **Tawny Pipit** *Anthus campestris* Atanasovo lake, Burgas, Bulgaria, 17:29, 21 September 2007. Four migrating at close range. Background: Mallard *Anas platyrhynchos*, European Bee-eater *Merops apiaster*, Tree Pipit *Anthus trivialis* and Common Starling *Sturnus vulgaris*. 070921.MR.172951.11

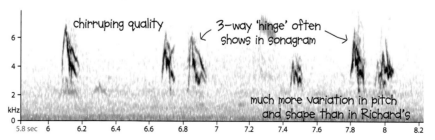

CD2-09 **White Wagtail** *Motacilla alba* Hanko Bird Observatory, Uusimaa, Finland, 21 September 2006. Typical flight calls while migrating at very close range. Background: Great Tit *Parus major*, Common Chaffinch *Fringilla coelebs* and Eurasian Siskin *Spinus spinus*. 06.003.DF.00834.01

Grey Wagtails look like darts when they hurtle past high overhead. Their flight calls often sound like a more piercing version of the disyllabic call of White Wagtail, with shorter, higher-pitched notes and slightly longer gaps between them.

really *chichik* because the second syllable isn't that different from the first. We both find this type of birdie talk exasperating. Here is a very typical recording of White Wagtail flying past (**CD2-09**), which we used in a recent paper comparing these calls in Dutch Birding (Robb et al 2010), followed by a recording of a large flock (**CD2-10**). Compare them with a smaller flock of Pied flying over Durlston (**CD2-11**). Although White and Pied Wagtails' *chichik* calls are not safely distinguishable, Pied Wagtail often uses a rasping call while migrating that we have never heard from a White Wagtail (**CD2-12**).

Pied Wagtail *Motacilla yarrellii* Durlston, Dorset, England, 09:02, 8 October 2008. Flight calls of a migrating flock, with one individual passing at particularly close range. Background: Rook *Corvus frugilegus*, Carrion Crow *C corone*, Common Chaffinch *Fringilla coelebs*, European Goldfinch *Carduelis carduelis* and Eurasian Siskin *Spinus spinus*. 081008.MR.090228.02 **CD2-11**

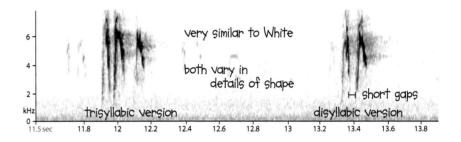

CD2-10 **White Wagtail** *Motacilla alba* Burgas lake, Burgas, Bulgaria, 18:58, 20 September 2007. A large flock of migrants flying along the shore of a lake, possibly looking for a suitable reedbed in which to roost. Background: Mallard *Anas platyrhynchos*, yellow wagtail *Motacilla* and a frog *Rana*. 070920.MR.185805.02

Pied Wagtail *Motacilla yarrellii* Durlston, Dorset, England, 09:21, 9 October 2008. Rasping calls and flight calls of several while migrating. Background: Herring Gull *Larus argentatus*, European Robin *Erithacus rubecula*, Eurasian Magpie *Pica pica*, Carrion Crow *Corvus corone*, European Goldfinch *Carduelis carduelis* and Eurasian Bullfinch *Pyrrhula pyrrhula*. 081009.MR.092148.01 **CD2-12**

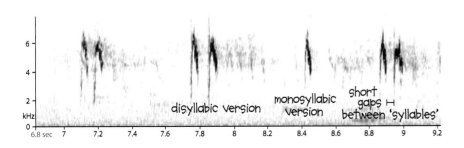

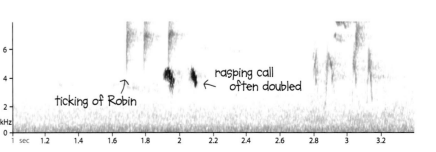

Listening to this recording of a single migrant passing at close range, it is apparent that they also have monosyllabic and trisyllabic calls (**CD2-13**).

To me, a flock of of migrating Yellow Wagtails is a sound of late summer. They move through in August and September and are rare by October. The monosyllabic flight call is a wedge of sound, thick at the front and narrowing to a whistle at the end. In autumn, there is a possibility that some of our yellow wagtails may be Blue-headed Wagtails from the continent, which have indistinguishable flight calls. The migrant in the recording was certainly of the British taxon *flavissima*, although it was actually recorded in Holland in spring (**CD2-14**).

CD2-13   **Grey Wagtail** *Motacilla cinerea* de Nolledijk, Zeeland, Netherlands, 09:44, 3 November 2006. Single, double and triple flight calls of a passing migrant. Background: Dunnock *Prunella modularis*, European Robin *Erithacus rubecula*, Fieldfare *Turdus pilaris*, Goldcrest *Regulus regulus*, Eurasian Magpie *Pica pica*, Western Jackdaw *Corvus monedula*, Common Chaffinch *Fringilla coelebs*, Eurasian Bullfinch *Pyrrhula pyrrhula* and Common Reed Bunting *Emberiza schoeniclus*. 061103.MR.94409.12

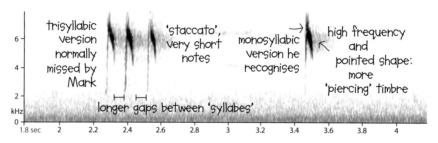

CD2-14   **Yellow Wagtail** *Motacilla flavissima* IJmuiden, Noord-Holland, Netherlands, 20 April 2003. Loud flight calls of a flushed adult male on spring migration. Background: gulls *Larus*. 03.010.MR.04705.11

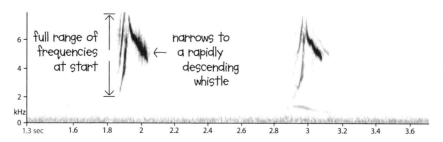

144

If pipits and wagtails are the bread and butter of learning flight calls, larks are the jam. Every time I hear a Skylark migrating, it's a treat. We usually recognise them by a fruity *chirrup*. There are so many variants of this call that it often seems as if each one could be a fragment of song. Here is one calling beautifully on the day of my exam (**CD2-15**). If Skylark is a treat, a migrating Woodlark's musical calls can make a morning (**CD2-16**). As for Horned Lark, we keep a defibrillator besides the toilet block at South Haven just in case we hear this very special bird flying up the beach (**CD2-17**).

It may come as a surprise to some that we see woodpeckers migrating. In October, one or two Great Spotted Woodpeckers can be seen undulating past in a single day. They sometimes pass silently, but here in Poole most of them give this call (**CD2-18**).

CD2-15 **Eurasian Skylark** *Alauda arvensis* Ballard Down, Dorset, England, 07:53, 12 October 2009. Four migrating on a windy morning, giving a lot of low, bubbling calls. Background: Meadow Pipit *Anthus* pratensis, Dunnock *Prunella modularis*, Common Blackbird *Turdus merula*, Long-tailed Tit *Aegithalos caudatus*, Carrion Crow *Corvus corone*, Common Chaffinch *Fringilla coelebs* and Eurasian Bullfinch *Pyrrhula pyrrhula* 091012.MC.075338.23

Horned Lark *Eremophila alpestris* IJmuiden, Noord-Holland, Netherlands, 17 October 2001. Typical flight calls of a single individual on migration flight. Background: Eurasian Whimbrel *Numenius phaeopus*, Eurasian Skylark *Alauda arvensis*, Rock Pipit *Anthus petrosus*, Common Blackbird *Turdus merula*, Song Thrush *T philomelos* and House Sparrow *Passer domesticus*. 01.041.MR.12242.12 CD2-17

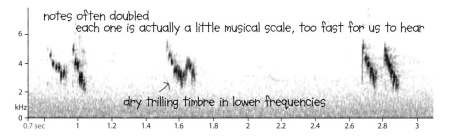

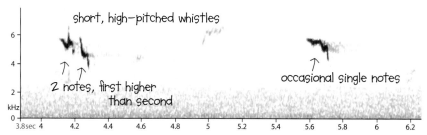

CD2-16 **Woodlark** *Lullula arborea* Breskens, Zeeland, Netherlands, 10:44, 23 March 2006. Two migrating, using a variety of calls. Background: gulls *Larus* and European Greenfinch *Chloris chloris*. 06.002.MR.14322.13

Great Spotted Woodpecker *Dendrocopos major* de Nolledijk, Zeeland, Netherlands, 10:26, 7 November 2006. Calls of a bird that appeared to be migrating as it arrived, although it then landed in some trees instead of crossing the Westerschelde estuary. Background: Common Blackbird *Turdus merula*. 061107.MR.102647.10 CD2-18

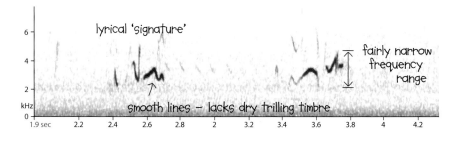

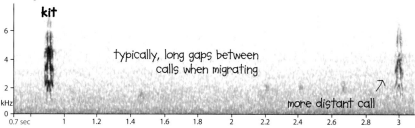

Hirundines pass a little later in the day than most migrants, and their calls are constantly in the air as the birds migrate. Barn Swallow flight calls are liquid, rising notes, on a background of cheerful song fragments (**CD2-19**). One evening when thousands were passing through the harbour, Mo and I saw a Red-rumped Swallow near Higher Bushey farm. Sadly, no one else got there before it moved on. Red-rumped Swallows can be picked up on call. The rippling quality and double length help to separate them from Barn Swallows if you are lucky enough to come across one (**CD2-20**). Flight calls of House Martin are hard, little two-part rattles (**CD2-21**), while Sand Martin flight calls are similar, but softer and more gravelly (**CD2-22**).

CD2-19   **Barn Swallow** *Hirundo rustica* Durankulak lake, Dobrich, Bulgaria, 19:07, 16 September 2007. A mass arrival of swallows on the Bulgarian coast, after a day of strong northwestern winds that had blown these migrants out over the Black Sea. 070916. MR.190705.12

Common House Martin *Delichon urbicum* Carnsore Point, Wexford, Ireland, 10:04, 24 August 2006. Calls of a migrant, heading out towards France or northern Spain from the southeast corner of Ireland. Background: Sandwich Tern *Sterna sandvicensis*, Collared Dove *Streptopelia decoacto*, Barn Swallow *Hirundo rustica*, Sand Martin *Riparia riparia* and Dunnock *Prunella modularis*. 060824.MR.100411.32   **CD2-21**

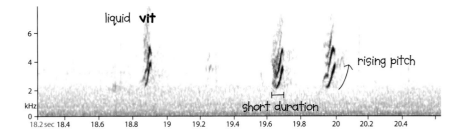

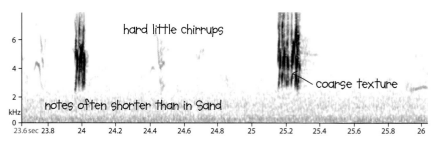

CD2-20   **Red-rumped Swallow** *Cecropis daurica* Atanasovo lake, Burgas, Bulgaria, 13:22, 22 September 2007. At least two migrating, one of which was an adult. Background: sparrows *Passer*. 070922.MR.132212.32

Sand Martin *Riparia riparia* Carnsore Point, Wexford, Ireland, 10:05, 24 August 2006. Calls of a migrant heading out over the sea. Background: Sandwich Tern *Sterna sandvicensis*, Collared Dove *Streptopelia decoacto*, Common House Martin *Delichon urbicum*, Eurasian Wren *Troglodytes troglodytes* and Dunnock *Prunella modularis*. 060824.MR.100553.12   **CD2-22**

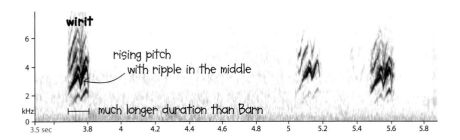

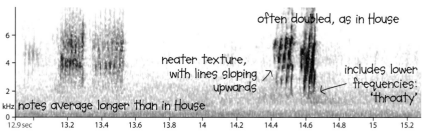

CD2-23 **Song Thrush** *Turdus philomelos* IJmuiden, Noord-Holland, Netherlands, 09:55, 13 October 2001. Flight calls of a passing migrant. Background: Eurasian Skylark *Alauda arvensis*, Meadow Pipit *Anthus pratensis* and Common Chaffinch *Fringilla coelebs*. 01.017.AB.01606.02

Migrating Song Thrushes have very short calls. Their extreme brevity and high pitch make them difficult for some of us to hear. If it hadn't been for the calls of the birds migrating on the morning we saw 6,000, though, we might have assumed they were Redwings. In **CD2-23**, a recording of birds migrating along the Dutch coast, they have been brought closer by using a parabolic dish. While many arrive to spend the winter in Britain, others winter much further south. In the next recording (**CD2-24**), you can hear Song Thrushes starting the sea crossing to Africa from the southwest corner of Europe. Their tiny flight calls are a little more varied than usual here, perhaps because they have just noticed that a Long-eared Owl is migrating along the same route. The whole scene was illuminated as the birds passed a floodlit fortress.

Redwings have flight calls that are equally high pitched, but long, descending and rapidly modulated, which gives them their characteristic *zzzzz* quality. In this recording (**CD2-25**) you can hear a mass exodus from Helgoland in the southern North Sea. After crossing the Low Countries and the English Channel, some of these birds could have reached Poole a day or two later. Blackbird's migration call is more like a slow cicada. They are less descending in pitch than Redwing, and have a slower modulation. In this dish recording (**CD2-26**), you can hear natural-sounding calls at a distance, followed by a couple of very close ones that are not how we usually hear them.

Redwing *Turdus iliacus* Helgoland, Schleswig-Holstein, Germany, 19:22, 12 October 2007. Departure of nocturnal migrants from a North Sea island. Background: Eurasian Skylark *Alauda arvensis*, Common Blackbird *T merula* and Song Thrush *T philomelos*. 071012.MR.192201.12 CD2-25

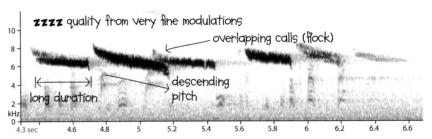

CD2-24 **Song Thrush** *Turdus philomelos* Sagres, Algarve, Portugal, 22:05, 16 October 2009. Excited flight calls of two nocturnal migrants flying over a floodlit fortress, the last building in Europe, as they notice a Long-eared Owl *Asio otus* migrating on the same track. Background: surf. 091016.MR.220506.11

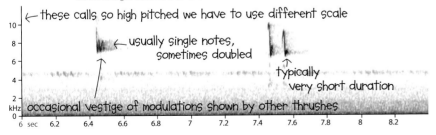

Common Blackbird *Turdus merula* IJmuiden, Noord-Holland, Netherlands, 31 October 2002. Two migrating, passing at very close range. Background: Eurasian Skylark *Alauda arvensis* and Western Jackdaw *Corvus monedula*. 02.052.MR.00209.03 CD2-26

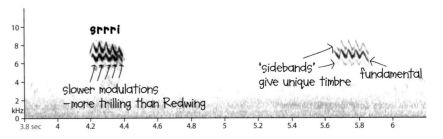

The latter three thrushes are mainly nocturnal migrants, and Redwing in particular can often be heard at night, but there are two thrushes that are more often heard migrating during the day. Both have different, much lower-pitched flight calls. Mistle Thrushes have a short harsh rattle, a bit like the sound of drawing one's finger across a comb (**CD2-27**), while Fieldfares give a great variety of goblin-like chuckles and *queep* calls as they fly above the Redwings in small flocks (**CD2-28**).

In the past, Starlings roosted in large numbers at South Haven. In recent winters they have preferred to collect around the Royal National Lifeboat Institute along Holes Bay and around Selsdown Bridge, sometimes in tens of thousands. These giant roosting flocks come and go in smaller groups, often leaving in giant concentric circles as they spread out to forage (see chapter 13). Small flocks pass South Haven looking a bit like Redwings. When migrants pass you at close range, you are more likely to hear their wings than the low-pitched flight call (**CD2-29**).

CD2-27   **Mistle Thrush** *Turdus viscivorus* IJmuiden, Noord-Holland, Netherlands, 17 October 2006. Two migrating, flying away from the recordist. Background: European Robin *Erithacus rubecula*, Western Jackdaw *Corvus monedula* and Common Chaffinch *Fringilla coelebs*. 061017.MR.90011.22

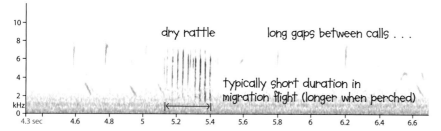

CD2-28   **Fieldfare** *Turdus pilaris* de Nolledijk, Zeeland, Netherlands, 10:43, 3 November 2006. Calls of a migrating flock. Background: Eurasian Wren *Troglodytes troglodytes*, Dunnock *Prunella modularis*, European Robin *Erithacus rubecula*, Redwing *T iliacus*, Western Jackdaw *Corvus monedula* and Common Chaffinch *Fringilla coelebs*. 061103. MR.104302.21

Common Starling *Sturnus vulgaris* de Nolledijk, Zeeland, Netherlands, 09:20, 7 November 2006. Flock of a couple of hundred migrating. As usual, only a few calls are heard and it is the wing sound (yellow) that dominates. Background: Common Pheasant *Phasianus colchicus*, Eurasian Wren *Troglodytes troglodytes* and Common Blackbird *Turdus merula*. 061107.MR.92056.31   **CD2-29**

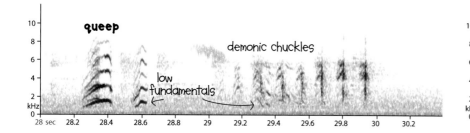

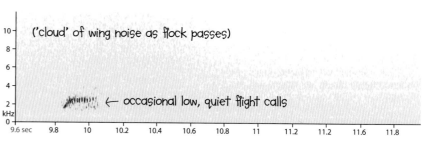

Tree Sparrows are rare in the harbour, but we occasionally get the odd one or two migrating. A variety of calls can be heard as they fly past, most of which are higher-pitched than the equivalent calls of House Sparrow. The one to listen out for is the main flight call, a relatively deep, wooden-sounding *tuv* (**CD2-30**). House Sparrows are resident here, and they could pass a migration watch point at any time. Their flight call is a much longer, disyllabic and nasal-sounding *chuwiv* (**CD2-31**). In flocks, the length of individual birds' flight calls influences the collective sound. The Tree Sparrows' shorter calls leave gaps in the flock sound, whereas House Sparrows, with longer calls, can attain a saturated flock sound with fewer birds.

CD2-30   **Eurasian Tree Sparrow** *Passer montanus* Breskens, Zeeland, Netherlands, 09:15, 23 March 2006. A migrating flock passes at very close range. Background: Mallard *Anas platyrhynchos*, Great Tit *Parus major* and Common Reed Bunting *Emberiza schoeniclus*. 06.002.MR.11504.12

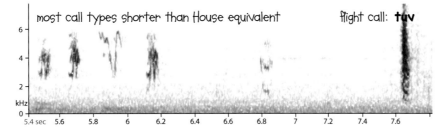

CD2-31   **House Sparrow** *Passer domesticus* Batalha, Alentejo, Portugal, 17:17, 14 March 2010. Small groups taking off in dribs and drabs from a pre-roost gathering. Background: European Stonechat *Saxicola rubicola*, Cetti's Warbler *Cettia cetti* and Zitting Cisticola *Cisticola juncidis*. 100314.MR.171734.22

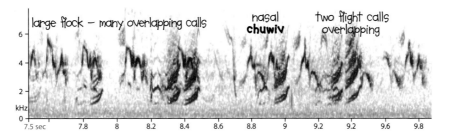

Bearded Reedlings are always entertaining to watch, especially when they migrate. Magnus often saw them attempting this along the Dutch coast. When they finally get going, after many false starts, their progress seems painfully slow on short, unsuitable wings. Their calls are unmistakable, and we once had a troop take off from the reed bed at South Haven sounding just like these ones in the Netherlands (**CD2-32**). Each note is a *ping* with a buzzing 'tail'.

Bearded Reedling *Panurus biarmicus*, Swineham Point, Dorset, 23 May 2010 (*Nick Hopper*)

Hearing a good bird before you see it is a common experience for a birder. This was best summed up for me when Ewan, Shaun, Graham Armstrong and Iain Prophet were at Lytchett Bay, standing on the bank looking into the field for Jack Snipe.

Graham heard a sound he recognised, turned round, pointed into the sky calling "Waxwing", and then they all watched it fly over towards the water works. "You could even see the yellow band on its tail when it flew off, calling as it went," said Shaun **(CD2-33)**.

CD2-32 **Bearded Reedling** *Panurus biarmicus* IJmuiden, Noord-Holland, Netherlands, 10:00, 27 October 2005. A small flock attempting to migrate. Background: Meadow Pipit *Anthus pratensis*. 05.028.MR.02507.31

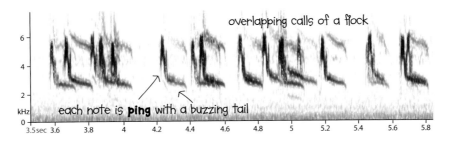

CD2-33 **Bohemian Waxwing** *Bombycilla garrulus* Castricum, Noord-Holland, Netherlands, 09:50, 14 November 2005. Calls of a passing migrant. In this recording you can hear the Doppler effect (think of a passing train): the first two calls are given while approaching the observer, and sound higher pitched, while the last two are departing and sound lower-pitched. Background: European Robin *Erithacus rubecula*, Fieldfare *Turdus pilaris*, Song Thrush *T philomelos*, Redwing *T iliacus*, Common Starling *Sturnus vulgaris*, Eurasian Siskin *Spinus spinus* and Parakeet Crossbill *Loxia curvirostra* type X. 05.031.MR.10136.13

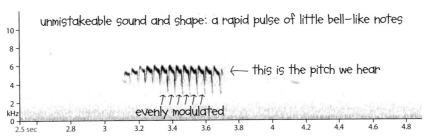

Chapter 15: With this ring

When I think of Aquatic Warbler, I just sigh. I think I'm the only Poole pub regular who has never seen one. I just tried a hopeful text to Shaun. "Have you ever seen or ringed an Aquatic in Poole Harbour?" "Yes, many at Keysworth," was the reply. I'm resigned to never seeing one in Poole Harbour.

Ticking birds that have been caught for ringing is slightly frowned upon. Ringers keep a 'ringing list', and birders worry about listing something in the hand. In Poole Harbour, Steve Smith came up with a simple guideline when we were comparing lists. The only species we could tick in the hand were Grasshopper Warbler (**CD2-34** and **CD2-35**) and Aquatic Warbler. Any other species had to be free flying. Ridiculous as it may seem, while the ringers were catching 21 of the stripey little blighters in 1992, I was searching the harbour's sedge beds pishing and generally believing I could find one without resorting to hanging around the ringing station. I even searched the opposite shore of the Piddle at the crack of dawn on various late August mornings, hoping for a crumb from their table. By the time I had lowered my standards and started to visit the ringers, it was all over and they were catching nothing.

CD2-34   **Common Grasshopper Warbler** *Locustella naevia* Keysworth, Poole Harbour, Dorset, England, 16 August 2000. Two *tak* calls of an adult female in the hand. Background: Mark discussing sounds with the ringers, and in the distance, ringer's lure tape with Aquatic Warbler. 00.017.MC.02903.30

Aquatic Warbler *Acrocephalus paludicola*, adult, trapped at Bloemendaal ringing station, Noord-Holland, Netherlands, 23 August 1997 (*Arnoud B van den Berg/Vrs van Lennep*)

Common Grasshopper Warbler *Locustella naevia* Keysworth, Poole Harbour, Dorset, England, 18 August 2000. Juvenile calls: some harsh distress calls in the hand, then a *plit* call on being released. At the time, the ringer commented that he regarded this call as typical of juveniles when released. Background: commentary from Mark, and as always, ringer's lure tape with Aquatic Warbler. 00.018.MC.01010.31   CD2-35

Finding or catching Aquatics all comes down to the weather. Ian Lewis illustrated the point in the 1995 bird report. "In the early part of August an area of low pressure remained North of Britain producing a north westerly air flow. Then on the 6th high pressure with weak easterlies settled over the south and three birds were trapped the following day. From the 7th to the 22nd the wind remained mainly in the east and a further nine birds were trapped. On the 13th a front lay over southern England with a low to the north and a high pressure to the south. Any birds migrating from the continent encountering these conditions would probably make landfall as indicated by the four Aquatics trapped on the next morning" (Ian Lewis in Ashby 1995).

At that time we knew these warblers were breeding in Poland, Belarus and Hungary, but the wintering grounds were a mystery. An Aquatic Warbler had been trapped by ringers in Djoudj National Park in northwestern Senegal on 8 February 1993, but it wasn't until 2007 that a Birdlife International team confirmed that this was one of their most important wintering grounds. The way they did it was very clever. They got ringers to collect feathers from adult birds caught in Poole and other European ringing stations, knowing that certain feathers would have been grown on the African wintering grounds. They compared the patterns of the feathers' isotopes with the patterns on isotope maps of West Africa and found what looked like a perfect match in Djoudj. Sending in a team, they estimated that a third of the world's population was wintering in the park, in an area of just 100 km² (van den Berg 1993, 2007; BirdLife News February 2007).

Ringing stations are powered by sound. At Keysworth, the private estate on the northern banks of the River Piddle, the Stour Ringing Group used to broadcast birds songs to the skies during consecutive autumns from 1991 to 2000. Grasshopper, Reed, Sedge and Aquatic Warblers were all played from a multitude of tape machines. This effort bagged them some impressive totals, including 82 Aquatics, most of which were caught in the first seven years.

The Stour Ringing Group is organised by amateurs, each of whom used to take their annual holiday to man the station at Keysworth or got up at dawn to fit ringing in before work. When Aquatics became rarer, their enthusiasm started to wane. Then the Keysworth estate changed hands to a less sympathetic owner and the ringing station had to be closed. Shaun wanted to set up a station in Lytchett Bay. Having the necessary permissions to tape lure, he set up a tape to start 45 minutes before dawn on chosen mornings. Bob Gifford provides the tapes for the Stour Ringing Group and has made and installed the broadcasting equipment.

The sounds on a ringer's tapes are selected with all the attention a chap might employ when choosing music for a lover. Made on dark winter evenings, they lay bare the hopes and dreams of the maker. So, for example, along with the warbler species

that are the staple catches in a reed bed, in goes a bit of Pallas's Grasshopper Warbler, Bluethroat and Scarlet Rosefinch, and this is topped off with a good strong helping of Aquatic Warbler. For the ringers among our readers, Magnus and I made our own version. Each sound has been chosen to best create the feeling of a party going on (**CD2-36**).

Magnus and Mark's jammy ringers' tape lure, with the month September in mind. CD2-36
Featuring:
Bluethroat *Luscinia svecica azuricollis* Sierra de Candelario, Castilla y Leon, Spain, 09:35, 1 June 2011 (110601.MR.093546.01);
Pallas's Grasshopper Warbler *Locustella certhiola* Chernava Rechka, Tomsk, Russia, 11:00, 11 July 2011 (110711.AB.110000.01);
Common Grasshopper Warbler *Locustella naevia* Biebrza marshes, Podlaskie, Poland, 20:00, 9 May 2005 (05.009.MR.00723.01);
Marsh Warbler *Acrocephalus palustris* Polder Achteraf, Noord-Holland, Netherlands, 04:45, 13 June 2006 (060613.MR.045557.01);
Eurasian Reed Warbler *Acrocephalus scirpaceus* Giethoorn, Overijssel, Netherlands, 04:19, 7 June 2006 (060607.MR.41910.01);
Sedge Warbler *Acrocephalus schoenobaenus* Tienhovense Plassen, Noord-Holland, Netherlands, 02:23, 16 June 2006 (060616.MR.22310.00);
Aquatic Warbler *Acrocephalus paludicola* Biebrza marshes, Podlaskie, Poland, 01:00, 15 May 2005 (05.013.MR.00415.00);
Great Reed Warbler *Acrocephalus arundinaceus* Oostelijke Binnenpolder, Noord-Holland, Netherlands, 02:54, 5 June 2006 (060605.MR.25410a.01);
Common Rosefinch *Carpodacus erythrinus* Jalman meadows, Tuv Almag, Mongolia, 06:06, 25 May 2008 (080525.MR.060618.10);
Yellow Warbler *Setophaga petechia* Fairbanks, Alaska, USA, 12:00, 19 June 2004 (04.020.AB.01951.01).

Aquatic Warbler song is fairly repetitive, so after a few mornings of passive listening while the nets are being checked and the birds ringed, you become familiar with it. At 08:30 on 16 August 2005, Bob and Shaun were packing up to leave the ringing site, and knowing that they weren't coming back the next day, Bob disconnected the battery from the timer and speakers. As they left, a familiar song started from the reeds. Nothing registered for about 30 seconds. Then absent-mindedly, Shaun shouted to

Bob to disconnect the Aquatic tape. "I have", shouted Bob. "It's coming from the other side of the reed bed." An Aquatic Warbler singing? Shaun couldn't believe it. They rushed over to the reed bed and scanned, but there was no sign, and frustratingly the bird had gone silent.

He came to the conclusion that it had to be me hidden in the reeds playing the song to trick him. He still suspects that, although he has put Aquatic Warbler on his Lytchett list. I promised to come clean in this book.

I find it just as hard predicting a whole series of other warblers in Poole Harbour. Take Wood Warbler, which is always difficult to pin down in the spring, the only time of year when we have a real chance of finding it. There's a small wood between the Arne road and The Moors that has sprung up around the high, moss-covered banks of a Saxon ruin. Sometimes in spring, less often nowadays, a male Wood Warbler will stop by to sing there for a few days. At one time they bred in Slepe Copse, and over the years I've heard several sing on the wooded slopes of Nine Barrow Down.

Recent research has shown that the number of Wood Warblers in a particular wood is correlated with fluctuations in the size of rodent populations, rather than the availability of food. Apparently, returning males can quickly sense whether the woodland has a high mouse population and, if it has, they move on to inspect other woods until they find a suitable one to start singing and attracting females. Since Wood Warblers nest on the ground, their eggs could be eaten, not only by mice but also by their predators. It must have been a bad mouse year in 1988, because three pairs stayed on to breed.

The six most common breeding warblers in Poole Harbour include three summer visitors - Reed Warbler, Common Whitethroat (**CD2-37**) and Willow Warbler (**CD2-38**) - as well as Dartford Warbler, Blackcap and Chiffchaff (**CD2-39**), which can be found all year round. Poole is unusual in that many of its warblers overwinter. Cetti's Warbler (**CD2-40**), Blackcaps and Chiffchaffs all started wintering in Poole, surprisingly during the colder '70s, and recent warmer winters have helped them expand their range. In the case of Cetti's, they are thought to have arrived here by way of Kent.

Common Whitethroat *Sylvia communis* Middlebere, Poole Harbour, Dorset, England, 05:40, 14 May 2010. Song of a male. The first strophe is in flight, then as a second strophe it does a perfect imitation of a Eurasian Skylark *Alauda arvensis*. Background: Mallard *Anas platyrhynchos*, Common Redshank *Tringa totanus*, Collared Dove *Streptopelia decaocto*, Green Woodpecker *Picus viridis*, Barn Swallow *Hirundo rustica*, Eurasian Wren *Troglodytes troglodytes*, Eurasian Blackcap *Sylvia atricapilla*, Common Chiffchaff *Phylloscopus collybita*, Common Chaffinch *Fringilla coelebs* and European Goldfinch *Carduelis carduelis*. 100514.MC.054042.02   **CD2-37**

Willow Warbler *Phylloscopus trochilus* Sunnyside Farm, Poole Harbour, Dorset, England, 08:50, 24 April 2010. Song of an adult. Background: Northern Lapwing *Vanellus vanellus*, Common Blackbird *Turdus merula*, Common Chiffchaff *Phylloscopus collybita* and Common Chaffinch *Fringilla coelebs*. 100424.MC.085018.11   **CD2-38**

Common Chiffchaff *Phylloscopus collybita* and steam train, Corfe Castle, Poole Harbour, Dorset, England, 09:00, 1 June 2008. Song of an adult, with *trr-trr* notes in between strophes (equivalent to the *CHUvit* of Siberian Chiffchaff). From 2:00, the train and Song Thrush *Turdus philomelos* carry on as children play nearby. Background: Eurasian Wren *Troglodytes troglodytes*, European Robin *Erithacus rubecula*, Common Blackbird *T merula*, Common Chaffinch *Fringilla coelebs* and European Greenfinch *Chloris chloris*. 08.013.MC.11310.20   **CD2-39**

Cetti's Warbler *Cettia cetti* Middlebere, Poole Harbour, Dorset, England, 09:48, 29 April 2011. A single explosive song from a distance. Background: Canada Goose *Branta canadensis*, Common Cuckoo *Cuculus canorus*, Song Thrush *Turdus philomelos*, Eurasian Reed Warbler *Acrocephalus scirpaceus*, Common Chiffchaff *Phylloscopus collybita* and European Blue Tit *Cyanistes caeruleus*. 110429.MC.094801.01   **CD2-40**

Poole Harbour has a third of Dorset's Cetti's Warblers, and 6% of the British population. There are around 30 singing males from the Corfe River valley round to Lytchett (which has 11 pairs), and Hatch Pond where there are three singing males.

A wintering Yellow-browed Warbler was found just around the corner from Sainsbury's by Jill Bale, one of our more persistent lady birders. It spent its time in the back gardens and scrubby edge along the west side of Poole Park. My dentist's practice overlooks a neat shrub-bordered garden there, and I'm proud to say that while having a tooth capped I managed to squint through the goggles, past the drill and beyond the reflection of two white coats, to get a glimpse of the Yellow-browed feeding in his garden.

Common Firecrest *Regulus ignicapilla*, Studland, Dorset, 28 October 2011 (*Nick Hopper*)

Yellow-browed Warblers are best found by call. There have been more than 10 now in autumn, and another one wintered in 2003/04 in the bushes along the edge of Border Drive at Lytchett. If you would like to find one of the 'autumn' warblers like Pallas's Leaf Warbler or Yellow-browed Warbler you have a difficult choice. I found the first Pallas's for the harbour while birding on the end of Pilot's Point with my daughter Claire (then aged 9) on 25 October 1999. She still remembers it fondly. I was teaching her to make the Stonechat's tongue-clicking call, and as she did it a Pallas's flew up on to a piece of gorse next to us, had a look, and dived into cover. Nick found another rather obliging bird at the start of the path to Old Harry in 2007 after trying to relocate a Yellow-browed he had found half an hour earlier. The same rather, shall we say, sensitive site has now hosted quite a few Yellow-browed.

So, to find these you have a choice: visit the dentist, hang around on the edge of a nudist colony with a child, or spend the day with binoculars looking in a tree directly above the ladies' toilets in Studland village, on the way to Old Harry.

The final sound in this chapter is a biological curiosity. It's a song made by a Firecrest but it sounds a bit like a Goldcrest (**CD2-41**). Firecrests arrive here in the autumn and often overwinter. In 2012 a pair built a lovely nest on Brownsea near the heronry. Because they are not regular breeders a young male that stays on to attempt breeding will have no other males to sing against. This encourages a phenomenon known as mixed singing where the stranger picks up phrases of its closest relative. Some times over a period of three years the mixed singer may adopt the complete song of the more common species, in this case Goldcrest. These birds aren't hybrids, rather they are confused. There is another bird that turns up in Poole that gets everyone confused. Siberian Chiffchaff.

CD2-41 **Common Firecrest (mixed singer)** *Regulus ignicapilla* Studland churchyard, Poole Harbour, Dorset, England, 11:14, 4 April 2008. Song with characteristics of both Goldcrest *R regulus* and Firecrest. Nothing in the appearance of this bird suggested that it was a hybrid. Background: Eurasian Wren *Troglodytes troglodytes*, Dunnock *Prunella modularis*, Common Blackbird *Turdus merula*, Common Chiffchaff *Phylloscopus collybita*, Western Jackdaw *Corvus monedula*, Carrion Crow *C corone* and Common Chaffinch *Fringilla coelebs*. 080404.MR.111428.23

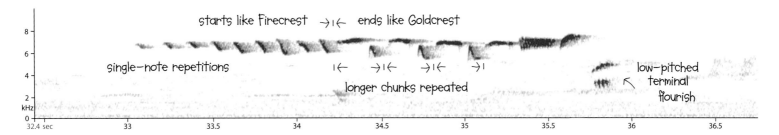

Chapter 16: Drab

I once asked bird artists Killian Mullarney and Lars Jonsson how many birds they identified first by sound. Both are authors of field guides, and both are excellent field birders with a strong visual bias. Killian said, "I detect about 80% of birds by sound, then if they're interesting I follow them up", while Lars said, "I identify around 60% of birds by sound first." This is in my opinion the best kept secret in birding.

In *The Sound Approach to birding* (2006), I showed how sonagrams can help us in the struggle to make sense of bird sounds. The simple 'shapes' of four calls commonly used by adult Common Chiffchaff, Siberian Chiffchaff, Iberian Chiffchaff and Willow Warbler offered a straightforward introduction to sonagrams. Further inside the book, I made an attempt to explain a call given by Common Chiffchaffs, often in the autumn and occasionally year round.

If you find a Siberian Chiffchaff in Holland, the Dutch rarities committee has decided that songs and calls can be used as the definitive means of identifying it, just as Eastern and Western Bonelli's Warblers are best separated by calls, or Iberian Chiffchaff and Common Chiffchaff. The British rarities committee decided in 2008 that Siberian Chiffchaff occurred too frequently to be vetted by them, and now if you find one you send your record to the local committee. Ours in Dorset accepts Siberian Chiffchaffs if heard to give diagnostic songs or calls. Birds that are silent are described as "having the characteristics of…"

So that's that then. But somehow it's not. We still have difficulty getting people to be less concerned about obscure field marks on Siberian Chiffchaffs, when sounds are the obvious key to identification. There seems to be confusion and it's coming in part from ornithologist Alan Dean, who has published various papers on the subject in *British Birds* and contributed many postings to internet forums.

It's difficult to work out exactly what worries him, but it's fairly obvious that he would prefer some visual features to be regarded as the primary, and most reliable means of identifying Siberian Chiffchaff. To that end, he published a paper in *British Birds* including a selection of colour swatches from Smithe's *Naturalist's color guide* (1975), asking observers to match the upperpart colour of Siberian Chiffchaffs to the swatches (Dean 2008). The colours range from 'pale neutral grey' through 'buff-yellow' and on to 'drab'. Reading Alan's internet contributions, he worries that we are misidentifying Common Chiffchaffs from Scandinavia *P c abietinus*.

Somewhere on the western edge of Siberia, the range of Scandinavian *abietinus* comes to an end and Siberian Chiffchaff's range begins. Although I've never met Alan, I offered him a visit

Siberian Chiffchaff *Phylloscopus collybita tristis*, 'grey-and-white', De Bilt, Utrecht, Netherlands, 16 February 2007 (*Arnoud B van den Berg*). Thanks to its calls, of which some 20 were recorded for the Sound Approach archives, this winterer was accepted by the Dutch rarities committee. It stayed until 9 April.

to this area with a sound recordist to find out how eastern *abietinus*, hybrids and western *tristis* really look and sound. He turned the offer down. Perhaps he thought that I was going to send him to Siberia without a return ticket.

Shaun found the first calling Siberian Chiffchaff for Poole Harbour on 22 November 1998, in the wood behind Knoll Beach car park on Studland. In the 2002 Dorset bird report, James wrote a review of Siberian Chiffchaffs, splitting the records between those that had been heard to vocalise (14 records) and those that hadn't (eight).

More recently, Iain Prophet found what he presumed to be a Siberian Chiffchaff in the outflow bushes behind PC World in mid-February 2009. He hadn't heard it call, so Nick, who had made it his mission to find and hear calling as many as possible in the harbour, was quick to follow up on the report. The whole area was busy with wintering chiffchaffs, and by the time Nick finished he had identified three *tristis* there, all giving the classic *tristis* call. The first was a classic brown bird, but the other two were sporting the so-called 'grey and white' plumage, regarded by Alan Dean as incompatible with *tristis*.

Worrying that he should back up the identification further or face a barrage of abuse from some of the more plumage-orientated old guard, Nick persuaded Shaun to try and catch them to procure a feather or two for DNA analysis. Their attempt was unsuccessful. While trying, however, they were delighted to hear one of the 'grey and white' birds singing a perfect *tristis* song. This bird stayed the longest of the three, and continued to sing on and off for the remainder of its four-week stay, becoming quite popular and even being given a name.

Siberian Chiffchaff *Phylloscopus collybita tristis*, Wessex Gate Retail Park, Poole, Dorset, 11 March 2009 *(Nick Hopper)*. The bird was named 'Patch' as it was easily identified by its plumage.

In the Urals, there is a narrow 'contact zone' where *abietinus* and *tristis* meet and their breeding ranges overlap, with some hybridisation going on. In order to sidestep this much-exaggerated problem, Arnoud visited Sergey Gashkov, a birder and sound-recordist who works at the Zoological Museum of Tomsk State University in Tomsk, Siberia, 1600 km east of the contact zone. There he recorded the full vocabulary of Siberian Chiffchaff. Magnus analysed Arnoud's recordings when he got back, and I've asked Magnus to take you through the full repertoire of *tristis*. Here are his thoughts...

CD2-42 **Siberian Chiffchaff** *Phylloscopus collybita tristis* Kolarovo, Tomsk, Russia, 12:19, 6 July 2011. Calls of an adult in the presence of a Red-backed Shrike *Lanius collurio*. Presumably, the chiffchaff had a nest or young nearby. Background: Blyth's Reed Warbler *Acrocephalus dumetorum*. 110706.AB.121933.21

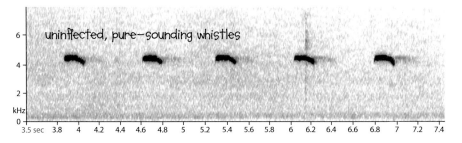

CD2-43a **Siberian Chiffchaff** *Phylloscopus collybita tristis* University campus park, Tomsk, 0:00-0:17 Russia, 07:30, 1 July 2011. Calls of an adult, probably at a nest. Background: song of Siberian Chiffchaff, Great Tit *Parus major*, Willow Tit *Poecile montanus* and Eurasian Magpie *Pica pica*. 110701.AB.073020.01

CD2-43b **Siberian Chiffchaff** *Phylloscopus collybita tristis* Kolarovo, Tomsk, Russia, 14:45, 6 July 0:18-0:34 2011. Calls of an adult near its fledged brood, perhaps alarmed by the presence of people. Background: Blyth's Reed Warbler *Acrocephalus dumetorum*. 110706. AB.144504.02

CD2-43c **Siberian Chiffchaff** *Phylloscopus collybita tristis* Kolarovo, Tomsk, Russia, 14:27, 6 July 0:35-0:53 2011. Calls of a pair of adults, with occasional husky calls of fledgling. Background: Steppe Buzzard *Buteo buteo vulpinus*, Blyth's Reed Warbler *Acrocephalus dumetorum* and Eurasian Magpie *Pica pica*. 110706.AB.142700.02

"As we described in *The Sound Approach to birding*, the typical call of adult Siberian Chiffchaff is very different from Common Chiffchaff, being an uninflected, pure-sounding whistle (**CD2-42**). These calls may be considered to have a plaintive, sad-sounding quality, and this together with the subdued plumage tones may be why Blyth chose the name *tristis* (sad) when he first described Siberian Chiffchaff in 1843.

While *tristis* calls usually sound uninflected to our ear, sonagrams seldom show a simple horizontal line. Typically, they are shaped more like a crescent or arch: slightly rising at the start, flatter in the middle, and descending at the end. There may be subtle deviations from this, most of which are not particularly audible. In **CD2-43**, you can hear a medley of three call sequences recorded near Tomsk, which show how little variation there exists in adult, breeding-season calls. We are not aware of any call differences between males and females, and the limited range of variation in adult calls suggests that if any exist they must be very subtle.

As we showed in *The Sound Approach to birding*, juvenile Common Chiffchaffs in summer can occasionally give very *tristis*-like calls. We have not heard these any later than mid-August. So

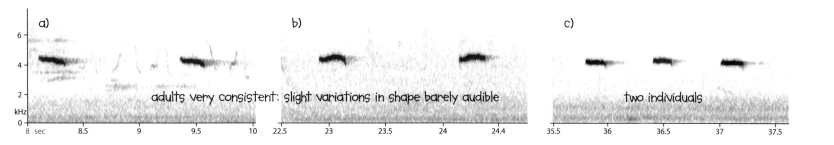

by the time *tristis* arrive in northwestern Europe in late autumn, chiffchaffs with *tristis*-like calls should indeed be Siberian. Arend Wassink's photographs of Siberians trapped in Kazakhstan (van den Berg & The Sound Approach 2009) show that the variation in the plumage and bare parts colouration of Siberian is considerable. Many birders, however, continue to believe in a mythical population of 'eastern *abietinus*' with *tristis*-like calls. I think I know how this may have come about.

When birders started visiting the Middle East en masse from the '80s, they commonly encountered birds with calls similar to *tristis* but an appearance much closer to *abietinus*. These birds were not, however, 'eastern *abietinus*'. Instead, they belonged to another branch of the chiffchaff genetic tree. In western Asia there are Common Chiffchaffs with calls very similar to *tristis*. I am not talking about the warm brown Caucasian Chiffchaff *P lorenzii*, sometimes referred to as 'Mountain Chiffchaff', which

replaces Common at high altitude in eastern Turkey and the Caucasus. Instead, I am talking about lower-altitude chiffchaffs much closer genetically and in their appearance to *collybita* and *abietinus* Common Chiffchaff than they are to either Caucasian Chiffchaff or Siberian Chiffchaff (Helbig et al 1996). These Common Chiffchaffs have been ascribed to three different subspecies: *brevirostris* in Anatolia, *caucasicus* in the Caucasus and *menzbieri* in northern Iran.

We have not recorded *menzbieri*, but we do have recordings of adult *brevirostris* from Turkey and *caucasicus* from Armenia. *Brevirostris* have calls that descend very slightly (**CD2-44**), but typical calls of *caucasicus* sound indistinguishable from *tristis* to our ears (**CD2-45**). Their songs on the other hand sound nothing like *tristis* at all, and show only slight differences from *collybita* and *abietinus* Common Chiffchaffs. None of these western Asian chiffchaffs are thought to migrate as far as *tristis*,

CD2-44   **Anatolian Common Chiffchaff** *Phylloscopus collybita brevirostris* Soğuksu national park, Kızılcahamam, Turkey, 9 May 2001. Calls of a presumed female, while a male sings in the background. Background: Coal Tit *Periparus ater* and Eurasian Nuthatch *Sitta europaea*. 01.018.MR.01621.11

Caucasian Common Chiffchaff *Phylloscopus collybita caucasicus* Dilijan, Tavush, Armenia, 12:34, 2 May 2011. Calls of a presumed female, alarmed by the presence of the recordist while nest-building. Background: Dunnock *Prunella modularis*, Green Warbler *Phylloscopus nitidus*, Eurasian Nuthatch *Sitta europaea* and Coal Tit *Periparus ater*. 110502.MR.123442.1   **CD2-45**

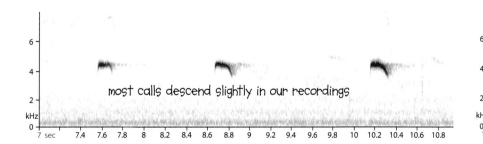

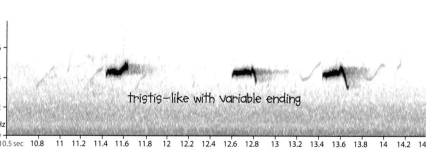

so they are unlikely to reach western Europe as *tristis* do. It is worth remembering that Green Warbler *P nitidus* breeds in the same part of the world, migrates further and is much easier to recognise, but has still been recorded only once in the UK.

Now we know that Siberian Chiffchaff is not the only chiffchaff with classic '*tristis*-like calls', let's flip the problem over and examine whether good Siberians ever have calls that deviate from the classic type. As we saw, there seems to be no evidence of this from adults recorded near Tomsk in July. However, juveniles just out of the nest do sound quite different from adults. As in other closely related *Phylloscopus* warblers, the calls of very young juveniles are quieter and huskier than adult calls. They have two main call types: contact calls that inform the adults and their siblings where they are, and begging calls that the contact calls change into when an adult arrives with food. Both of these call types can be heard in **CD2-46**.

Siberian Chiffchaff *Phylloscopus collybita tristis* Tugojakovka river, Tomsk, Russia, 07:22, 7 July 2011. A brood of three or four fledglings giving contact calls while the male sings, then begging calls when an adult comes to feed them from 00:18. Background: Great Spotted Woodpecker *Dendrocopos major*, Rufous-tailed Robin *Larvivora sibilans* and Common Rosefinch *Carpodacus erythrinus*. 110707.AB.072203.10

CD2-46

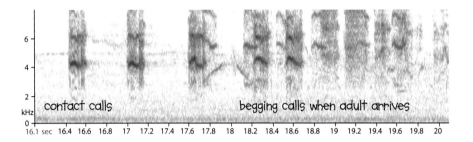

Interestingly, calls of very young *tristis* have variable inflections. They are typically flat or slightly descending, but sometimes rise audibly in pitch. In **CD2-47**, you can hear examples of descending and rising juvenile contact calls from Tomsk in mid-July.

CD2-47a
0:00-0:22

Siberian Chiffchaff *Phylloscopus collybita tristis* Kolarovo, Tomsk, Russia, 14:53, 6 July 2011. Contact calls of fledglings waiting to be fed by an adult, which can be heard at a distance. In this recording, most of the calls have a slightly descending inflection. Background: Barn Swallow *Hirundo rustica*. 110706.AB.145337.01

CD2-47b
0:22-0:46

Siberian Chiffchaff *Phylloscopus collybita tristis* Tugojakovla river, Tomsk, Russia, 07:14, 7 July 2011. Calls of fledglings waiting to be fed. Background: Great Spotted Woodpecker *Dendrocopos major*, Golden Oriole *Oriolus oriolus*, Eurasian Siskin *Spinus spinus* and Common Rosefinch *Carpodacus erythrinus*. 110707.AB.071404.31

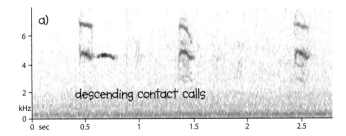

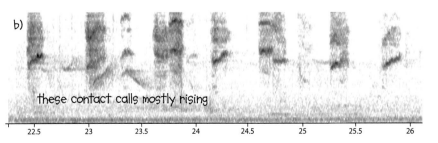

In Western Europe, we don't see Siberian Chiffchaffs until October, by which time their calls are no longer husky and usually sound very similar to adults. However, autumn Siberians don't always give classic *tristis* calls, and often show more inflection than we would expect. Perhaps we should not be surprised if some of the plasticity in calls of very young juveniles is retained in birds only three months older. Plasticity, as we explained in *The Sound Approach to birding*, is the greater variation audible in young birds still learning their sounds.

Like the fledglings from Tomsk, autumn vagrants not only give flat and slightly descending calls but occasionally also variants that are inflected upwards. Here is an example of a first-winter Siberian with very good credentials (it even sang), giving rising calls in October. It was recorded by Pim Wolf in the Netherlands (**CD2-48**).

Contact calls are not the only sounds with which we can readily identify a Siberian Chiffchaff. Fortunately, migrants and wintering birds sometimes sing, and their song is highly distinctive. As mentioned already, they have been heard singing in Poole Harbour in winter. Here is an example of adult song, one of the most characteristic sounds of the Siberian forests, recorded in Tomsk in early July (**CD2-49**). Note that it contains many rising notes, usually lacking in Common Chiffchaff songs, giving it a much more fluent and melodious character.

CD2-48 **Siberian Chiffchaff** *Phylloscopus collybita tristis* Westkapelle, Zeeland, Netherlands, 12 October 2005. Calls of a first-winter (the one that can be heard singing in CD2-51). Some of these calls have a strongly rising inflection. Background: Common Chaffinch *Fringilla coelebs* and Brambling *F montifringilla*. Pim Wolf.

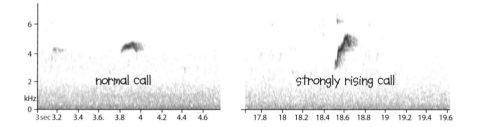

CD2-49 **Siberian Chiffchaff** *Phylloscopus collybita tristis,* Tom river, Kolarovo biological station, Tomsk, Russia, 08:00, 4 July 2011. Song of an adult. Background: Pied Flycatcher *Ficedula hypoleuca* and Common Chaffinch *Fringilla coelebs*. 110704.AB.080001.02

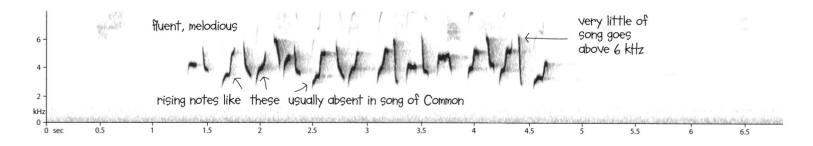

CD2-50   **Siberian Chiffchaff** *Phylloscopus collybita tristis* Tom river, Tomsk, Russia, 09:41, 1 July 2011. Subsong of a very young fledgling. The two 'strophes' here were taken from different recordings made within 30 seconds of each other. Background: song of an adult, and Common Rosefinch *Carpodacus erythrinus*. 110701.AB.094136.12 & 110701.AB.094157.12

Juveniles start attempting to sing almost as soon as they leave the nest. Their attempts might not immediately be recognised as song, but compare the pitch and rhythm of the husky sounds in **CD2-50** with the adult song in the background. By the time they reach Europe, these subsongs have developed into something much closer to adult song. If you are lucky enough to hear a first-winter singing, you will probably hear some plasticity, hesitation, and sometimes a whispering quality that gives away its age. In **CD2-51**, you can hear subsong recorded from the same Dutch first-winter with odd, upward-inflected calls that you already heard.

Sergey Gashkov, Evgeniy Karachakov and Arnoud, well protected against ticks and musquitos, in nesting habitat of Siberian Chiffchaff *Phylloscopus collybita tristis*, Tom river, Kolarovo, Tomsk, Russia, 3 July 2011 (*Cecilia Bosman*)

CD2-51   **Siberian Chiffchaff** *Phylloscopus collybita tristis*, Westkapelle, Zeeland, Netherlands, 12 October 2005. Subsong of a first-winter (the one that can be heard calling in CD2-48). Background: Great Spotted Woodpecker *Dendrocopos major*. Pim Wolf

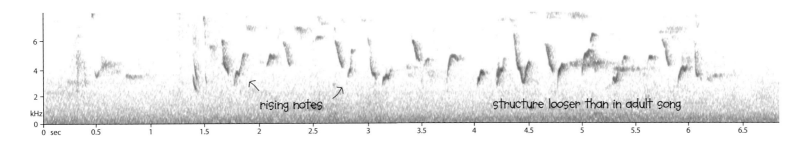

Sergey Gashkov in Siberian Chiffchaff *Phylloscopus collybita tristis* habitat, Tom river, Kolarovo, Tomsk, Russia, 3 July 2011 (*Cecilia Bosman*)

CD2-52 **Siberian Chiffchaff** *Phylloscopus collybita tristis,* Tom river, Kolarovo biological station, Tomsk, Russia, 05:28, 4 July 2011. Song of an adult, with *CHUvit* notes in between strophes. Background: chiffchaff food (insects), Garden Warbler *Sylvia borin* and Siberian Rubythroat *Calliope calliope*. 110704.AB.052802.11

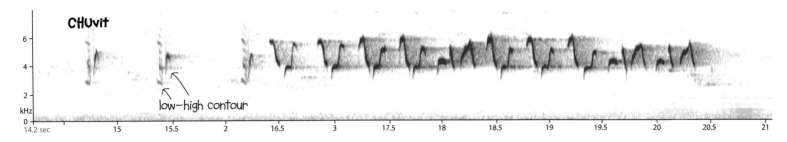

One neglected aspect of chiffchaff sounds is the little call-notes that are often heard between the strophes. In *tristis*, these notes can be described as *CHUvit*, having a characteristic low-high contour that distinguishes them from equivalent notes in European chiffchaffs (**CD2-52**). In *collybita* and *abietinus*, the notes heard between strophes are simpler, and sometimes just a single note or 'syllable'. If there are two then the second is usually very similar to the first. In autumn subsongs of *tristis*, these notes are likely to be present (as indeed one was in **CD2-51** at 0:01), and once in the Netherlands, I recorded some from a bird that was not singing at all (**CD2-53**). I suggest that birders listen for *CHUvit* calls as an additional means of identifying Siberian Chiffchaff.

What about the possibility of vocal impostors, *abietinus* or hybrids from the narrow contact zone that have adopted calls or songs of *tristis*? According to a recent study, such birds are not unusual in the contact zone (Marova et al 2009). However, I suggest we should not worry too much about this, and keep things in perspective. The contact zone was revealed in the same study to be less than 65 km wide, compared to a total east-west range of more than 4,000 km. So hybrids and chiffchaffs that have learned the wrong calls must make up a very small number compared to the huge total population of *tristis* in the Siberian taiga. Any bird calling or singing like *tristis* in late autumn in western Europe is more than likely to be one. And if the bird itself is telling us it's a *tristis* then that's good enough for me."

CD2-53 **Siberian Chiffchaff** *Phylloscopus collybita tristis* Harlingen, Friesland, Netherlands, 16:45, 2 January 2004. Contact calls and *CHUvit* calls of an individual approaching its roost. Background: traffic, children playing and Common Blackbird *Turdus merula*. 03.039.MR.12123.11

Chapter 17: The great Western

If you think the Poole birders you've read about have been dedicated to Poole Harbour, then I've given the wrong impression. On 28 September 2004, James Lidster was sitting at home not far from Lawrence of Arabia's cottage at Bovington, having moved from Poole into the centre of Dorset, all the better to access Portland. Nick had decided to go one better and move to Portland just in time for the autumn rarity season. He had hired and loaded a van and was just heading down through Weymouth. Shaun was even further away, having touched down in Copenhagen on a trip to celebrate Marie's birthday. The first text from Brownsea arrived mid-afternoon, just as they were buying tickets to go to the Danish Royal Opera House to see a performance of Madame Butterfly.

What was the subject of Shaun's text? Colin Williams and Chris Thain, Brownsea wardens, had seen a 'funny' wader on Brownsea lagoon. Colin started phoning around to get advice. Drawing a blank, he found Mo and I discussing soft furnishings in a shop at Branksome.

You know the kind of conversation we were having, the kind that starts with which cushions go best and should they be velvet or chenille. Faking an opinion, especially between drab and pale neutral grey, is almost as much fun as using Alan Dean's colour swatches to identify a Siberian Chiffchaff. You can imagine the relief when I heard Colin say, "Well, Mark we've got this funny wader".

Mark: "What's funny about it?"

Colin: "It's a bit like a Dunlin but smaller."

Mark: "As small as a stint?"

Colin: "It is a bit like a Little Stint, but the bill's not right."

Mark: "What's the bill like?"

Colin: "A Dunlin. It could be a runt Dunlin."

Mark: "OK, can you see it now?"

Colin: "Yes, it's quite close. It's roosting in with the other waders."

The conversation continued as my knowledge of unusual wader features was put to the test. I've been called to look at stints in September on Brownsea lagoon a few times over the years, and it usually proved to be a long and frustrating job. The island is only open to the public between 10:00 and 17:00, and the changing light combined with long distances conspire to build and dash hopes. Up until now the birds had always ended up being juvenile Little Stints.

A juvenile Little Stint can be identified by the colour of the feathers on the folded wings, and especially by a line or often two of white edged feathers called the mantle V. With a close view, you can sort it out fairly quickly. Western Sandpiper would be a dream bird, and that has a couple of lines of red scapulars (rufous, really). The conversation continued:

Mark: "Can you see its back?"

Colin: "Quite streaked."

Mark: "And either side of that - is there any red?"

Colin: "Yes there is."

It makes me shiver now writing it down.

For me, what makes a good bird is the number of people who enjoy it. So being involved in the identification and sharing the eighth British record of Western Sandpiper, with the 1,620 birders who came to see it and all in Poole Harbour, simply couldn't be beaten.

The masses of birders also helped the local economy, paying £3,000 in entrance fees and donations to the Dorset Wildlife Trust. The ferrymen got £10,000 for boat tickets, the National Trust made £10,000 in landing fees, and another £10,000 in the café for bowls of soup and rolls.

Mo and I helped with getting the visitors onto the bird. A couple of years later, I was walking up the aisle of a train when I passed a smiling chap I didn't recognise. Suddenly he pointed at me from his seat. A little shocked, I recoiled, then with a beaming smile he blurted out, "Western Sandpiper." It made my day. The two Dorset Wildlife Trust wardens enjoyed deserved praise for finding the bird and their

Western Sandpiper *Calidris mauri*, juvenile, Brownsea Island, Dorset, 8 October 2004 (*Iain H Leach*)

Western Sandpiper *Calidris mauri*, twitch, Brownsea Island, Dorset, October 2004 (*Anonymous*)

organisation of the twitch, and also because Brownsea lagoon and its amazing array of birds looked so absolutely perfect.

It's not surprising that Brownsea looked good. The largest flock of Avocets in Britain and at least 700 Black-tailed Godwits use it for roosting. Add Britain's only pure pair of breeding Yellow-legged Gulls, more than 1% of Britain's breeding Common and Sandwich Terns and one of only six pairs of Roseate Tern outside Northumberland.Top it off with up to 27 roosting Spoonbills and nationally important numbers of Little Egret, cormorant and Dunlin, and for its size it has to rank as one of the most important wetland sites in Britain.

The National Trust manages another great place for watching waders in the harbour: Middlebere. They have built hides there and converted the farm buildings into holiday cottages. As I write this, it's springtime and Mo and I are staying in the farmhouse, even though it's only 'around the corner' from home. The main hide gives great views of the Middlebere channel and across to Arne. Spring migration of waders is well underway.

Timing is important for seeing waders here. Get it right and you will be well rewarded. Visitors to Middlebere regularly ask why the tide always seems to be out, even when it is in everywhere else. This is because the mud is so thick here that as soon as the water levels begin to drop, the mud immediately appears. It then quickly dries out and the birds soon move on or else disappear out of sight into the main channel.

Today, 12 May 2010, that's what is happening. Among the waders there are over 400 Black-tailed Godwits that should really be in Iceland by now. Icelandic Black-tailed Godwits are one of the

reasons Poole Harbour is so important for conservation. We look after more than 6% of the entire wintering population through the winter.

These birds love coming here because not only are there extensive mud flats, but also regularly flooded fields extending right up the Frome valley. Our winter population is currently around 2,500 birds. If you want to see them all in one go, Brownsea lagoon at high tide is your place. At low tide they split into two main feeding populations, a southern one based around South Lake and a northern one based at Holes Bay, making occasional visits to Lytchett. During periods of high rainfall, all intertidal areas are abandoned for the waterlogged areas of Bestwall and the Frome valley, the godwits returning when the water goes back down.

By March, when you think you have worked out these feeding patterns, migrant birds begin to arrive, putting the whole feeding strategy into turmoil. With impatient birds constantly flying around looking for available mud, any site can get a visit. To conserve energy, the roosting strategies also change with birds mostly staying on site. The local *Spartina* is regularly made use of, although for some this is still too far to go. In a race to build up fat reserves, many birds will continue to feed as the tide rises up their legs. When it reaches their bellies some will then just float on the water until the tide goes back down. Numbers peak in April, when most sites record their highest counts. Then all of a sudden they are gone. During our 2007 survey, huge numbers in April became just 27 birds in May.

So what are our 400 birds still doing at Middlebere in mid-May 2011? Perhaps they are just late. Only time will tell, but we do seem to be getting more and more first-year birds spending the summer here. In 2007 just six birds stayed through the summer, and in recent summers this has risen to 150.

Suddenly they all take off. We look into the sky for a Peregrine but there's nothing. The godwits settle again but seem very interested in something in the channel. They're peering into it, occasionally spooking and flying up in small groups. Something

Bar-tailed Godwits *Limosa lapponica*, Shore Road, Poole, Dorset, 11 March 2010 (*Nick Hopper*)

is moving up the creek and although we can't see it, we can follow its progress as it moves upstream, causing little disturbances on the way.

The godwits are just a mass of mud-brown backs in winter, but now in summer plumage their deep brick-red underparts are eye-catchingly vivid. They are craning their necks to get a look at whatever is in the creek. 132 Dunlin then flush and fly round before settling among the godwits' legs.

Bar-tailed Godwits are much more local. They eat Lugworms and King Ragworms, which are really only found in the sandy mud in the east of the harbour, along Shore Road, off Green Island and on the mud between Brownsea and Brand's Bay. At high tide, they all roost in a tiny group on the edge of the 'lawns' of Brownsea lagoon.

Before the Holes Bay road was built in 1990, there used to be two gangs of Dunlin: one based in Holes Bay that exploited the north of the harbour and another based in Brand's Bay that fed in the southern half. 90% of Dorset's Dunlins can be found in the harbour, and they used to roost on Pilot's Point, one time setting a county record at 8,300. One of the results of global warming is a lot of extra dog walking throughout the winter along the beach at Studland and, nowadays, the main roost site is Brownsea lagoon, and the population is estimated to have been around 3,000 to 4,000 for the last few years.

Over 10,000 Dunlins have been ringed in the harbour. The Stour Ringing Group used to catch Dunlins in the entrance to the Middlebere channel, one of which was recovered, decapitated, from an Arctic Fox burrow in the northwest of Iceland.

In September 1975, one of the Dunlins that veteran ringer Chris Reynolds caught was found to have a Polish ring. It had flown from Gdansk to Brownsea in 13 days. Juvenile *alpina* Dunlin from northwest Siberia and northern Scandinavia arrive in Poole in September. The adults moult in The Wash or Waddensea and start to arrive here from October, and continue to arrive right up until January, starting the return journey to the breeding grounds in early spring. *Arctica* that breed in northeast Greenland and *schinzii* from southwest Greenland, Iceland, Britain, southern Scandinavia and the Baltic pass through Poole in July and August on their way to northwest Africa, where they moult and winter.

I'm not sure whether the 132 that have just landed among the godwits are *arctica* and *schinzii* returning, but with their bright backs and dark bellies, I assume so. By now we can see that it's a Common Seal moving up the channel that's creating all the fuss. As it turns round to head back to its usual haunt off Round Island, it spooks a couple of Oystercatchers. We have 20 or so breeding pairs of Oystercatchers nesting, mainly on Brownsea. In addition, around 1500 Oystercatchers arrive here in autumn from Iceland, Scotland and the north of England. Poole Harbour is one of the most important wintering areas on the south coast for this species.

As winter progresses, birds filter down the east coast from Norway too, arriving here between November and January. They stay till late, waiting for the arctic summer. Alan Bromby of Brownsea Island and Chris Reynolds have ringed over 1,500 Oystercatchers here over several decades. One of them became Britain's only foreign recovery when it appeared as a vagrant in Greenland.

Eurasian Curlew *Numenius arquata* Middlebere, Dorset, England, 31 August 2002. Restless Curlews calling at dusk, shortly before taking off on a migration flight. Background: Eurasian Oystercatcher *Haematopus ostralegus*, Black-tailed Godwit *Limosa limosa*, Common Sandpiper *Actitis hypoleucos*, Common Redshank *Tringa totanus* and Yellow-legged Gull *Larus michahellis*. 02.040.MR.01824.01 **CD2-54**

Middlebere is lovely at night in late summer, especially at full moon. Waders gather here and at points along the Wareham Channel, and as the sun sets they start calling to each other. Within an hour, many of them fly out of the harbour to resume their southbound migration. Magnus and I first recorded migrant waders leaving across the heath in 2002. Here is a group of Curlews that Magnus recorded, calling wildly, outside the Middlebere hide at dusk (**CD2-54**). Listen to the next recording he made, and you will hear how the chaos reaches a crescendo before they all take off (**CD2-55**). This chaos is conveniently echoed by the physical structure of the sound. In the classic Curlew flight call, a clear rising note actually emerges from chaos, as you can see on the sonagram. After this recording was made, two flocks passed me in the dark on the top of Hartland Moor.

Eurasian Curlew *Numenius arquata* Middlebere, Dorset, England, 31 August 2002. Excitement building up to the moment when the flock takes off on its migration flight. Background: Eurasian Whimbrel *N phaeopus*, Common Redshank *Tringa totanus* and Yellow-legged Gull *Larus michahellis*. 02.040.MR.02101.01 **CD2-55**

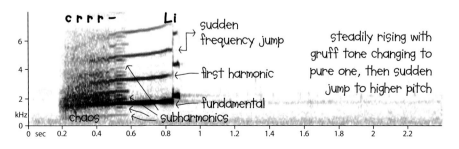

By using a parabolic reflector, I was able to track the first group along the woodland bordering the north of Hartland Moor, and then they headed in the direction of Lulworth. The second group seemed to head for the gap in the hills where Corfe Castle was built. Later I heard that Bob Gifford, who was staying in the ringing hut that night, had heard Curlews passing Chapman's Pool as they headed out over the English Channel.

At the end of the last recording there is a Whimbrel's flight call, a series of short clear notes very different from the Curlews' flight calls. In the late '70s, flocks of Whimbrel would arrive at dusk in spring, using the harbour as a staging post before moving on towards their breeding grounds in Iceland and Scandinavia. On one evening, I remember watching about 200 calling birds coming in to roost. Between 20 April and 13 May 1975, 2,070 birds were counted, many roosting on The Moors. **CD2-56** is a recording of a small flock heading north in spring, made at midnight in the south of the Netherlands. A classic series of short piping notes can be heard as they take off in two waves.

On that first evening at Middlebere in August 2002, we also heard several species of *Tringa* sandpipers or 'shanks. In **CD2-57** you can hear a single Greenshank that migrated shortly before the Curlews. We had a good time making those recordings, and eight years on we also recorded a party of Greenshanks getting ready to migrate (**CD2-58**). This time, you can hear them getting very excited, before twos and threes take off. Unlike the Curlews, they flew along the southern shore of the Wareham Channel.

Eurasian Whimbrel *Numenius phaeopus* Landschotse Heide, Noord-Brabant, Netherlands, 23 April 2005. A flock of about 20 spring migrants taking off in the middle of the night. Background: Eurasian Curlew *N arquata*. 05.004.MR.14318.11 CD2-56

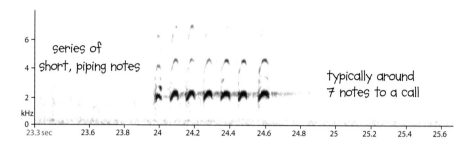

Common Greenshank *Tringa nebularia Middlebere*, Dorset, England, 31 August 2002. Typical calls, speeding up as the bird takes off on its migration flight. Background: Eurasian Curlew *Numenius arquata*. 02.040.MR.01352.01 CD2-57

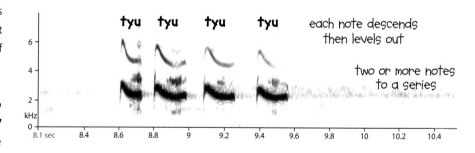

Common Greenshank *Tringa nebularia* Middlebere, Dorset, England, 19:26, 23 August 2010. Calls of two or three taking off on a migration flight. Background: Canada Goose *Branta canadensis*, Mallard *Anas platyrhynchos* and gull *Larus*. 100823. MC.192600.22 CD2-58

Next listen to a flock of Redshanks recorded by Killian at Tacumshin in Ireland (**CD2-59**). Redshanks stress the first element of their flight call, which can help separate their multi-note calls from those of Greenshank and Whimbrel. Redshank's multi-note call is shorter, faster, more continuous and less piping than Greenshank. Another call, which is a single long note, can sound slurred and has no equivalent in Greenshank.

Identifying Spotted Redshank by sound is very easy by comparison, as it has a completely different flight call (**CD2-60**). If you don't already know this call, I recommend it for impressing your friends. Normally described as *chu-it*, it can only be confused with Pacific Golden Plover, which has never knowingly been heard in Poole Harbour. You can often hear Spotted Redshank along the edge of Holes Bay in winter.

CD2-59   **Common Redshank** *Tringa totanus* Tacumshin, Wexford, Ireland, 9 September 2002. Calls of a relaxed flock. Background: domestic cows *Bos primigenius taurus*, Black-headed Gull *Chroicocephalus ridibundus*, Dunlin *Calidris alpina* and Meadow Pipit *Anthus pratensis*. 02.009.KM.04340.01

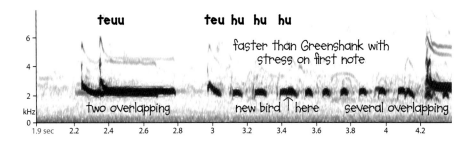

CD2-60   **Spotted Redshank** *Tringa erythropus* Middlebere, Dorset, England, 24 April 2005. Typical *chu-it* calls, in this case given by a standing bird. Background: Common Shelduck *Tadorna tadorna*, Black-tailed Godwit *Limosa limosa* and Common Blackbird *Turdus merula*. 05.004.MC.14250.32

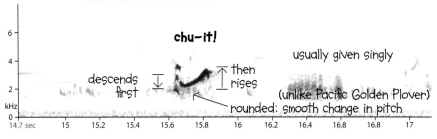

Common Sandpiper's flight call is very high-pitched, fast and piercing (**CD2-61**). Some years ago, I was foolish enough to let James stay at my house, and he added Common Sandpiper to my garden list by hearing it flying overhead at night. Wood Sandpiper (**CD2-62**) has slightly lower-pitched and less tinny flight calls than Common Sandpiper. The notes sound more or less identical, whereas in Common Sandpiper flight calls, each note is slightly lower than the one before. I once heard a Wood Sandpiper calling as it headed out across Hartland Moor, and Nick would also like you to know that he has heard one calling over his garden in Stoborough.

Green Sandpiper is another species that we hear flying out from Middlebere at dusk, although the three in **CD2-63** were recorded by Magnus in the Netherlands. The flight call is at a similar pitch to Wood Sandpiper, but each note is clearly rising in pitch, and the first note usually sounds longer than the others.

Water Rails also migrate in and out of Poole Harbour each winter, so here are the three common rail flight calls for you to listen to. This Moorhen flight call recorded by Peter Nuyten (**CD2-64**) has often been mistaken for a Barn Owl in Britain, and for a Long-eared Owl in the Netherlands. Coots make this toy trumpet sound while flying around at night from February to October at least (**CD2-65**). Water Rails can give a variety of calls in flight, but the one heard most often is a clear sharp whistle with a wavering or modulated quality (**CD2-66**). This flight call can be heard both in spring and autumn.

CD2-61   **Common Sandpiper** *Actitis hypoleucos* IJmuiden, Noord-Holland, Netherlands, 13 September 2003. Two juveniles in flight. Background: Lesser Black-backed Gull *Larus fuscus*, Meadow Pipit *Anthus pratensis*, Dunnock *Prunella modularis*, Common Chiffchaff *Phylloscopus collybita* and Western Jackdaw *Corvus monedula*. 03.035. MR.04220.02

Wood Sandpiper *Tringa glareola* Salalah Beach, Dhofar, Oman, 29 October 2002. Typical calls of a solitary individual in flight. Background: Kentish Plover *Charadius alexandrinus*. 02.011.KM.01830.32   CD2-62

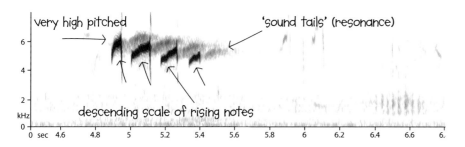

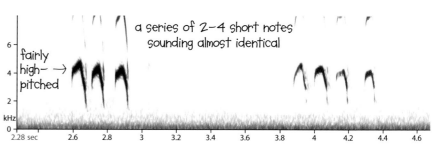

176

CD2-63 **Green Sandpiper** *Tringa ochropus* Nieuwe Keverdijkse Polder, Noord-Holland, Netherlands, 12 August 2005. Three taking off on migration flight at dusk. Background: Mallard *Anas platyrhynchos* and Barn Swallow *Hirundo rustica*. 05.022.MR.01910.23

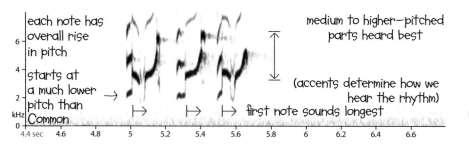

each note has overall rise in pitch

starts at a much lower pitch than Common

medium to higher-pitched parts heard best

(accents determine how we hear the rhythm)

first note sounds longest

Eurasian Coot *Fulica atra* de Weerribben, Overijssel, Netherlands, 01:25, 28 April 2006. Calls while flying around at night. Background: Greylag Goose *Anser anser*, Eurasian Great Bittern *Botaurus stellaris*, Savi's Warbler *Locustella luscinioides* and Sedge Warbler *Acrocephalus schoenobaenus*. 060428.MR.12547.03 **CD2-65**

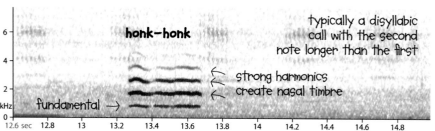

honk-honk

typically a disyllabic call with the second note longer than the first

strong harmonics create nasal timbre

fundamental →

CD2-64 **Common Moorhen** *Gallinula chloropus* Ameland, Friesland, Netherlands, 00:56, 24 April 2010. Flight calls during the night. Background: Lesser Black-backed Gull *Larus fuscus*, Short-eared Owl *Asio flammeus*, Eurasian Oystercatcher *Haematopus ostralegus* and Common Nightingale *Luscinia megarhynchos*. 100424.PN.005626.24

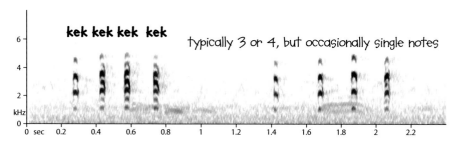

kek kek kek kek

typically 3 or 4, but occasionally single notes

Water Rail *Rallus aquaticus* de Weerribben, Overijssel, Netherlands, 4 May 2003. Calls in flight during the night. Background: Marsh Frogs *Rana ridibunda*, 03.013.MR.02700.11 **CD2-66**

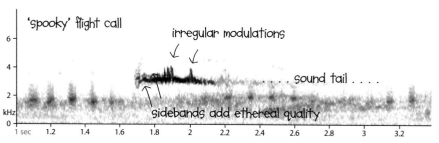

'spooky' flight call

irregular modulations

. . . . . sound tail . . . .

sidebands add ethereal quality

Chapter 18: How much is that doggie in the window?

The ship's entertainer was singing *How much is that doggie in the window?* Mo, Dick Forsman and I were cruising the Finnish Gulf on the *Kristina* for four days. I was hoping to record the Velvet Scoters breeding on one of the islands, while Dick was employed to get everyone up at 04:30 to watch the arctic migration of ducks and geese through the myriad of small islands and promontories. It was May 2009.

My mind started to wander as I thought about my own part-time occupation as an amateur cruise entertainer. I'm one of the guides on the RSPB bird boats around Poole Harbour. It's my job to give a commentary on the two-hour trip. You know the kind of thing:

"On the left as we look forward is Brand's Bay." (I've never mastered port and starboard.) "I think… yes there are three Eider, you can just make them out. All brown, so females or immature males, big, chunky… take a line towards those house boats… a rare vagrant until the '50s, the most ever seen was 135 in February 1989… 10 or 20 immature birds can turn up here in the summer, probably Dutch birds from the Waddensea, but most of the time we only have a few… Flying across the back of the boat now… Lately these three or four have been wintering in Brand's Bay…"

"Black-necked Grebe on the left of the boat as you look forward… It's just dived. Over there you can see the harbour mouth and how narrow it is… Male Goldeneye flying directly in front of the boat… Imagine how fast the water from this, the second largest natural harbour in the world, pours out through there… Raven over Brownsea…"

"The harbour mouth is only 400 metres wide, although 20 metres deep in places. This stops the harbour being an estuary… When a colleague from work first came down here he decided to swim across, stripped and dived in. He waded ashore 13 miles down the coast at Christchurch and was bought back in his wet underpants to his motorbike by the police… Great Northern Diver very close, just dived. Up again with a small flat fish, probably a Dover Sole."

Coming out of my daydream, I realized that the Finnish organist was actually singing *My bonnie lies over the ocean*. I picked at my pickled herring and looked out of the window at the endless flocks of Eider. These come complete with White-tailed Eagles, always breathtaking in all regards, and I could see one sitting on its nest as we sailed past. I would give anything to see a White-tailed Eagle in Poole Harbour. Imagine the excitement of that on a Poole bird boat. It's not such a fantasy. Nick had what was undoubtedly one over Hartland Moor a couple of years ago. Two Buzzards were mobbing it, and each was dwarfed by

European Otters *Lutra lutra*, Little Sea, Studland, Dorset, 23 August 2010 *(Arnoud B van den Berg)*. At the same site as CD2-67.

the eagle. The bird was such an awesome sight that for once Nick was speechless. We got there just too late and found him sitting on the tailgate of his car. He looked as if he had seen a ghost rather than a Dorset mega. I wonder if I'd have been able to cope. White-tailed Eagles do winter occasionally in southern Britain. Nick's bird was probably the youngster that had been wintering in Hampshire. That bird had been ringed and was from Finland.

The Finnish cruise was rather like a grown up version of Poole Harbour's winter bird boat, the birders thick with winter clothing, furry hats and heavy boots. By now we were steaming through hundreds of Long-tailed Ducks. They were feeding up before flying north to breed on the tundra. Some had been stuffing themselves for a month and as they settled, we could see a big splash and a plume of water. The females have to live off this fat for a month or so once they make it to the nesting grounds. Perhaps the beautiful male that wintered in Poole this year was somewhere in these flocks. A highlight for the bird-boaters on winter Sundays, we often find them somewhere around Green Island, feeding on cockles.

Poole Bird Boats evolved in 1984 from a trip that the RSPB Poole group leader Mike Diamond ran each year to watch waders. The idea was to look for Black-tailed Godwits and Curlews, and to search for wintering birds like Greenshanks. In 1992, with a little guidance from Jackie and Nick Hull and a fair bit of organisation from Colin Burt, these trips evolved into 'the bird boat', raising thousands for the RSPB.

I still enjoy doing the commentary, both for the mischief and to turn others on to birding as part of the RSPB's *Aren't birds*

brilliant campaign. The boats go in all weathers except fog. They even go in southwest gales when it's blowing rain into our faces. On those days *Misery loves company* could be a more appropriate slogan, although it only takes a Grey Phalarope to whizz past the boat or a Little Auk to sit off Brownsea to make birds brilliant again.

Public speaking from a wheelhouse while identifying whatever flies past can be tricky. There's a gunslinger, showing off element to it all until one of the passengers catches you out. Once, as we passed Brownsea's Pottery pier, I told everyone that you don't get Goosanders on the open water just 30 seconds before a lovely lady pointed out a male flying right over the back of the boat.

Terry Elborn also leads bird boats and gets great pleasure in showing people anything to do with the natural world. He seemed to grow up at the bird pub, although I suppose he must have been 18 when he first came. Wanting a career in nature conservation, he first gained experience suggesting ways of making Broadstone golf club wildlife friendly, while working there as a greens keeper.

Over the years, Terry has had a run of bad luck. Every time he goes away, something good seems to turn up. He has even gained notoriety in the papers as the unluckiest birder in Britain. He has managed to arrange visits to his parents to coincide with some of Dorset's finest rarities, including Red-flanked Bluetail and Siberian Rubythroat. Things reached a particularly low point when a golfer told him about a Great Bustard he had seen on one of the fairways at the golf club, just before Terry's return to work. Ever sympathetic, it got so bad that the rest of us would ask him when he was planning to go away so we could book time off for twitching.

Terry is now the Natural Habitats Officer for Poole. For us birders, his greatest bit of habitat management was when he waded out in his wellies and created 'the Elborn cut' through the reeds at Hatch Pond. Before that, Bitterns were very awkward to see here.

Bitterns haven't been known to breed in Poole Harbour since 1900, and they remained scarce until Shaun found one at Hatch Pond on 6 December 1997. As breeding Bitterns in Britain (try saying that after a couple of shandys) have become more successful, so we've seen more wintering at Hatch Pond.

Over the years, with a passion bordering on obsession, Ewan has watched Bitterns there most winter evenings. On 3 November 2006, this loyalty rewarded him with the rather unexpected and somewhat privileged sight of an Otter eating a fish. Although Hatch Pond is Terry's pride and joy, it happens to be on the edge of an industrial estate, so hardly a classic Otter wilderness. Trevor Warrick, a pub regular, put the general reaction well: "Ewan's claim of Otter inevitably came under close scrutiny. We wondered if he'd seen a mink, but he claimed that the beast was 2-3 feet long, which is far too big for that species. Another point of concern was: how did it get there? The nearest suitable habitat was likely to be Holes Bay, but the watercourse that flows out of Hatch Pond towards the harbour is largely culverted, so the Otter would have had to come over land. It would have had to cross several very busy roads, which seemed unlikely, and would have had the opportunity to pick up an iPod at PC World, a Whopper at Burger King and some very reasonably priced quality food items at Lidl on its way. An Otter at Hatch Pond? Yeah, right."

"As I wandered around the edge of the pond I saw some dodgy-looking characters lurking amongst the trees. They were Ewan, Ian Lewis, Terry and another guy I didn't know. Ewan had been there from soon after 3pm and there had been no sign of either the Bittern or any swimming mammals, be they mink, Otter or whatever. Ewan said that he had heard some unfamiliar whistling sounds up to a week previously, which he now thought were from the Otter."

"Ewan's time by the pond that afternoon had not been entirely fruitless. There were at least 3 Cetti's Warblers and 2 Kingfishers about, also over 100 Magpies had come into the roost before I got there. Despite these ornithological highlights, Gryllo (Ian Lewis) had to leave just after 5pm, and I must admit I was on the point of going too, when Terry shouted 'I've got something swimming out from the main channel. It looks huge. I think it's an Otter'. I quickly got my bins onto it and as I watched, the Bittern flew through my field of view and landed on the floating vegetation in front of the reeds. The light was fading fast, but there was still enough to pick out a fair bit of detail."

"Later, Terry picked out a bird in the sky. It was the Bittern. We all thought it was going to leave, but instead it started circling around over the pond calling - at least 5 or 6 times. Being 4th November, there were already fireworks going off all over the place in the cold, clear sky. A Bittern circling overhead calling in urban Poole, to the background sound of bangers and rockets, is something I will never forget."

Eurasian Bittern *Botaurus stellaris*, Hatch Pond, Dorset, 1 February 2010 (*Mike Coleman*)

Trevor was describing the first record of the return of Otters to Poole Harbour. Now, if you are very lucky, you can see Otters on the rivers, Brownsea lakes or lagoon, or catching carp at Little Sea. Listen out for the Otters' unusual calls, which I was lucky enough to record at Little Sea (**CD2-67**).

CD2-67 **European Otter** *Lutra lutra* Little Sea, Poole Harbour, Dorset, England, 19:18, 13 May 2010. Whistle calls while swimming, recorded at very close range. The age and sex of this animal are unknown, but a young otter looking for its parents makes the same sound. Background: Mute Swan *Cygnus olor*, Common Wood Pigeon *Columba palumbus*, Common Blackbird *Turdus merula*, Eurasian Reed Warbler *Acrocephalus scirpaceus*, Common Chiffchaff *Phylloscopus collybita*, Common Chaffinch *Fringilla coelebs* and Common Reed Bunting *Emberiza schoeniclus*. 100513.MC.191800.11

The Bitterns leave Hatch Pond around the middle of March, and several birders have been lucky enough to hear them go. Last year there were four Bitterns, and at 18:42 on 14 March 2010, Joe Kaplonek had found two feeding before he noticed two more circling high above the lake calling. One of the feeding birds also took flight and they circled, calling to each other for around four minutes, until two flew off high to the north. They weren't seen the subsequent evening so presumably he had witnessed them leaving for their breeding sites. The previous year they had left one day earlier. Then in 2012 we realised that more Bitterns were leaving Hatch Pond than were wintering there. It became obvious that Hatch Pond was one of a series of staging posts for Bitterns returning east for their breeding grounds. Bitterns could be seen when the weather was suitable in evenings throughout March. A similar evening flight in the Netherlands was recorded many years ago by Arnoud, although this after the breeding season, not before it. You can hear the Bitterns' flight calls in **CD2-68**.

Eurasian Bittern *Botaurus stellaris* Lauwersmeer, Friesland, Netherlands, 23:20, 1 July 2001. Flight calls by two individuals an hour after sunset. They passed directly overhead about 20 m apart, then gradually disappeared. Background: Common Moorhen *Gallinula chloropus*, Eurasian Coot *Fulica atra*, Common Grasshopper Warbler *Locustella naevia* and Eurasian Reed Warbler *Acrocephalus scirpaceus*. 01.010.AB.00000.11

Returning to the bird boat, Terry loves to get visitors to see the local seals. After a lot of discussion down the pub about which ones have dog's heads (and come to that which dog), we think the animals most often seen in the harbour are Common Seals. I don't think I've seen a Grey Seal actually inside the harbour. I've only recently understood that, viewed from the front, Common Seal's flatter oval head and v-shaped nostrils can be easily told apart from Grey Seal's vertical oval head and parallel nostrils.

Not all bird boats are for the public. Retired teacher and keen birder Phyl England organises bird boat trips for local school children, which I lead whenever possible. She visits the schools and teaches the children what to expect, while I recite doggerel about common cormorants (or shags) laying eggs in paper bags (Isherwood 1959). I'm tall and Phyl is short. Were we to put on pirate costumes, we could do a good impression of Captain Hook and Smee. I love sneaking out from the office for two hours, having no responsibilities except to provide some information and a bit of entertainment. The children's boats are one of the highlights of my winter.

Shags prefer the Brownsea roads, the deep stretch of water straight off the sea defences where the boat lingers while we scan the lagoon. No matter how casually I mention the bird's name, it always raises a giggle, even with the teachers.

European Shag *Phalacrocorax aristotelis*, diving, Shell Bay, Studland, Dorset, 8 December 2009 (*Nick Hopper*)

Derek Ball and his wife Kay normally take turns showing the birds to the children. Until I read his article *Losing my virginity* (Ball 2008), I hadn't realised that Derek had been inspired by a bird boat outing to take up birding (and I am now rather flattered). As he put it, "because I was a virgin bird watcher, nearly every bird was a lifer! As Mark would say, I 'had my first Shag in Poole Harbour!'" Shags, being fish-eating birds, get caught up in fishermen's nets left overnight in Poole bay and drown, only to be brought to the surface when the embarrassed fishermen lift the nets a little later in the day. More and more of them seem to be fishing inside the harbour. Perhaps the ones with a preference for fishing outside the harbour are dead!

Three channels come off the Brownsea roads. The closest to Brownsea is the Upper Wych Channel, which goes along the southern shore. It's at the beginning of the commercial oyster beds, two huge 30-acre patches. The little ones are grown on the sides of the old blue ferry moored alongside Brownsea's shore, just below the heronry. When the Oysters are big enough they are dropped into an area that stretches west to Round Island in one direction and Green Island to the other. Mussels are also grown along the edges of the oyster beds, and the whole area is populated with crabs. Mussels are the preferred food for Goldeneye, which feed either side of the Wych channel, sometimes with small numbers of sea duck. Velvet Scoters also like mussels, and a couple can spend their winter at a spot equidistant from Poole Quay, Hamworthy and Brownsea. The shell fisherman used to grow Manila clams until about 12 years ago, when they populated the whole of the harbour, supporting a rather dubious industry of 40 boats. Common Scoters like to go for the clams, their fragile shells making them a bit easier to open.

The second is the Middle Ship channel, dredged to a depth of six metres for the ferries and cargo boats. This is one of the Great Northern Divers' favourite places. However, they can be found in many other places, and some can even be seen going into summer plumage in May off Branksome. Nick had five birds on a visit to Branksome one year, some looking very smart indeed. Great Northern Divers are great fishermen, and their winter itinerary is influenced by the amount of flatfish and crabs in the harbour. The adults moult from late January, and become flightless until they prepare to return to Greenland and Iceland in April, so around Christmas they have to make a decision as to whether there is enough food to last through the next few months. The juveniles are more mobile.

The furthest channel from Brownsea is called the North Channel and is used more by pleasure craft, especially boats heading for Salterns marina. Adult Black-throated Divers really like the sandy parts in some bays and near the entrance to the harbour. Their distribution seems to be influenced by the state of dredging and sand restoration projects along the shallower beaches. One day we found three Black-throated Divers feeding in the North Channel from the bird boat. North Channel is only dredged to four metres, but it has one major advantage: I can see into it from my platform at home. So on that day I was able

to quickly cycle home, rush upstairs to the verandah and get them on my garden list. The North Channel is also a favourite with Mediterranean Gulls, and from it you can also peep into the edges of the marinas to watch Red-breasted Mergansers and the occasional Goosander.

The harbour is full of old names like Salterns that relate to salt production. Wych is a name for areas where brine springs or wells are used for salt production, and no doubt if we dug down through the oysterbeds we would find the remains of salt pans. Wych channel goes right down to Shipstal on the end of Arne, sweeping west of Long and Round Island where flocks of cormorants feed on the flounders in early winter.

There are normally plenty of wintering Great Crested Grebes about as we take the Wych channel down towards Arne. Ringing recoveries suggest that the ones wintering in the harbour are mainly local breeders, and theoretically from February to April they should all be females, since the females depart for breeding lakes or rivers 50 days later than the males. There's also a chance of getting Black-necked Grebe and Slavonian Grebe, sometimes off Arne or maybe between Green Island and the entrance to Brand's Bay, but Red-necked Grebe is less likely.

The highlight of the boat trip is Brownsea lagoon. It started life as St Andrews Bay until it was poorly walled up and drained in the 1700s. The sea defences regularly failed, however, and were constantly in need of repair. That was until Colonel Waugh bought the island in 1852 for £13,000. He had been walking on Brownsea considering its purchase with his wife, when they discovered small outcrops of fine clay suitable for making porcelain. Charles van Raalte writes that a civil engineer then

Pied Avocets *Recurvirostra avosetta*, Brownsea lagoon, Dorset, 13 September 2011 (*Nick Hopper*). The ringed bird was only four months old, being ringed as a chick at Oxfordness, Suffolk, on 29 May 2011, and perhaps not surprisingly it was seen the next spring in the Netherlands at Ezumakeeg, Lauwersmeer, on 28 April 2012.

made a report estimating there to be 30 to 40 million tons of clay worth between 15 to 20 million pounds. "Here we have a retired Indian colonel, probably the most unsophisticated type of businessman in existence, placed face to face with the scientific reasoning that millions lay within reach of his hands" (van Raalte 1906).

Colonel Waugh then started to behave like the millionaire he thought he was, borrowing from a bank for which he became chairman with the mineral rich island as collateral. (On a more modern note, this is similar to Icelandic banks lending to their own directors to buy British companies, which led to similar

results.) He restored the castle and clad it with a gothic façade of Portland stone. As he didn't like the sea lapping at the back door, he filled in the river that went into St Andrews Bay. As if these changes were not enough, he built the clock tower, church, farm buildings, laundry, school house, a pier and a tramroad and a village of cottages at Maryland "for the workfolk". According to van Raalte, "he opened clay pits and established pottery works, and started a concern called the Branksea Clay & Pottery Company with offices in London, and withal he entertained in more than princely style at the castle." Finally, between 1853 and 1856, Colonel Waugh made a substantial sea wall when he paid for hundreds of barges of clay to be sunk in the deep parts of the bay, and bought over a million and a quarter bricks to build the wall. To provide the funds necessary for carrying out the scheme, Waugh borrowed from his bank £237,000 at 10% interest.

But there was no clay of any standard. Van Raalte suggests that the island may have been 'salted' with the clay to aid the sale. Waugh disappeared to Spain and his wife, who was deaf, stayed behind. Once when faced with a group of Poole folk, she mistakenly thought they wanted money, when in reality they wanted Waugh to be Mayor. She gave the game away by asking for time to pay. Anyway, it's an ill wind, and soon what is now the bird-covered lagoon was a series of broad meadows reclaimed from the sea, with cattle grazing and the pasture divided by little canals.

Van Raalte, who bought Brownsea in 1901, recorded the birds as well as the fortunes of previous owners. His Brownsea list of 190 species included birds that would need a lot of corroboration today: Bufflehead, Hooded Merganser, King Eider, Noddy, Ross's Gull, Night Heron, Purple Heron, Little Bittern, Killdeer, Kentish Plover and Dotterel.

Predictably, the sea wall started to leak, and over time the pastures turned into a brackish lagoon with a grass 'lawn' and several *Spartina* islands that you can see today. It is one of the most spectacular sites in Britain to see birds at any time of year, and as we will see, vitally important for many of the harbour's birds.

On the bird boat, once everyone has ticked the Spoonbills, it's the Avocets that most people want to see there. The lagoon is the most consistent site in the harbour and Britain for seeing them in the winter. Arriving here for the first time in the winter of 1948, they reached national importance in 1978 with just 21 birds. Most of our Avocets breed in the Netherlands, and some at least are birds that used to winter on the Exe. On 5 December 2002, a flock of 1,155 became the largest ever counted in the UK, and a count of 1,500 in October 2009 made Brownsea the most important wintering site in Britain. The Avocets' favourite feeding area is Wych lake off Fitzworth, where they eat the mud shrimp *Corophium volutator* (Thomas et al 2004).

As we steam away from the lagoon between Goathorn and Green Island, Goldeneyes become more common. 185 pairs nest in Scotland, and while they may well winter with us, ringing records suggest that some of our Goldeneyes come from Finland, where they have been increasing as a breeding bird. Overnight they used to roost together on Little Sea, but the Otters seem to have put a stop to that. Now they prefer Brand's Bay, Fitzworth or very occasionally Poole Park.

It's not only the Otters that make them hard to count. In *Important Birds of Poole Harbour*, Bryan Pickess & John Underhill-Day (2002) pointed out that there were some anomalies in the counts of Goldeneye. The responsibility for recording the status of birds in Poole Harbour lies mainly with the BTO. They in turn rely on amateur bird surveyors like me to actually count the birds. The largest survey the BTO runs is the Wetland Bird Survey (WeBS), and it has been going since 1947. What Bryan had noticed was that in November 2002, there were 152 Goldeneye roosting on Little Sea, which was three times the WeBs count for the whole of the harbour for that month.

Chapter 19: Come hell or high water

Come rain or shine, once a month during the non-breeding season, 3,000 counters stand along the water margins of the 2,000 WeBS sites in Britain, and count the ducks and waders in synchrony. It's a massive undertaking, generating what is an industrial quantity of data. Over the last decade, Andy Musgrove and his team at the BTO turned this survey round from something that was producing results three years late, to one that is bang on time, and now the challenge is to repeat that year after year. Starting in 2007 they changed WeBS from an entirely paper-based survey to one that is now predominantly online. Just to add to the challenge, they aim to produce a full national report 12 months after the end of the last count.

I'm hoping now that I have you imagining a group of bird surveyors co-ordinated in perfect harmony, like a flock of Dunlin veering across the sky... and it's true if you add a little group of stragglers trying to catch up. We are those stragglers. All over Britain, bird counters go out at the same time, at high tide. Here in Poole, however, we go out at low tide.

Traditionally, this is because where other sites have easily visible roosts, in Poole Harbour and all along the Solent the roosts are on *Spartina*-covered islands. Consequently, you can't see the waders hunkered down in the grass. That's how it used to be, but the *Spartina* is dying. Its lightning-fast colonisation (described as hybrid vigour) peaked in 1924, and between then and 2004 the amount of mud flat covered by *Spartina* within the harbour halved. The decline of *Spartina* continues, but we still go out at low tide.

Well, we hope it's going to be low tide. We get a tidal surge caused when the Isle of Wight delays a body of water that rushes in through the harbour mouth about 40 minutes after the normal high tide, just when everything else is trying to rush out. Called the 'cork effect', this creates a double high tide both here and at Christchurch harbour.

Because Poole Harbour is a large shallow basin of water, high-pressure weather systems can affect the height of the tide. In addition, strong westerly wind can push the water out while an easterly can hold the water in. Just to add to the confusion, the narrow harbour mouth creates a delay as the water passes between the islands where it slows down. All this means that high tide at the harbour entrance can be up to an hour and forty minutes before high tide at Wareham. In other words, you can be watching waders at low tide at Brand's Bay at 13:00 while a friend at Middlebere has to wait till 14:40 for the same amount of mud.

That's assuming that the water has covered the mud at Middlebere at all. The shallow nature of the harbour means that higher parts of the harbour seabed like Middlebere can

Common Redshank *Tringa totanus*, Poole, Dorset, 27 August 2011 (*René Pop*)

be left exposed at high tide. It's not just the shallows. The deeps also cause problems. To count the waders in Lytchett Bay, you have to be there at the magic moment when the mud is uncovered but the creeks are full, otherwise all the waders have disappeared into the deep channels and can't be seen. Pity the amateur WeBS organiser trying to fit in an ideal tide on a Sunday after church.

I had only just got to grips with the idea of the tidal range being greater when the earth, moon and sun are in alignment (spring tides twice a month) and, conversely, reduced when the same heavenly bodies are furthest out of line (neap tides), when I learnt about our local amphidrome. Like a mythical destination from a pirate film, tidal systems rotate around amphidromes, and consequently the tide neither rises nor falls at the centre of one. This has to do with the Coriolis effect, which most famously determines the direction water spirals down a drain (anti-clockwise in the northern hemisphere). The closest major amphidromes to Poole are in the Atlantic and North Sea (halfway between Holland and Norfolk), but there is a minor one on the edge of the New Forest. Obviously there's no tide in a forest, but if water did cover it the tide there would never come in or go out. All the smaller harbours along the Solent, like Christchurch, have a tiny tidal range because of their proximity to the amphidrone.

Across the channel at Cherbourg the tidal range is 12 metres, so the tide goes a long, long way out there, but inside Poole Harbour the range is only two metres between high and low water during spring tides, and as little as 30 cm during neap tides. All this means that for 16 out of 24 hours, the mud in Poole is submerged. Great for the small boats of bait draggers who chug round and round in circles dragging the worms up to sell to fisherman, but a bit tougher on the waders.

All the talk of sea levels rising a meter because of global warming melting ice in the Arctic means that our pub conversations are often about the possible consequences for Poole Harbour, and especially about the state of repair of the sea wall around Brownsea lagoon.

While water levels have been predicted to rise around 29 cm on the southwest coast by 2050 (UK government 2010), there has been little sign of this so far. Over the past 25 years, we have only seen a rise of a centimetre inside Poole Harbour. With the effect of the New Forest amphidrome, dredging of main channels, long shore drift, silt from rivers, and dramatic changes in the distribution of *Spartina* it is difficult for us to agree about its significance. All the studies show that ice on Greenland is melting at an unprecedented rate. While resulting rises in water levels are fairly slow at present, they are expected to be much faster by around 2025.

Down at the pub I suggested that when world water levels have risen dramatically by a meter, the close proximity of the New Forest amphidrome will mean that we only get a couple of centimetres while the parts of France with a huge tidal range will disappear in a biblical flood. This idea got me a few hearty English laughs but as amphidromes have no effect on general increases in sea level, only its tidal range, the idea was soon rubbished.

At present, the shoreline policy within Poole Harbour is to remove sea defences. Ian Alexander, a birder and pub irregular,

Icelandic Black-tailed Godwits *Limosa limosa islandica*, Poole, Dorset, 27 August 2011 (*René Pop*)

works for Natural England, one of the agencies responsible for this policy. Cyril Diver's natural vision for our area lives on in Ian and his colleagues, and as he talks you can feel the passion he has for this countryside. He takes climate change seriously, and when he's not striding round Bestwall working out exactly what will be inundated when water levels rise, he can be seen in the local Waitrose removing the unwanted plastic packaging from his purchases with his penknife. Predicting the effects of climate change is one very big step beyond weather forecasting, and Ian hits the nail on the head when he says: "You can't plan for climate change, Mark, only prepare."

Black-tailed Godwits *Limosa limosa* and other waders, Brownsea lagoon, Dorset, 4 October 2009 (*Claire Lodge*)

OK, it's time I came clean, here tucked deep inside the book. Having watched Poole and Bournemouth councils spend millions creating artificial reefs, and pumping sand back onto the popular beaches, there's a similar project I'd like to see adopted. I like the way the Dutch look at things. Their dykes reclaim the sea to create reserves that in turn hold masses of singing Marsh Warblers. Now you're talking! I prefer a vision of Poole where we create dykes to control flooding, creating new bird habitats while protecting homes. In this utopia, two new dykes would be built between Brownsea and Furzey, forming another huge lagoon. Alternatively, linking Furzey and Green Islands with dykes and a lagoon would effectively recreate 'South Island', which existed until Iron Age times (Dyer & Darvill 2010).

I suggested this to Ian and he frowned. "Hardly preserving a natural England, Mark." I pointed out that it was interesting how aware he was of the chaotic reality of Poole Harbour's nature, and yet through his work and training he maintained an 'unspoilt' and tranquil vision for others. He replied: "The pace of present change is high by most historic standards and we are changing so many things simultaneously. It seems to me to be a fairly irresponsible experiment."

One of the reasons why counting the waders in the harbour is so essential, especially in Brownsea lagoon, is that internationally important numbers of birds like Avocet and Black-tailed Godwit bring with them responsibilities. Should the lagoon wall be breached by rising sea levels, the Environment Agency would have to find and fund a solution. This makes me very worried. Can my pantomime villains at the Environment Agency really be trusted to look after something as important as Brownsea's sea wall?

That's why accurately working out what the tides are doing and correctly counting the waders isn't just an intellectual challenge but a vital one. At the pub, county bird recorder Kevin Lane started to wonder if the WeBS counts were showing an accurate picture. While editing the Dorset bird report, he had noticed that, according to the WeBS figures, Poole's birds were no longer reaching nationally significant numbers. A glance through the 2008 report shows why Kevin was worried. To be nationally significant, you need more than 981 Dark-bellied Brent Geese, and the WeBS count of 721 in 2007/08 fell short for the first time. With Pintail, the national threshold is 279 but the highest WeBS figure was 155 birds. The same could be said for Teal and Black-necked Grebe. Shelduck had already slipped from being internationally important and barely scraped through as nationally important.

At BTO HQ they knew something was up. A joint Dorset Bird Club/BTO 'Birder's conference' was organised for October 2010

and the BTO's Neil Calbrade gave a lecture explaining the problem. Looking at his graphs covering the previous five years, you could see that Poole Harbour had the highest number of incomplete counts in Britain.

What had happened to the counters? More than once, we were sent us to do a count in the dark, or at the wrong state of tide. Over a year or two, half the counters quit, and it's not easy getting counters. In neighbouring Hampshire, the WeBS organisers overcome any shortage of counters by arranging the dates to fit in with the availability of the people. Christchurch birder Mark Andrews spotted the problem with this and gave an example. "With a known movement of Black-tailed Godwits between the Lower Avon Valley and Poole Harbour, my feeling is that the figures could be potentially meaningless when the counts are a week apart."

John Day was at the conference. John lives at Arne, having been a senior warden there for the RSPB. He has instigated, coordinated and written a series of important reports on the birds of the harbour, published by the Poole Harbour Study Group. If you were looking for an elder statesman, John would be your man. He stood up and told the conference, "The mean peak counts for Poole Harbour over the last five years for which data is available show that the numbers have now slipped below the 20,000 threshold for an internationally important assemblage of waterfowl. If this continues for another five years, and especially if Avocet or Black-tailed Godwits are undercounted, the area could lose the protection that this designation affords." And on that bombshell he sat down.

Chapter 20: I love it when a plan comes together

There must be something about Nick and me that doesn't inspire confidence. I admit that my son's careers officer once likened me to small-scale wheeler-dealer Del Boy, and Nick did at one time sell classic cars for a living. As long ago as 2006, we nagged the BTO and anyone else that would listen that the WeBS numbers weren't up to scratch. We met Andy Musgrove, the BTO's head of monitoring, even bought him lunch at The Blue Boar. An extraordinary general meeting was held with all the counters present, but after careful consideration it was decided that nothing needed to change.

So Nick and I decided to run our own survey alongside the WeBS counts. We recruited professional bird surveyors Neil Gartshore and Dave Chown to count alongside Nick. Nick worked out the optimum state of the tide for each part of the harbour. He used Dave Collins' survey from 22 years ago as his template. During the same time, Neil was also working on a Nature Conservancy study, surveying wader habits after dark. So he was purposely sent out at night, but unlike the WeBS counters he was issued with night vision optics.

The single biggest discovery we made was that one person counting the birds on Brownsea lagoon at high tide gave a better idea of peak numbers than the maximum winter WeBS counts for the whole harbour. WeBS counts at low tide gave a maximum of 2,350 Dunlin, while our survey saw 3,001 in one count on Brownsea lagoon. It was the same for three other species: Red Knot - WeBS 43, Brownsea lagoon 143; Grey Plover - WeBS 53, Brownsea lagoon 235; and Ringed Plover WeBS - 43, Brownsea lagoon 74.

Under the guidelines for WeBS observers, gull counts are optional. Our own co-ordinated count of 4,500 Herring Gulls reached the threshold for national importance, while the highest WeBS count for the same period (896) did not. We also used surveyors who could identify Yellow-legged Gulls in all plumages, finding 170 at two sites, while the highest WeBS count was 19 birds in 2008/09.

Meanwhile, the Nature Conservancy's night study compared bird numbers during night and day on the northern shores. It highlighted a few species, like Ringed Plover, Grey Plover, Dunlin and Common Snipe, of which more fed at night than during the day. Most excitingly, four Jack Snipe that we never see feeding during the day were spotted in Holes Bay at night.

Strangely, Studland Bay (just outside the harbour proper) has never been included in the local WeBS counts. It's great for Black-necked and Slavonian Grebes, although they also get into Brand's Bay off Arne, and between the islands.

Studland Bay has 250 acres of eelgrass, and in 2004 it was found to hold a population of 40 adult Spiny Seahorses *Hippocampus guttulatus*. The government is to set up a network of 43 Marine

Sanderlings *Calidris alba* and Dunlins *C alpina*, Shell Bay, Studland, Dorset, 19 May 2011 (*Nick Hopper*)

Conservation Zones, and was considering Studland Bay as one of the 13 of these sites that shouldn't be disturbed at all. The Daily Telegraph wrote an article about the fuss it has caused (*Sailors vs seahorses: the battle of Studland Bay*, Saturday 19 November 2011). It describes a battle between the local boat owners who have been mooring boats here since time immemorial and the marine conservationists who believe this damages the eelgrass meadows and therefore the breeding conditions for the sea horses. The locals think the eelgrass has expanded over the past years and that they should be able to continue, while the conservationists argue that the density of sea horses is low considering the habitat and that there should be at least 200 adults. In the end, the designation has been delayed due to a lack of data.

Could Black-necked Grebes actually be part of the problem? Pipefish, which are closely related to seahorses, are known to be among their prey. Fully grown Spiny Seahorses are approximately 17 to 18 cm from the top of the coronet to the end of the tail, so presumably too big. Although they breed more frequently from the spring, they can breed throughout the year, so perhaps their 'seafoals' might form part of the grebes' winter diet.

Over the past five years, Black-necked Grebe numbers have been rising spectacularly at Studland. In 2011, Stephen Morrison started to watch the evening roost off Studland beach and counted 80 birds. That is the largest flock in Britain, where a flock of five is nationally significant. It is also four times the size of the other significant flocks at Langstone harbour in Hampshire and the Carrick roads in Cornwall. Stephen takes great care to get the numbers right.

"Watching the grebes come in to roost in the evening, I often pick up a number of birds coming in from the north-east and east from beyond the Training Bank and I can only think that during the day they have just been beyond the detection range for me even in calm conditions. With large numbers, and despite the greatest of care and skill, it is not too difficult to overlook those birds that insist on staying under the water for longer than they should. (I remember once having to wait 20 minutes to determine that there were actually 5 birds in a small flock, and not 4, when watching off Pilot's Point.)"

When Durwyn Liley did a study of the disturbance to the grebes in Studland Bay in 2005/06, he noticed that many of the grebes didn't fly between the spots but swam. As adult Black-necked Grebes are virtually flightless for most of their stay with us, it's likely that any Black-necked Grebe you might see flying will be a first-winter bird. Strong easterlies upset the grebes' and the seahorses' habits, and it is then that the grebes all move to feed off the south shore of Brownsea.

As for Slavonian Grebes, according to ringing recoveries, 'ours' are from Finland, Sweden or Norway. They hang about off the shore of Bramble Bush Bay or off Arne more often than Black-necked Grebes. There used to be 22 on average, but now numbers are much lower, with only three or four in recent years. Sadly, we have no idea why, and the WeBS counts have missed most of them.

Some species are considered too secretive to be counted as part of WeBS. Water Rails for example. If you look in British Birds journal's rare breeding birds report for 2008 (Holling & the Rare Breeding Birds Panel 2010), you will see that it only received reports of six territories of Water Rails in Dorset. Various other reports over the years suggested between 13 and 30. In 2004, Dave Chown squelched through our reed beds on a specially designed survey, playing taped Water Rail calls and counting responses. He surveyed 13 of Poole's reedbeds on seven mornings between 27 March and 20 April.

Dave found 211 pairs of Water Rail and 63 'single' birds, and he still thought this was a minimum. The 'single' birds could have included breeders, and because surveying had to go on into the day when Water Rails are less responsive, Dave thought some pairs must have been overlooked. So in a godlike seven days, Dave increased Britain's total of Water Rail territories by 21%.

Why does Poole have so many? Once the young Water Rails have fledged they are not thought to travel far, and if we take the pessimistic view that half the pairs successfully rear four young, that would take the population to 750. Large numbers of migrant German, Danish and Slovakian Water Rails are known to arrive here to winter. If you add that to our resident families, it wouldn't be unreasonable to have 1,500 individuals here in January. I should add that although these numbers add significantly to Britain's Water Rail population, Dave suggests that it isn't only Poole that doesn't know how many Water Rails it hosts.

Through his survey, Dave also gained some interesting insights into the harbour's ecology. "Water Rails were particularly numerous in areas where deer tracks were frequent (for example, the whole of the East Holton and Holton Heath)." He noticed that the Water Rails appeared to use the tracks to move around their territories. "By increasing the extent of standing water and bare mud in reed beds, deer tracks probably provide improved foraging conditions for the rails" (Chown 2004). And there is more to this web of ecological relationships than just deer and rails. The grass itself is *Spartina*, accidently introduced from North America, and native Redshanks are suffering because of its decline.

Japanese Sika Deer were first introduced to Brownsea Island in 1896. Being able swimmers, they started to leave the island, deserting it completely in 1934 during the big fire. As you may remember, by this time *Spartina* had arrived, hybridised and quickly colonised a third of the harbour, creating the most dramatic change in 400 years. Sika Deer have sturdy digestive systems and like to eat the *Spartina*. Now we had alien deer taking advantage of an alien grass.

The fact that both are aliens is important, because as a rule conservationists are purists and try to control non-indigenous flora and fauna. Sika don't only eat the *Spartina*, they also eat crops, damage trees and become a nuisance in gardens and nature reserves. On the other hand, they trample the edges of the salt grass, allowing indigenous grasses to return. The tenant farmers hate them, especially those where their landowners lease out the deer shooting. They find themselves growing crops for the Sika Deer to give a bit of sport to the shooters, who pay the farmers' landlords for the privilege of selling the 'venison'.

A rough estimate puts Purbeck and Poole Sika numbers at 5-7,000, one of the highest densities in Britain. Between foresters, conservationists, the army and landowners, I'm told that 1,000 a year have been culled over the past few years. The intention is to carry on shooting them, "until they are no longer a nuisance". I don't like shooting, but suspending my natural wish to put all the perpetrators on my little list, it's interesting to explore this decision to 'cull' Sika Deer a little more scientifically.

It is thought that in the absence of predators, Sika populations increase roughly 10% a year. If 1,000 a year are being killed (between 14% and 20%), this will bring down the numbers (May & Humphreys 2005). In Japan, however, they calculate that the unpredated annual increase rate of Sika deer is far higher at 16–21% (Matsuda et al 2002). If the Japanese figures are right, the current rate of shooting will have no effect on the deer, which could be good news for Water Rails but perhaps bad news for Redshanks.

As far as we can work out, Redshanks really flourished from 1900 when the *Spartina* started to cover the mud flats and provided more nesting opportunities. Breeding numbers in the early 20th century were suspected of reaching 100 pairs several times, but dropped to just six pairs after the cold winters of the early '60s. Because of this, we realised that the Redshanks breeding in the harbour were sedentary. By the middle of the '80s, numbers had recovered and we had some of the highest breeding densities in Britain, rising to 103 pairs by 1994 (1% of Britain's breeding population). But by 2002, Redshank breeding numbers had dropped again.

As we saw, the amount of mud flat covered in *Spartina* halved between 1924 and 2004. So we have more Sika feeding in half the area, and only half the space for the Redshanks' nests. Meanwhile, as other nature reserves like Sunnyside farm and The Moors become wetter, some Redshanks are returning to breed in their more natural habitats.

A 2004 study showed that breeding Redshank numbers in Poole Harbour were down to 69 pairs, a reduction of 19% in the eight years since 1997 (Cook 2004). There was a strange disparity between the north (Keysworth and Holes Bay), where numbers had halved, and the south (from Brand's Bay to Swineham), where the population had increased by five pairs to 51 pairs.

One of the reasons suggested for the Redshanks' decline was that the deer tracks made it easier for predators - perhaps Red Foxes, or Brown Rats - to find the nests and eat the young. But the deer are just as prevalent all around the harbour and you are more likely to see a fox at Middlebere than in Holes Bay. Interestingly, areas that had the highest Water Rail counts had the biggest declines in Redshank breeding numbers. Water Rails are carnivorous, and perhaps young Redshank are tasty.

While all these surveys are very interesting, none so far have told us whether or not WeBS should be counted at high tide. Although the lagoon high tide roosts were producing higher numbers, we now know that the WeBS were being dramatically under-counted. Seeing the figures at the conference inspired Shaun, Nick and me to organise a 'Big winter bird count' (BWBC). Based on the Western Hemisphere 'Christmas bird count', we invited local birders to give up any part of their day on 8 January 2011 to count any and all the birds in the harbour area. The idea was simply to provide a snap shot that might illustrate where future counts needed to be made. Having by now concluded his studies of Poole's birds, Nick had a good idea of where everyone should go and when. 46 birders took on the challenge to record as many species in the Poole Harbour area as was collectively possible - with targeted searches for Great Grey Shrike, which was found, and Lesser Spotted Woodpecker, which was not. In

Common Shelduck *Tadorna tadorna*, Brownsea lagoon, Dorset, 13 September 2011 (*Nick Hopper*). 'Numbers at Poole of national importance.'

addition, we were to do a high tide count of all wildfowl and waders, and roost counts of grebes, Goldeneyes and Starlings.

It turned out to be a wonderful day. Collectively, we found 143 different species and counted a minimum of 114,269 birds. Now admittedly 62,000 of those were Starlings, but considering Poole town has a human population of 138,000, it was still a fair few.

Among a series of interesting records, Peter Hadrill had six Marsh Harriers coming out of their roosts in the Wareham Channel, and 31 Woodcocks were found by all the counters, which is nationally significant. There were nine Firecrests scattered through the harbour, a record 410 Gadwall, 121 Magpies roosting at Hatch Pond, 10 Golden Pheasants, 18 Sparrowhawks, four Peregrines, two male Hen Harriers and a couple of Merlins.

Our various surveys enabled us to reach several conclusions. First, since Dave Collins' 1984 survey, the lagoon had become the most important roost site in the harbour. Second, that the important bird populations had not dropped out of national significance: they just weren't being counted properly. Third, our counters still found it hard to see waders at high tide. Redshank numbers for example were half what we knew them to be at low tide.

We reckon that just on the BWBC, Avocet numbers at 1,249 were above their international threshold which is 730, while there were 1,270 Black-tailed Godwits (international threshold 470). 1,741 Shelduck however were only nationally important (international threshold is 3,000). And the birds that had concerned Kevin - Dark-bellied Brent Goose, Common Teal, Pintail and Black-necked Grebe - were all found in nationally important numbers. With nationally significant numbers of Great Cormorant, Water Rail, Greenshank, Herring Gull, Yellow-legged Gull and Mediterranean Gull, and most importantly a total of wildfowl, waders and gulls using the harbour in winter nearer 30,000 than 20,000, Poole Harbour's status as an internationally important assemblage of waterfowl seems assured.

As for the issues with WeBS in Poole, it seems that while computerising the processing of data, the BTO organisers hadn't maintained their high standards of data gathering. Now, however, we have all got our act together. The RSPB are providing an organiser (Paul Morton) with backing from the Dorset Bird Club. Birders have been recruited to count all the areas, using knowledge gained from our own 2007/08 survey and the BWBC.

Stragglers Shaun, Nick, Mo and I will be attempting to rejoin the wheeling flock of counters next time on Sunday at 15:00.

Chapter 21: Dancing with the moonlit knight

When you are impatient for spring, and you think you have the flu but really it's just winter reaching right to your soul, and you read of Woodlarks breeding from February and singing on moonlit nights, you want to experience it… badly.

There's something about birds that sing at night, even as I write, I feel the itch to find one. The song is so beautiful, and it is often delivered in flight. In this example, it was recorded in the morning after rain using a parabola (**CD2-69**), but with luck you might hear the same sound floating around above your head in pitch darkness.

When they sing from perches or from the ground, male Woodlarks can sing much more simple songs, which are musical all the same (**CD2-70**). I have also read that female Woodlarks sing. Killian and I watched a pair feeding on the ground.

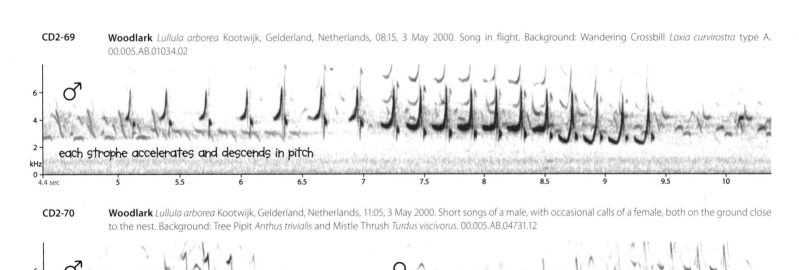

CD2-69 **Woodlark** *Lullula arborea* Kootwijk, Gelderland, Netherlands, 08:15, 3 May 2000. Song in flight. Background: Wandering Crossbill *Loxia curvirostra* type A. 00.005.AB.01034.02

each strophe accelerates and descends in pitch

CD2-70 **Woodlark** *Lullula arborea* Kootwijk, Gelderland, Netherlands, 11:05, 3 May 2000. Short songs of a male, with occasional calls of a female, both on the ground close to the nest. Background: Tree Pipit *Anthus trivialis* and Mistle Thrush *Turdus viscivorus*. 00.005.AB.04731.12

much shorter strophes when singing from ground

Woodlark *Lullula arborea*, juvenile, Morden Bog, Dorset, 16 June 2011 (*Nick Hopper*)

CD2-71 **Woodlark** *Lullula arborea* Morden bog, Dorset, England, 05:09, 16 June 2010. Song of a female in flight. Background: European Stonechat *Saxicola rubicola*, Common Chaffinch *Fringilla coelebs* and Yellowhammer *Emberiza citrinella*. 100616.MC.050900.04

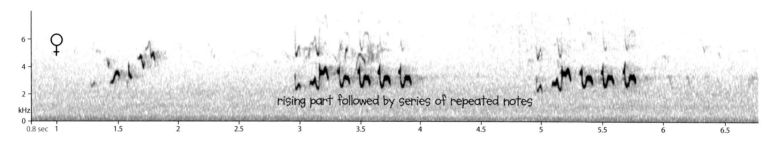

CD2-72 **Woodlark** *Lullula arborea* IJmuiden, Noord-Holland, Netherlands, 29 September 2002. Subsong of an individual, foraging in a flock during autumn migration. Background: Dunnock *Prunella modularis*, European Robin *Erithacus rubecula*, Great Tit *Parus major* and Common Reed Bunting *Emberiza schoeniclus*. 02.042.MR.10519.12

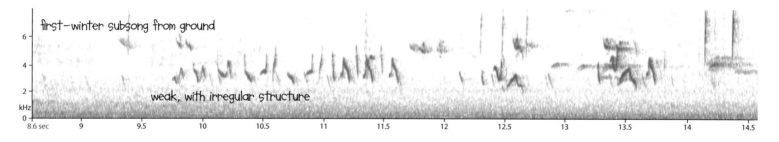

CD2-73 **Woodlark** *Lullula arborea* IJmuiden, Noord-Holland, Netherlands, 28 September 2002. A variety of calls including harsh threats from one of two individuals squabbling. This was a foraging flock of about 12 migrants. Background: Meadow Pipit *Anthus pratensis* and Eurasian Magpie *Pica pica*. 02.041.MR.14805.12

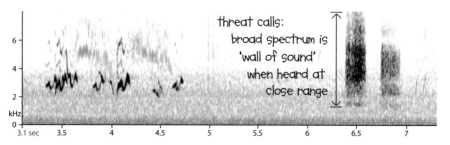

The male flew to its song perch and the female flew past us singing (**CD2-71**). In autumn and winter, it is sometimes possible to hear Woodlark subsong, which can give away the location of an otherwise unnoticed flock (**CD2-72**).

Woodlarks calls are often reminiscent of their songs, and can be highly variable. Listen to the calls given by this foraging flock in a brief recording of migrant Woodlarks in autumn (**CD2-73**). The

harsh call at 0:06 is a threat call, which has a very similar harsh quality across a wide range of passerine species.

One particular call, often used in alarm, is a bit monotonous (**CD2-74**). When flushed, Woodlarks often give a quiet, bubbling call before they launch into anything louder (**CD2-75**). Calls given while migrating are quite variable, but can always be recognised by their musical quality and, when present, by

CD2-74   **Woodlark** *Lullula arborea* Azrou, Middle Atlas, Morocco, 10:28, 26 March 2002. Calls of a pair, almost in alternation. The higher-pitched calls sometimes overlap with fragments of song from the other individual. So, presumably the lower-pitched whistles belong to the male and the higher-pitched calls to the female. 02.004.AB.03257.01

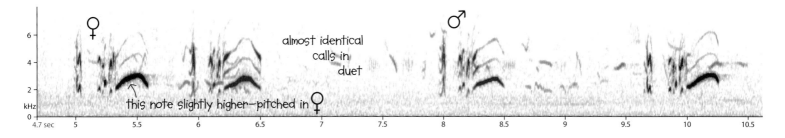

CD2-75   **Woodlark** *Lullula arborea* IJmuiden, Noord-Holland, Netherlands, 29 September 2002. *Pu-pu-pu* calls of a flock of eight autumn migrants when flushed. Background: Meadow Pipit *Anthus pratensis* and Dunnock *Prunella modularis*. 02.042.MR.10827.01

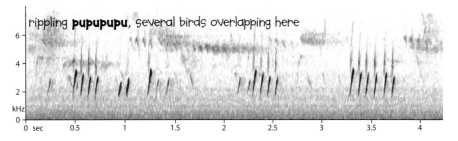

those quiet bubbling notes, interspersed between the louder more musical notes (**CD2-76**). There was also an example of two migrating Woodlarks under *A flock of birds forever in flight* (**CD2-16**).

Juvenile Woodlarks have tiny, high-pitched calls, which remind Killian and me of a Meadow Pipit (**CD2-77**). This bird was photographed by Nick and sound-recorded by Killian, and is celebrated again in Killian's plate.

CD2-76   **Woodlark** *Lullula arborea* de Nolledijk, Zeeland, Netherlands, 11:03, 8 November 2005. Calls of a single individual while migrating, including quiet *pu-pu-pu* calls. Background: Common Chaffinch *Fringilla coelebs*. 05.030.MR.13314.22

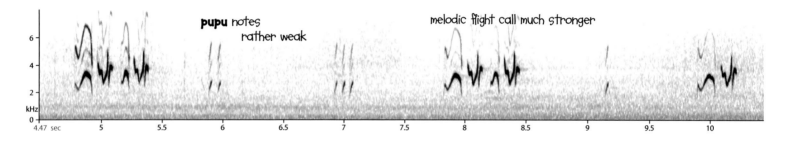

CD2-77   **Woodlark** *Lullula arborea* Morden bog, Dorset, England, 04:33, 17 June 2010. High-pitched, three-note calls of a juvenile and typical whistles of an adult. Background: Common Blackbird *Turdus merula* and European Robin *Erithacus rubecula*. 100617.KM.043300.02

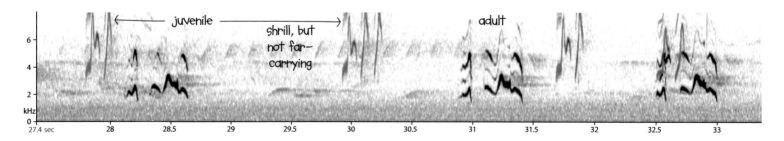

WOODLARK

song flight

Woodlark is smaller and shorter-tailed than Skylark

Skylark

Woodlark has paler stripe on underwing than Skylark

prominent pale tips, even in flight

broad, creamy supercilia meet at nape; distinct dark frame to ear coverts

slender

Woodlark

Skylark

compared to Skylark, Woodlark is shorter tailed, has a stronger head-pattern and diagnostic bold black-and-white markings on the wing

juv

Skylark juv

juv Skylark is sometimes surprisingly pale on nape, but pale patch is more spotted than in juv Woodlark

juv

adult

prominently pale-tipped alula and primary coverts diagnostic

autumn through to late winter (fresh)

adult in summer (worn)

Chapter 22: Bill Oddie, Bill Oddie, rub your beard on my body

Cycling to work along Baiter, I had noticed a flock of crows. Normally a 'flock' is an identification feature for Rooks while 'not in a flock' identifies Carrion Crows. So this little gathering caught my attention. It seemed as if these Carrion Crows were standing on the grass around the cycleway, waiting for the tide to turn so they could go fishing for winkles and cockles. Then they would fly up and drop the shells onto the tarmac to break them. Lately, the cycle path had been getting very crunchy to ride on.

Around the same time, Stephen Moss (author, columnist and birder) was one of the two producers responsible for coordinating the various live strands of *Autumnwatch*, the BBC TV programme that at that time starred Bill Oddie. The programme was to be based on Brownsea Island, and as part of Stephen's research he had contacted me. Over breakfast at The Sandbanks Hotel, I gave him a digest of interesting bird things that happen here in late autumn. Almost as an afterthought, I mentioned the cockling Carrion Crows.

Stephen sent his team in to film them. When the sequence was broadcast the next evening, Bill was chatting away to the camera when he mentioned that it was the first time he had seen Carrion Crows cockling. Intrigued, I looked it up in Witherby et al's *The handbook of British birds* (1938-41), which stated that the "Habit of smashing molluscs, crabs, … and other hard-shelled articles of food from a great height is well known." So I hadn't made a new discovery.

Why had both Bill and I missed this behaviour before? It's probably because they are still recovering from the most severe persecution of any of our native birds. All the corvids were shot, poisoned or trapped routinely. Carrion Crow numbers have now recovered dramatically, with very few of us noticing. Between 1964 and 1977, Carrion Crow numbers in Britain doubled and in the 30 years since then, with a decline in shooting and trapping, no doubt they have doubled again. This means that we are seeing behaviour like cockling that was probably common in Poole Harbour when numbers were higher in past centuries.

Bill has been a household name in Britain since he first appeared as a comedian in television and radio in the '60s. My family first met him when he stayed at our home while giving a talk for the Dorset Bird Club. My son Simon (7 at the time) was delighted and hung off his every word. The next morning when Simon hadn't done his homework, Bill wrote him a note: "I'm sorry Simon didn't do his homework. It was because he came to hear me give a talk. Yours, Bill Oddie." At first the teachers thought it was just an imaginative excuse, then when they realised it was genuine they wanted to keep the note. Simon was desperate to keep it, so after some negotiation he got it back and we still have it today.

Carrion Crow *Corvus corone*, Baiter, Poole, Dorset, 4 March 2010 (*Nick Hopper*). Opening shell.

Carrion Crow *Corvus corone*, Baiter car park, Poole, Dorset, 12 April 2010 (*Nick Hopper*). Dropping shells on tarmac.

Bill stayed an extra day and we went birding at Durlston Country Park. I introduced him to Hamish Murray, who lived up to all of my stories of his canny frugality by being caught in the act of steaming an unfranked stamp off an envelope for future use. As he had the kettle on, we were able to beg a cup of tea.

Bill and I have met occasionally since then. If he was a bird he would probably be a Jay, garrulous yet elusive. I once spotted him in the summer from an office window in Carnaby Street and shouted down. Catching up on the street, I told him of one of my customers, whose ambition was to make the famous Reading football club chant 'Bill Oddie, Bill Oddie, rub your beard on my body' a reality. He blushed and carried on with his mission to spend his birthday money.

At the Bird Fair I've watched, impressed, as he does the rounds in the optics tent, asking all the binoculars and telescope companies why they can't abandon their support for shooting interests.

On Brownsea Island, local author Dominic Couzins and I watched the rehearsals. Bill was sharp and very funny. I'm not sure who had come up with the idea of Simon King spending part of the night looking for Conger Eels off Brownsea pier. As he enthused about his task, held his mask and tipped off the boat backwards into the grey-brown soupy water of an ebb tide, they cut to footage shot earlier of an Avocet wrestling with a worm. Bill pointed out that this might be as close to a Conger Eel as the viewers would be getting this evening. Next came a man with a poem about our lives being like autumn leaves, whereupon Bill said, "And now on to a piece about feeding the birds in our gardens before we die." None of Bill's best jokes were in the finished programme.

Across from Brownsea, at South Haven, I've seen family parties of Rooks and Carrion Crows making their way into the harbour. I had often suspected that some corvids move through the harbour as winter approaches, or stay for the winter. Then one

November morning while I was in London doing something important, Mo was watching a large passage of Wood Pigeon from the top of our house when she saw a single flock of 600 Jackdaws flying low over the pines of Brownsea and then west across the harbour. I was a bit gripped.

It was this observation that led me to ask Nick to survey the corvids. He read Crow Country (Cocker 2007) and was inspired. We wondered if there were communal corvid roosts like Cocker described, inside the harbour. Nick worked through the autumn and winter to track down all the roosts, starting by searching out the rookeries. Visiting Studland on winter afternoons, he discovered what looked like a roost at the edge of Greenlands farm. He watched the large numbers of birds that gathered in the nearby fields. As it got darker, their feeding was interspersed with short swirling flights. When it was nearly dark, the birds started to assemble in the pines on the eastern edge of the plantation, chattering away and doing little 'dread' flights in and out, until eventually all went quiet and Nick assumed he had found the roost.

As darkness fell, he started to walk back to his car when suddenly there was a great cacophony. The whole flock got up together and sped off into the darkness. So he still didn't know where the roost was, and was back the next evening waiting at Goathorn, the last place he had seen them. This time his luck was in and he found the roost. It was even noisier here, with birds squabbling and jostling for position. This roost turned out to be the most impressive gathering in the harbour. In midwinter it peaked at 1,200 birds, of which 70% were Jackdaw and 30% Rooks and Carrion Crows (not easy to tell apart in the dark). Birds from Ballard and Bushey made up most of the roost. I tried to record this event, but managed to be in the wrong place at the wrong time. Then as I was answering the call of nature, this huge flock approached and I just managed a recording (**CD2-78**). For comparison, here are typical calls of Carrion Crow (**CD2-79**) and Western Jackdaw (**CD2-80**), also recorded in Poole Harbour.

CD2-78   **Rook** *Corvus frugilegus* and **Western Jackdaw** *C monedula* Goathorn, Poole Harbour, Dorset, England, 16:18, 18 January 2011. A mixed flock dominated by Rooks but also including a significant number of Western Jackdaws. Carrion Crows are much harder to pick out. Background: Common Blackbird *Turdus merula*. 110118.MC.161800.23

CD2-79   **Carrion Crow** *Corvus corone* Arne, Poole Harbour, Dorset, England, 07:00, 20 April 2008. Typical loud 'structured calls', an exchange between one individual close by and two or three at a distance. Carrion Crows sound more strident than Rooks, and their calls tend to be higher-pitched. Background: Common Wood Pigeon *Columba palumbus*, Barn Swallow *Hirundo rustica*, European Robin *Erithacus rubecula*, Common Blackbird *Turdus merula*, Common Chiffchaff *Phylloscopus collybita* and Goldcrest *Regulus regulus*. 08.011.MC.01645.01

CD2-80   **Western Jackdaw** *Corvus monedula* Slepe Copse, Poole Harbour, Dorset, England, 08:38, 5 May 2010. Two or three individuals at a potential breeding site. *Chak* calls and crowing. Background: Great Spotted Woodpecker *Dendrocopos major*, Eurasian Wren *Troglodytes troglodytes*, Eurasian Blackcap *Sylvia atricapilla* and Great Tit *Parus major*. 100502.MC.083842.01

After Nick had done a few early morning visits, it became apparent that there was also a precise ritual for leaving the roost. While still dark, the chattering and calling starts. At the first sign of any light, there would be a dramatic increase in the volume, as Jackdaws and Rooks erupt out of the roost together in a single flock and swirl around the tree tops. They would then split into groups. Jackdaws would speed ahead, with the Rooks following on at a more leisurely pace. The 'eruption'

Carrion Crow *Corvus corone*, Baiter, Poole, Dorset, 12 April 2010 (*Nick Hopper*). 'Winkling.'

210

times were quite predictable, being triggered by light levels, with birds 'lying in' on mornings with a lot of cloud cover.

Nick found three more corvids' roosts in the harbour: Upton Heath, Arne and Keysworth, and two more outside the area that were also used by Poole's birds, one at Stony Down Plantation just north of Corfe Mullen tip, and the other a few miles up the Piddle Valley. Checking the Keysworth roost proved difficult. The owner of Keysworth wanted over 300 pounds a visit, donated to the local church. So Nick had to peep into the trees near the waterworks from across the river Piddle. This roost was unusual, as its occupancy peaked during the autumn. In mid-December a total of 1,420 Jackdaws and 685 Rooks were counted at all four main roosts. Towards the end of January, the numbers fell, and by late February numbers fell again.

To give you an idea of the recent increase in Magpie numbers, the largest known roost is at Hatch Pond. In 1995 there were 74 birds, but each year the number crept up a little. By 1 December 2008 it had reached 193, a new Dorset record. The 'Songbird Survival Trust' believes these rises in corvid numbers have a negative effect on farmland birds. This is a cheeky group of landed gentry and farmers who want to return to heavy control of "predators, such as cats, corvids (which include crows, jackdaws and magpies), raptors, grey squirrels, rats and foxes". They would like to see the government controlling these 'vermin', and blame its reluctance in part on "relentlessly sentimental wildlife programming". So I think it's unlikely that any of them saw our flocks of Carrion Crows innocently feeding on cockles on *Autumnwatch*.

To prove their point, *Songbird Survival* funded a sophisticated piece of analysis that appeared in the *Journal of Applied Ecology* (Newson et al 2010). No doubt to their disappointment, it showed that neither Magpies nor Carrion Crows, nor indeed most of the other 'vermin', had played a major role in the collapse of songbird populations. So if the increase in corvids is not causing the problems facing Poole's farmland birds, what is?

Chapter 23: An obsessive Hobby

While we are dealing with my anxieties, we might as well cover this one. I think I have a deaf spot when it comes to Hobby calls, but I can't be sure. Let me show you what I mean. Imagine that you are walking with me from the hide at Middlebere along the track towards Hartland Moor, then along the old tram track up to Soldier's Road. There are 10 sounds that you hear. Without turning the page, have a listen to each sound (**CD2-81**). Hobby is featured twice, an adult male and a pair. Each of these species has been seen or heard over the years along this route, some more often than others. If you can identify more than half, you are doing better than anyone did when we tried this at the pub.

Eurasian Hobby *Falco subbuteo*, first-summer, near Sherford Bridge, Dorset, 16 June 2010 (*Mike Coleman*). Each year in June, first-summer Hobbies appear in the south of England. The one in this picture can be distinguished from an adult by the tar-brown upperwing with indications of retained scaling, and also the distinct barring to the undertail. These first-year birds need to be taken into account when doing a Hobby census.

CD2-81a
0:00-0:21
Common Greenshank *Tringa nebularia* Middlebere, Dorset, England, 31 August 2002. Calls of a migrant preparing to take off. Background: Eurasian Curlew *Numenius arquata*. 02.040.MR.01249.22

CD2-81b
0:22-0:42
Osprey *Pandion haliaetus* Raso, Cape Verde Islands, 13:13, 21 March 2007. Calls of a pair. Background: Raso Lark *Alauda razae*. 070321.MR.131303.31

CD2-81c
0:43-0:58
Lesser Spotted Woodpecker *Dendrocopos minor* Castelo Branco, Portugal, 08:38, 1 July 2010. Song. Background: Spanish Imperial Eagle *Aquila adalberti*, Spotless Starling *Sturnus unicolor* and Spanish Sparrow *Passer hispaniolensis*. 100701.MR.083808.20

Eurasian Hobby *Falco subbuteo* Lentevreugd, Zuid-Holland, Netherlands, 22:18, 30 June 2004. Staccato calls of a pair circling over a marsh at dusk. Background: Egyptian Goose *Alopochen aegyptiaca*. 04.021.AB.02533.13

CD2-81i
3:21-3:52

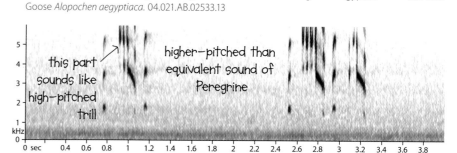

CD2-81d
0:59-1:53
Eurasian Hobby *Falco subbuteo* Hoge Vuursche, Utrecht, Netherlands, 3 August 2004. An adult calling to a fully grown juvenile on the nest, perhaps encouraging it to take its first flight. Background: Common Buzzard *Buteo buteo*, European Blue Tit *Cyanistes caeruleus* and Short-toed Treecreeper *Certhia brachydactyla*. 04.039.MR.11412.01

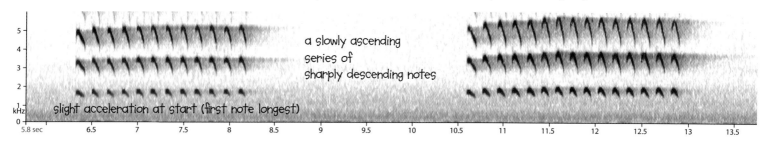

CD2-81e
1:54-2:14
White-tailed Eagle *Haliaeetus albicilla* Pyhäjärvi Lake, Yläne, Finland, 7 March 2003. Calls of a five-year-old female at a feeding station. Background: 03.004.MC.01300.01

CD2-81f
2:16-2:31
Eurasian Wryneck *Jynx torquilla* Białowieża, Podlaskie, Poland, 09:30, 28 April 2003. Song of a pair. Background: Common Starling *Sturnus vulgaris* 03.013.MC.04200.01

CD2-81g
2:32-3:10
Common Kestrel *Falco tinnunculus* Cesaro, Sicily, Italy, 18:27, 3 May 2010. Calls of an adult flying close to the pinnacle it was breeding on. Background: Eurasian Wren *Troglodytes troglodytes*, Common Nightingale *Luscinia megarhynchos*, Common Blackbird *Turdus merula* and Corn Bunting *Emberiza calandra*. 100503.MR.182740.01

CD2-81h
3:11-3:20
Green Woodpecker *Picus viridis* Arne, Poole Harbour, Dorset, England, 20 April 2008. A yaffle or 'laughing' call. Background: Common Teal *Anas crecca*, Eurasian Wren *Troglodytes troglodytes*, Song Thrush *Turdus philomelos* and Willow Warbler *Phylloscopus trochilus*. 08.011.MC.00350.01

Peregrine Falcon *Falco peregrinus* Soldier's Road, Poole Harbour, Dorset, England, 17:00, 24 January 2004. An interaction between two birds at dusk, with *keCHEK* calls. One of them had prey and the other was seen flying off towards a roost. 04.003.MC.00050.41

CD2-81j
3:53-4:22

The last two don't sound much like the others, but show that there is even potential for confusion between Hobby and Peregrine. I actually recorded that pair of Peregrines interacting at dusk one winter on Soldier's Road, where you can see Hobbies a few months later.

Maybe I just don't hear enough of the real thing, and yet with about half a dozen pairs of Hobby in the harbour I get to see them often enough. The adults arrive in May, while some yearlings pop back in June for a bit of prospecting. Other young Hobbies stay on their wintering grounds, or else move north but not far enough to reach Poole Harbour.

So how can we tell Hobbies apart from some of the species that give similar sounds? Wryneck can sound very similar indeed, and although they are rare in the harbour, the potential for confusion does exist. Magnus tells me that the more Wryneck-like examples of Hobby in our collection all start with an acceleration, coinciding with a slight rise in pitch. In other words, at the start of a call the notes become progressively shorter and higher-pitched before stabilising. You can hear this clearly in **CD2-82**, a male and female calling in turn having recently returned to their breeding grounds. In Wryneck, there is a slight rise in pitch too, but none of our recordings show an obvious acceleration. If anything there is sometimes a slight

CD2-82 **Eurasian Hobby** *Falco subbuteo* Aksu-Dzabagly zapovednik, South Kazakhstan, Kazakhstan, 5 May 2000. Courtship of a pair. Background: Water Pipit *Anthus spinoletta* and Eurasian Magpie *Pica pica*. 00.021.MR.04414.11

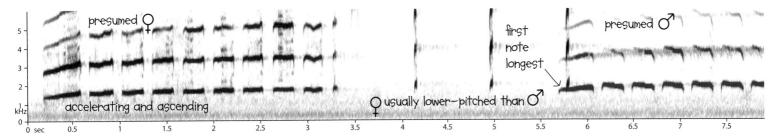

CD2-83 **Eurasian Wryneck** *Jynx torquilla* Białowieża, Podlaskie, Poland, 08:10, 28 April 2003. Courtship of a pair. Background: Eurasian Blackcap *Sylvia atricapilla*, Common Chiffchaff *Phylloscopus collybita*, Eurasian Starling *Sturnus vulgaris*, Common Chaffinch *Fringilla coelebs* and Hawfinch *Coccothraustes coccothraustes*. 03.013.MC.02400.01

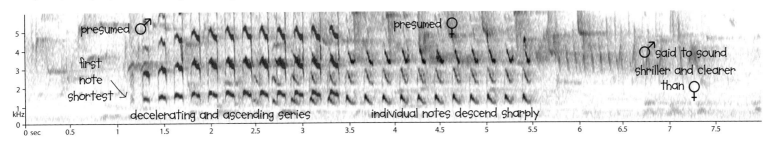

deceleration, the first note or two being noticeably shorter, as if the bird stutters to get started. You can hear this from a male and female calling in alternation in **CD2-83**.

Of the other species you listened to, Kestrel is a common relative of Hobby, allowing plenty of opportunities both for mistakes and learning. Some of the faster call types of Hobby are similar in pitch and repetition rate to Kestrel calls, and one way to tell them apart is to listen carefully to the individual notes. In Hobby, each note in the faster call type descends sharply in pitch (**CD2-84**). This is not the case with Kestrels, where if anything, each very short note sounds as if it rises rapidly (**CD2-85**). In fact the pitch then goes down again, but this is hardly audible. As the example shows, Kestrels also tend to have a slightly harsher timbre.

CD2-84   **Eurasian Hobby** *Falco subbuteo* Hoge Vuursche, Utrecht, Netherlands, 3 August 2004. Calls of a juvenile female followed by a more distant alarmed adult. 04.039.MR.10840.00

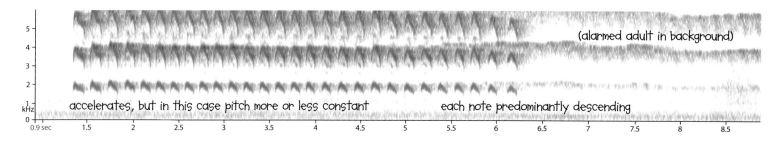

CD2-85   **Common Kestrel** *Falco tinnunculus* Merja Zerga, Moulay Bousselham, Morocco, 06:35, 7 October 2006. Calls of a female, given during a display flight with fast and fluttery wingbeats. Background: Eurasian Collared Dove *Streptopelia decaocto,* Common Bulbul *Pycnonotus barbatus,* Common Blackbird *Turdus merula* and European Goldfinch *Carduelis carduelis*. 06.014.AB.03703.01.

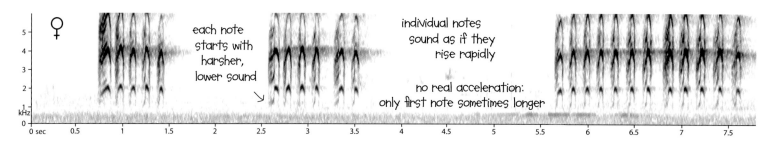

Eurasian Hobby *Falco subbuteo,* first-summer, near Sherford Bridge, Dorset, 4 June 2010 (*Mike Coleman*). Superficially similar to adults, first-summer Hobbies are best identified by the brownish, juvenile upperwing and the distinctly barred juvenile tail-feathers (best seen from below). Note also on this bird, that the reddish colour below is restricted to trousers only and that the trousers are boldly marked, although both of these features vary individually.

CD2-86   **Eurasian Hobby** *Falco subbuteo* Hoge Vuursche, Utrecht, Netherlands, 3 August 2004. An adult responding to at least three intruders of the same species flying high overhead. Background: Great Spotted Woodpecker *Dendrocopos major*, Great Tit *Parus major* and Eurasian Nuthatch *Sitta europaea*. 04.039.MR.02406.11

Eurasian Hobby *Falco subbuteo* Hanko, Uusimaa, Finland, 07:00, 30 July 2006. High-pitched calls of an adult perched in a tree, with some weaker, faster juvenile calls towards the end. Background: White-tailed Eagle *Haliaeetus albicilla*, Eurasian Blackcap *Sylvia atricapilla*, Spotted Flycatcher *Muscicapa striata*, Common Chaffinch *Fringilla coelebs* and Yellowhammer *Emberiza citrinella*. 06.002.DF.13256.21   **CD2-88**

Hobbies also have a very short *kip* call that is shared by several other falcon species. In **CD2-86** it is given by an adult, as a response to several other Hobbies flying over its territory. Very young Hobbies still on the nest can be identified by the weaker, scratchier quality of their calls (**CD2-87**). The sound we hear most often from Hobbies is a far-carrying, insistent *pee-pee-pee*, as in **CD2-88**, although we don't usually hear it with White-tailed Eagles in the background. I should explain that it was Dick Forsman who made the last two recordings, near his holiday home in the southwest corner of Finland. I wouldn't mind hearing either of these raptors more often in Poole Harbour.

CD2-87   **Eurasian Hobby** *Falco subbuteo* Hanko, Uusimaa, Finland, 07:00, 30 July 2006. A juvenile calls weakly from the nest. Background: White-tailed Eagle *Haliaeetus albicilla*, Common Gull *Larus canus*, White Wagtail *Motacilla alba* and Common Chaffinch *Fringilla coelebs*. 06.002.DF.14454.21

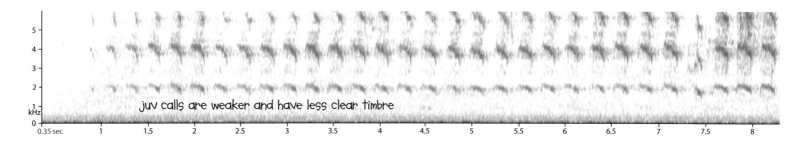

juv calls are weaker and have less clear timbre

HOBBY

catching and eating dragonfly on the wing

first-summers always retain entire set of juvenile flight-feathers, while amount of moulted scapulars and upperwing coverts vary individually

alternates relaxed gliding flight with exhilarating bursts of acceleration

uniformly dark slate-grey upperparts in adult

underparts, including thighs and vent, buff

unbarred central tail-feathers

rust-red

slim body, long wings

first-summer

juv

unbarred tail (from above) often looks rather pointed

Merlin (juv)

juv

Peregrine (ad)

scaly upperparts

Merlin has shorter wings, more strongly barred tail and less clear-cut head pattern

well-defined 'L-shaped' white cheek-patch distinctive

Peregrine usually looks much broader with less attenuated shape

juv

lacks red thighs and vent of adult

first-summer

acquires adult-like plumage at individually variable rate, between first- and second-winter

Chapter 24: The silent spring of the Anthropocene

On 13 June 2009, the Poole birders could be heard belting out *Jerusalem* in Lytchett Minster Church in celebration of Ian and Margaret Lewis's wedding. Ian was a widower, and his first wife Janet lay in the churchyard. Janet had died suddenly, plunging Ian into unanticipated circumstances, but renewal and adaptation is a human strength and as the couple walked down the aisle Ian radiated with newfound happiness.

The weather should be a safe conversational gambit to strike up at an English wedding reception in June, but not now. The birders talked intensely about conservation in Poole Harbour and the birds' future, with the climate changing and the likelihood of all of nature being plunged into unanticipated circumstances.

The first Met Office regional weather forecast for southern England was made by Admiral Fitzroy (Darwin's companion, the captain of the Beagle) and published in *The Times* on 1 August 1861, when it forecasted "Fresh Westerly; fine" for southern England. The forecast for 1 August 2009 at the time of writing is almost identical. Predicting the weather must have been even more contentious then than today, because Fitzroy was mauled badly by dissatisfied readers, and *The Times* dropped weather forecasts in 1864. The next year Fitzroy got up one morning, went into the bathroom and cut his throat.

With or without forecasting, extremes in the weather have been making the news for centuries. In 1862 it was so wet and cold here that a large number of Barn Swallows died in a very cold June for want of their usual supply of insect food, yet in 1868 there were eight months of extraordinary heat and so many flies that people complained. A hurricane in 1866 blew down the elms in Studland village churchyard, and the Rooks that are there today didn't breed for nearly 40 years.

For Poole, Bournemouth and Christchurch, merging along Poole Bay to create one big tourist destination, sunny weather is economically vital. Dorset has a billion pounds a year of tourist income, and in our conurbation a sunny weekend adds a million pounds to the local economy. Historically, Poole and Christchurch grew in the 1600s and then in the early 1800s, Bournemouth was built on the huge expanse of heath between them.

This Victorian new town grew as tuberculosis sufferers and others left smoggy London to take the air. Growth was fast. In 1826, James Harris was shooting 'Blackcock' on the heath where 40 years later invalids were being pushed in bath chairs along the lower pleasure gardens. Most of the tourists were sick, and good official figures for temperature and sunshine were essential for the resort's success. This had an effect on

Ian and Margaret's wedding, Lytchett Minster, Dorset, 13 June 2009 (*Janis Dreosti*). Featuring from left to right: Ewan Brodie, Christine Arnold, Anne Heeley, Guy Dutson, Margaret Lewis, Ian Alexander, John Lockwood, Ian Lewis, James Phillips, Mo Constantine, Jean Obray, John Dowling, Roger Howell, Mark Constantine, Sue Howell, Tim Kellaway and Trevor Warrick.

Barn Swallows *Hirundo rustica*, at Nick's garden, Nutcrack Lane, Stoborough, Dorset, 3 June 2011 (*Nick Hopper*)

the systematic weather recording in Bournemouth and Poole. According to a recent book, "the location of the metrological instruments changed during Bournemouth's history in an attempt to maximise a favourable climate" (Sloane 2010).

Microclimates could influence where the invalids stayed, and different areas would spin the climate in their area to make it sound the most favourable. During the '60s, the official site for the sunshine recorder was Meyrick Park. Then a trial was run on

Bournemouth pier, where any seawatcher could have told them that 'sea fog' was going to be a problem. The difference was 21.3 hours, far too great a variance in the annual competition between resorts for the sunniest seaside town. The recorder was duly moved to Poole at Wallisdown and then to King's Park in Bournemouth.

Having made it this far you will know that climate change has always been with us, and that the birds we enjoy today are a reflection of the current climate. So on behalf of birds, we don't have to consider whether the climate is changing but rather keep an eye on which way it's going and try to work out how much it's going to change.

At the time of the wedding, I read a desperate article in the RSPB's *Birds* magazine, in which the present era was described as the "Anthropocene", created by man with "vast emissions of carbon dioxide". It told readers that mankind was facing "the Four Horseman of the Apocalypse" and continued, "The Anthropocene threatens to be a truly terrible time for a person to be alive… unless we act very radically and very quickly to change things" (McCarthy 2009).

Allowing for a little local massaging of the figures that I mentioned, here are some data about how our temperature has changed over the years. At the beginning of the last century, the average annual temperature here was 10.36°C, and it slowly crept up to 10.58°C in the 1940s. It then cooled for several decades, dropping half a degree to 9.98°C and didn't manage to climb again until 1995. In the last decade, we have seen a dramatic rise, as local temperatures increased on average by 1°C to 11.47°C. The increases in local air temperature in the last

two decades have been measurably larger than those in sea temperature, and while unlikely to herald conquest, war, famine and death, this is known to create stronger onshore winds.

The way in which the 'Anthropocene' differs from past eras is that this time we are thought to be directly responsible and should, theoretically, be able to shape the way and the speed of how the changes happen. If the changes are too fast, the general thinking is that birds may not have the time to adapt.

With the weather becoming political, we expect the government to do something about it. Two of the guests at Ian and Margaret's wedding were better informed than the rest of us as to what was happening. We've already met one of them, Ian Alexander. Keen birder James Phillips is another ecologist and Ian's colleague at Natural England. On farmlands and in our woods, James is trying to recreate the kind of conservation success that has already been achieved with waterbirds. Unfortunately in these habitats, the frightening prediction in Rachel Carson's *Silent Spring* (1962) of a countryside without bird song is fast becoming a reality.

At the wedding reception, I took the opportunity to ask why Poole's farmland wasn't as good as it used to be for birds. Ian explained that since the mid-'40s, when the UK was genuinely short of food and had been close to collapse, the government had stepped in to support increased productivity, and farm production had gone up.

"Even when we had sufficient food, farmers strove to become more and more 'efficient', especially labour efficient. We stripped the countryside of most of the labour that historically cared for it and replaced it with oil-consuming machinery until we reached the point where some of our meals use more fossil fuel calories to produce than the food calories we consume." I ate my vegetarian quiche and my eyes widened. With a sweeping gesture towards the buffet, he went on, "We are effectively eating oil. And it is fossil fuel derived inputs, the fertilisers and pesticides, that create the ecological damage."

Ian was preaching to the converted of course. For many years I've been looking forward to us all consuming less oil, wasting less food, creating less air pollution and throwing less away. The prospect of less noise both from planes and car tyres, and listening to bird songs free of both is tantalising. Now with everyone worried about climate change, the society I've always dreamt of is so much closer. Major change in our climate could be 50 years away or 50 weeks, depending on which information you read. Still dreaming, I'm transported back to Ben Pond's countryside with heath untouched and Black Grouse, Corn Crake, Stone-curlew, Yellow Wagtail, Red-backed Shrike, Chough,Tree Sparrow and Cirl Bunting still present, all to be lost over the intervening 60 years.

I've never seen or heard a Quail or Grey Partridge in Poole Harbour, and I asked Ian why we didn't find them anymore. He reminded me that at the beginning of the silent spring, pesticides were directly and very visibly toxic to wildlife, killing individuals or disrupting their breeding so that populations plummeted.

Ian explained that nowadays we are better at designing and screening chemicals for direct toxicity, but the problems have shifted to the disruption that the chemicals cause in the ecosystem. "Basically, partridge chicks need insects for the first couple of weeks after they hatch and this invertebrate prey, in turn, needs a range of host plants on which to feed, by and large the very plants that the herbicides have removed from the farmland. No 'weeds', no invertebrates feeding on the weeds, no food for partridge chicks, no partridges."

A lot of James's work involves encouraging local landowners and farmers to try wildlife-friendly farming. He chipped in,"On top of that there just hasn't been the nesting habitat or food through the late winter and early spring for farmland birds. The loss of spring-sown crops and weedy stubble hedges and the little margins mean that birds have fewer places to nest, produce fewer offspring and can't survive the winter."

Ian and James know that we can reverse these effects in years not decades. Part of their job is to help our farmers to do just that, and in 2010 in Dorset alone, the government distributed £19 million of grants to farmers, especially to look after our wildlife. They are part of the effort to reverse the silent spring effect. After 70 years of indoctrination, however, asking farmers to love their 'weeds' and 'pests' must be tough.

James pointed out that the species disappearing most rapidly in Poole were Lapwing, Skylark, Linnet, Yellowhammer and Reed Bunting, and that all could be brought back from the brink. A birder's gleam lit up his eye. "We have the grants available to encourage farmers to replicate the key habitats with wild bird mixtures or pollen and nectar mixes, beetle banks, conservation headlands, weedy over-winter stubbles, skylark plots, summer fallow and flower rich margins."

Ian went on: "While I agree that we need to be taking action to defend what we still have, we could and should aspire to regain the birds and plants we have lost." James added, "In Poole that could be Corn Buntings and Yellow Wagtails."

I find it hard to understand how farmers have been allowed to lay bare the countryside. In the 1930s, my Grandad owned a grocer's on South Street in Dorchester, the county town of Dorset, and he made his living servicing the farmers' needs, staying open until 23:00 and opening on Sundays. Nowadays the farmers service the grocers. If you add up the incomes of all Britain's farms, in 2008 this amounted to £8.7 billion while just one of the supermarkets with a branch in Poole, Tesco's, turned over £68 billion, making nearly a £1 billion of profit in a quarter. It is demand from supermarkets like Tesco's that encourages farmers to rely on techniques that are unfriendly to birds.

Theoretically, Poole Harbour shouldn't be suffering as many problems with birds and farmland as other parts of Britain, as a large part of the farmland on the shores is owned by nature conservation groups and leased to farmers.

Shaun, who has been keeping account around the farm at Lytchett for 20 years, reminded us all that the pair of Little Owls that bred from the early '70s had disappeared by 2001. Not only have there been none since, but the pattern has been replicated around Poole Harbour, where the species no longer breeds. He suggested that 'cleaning up' of the farms and their surroundings had been responsible. Another farmland bird lost from Lytchett is Yellowhammer, which last bred there in 1993. In this case it still breeds at Lytchett Minster just round the corner, so it really should have returned under RSPB's stewardship but hasn't.

While we do have one organic farm at Rempstone, The National Trust and the RSPB have allowed their tenants to farm conventionally, using pesticides and producing crops with a big appetite for fertiliser. So even the nature reserves aren't organic. Most of what we consider natural is kept that way through a lot of management, and while not as widespread as in farming, 'weed killers' are used to maintain heathlands, killing plants like rhododendrons, Gaultheria and bracken. Ian explained how few insects there are now in comparison to the '40s and '50s. "You'll know when we've got it right, Mark. You wont be able to cycle across Hartland without getting flies in your teeth and eyes."

Chapter 25: Completely cuckoo

We continued from Ian's reception on to the pub, and over a beer the conversation moved on to what should be another safe subject in Dorset: what date did you hear your first cuckoo this year? Down the road in Wareham, tradition has it that cuckoos hibernate in hollow trees. Each year the first cuckoo in Dorset to wake up and call is in Purbeck, where on 17 April he goes to Wareham's spring fair and "buys hisself a pair of breeches" (Legg 2000). Ian Lewis explained that when the weather is bad, birds arriving earlier die, while those with the habit of coming later survive, and so birds adapt to the changing climate. Cuckoos are 10 days earlier now in Purbeck, arriving sometime between 3 and 9 April, so the risk of arriving earlier is not as high as it used to be.

I knew cuckoos didn't hibernate in trees, but until recently I did believe that females were able to vary the pattern of their eggs to match those of the potential host, say one year Reed Warbler and another year Meadow Pipit. I'm not sure what I thought was going on (tiny fairies with paint brushes?), but it's not true. Common Cuckoos lay eggs with genetically predisposed patterns that fit their specific host. This means that female cuckoos can be divided into 'host specific races', and pass their preference on to their female young, who lay their eggs in nests of the same species that brought them up. Research into Hungarian cuckoo calls by Fuisz & de Kort (2007) suggests that male cuckoos in marshes call differently from males in forests.

Meadow Pipit *Anthus pratensis*, Hartland Moor, Dorset, 3 May 2010 (*Nick Hopper*)

Common Cuckoo *Cuculus canorus*, Chardara, Kazakhstan, 3 September 2009 (*René Pop*)

If this proves correct, it could mean that males also belong to 'host specific races', some for example pairing with females that lay in Reed Warbler nests, and others with females that lay in Meadow Pipit nests. So perhaps when we hear 'the' cuckoo we are not listening well enough.

Listen to a recording of a classic 'reedbed cuckoo', singing along with a group of Reed Warblers (**CD2-89**). For a little light entertainment, compare it to this 'forest cuckoo' recorded in Poland (**CD2-90**). The main difference you will hear between these two examples (the higher pitch of the reedbed cuckoo, especially in the second note) is exactly what Fuisz and de Kort found.

At Ian's wedding, it soon became apparent that none of us was noticing as many cuckoos as we used to. British cuckoo numbers dropped by 58% between 1970 and 2008 (Eaton et al 2010), and I suggested to the others that it wasn't so bad

in Poole. Terry thought that as Meadow Pipits had gone from his patch, so had the cuckoos. Shaun remarked that he only heard migrant cuckoos a couple of times a spring at Lytchett. We talked through the usual confusing array of reasons for the decline, including global warming, with flowers and the insects that depend on them appearing earlier and the host species breeding earlier. Someone added that increasing desertification in Africa was causing problems on the wintering grounds. Intensive farming in Britain was also blamed.

Cuckoos mainly eat caterpillars, especially the hairy ones avoided by other birds. They like tiger moths *Arctiidae*, which declined by 45% in Britain from 1966 to 2005. These in turn depend on common weeds like dandelion *Taraxacum*, nettles *Urtica*, dock *Rumex*, and brambles *Rubus*. We suspect that there may be an echo of Grey Partridge here: twice the productivity for supermarkets, half the weeds, half the hairy caterpillars, half the food for cuckoos, half the cuckoos?

CD2-89　'Reedbed Cuckoo' *Cuculus canorus* and **Eurasian Reed Warbler** *Acrocephalus scirpaceus* Middlebere, Poole Harbour, Dorset, UK, 04:32, 8 May 2010. Song of a male, to the accompaniment of reed warblers, the probable guardians of its offspring. Background: Common Pheasant *Phasianus colchicus*, Common Wood Pigeon *Columba palumbus*, European Robin *Erithacus rubecula*, Common Blackbird *Turdus merula*, Common Whitethroat *Sylvia communis*, European Blue Tit *Cyanistes caeruleus* and Long-tailed Tit *Aegithalos caudatus*. 100508.MC.043200.02

'Forest Cuckoo' *Cuculus canorus* Białowieża forest, Podlaskie, Poland, 20:30, 3 May 2005. Much lower-pitched song of a cuckoo in a forest habitat. Background: European Tree Frog *Hyla arborea*, Eurasian Woodcock *Scolopax rusticola* and Song Thrush *Turdus philomelos*. 05.006.MR.04331.01　**CD2-90**

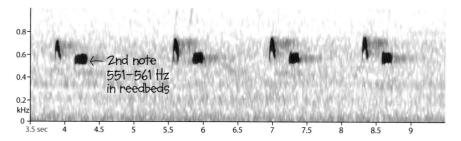

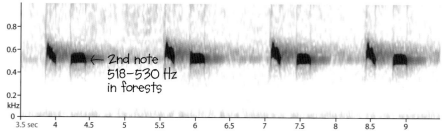

Common Cuckoo *Cuculus canorus*, Zhabagly, Kazachstan, 18 September 2009 (*René Pop*)

Living in the town, we don't notice the decline. With farmers hiring in contractors who harvest the crops, sitting oblivious inside giant soundproof tractor cabs, it becomes easier to understand how the silence in the farmland has crept up on us. If we want to be part of a future where we still hear cuckoos, we must change our demands on supermarkets, forcing farmers to adopt more wildlife-friendly practices, and we need to do it today.

When I first went birding around the harbour, telling Willow Tit from Marsh Tit was an issue. Not anymore, because Willow Tit has disappeared. In *A climatic atlas of European breeding birds*, Huntley et al (2007) predicted it would move north with the warming climate. We don't know how much further north, but in 1997 someone did estimate that natural habitats and agriculture would move northwards by 50-80 km a decade. Within 90 years, Huntley et al anticipated fewer Gannets breeding in the English Channel, the loss of Fulmar and Black-legged Kittiwake here, and a northward shift in the range of Shelduck so that Poole Harbour may become the last breeding site in southern England.

Sea levels rise as water warms, and while one centimetre rise in 30 years may seem modest, the massive gull colonies of Holton Heath only need to flood once each spring to force the gulls to move elsewhere. Such apparently modest flooding can also devastate the thriving diversity of invertibrates breeding in the ditches, and the ducks and waders that feed on them. Meanwhile, dwindling or northward shifting fish stocks could affect the tern colonies.

It makes little difference to the average bird in the tree, or come to think of it, the average birder in the street what has caused the warmer weather. It only matters that it exists. Remove the tree or kill all the insects on it, however, and you have a real problem. As the temperature increases so the flora changes, tides reshape the land, winds change speed and direction and birds have to make do. Nick (a very typical birder) likes to joke, "It won't be long before we get our next Mediterranean period, but this time we've got to pay tax on it," before parodying the parochial English response to warmer weather, "Bring it on!" If you are able to blinker yourself to the tropical end of the problem and read of the birds Huntley et al believe will be here in Poole, it's tempting to agree with him.

"Bring it on," is also how the birders at Ian and Margaret's wedding responded when Nick and I told them about the breeding forecasts in Huntley et al's *Atlas*. Breeding Little Bitterns, Night Herons and Purple Herons, yes please! Honey Buzzards should become commoner, and we can look forward to seeing more and more Black Kites. We might get vagrant Egyptian Vultures and Bonelli's Eagles on a regular basis. Goshawks could resume regular breeding, preying on Turtle Doves escaping the heat in France. Quails could breed again, as could Spotted Crakes, Corn Crakes and Little Bustards, and we could have the occasional breeding pair of Black-winged Stilts or Kentish Plovers.

We could look forward to Crested Larks singing in the dunes and Black Redstarts breeding around my offices. Migrant Rock Thrushes exploring the old stone workings around Corfe Castle, being expelled from the turrets by territorial Blue Rock

Thrushes. Cisticolas 'zitting' on the edge of the saltmarsh, and Savi's Warblers reeling at Lytchett. Crested Tits, Short-toed Treecreepers, Long-eared Owls and Scops Owls calling in the conifers. Migrant Moustached Warblers overshooting from northern France, meeting Melodious Warblers that used to breed no further north than there. Sardinian Warblers starting to take over any niche left vacant by our Dartford Warblers and Common Whitethroats. Elsewhere, the occasional Western Orphean Warbler singing from an orchard in Wareham, to the accompaniment of Golden Orioles breeding in trees along the Piddle...

[We had forgotten to mention termites, and at this point I revealed that malarial mosquitoes would be able to breed permanently again in Poole, although a recent study had concluded that the drainage of much of the marshes made this unlikely.]

...Rock Sparrow, Serin and Hawfinch becoming year-ticks, migrating past South Haven, and Nick's flight call detectors at Stoborough regularly picking up Cirl Bunting, Rock Bunting and Ortolan Bunting passing at night. Alpine Swift nesting on the Barclays building, and Pallid Swift on the cliffs near Old Harry. Bee-eaters breeding on the Piddle at Trigon and Wrynecks calling from the bushes at Rempstone. Great Grey Shrike and Woodchat Shrike peering down at us from roadside wires and last but not least, Hoopoe everywhere... OK, they didn't actually suggest that all these birds would be where we put them, but it's good to dream. After all, the ways of nature are always full of surprises...

At this point Ian Alexander, overhearing us drifting slowly off into cloud cuckoo land, popped in a little caveat. "Adding large volumes of fresh water to the Arctic reduces the salinity, which stops the water in northern latitudes sinking, and it is this sinking water that powers the Gulf Stream. If the Gulf Stream slows (or, less likely, stops) then we may see a different chain of events – and that could be the beginning of a series of cold winters."

Chapter 26: A new England?

Looking out of the window along the clifftop above Burton Bradstock beach in the most western part of Dorset, Billy Bragg could see flocks of birds where normally there were none. He watched spellbound as a mass movement of Lapwings travelled east up Chesil Beach, and they weren't alone. There was a host of smaller birds too. It was a sign of hard times, a phenomenon of biblical proportions. He phoned fellow musician and birder Simon Emmerson and described what Simon realised were Redwings and Fieldfares. Billy was reminded of a story he had heard while making a documentary about Woody Guthrie. He had visited Pampa near Amarillo, where he interviewed a woman who had witnessed the big dust storm that hit the Texas Panhandle on Black Sunday (14 April 1935). She told him that the first sign was thousands of birds flying fast and low, ahead of the dust cloud.

At 13:00, Simon sent us an email describing what Billy had seen and adding, "I'd get down there myself but we are totally snowed in up here in the hills, with all exits from the village blocked by abandoned cars. Armageddon time!" Fieldfares, Redwings, Skylarks, Lapwings and even the odd Snow Bunting were fleeing east from Devon and Cornwall. Displaced by snowstorms, they flew into the strengthening easterly wind and towards us.

Meanwhile further east, Hamish, also unable to move his car, had walked up to Durlston where he counted a staggering

34,000 Fieldfares moving north-northeast. Steve Smith could see the birds heading north over Swanage. He was getting late for work but managed a five-minute look across Studland Bay, where streams of Fieldfares and Skylarks were battling across the choppy water, into the freezing easterly wind.

On hearing the news, I rushed out onto my platform and was confronted with a whiteout. Every so often a flock of 40 or so Fieldfares materialised, then shot over very close to the roof. I could have reached out and touched them. I couldn't see if we were enjoying very large numbers because of the blizzard, but just down the road birders that had made it to Mudeford Quay during the afternoon saw 33,000 Fieldfares, 12,000 Redwings and over 30,000 Skylarks.

Shaun got very excited, pointing out that this could be the last cold weather movement we would ever see. He obviously hadn't had a beer with Ian Alexander lately. As Ian suggested, despite the sub-zero temperatures and frozen pipes locally, globally speaking 2009 was still the fifth warmest year on record, and according to NASA, 2010 tied with 2005 as the warmest. This was despite yet another cold British winter complete with cold weather movements.

To see one of these cold weather movements, you have to react very quickly to fast moving news. Billy saw the birds at the western end of the county in the morning, and most of the

Snow Bunting *Plectrophenax nivalis*, Studland Bay Beach, Poole, Dorset, February 2010 (*Steve Trewhella*)

movement had cleared Christchurch in the east by 16:00. If you were preoccupied with more mundane tasks like getting home in a snowstorm you missed it.

The cold arrived very quickly. One minute John Down was watching a December swallow flying over Wareham, when suddenly we were in the middle of a reassuringly old fashioned British winter. Late December brought surprise snow and trapped Christmas shoppers in their cars. Swine flu disappeared from the headlines, as the arctic temperatures swept across Europe. Copenhagen's climate conference was suddenly looking rather irrelevant, and an icy Polar Bear that was supposed to melt in Trafalgar Square remained resolutely frozen. By 18 December 2009, most of Britain including Cornwall was covered in snow.

Eurasian Oystercatcher *Haematopus ostralegus* and Common Redshank *Tringa totanus*, Shore Road, Poole, Dorset, 10 January 2010 (*Nick Hopper*). 'Oystercatcher and Redshank feeding in snow, both ringed.'

In Poole at first we were the exception. Nick was out and about finding odd birds in odd places, all seeking refuge. One of his emails ended, "This could be the all time classic cold weather movement scenario for Poole Harbour. I can almost feel a whole new chapter coming on!!"

On 23 December, after a work's Christmas lunch, I was sitting looking out and spotted a Black Redstart tucked up on a roof behind my office. My thoughts went to bird racing. Terry had been emailing us all, asking if we were going to do one, since mid-November. I hadn't really decided if I was on for a race. Still, a tame Black Redstart could come in handy.

New Year's Eve was very sedate with a dinner, champagne, lots of birders' chat and off to bed by 01:00. The next morning I woke to Blackcaps chasing each other off the fat balls, Goldfinches squabbling over the niger feeders, Jays sneaking in to gobble the peanuts, and Bullfinches whistling sweetly from the bushes (**CD2-91**). I didn't want to get into a traditional New Year's Day debate with Mo, so I strategically suggested she had a lie in while I cycled around Holes Bay. We could then meet at the quayside at 11:00 to join the other birders for our traditional New Year's Day Bird Boat trip around the harbour.

CD2-91   **Eurasian Bullfinch** *Pyrrhula pyrrhula* Poole, Dorset, England, 15:32, 2 April 2008. Singing in Mark's suburban garden on a windy day. Background: European Robin *Erithacus rubecula* and European Blue Tit *Cyanistes caeruleus*. 080402.MR.153248.01

We had a lovely boat trip. The weather was perfect, pretty cold but dry and bright. Nick had drunk too much champagne the night before so didn't make it out of bed. Ewan, Roger, Terry and

James Phillips, however, were all there. Together they are our arch rival bird racing team, and they are not regulars on the bird boat. I should explain that by this point we had decided to do a January bird race, but instead of the usual sprint around Dorset, we were limiting ourselves to the confines of Poole Harbour. Not knowing the harbour well, Roger's team had declined the invitation to compete. I wondered why they had all, seemingly coincidentally, decided that it would be a nice idea to join the bird boat. They weren't secretly scouting, were they?

As it turned out, they were being even more cunning than that! On the boat, Roger shared soup with Shaun (one of our team members) and innocently asked whether he might feel like a boy's night out at Prezzo Pizza with James and Terry. The next night Shaun was half way through his pizza when he realised that the conversation was all about the birds in Poole Harbour. There was something going on. "You guys are planning to do the bird race, aren't you?" There were a few smiles and then they came clean. Terry explained that as they had easily set the county winter day record at 129 in 2008, they were now looking at other records to challenge. James chipped in that if they could have agreed about the Greenshank seen from Evening Hill on Brownsea lagoon (a mile away), it would have been 130. James and Roger then admitted they were looking to secure the double - Dorset and Poole Harbour winter records - so they were giving Dorset a rest to concentrate on beating the Poole Harbour record held by our team and then standing at 119. They were the most competitive team Shaun had ever met, and absolutely revelled in their victories. When he looked surprised, Roger smiled and repeated that they really did intend to take the Poole record.

The race was to take place on 9 January, and Shaun knew he hadn't really got the team together, had no strategy and had done no scouting. When he got home, he sent Hamish, Nick and me an email. "Are we up to the challenge? Roger's team wants to break our record. Are we all up for taking them on? Look forward to hearing ideas!"

Nick answered first: "Consider the gauntlet thrown down! No way are those guys beating us on our own patch! I will be out today." Hamish also replied, "Let's do it!"

A great tradition, bird races are often sponsored and there's a prize cup named after Hamish's marvellous birding dog Douglas (since deceased) for the team that sees the most species in Dorset in a January day. There are normally between six and eight teams in a bird race, with varying levels of experience.

I was now really up for competing, and suggested that we hired the bird boat. Nick liked the idea but Shaun thought it could waste a lot of time. Hamish agreed. He wasn't sure about the added value of a boat trip. "Perhaps I've still got too vivid a memory of the last time we took a boat to Brownsea in a bird race!"

I have to admit, most of my efforts to get bird race teams around the harbour have been a disaster, and most have involved Hamish. The two of us have been bird racing around Dorset since August 1980. In that first year, our effort to see 100 species in the county ended with 91, but after a few more goes we eventually managed to set a record Dorset day of 123 on 5 May 1984. On that day I really thought I had it sorted. Phil Greaves, a fireman, had contacts in the coastguard. He persuaded them to pick us up in an open inflatable powered by two huge outboards. The team at the time was Tasie Russell, Dick Burt, Hamish and me. Phil was there to pick us up from the pier at South Haven to go to Brownsea, then take us right across to Holton Heath. We reached Brownsea OK, but I hadn't realised that on a windy day buckets and buckets of freezing cold seawater will pour over you and your optics at high speed.

I vividly remember trying to be as insignificant as possible to avoid both the freezing deluge and Hamish's gaze. As we tried to reach the Holton shore, Phil, wanting in some way to make amends, jumped deep in the cloying mud and tried to manoeuvre the boat so that we could step ashore. It was impossible, so we all had to do a bit of mud wrestling.

I had a borrowed Range Rover waiting. We changed what clothes we could but it was miserable. Nothing was said and we continued the race. Eight hours later we all stood shivering in the darkness at Martin Down in the north of the county hoping for a Stone-curlew to call. In the darkness I confessed, "I'm really cold". "Good," was Hamish's quiet reply out of the dark. So for this latest bird race I was thinking that the expensive yet sedate big old yellow two-deck bird boat would be more appropriate.

Snow and ice were now everywhere in Britain, and this was creating further cold weather movements. I suggested to the others that the team that kept warm and healthy would gain the advantage. Nick admitted he already had a touch of 'man flu' so would stay indoors for a couple of days. We discussed a strategy that used our local knowledge and avoided being out in potentially icy conditions too early in the morning or worse, stuck in ditches. During the last autumn race Nick had reversed into a ditch at Arne at 04:00. Both front wheels were off the ground and all looked lost when Kevin happened to come by. He kindly drove Nick to Sandford where he was able to blag a piece of rope off a guy in a van. Only with Kevin's car pulling and three people pushing did he and Magnus manage to get back in the race. Later Kevin got a lot of grief from fellow racers for that act of kindness, as Nick and Magnus went on to win the bird race, setting a new autumn record.

If we could keep calm and warm, I thought we could trust Roger's overenthusiasm to see him come unstuck. We secretly started scouting like fury, but there wasn't enough time. Langton Steve Smith, seeing that the schools were closed and there were warnings to wildfowlers, suggested a postponement. Not really knowing what it would mean for our opponents, we suggested rescheduling for the following Sunday. It certainly helped us, as it gave us more time to catch up on scouting and, as it turned out, put Roger's carefully laid plans into turmoil.

The first thing we did was re-book the big yellow boat. We hoped for a bit of 'Shock and Awe'. Hopefully, seeing the four of us perched on top of it as it manoeuvred around the harbour would be such a spectacular display of force that it would paralyse Roger and his team, and they would give up and go home.

Our scouting started in earnest, and potentially the most elusive bird would be the Snow Bunting that had taken up residence on the customs dock opposite the quay by the bonded warehouse (the mysterious 'workshop M'). It was legally off-limits, and remained that way despite our pleading with the authorities. I tried with my scope from Poole Quay, and from the balcony up the steps by the Italian Gossip restaurant.

Rob, the skipper of the boat we were to hire, happened to be moored at the quay for some welding work. He could see me lugging my scope up the steps to sit next to the sea music sculpture, trying to get an angle on the dock, desperate to see this Snow Bunting. Eventually he took pity on me and promised that when the welding was done, he would take me across to the dock. We tried this, but no matter what, I couldn't see it. My lucky Black Redstart was there though, with a regular Kingfisher hidden amongst the rocks, out of sight for anyone on the quay.

If you want to win a bird race, you can't wait until dawn to get started. Roger, ever the competitor, would have roused his team and got them going by 04:30. The sun was unlikely to join any of us until 08:00 most years, and on a rainy morning, first light could be even later. Low tide was to be 11:12 at the Quay, and wouldn't last for too long so we also needed to think about that.

As we had hoped, Terry later told us his team did not set out with great confidence, because the tides and timing for the previous weekend had been ideal. "This weekend, however, things were not going to be straightforward, and we had lost our lift to Brownsea. Permissions had been granted for a Saturday landing, and access to the island was not possible on the Sunday."

Their start didn't go well. They missed the Greylags in the dark at Poole Park and didn't connect with the Barn Owls at Middlebere. At least they had a Tawny Owl, which was a start and a Woodcock, which should have been a help for later in the day. They then hit 'the Bridges of Branksome', ticking off Gannet and Red-throated Diver. A half decent seawatch for this site was quickly followed by Goosander off of Evening Hill.

They dipped on the roosting Purple Sandpipers and Sanderlings on the Sandbanks Groynes, but once they got to Studland things improved, the highlights being both Slavonian and Black-necked Grebes, Great Northern Diver, Long-tailed Duck, Common Eider, Common Scoter, Red-crested Pochard, Linnet, Yellowhammer, Dartford Warbler and of course the all-important Ring-necked Parakeets.

Their list grew in leaps and bounds at what was probably their best stop of the day: Wytch Causeway. As Terry recounted, "This started with a Hen Harrier on the deck, being mobbed by a Carrion Crow. It soon took flight and quartered across the marsh in such brilliant crisp winter sunshine. What a buzz! These are the moments when a bird race becomes a hinderance, as it becomes very hard to leave certain sites and birds behind! Still, just being out and enjoying such magical birds in these precious places is always a delight." Further gains for their team there included a Spoonbill roosting on the spit, a Green Sandpiper on the marsh, along with a Water Pipit and a host of the more usual species scattered across the distant water and saltmarsh.

Being so far round the harbour, they had missed seeing us on the bird boat. Damn! We had arranged for Kevin to join us to take some photos, knowing he would enjoy it, and most importantly as an impartial witness to counter any suggestions of stringing.

From our boat, we checked out the rocks at the harbour mouth where eight Purple Sandpipers and 13 Sanderlings were roosting, then headed down the channel towards Goathorn, picking up Long-tailed Duck, Slavonian Grebe and a Scaup.

I have to be honest. Only one bird boat in 10 sees Golden Pheasant, so we just hung off Furzey Island to try our luck. Shaun got impatient and I had to ignore the general "How long do you intend keeping us here?" mutterings, until there, in all their glory, four Golden Pheasants started running around the edge of the lawn. We then took the boat slowly past Brownsea lagoon, picking up Spoonbill, Spotted Redshank and Red Knot.

Sailing our way gradually towards Poole Quay and, we hoped, our trump card, we took in Salterns Marina, where we saw another Slavonian Grebe, and Liliput where we ticked a nice male Goosander. Kevin takes up the story: "As we headed towards Poole Quay, two Great Northern Divers swam alongside the boat... I then casually mentioned that the Snow Bunting apparently sometimes sat up on the fencing, at which point Shaun said 'what's that bird on the fence?' Sure enough it was the Snow Bunting, which lingered just long enough for me to get it in the scope before dropping down behind some metal girders. That was the last we saw of it. Then Hamish picked up the serendipitous Black Redstart flitting amongst the rocks."

Roger's team had also been busy, clocking up Raven and Grey Wagtail before Arne produced the key woodland species. At this point, finally, the overenthusiasm that I was praying for kicked in. Or as Terry put it, "Well... then we took a bit of a plunge as we tested the semisubmersible capabilities of my car! We arrived at East Holme to find the ford crossing somewhat full. There we sat and pondered, whilst Roger rubbed his hands together and said, 'it's time to get my own back.' He was referring to a race about 8 years ago when he drove down a flooded road, during which a large quantity of water soon joined us in the car!"

Golden Pheasant *Chrysolophus pictus*, male, Rose Cottage, Brownsea Island, Dorset, 1 December 2008 (*Kevin Lane*)

"James assured me that all would be fine as a car had come from the other direction. I still wasn't going to go for it, but then a moment of madness saw a bow wave over the bonnet and half way up the windscreen! At this point I said to James, 'What made you think that other car had come through? It could have just been sensible and turned around?' He replied with a slight giggle in his voice, 'Oh yes, I guess it could have done.'

We then spent the next 10 minutes or more trying to get the car going, sending huge plumes of smoke through the village, which Roger referred to as something out of Harry Potter."

"Anyhow, all this was to be worth it, wasn't it...? No such luck. We added not a single bird to the list. We did have another Goosander, which on any other race would have made it well worthwhile. Still, nice record nonetheless. Stupidly, we only looked down the Frome valley and not up, as this was where the Bewick's were!"

Things didn't get much better for Roger's team, and it took over an hour before they added another species, a Firecrest at Creekmoor. They could only manage another four species in the next hour and a half. Thankfully for Terry and Ewan, their home patch, Hatch Pond, gave them two of those, which were Chiffchaff and… stunning views of one of the Bitterns sitting out in the open. Holes Bay gave up Common Sandpiper in seconds, but the Red Knot that they had seen on both the two previous days was missing.

Swineham got them going again with great views of Marsh Harrier and Scaup, along with some pinging Bearded Reedlings and a calling Cetti's Warbler. They shot off to Middlebere in the hope of a Barn Owl. No luck, so they left for a second shot at the Greylags in Poole Park, passing us on the way out. Within minutes we were watching the Barn Owl flying around the buildings!

Shaun, Nick, Mark and Hamish on bird boat, Brand's Bay, Dorset, 17 January 2010 *(Kevin Lane)*. 'On the bird boat, hoping for a bit of Shock and Awe.'

The finish line was my home, and all the teams had to be there by 18:30, with a bird deducted for every minute late. The kitchen bustled, but no one was divulging how many species they had seen.

We had recently come up with a new way of revealing the scores. Everybody puts their hands up at the start, as Shaun starts shouting out ascending numbers into the packed room. As your score comes up, you put your hands down. This ultimately leaves the winning team with their hands in the air. He started. "90… 91… 92…" and by the time he got to 110 there were only two teams left: Roger's and ours.

Shaun continued, "111… 112… 113… 114…" All hands remained resolutely aloft. "115… 116…" Finally all the hands in Roger's teams went down. We had beaten them!
But wait for it. "117… 118… 119… 120…" Now the old record had gone. "121… 122… 123…" and finally our hands went down. One hundred and twenty three! The look on Roger's face was of utter disbelief. There is an old Chinese proverb that says, "Fortune doesn't change a man. It only unmasks him." Whatever Roger's team had been full of in previous years now flowed across the room and filled us.

The weather had been perfect, helping us to achieve a great score. All in all, it had been one of our best birding days in the harbour ever with highlights including Snow Bunting, Black Redstart, Golden Pheasant, Goosander, Firecrest, Long-tailed Duck, Red-crested Pochard, Red-throated Diver, Barn Owl, Lesser Redpoll, Hen and Marsh Harriers, Chiffchaff, Bittern and Bewick's Swan. Despite reaching 123, we had missed two

Jubilant Mark, bird boat at Poole Quay, Poole Harbour, Dorset, 17 January 2010 (*Kevin Lane*). 'Next year.'

birds carefully scouted at Wytch Causeway: Green Sandpiper and Water Pipit. We remembered seeing Roger's team leaving just as we arrived. At the time we joked that they had probably scared them off.

Homemade soup was served and the conversations flowed back and forth. Terry was asking whether at 123 this record would even be worth chasing in the future. I could hear him say, "Would have been great though, wouldn't it, if it had been on the Saturday and we'd passed each other, neither team knowing that the other was involving a boat! Ah well, records are there for breaking."

As everyone was leaving, Roger smiled and said, "See you next year."

Chapter 27: It's all right Mark, we believe you

I've lived in Poole most of my life. You would think that living in such a beautiful spot would have produced a mild natured man, content in his rustic idyll. Sadly not, and as friends sometimes complain, I'm just a bit combative. Especially when it comes to year listing in Poole Harbour.

If I can now take you back to 2000, the start of a new century, my ambition was a new start for the harbour. In 1994 Nigel Symes had won the coveted egret feather by recording 167 species in or from Poole Harbour, and in 1995 he won the feather again. Shaun took the year listing trophy in 1996 and 1997 with 187. Since then, Mo and I had matched his record, but now I wanted to beat it. I didn't just want to beat it. I wanted 200 birds in Poole Harbour in 2000.

Year listing gets you out. It's easy to sit indoors and sneer at listing but it does give the year purpose. Sometimes too much purpose.

I had been cutting out and marking up maps with all the Wryneck records, Red Kite sightings, flight lines of Spoonbills, Hoopoe sightings, Spotted Crakes, and where Aquatic Warbler had been caught.

I was looking for insights into routes used by migrants passing through the area. I bought the new tide table and fisherman's bait guide (the waders feed where the "bait" is), noted the states of the moon and the dates for the bird boats. Mo renewed our pager subscription and National Trust, RSPB and Dorset Naturalist Trust membership to give free parking, easy access to Brownsea, and to support the organisations responsible for some of Poole's best habitat.

200 kg of wholesale bird table seed, ground food, niger seeds, cakes of fat, and peanuts arrived at the house. Ewan attracted flocks of Bramblings to his garden by grinding up peanuts, so our liquidiser was transferred to the shed. I was toying with the idea of playing reassuring finch sounds by the bird table. When I told Mo, she suggested I put out a menu.

New Year's Day for me is the most exciting day of the year, better than my birthday, Christmas day, and certainly much better than New Year's Eve. When I reflect, I have enjoyed my birthday parties almost as much as New Year's Day birding, especially my 50th (50 hours of fun), when Shaun shouted the immortal words "I've never drunk till dawn before." New Year's Eve on the other hand is party time for amateurs, and I prefer to enjoy it quietly.

For me a big bird year traditionally starts with a brisk, bird filled January the first. Mo doesn't see the point of running around in the dark trying to tick a bird you are going to see or hear all year. Having suffered cold and miserable January the firsts standing in freezing easterlies in the dark, waiting for a glimmer of dawn to see Purple Sandpipers feeding on the steps beside

Eurasian Spoonbills *Platalea leucorodia*, flying past the Barfleur ferry operating between Poole and Cherbourg, Brownsea lagoon, Dorset, 13 September 2011 *(Nick Hopper)*

Purple Sandpiper *Calidris maritima*, North Haven, Poole Harbour, Dorset, 16 March 2010 (*Nick Hopper*)

the Sandbanks car ferry, she believes it's responsible for some of my worst craziness.

It's just the difference of a few hours, I argue. Instead of celebrating the arrival of the new year at midnight, it's a celebration at six. Mo says it's not six, it's some hideous time around four or four thirty. Don't get the wrong idea though. Mo is as competitive as any of the male birders, and at the time of writing has seen more birds in the harbour than any of them.

I can't remember what sort of New Year's Eve party we had that year, but I know the party was at our house, because our first

record in the diary was a Collared Dove that was flushed by all the fireworks going off. We went to bed quite late because the next one was a "Robin singing 3am".

Up at dawn, and as it was to be for much of the decade, the weather was mild. We wandered around the garden looking for Blackcaps. In a survey, a third of Dorset's wintering Blackcaps were found in Poole gardens, up to nine of them in ours. They are thought to be from Belgium and Germany, and researchers there have discovered that the Blackcaps we have wintering in southern Britain are slightly different from those that winter in Spain. They have rounder wings and longer, narrower beaks.

The males return to their central European breeding grounds earlier to claim territory and mate with females that have also wintered here. It seems that they are evolving into two distinct populations of Blackcap.

A walk down the track to the Middlebere hide, and we had ticked Graham Armstrong, Andy Humber, Phil Read, Jackie and Nick Hull, George Dunklin and the chap from the record shop out with his family. I told them all we were doing a year list and to please call my mobile if they found anything. Only 40% of local birders had mobiles then, and regular emails wouldn't really get going until the next year. Always a great place, at Middlebere we saw Hen Harriers, a wintering Green Sandpiper and a rather jammy male Merlin dashing between the cottages.

Mo Constantine, Poole, Dorset, 21 August 2006 (*Arnoud B van den Berg*)

On January the first, it's traditional to try and see a Woodcock. You used to need cold weather, but Nick discovered a good site for winter flight views. At dusk he would wait beside the gate into the forest at the start of Soldier's road, and watch Woodcock flying from the pines overhead into the wet fields and heath to feed.

They are one of our long distance migrants, shot at in every part of their range. A Woodcock caught and ringed at Lytchett in December was shot the following April, half way between Moscow and the Ural mountains, some 3,000 kilometres away. Anyway, we got our traditional tick around 17:30 as the sun was setting. Just as we were starting to shiver, a Woodcock called and flew over our heads, silhouetted against the dying light.

Sunday 2 January saw Mo videoing a big flock of ducks on Little Sea with the idea that we would pop home and put them on our big telly screen for identification over a nice cup of tea. What if we did find a good duck and hadn't actually seen it? We couldn't really count it on our year list. For insurance, we looked through and found a Scaup and a Ruddy Duck.

Ruddy Ducks are rare here and suffering a fiercely unpopular extermination programme. They were first seen locally when four turned up on 6 January 1979 at Poole Park, after the inland lakes had frozen. Since then, there have been around 30 records, and like our bird, which stayed for a month, they arrive during cold snaps or on a Saturday or Sunday morning when wildfowling disturbs them from their normal haunts. Now when one turns up, there is an unspoken news blackout to protect the few that remain.

6 January saw us at the Harrier Hide, watching a Barn Owl hunting over Wych creek. A few Rock Pipits winter there and at Lytchett Bay, and are occasionally trapped and ringed. Rees Cox was analysing one of the Holton Heath Barn Owl pellets when he discovered one of their rings inside it. Walking back to the road afterwards, four or five Woodcock flew over the track, calling as they headed into the fields from the wet bog, and Mo gave me that "I told you about January the first" look.

Telling Snipe from Jack Snipe and Woodcock by call at night is a dark art, and it comes in handy when you compete on year lists or bird races. Magnus had studied this, and sent me a little monograph 12 years ago. I suppose I should share it (especially as he has updated it):

"Dear Mark,

*Here are my thoughts on separating Snipe and Woodcock flight sounds, I've included Jack Snipe for completeness. Common Snipe flight calls are well known to anyone who has walked through certain kinds of marshy ground at the appropriate time of year. Typically, a snipe we had not yet noticed because of its camouflage takes off at our feet with a whirring of wings, then gives a series of calls as it twists and turns away from us, towering high before descending into another part of the marsh, or disappearing as a spec in the distance. The calls we hear have a harsh, scratchy quality, a duration of around a tenth of a second, and an intonation that rises noticeably at the end, which is also the loudest part of the call. This ending is important, because Woodcock and Jack Snipe calls don't have it. In **CD2-92** you can hear calls given by a*

Common Snipe that was not flushed, but actually approaching the microphone.

*The call most often given by Woodcocks in winter is similarly short, but keeps the same pitch from start to finish. An even simpler difference to remember between Common Snipe and Woodcock flight calls is the repetition rate. Common Snipe tend to give calls in sequences, at a rate of roughly one call per second, occasionally a bit more than a second, or nearly two. Woodcock usually repeats its winter flight call much more slowly, at about one call every four seconds (**CD2-93**), or gives just a single call.*

*Woodcocks are less likely to call when flushed, and so their flight calls are less well known. The best time to hear them in winter is when they are leaving the woods about half an hour after sunset. They will probably follow the same route every day, and once you locate it, you can go and check when they arrive in autumn, how their numbers change with winter temperatures, and when their numbers dwindle or they start displaying at the end of winter. The call described above is not their only winter call. If you are lucky, you may hear them giving a very strange 'throbbing' sound. I made several recordings of this sound in the Netherlands, all along the same flight route in January but over a period of four years. The first time I recorded it, I thought it might be the sound of a damaged wing beating, but in some recordings the wingbeats can be heard too, and they are about twice as fast (**CD2-94**). So the throbbing sound does appear to be a rapid series of calls. It is not very loud, has a reedy quality, and a 'pulse rate' of about four throbs per second.*

Occasionally, Woodcocks in late winter can be heard to give a 'sneeze', which is identical to one of the sounds given during their

CD2-92 **Common Snipe** *Gallinago gallinago* 20:50, 18 March 2008, Tory Island, Donegal, Ireland. Flight calls of a bird approaching the microphone. Background: Atlantic Ocean and Northern Lapwing *Vanellus vanellus*. 080318.MR.205016.01

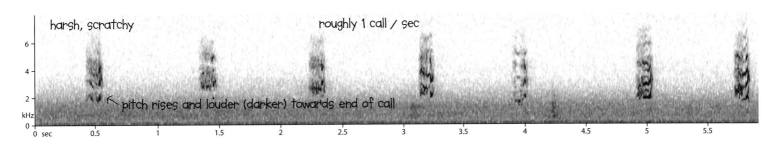

CD2-93 **Eurasian Woodcock** *Scolopax rusticola* 18:01, 14 January 2005, Oostkapelle, Zeeland, Netherlands. Flight calls while leaving the woods at dusk, on the way to nocturnal feeding grounds. Background: Tundra Bean Goose *Anser serrirostris* and Western Jackdaw *Corvus monedula*. 04.045.MR.14901.11

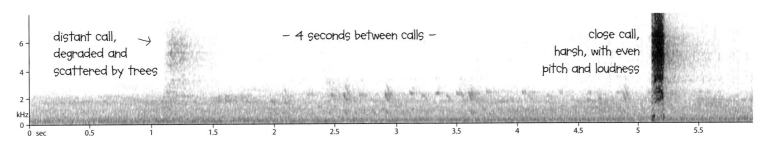

CD2-94 **Eurasian Woodcock** *Scolopax rusticola* 17:51, 14 January 2005, Oostkapelle, Zeeland, Netherlands. 'Throbbing' of a Woodcock leaving the woods at dusk, on the way to nocturnal feeding grounds. Background: Western Jackdaw *Corvus monedula*. 04.045.MR.14308.11

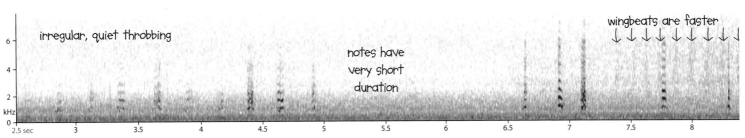

'roding' display. I have only recorded it twice given singly, so I am not sure about any possible repetition rate. However, in roding displays, this sound is heard about once every four seconds. In the example in **CD2-95,** there are some very faint low sounds before the sneeze with a rhythm and pitch similar to the deep, grumbling first part of the roding sound, so perhaps this was half-hearted roding from a bird not yet in the mood or condition to give a full display.

CD2-95   **Eurasian Woodcock** *Scolopax rusticola* 19:18, 12 March 2006, Oostkapelle, Zeeland, Netherlands. Single 'sneeze' of a presumed male, preceded by some very faint low sound. This may be an incipient 'roding' display of a bird not yet in full breeding condition. 06.001.MR.04328.01

In roding displays, the combination of the deep grumbling and the sneeze is given about once every four seconds. With its similar repetition rate, it seems very possible that the snipe-like winter call of Woodcock is related to this sneeze. Perhaps the sneeze, which includes some incredibly high frequencies, can only be given by adult males approaching breeding condition. During the breeding season and occasionally in late winter, Woodcocks often engage in courtship chases, in which the sneeze can be heard in combination with a lower-pitched sound, which is presumably given by females **CD2-96**). In such cases, the repetition rate of the sneeze notes is irregular, but typically much faster than in roding.

Eurasian Woodcock *Scolopax rusticola* 19:24, 12 March 2006, Oostkapelle, Zeeland, Netherlands. A chase flight involving three birds, with two of them giving very high-pitched 'sneezes', so presumably two males chasing a female. 06.001.MR.04924.01   CD2-96

Flight calls of Jack Snipe are similarly poorly known. For many birders, a lack of a flight call when flushed seems almost diagnostic for Jack Snipe. However, careful attention reveals that they often call when taking off, especially if there is more than one present. In my experience, if you do hear one calling as it takes off at your feet, you can be almost certain that there is another nearby. Those who have never noticed the flight call of Jack Snipe can be easily forgiven, because it is a weak sound, quieter than a Common Snipe, and the whirring of wings as a Jack Snipe takes off can drown it out. If you don't stop moving immediately, the sound of your feet in the marshy vegetation could also quite easily mask the call, which is usually only given once or twice. Besides being quieter than

CD2-97   **Jack Snipe** *Lymnocryptes minimus* 30 October 2002, IJmuiden, Noord-Holland, Netherlands. Two birds calling when flushed, part of a group of 14 that were concentrated in a small area. Six of them called as they took off in ones and twos. Background: Meadow Pipit *Anthus pratensis* and European Goldfinch *Carduelis carduelis*. 02.051.MR.13750.22

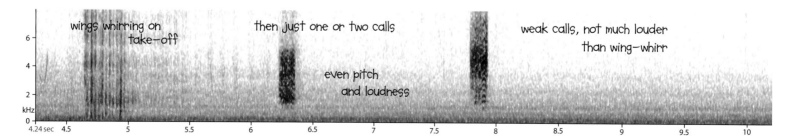

Common Snipe, calls of Jack Snipe are lower-pitched and lack a distinctive ending. In **CD2-97** *you can hear how two Jack Snipe called when taking off.*

The commonest way to find a Jack Snipe is to flush one, whether accidentally or deliberately. If you know an area where there are likely to be Jack Snipe hiding by day, a good way to count them without disturbance is to wait till dusk, when they take off and fly to their feeding grounds. At this time, they are highly likely to call when taking off. The Jack Snipe in **CD2-98** *was recorded passing in a group of Common Snipe at dusk. Now you know what to listen for, see if you can pick it out.*

Bye for now,

Magnus"

CD2-98   **Jack Snipe** *Lymnocryptes minimus* and **Common Snipe** *Gallinago gallinago* 25 March 2004, Texel, Noord-Holland, Netherlands. Three calls of a Jack Snipe flying over at dusk in a group of Common Snipe. Background: Common Blackbird *Turdus merula*. 04.009.MR.14740.12

Our home in 2000 contained our three teenage children and their friends and music mixing from every room. My contribution was a series of bird clocks all broadcasting a different bird sound on the stroke of every hour. I felt I was winning, then on Thursday 13 January on coming back from birding we found our teenage niece Anna sitting on our doorstep, having run away from home to live with us. At the same time there was a nice Brambling feeding on 'Ewan's' scrambled peanuts on our lawn. We didn't have much time to sort her out though (she stayed for a few years, bringing her own music, boyfriends and taste in alcohol), because Ewan had something else special for us.

While putting away an all day English breakfast in a beach café at Sandbanks, he'd noticed a Great Skua doing much the same. A juvenile, it was on the water eating a Herring Gull. After a while it flew to Pilot's Point, where it preened for five minutes, then it was flushed by a walker and flew over our heads towards Brownsea and beyond. This monster took our list to 122.

Twitching now started in earnest, and we enjoyed being shown stuff. An Iceland Gull turned up at Hatch Pond on 22 January, a Saturday. We chased it... no luck, searched for it most of the next day... no luck. Then hooray. Stan found it a week later in Poole Park, looking Persil white sitting on the mud, so we cycled down and twitched it.

We met George Green at Middlebere, who told us there were Goosanders on Little Sea. Always a difficult bird, when we got there... nothing. Then a smart drake drifted out from behind the central spit where it had been sheltering from the westerly wind. By the end of the first month, we had seen 135 species in the harbour and the pace kept up like this until by mid-February we had seen 152.

Spring arrived, and we tested out some of my theories. Over the past few years, we had all visited Ballard Down but hadn't found many local rarities. When I looked at my maps, Ballard had six, the most spectacular being a Gyrfalcon found on 5 February 1912 after a blizzard. Chatting with Stephen Smith, he pointed out that that Ballard faced east. We looked at the map together, and he suggested that the huge ridge of hills around the harbour was forming a barrier. Looking at the marked maps, wherever there was a gap in the hills there was a little cluster of rarity dots.

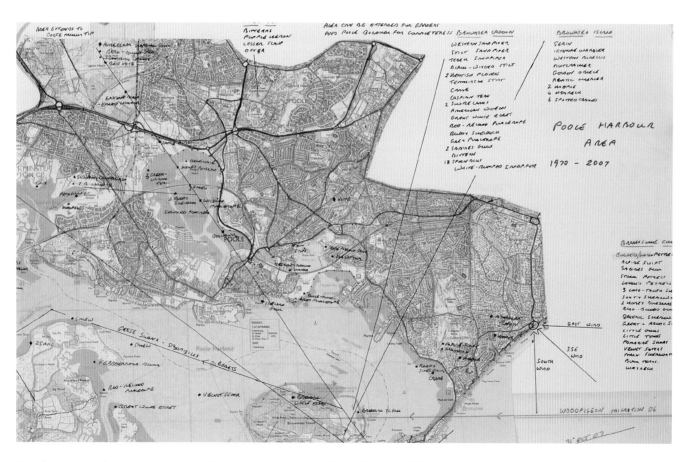

Part of Mark's map of rarities and migration paths for Poole Harbour, Poole, Dorset, 20 August 2009 (*Arnoud B van den Berg*)

Stephen theorised that when flycatchers, redstarts and other spring migrants came into the harbour through the Ulwell gap, they saw heathland stretching out in front, and for some it was unappealing. He suggested that the green grass and trees of Greenlands farm might concentrate migrants in the same way as an oasis in the desert.

I wondered if it could have the same effect on rarer birds, and worked out that a Montagu's Harrier, three Hoopoes, five Wrynecks, a Golden Oriole, an Icterine Warbler and a Rosy Starling had all been found in this area. Drawing a line from where the American Robin was found at Redhorn Point to the Arctic Redpoll spot on the edge of Spur Heath, and then to Brands Ford where six Bee-eaters were seen, created a rarity area that we called the Smith triangle. This theory was to substantially improve birding in the harbour. To prove the point, at Greenlands farm in the heart of the Smith triangle a lovely female Ring Ouzel sat out and looked beautiful, while a male hid in the bushes on 2 April.

I'd worked out that Montagu's Harriers turn up in Poole Harbour between 5 and 23 May. Add a little Smith triangle theory and bingo: on 6 May as we sat drinking a thermos of tea, Mo spotted a second calendar-year female floating over the heath at the entrance to Greenlands farm.

The 187th species was Manx Shearwater, with 10 seen from Branksome Chine on 1 June, a new bird for my harbour list. Now that all the summer visitors were ticked, things slowed down and every new bird was hard won. I had a list of potential birds and rated them A, B or C dependant on their rarity. However, the next new bird was completely off the radar.

Rosy Starling *Pastor roseus*, juvenile, in flock of Common Starlings *Sturnus vulgaris*, Greenlands farm, Studland, Dorset, 3 October 2010 (*Nick Hopper*)

On 25 June, the day after Mo's birthday, we were catching up with our work. I hadn't really chosen the best year, as my business partner Andrew Gerrie had recently domiciled in Australia. He was due in for an overdue visit, but just as he arrived we had to excuse ourselves. A first-summer male Eastern Black-eared Wheatear had just turned up on Upton Heath! We rushed over there and saw it. Fortunately, our definition of Poole Harbour had been extended to include the heath, so it was just inside the area.

August is one of the best months in the harbour, and on Sunday 6 August Graham phoned us, having found a Wood Sandpiper on the ornamental lake in front of North Bestwall House at Swineham. It's tricky peering over the shrubbery into the lake, as it looks as if you are trying to see someone in the house through your scope. In the end, we had to climb on top of a stile before we could find it tucked into the western corner of the lake, almost behind an island.

At Swineham there were over 100 Yellow-legged Gulls, and we flushed a Green Sandpiper. Wandering further, Mo found a Little Ringed Plover on the edge of the pit, then I saw a Ruddy Shelduck on the bank. Was it the wintering bird or a visitor? At this time of year it stood a better chance of being a genuine vagrant. We wandered off to Soldier's Road then round to Greenlands farm. My son Jack phoned with news. "A Tawny Pipit in a field at Ower." Wow, that would be the first for the harbour... We were there in minutes and joined the finder, Paul St Pierre.

There had been a fall, so we birded the area and found a few Spotted Flycatchers, a Pied Flycatcher and a Turtle Dove. Autumn had started with a bang, and one of the best days of the year saw us reach 191.

It's traditional to see Curlew Sandpipers on Brownsea lagoon when adults pass through in the last days of August. Our first turned up on 27 August (taking us to 198). Shaun had organised a Big Bird Day for 3 September. We started at 03:30, but everything was overshadowed by a rarity. At around 09:00, Mo and I were seawatching lazily on the south side of Ballard, about 250 m up from Old Harry, when a Black Kite flew into view, being mobbed by a Carrion Crow. I didn't get excited, because

James Lidster had told me that there was an escaped Black Kite doing the rounds and I assumed this was it. I calmly noted the heavy moult, thinking "It's an adult". It flapped off, and despite us calling all the other guys, some of whom were close by, only Mo and I saw it. James explained later that it couldn't have been the escaped bird, but I can't remember why. That evening we caught up with a Ruff, the 116th bird for the day and most importantly the 200th bird of the year.

The next day, after two hours of searching, Mo rediscovered and I glimpsed the Wryneck that Graham had found on Rempstone heath, when it flew out of the heather and briefly perched on a post.

Now comes something very odd... At this time we didn't know about any mass migration through the harbour, and on 30 September we left for a fortnight on Scilly with The Sound Approach. I had sketched out the ideas that would form the book *The Sound Approach to birding* (2006) for discussion. Not birding the harbour in October now 10 years on looks very foolish. I missed the great Honey Buzzard migration of that year, and also the Cliff Swallow at nearby Portland. (Arnoud can still remember the expression on my face when I heard the news. I was actually watching a Cliff Swallow on St Mary's at the time!)

We had to wait until 2 November for a southerly gale, which produced a sighting of two British Storm Petrels in the waves off Branksome Chine, taking our very full list to 205. Towards the end of the year, work took over. On 7 November, Mo and I were at a large meeting when Shaun phoned to tell us that Hugo Wood-Homer had found a Long-billed Dowitcher at Wych lake, from the Harrier hide where we had been watching the Barn

American Cliff Swallow *Petrochelidon pyrrhonota*, juvenile, Hugh, St Mary's, Scilly, 28 September 2000 *(Arnoud B van den Berg)*. 'The one in England that Mark did see...'

Owl at the beginning of the year. We shot down there, and as we searched unsuccessfully three male Hen Harriers headed to their roost. The next day we were in London. We finally saw it on 9 November.

The weather turned very nasty, and after 12 fruitless days of seawatching, a dark-morph immature Pomarine Skua flew west past Branksome Chine with 12 Little Gulls taking our final score to 207. Now I had to clean the list. As Poole Harbour is in Dorset, we have to use the British Ornithologists' Union list, which doesn't include White Wagtail and Pale-bellied Brent Goose. Green-winged Teal has since been accepted as a full species, but wasn't one back then. That's minus three.

When a record is rejected it feels like a kick in the teeth. No matter how it is explained, "Liar liar pants on fire" rings in your ears, followed by indignation and often a long period of sulking. It's a measure of the birder how he copes with it.

Now if you look in British Birds 93 (11, 2000) you will see: "We were not convinced that the identification was fully established"; "rejected…" "Black Kite, Ballard Down 3rd September 2000."

I may have ranted about this decision. I may even have sulked. Finally today, to lay a ghost to rest, I phoned Nick and then Shaun and asked what they thought of our Black Kite record.

My heart was in my mouth, but both said, "It's all right Mark we believe you".

Postscript: The Rosy Glow

An English pub sometime in the future. In this little fantasy our group of birders have met to compare their diaries from 2008 when they all spent a year trying to see 200 species in Poole Harbour. Lit with lanterns, our faces could be as easily from 1830 as 2030. Shaun has a thick diary in front of him. Ian Lewis has just brought a round of drinks. Nick Hopper, Mark and Mo are sitting at one end, Kevin, Terry and several new faces at the other.

Shaun: *"I've brought my 2008 diary down. How about you lot? I was thinking about what motivated me to do a year list that year. I think I just wanted to join the Poole Harbour 200 club."*

Nick, who has brought his notebooks: *"It kicked off for me at 3:50 in the morning with a Robin singing, and unless there was somebody here even sadder than me it put my yearlist at the top of the table. A position that I never relinquished!"* He looks out of the window at the rain. Elderly masons are going into the lodge on the other side of the road. *"My January 1st daylist went well and I reached a creditable 116, very close to the winter harbour record at the time. I remember hearing Woodlark singing in the dark at East Holme, and seeing male and female Hen Harrier on the deck, Barn Owl, Firecrest, Bewick's Swan, Spot Red, Spoonbill, Velvet Scoter, Long-tailed Duck, Kingfisher and Woodcock. Now if that's not an advert to come to Poole Harbour for a winter day's birding then I don't know what is."*

Shaun, grey, with a discreet hearing aid, nods sagely and starts to read aloud from his diary in a Geordie accent: *"Tuesday January 1st, 2008 Poole Harbour Bird Boat. For once, Captain Constantine's bird boat was greeted with calm waters and clear skies. Poole Harbour is really on the up and there were birds everywhere. We were all there to start our friendly big year, all except one (nods towards Nick). We saw Sandwich Tern, 11 Spoonbills - that was before they started to breed - 6 or 7 Long-tailed Ducks, and 3 Eiders."*

Mark: *"Yes, it was a good start to the year but things got a bit frustrating after that. I remember desperately trying to catch up with your Egyptian Goose at East Holme, Kevin."*

Mo: *"Without luck."*

Kevin: *"Did you see the Cattle Egret?"*

Mo: *"No, we didn't see that either."*

Mark: *"We did manage to see Goosander, though, after sneaking about on the south side of the Wareham Channel one day. There were still conifers covering the heath back then, rather than today's biomass crops of dense brushwood. But we lost ground again when we missed the 12th January bird race, flying to Amsterdam instead."*

Great Bustard *Otis tarda*, Holmebridge, Frome valley, Poole Harbour, Dorset, 29 December 2008 (*Nick Hopper*). Unfortunately for Nick, this Salisbury Plain bird could not be counted.

Nick: *"I don't know why you had to go to the Dutch Birding Day. We had a real chance of getting 120 species that day and a new harbour record, not to mention adding valuable species to the year list, species you needed to keep in the hunt. I did begin to wonder how committed you really were to a year list. Weren't you worried we'd beat your record?"*

Mark: *"I was encouraging you with a bit of a head start."*

Shaun: *"What about the Pink-footed Goose at Swineham? Was that before or after the bird race?"*

Nick: *"That was a couple of days after. I remember seeing it asleep on one of the gravel pit islands, which was a bit of an anti-climax. It looked pretty plastic really, but a tick's a tick!"*

Shaun: *"I seem to remember there was a bit more excitement involved in your next tick, which none of the rest of us saw. Holton Heath, 17th January..."*

Nick, gloating: *"Oh yeah, you mean James's Franklin's Gull. Yeah, you could call it exciting, it damn near killed me! After driving like a maniac then nearly giving myself a heart attack from running, I just got there in time to see it before it lifted off and flew into the murk, never to be seen again."*

Shaun: *"It wasn't the only good gull. According to my diary we had the 8th Ring-billed Gull for Lytchett Bay on 16th March. I distinctly remember you playing the daft laddie that day."*

Nick: *"Who, me?"*

Shaun: *"We were both watching the bird when Kevin rang you to say he'd seen it on the pager, and did you know about it? You had obviously forgotten to ring him, and I remember you squirming as you made out that you hadn't heard the news, then thanked him for ringing, before quickly legging it before he got there."*

Kevin, smiles and shakes his head.

Nick: *"Yeah, sorry about that Kevin. I'm glad you got there in time to see it. I did make up for it by telling everybody about a private and hitherto unknown guaranteed Golden Pheasant viewing area. Doing survey work in the harbour gave me an 'access all areas' pass, and one day I was at Goathorn counting waders when I realised that from a certain position, I could see to the back of the lawn on Furzey Island. I set up the scope and immediately found two stunning males."*

Steve, just arriving and pulling up a chair: *"Well that would have been good gen if we had been allowed in."*

Nick, with a cheeky smile on his face: *"Come on Steve, don't be like that!"* He cups his hand and whispers *"Bad loser"* to Mark, then turns back to Steve. *"I didn't hear you complain a couple of days later when I rang you with a Balearic Shearwater that I had found lingering in Studland Bay. Wasn't that the first March record for Dorset? Anyway, it certainly was a cracker, showing really well. I remember at the time I was just scanning the bay for grebes when it glided through my scope. It wasn't too long afterwards that you found a Nightingale at Old Harry, was it Steve? I don't remember you being in a hurry to get the news out about that."*

Steve, looking quite sprightly considering his age: *"That's just because I didn't see it. I remember I'd just heard my first Lesser Whitethroat of the spring - one of my favourite UK birds, that - and then a Nightingale started singing in the front wood. I tried to flush it, but it refused to break cover."*

Mark: *"Why do you make such a big effort to see these birds when you've already identified them by their song?"*

Steve: *"It's just 'my approach'. I will tick things however identified, but for a significant list I like to have seen the bird."*

Nick, smirking: *"Yeah but your year list wasn't actually that significant was it, Steve!"*

Mark: *"How about viz mig. You have to use calls then?"*

Steve: *"It wasn't an issue that year and anyway, Nightingale was the only bird that I didn't see. I would have preferred not to have ever seen crap pigeon. I really don't like crap pigeons."* Screwing his face up at the thought of feral pigeon, he takes a swig of lemonade and lime.

Nick: *"You'd have hated identifying the Phantom Crossbills that me and Kevin had in the old Rempstone Forest."*

Steve: *"You can't count those."*

Mark: *"You can now. They were split by the BOU. Not that there's any hope of seeing those again, now that the pines have all been felled and replaced with biomass crops."*

Shaun: *"Hardly anyone had heard of biomass boilers then, now we are all heating our homes and workplaces with them."*

Nick: *"I'm not. Living on the edge of the heath, I'm burning peat."*

Shaun: *"It's illegal."*

Nick: *"It's not in Stoborough, and it's a lot easier than chopping wood."*

Terry: *"Well it's illegal at Canford. My staff spend a lot of time chasing off illegal peat diggers. That and catching poachers".*

Shaun, returning to his diary: *"So, on the 5th May, Nick, you saw a Garganey on Swineham and that took you to 183. Steve, you were at 175. You two"* (points to Mark and Mo) *"were at 170, Kevin you were at 165, I was on 162, Iain Prophet 155 and Graham 150."*

Kevin: *"Let's have a look."* Shaun passes the diary. *"I've been trying to gauge why I stopped at the end of May. I thought it was 'cos I missed a load of stuff when I was in Spain, but looking at these records that wasn't the case. I think it was actually a combination of work and holidays. I missed the East Holme Woodchat 'cos of this. When I got back from Scotland, I had another busy week at work and no opportunities for skiving. So I missed two thirds of May. Then things wound down for the summer, and I was way off the pace. Naffed off, this is likely to be when I gave in. I think I used the excuse that now I was County Recorder, I needed to be showing my face around the county more, which of course was complete bollocks!"*

Paul Morton (one of the younger new faces): *"Nick, wasn't it in May that you had your eagle? I often wondered what happened there."*

Nick, rather reluctantly takes up the story: *"It was just after 1pm and quite a nice day, so decided to stop and do some raptor scanning at Hartland Moor. After literally a couple of minutes, I picked up this raptor being mobbed by jackdaws or something. Given this, I assumed it was going to be a buzzard but when I got my bins on it I realised that the smaller birds were the buzzards! What the hell was that thing they were mobbing? It was massive…!"* He fishes out another A6-sized Alwych notebook. *"By the 12th I had started my second notebook of the year, something which in the past I could have taken a year or two to fill, but I really was a man on a mission!"*

Paul: *"Did you decide what it was?"*

Mark: *"It was the immature sea eagle that had been hanging around all winter in Hampshire."*

Shaun: *"Nick didn't think the description was good enough, so he decided to submit it as an 'eagle sp', Paul. There was another guy just down the road at Wareham Moors who also saw it. He thought it was a White-tailed Eagle. And anyway Kevin really packed in because of my Woodchat. He's as good as admitted it. I remember it as if it was yesterday. I'd had a late start. Just about to go shopping, ignoring the previous evening's Little Bittern at Lodmoor. Checked Birdguides just to make sure it was not showing well. It wasn't. But then I read 'Portland – Thrush Nightingale, singing by the Obs'! Even though I knew I shouldn't, off I went, arriving one hour after it went silent. Off to Lodmoor, no sign of Little Bittern, Red-rumped*

Swallow or Golden Oriole. All Dorset ticks, all had been seen that morning and there were more birders than birds. Decided to drive to Arne Moors to look for my own birds. As I drove past East Holme, something said, 'Go and check the fields.' Thoughts of White Stork seemed optimistic. Stopped at the first pull in. An egret with the cattle! Wondered if it might be another Cattle Egret. No, it was a Little, but what was that on the fence in front of me? A cracking male Woodchat Shrike! All the Poole year listers rushed back from Portland and it was enjoyed by all."

Steve: *"I wouldn't have given up, although I did get a bit frustrated with your Stone-curlew, Nick."*

Nick: *"Yes, that was one of my most unexpected finds. Given that it was nearly June, I figured my best bet would be to cover as much ground as possible because birds at this time of year would more than likely be singing anyway. I decided to take my bike and start off by cycling around Ballard. This proved to be easier said than done as it was very hilly, and the grass was long. More pertinently, it was wet! So cycling turned out to be much more of a struggle than I thought. I was about half way round when I heard this curlew-type call. I stopped and could see this bird heading toward me, and I remember being astonished to see a short bill. It was a Stone-curlew! That was a great moment. It flew to the ploughed fields where I lost it in the dip, but as it had stopped calling by this time I presumed it had gone down. Some quick phone calls and then I thought it best to wait for the cavalry. You lot arrived,"* (pointing to Mark, Mo and Steve,) *"but we couldn't refind it. You didn't appear to be in the best of moods, Steve. I remember you saying that we should ban people from coming out on week days when others don't have a chance of twitching."*

Steve: *"I had a massive amount of work I had to do, whereas you were full time bird surveying. I remember saying at the time that it wasn't really a level playing field."*

Nick: *"You managed to get there ok so what are you moaning about?"*

Steve: *"In the end, you do have to consider chasing things when you'd rather be finding your own birds. The reality of year-listing is the harder you try, the more times you are going to go for something that simply isn't there."*

Shaun, looking in the diary: *"Considering you had packed in your year list, Kevin, you found some great birds. Pec Sand for a start."*

Kevin: *"Yeah, I was meant to be taking the firm's banking to Nat West in Broadstone but somehow ended up in Wareham when I found that. After visiting the bank, I thought I'd sneak in a bit of birding. Walking out to Swineham, I thought I may as well count the Great Crested Grebes, and there it was."*

Shaun: *"I executed a smash and grab raid at Swineham that evening, replicating behaviour I have deplored in others for years. I left work at 8:15 after a late meeting. Arrived at the rugby club at 8:30. My bike was strategically placed in the boot, and I was soon tearing past the Bestwall Park signs prohibiting breathing, amongst most other human activities. Ditched the bike at the sluice and was hurrying along the top bank when I met three young fishermen who asked if I'd come to see the Pectoral Sandpiper! Yes, I replied, asking if they knew where it was. Hey! The hour was late and it had been a long day... One of them kindly took me to the exact spot. Pointing helpfully, he said, 'It was just on the end of*

that spit against the clump of rushes when the last bloke saw it.' I raised my bins and there it was. Excitedly I thanked him, mounted the scope, focussed, just in time to see it fly out of view. The joys of Poole Harbour listing."

Steve: *"The most surprising call of the year I got was from Peter Williams about a probable Lesser Grey Shrike – and did I want to check it out? Silly question. After a short search through neighbouring fields, it was relocated on the now famous yellow farm machinery."*

Shaun: *"Sunday August 3rd , 2008. I was watching England play South Africa at Edgbaston when Steve called to say a 'grey' shrike had been found at Corfe Meadows."*

Mark: *"That was my favourite. I always like major twitches and that was in such a lovely spot. I've been down there a lot since."*

Shaun, reading from his diary again: *"Wednesday September 10th, 2008 was my red letter day. At 07:55 I found a juv Rose-coloured Starling at Lytchett Bay. Unfortunately the bird is on private land. It was last seen at 08:13 when it flew towards Holton Lee (also private in those days, you could only get in with a permit) among a small group of about 20 Starlings. In my excitement I nearly forgot to mention that an Osprey caught a fish just after 07:30. I don't want to seem ungrateful, but Mark and Terry gripped me off with a Black Tern on my local patch tonight, a species that still eludes me at Lytchett."*

Kevin, who has now fished out his own diary: *"Wryneck was fun. Graham rang me to say he had just flushed a one off the path that goes up to the top hide. I can't remember it all, but I spent a good* *while looking. Then on Sunday 14th September, Neil Gartshore found another one on Ballard and Nick & I tried for well over an hour to relocate it. Nick spotted Shaun cycling up the field towards us, rang him & suggested he moved over to the grockle-free left hand side of the long field, as nobody had walked down that edge for about 45 min. Less than 1 minute & 40 yds of cycling & Shaun had flushed the Wryneck. We raced down & it showed really well, sitting fully in the open for about 5 minutes."*

Nick: *"That was 199, and I think it was the next day that I hit the magic 200 with Little Stint on Brownsea."*

Steve: *"I missed the Wryneck but caught up a bit while taking a leak in the bushes at Studland. I heard a flock of Long-tailed Tits, but the second bird I looked at was a Yellow-browed Warbler, which performed for the next 45 seconds before diving into cover."*

Mark: *"I think that's when it all went badly wrong. Mo and I had missed that, and then on October 7th I had just got my bum on a train seat as it set off for London when my phone rang and I could see from the display that it was Graham Armstrong. I said, 'Please don't tell me it's a good bird Graham.' 'I'm afraid it is Mark. I'm watching a juvenile Sabine's Gull sitting on the water here off Branksome.' That hurt!"*

Kevin: *"Seems like there were only a few birds around that day, but those that were being seen were quality. I missed the juv Sabine's but had great looks at a Leach's Petrel at ten past one, slowly moving west."*

Shaun: *"Then I saw a Sooty Shearwater."*

Mark: *"Which would have been a Poole Harbour life bird and you all gave me a ring. Still, it could have been worse. Nick was getting the same gripping phone calls whilst on Scilly. I seriously thought about retiring from birding altogether, but I remember that you, Nick, couldn't eat,"* (Nick is looking very uncomfortable) *"and had to come home early from the Scillies to see the doctor. Mind you, I reckon if you found a Shore Lark on Studland beach while I was on a train to London tomorrow, that would be the end of me."*

Nick, getting up to go to the loo: *"I'll see what I can do!"*

Mark, turning to Paul and the new faces: *"Poor old Nick then went extremely quiet and we only be saw him here and there in the odd place around the harbour. He kept himself very much to himself, just a nod, no conversation. He didn't come down the pub and we started to talk seriously about him."*

Shaun, being a Newcastle United fan, had experienced these feelings before: *"He was depressed."*

Everybody nods solemnly.

Nick, having returned to hear the end of the conversation: *"Still, by the 3rd of December I was back into it. I was at the middle viewpoint by the main road at East Holme counting the Greylags, as there seemed to be rather a lot, when Iain Prophet rang to say he was at Swineham and had just seen the back end of 3 wild swans heading west. He thought they looked like Whoopers and was wondering if I was out and about. Just as he'd finished getting the words out I caught the back end of the same 3 Swans, still going west. I told him that I was going to the bridge on the off chance that they had come down. On arrival, things didn't look promising,* until a swan walked out from behind one of those shooters screens. I put the bins up and hey presto it had yellow in its bill. Not only that, but it had the right pattern for a year tick! The other two soon followed it out so I called back. 'Iain get your arse down here. They've landed and they're Whoopers!'"

Kevin, reading from his diary: *"7th December. This morning I was tempted away from the Harbour by a report of a possible Rough-legged Buzzard at Tadnoll Heath. It was beautifully crisp and frosty on the heath, with temperatures dipping to -5°C, but nothing interesting showed up raptor-wise, so I opted for a walk at Swineham. The walk out along the pits was pleasant. The freeze had persuaded a Water Rail to feed out in the open and a Snipe did the same, while 4 DEFRA-dodging Ruddy Ducks were also merrily swimming around and not looking in the least bit like they fancied a holiday with their cousins in Spain.*

Pausing at the spot where I had located the Pectoral Sandpiper back in July (something that I now do unfailingly on every visit), I scanned across the water to a group of Tufted Ducks bobbing about by the island in the middle of the pit. There amongst them was something different – a duck with a prominent white eye-ring, tri-coloured bill pattern and a squat shape. I instinctively thought 'Ring-necked Duck'. However, I'd only previously seen drakes of this species and some of the features I could see didn't quite tally with my mental picture of a female bird.

I rang Shaun and talked him through my doubts. He quickly dispelled them and said he was on his way. Phone calls and texts then flew out to make sure everyone else knew about the bird. After what seemed like an age of standing on the seawall waiting for others to arrive, Shaun rang back – he had been watching the bird with Nick for the past 5 minutes from further back along the pit. Speedily making my way over to Shaun and Nick, I was just in time to see the duck waddle out onto a straw bale that was floating in the water, revealing a distinct lack of leg rings."

Looking up from his diary: *"For you lot, this bird was a valuable year tick at a time of year when things were winding down. For me it was my 187th harbour species that year, and left me pondering what could have been had I not wound down my year-listing back in May."*

Nick, changing the subject: *"I was having a spot of lunch with Claire at the Holmebridge pull in. It's always a favourite place to stop, as you can look up and down the valley whilst eating. On this occasion lunch didn't get finished. I looked up just in time to see this large bird flying beyond the trees with a very large pale wing flash and a dark trailing edge. 'What the **** was that?' I said to Claire. The rhetorical question is always answered. 'I don't know, do I.' Although Claire is a non-birder, I always manage to say something like, 'Did you see that?' or 'What the hell was that?' Anyway, what it appeared to be was a Great Bustard, but the problem was that I got a very brief view, and there was a record number of other large birds with pale wing flashes and dark trailing edges kicking around, i.e. Greylag Geese. It wasn't a Greylag, was it? I was convinced it was a bustard, but the nag was the size just didn't seem to ring true. My anxiety didn't last long, as the bird made another flypast, this time in full view straight down the middle of the valley. 'Shit, it is a Bustard!' followed by, 'Shit, it's got a wing tag!'"*

Shaun: *"I was out looking for Mark's flyby Whoopers from the day before when I bumped into you, Nick".*

Nick: *"Of course, it had gone by then."*

Steve: *"Not that either of you could tick it."*

Nick: *"I didn't mind not ticking it. It was a fantastic bird to see. It then came back and turned out to be quite a small female, which is probably why it didn't seem as impressive as I thought it should have done. I photographed the bird and got the tag number, red with a white 28 on it. Luckily Shaun hadn't gone too far and was also able to get great views."*

Kevin: *"...which brought us to mid afternoon on New Year's Eve, when I was heading down to Poole to pick up a friend from the train station. Being early, I thought I'd pop past Poole Park to have a squint at the lake. I parked up near the 'Yellow browed Warbler corner' and had a scan across the water. The usual assortment of swans, geese and gulls were present. As my bins reached the area near the model boat zone, I found a small flock of Goldeneye, with an attendant group of Black-headed Gulls. One of the gulls made me do a double take, and I couldn't quite believe I was looking at a fine drake Smew.*

Nick Hopper, Poole, Dorset, 21 August 2006 (*Arnoud B van den Berg*)

Most of you had a fighting chance of getting down to the lake before dusk and gaining a priceless final year tick of 2008. I had a choice between keeping an eye on the bird for you lot and then picking up a very grumpy friend or leaving and hoping it stayed put. I went for my friend, and by the time I arrived back home all your negative phone calls began to arrive. It was nowhere to be seen. I got back in the car and raced down to Poole Park but you were right, it wasn't there.

The light was beginning to fade and I was on the verge of giving up, when Nick called. He'd refound it off nearby Baiter Point. We all redeployed to Baiter, and there was a collective cheer as we got onto the bird. I seem to remember you doing a little jig in the car park Shaun!"

Shaun, beaming: *"I'd made it to 200."*

Mark Constantine, Poole, Dorset, 21 August 2006 (*Arnoud B van den Berg*)

Nick: *"And I'd got 210, a new record for the harbour."*

Shaun: *"In all there were 225 species recorded. There were 3 species of BBRC rarities: 14 Cattle Egret including 6 together, the Franklin's Gull, and the Lesser Grey Shrike. And there were 14 Dorset rarities. These also included my Leach's Petrel, the 3 Whooper Swans, the Pink-footed Goose, Kevin's Ring-necked Duck and Nick's White-tailed Eagle. Then there was Kevin's Pectoral Sandpiper, two Ring-billed Gulls, Grahams Sabine's Gull, a Willow Tit, and my own Woodchat Shrike and Rose-coloured Starling. A Honey Buzzard and a Red-footed Falcon were also seen in the harbour but we all missed those. I worked out that 74% of these birds were found by just the 7 birders participating in the year listing, which goes some way to show that concentrated effort on a patch (even one as large as Poole Harbour) can produce results."*

Mark: *"I can add a bit more to that. You remember Martin Cade's comments on county rarities in the bird report, when he pointed out that between 1983 and 1992 Poole only had 6% of the rarities?"*

Shaun: *"I remember you telling me about how much it wound you up."*

Mark: *"Well, if you take 1999 to 2008 and count up the finds of all the county rarity hunters, there were 135 BB rarities. Working out the figures, Portland dropped from 41% down to 35%, Weymouth and Christchurch are much the same at 18% and 17% while Poole more than doubled, going from 6% to 13%. Even more encouragingly, if we take the years 2006-2008, there were 20 rare birds found in Dorset. Of these, 20% were in Poole and only 15% found on Portland, which is surprising considering its geographic advantage, the presence of a ringing station, and them having such a large numbers of observers in such a tiny recording area."*

Conclusion

This book is dedicated to Ian Wallace. My chosen birding teacher was the logical clear thinking Peter Grant, and if he was on my mind my heart always belonged to Ian Wallace. There were three light-hearted books that informed birders of my generation, Bill Oddie's *Little Black Bird Book*, Richard Millington's *Twitchers Diary* and Ian Wallace's *Discover Birds*. They were all published within 18 months of each other. *Discover Birds* was intoxicating with Ian's supercharged bird illustrations, where everyday bird flocks mixed with dream birds, all sold with urgent prose. Ian became the 'godfather of modern birding', writing a series of high-octane articles and books that willed you back into the field.

Catching the Bug is our snapshot of birding the harbour, and was coloured with anxiety about climate change and potential rising water levels. Reading this in the future, you will know what happened. We figure that if we have been successful and infected you with that same bug, then there will always be someone to look after the birds of Poole Harbour, whatever the weather.

References

Alerstam, T. 1990. *Bird migration*. Oxford.

Alexander, H G 1969. *A checklist of the birds of Purbeck*. Unpublished.

Alexander, H G 1974. *Seventy years of birdwatching*. Berkhamsted.

Ashby, V (editor) 1995. *Dorset Birds 1995*. Dorset Bird Club.

Austen, J H 1885. *A systematic catalogue of the birds of the Isle of Purbeck*. Papers of the Purbeck Society: 61-75. Wareham.

Ball, D 2008. *Losing my virginity*. The Hoopoe, Dorset Bird Club Newsletter 66 (Autumn & Winter).

van den Berg, A B 1993, 2007. *WP reports*. Dutch Birding 15: 82-90; 29: 106-119.

van den Berg, A B, Constantine, M & Robb, M S 2003. *Out of the blue. Flight calls of migrants and vagrants*. CD & booklet. Amsterdam.

van den Berg, A B & The Sound Approach 2009. *Calls, identification and taxonomy of Siberian Chiffchaff: an analysis*. Dutch Birding 31: 79-85.

Bibby, C 1977. *Ecology of the Dartford warbler* Sylvia undata *(Boddaert) in relation to its conservation in Britain*. PhD thesis.

Bromby, A 1983. *Poole Harbour*. Chapter 8 in: Prendergast, E D V & Boys, J V (editors), *The birds of Dorset*, London.

Burton, J 1995. *Birds and Climate Change*. London.

Cade, M 1993. *Rare birds in Dorset 1983-92*. Dorset Birds 1993. Dorset Bird Club.

Carson, R 1962. *Silent spring*. New York.

Chandler, D 1995. *The Campaigns of Napoleon. The mind and method of history's greatest soldier*. New York.

Chown, D 2004. *Important breeding birds of Poole Harbour, part 1, Water Rail*. Poole Harbour Study Group, report 7.

Clements, J F 2007. *The Clements Checklist of Birds of the World*. Sixth edition. New York.

Cocker, M 2007. *Crow Country*. London.

Collins, D R 1986. *Poole Harbour RSPB Ornithological Survey 1984 - 1986*. Sandy.

Constantine, M & The Sound Approach 2006. *The Sound Approach to birding*. Poole.

Cook, K 2004. *Important breeding birds of Poole Harbour, part 2, Redshank*. Poole Harbour Study Group, report 7.

Cooper, I 2004. *Purbeck revealed*. Bath.

Cornisch, C J 1895. *Wild England of today and the wild life in it*. New York.

Cramp, S (editor) 1992. *Handbook of the birds of Europe, the Middle East and North Africa 6*. Oxford.

Cramp, S & Simmons, K E L (editors) 1977. *Handbook of the birds of Europe, the Middle East and North Africa 1*. Oxford.

Dean, A R 2008. *Colour nomenclature and Siberian Chiffchaffs*. British Birds 101: 144-150.

Diver, C 1947. *Conservation of Nature in England and Wales*. Command 7122. UK government White Paper.

Dixon, B 1966. *Wildfowl in Poole Harbour*. Dorset Natural History and Archaeological Society 88: 76-83.

Dyer, B & Darvill, T (editors) 2010. *The book of Poole Harbour*. Wimborne Minster.

Eaton, M A, Appleton, G F, Ausden, M A, Balmer, D E, Grantham, M J, Grice, P V, Hearn, R D, Holt, C A, Musgrove, A J, Noble, D G, Parsons, M, Risely, K, Stroud, D A & Wotton, S 2010. *The state of the UK's birds 2010*. RSPB, BTO, WWT, CCW, JNCC, NE, NIEA and SNH, Sandy.

Ericson, P G P & Carrasquilla, F H 1997. *Subspecific identity of prehistoric Baltic Cormorants* Phalacrocorax carbo. Ardea 85: 1–7.

Follett, J C (editor) 1964. *Bird report for 1963*. Dorset Natural History and Archaeological Society 85: 47-69.

Fuisz, T I & de Kort, S R 2007. *Habitat-dependent call divergence in the common cuckoo: is it a potential signal for assortative mating?* Proceedings of the Royal Society B 274: 2093-2097.

Goostrey, A, Carss, D N, Noble, L R & Piertney, S B 1998. *Populations introgression and differentiation in the great cormorant* Phalacrocorax carbo *in Europe.* Molecular Ecology 7: 329-338.

Green, G P 1984. *Summary of the Dorset Bird Report 1983.* Dorset Natural History and Archaeological Society 105: 178.

Hawker, P 1859. *Instructions to young sportsmen in all that relates to guns and shooting.* 11th edition. London.

Hawker, P 1893. *The diary of Colonel Peter Hawker, 1802-1853, volume 1.* London.

Helbig, A J, Martens, J, Seibold, I, Henning, F, Schottler, B & Wink, M 1996. *Phylogeny and species limits in the Palearctic chiffchaff complex: mitochondrial genetic differentiation and bioacoustic evidence.* Ibis 138: 650-666.

Holling, M & the Rare Breeding Birds Panel 2010. *Rare breeding birds in the United Kingdom in 2008.* British Birds 103: 482-538.

Humphreys, J & May, V (editors) 2005. *The ecology of Poole Harbour.* Amsterdam.

Huntley, B, Green, R E, Collingham, Y C & Willis, S G 2007. *A climatic atlas of European breeding birds.* Barcelona.

Isherwood, C 1959. *The common cormorant.* In: *Poems past and present.* Fourth edition. Don Mills.

Kortland, A 1938. *De uitdrukkingsbewegingen en -geluiden van* Phalacrocorax carbo sinensis. Ardea 27: 1-40.

Kortland, A 1995. *Patterns of pair-formation and nest-building in the European Cormorant* Phalacrocorax carbo sinensis. Ardea 83: 11-25.

Ladle, L & Woodward, A 2009. *Excavations at Bestwall Quarry, Wareham 1992-2005, volume 1: the prehistoric landscape.* Dorset Natural History and Archaeological Society Monograph 19. Dorchester.

Legg, R 2000. *Corfe Castle Encyclopedia.* Wincanton.

Lindholm, A 2011. *Crossbill call types in Finland 1998-2009.* Caluta 2: 7-18.

Mabey, R 1972. *Food for free.* Glasgow.

Marion, L 2009. *Recensement national des hérons coloniaux de France en 2007: Héron cendré, Héron pourpré, Héron bihoreau, Héron crabier, Héron garde-bœufs, Aigrette garzette, Grande Aigrette.* Alauda 77: 243-268.

Marion, L & Le Gentil, J 2006. *Ecological segregation and population structuring of the cormorant* Phalacrocorax carbo *in Europe, in relation to the recent introgression of continental and marine subspecies.* Evolutionary Ecology 20: 193-216.

Marova, I M, Fedorov, V V, Shipilina, D A & Alekseev, V N 2009. *Genetic and vocal differentiation in hybrid zones of passerine birds: Siberian and European Chiffchaffs* (Phylloscopus [collybita] tristis and Ph. [c.] abietinus) *in the southern Urals.* Doklady Biological Sciences 427: 384-386.

Matsuda, H, Uno, H, Tamada, K, Kaji, K, Saitoh, T, Hirakawa, H, Kurumada, T & Fujimoto, T 2002. *Harvest-based estimation of population size for Sika deer on Hokkaido Island, Japan.* Wildlife Society Bulletin 30: 1160-1171.

May, V J & Humphreys, J (editors) 2005. *The Ecology of Poole Harbour.* Proceedings in Marine Science 7: 175-188.

McCarthy, M 2009. *Think about it.* Birds 22: 36-40.

Moore, P (editor) 2003. *For nature, not humans: recollections of Brownsea Island under the ownership of Mrs. Bonham Christie.* Poole.

Mullarney, K, Svensson, L & Zetterström, D 2009. *Collins bird guide.* Second edition. London.

Newson, S E, Rexstad, E A, Baillie, S R, Buckland, S T & Aebischer, N J 2010. *Population change of avian predators and grey squirrels in England: is there evidence for an impact on avian prey populations?* Journal of Applied Ecology 47: 244-252.

Norman, A 2005. *Enid Blyton and her enchantment with Dorset*. Wellington.

Olburs, C 2008. *The chinese cormorant* Phalacrocorax carbo sinensis *Blumenbach 1798, an alien bird*. Internet: www.fiskevatten.se

Oppenheimer, S 2006. *The origins of the British: a genetic detective story*. London.

Pickess, B P & Underhill-Day, J C 2002. *Important birds of Poole Harbour*. Poole Harbour Study Group, report 2. Wareham.

Pond, B 2009. *Longshoreman*. London.

Poot, M & Flamant, R 2006. *Numbers, behaviour and origin of Mediterranean gulls* Larus melanocephalus *wintering along the west coast of southern Portugal*. Airo 16: 13-22.

Prendergast, E D V & Boys, J V (editors) 1983. *The birds of Dorset*. London.

van Raalte, C 1906. *Brownsea Island*. London. (Reprinted by the Poole Historical Trust 2011.)

Rogers, M & the Rarities Committee 1994. *Report on rare birds in Great Britain in 1983*. British Birds 77: 506-562.

Shirihai, H, Gargallo, G & Helbig, A J 2001. *Sylvia warblers*. London.

Sloane, J 2010. *Bournemouth 1810-2010. From smugglers to surfers*. Wimborne Minster.

Smithe, F B 1975. *Naturalist's color guide*. The American Museum of Natural History. New York.

Taylor, T 2004. *Green Island*. *Time team* series 11, broadcast on Channel 4 on 8 February 2004.

van Tets, G F 1965. *A Comparative Study of Some Social Communication Patterns in the Pelecaniformes*. Ornithological monographs 2.

Thomas, N S, Caldow, R W G, McGrorty, S, Durell, S E A le V dit, West, A D & Stillman, R A 2004. *Bird invertebrate prey availability in Poole Harbour*. Poole Harbour Study Group, report 5. Wareham.

UK government 2010. Planning policy statement 25: Development and flood risk. www.communities.gov.uk/documents/planningandbuilding/pdf/planningpolicystatement25.pdf

Voelker, G & Light, J E 2011. *Paleoclimactic events, dispersal and migratory losses along the Afro-European axis as drivers of biogeographic distribution in* Sylvia *warblers*. BMC Evolutionary Biology 11: 163.

Watts, A 1968. *Instant weather forecasting*. London.

Weninger, B, Schulting, R, Bradtmöller, M, Clare, L, Collard, M, Edinborough, K, Hilpert, J, Jöris, O, Niekus, M, Rohling, E J & Wagner, B 2008. *The catastrophic final flooding of Doggerland by the Storegga Slide tsunami*. Documenta Praehistorica XXXV: 1-24.

Wernham, C, Toms, M, Marchant, J, Clark, J, Siriwardena, G & Baillie, S 2002. *The migration atlas*. London.

White, G 1789. *The natural history and antiquities of Selborne*. London.

Winney, B J, Litton, C D, Parkin, D T & Feare, C J 2001. *The subspecific origin of the inland breeding colonies of the cormorant* Phalacrocorax carbo *in Britain*. Heredity 86: 45-53.

Wise, A J 1981. *Birds of Brownsea*. Third edition. Dorset Naturalists' Trust.

Witherby, H F, Jourdain, C F R, Ticehurst, N F & Tucker, B W 1938-1941. *A handbook of British birds*. London.

Yalden, D W & Albarella, U 2009. *The History of British Birds*. Oxford.

Index

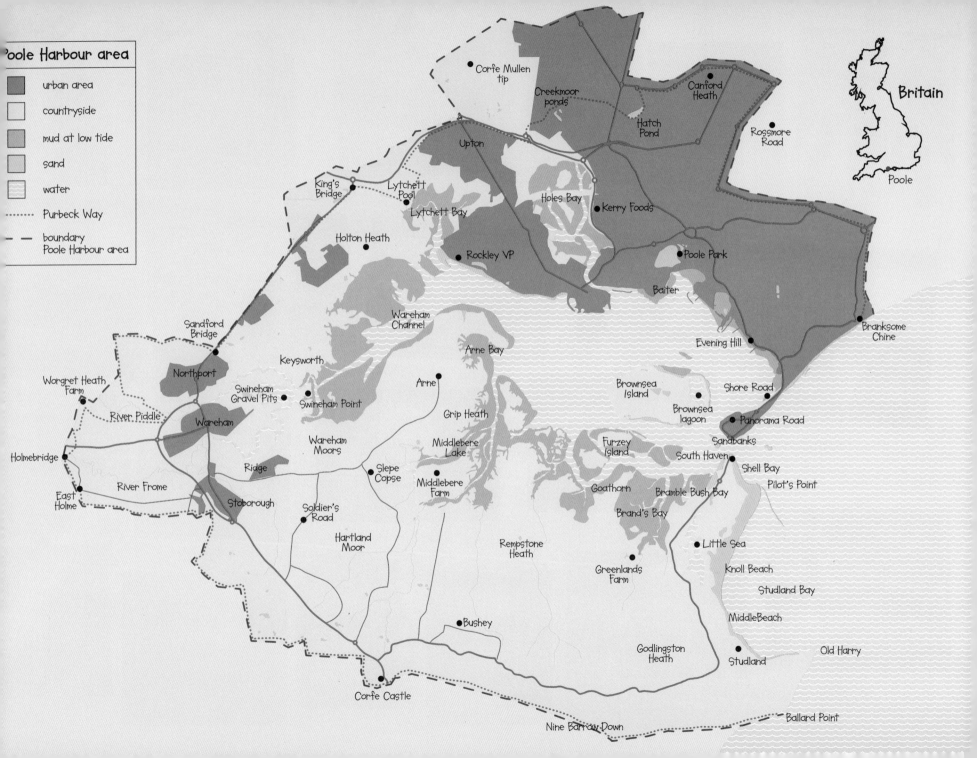

Poole Harbour area

- urban area
- countryside
- mud at low tide
- sand
- water
- ⋯⋯⋯ Purbeck Way
- — — boundary Poole Harbour area

Britain

Poole

Corfe Mullen tip

Creekmoor ponds

Canford Heath

Rossmore Road

Hatch Pond

Upton

Holes Bay

Kerry Foods

King's Bridge

Lytchett Pool

Lytchett Bay

Holton Heath

Rockley VP

Poole Park

Baiter

Sandford Bridge

Wareham Channel

Evening Hill

Branksome Chine

Keysworth

Arne Bay

Brownsea Island

Shore Road

Worgret Heath Farm

Northport

Arne

Brownsea lagoon

Panorama Road

Swineham Gravel Pits

Swineham Point

Grip Heath

Furzey Island

Sandbanks

River Piddle

Wareham

Middlebere Lake

South Haven

Shell Bay

Holmebridge

Ridge

Slepe Copse

Middlebere Farm

Goathorn

Bramble Bush Bay

Pilot's Point

East Holme

River Frome

Stoborough

Soldier's Road

Brand's Bay

Rempstone Heath

Hartland Moor

Greenlands Farm

Little Sea

Knoll Beach

Studland Bay

MiddleBeach

Bushey

Godlingston Heath

Studland

Old Harry

Corfe Castle

Nine Barrow Down

Ballard Point

Terry Elborn

Kevin Lane

Andy Humber

Durwyn Liley

Chris Thain

Colin Williams

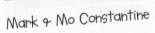
Mark & Mo Constantine

Jackie Hull

Ian Stanley

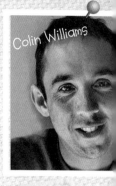
Ian Alexander   Paul Harvey

Tasie Russel

Trev Haysom   Derek Ball

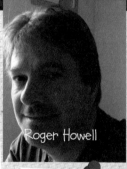
Bob Gifford   Roger Howell

Alan Bromby

James Phillips

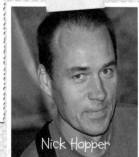
Nick Hopper

Dick

Kay Ball

Guy Dutson